# FROM PERSONAL DUTIES TOWARDS PERSONAL RIGHTS
Late Medieval and Early Modern Political Thought, 1300–1600

Continuing the historical investigation begun in *Consent, Coercion, and Limit*, Arthur Monahan examines Western political thought during the period c.1300–c.1600.

Focusing on the concepts of popular consent, representation, limit, and resistance to tyranny as essential features of modern theories of parliamentary democracy, Monahan shows a continuity in use of these concepts across the alleged divide between the Middle Ages and the Renaissance and Reformation. Each of the four parts of the book deals with a specific historical event or phenomenon that provides a focus for the political writings of that period. Part One examines the late medieval northern Italian city-state republics and the humanist depiction of their form of polity. Part Two reviews the legal (principally canonical) and political thought behind the development of a theory of popular consent and limited authority employed to resolve the Great Schism in the Western church. Part Three describes sixteenth-century Spanish neoscholastic political writings and their application to Reformation Europe and Spanish colonial expansion in the New World. Part Four examines the political thought of some of those who responded to new problems in church/state relations caused by the fracturing of medieval Christendom in the West: Luther, Calvin, and other Reformation writers; the Protestant resistance pamphleteers; and Richard Hooker.

Featuring an extensive bibliography, *From Personal Duties towards Personal Rights* will be of specific interest to intellectual historians as well as historians of political ideas and political theories and students in history, political science, and religious studies.

ARTHUR P. MONAHAN is Professor Emeritus of Philosophy, Saint Mary's University.

McGILL-QUEEN'S STUDIES IN THE HISTORY OF IDEAS

1   Problems of Cartesianism
Edited by Thomas M. Lennon, John M. Nicholas, and
John W. Davis

2   The Development of the Idea of History in Antiquity
Gerald A. Press

3   Claude Buffier and Thomas Reid:
Two Common-Sense Philosophers
Louise Marcil-Lacoste

4   Schiller, Hegel, and Marx:
State, Society, and the Aesthetic Ideal of Ancient Greece
Philip J. Kain

5   John Case and Aristotelianism in Renaissance England
Charles B. Schmitt

6   Beyond Liberty and Property:
The Process of Self-Recognition in Eighteenth-Century
Political Thought
J. A. W. Gunn

7   John Toland: His Methods, Manners, and Mind
Stephen H. Daniel

8   Coleridge and the Inspired Word
Anthony John Harding

9   The Jena System, 1804–5: Logic and Metaphysics
G. W. F. Hegel
Translation edited by John W. Burbidge and George di Giovanni
Introduction and notes by H. S. Harris

10 Consent, Coercion, and Limit:
The Medieval Origins of Parliamentary Democracy
Arthur P. Monahan

11 Scottish Common Sense in Germany, 1768–1800:
A Contribution to the History of Critical Philosophy
Manfred Kuehn

12 Paine and Cobbett:
The Transatlantic Connection
David A. Wilson

13 Descartes and the Enlightenment
Peter A. Schouls

14 Greek Scepticism
Anti-Realist Trends in Ancient Thought
Leo Groarke

15 The Irony of Theology and the Nature of Religious Thought
Donald Wiebe

16 Form and Transformation
A Study in the Philosophy of Plotinus
Frederic M. Schroeder

17 From Personal Duties towards Personal Rights
Late Medieval and Early Modern Political Thought, 1300–1600
Arthur P. Monahan

# FROM PERSONAL DUTIES TOWARDS PERSONAL RIGHTS
## Late Medieval and Early Modern Political Thought, 1300–1600

Arthur P. Monahan

McGill-Queen's University Press
Montreal & Kingston • London • Buffalo

© McGill-Queen's University Press 1994
ISBN 0-7735-1017-6
Legal deposit second quarter 1994
Bibliothèque nationale du Québec

Printed in Canada on acid-free paper

This book has been published with the help of a grant from the Canadian Federation for the Humanities, using funds provided by the Social Sciences and Humanities Research Council of Canada. Publication has also been assisted by grants from St Mary's University, Senate Research Committee, and the office of the Vice-President, Academic and Research.

**Canadian Cataloguing in Publication Data**

Monahan, Arthur P., 1928–
From personal duties towards personal rights: late medieval and early modern political thought, 1300–1600

(McGill-Queen's studies in the history of ideas; 17)
Includes bibliographical references and index.
ISBN 0-7735-1017-6

1. Political science—History. I. Title. II. Series.
JA82.M56 1994   320'.09   C94-900061-2

To Michael, Paul, Moira,
Corinne, Christopher, and Valery

# Contents

ACKNOWLEDGMENTS xi
PREFACE xiii
ABBREVIATIONS xxv
INTRODUCTION 3

PART ONE: CIVIC REPUBLICANISM AND RENAISSANCE LIBERTY

1. Italy: Fourteenth-century Political and Legal Developments 13
2. Bartolus of Sassoferrato 21
3. Baldus de Ubaldis 23
4. Fifteenth-century Humanist Political Thought 32
5. Sixteenth-century Humanist Political Thought 37

PART TWO: CONSTITUTIONALISM IN THE CHURCH

1. Introduction 50
2. John of Paris 65
3. Conciliar Thought in the Fourteenth Century 68
    Joannes Monachus 68
    Guilielmus Durantis 70
    The Academic Canonists 73
4. Conciliarism at the Time of the Great Schism and Basle 75
    Pierre d'Ailly 76
    Jean Gerson 90

Franciscus Zabarella  95
Nicholas of Cusa  98

5. Conciliarism after Basle  107
   Introduction  107
   John Major  109
   Jacques Almain  114

6. Conciliarism Secularized: George Buchanan  121

PART THREE: CONSENT AND LIMIT IN SPANISH NEO-SCHOLASTICISM

1. Spanish Scholasticism  128

2. Cardinal Cajetan (Tommaso de Vio)  142

3. Alonzo de Castrillo  145

4. Juan Luis Vives  146

5. Francisco de Vitoria  147

6. Juan de Mariana  161

7. Francesco Suárez  166

PART FOUR: EMERGING RIGHTS AS A BASIS FOR RESISTING AUTHORITY: REFORMATION POLITICAL THOUGHT

1. Introduction  185

2. Martin Luther  195

3. John Calvin  217

4. Theodore Beza  239

5. Peter Martyr Vermigli  249

6. François Hotman: The *Francogallia*  256

7. Mornay: The *Vindiciae contra tyrannos*  260

8. Richard Hooker  273

CONCLUSION  294
BIBLIOGRAPHY  301
INDEX  431

# *Acknowledgments*

INDEBTEDNESS TO THE SCHOLARSHIP of others, always a given in a work of this magnitude and pretension, is probably best expressed in the use made of it in the text, footnotes, and bibliography. As well, however, I wish to thank the staffs of a number of libraries for their unfailingly professional and friendly assistance: the British Library, the library of Trinity College, Dublin, and that of Saint Mary's University, Halifax. And in particular I should acknowledge the indefatigable and remarkably successful efforts of Douglas Vaisey at the Saint Mary's Library in filling bibliographical *lacunae* remaining after my original efforts. Finally, may I thank my editor, Claire Gigantes, for her admirable and amiable efforts at rendering my pedantic academic prose into more readable form.

I wish also to express appreciation to the Senate Research Committee, Saint Mary's University, for a series of research grants; and to the Social Sciences and Humanities Research Council of Canada for a subvention in aid of publication and the offices of the Dean of Arts and the Vice-President, Academic, Saint Mary's University, for similar support.

# *Preface*

THE STORY OF THE DEVELOPMENT of political thought in the Middle Ages must begin with an analysis of the most relevant source material: the Christian Scriptures and the works of authoritative Christian writers, both theologians and institutional Church authorities.[1] The standard approach to the subject has reflected this well-understood point, as the classic and conventional presentations of medieval political theory illustrate. But a simplistic understanding of method has sometimes produced a sterile and often distorted view of the political thought of medieval writers, the result of an excessively narrow analysis of, if not mere search for, concepts presumed to be essential elements in a proper theory of polity and therefore a legitimate object of search through the history of political thinking. The analysis has often been vitiated further by either or both of two other defects: first, the mistaken and mischievous notion, usually unacknowledged because largely unnoticed, that the concepts under examination contain a purely transcendental, ahistorical meaning intelligible today as it has been across the centuries; and secondly, an even more misguided assumption that political thought develops somehow in the disengaged minds of great thinkers independently of contemporary events.

It is no longer acceptable or even fashionable to employ so faulty a methodology. Nor am I aware of any instance in which earlier historians of political thought consciously did so. Nonetheless, it is worth drawing attention to this caricature of an appropriate intellectual frame of refer-

---

1. The rubric *sola Scriptura*, of course, became a rallying cry only with Luther's sixteenth-century Reformation views; but even here there was an inevitable tendency to follow the authoritative statements of the new religious leaders as well as the Church Fathers. See *infra*, pp. 197ff.

ence. For the difficulty of eliminating distorting perspectives that surround the thought and attitudes of earlier thinkers is a persistent challenge; and the more removed in time and the more unlike us our predecessors may have been, the more difficult it is to get their views right.

Medieval political thinkers have been almost paradigm victims of this sort of distorting interpretive activity, for several reasons. The standard and traditional literary models in which medieval writers expressed their views were deliberately and, to modern literary tastes, even excruciatingly abstract in form; their authors employed considerable rigour in omitting any reference to personal interests and their contemporary political and social scene. Also, however much common sense and an intuitive notion of history might indicate that essential elements of the Western intellectual tradition had some origins in medieval Europe, a significant segment of contemporary scholarship and current Western intellectual attitudes, especially in the social sciences, still finds it difficult to acknowledge and understand this basic fact. It is as if, having in many respects left behind the religious and theological trappings with which Western society was both adorned and encumbered for so many centuries, we are ashamed of our past and, unthinkingly perhaps, prepared to ignore it where we do not actually deny it.

A third factor closely allied to the second is the notion that an adequately "scientific" approach to any field of intellectual enquiry involves a careful delineation of the bounds of rational discourse and a corresponding exclusion of whatever smacks of the irrational or subjectively emotional, elements assumed to have no place in properly scientific discourse. Where the presence of religious concerns seems overwhelming, something frequently judged to be the case in medieval writings, the inference is then drawn that all one can do is reject the whole body of thought as contaminated beyond hope of cleansing. Much of what remains of the traditional humanities in contemporary higher-education curricula continues to suffer from this superstitious attitude towards an acceptable mode of intellectual discourse, even though nostalgia for the classical liberal-arts curriculum still serves as a basis for retaining some of its vestiges. As long as excessive emphasis on a positivist methodological model persists, however, we shall continue to suffer from an inability to profit adequately from the lessons history can teach us.

What weakened earlier and even some current writing on Western political thought, as already suggested, was not so much the deliberate application of mistaken methodological assumptions as their largely unconscious implementation. Unfortunately, this has been true not only for medieval political thinkers but for modern ones as well. John Locke, for example, has only recently been accorded the benefit of having his political thought presented adequately within an appropriate historical context, thereby showing his considerable involvement in the political realities of Restoration England.[2] Hobbes is undergoing similar revisionist refurbishment, but the process is still incomplete.[3]

It is now commonplace for historians of all stripes and areas of specialized study to become circumspect about the methodology they employ and to address directly the issue of how, if at all, to justify the validity of their approach and conclusions. Much of this self-awareness among historians and social scientists in general has been caused by the pervasiveness and thrust of the methodology of the empirical sciences, and by conscious efforts to conform to this paradigm of scientific knowledge, a move begun in the second half of the nineteenth century with the first flowering of scientific history and the correspondingly anxious and ultimately anxiety-producing efforts to discover the laws of history.

Today's conventional model of academic discourse is even more self-conscious as regards method; but it reflects contemporary philosophical more than scientific models. Of course, there is a sense in which philosophical thought and methodology also aspire to be scientific, but, except in certain rapidly shrinking areas of philosophy in the English-speaking world, the classical distinction between philosophy and science is still generally accepted. European intellectual circles in the decades since the Second World War, however, have spawned a new set of increasingly and deliberately comprehensive theories designed to circumscribe, as well as prescribe for, the whole of human knowledge. Often annoyingly prolix and intellectually opaque in formulation, a number of new "isms" have been articulated by post-war and self-described post-modern European thinkers, to produce what has been called "the return of grand theory in the human sciences."[4]

2. See Dunn, *Political Thought of John Locke*; Tully, *Discourse on Property*; Ashcraft, "Problem of Methodology," *Revolutionary Politics*, and "Two Treatises and the Exclusion Crisis."

3. See Baumgold, *Hobbes's Political Theory*; Kavka, *Hobbesian Moral and Political Theory*; Hampton, *Hobbes and the Social Contract Tradition*; Johnston, *Rhetoric of Leviathan*; Mathie, "Justice and Equity," and May, "Hobbes on Equity and Justice," in Walton and Johnson, eds., *Hobbes' Science of 'Natural Justice'*; Carmichael, "Right of Nature in *Leviathan*"; and for a games-theory approach to Hobbes, Gauthier, *Logic of Leviathan*.

4. Cf. Skinner, ed., *Return of Grand Theory*. But see also the rather tart assessment of this collection of essays by Frederick Crews in *The New York Review of Books* 33. no. 9 (1986): 36–42.

These focus on and contain an analysis of human thought and language that aims to show the inevitable structuring, modelling, and ultimately distorting effects produced on the data of consciousness by the human mind's efforts to give form and expression to what impinges on it from without. Constructionism, deconstructionism, semiotics, and the various forms of hermeneutical formulations all describe the inevitable and allegedly unbridgeable gap between the reality in which we exist and the knowledge that constitutes and expresses our understanding of it. Long gone, at least among serious Western intellectuals, is anything in the way of a theory of knowledge remotely akin to the ordinary mortal's unreflective, commonsense notion that things really are the way we perceive them.

Much of the attraction of these various epistemologies undoubtedly involves the fact that they suggest, upon minimal reflection even by ordinary readers, that we all necessarily organize and structure our knowledge to give it coherence for ourselves and others to whom we may wish to express it. The knowing subject in some sense does "intervene" between reality and our own structured experience of it. We all must acknowledge this basic epistemological insight whenever attention is drawn to it. Does this mean, however, that all our knowledge is so irremediably subjective in both formulation and expression as to be radically incommunicable to any other human being, if not simply unintelligible; that no one else can identify the meaning contained in the language we employ to express "our" knowledge, even when that other person might employ the same language to express their own experience?

The most dramatic way of responding affirmatively to this question is to maintain that words and statements are susceptible of any number of distinct meanings; hence no one meaning is "correct" for any verbal expression or written text. But however startling and insightful such an intellectual posture may appear, it is in the final analysis silly and even self-contradictory, at least insofar as its formulation for the purpose of communicating a truth about the nature of human knowledge is self-denying.

We do need to be mindful of the need to acknowledge and measure the limitations and structure we impose on our own knowing and on its expression through the language we employ. We must do all we can to recognize the limited character of our knowledge and the equally limited and irremediably problematic nature of the language we use to express it, language that may seem to, but does not always, communicate identical content to someone else who thinks they understand it. Self-consistency of theory regarding the fundamental issue of knowledge and truth value, however, admits of only two positions. The first entails basic, total silence in recognition of the "fact" that knowledge formation and communication are simply impossible. As Plato's sophist opponent Gorgias is alleged to have put it: nothing exists; if anything does, it cannot be known; and if anything can be known, it cannot be communicated.[5] The other option is to accept that human knowledge is "realistic" at some basic level, that it does involve somehow an apprehension of the external world of objects human beings share a common ability to grasp, and that we can communicate with one another through common and mutually intelligible language.[6]

This second view does not rest on any simple-minded assumption that a universal language exists, or can be developed, to express in a comprehensive way the transcendental content of the indefinite range of human concepts and ideas. Still less does it entail the Platonic metaphysics of ideas as themselves the ultimate realities whose unchanging contents are the object of every genuine human act of knowing. An appropriately sophisticated theory of knowledge must balance claims to truth against the recognition that this "true" content is always grasped imperfectly and expressed in language that further limits the adequacy of our grasp while carrying the additional risk of a second distortion when communicating with others.

On the other hand, reflection on the nature of human thought and language suggests that there is a certain hierarchy among ideas and the terms used to express them. The mind produces a variety of ideas in the activity of comprehending, some of which convey a broader rational content than others. More universal or abstract ideas, scientific in the Aristotelian sense, are of this sort; and the more universal their logical extension, the greater their organizing potential for the formulation of intellectual theory. This is why a history of ideas ultimately makes sense. Some ideas, the most important elements in the intellectual baggage humans carry in their collective journey through existence, have a history. They do; and yet in a sense they do not. Really fundamental con-

5. Sextus Empiricus, *Against the Logicians*, p. 65.
6. Cf. the nuanced position that rests a realist approach on at least the adequacy of an assumption, in Dunn, "Practising History and Social Science on 'Realist' Assumptions," in Hookway and Pettit, eds., *Action and Interpretation*. Cf. also Taylor, "Philosophy and Its History," pp. 17–30. For a more extensive presentation of Taylor's views, see his collection of essays, *Philosophy and the Human Sciences*.

cepts, being omnipresent, are somehow transhistorical; at the same time they exhibit a kind of unfolding by way of specification as individual human beings achieve a fuller understanding of their meaning in different conditions of actual need and circumstance. Ideas of this kind are simply the essential ingredients that the human mind employs for thinking about reality.

This is not to say that humans are ever required to think about any given issue; the human mind is not "determined" to think about any given question, even though failure to do so can lead to human misery and even destruction. There are many issues about which, arguably, we should be thinking profoundly but do not consider at all, and we are the worse off for the omission. The point is that, if humans ever have raised a specific question, or if they begin at some phase of human historical development to raise a specific question, certain conceptual ingredients—call them core concepts—are essential to the relevant thought process. They are the rational building blocks used by the human mind to address the issue, and they constitute its basic intellectual frame of reference.

Kant satisfied himself that the space/time forms of pure intuition and the twelve pure categories of mind expressed a fundamental conceptual structure for the whole of human knowledge, although the transcendental character of his theory, as he himself insisted, can be appreciated without accepting his identification and enumeration of its basic elements. In a comparable manner, H. L. A. Hart and Lon Fuller have spoken about the necessary "forms' for a coherent theory of law, a set of concepts apparently inseparable from any rational effort to think about law.[7] In their view, what Kant would call the "matter" or content of one specifically articulated system of law might differ from that of another—for example, the matter of Roman from that of Chinese law—but a necessary similarity, even an identity, exists in respect of form. Every system of law will contain "formal" elements such as an identification of the locus of coercive power, a means of identifying what a law is and of interpreting its meaning, etc.; lack of these elements signals the absence of a theory or system of law as such.[8]

Similarly, it can be argued that a rational theory about human beings living together in some form of community or society will contain similar

7. Hart, *Concept of Law*; Fuller, *Morality of Law*.
8. Fuller is particularly effective on this point with his discussion of the commands of a forgetful ruler. Fuller, *Morality of Law*, pp. 33–38; cf. Hart, *Concept of Law*, pp. 77–96, especially 89–96.

key elements. A comprehensive intellectual awareness by members of a political community of what is involved in their living together, their notion or theory about "where they are" politically and socially, is not *de facto* essential. But they must have some notion of what they are involved in, what they are doing; otherwise they are not functioning consciously at all: they literally do not "know" what they are doing.

When humans become conscious of themselves *in situ*, so to speak, another integral feature of human behaviour comes into play: interest in and concern for self-regulation and efficiency. As Aristotle understood so well and, for the first time in the history of human intellectual self-awareness, expressed so carefully, self-regulation has two features. First, humans aware of what they are doing are drawn naturally to consider how best to perform a given activity, how to act most efficiently; the second, more difficult feature concerns the purpose behind the activity itself: *why* do X, as distinct from *how* to do it effectively. A fundamental and often problematic distinction between the descriptive and prescriptive meanings of "natural" may illustrate the point. Humans are often said to be "naturally" selfish, meaning that we actually do perform acts directed exclusively to self-interest. On the other hand, we are also called "naturally" unselfish or self-sacrificing, in the sense that it is ethically proper to so behave in certain circumstances. Individuals, at least sometimes, do act from self-interest; and individuals are obliged, at least sometimes, to act out of interest for others.

The contention that certain fundamental features of human social behaviour and human society are essential to the structure of any functional set of relationships among human individuals living together in an integral and self-sustaining community also seems historically verifiable. Humans knowingly engaged in this form of activity can be said to realize and recognize the fundamental features, the "how" and "why" (efficiency and purpose), of the project itself. Giving expression to this awareness yields what we call political thought.

Accordingly, an appropriate method for presenting the history of political thought will identify certain fundamental elements in political society and examine what various societies and communities and their prominent thinkers have understood by them. The material under examination can be expected to differ somewhat across a wide range of specification because of the broad nature of these elements; it may even appear that different persons or groups in different times and circumstances had opposed, even contradictory, perceptions of what is involved in one or another basic notion. It is an error, however, to ignore or reject the point that common threads run through the continuum of human social and political history. At the least, such an attitude signals failure to keep a sufficiently open mind and the mistake of concluding that others think differently than we do simply because their understanding of a particular notion seems directly at odds with our own: X did (does) not have a "real" notion of Q because either they do not use Q at all or, if they do, do not mean by it what we do.[9]

Some have argued, for example, that the modern notion of "state" did not exist in the Middle Ages because the term did not appear there in its modern meaning.[10] The absence of any earlier intellectual awareness of what the modern term connotes does not follow, however; some other term might have been doing at least partial service in conveying what we now understand by "state." Foreshortening of historical and, therefore, intelligible perspective is often the result of unconscious contemporary conceptual egocentrism. It makes more sense in the long run and yields a more comprehensive account of human intellectual development to post notices identifying basic common denominators in the many examples of political thinking across history, and to clarify and compare various ways individuals in concrete and differing circumstances specified their understanding of essential features of the human condition.

Elsewhere I have employed three basic concepts in political thought that are crucial for any coherent theory of polity: consent, coercion, and limit.[11] This approach has been challenged on the not implausible grounds that these notions are too broad and too vague, and with the suggestion that power and right would be more useful concepts.[12]

---

9. A measure of how far modern scholarship has come in tracing key concepts in the history of political thought, and of how much farther it has yet to go, can be found in Ball, Farr, and Hanson, eds., *Political Innovation*. This recent collection of essays examines notions such as state, representation, rights, and property. The various contributors start with the Greek understanding of items in their glossary and make some mention of Roman contributions and medieval theories in a few specific instances. But the general impression is that little is known about the medieval history of these terms or its relevance, and there is a tendency to jump from the Greeks to Calvin and the Levellers, and to scant any notion of a general continuity across the classical, medieval, and modern periods.

10. Even Skinner holds the view that one cannot be certain about the conscious adoption and use of a given term until it is used in an earlier text with the meaning we now give it. Skinner, *Foundations*, 2:352. He also singles out the modern concept of state for specific consideration: ibid., 1:ix and note 1; and 2:349–58. Skinner's views on this subject, however, have undergone significant change: see his article, "The Modern State."

11. Monahan, *Consent, Coercion, and Limit.*

12. T. N. Bisson, review of Monahan, *Consent, Coercion, and Limit*, in *American Historical Review* 94 (1989): 111.

Perhaps. But, unlike consent and limit, the suggested alternatives are peculiarly modern conceptual tools. And because they are not found as such in the lexicon of medieval political terms, focusing on them can lead to a needless denigration of the quality of medieval political thought, and even a distortion. In fact, of course, the modern concept of power is reflected in the seemingly more concrete medieval concept of coercion, with its distinctions between physical and spiritual forms and external and internal forums, while the notion of sovereignty is found at least indirectly under the medieval concept of limit as a qualifier of authority and in the formula *princeps legibus solutus*, "the ruler is above the law." The notion of right, however, is much more difficult to deal with in trying to argue for an historical continuum from medieval to modern thought paradigms. The term right (*ius*) existed in Roman private law and was commonplace in medieval philosophical, theological, and legal texts; but its gradual shadings of meaning as political ideology developed towards current notions can be tricky to delineate. There is, as well, the issue of consensus regarding the modern meaning of the term.[13] As already noted, denial that modern notions existed in the Middle Ages can be countered with the suggestion that comparable medieval notions appeared under a different rubric and related differently to more fundamental conceptual structures than apparently important present-day concepts do.

Earlier academic writers were, for the most part, far less self-conscious and inclined to make a profession of how they intended to go about their task. In the current dispensation of scholarly publication, however, one is expected to give an account of one's methodology and, to reiterate, there are good, even compelling, epistemological reasons for this. The simple view that knowledge is somehow conditioned by the structure and form of our minds and experience and that language adds further structure to what we say and write are points accepted by all. Accordingly, we probably do not need all the complex lessons that are read to us by various contemporary ideologues of language structure and hermeneutics; the methodological cautionary tale to be understood and assimilated by historians has long been recognized to be very complex, as attested to by a general unwillingness to accept either the simple-minded assumption that what one says is true only to the extent that it

13. Richard Tuck, for example, argues that the early and high medieval era was one of two periods in our history where explicit advocacy of a natural rights theory can be found, the other being the run-up to and aftermath of the English Revolution. Tuck, *Natural Rights Theories*.

exactly mirrors reality, or the equally simple-minded scepticism about anyone being able to "re-present" reality at all. The rapidly burgeoning science of hermeneutics and the lively renewal of philosophical interest in theory of knowledge exemplify this: it is even common now for some to enquire whether "objective" philosophy is even possible[14]

A current standard for historico-political writing has been set by Quentin Skinner, whose first-rate account of the foundations of modern political thought was preceded by extensive and sensitive discussion of the problem of method.[15] This is not the place to offer either an account or a critique of Skinner's theory of methodology, but I am inclined to accept it for the most part, particularly in two fundamental respects. Skinner maintains that political writings, especially those exhibiting signs of novelty, are deliberate efforts to react to existing political and social conditions and aim consciously at a specific audience: new political thought rarely, if ever, originates in a purely speculative context. Accordingly, understanding texts that either directly or indirectly reflect political thought requires knowledge and appreciation of the historical realities in which this thought was produced, an appreciation of the form of discourse in which it is presented, and a grasp of the contemporary meaning of the terms in which it is expressed. Even great thinkers who may have been aloof from the actual political and social events of their own day—their number is almost certainly fewer than we suspect—would have been conditioned by the realities of their own time and the form and terms of its conventional discourse. Current social, economic, and political conditions necessarily influence thought in any period, whether or not this fact is acknowledged, and whether or not the influence is consciously felt, a truism that might be thought virtually self-evident had it, too, not been ignored so often, particularly by writers of intellectual history.

---

14. See Rorty, *Philosophy and the Mirror of Nature*, and his "Pragmatism and Philosophy," in Baynes et al., eds., *After Philosophy*, and other essays in this interesting collection. See also a variety of answers to the question whether even the hard sciences describe reality "as it really is," in McMullin, ed., *Construction and Constraint.*

15. Skinner, *Foundations.* Skinner's views on methodology were set out in an earlier series of articles: "Conventions and the Understanding of Speech Acts"; "Limits of Historical Explanations"; "Meaning and Understanding in the History of Ideas"; "Motives, Intentions and the Interpretation of Texts"; "On Performing and Explaining Linguistic Actions"; "'Social Meaning' and the Explanation of Social Action." Cf. Tully, ed., *Meaning and Consent,* especially Tully's own contribution, "The Pen Is a Mighty Sword," and Skinner's latest formulation of position and response to his critics, pp. 231–88.

A second important Skinnerian idea concerns specific terms of discourse: their actual use provides clear evidence that the ideas they express have been recognized in the thought structure of the time; explicit use of a particular concept or term shows that it is consciously employed as an intellectual tool. Skinner's example is the concept of "state."[16] As he contends, the notion became a conceptual building block in political theory no later than the first time it was given the specific meaning now associated with it. This point too would seem virtually self-evident were it not that so many writers of intellectual history have appeared unable or unwilling to accept it. A qualification can be added, however, to Skinner's cautionary point about a reading of modern notions back into historical contexts that are too early, and whose ideology and language offer no warrant for doing so. The earliest use of a term with its current meaning does signal the beginning of the thought structure in which it is similarly employed; but this does not by itself establish that the general notion to which the term is connected, and for which it performs a specific function in current ideology, was not served at least in some loosely parallel though less specific way by an earlier form of language or terminology.

A further methodological note suggested but not explicitly emphasized by Skinner is that history must be read "forward," not backward. A surprising number of interpreters of the ideology of the past have had a terrible time with this commonsense nostrum, and much twentieth-century intellectual history has failed to take it seriously enough. Earlier writings simply cannot adequately be understood in terms of what their language and set of conceptual tools might convey to a modern reader. A text's meaning is the one it had when it was written, and this may not be the meaning conventionally given the same set of words today.

The two points in this contention, especially the second, must be emphasized. Reading history "forward" entails the view that the proper perspective from which to understand a document is that of the period in which it was written *and* that of the earlier period from which it emerged: the period before a text was written is a crucial feature of its context. Initial assumptions concerning the meaning of a text, then, relate to what its terms meant at the time they were being used and earlier, not to their meaning today. To understand what Locke meant by property, for example, requires an appreciation of what that term meant when Locke employed it, and what it meant in the earlier Western intel-

16. Skinner, *Foundations*, 2:352.

lectual tradition in which he was operating.[17] This is not to deny that Locke may have given it a novel meaning. Indeed, what happens when great thinkers produce new paradigms of meaning is precisely that they appropriate into their language of discourse an element not previously realized or understood.

Sometimes the addition is made by way of completely new terminology, the coining of new language. But usually intellectual novelty occurs through clarification of or addition to the meaning of terms in current use; new theories and doctrines are normally developed in this way. Nonetheless, and once more the point is obvious but not unimportant, understanding the novelty and value of a "new" doctrine is better achieved from the perspective of where it came from rather than from where it ended up. To repeat the same general example, careful study of seventeenth-century political thought is better done by examining its medieval forerunners than its twentieth-century successors. One reviewer has praised Skinner's *Foundations of Political Thought* by suggesting that its author did for his subject what Étienne Gilson did for modern (i.e., Cartesian) philosophy: he added greatly to its understanding by investigating its medieval roots. This work has a similar purpose and employs a similar approach.[18]

---

17. Cf. Coleman, "*Dominium*," and "Medieval Discussions of Property." Tuck's recent work, *Natural Rights*, is wonderfully problematic in this respect when he connects the modern concept of natural rights with C. B. MacPherson's interpretation of seventeenth-century English political thought, principally Hobbes and Locke, in terms of "possessive individualism" and reads both concepts back into the thirteenth century. It is now commonplace to accept that MacPherson's modern intellectual chisel was innapropriately applied to the marble slab of seventeenth-century political thought, and Tuck himself has been criticized for finding natural rights in a medieval context where they may not have been spoken of at all. Cf. *supra*, note 13, and Tierney, "Tuck on Rights."

18. I do not mean to be insensitive to two other issues made problematic by recent authors: that of adequately tracing an intellectual tradition (cf. Hemming, "Archaeology, Deconstruction and Intellectual History," in Capra and Kaplan, eds., *Modern European Intellectual History*); and the narrower issue of establishing the influence of one writer on another (cf. Condren, *The Status and Appraisal of Classic Texts*).

*Pace* Condren, however, the term "influence" need not be evaluative when asserting connection between doctrines and texts; at least this is not how I employ it. I accept that lines of doctrinal affiliation cannot be established a priori but only on the evidence and may denote nothing more than that a later writer found an earlier doctrine useful for his or her purposes. Cf. Alberigo, *Chiesa conciliare*.

# *Abbreviations*

| | |
|---|---|
| *CIC* | *Corpus iuris canonici* |
| *Cod.* | *Corpus iuris civilis* |
| *Const.* | *Constitutiones* in *MGH* |
| *Dig.* | *Digesta* in *Corpus iuris civilis* |
| *Dist.* | *Distinctiones* |
| Goldast | Melchior Goldast, ed. *Monarchia s. Romani imperii* |
| Gratian | *Decretum Gratiani* |
| *Inst.* | *Institutiones* in *Corpus iuris civilis* |
| *Leg.* | *Legum* in *MGH* |
| *MGH* | *Monumenta Germaniae historica* |
| *PL* | J.-P. Migne, ed. *Patrologia cursus completus, series latina* |
| *ST* | Thomas Aquinas, *Summa theologiae* |
| *Sent.* | A commentary on Peter Lombard, *liber Sententiarum* |
| *Sext.* | *Liber sextus decretalium Bonifacii papae VIII* |

FROM PERSONAL DUTIES TOWARDS PERSONAL RIGHTS

## *Introduction*

THE TASK OF AN HISTORIAN of late-medieval political thought is not unlike that of the zealous and erudite canonical glossators of the fourteenth century who strove to formulate an ecclesiology. A vast cornucopia was available from which to extract earlier views on the nature and structure of the Church, and of the character and authority of the various elements of which it was constituted: pope, college of cardinals, bishops and other ranks of clergy, the laity, the Roman church and the Church universal. Withal, however, the sources were not only polyglot but even contradictory. The plethora of papal decretals and other canonical legislation that had blossomed in the two centuries after Gratian's *Decretum* was published in the 1140s, and, even more significantly, the mountains of glosses and interpretive literature to which the new ecclesiastical legislation gave rise, provided a trove from which many precious stones could be mined. By no means, however, were all of these sources mutually consistent or even obviously interconnected.

How, then, to make coherent sense of such disparate material? How, moreover, to present a general picture and identify at least the major outlines of an historical continuity? Any attempt might assume a false principle of interpretation, namely, that there was something in the way of a consistent picture or pattern. Better, perhaps, just to point to what was there.

Political thought in western Europe in the fourteenth century can be found in a variety of sources and was stimulated by a variety of events. From largely if not exclusively academic sources came a continuing supply of treatises, tracts, and occasional individual random thoughts from various representatives of university-based scholasticism. Commentaries on the *Politics* of Aristotle appeared in a regular stream, as did additions to the standard "mirror for princes" genre of public advise to various rulers. There were items triggered by various political incidents involving the issues of church/state relations or imperial efforts, frequently in northern Italy, to exercise political hegemony over a portion of the traditional *imperium* that had somehow escaped the ministrations of the *dominus mundi*. And there were numerous interpretive writings on both civil and canon law as well as the legislation itself.

My continuing emphasis will be on the contents of literary source material the meaning and intelligibility of which require, however, that it be set in its historical context, insofar as this is possible. Accordingly, while the preface offered a general account of the methodology employed in this study, the introduction provides a brief overview of the events and activities an historian can use to give structure and coherence to the political thought of a given period. There is an arbitrariness in the very nature of such an enterprise: interpreters can only begin where they begin, and they must begin somewhere. But distortions inevitably follow from beginning at any given point in the historical continuum: any suggestion that a basic conceptual element in political theory had an absolute beginning in time is as problematic as it is difficult to establish on an acceptable evidentiary basis. At the same time, however, one must be cautious about assuming that there is nothing new under the sun. Political realities do develop and are formulated from time to time, and it is possible in certain circumstances to identify and clarify such events. While the tendency to see and identify something new in the history of thought, particularly something recognized as new from the vantage-point of historical hindsight, needs constantly to be restrained; a balance must be struck between judging as new something that in reality is an extension or reformulation of something already present, and recognizing a genuinely novel element that does not match exactly what we have come to think of as conventional from the perspective of modern thought. In this connection, there is the further temptation to begin with the assumption that what is modern is better than what is old or ancient, thereby heightening the tendency to read back into history matter that never really existed there.

The first feature of an historical account is chronological sequence. I have given it a primary role, doubling back so to speak only infrequently to make the presentation more coherent. But because the work is a history of thought rather than of events, no serious effort has been made to apply any but the broadest strokes to the historical canvas. The myriad of detail needed for an adequate factual account of our period must be sought elsewhere; even the bibliography aims only to provide references to historical data of the most general kind, along with signs of where to look for a more finely detailed picture of individual persons and particular events. Generalizations about historical realities in the three centuries under survey have some explanatory value, nonetheless, as long as they are not pressed in too simplistic a fashion and are used only as background to offset any tendency to consider political ideologies in a transcendental, ahistorical vacuum. As long as they are valid within the limits of their mode of expression, generalizations can serve to highlight at least the broad frame of reference within which individual writers and their texts should be located and understood.

They are also necessary as a product of the human mind's natural activity of division and classification. The generalizations employed are of two kinds: large-scale events themselves—that is, events that clearly appear with the vision of historical hindsight to have had a considerable impact on those affected by them—and what might be called intellectual and ideological currents that also appear from this distance to have had a widespread influence on people as a whole.[1] Two far-reaching events, both religious rather than secular in character, frame the major divisions of this work: conciliarism in the Christian church as it developed from late medieval canonical and legal thought and came into practical focus in resolving the scandal of the Great Schism in the late fourteenth century; and the Reformation of the early sixteenth century that set in motion theological and other forms of ideological development whose

1. I wish to avoid the combination of language analysis and sometimes excessive zeal in trying to offer an exclusively fact-based account of political thought that has led some to question whether one can speak meaningfully of such a thing as intellectual history, or of one political thinker "influencing" another. If the only point here is that political thinking does not (cannot?) occur anywhere but in an historical context, that no human beings, not even great thinkers, exist in an historical vacuum, fait enough. But in accepting this simple truth, one does not have to retire the perfectly serviceable term "influence" on the grounds that its users are not sufficiently attentive to the impact of an individual's historical situation on what she or he thinks and writes. This is not what I mean when I use the term "influence"; nor is it what Skinner means when he employs it, as he does, without apparently violating his own strictures about the need to avoid the pitfalls of a history of ideas that is not grounded in fact. It might also be observed, however, that in several instances, his assessment of one thinker's influence on a successor does not seem well supported by the facts: for example, where he finds the Spanish neo-scholastics, specifically Vitoria, Bellarmine, and Suárez, to have blended Ockhamist with Thomistic notions about papal authority in the temporal sphere, and where he speaks in passing of Aegidius of Rome as a "close disciple" of Aquinas. The reference to church/state theory is at *Foundations*, 2:175; that to Aegidius at *Foundations*, 1:62.

consequences exercised the greatest impact on the history of Europe prior to Marxism and the Russian Revolution.

Attention is also paid to two other historical phenomena that are more difficult to specify precisely in terms of how they affected political thought in the West: continuation of the medieval scholastic tradition of political thinking among fifteenth- and sixteenth-century Spanish theologians stimulated in some sense by the Spanish conquests in the Americas and expressed as well in the Counter-Reformation movement; and the development and expression of political thought among humanist thinkers of the late fourteenth through the sixteenth century, focusing on the particular political realities of the northern Italian city-state republics. This latter area is particularly difficult to assess largely because so much has been made of the humanists' self-advertisement of their notions of liberty and freedom, which sound remarkably modern and liberal as slogans, but whose (to us) conventional meaning gives only a distorted echo of actual conditions in the republican communities in which they arose. The same might be said about the claims that are conventionally made concerning the emphasis on freedom and the individual as major features of the Reformation movement. However, while Reformist political writers and activists in no way advocated the political rights and freedoms of the individual we now associate with constitutional democracies, their theologies and ecclesiologies did provide a form of discourse and generate a psychological atmosphere, particularly in their devastating attack on the institutional church and articulation of the genuinely felt oppression of ordinary lay members, that unquestionably contributed to the awareness and exercise of personal independence.[2]

A major problem in trying to set the historical context for late medieval political thought is giving a coherent account of the fourteenth-century scene that does not do violence to the realities of the time by suggesting a greater degree of homogeneity than was actually present. The difficulty is twofold. On the one hand, a late twentieth-century perspective on Europe and indeed the world sees the globe and its various regions joined together in a kind of grand unity that is not, of course, necessarily political. While acknowledging a plurality of different nation

---

2. A good place to begin the examination of the impact of Reformation theology and the "revolt" against the medieval church is Ozment's brilliant work, *Reformation in the Cities*. He begins with a fine survey of the *status questionis* with regard to various scholarly interpretations of the causes of the Reformation (pp. 1–14) and an overview of lay religious attitudes prior to Luther's stand against Rome (pp. 15–46).

states and geographical groupings, we tend nevertheless to perceive our world as a whole and are inclined inappropriately to project this view back on earlier periods of history: persons living in medieval times had no such perception.

At the same time we have little appreciation of the form of unity existing in medieval western Europe, for which certain present-day conventional political and ideological concepts like national sovereignty and ethical and religious pluralism totally unfit us. From the thirteenth to the beginning of the sixteenth century, western Europe exhibited a theological and socio-ecclesiastical unity that, among other things, also expressed itself in an intellectual and ideological unity quite outside current conventional modes of thinking. Thus, efforts to describe the late medieval intellectual scene are frequently distorted by either favourable or critical preconceptions about the value of political and ideological unity. On the one hand, we cannot generalize about actual political conditions from one part of Europe to another, or even assume that persons in one area were knowledgeable about conditions elsewhere. On the other, we have trouble appreciating the uniformity in attitudes and thinking of ordinary medieval people, which was based on their common acceptance of a single religion and its institutional dominance and pervasiveness, as well as the uniformity in thought spread by the medieval lingua franca, Latin, and shared generally by academics and intellectuals who accepted a common view of the world that has no modern parallel.[3] In detailing political and intellectual conditions in the areas covered in this book, it is important not to assume too great a uniformity. But at the same time it must be accepted that both general and specialized expressions of current thinking would have been well circulated and common knowledge to intellectuals from one end of the region to the other.

At the other extreme in trying to gain some understanding of what they were about, we can legitimately ask questions of our medieval forbears that they did not necessarily ask themselves. They may not have expressed precisely the same views or ideologies as their twentieth-century successors; but it is our intellectual frame of reference that controls the structure and mechanics of how we understand the past, for this is the

---

3. Perhaps the closest modern counterpart is the bureaucratic European Community language, "Brussels." It, too, is virtually a closed book to ordinary people who do not use it, while its value as a linguistic currency that cuts across national and linguistic borders often blinds its élite bureaucratic users to its limitations in meaning and intellectual sophistication.

only way we can understand it. Accordingly, writing history can be as difficult as it is useful, although arguably it can never really be as useful as various historians have, over the centuries, somewhat naively maintained. The lessons of history are taught in the present. To learn them at all we must do two things: offer as accurate a description of the past as it is possible to provide from this distance without reading contemporary concerns and thought patterns into it; and simultaneously address our own questions to the past so that it can teach us, if we are prepared to learn.

Western Europe in the fourteenth century saw the beginnings of what we understand today as nation-states in France and England and, somewhat later, in Spain. In central Europe and the Italian peninsula, however, the scene was much different and reflected more a continuation of feudal conditions and vassalage in small and relatively isolated pockets under the marginal, if not largely symbolic, control of distant political jurisdictions. Though some efforts had been made in the preceding two centuries to organize northern Italy into a single political entity under the Holy Roman emperor, the *regnum Italicum*, there existed in fact a much less centralized form of political organization with one further regional peculiarity: city-states, particularly in Tuscany and Lombardy. Their forms of polity and the way they were articulated and justified intellectually differed considerably from the more general and abstract formulations of political thought that had become an integral part of the academic output from the newly emerging universities in western Europe, where academic inheritors of the Christian intellectual tradition so dominated by St Augustine were attempting to correlate it with the more recently acquired and vastly superior rational formulations of Aristotle's *Ethics* and *Politics*.[4]

An earlier work of mine provided a general account of the history of medieval political thought up to the end of the thirteenth century, with a brief excursion into the fourteenth to consider Marsilius of Padua, William of Ockham, and Dante. The first two have been credited with striking innovations in constitutionalism and the theory of popular sovereignty, even though both were conventionally medieval in many of their basic political premises and principles.[5] This is not to say, of

---

4. Attention has also been drawn recently, and properly, to Ciceronian influences on medieval political thought from the *De legibus* and *De officiis*. See Nederman, "Nature, Sin and Origins of Society"; cf. Wood, *Cicero's Social and Political Thought*.

5. Monahan, *Consent, Coercion, and Limit*.

course, that they had nothing to show us in the way of modern notions of political theory, but rather that a number of important concepts in modern constitutionalism and the limitation of sovereign authority owe much to general medieval political speculation.

I have not found it necessary to repeat conclusions about the modernity of Marsilian and Ockhamist political thought here, although their views are essential background material for the present study, and I have made some reference to Marsilius's republicanism. At the same time it must be recognized that they were the contemporaries, or at least proximate forerunners, of many thinkers whose views are treated at the beginning of this work. This is especially true of the early humanist political writers who, like Marsilius, reflected views concerning the best form of government developed in the northern Italian city-states, and of fourteenth-century canonists who, like John of Paris, developed the conciliar theory that was re-expressed in later constitutionalist ideology. Several late thirteenth-century figures, themselves Italian in background, who might on chronological grounds have been mentioned in my earlier volume, are included here to show their continuity with later humanists and legists. Stressing ideological continuity, it should be noted, sometimes results in a presentation that does not follow a simple chronological sequence.

Similarly, one might treat the Spanish neo-scholastic tradition as a continuation of its thirteenth-century flowering with Thomas Aquinas and his immediate followers. But in an effort to place political thinking in its appropriate context, I present this material as part of the theological debate among Spanish academics on the moral legitimacy of the Spanish conquest in the Americas and also locate it in the Reformation debate concerning the legitimacy of resistance to political authority in defence of religious commitments.

As already mentioned, it is the so-called humanist political thinking of the late medieval period that proves most difficult to place within an historical context. In many ways, it seems closely aligned with modern republican and democratic thought because it touted the value of a political community in which all citizens played an active role. But at the same time it did not precisely reflect the virtue modern thinkers find in democratic forms of polity. The main difference is what I see as an excessive emphasis in Italian humanism on political glory and greatness that is directly connected to its concept of freedom, a form of republican triumphalism that infers the freedom of its citizens from a state's power.

Any intellectual history also must address the problem of how to correlate what is essentially an intellectual formulation, expressed and expressible in a two-dimensional form, with the facts of history, which constitute a kind of third dimension of contingent data that is different in character from the rational mode of scientific thought. What is required is somehow to provide a three-dimensional account when two of the dimensions do not easily coordinate with the third. Historical data are in a different category of knowledge than concepts or ideas; hence the difficulty of coordinating the two categories involves the added difficulty of attempting any epistemological explanation and justification. This is why intellectual history sometimes appears as a transcendental form of discourse without any genuine connection with the real world, and why an exclusively positivist methodology implies the impossibility of intellectual history. An inadequate history of political ideas results from any totally deductive formulation that offers judgments about what a particular political thinker "must have meant," since this meaning seems invariably to derive from other stated views. A purely historical account, on the other hand, at least insofar as it tells a concrete and individualized story, lacks the character of science or ideology precisely because it is not universalizable. A sound history of political ideas must bridge the gap or "halve the difference" by offering an account of ideology grounded in the historical context of the era and the conditions under which it was produced, while also expressing basic notions that are a necessary feature of the nature of human thought on the subject matter at issue. I want to argue that the human mind employs certain essential conceptual elements whenever it undertakes to formulate political theory, and that it is intellectually valuable to try and discover these elements in actual cases of expressed political thought grounded in the political realities experienced by their authors.

A number of other difficulties arise for the intellectual historian of politics. Proceeding in the first instance from a set of texts may seem to scant the history of actual political institutions whose development would have had a direct impact on political thinking at the time: the changing relationships between monarch and parliament (or estates general) and monarch and courts in England and France are cases in point. The intent to offer a coherent history of ideas and the need to draw some boundaries around the material that can be included in a single monograph have led me simply to stipulate these and other historical data as essential background, and leave it at that. Relevant historical details do appear in the various specific accounts of doctrine or ideology.

Further, there is the issue of where to locate obviously significant literary sources that fall outside the general categories under which the contents are organized. Seyssel's early sixteenth-century *History of France* is one example of this. In order not to err by omitting such important elements in Western political thought, I have included them without making any particular issue or defence of their placement in the manuscript. Seyssel thus appears here as a forerunner both to Hotman's *Francogallia* and Mornay's *Vindiciae contra tyrannos* and will appear more extensively in a subsequent volume as background to the treatment of Jean Bodin. I have made no effort to be encyclopaedic by including references to every author and text that might be generally related to the subject of late medieval political thought. Lesser figures who deserve some mention such as Erasmus, Sir Thomas More, Robert Bellarmine, John Colet, and John Knox appear in conjunction with other more significant political thinkers.

In a survey that spans some three centuries, there is always the problem of where to stop. Broadly speaking, this account runs from the early fourteenth to the end of the sixteenth century. It thus excludes Jean Bodin, whose death occurred four years before my arbitrary cut-off date and whose writings constitute the most formidable and influential contribution to late sixteenth-century legal and political theory. It also excludes Thomas Hobbes, whom I had originally thought to include in this book, highlighting any debt the author of *Leviathan* owed to medieval political thinkers for a doctrine he himself described as the first scientific treatment of a theory of polity. To have done so, however, would have greatly enlarged the present work, and I have chosen instead to banish both Bodin and Hobbes to a later work whose primary focus will be theories of polity that are recognizably "scientific" in the Hobbesian and late sixteenth-century meaning of the term.

As the title of this work suggests, political theory in the period covered shows a deepening awareness of the place of individuals in society. From being perceived essentially as units in a corporate whole, subordinate to the whole and therefore apparently lacking what might be called personal integrity, they began in both Spanish neo-scholastic political thought and various forms of Protestant resistance theory to acquire, without fully achieving, a status in their own right by which they were guaranteed protection against political authority, however legitimate, that coerced their behaviour in respect of something as fundamentally personal as religious convictions. The medieval concept of popular consent as an essential feature of a legitimate polity takes on a more comprehensive and deliberately articulated meaning when it is extended to political regulation of religious convictions and practices, whose uniformity was fractured permanently by the Protestant Reformation. This is what I shall argue in the conclusion, after presenting the data such a judgment rests on in the four parts that follow.

PART ONE

# Civic Republicanism and Renaissance Liberty

## 1. ITALY: FOURTEENTH-CENTURY POLITICAL AND LEGAL DEVELOPMENTS

THERE ARE TWO REASONS for beginning this examination with the Italian city-states. Firstly, a simple form of republican constitutionalism did develop in these communities in the medieval period even though it did not last long. Secondly, its advocates stressed a conceptual trace element integral to any constitutionalist and democratic theory of polity: popular consent. The history of the medieval northern Italian city-states provides the most graphic illustration of the fact that conscious formulation of political thought usually rests on perceived needs and concrete historical circumstances. The actual practice of genuinely popular and direct democracy—i.e. all-citizen assembly—in northern Italy dates from slightly different periods in individual city-states and didn't last in any of them for any appreciable period of time, as far as one can gather from available evidence. Moreover, during its relatively brief heyday in the thirteenth and early fourteenth centuries, Italian urban democracy and republicanism produced little, if anything, in the way of written political thought or even historical records. Hence conclusions about the state and nature of political thought at the time are necessarily tenuous and somewhat problematic.

Economic development was the primary impetus behind the efforts of various Italian and other European urban communities to move away from the essentially rural basis of existing feudal relationships between authority and individuals. The feudal system of landholding, owning, and use rested on a contractual relationship between individuals, that of lord and vassal, into which the realities of production and distribution of nonagricultural products, mercantile development, and trade did not fit easily. Neither did the energies and values embodied in group economic activity. Accordingly, it was economic change and the revival of trade that led to the call for new forms of political arrangement. The movement away from feudal conditions sought to achieve "freedom" from the conventional relationship existing between lord and vassal. Otto of Friesing had remarked on this peculiar feature of the new political and social organization in northern Italy as early as the mid-twelfth century and located it in the rising urban communities. He noted in the citizens of these communities what seemed to him a quite subversive "desire for liberty," and what the townspeople meant by liberty was freedom *from* feudal obligations: having a legal status such that they would no longer be bound by the conditions and obligations connecting a serf or vassal to his feudal lord.[1] To the townsperson, this constituted personal liberty or freedom.

Beginning in the twelfth century, then, and throughout the thirteenth—even earlier in the cases of Pisa (1085), Milan (1094), and Arezzo (1098)—various northern Italian cities in Lombardy and Tuscany succeeded in establishing their independence from surrounding larger units or from the traditional structures and authority of their own communities. Where very early in the period the larger *de facto* unit might simply have been a local feudal lord, the ultimate antagonist from the twelfth century on would have been the Holy Roman emperor, whose claims to sovereignty and authority over Italy went back to Charlemagne's imperial coronation at Rome in 800. Various emperors had tried to enforce these claims militarily in the twelfth and thirteenth centuries and the attempts continued up until the mid-fourteenth, by which time papal territorial ambitions had also to be reckoned with as the papacy embarked on a policy of political domination over segments of the Italian peninsula. Thus, actual danger to the political independence of Italian city-states came sometimes from the imperial and sometimes from the papal side, and the cities themselves were tempted periodically to try to cast their lot with one side as a defence against the other. What the individual cities cherished most, however, was independence from any political domination and the unchallenged right to govern themselves.

The first efforts to achieve this form of freedom were made at the

---

1. Otto of Friesing, *Deeds of Frederick Barbarossa*, p. 127; cited in Skinner, *Foundations*, 1:3.

behest of individual members of a group that recognized the need for, and advantages of, new political arrangements. Naturally enough, this was likely to emphasize both the equality and identity of claims made by individual members of the group or community to share in any new dispensation. Agreement or consent among all individuals also would have been a prerequisite in some sense, and the corresponding need to formulate a procedure or mechanism for expressing consent would have been obvious. The model of direct participatory democracy was the apparent first choice in many of these urban communities, so that the notions of liberty and popular consent became connected directly to a republican form of polity.[2]

Direct participatory democracy, however, soon gave way to a more efficient method for expressing popular support on an increasingly complex range of matters of general civic interest and concern. Actual involvement by every individual citizen in determining things came to be limited both in frequency and specific subject matter. Formal meetings of the entire citizenry became relatively infrequent, and lawmaking and governing were correspondingly delegated to smaller groups or councils that were themselves elected in various ways by the community as a whole. A system of *podestà* rule had developed quickly in many cities in Tuscany and Lombardy by the late thirteenth century: the cities hired an administrator on a fixed-term basis, often six months, who ruled according to policies and procedures established by the citizens themselves, to whom he was fully accountable.

Not until early in the fourteenth century did writers begin seriously to extol the freedom of the Italian cities. By that time, pure democratic forms had largely been replaced by one-man administrators and limited-term rule, the *podestà*; various forms of tyrannical regime soon followed in most Italian city-state jurisdictions. Meanwhile, the original notion of freedom from feudal contractual obligations had expanded to include the concept of individual consent to the obligations imposed by political authority; in other words, some form of republicanism. And the authority from which independence was declared had become further specified. In the immediate instance of current political and legal realities it was independence from the authority of the Holy Roman Empire or, insofar as it tried to exercise secular authority, the papacy. The advocates of freedom, then, stressed political integrity and a kind of sovereignty: the city-state laid claim to a right to exercise independent political power

---

2. Cf. Monahan, *Consent, Coercion, and Limit*, pp. 148–54; Skinner, *Foundations*, 1:7–12.

on its own behalf, free of interference from any external political sources. Historically, the actual achievement of independence usually came first, and its rational justification later. One ironic aspect of the Italian urban experiments in republicanism in the fourteenth century was that the political thought they embodied was articulated only after the political realities and models it praised and defended had been largely superceded by much more straitened conditions of political tyranny and absolutism, which were apparently accepted as the only realistic bulwark against factional strife and community chaos.

In the event, advocacy for city-state independence tended to find uniform expression in an insistence on the right to self-government, which, in its most comprehensive model, included some form of republicanism, exercise of political authority by the body of citizens themselves. The conceptual distinctions between monarchy, aristocracy, and democracy derived from Plato and Aristotle, however, often were not particularly clear in respect of the actual mechanism of government in place.[3] Nor did the political realities of individual polities always accurately reflect the details of independent republicanism touted by particular writers. Nevertheless, these writings, as understood by their authors' contemporaries and successors, had a significant impact on the development of Western political thought.

Chroniclers and advocates of freedom residing in the late medieval Italian city-states expressed their claims for the most part in rhetorical rather than logical terms; but there were interesting exceptions. The fundamental issue they usually addressed was the need to counter the accepted view of how political authority should operate. This view, which rested on either history or conventional political ideology, saw the communities in question as legally subject to a given external authority. In such circumstances any claim to independence could obviously be made more effectively where the conventional external authority had either little real stake in, or minimal ability to continue, the legal *status quo*. In any event, what interests the historian of political thought is the historical context in which the case for independence was made. This context shows clearly that the case itself was given a legal frame of reference: claims for independence of the city-states were initially expressed in terms of a right to operate outside the legal jurisdiction of the empire or papacy, and to make and be bound by their own laws.

---

3. See Ptolemy of Lucca's *De regimine principum* and humanist descriptions of Florence as a superior polity, *infra*, pp. 18–19; 34–37.

Genuine difficulties were involved in the effort to establish a legal basis for such claims within the context of current civil law, based as it was on the Roman Code. A literal acceptance and intepretation of the Code, the standard posture adopted by medieval civilian glossators, accepted the emperor as *dominus mundi*, the source and reservoir of all legal rights. Claims to this status by the reigning emperor went back to Charlemagne's establishment of the empire itself, and similar legal claims had been made by a succession of later emperors. Though not pressed in the original ninth-century conditions of relative political chaos, they had been carefully revived when Otto I linked the Italian kingdom with his German possessions. A series of military campaigns to enforce these claims began with Frederick Barbarossa's first expedition to Italy in 1154 and was renewed by a succession of emperors down to the fourteenth century. During the period when northern Italian cities were experimenting with forms of democratic republican government and mechanisms for practising popular consent, at least part of their instability was caused by the various imperial efforts to exercise political control in the region.

By the late thirteenth century a number of Italian writers had begun to express their familiarity with and sympathy for the contemporary political scene in northern Italian communes like Florence and Padua. Remigio de' Rigolami (?–1319) offered a straightforward and somewhat novel account of republicanism that clearly reflected his Italian background. A Florentine who had studied at Paris in the 1260s, probably under his Dominican confrère Thomas Aquinas, Rigolami taught for many years at the Dominican college in Florence, where one of his pupils may have been Dante Alighieri. He was a prolific writer of theological tracts and sermons as well as the author of two political treatises, *De bono communi* (1302) and *De bono pacis* (1304), that reflected his Aristotelian and Thomistic background, but were specifically adapted to the contemporary city-state scene in northern Italy.[4]

Remigio favoured a republican form of government and traced its origins back to the republic at Rome, which he preferred to the imperialism of the Caesars, praising Cato and Cicero as advocates of republi-

---

4. Extracts from Remigio's *De bono communi* are translated into English in Minio-Paluello, "Remigio Girolami's *De bono communi*"; the *De bono pacis* has been edited by Charles T. Davis in *Studi Danteschi* 36 (1959): 123–36; and two Latin editions of both the *De bono communi* and the *De bono pacis* have been published recently: Matteis, *La "teologia politica communali" di Remigio de' Girolami*, and Ponella, in *Memorie domenicane*, the latter being far superior. I am preparing an English translation of these texts.

canism.⁵ He also presented his theory of the common good as the purpose of government with specific application to a city-state, emphasizing that its appropriate form was the peace of the community, a concept also emphasized by Dante and subsequently made famous by Marsilius of Padua in the *Defensor pacis*, and by Bartolus of Sassoferrato.⁶

Another turn-of-the-century advocate of Italian republicanism was Ptolemy of Lucca (?–1327), also a student and associate of Aquinas at Paris, who spent much of his ecclesiastical career in his native Italy where, late in life, he became bishop of Torcello (1318). His major political work, probably written in the years 1300–05, was a treatise in the standard "mirror for princes" form, *De regimine principum*, which quickly became attached to Aquinas's uncompleted work given the same name in the manuscript tradition connecting them; and the combined Thomistic and Ptolemaian text circulated for centuries as the work of Aquinas.⁷ Ptolemy's doctrine differed from his Dominican Master's, however, in that it generally favoured republicanism over monarchy as the best form of government, and Ptolemy took particular pains to laud its contemporary Italian form. Advocating an elective form of polity and designating kingship as despotic, Ptolemy conceded that a free and self-governing administration might not become established in regions "more suited to servilitude than liberty"; but he extolled those parts of the world whose people "have virile spirits, courage in their hearts and confidence in their intelligence," where republicanism was the best and most natural form of government. He also declared that "this form of polity flourished above all in Italy," whose people held freedom in such high esteem that "no one is able [there] to wield perpetual power or rule tyrannically";⁸ he made specific reference to the Roman tribunes as representatives of the people, a point made much of later by Calvin in his enigmatic remarks about possible resistance to religious persecution by

---

5. Remigio, *De bono communi*, p. 68, cited in Davis, "An Early Florentine Political Theorist", p. 666.

6. The view that the purpose of any civil authority is the common good was, of course, universal among medieval political theorists and went back to Plato and Aristotle. For Marsilius, cf. *infra*, pp. 19–21, and for Bartolus, *infra*, pp. 21–23.

7. Ptolemy's work remains attached to the Thomistic text even in one recent modern edition, without any clear indication of the difference in authorship: see "De regimine principum," in Thomas Aquinas, *Opuscula omnia*, ed. Perrier. Another modern edition, however, puts the record straight: Thomas Aquinas, *Opuscula philosophica*, ed. Spiazzi, p. 280B. My translation of the Ptolemy text will appear shortly.

8. Ptolemy, *De regimine principum*, pp. 187, 381.

political authorities.[9] Even Aegidius of Rome, certainly no advocate of either popular sovereignty or republicanism, acknowledged that both flourished in the Italian city-states of his day.[10]

At the time, however, the most outspoken advocate of a form of polity based on popular sovereignty and a constitutional limitation on political authority was Marsilius of Padua, whose best model would have been his own city-state of Padua.[11] The impact of his *Defensor pacis* on later European political thought, while obvious in many ways, still requires exposition.[12] The work was damned from the moment of its appearance by ecclesiastical authorities for its direct subordination of church to state and later praised for precisely the same thing. But that it was something of a *livre de circonstance* has led to a number of oversimplified assessments of the work, both for and against, and until recently insufficient attention has been paid to its contents.[13] Similarly, careful attention has yet to be paid to its influence on later Western political thought.[14]

Though couched in universal terms, Marsilius's assertion of claim for political independence from higher authority was clearly an attack on church pretensions to temporal power in Italy and elsewhere. Such claims to ultimate authority over the temporal sphere by the papacy and institutional Church as a whole had reached their zenith with Boniface VIII and, regardless of the sophisticated interpretations some theolo-

9. Cf. *infra*, pp. 229–30.
10. Aegidius of Rome, *De regimine principum* 3.2.2.; cf. Monahan, *Consent, Coercion, and Limit*, p. 193 and note 301.
11. Marsilius's political views were examined briefly in my earlier work, *Consent, Coercion, and Limit*, pp. 209–29. I have greater reservations now concerning Wilks's interpretation of Marsilius as a closet imperialist and his downplaying of Marsilius's advocacy of city-state republicanism. Marsilius did concede that political authority could be exercised legitimately by a single ruler and clearly sought support from the current emperor, Ludwig of Bavaria; but the details in the *Defensor pacis* show that a city-state was the principal model to which he applied Aristotle's description from the *Politics* of a Greek city-state. See Wilks, "Corporation and Representation," pp. 251–94.
12. Cf. *infra*, note 14.
13. Two modern translations of the *Defensor pacis* have been published in the last thirty-odd years, one in English and the other in French, both accompanied by a lengthy analysis of its contents: Gewirth, *Defender of Peace*, and Quillet, *Marsile de Padoue*.
14. The conventional view is that Marsilius's *Defensor pacis* was known and presumably played an "influence" role in sixteenth- and seventeenth-century English views of the relation of church and state in both its Anglican formulation and in Hobbes's doctrine of the "leviathan", but actual evidence is thin: see Skinner, *Foundations*, 1:101. The first English translation of the *Defensor pacis* was produced in 1535 by William Marshall on a commission by Archbishop Cromwell. cf. Condren, "Democracy in the *Defensor pacis*."

gians and canonists were to give these claims in trying to maintain that ecclesiastical authority was essentially spiritual in nature and that real and appropriate jurisdiction still remained in the hands of temporal rulers, few, if any, contemporary rulers were completely persuaded by such disclaimers. More to the point was the fact that the Roman pontiffs of the day and for centuries to come were more than willing to claim and actually exercise temporal jurisdiction over regions in Italy, as well as engage in warfare and the other pursuits of political and diplomatic chicanery ordinarily regarded as "the things that are Caesar's," not God's.

Arguably, then, Marsilius's purpose in writing the *Defensor pacis* was more to deny the Church grounds for the exercise of power, whether directly or indirectly, over temporal polities like Padua in northern Italy, than to present a formal theory delineating the purely spiritual character of ecclesiastical and papal hegemony and its essential and complete subordination to temporal rulers. Nonetheless, in rejecting contemporary papal absolutist claims, Marsilius presented an image of the Church that would be developed much more fully by Luther and other sixteenth-century reformers, viz., that of a purely voluntary and apolitical, seemingly noninstitutional entity or association, a *congregatio fidelium*. However, he did not anticipate the more thorough Reformation rejection of the episcopal and clerical structure of the Church in favour of a simple community of believers, all equal and in equally direct communication with God through faith in the Scriptures alone. Marsilius was not concerned with dismantling the medieval institutional church; he wanted only to strip it of all temporal authority and power. John of Paris, it might be noted here, also upheld the idea of the purely spiritual nature of the Church.[15]

In effect, the Marsilian attack on the Church's pretensions to authority over temporal polities like the northern Italian urban centres was much the same as that of Bartolus of Sassoferrato, who argued against imperial jurisdiction over the same territories a few years later. Both offered grounds for insisting on the independence of city- (or nation-) states from external political authorities, although Bartolus was more explicit than Marsilius in his acknowledgement of papal superiority in spiritual matters. Elements in both their theories were later harnessed to other political ends, specifically, to a more modern theory of representative democratic polity inasmuch as both located political authority in

---

15. See *infra*, p. 196, and Monahan, *Consent, Coercion, and Limit*, pp. 198, 204.

the people as a whole and advocated a republican form of government, notions they derived from Aristotle's *Politics*.

## 2. BARTOLUS OF SASSOFERRATO

Italian jurists and writers on legal matters also accepted the challenge of spelling out the rational grounds on which claims could be made by various Italian urban communities for their preferred mode of governance. The first to do so was Bartolus of Sassoferrato (1314–57), founder of the post-Glossator school of civilian jurists. Referred to as "perhaps the most original jurist of the Middle Ages,"[16] he studied at Bologna and subsequently taught Roman law at several universities in Tuscany and Lombardy. He set the terms of reference for his own legal theorizing by enunciating the methodological principle that law should reflect existing conditions and express the realities of actual political communities, rather than "turn the clock back" to earlier political arrangements. The principle, of course, was directly self-serving, and Bartolus proceeded to make it serve him well. He began with a point made earlier by political writers like Thomas Aquinas and John of Paris that had become a commonplace by the early fourteenth century: a plurality of different polities existed in the world, and they were not all subject to a single authority according to some abstract hierarchical principle. Efforts to describe the Holy Roman Empire as a comprehensive jurisdiction or to claim universal territorial dominion for it had never been much more than rhetoric, despite legal justification available through an appeal to Roman law and historical precedent. The medieval emperor did not exercise jurisdiction over the whole of the territory originally controlled by ancient Rome; even the original Caesars did not govern the whole world. Moreover, imperial efforts to exercise *de facto* jurisdiction in medieval Italy had never been very successful even in the short term.

By stating that a plurality of independent polities existed worldwide, Bartolus provided grounds for the claim that the various city-states in northern Italy could be numbered among them. He contended that such was indeed the case and proceeded to move from the *de facto* situation to *de iure* ground on which they could rest their right to sovereignty, using the concept of custom to bridge the gap between actual and juridical reality and combining it with popular consent to forge an

16. Skinner, *Foundations*, 1:9.

impressive ideological instrument for justifying republicanism as an appropriate form of city-state polity. Quite simply, Bartolus contended that an actual political structure acquired legal status *ipso facto* by existing "for a very long time."[17] Communities exercising powers of lawmaking and self-government over a long period acquired thereby the right to continue to do so, that is, to operate independently of a higher authority such as the emperor, even though it could still be maintained that in some sense the larger-scale legal arrangement continued in existence.[18] Bartolus was careful not to reject the claim for imperial jurisdiction based on Roman law; he contended instead that facts ballasted by custom outweighed the literal contents of the Code and thus made possible a general claim by any newly emerging nation-state for withdrawal from the empire. This line would be taken by other groups in the fourteenth century and later, and it had been at least partially delineated a few decades earlier by French publicists arguing independence from papal jurisdiction by Philip the Fair in his quarrel with Boniface VIII.[19]

Bartolus's claim appealed to certain historical realities and even legal facts as they pertained to the Holy Roman Empire. Many Italian city-states had been exercising *de facto* independence from the emperor for some time, and most of these had at least a quasi-legal basis for their behaviour—an agreement of sorts with one or another of the emperors with whom they had negotiated a form of actual independence in return for payment of some kind. Legal form, he argued, could be given to this *de facto* independence by asserting that actual sovereignty rested in the communities themselves; for sovereignty could only arise in fact insofar as authority to establish it existed in the people from the beginning: the historical record did not show any emperor having granted it.

The formal legal issue of imperial authority over the cities of northern Italy had been raised at the time of Barbarossa's unsuccessful efforts to subjugate them in the mid-twelfth century. The Diet of Roncaglia had set

---

17. See Canning, *Political Thought of Baldus*, pp. 65–67 and *passim*. Canning's work shows the connection between Bartolus and his pupil, Baldus de Ulbadus, as regards their views on the sovereignty of some fourteenth-century Italian city-states. Canning also points out that the argument moving from the *de facto* to the *de iure* had been applied to the relationship between kings and emperor since at least the beginning of the thirteenth century. Canning, *Political Thought of Baldus*, p. 66.

18. Skinner, *Foundations*, 1:9 and 11.

19. As Skinner points out, it was but a short step from Bartolus's position to the formula *rex est imperator in regno suo*: Skinner, *Foundations*, 1:11. However, Skinner errs in the time sequence between the Philip/Boniface dispute and the Bartolus formulation (ibid.); the former was the earlier.

the terms of the relationship between the empire and the cities over which the emperor had failed to win complete control. The terms of settlement had been formulated in part by the four most eminent Bolognese legists of the day. They had sat on the commission that drew up the Diet's decrees, and each had agreed that the emperor possessed full sovereign rights over the cities in question: he was "the supreme ruler at all times over all his subjects everywhere [and enjoyed] the power to constitute all magistrates for the administration of justice ... and to remove them if they neglect their duties."[20]

With so clear a statement of imperial jurisdiction it is little wonder that Bartolus stressed the notion of customary law, a concept universally accepted by medieval legists and theologians if not always clearly explicated. And as noted, he made popular consent one of its essential features, though he obviously considered customary consent to have been passive or tacit; the people consented to the law of custom simply by following it, although it might be presumed to have been agreed to actively at an earlier time. By ingeniously giving a primary function to popular agreement or consent in customary law, Bartolus was able to describe custom as having the same status as statutes that actually had been given formal legislative validity by a process in which popular consent was also an essential feature. Thus, both custom and positive law rested on consent and differed only in the form in which popular agreement was expressed: custom expressed consent in a tacit or passive form, while positive statutes did so in an active form. Accordingly, custom had the same legal force as positive law. And Bartolus coordinated consent and legality in the case of sovereignty for the city republics by arguing that custom showed the cities to have enjoyed the status of being "free" for some time; hence one could infer that the people had consented to this condition and thereby validated it. And having done so, they validated their community's independent status as legal, free, and sovereign within the empire. Bartolus spoke of the city-state as a ruler in respect of itself: *civitas sibi princeps*.[21]

### 3. BALDUS DE UBALDUS

Once scarcely considered in studies of the development of thought in the Middle Ages, Baldus de Ubaldus (1326?–1400) is now recognized as

20. "Decreta Curiae Rancogliae," in *MGH, Constitutiones*, 1:245–46.
21. Canning, *Political Thought of Baldus*, p. 96. Canning cites Baldus, ad D.4.4.3, n. 1, fol. 133r, and D.49.15.7: p. 97, n. 15; cf. n. 16. Cf. *infra*, n. 20.

both the greatest jurist of his day and a signal contributor to the development of the theory of popular government. A student of Bartolus of Sassoferrato, he was born in one of the northern Italian city-states, studied both canon and civil law in Perugia and possibly Pisa, and spent his life teaching and practising law in Perugia, Pisa, Florence, Padua, and Pavia. He was at the University of Padua when he died on 28 April 1400.[22] Like most contemporary civil and canonical legists, he was more practitioner than theorist, and this was where he made the greatest contributions to his profession. Following the general path set down by his master Bartolus, Baldus's basic intention was to employ the law to accommodate contemporary conditions, rather than require existing political and legal realities to express the literal intent of statutes of the Roman Code. His attitude was shared by the school of contemporary canonical commentators also known as post-Glossators to distinguish them from earlier canonists (the Glossators) who had insisted on implementing the Code directly.[23]

Like most of the thinkers I shall discuss, Baldus did not engage in political writing as such; his works were entirely juristic in nature but they are nonetheless valuable as political thought. Baldus was interesting in that he was a genuine practitioner of the very law on which he was commenting, and he proved to be an innovator here as well. He frequently served particular city-state constituencies as a legal expert, advisor, and sometimes as a negotiator. His written legal output was prodigious, something in the order of seven million words in all, perhaps the largest body of written text by any medieval jurist. However, except for a few *consilia*, that is, written legal opinions on specific issues which Baldus produced literally in the hundreds, and one commentary on the Code, there is no modern or critical edition of the many volumes of his writings. Unlike Bartolus he wrote no professedly political tracts, preferring

---

22. For a fine recent treatment of Baldus, see Canning's *Political Thought of Baldus*. It contains an up-to-date list of both manuscript and printed sources for Baldus's writings. See also by the same author "The Corporation in the Political Thought of the Italian Jurists"; "A Fourteenth-Century Contribution to the Theory of Citizenship"; "Ideas of the State of Thirteenth and Fourteenth-Century Commentators on the Roman Law." Canning indicates that biographical details on Baldus are not nearly as certain as had previously been thought: *Political Thought of Baldus*, pp. 3–4.

23. An important point made by Tierney in his classic study of conciliarist thought was that as early as the thirteenth century, the Decretalists aimed to express a canonical position that "worked," rather than simply impose earlier legal formulations on existing ecclesiastical conditions: their development of corporation theory was an obvious case in point. See Tierney, *Foundations of the Conciliar Theory*, p. 104; cf. *infra*, p. 52.

apparently to put directly into practice his master's principle of making law fit current realities rather than the other way about. He was not interested in acting as theoretical apologist for one type of government over another, but sought to provide juristically acceptable explanations for the forms of government, jurisdiction, and political organization he knew and represented. It is very clear from his written work that he was the kind of legal advocate we might expect ourselves to find to represent specific interests, someone who would put the best case for the particular interests he had been retained to represent. This was Baldus. Often representing particular city-states in their dealings with other constituencies—other city-states, the empire, the papacy—he advocated self-determination or sovereignty for his client by posing the legal and political basis for a city-state's independence in opposition to claims grounded in a traditional interpretation of Roman law that gave all the rights of a classical Roman emperor to the medieval imperial officeholder. Traditional and conventional legal thinking held that a city-state or any other would-be independent constituency could lay claim to independence from the empire on the sole theoretical basis that its independence had specific legal sanction—an approach that offered no prima facie legal capital for Baldus in arguing the case for his city-state clients.

Along with Bartolus, Baldus accepted on theoretical legal grounds that the emperor was a universal ruler, but without construing universal in any essentially geographical way; universality did not necessarily entail geographic universality. Further, however, and again following his master, Baldus was careful to distinguish between theory and practice, and he also established more than the distinction between *de iure* and *de facto* by providing a legal basis for the actual state of affairs in northern Italy. He asserted that, whatever legal theory, as expressed in various statutes of the Code, was enshrined in Roman classical law, the current emperor simply did not exercise actual political authority over identifiable areas and regions; many northern Italian cities in fact were independent of imperial control. The reality was that various cities had been trying for some time to confirm their actual independence from the empire through some form of agreement giving them a kind of vicariate status wherein the emperor's authority and ultimate sovereignty was of a legitimizing rather than ruling kind.[24] Accordingly, northern Italy in the fourteenth century was a scene of competing, independent territorial powers, each with some form of grant from the empire. From as early as

24. Canning, *Political Thought of Baldus*, p. 19.

the mid-thirteenth century, *signori* had supplanted communal forms of government in most city-states and the number of democratic republics was diminishing steadily.

In the formality of argument, Baldus conceded that the emperor was "lord of the world" and God the ultimate source of imperial authority. Offering a sophisticated elaboration of this point, however, he asserted that the way the emperor held authority from God involved the age-old and much invoked *lex regia*.[25] The emperor held power from God, but through the Roman people; his legal status as emperor derived from the *lex regia*, by which the people had transferred political authority to him. Baldus asserted that the reality of universal imperial power rested on historical fact and described a four-stage process of its transfer from the people. Rulership rested originally in the Roman people by divine permission: in the beginning God gave sovereign power to the people by allowing them to possess it. The *populus* then transferred it to the emperor, who thus possessed sovereign authority in virtue of this popular concession. The third step was Christ's formal confirmation of the imperial jurisdiction ("render to Caesar"), while in the fourth and final stage, that in which humans now found themselves, the emperor's power was confirmed by the Church: as God's established divine instrument on earth the Church institutionalized imperial power by validating imperial elections through a papal coronation procedure.

Thus, Baldus was content to rest his case on existing political and apparently legal conditions and circumstances, while having no trouble accommodating the contemporary claims and circumstances of both empire and papacy. He maintained the divine origin and character of emperor and pope and acknowledged the universal jurisdiction of both, though of course in different spheres and with a nongeographical understanding of universal in the case of the emperor. He also accepted the typically medieval notion of a hierarchy of powers between papacy and empire or other forms of temporal authority. He even repeated the standard canonical claims for papal jurisdiction over temporal matters, but in a way that maintained the concept of imperial temporal sovereignty. He also accepted canonical views on the pope's role in appointing the emperor, while following the civilian position that papal

---

25. No such law ever existed as actual legislation. The *lex regia* was an *ex post facto* juristic construction to explain the legal origins of imperial power; it held that the Roman emperor's power derived from the people as its original source. See *Inst.* 1.2.6; d. Const. "*De auctore*"; d.1.4.1; 1.9.1; 1.17.1.1. Cf. Canning, *Political Thought of Baldus*, p. 25 and note 27.

confirmation in the coronation ritual dating back to Urban IV's crowning of Charlemagne in 800 was not essential in conferring imperial authority: for Baldus an emperor came into office because he was chosen by the electors. Baldus, moreover, was conservative in interpreting the *lex regia*. While viewing it as an historical act, he maintained that the people's action in relinquishing power to the emperor was irrevocable. Withal, however, the *lex regia* explained the human origin of imperial power just as the current papal practice of performing the imperial coronation exhibited its divine verification, but it provided neither a universal nor general model for how all governmental authority should be instituted.

Baldus appealed to another legal concept, *ius gentium*, as the basis for any general or universalizable feature of temporal polity. As he saw it, the problem was to accommodate the sovereignty of an individual territorial state within the two universal jurisdictions of empire and papacy. His solution was to emphasize the distinction between the *de iure* character of the universal jurisdictions of emperor and pope and the *de facto* conditions of various particular national or regional states, *de facto* in that he attributed legal validity to these conditions. Baldus did not deny *de iure* authority to either emperor or pope, as some Neapolitan jurists had done in respect of imperial authority by invoking the formula that "the king is emperor in his own kingdom." Rather, he employed imaginatively the standard medieval theological distinction between God's absolute and ordinary powers (*potestas absoluta et potestas ordinaria*).[26]

For Baldus, the emperor could legally exercise sovereign power over various smaller political units under imperial jurisdiction, but did not. Instead, in exercising his *potestas ordinaria*, he recognized existing forms of law, the most critical of which was the *ius gentium*; and by doing so he accepted that these smaller polities exercised their own sovereign power. The emperor agreed to follow existing laws and exercise only his "ordinary" rather than his "absolute" power, even though he could set aside existing legalities if he were to exercise the latter. Aegidius of Rome had used the same distinction almost a century earlier to explain the papacy's *de iure* power over all forms of temporal authority, arguing that the pope, by virtue of his superior spiritual status, had "both swords" and *de iure* could exercise both spiritual and temporal universal authority. According to Aegidius, however, he normally chose not to do so, prefer-

---

26. See the later use made of this distinction in discussion of the theory of the absolute right of kings: *infra*, pp. 287–88.

ring to operate according to his ordinary rather than absolute power, thus behaving as God does in the physical universe by allowing the natural laws of physics to function and intervening only rarely by performing miracles. Similarly, the pope allowed temporal rulers to exercise authority in the application of (their) ordinary laws and intervened only in very serious matters for which he was especially competent.[27] For Baldus, of course, one limit always operated even on the emperor's exercise of absolute power, viz., higher norms imposed from the three more transcendental types of law: *ius naturae, ius gentium,* and *ius divinum,* a limitation every medieval political writer placed on every type of authority, temporal and spiritual.

Another important feature of Baldus's treatment of the sovereignty of independent city-states was his theory of consent, which had such an important role in the later development of political thought. Again following Bartolus, he accepted the *Codex iuris civilis* as the basic legal context, an approach that seemed to offer little scope for his purpose. But Baldus stressed the same point Bartolus had seen so clearly: that popular consent was an essential ingredient in lawmaking activity and could therefore function as an adequate alternative to the will of a political superior (such as the emperor) in the provision of cause for legal and political fact. Baldus also followed Bartolus in emphasizing the role of popular consent and custom as critical foundation stones for the legal independence of city-states from imperial jurisdiction.[28] For Baldus there were two sources for political sovereignty or jurisdiction: privilege from the emperor or *princeps,* and prescription through custom. Here Baldus roughly reflected the twofold distinction employed earlier by Thomas Aquinas and others with regard to the two sources of political authority, God and the people. Consent was the cause and substance of law in both its basic forms, custom and statute. Custom was law produced through tacit consent, while statute law was made by express consent, and the only difference between them was the form of consent given them by the people.

There was still, of course, the theoretical question of whether the legal status of popular consent through custom required agreement from the higher imperial power. And while Baldus did not address this issue directly, it is clear that he considered the people able to legislate on their own behalf without specific authorization from a higher authority. The

27. Aegidius of Rome, *De potestate ecclesiastica,* 3.7, pp. 248–52.
28. See *supra,* p. 23.

power to do so was innate, inherent in the *populus* that was itself a legislative entity. Baldus's argument aimed at establishing political autonomy for individual city-states in fourteenth-century Italy, but its basis in the *ius gentium* could be expanded into a general theory of sovereignty.

Baldus's overall position was that people possess an autonomous capacity to legislate through the exercise of their own judgment, an aspect of the power of jurisdiction derived from the *ius gentium* itself, although he accepted that this capacity could be obscured where the hierarchical structures of the *ius commune* (by which he meant Roman law) were operative. But he contended that popular rights of self-government under the *ius gentium* re-emerge wherever a people is freed from the restrictions of the *ius commune*, something that occurs in part even when the people's autonomy exists only *de facto* and fully when it exists *de consuetudine*. Here Baldus was very close to expressing a fully articulated doctrine of popular sovereignty; all that was needed was the final step of asserting non-recognition of any superior, the crucial stage in achieving sovereignty through the exercise of popular will.

Without inserting this essential feature of the modern concept of sovereignty into his theory, Baldus nonetheless stressed the *de facto* independence of Italian city-states in that they did not obey the emperor on a regular basis. He conceded for purposes of argumentation that statutes passed by a city-state would require the emperor's approval, were the emperor actually present and in a position to exercise authority in any meaningful sense; the emperor could thus be said still to exercise some form of control *de iure*. But this was quite irrelevant given the current circumstance that the emperor was almost literally nowhere to be found.

Theoretically, then, Baldus did not attribute full sovereign power (*plena potestas*) to city-states but assigned it instead only to emperor and pope. Moreover, he limited a city-state's power further with the traditional insistence that any form of political authority and positive law falls under the transcendental norms of natural and divine law. And while these limitations were exclusively moral and lacked coercive force, they were taken seriously by jurists, publicists, theologians, and philosophers of his day, as well as by rulers themselves who, largely speaking, did not exhibit the cynicism or machiavellian propensities we are wont to associate with people seeking to exercise political power. Baldus made no suggestion about how this normative structure was to be enforced, however, although he did accept the general notion of papal intervention in the temporal sphere *ratione peccati*. He also supported the right of city-states to resist interventions from outside political forces such as emperor or pope, on the grounds that city-state authorities had an obligation to protect the common good of their citizens, who themselves had the right to judge emperor or political pope in terms of how either furthered the citizens' common interests.[29]

Two other notions developed by Baldus are also worth mentioning in connection with his general political thought. First, he extended the Aristotelian concept of the individual human being as naturally social and political to the point of indicating that individuals were *eo ipso* naturally citizens in their own society: the status of citizenship was somehow integral to human nature. This meant that all individuals in a given polity should be considered equal and that all shared equally in citizenship status. Secondly, reacting to William of Ockham's discussion of the medieval notion of corporation in Ockham's argument with the papacy over the Franciscan concept of poverty and the legitimacy of Christians actually owning property, having *dominium* over material goods, he reasserted that the *populus* as a whole was somehow a natural entity. Ockham had rejected the papal view that religious communities and churches could own property with the blunt contention that the legal concept of corporation designated a fictive entity and not a real thing, given that only individuals were real substances. For his part, Baldus held that the people enjoyed natural rather than merely fictive rights.

Baldus needed to consider the community of individuals that constituted a polity as something more than a fictive entity if he was to advance the notion that the natural status of the *populus* was that of a common body possessing rights and abilities to perform legitimate actions on their own behalf. Again Baldus was clearly foreshadowing the modern concept of state, that of a legal entity possessed of rights. His unique contribution to political thought in this regard was to combine a fully articulated juristic view of corporation with an ultimately Aristotelian conception of the state as a collection of natural political entities. The result was a concept of a territorial state that was legally both more complex and more comprehensive than anything previously developed in medieval political theory. The *populus* was a commonweal conceived of as a specific type of corporation.

The essentially corporationist aspects of the legal theories of Bartolus and Baldus were reflected again in conciliarist thought in the late fourteenth and fifteenth centuries, as well as in various forms of sixteenth-

---

29. There is a partial anticipation here of the Lutheran resistance-theory argument that "lesser magistrates" and political authorities subordinate to the emperor can oppose imperial tyranny exercised against subjects in their charge. Cf. *infra*, pp. 210–11.

century resistance theory. One of the most interesting earlier Italian formulations of this corporationist view was offered by the Dominican preacher and writer Girolamo Savonarola (1452–98), a very influential supporter of the Florentine republic that was temporarily restored after the anti-Medici coup in 1494. Though expressed in eschatological and millenarian terms, Savonarola's position was basically that of Bartolus of Sassoferrato, Marsilius of Padua, and Ptolemy of Lucca, the last of whom he sometimes followed word for word.

Savonarola's most systematic statement in favour of Florentine republicanism was the *Trattato circa il reggimento e governo della citta di Firenza* (1498). Here he asserted that the traditional view of monarchy as the best form of government was not applicable to Florence, which needed a republican form of polity to provide "true liberty" for its citizens as their "most precious possession." He went on to offer what had by then become the conventional view—Bartolus and Marsilius's argument that the best method of preserving civic liberty was through a stable system of citizen councils whose authority was delegated by the whole body of the people. Savonarola argued in the traditional corporationist way that the only certain method for maintaining liberty was to accept the whole people as supreme authority in all political affairs.[30]

Another example of the continuing medieval corporationist and scholastic influence on later Italian political thought was Mario Salamonio's *Patritii Romani de principatu* (1544), written shortly after the 1512–14 crisis in Rome precipitated by the uprising against papal tyranny. Salamonio (c.1450–1532) was a member of a Roman patrician family and a leading jurist of his day, as well as a political activist. He was one of the first writers to emphasize that Italy's political problems stemmed from the combination of military weakness and excessive wealth that invited attack from external conquerors, a view expressed later by Machiavelli and Guicciardini. His basic political position stressed that effective political institutions had to be based on the whole body of citizens as the ultimate source of political authority, and he spoke of "the *imperium* of the Roman people [with] no *princeps* [or] true overlord in Rome [but] only a minister of the people."[31]

---

30. Girolamo Savonarola, "Trattato circa il reggimento e governo della citta di Firenza," pp. 446–50; 481; 488 and 471. Cf. Savonarola, "De politia et regno," pp. 576–99. For Savonarola's repetition of the text of Ptolemy of Lucca's *De regimine principum* 4.8, see Weinstein, *Savonarola and Florence*, p. 292, note and p. 293. I hope to publish soon an English translation of Savonarola's text *De politia et regno*.

31. Salamonio, *Patritii Romani de principatu*, fol. 55A–B. Cf. Skinner, *Foundations*, 1:148–52.

A final word on Baldus's influence. Scholarly jurisprudence of the type he practised continued to be very significant for both the study and practice of law in succeeding centuries, and was to exert considerable influence right into the seventeenth century, largely through its currency in legal education. Baldus was also referred to frequently by later political writers: Bodin mentions him often; there are references to his views among the later neo-scholastic writers, such as Suárez; and he appears in Grotius.

### 4. FIFTEENTH-CENTURY HUMANIST POLITICAL THOUGHT

Skinner makes much of the mistaken interpretation he attributes to Baron concerning the novelty of the "civic humanism," centred in Florence, of the fifteenth century. Baron's thesis was that the development of Florentine political thought, with its emphasis on liberty and civic involvement, dated from successful Florentine efforts, beginning in 1402, to defend itself against Milan and others and preserve the Florentine republic. According to Skinner, however, Baron overlooked two points: the extent to which "civic humanism" in Florence was anticipated elsewhere in northern Italy; and the links between fifteenth-century Florentine humanism and "the wider movement of Petrarchan humanism which had already developed in the course of the fourteenth century."[32]

On the first point, Skinner asserts that Baron scanted the extent to which the early quattrocento Florentine writers followed in the footsteps of the medieval *dictatores*. Following Kristeller, he sees an important element of continuity in the fact that both groups generally received the same kind of legal training and went on to occupy similar professional roles as teachers of rhetoric in Italian universities and as secretaries employed by cities and the Church. He cites Coluccio Salutati (1331–1406), the elder statesman of the fifteenth-century Florentine humanists, as a case in point.[33] He also mentions Leonardo Bruni (1369–1444), Pier Paulo Vergerio (1370–1444), and Poggio Bracciolini (1380–1459) as followers of Salutati who all made similar contributions to the expression of quattrocento Florentine political thought in a series of treatises that exhibit a remarkable similarity of

---

32. Skinner, *Foundations*, 1:71. Cf. Baron, *Crisis of the Early Italian Renaissance.*
33. Skinner, *Foundations*, 1:71.

content and approach and bridge the gap between the early fourteenth century and the works of Machiavelli and Guicciardini in the early sixteenth.[34]

Skinner is careful, however, not to overstress the similarities between these humanists and the earlier *dictatores*. Whereas the *dictatores* tended to discuss dangers to liberty in terms of factional problems, the later writers showed no such emphasis, probably because they considered that the constitutional difficulties of the Florentine republic had largely been solved by a relatively stable form of oligarchy. The dilemma over how to resolve the tension between individual freedoms and political stability seemed to have been overcome in favour of the second and at the expense of the first. By the time of Bruni, for example, and he seems typical in this connection, the assumption apparently was being made that if all individuals pursued their own interests "with industry" and "quickness in matters of business," the ultimate effect of this enlightened self-interest would benefit the republic as a whole,[35] a considerably different line from the earlier advocacy of political involvement as the touchstone of liberty.

Coluccio Salutati provides a clear illustration of this contrast. Trained in rhetoric in Bologna under Pietro de Muglio, he enjoyed a long career as a civil servant and chancellor in several Tuscan cities: Todi in 1367, Lucca in 1370, and ultimately Florence, where he served from 1375 until his death. As early as the 1360s he was voicing the need to base the independence of city-states on their citizens' willingness to act directly to defend their interests by taking up arms, rather than counting on mercenary troops to do their fighting for them. He returned to the same lament in 1383 in a letter describing affairs in Florence.[36]

Salutati conceived of liberty and independence in the traditional way, as denoting both independence from external forces and self-government; freedom from external interference coupled with the opportunity to take part in governing one's own polity. Of course, this view was not born with the humanists, as Baron tried to maintain, but continued a line of argument found in the thirteenth and fourteenth centuries among scholastics and legists such as Remigio, Ptolemy, and Bartolus.

---

34. Completed in 1513 and published two years later, Machiavelli's *Prince* predates Luther's posting of his Reform theses by only two years; and Guicciardini's *Maxims and Reflections* and *History of Italy* both appeared in the 1530s.
35. Skinner, *Foundations*, 1:74.
36. Salutati, "Epistolario," in Novati, ed., *Fonti per la storia d'Italia*, 2:85.

Salutati was a committed republican and asserted in no uncertain terms the superiority of this form of government over the more normal monarchical type. As Bruni did later, he mounted an explicit attack on monarchy in a public letter issued in 1378.[37] In extending public congratulations to Florence for its republican form of government, he contended that the city had been founded originally by Sulla's veterans from the last days of the Roman republic, rather than by the later imperial efforts of Julius Caesar. He also made clear that humanist writers like Petrarch supported the values of independent republican city-states. He praised Petrarch extravagantly for stressing the Ciceronian ideal of the *vir virtutis*, and for emphasizing rhetoric and the rhetorical form of education as the means of instilling the needed *virtus*; Salutati advocated a combination of the two as a basis for patriotism in a modern *regnum Italicum*. This advocacy, as well as Salutati's commitment to the republican ideal, can be seen in another public letter addressed in 1377 to the people of Rome, asking them to "recall the ancient *virtus*" in efforts to resist papal tyranny aimed at bringing about "the desolation of Italy."[38]

Salutati also heaped praise on Petrarch in a 1406 letter that spoke of the great fourteenth-century humanist as having "brought back the light" of Latin literature, thereby "recovering and reviving a form of study which had previously been almost dead."[39] At the same time, however, and perhaps somewhat quixotically, he was prepared to offer direct support to a single ruler in a late work, *A Treatise on Tyrants* (c.1400) and to caution against any justification of tyrannicide such as had been made in some thirteenth- and fourteenth-century scholastic works on politics. He even referred to Julius Caesar in favourable terms, denying that he was in any sense a tyrant.[40]

Leonardo Bruni (1369–1444) was another northern Italian early quattrocento humanist, political thinker, and agent who reflected the Italian city-state connection between training in the rhetorical and legal tradition and support for republicanism. After studying law and rhetoric at Florence in the 1390s he entered secretarial service with the papal curia in 1406, returning to Florence about ten years later to serve as chancellor of the republic until his death. Like Salutati, he was an outspoken advocate for the republican form of Florentine government, and he con-

37. Ibid., 2:386–93.
38. Ibid., 2:141, 143.
39. Ibid., 4:161. For his own part, Salutati discovered the full text of Cicero's *Familiar Letters* in 1392.
40. Salutati, "Treatise on Tyrants," pp. 81; 91–93; 94–100.

stantly insisted on the need for all citizens to do their share personally in any military defence of the values of their polity. He argued forcefully in his *Laudatio Florentinae urbis* that every citizen had to be ready "to bear arms for the preservation of liberty" and praised the earlier Florentines who had prevailed over Volterra in the mid-thirteenth century for having "acted by themselves without the help of any foreign auxiliaries, fighting on their own behalf and contending as much as possible for glory and dignity."[41]

Bruni was also explicit in his insistence that liberty entailed a constitution under which every citizen enjoyed equal opportunity to involve themselves in the business of government. His *Eulogy* praised the Florentine political organization for ensuring that "the people and their liberty dominate everything [such that] the maintenance of liberty is nowhere as well assured."[42] Elsewhere he asserted that the basic virtue in the constitution of Florence was that it made it "equally possible for everyone to take part in the affairs of the Republic [guaranteeing that] everything is directed to the greatest possible extent towards maintaining the liberty as well as the equality of all its citizens ... no one has to stand in awe of anyone else's power or capacity to do them harm ... the control of the city is always prevented from falling into the hands of one or a few people."[43] He also drew a bead on the monarchical form of government, arguing in his *Oratio in funere Nannis Strozae* that kings cannot expect to be well served because "good men are a source of greater suspicion to them than bad men, the reason being that virtue in anyone other than themselves is always threatening to them."[44] Popular government is "the only legitimate form ... [it] makes possible true liberty and equality before the law for the whole body of the citizens [and also] enables the cultivation of the virtues to flourish without any suspicions being aroused."[45]

Bruni also added a novel point to the conventional humanist panegyric on republican liberties, a point that found considerable resonance in later humanist and other political writings: the alleged connection between a polity's freedom and its greatness. He spoke in the *Oratio* of a

---

41. Bruni, "Laudatio Florentinae urbis," p. 200. The Latin text is in Baron, *From Petrarch to Leonardo Bruni*, pp. 217–63.

42. Bruni, "Laudatio," pp. 260; 262.

43. Bruni, "Oratio in funere Nannis Strozae," in Stephanus Baluzius, *Miscellanea*, 4:2–7, esp. 3.

44. Ibid., p. 3.

45. Ibid.

republic's special merit being reflected in "the hope of rising to public honours, of building up a career by one's own efforts, [which] is the same for everyone [the result being that men] rouse themselves and raise themselves up as soon as the honour is held out to them, whereas they collapse into idleness as soon as it is withdrawn ... as soon as a capacity for rising to honours and pursuing power is made available to a free people [it has] the effect of calling forth their talents."[46] Applying this principle directly to Florence, he concluded that "it is not at all surprising [that the city] is so outstanding for its talents and industry [since] this hope of honour is in fact held out, and these energies are in fact released amongst all the citizens of our city."[47] His effusive praise for the political *status quo* in Florence was also reflected in his agreement with Salutati that the city could only have been founded by republican Romans: because so well known for its republican liberties, "this colony must have been established at the time when the city of Rome flourished most greatly in its power and liberty, [when] the liberty of the people had not yet been stolen from them by any Caesar, Antony, Tiberius or Nero."[48]

The connection Bruni made between political liberty and civic power or greatness is a significant departure from previous formulations of political thought, where the purpose of political action had always been expressed in terms of the common good. While political power, wealth, and greatness are not in themselves incompatible with the common good as the end of political authority, stress on these values encourages the more aggressive and less attractive features of human motivation. Machiavelli pressed the same point without reservation in the *Prince*, and Thomas More was to point to exactly this moral in his indirect criticism of humanist political thought in *Utopia*.[49]

Another aspect of Bruni's thought that contrasted with earlier scholasticism was his rejection of the Aristotelian view that contemplation was the highest form of human behaviour. In his *Life of Dante*, he praised his subject for retaining an interest in the life of his city even while engaging in the most intensive studies and contended that it was a "false opinion [of] ignorant persons [to hold] that no one is a student save he who buries himself in solitude and ease ... to estrange and absent oneself from society is peculiar to those whose poor minds unfit them for knowl-

46. Ibid., pp. 3–4.
47. Ibid.
48. Bruni, "Laudatio," p. 235.
49. See *infra*, p. 46.

edge of any kind."⁵⁰ In contrast to the earlier *dictatores* and later, more cynical, humanist political writers who advocated the contemplative life, and unlike Salutati, who was an admirer of monarchy, Bruni addressed his remarks on leading a civic life to "the whole body of citizens."⁵¹ It was not until the complete collapse of the Florentine republic in the 1480s that one finds again an emphasis on the life of contemplation, for example, in Marsilio Ficino and Pico della Mirandola.⁵² But like Salutati, Bruni praised Petrarch as "the man who restored the *studia humanitatis* when such studies were extinct, and showed us the way to gain learning for ourselves."⁵³ Also in keeping with Salutati and following Petrarch, he offered an alternative to the Augustinian conception of human nature as ineradicably damaged by sin and therefore unable on its own to achieve the highest orders of virtue.⁵⁴

## 5. SIXTEENTH-CENTURY HUMANIST POLITICAL THOUGHT

During the fifteenth century, as affairs in the Italian peninsula became increasingly embroiled in imperial and other efforts at conquest, and in internal and internecine rivalry and strife, monarchy again became the preferred form of polity among humanist political writers. As life in the northern city-states and Rome became more and more choatic, the values of security and stability became more significant in the eyes of var-

50. Bruni, "Life of Dante," p. 84.
51. Bruni, "Dialogus," p. 78; cf. "Oratio," p. 3. Skinner notes Bruni's "implied rebuke" of Salutati's monarchism here, as well as Leon Battista Alberti's more explicit republicanism in "The Family": Skinner, *Foundations*, 1:109. Alberti's work is in *The Albertis of Florence*, pp. 27–326.
52. Skinner cites Ficino's "Introductio ad commentationes Platonis," in Ficino, *Opera omnia*, 2:116; 117; and Giovanni Pico della Mirandola, "Oration on the Dignity of Man," in Cassirev et al., eds., *The Renaissance Philosophy of Man*, p. 238. Skinner, *Foundations*, 1:117.
53. Bruni, "Dialogus," p. 94.
54. Skinner considers that this emphasis on the development of natural human goodness through education in rhetoric and humane letters—that is, Greek and Latin literature—was really novel among the early Italian humanists. But caution is called for here: Aristotle's optimistic conception of the naturally good human being expressed in his *Ethics* and *Politics* would also have exercised some influence by this itme through scholastic sources.
One clear and important non-Aristotelian point about humanist political thought was its emphasis on the good human life as active rather than contemplative. Only later, when all the northern Italian city-states except Venice had succumbed to new forms of *podesta-*type tyranny, did humanist voices begin to view withdrawal from civic affairs as the mark of the wise man.

ious political writers and ordinary citizens alike, and Plato's predictions in the *Republic* that popular government would give way to single-ruler tyranny as a solution to the chaos of equality and freedom were borne out. Except in Venice and Florence, *podestà*-type rule became the norm, and the "mirror for princes" genre again became the common literary vehicle for expressing political thought, with the humanist notion of *vir virtutis* as the princely image. Honour, glory, and fame were emphasized as the goals of political rule. It is not difficult to see how advocating achievement of these goals through a single ruler would be likely to lead, at least indirectly, to a lessening of emphasis on the common good as the object of political authority. The common good would be construed largely in terms of protection and peace for ordinary citizens, whose personal civic good would come to mean little more than being able to bask in the reflected glory and honour of their "prince." The most single-minded and self-serving expression of this attitude was, of course, Machiavelli's *Prince*, whose contents set its author apart in a dramatic way from earlier humanist writers, but whose format and style reflect a standard form of political treatise going back to the early Middle Ages.

The Peace of Lodi (1454) saw the end of the struggle in Italy between republicanism and "princely" forms of government. The triumph of the latter was decisive, extending virtually everywhere except for a short time at the end of century, when republican forces in Florence and Rome tried to take advantage of the current French incursion into Italy to reestablish a republican form of government. Venice, of course, was the other exception. In fact, the success of the Venetian republican form of government in preserving the independence and security of its citizens had already become a matter of interest to humanist political writers by the end of the fourteenth century. The standard account paid tribute to the structure of the Venetian political model for having retained the form it received under a constitution established in 1297: a standard three-tier form of Italian city-state polity with a great council that appointed most of its government officials, a senate that controlled financial and foreign affairs, and a doge who served along with his council as elected head of government. In effect, Venice was a republican oligarchy rather than a democracy; the "people" were its leading citizens who constituted the great council and appointed a single ruler. Though several popular uprisings occurred in the course of the fourteenth century, none was successful, and the general atmosphere and tenor of political stability made Venice unique at the time among other less-fortunate Italian city-states.

In their admiring descriptions of the Venetian republican model, however, humanist political writers presented it as a "mixed" form of government. The first to do so was Pier Paolo Vergerio in a letter to the chancellor of Venice in 1394. He remarked that Venice exemplified the view expressed in Plato's *Laws* that the best and most secure form of polity fused monarchy, aristocracy, and democracy.[55] Other examples of the admiration of Florentine republicans for their Venetian neighbours were Donato Giannotti's *Libro della repubblica de Viniziani*, drafted in Venice in 1525 and published in 1540 when Giannotti, a friend of Machiavelli and fervent republican, was in exile from his native Florence,[56] and *The Commonwealth and Government of Venice* (1543), a panegyric by Gasparo Contarini (1483–1542).[57] Both works rested on the basic assumption that Venice had a mixed form of government, echoing Serverino's reverence for the "democratic" character of the great council and treating the senate as aristocracy and the doge as monarch.

The temporary revival and ultimate swan-song of Florentine republicanism after the anti-Medici coup in 1494 saw the last and greatest series of humanist political writings that included the republican treatises of Guicciardini and Machiavelli, though the beginnings of a revival of Florentine republicanism had begun as early as the mid-quattrocento. Francisco Patrizi (1413–92) produced a major work of republican political thought in the 1460s, *De institutione reipublicae*.[58] This was followed in the 1470s by Alamanno Rinucci's tract *Dialogus de libertate*,[59] and Donato Acciavoli's commentaries on Aristotle's *Ethics* and *Politics*, as well as his history of the Roman campaigns against Carthage.[60] Ironically, perhaps, it was the period of the return of the Medicis after 1512 that saw the greatest flowering of republican thought in Florence in the writings of Guicciardini, Machiavelli, and Donato Giannotti.

---

55. Pier Paolo Vergerio, "On Good Manners," trans. W. H. Woodward, in *Vittorino da Feltre and Other Humanist Educators*, pp. 96–118. The notion of the perfection of a "mixed" form of polity was also noted by typical medieval political thinkers like Thomas Aquinas and John of Paris. Cf. Thomas Aquinas, *ST* 1-2.105.1; John of Paris, *Royal and Papal Power*, 19 *ad* 35, p. 100, cf. *infra*, p. 67. It also appeared in conciliarist thought in d'Ailly and Gerson: *infra*, pp. 81 and 92.
56. Donato Giannotti, "Della reppublica fiorentina," in *Opere*, 2:1–278.
57. Gasparo Contarini, "The Commonwealth and Government of Venice."
58. Francisco Patrizi, *De institutione reipublicae*.
59. Rinuccini, "Dialogus de libertate," pp. 265–303.
60. Baron, *Crisis of Early Italian Renaissance*, p. 437.

Though something of a closet republican, Francesco Guicciardini survived the return of the Medicis in 1512 better than Machiavelli, whose efforts to ingratiate himself with Lorenzo de' Medici led to the writing of *The Prince*, though he shared Guicciardini's republican leanings. Guicciardini served both Medici popes, Leo X and Clement VII, in a series of political appointments. His political writings span the period of Medici rule from 1512 to their permanent return as Florentine rulers in 1530. *Del modo di ordinare il governo popolare (The Discourse of Legrogno)* was written in 1512 when he was serving on a Florentine diplomatic mission to Spain. At the same time he began to sketch his *Maxims and Reflections*, completed and published between 1528 and 1530. He composed two other political works, *Dialogo del reggimento di Firenza* (1521–23), and the incomplete *Considerations on the "Discourses" of Machiavelli on the first Decade of T. Livy* (c.1530), before publishing his great *History of Italy*.[61]

Guicciardini took the standard humanist line in extolling the values of liberty in a city-state, but he gave his position a tendentious grounding in Roman republican history, as Salutati and Bruni had done earlier, and Remigio de' Girolami and Ptolemy of Lucca earlier still, and as Machiavelli did in his *Discourses*. He was more reluctant than Machiavelli, however, to view political liberty as a realistic ideal in existing circumstances and considered republicanism to have many defects, though it was the lesser of two political evils: he acknowledged that popular government was "better than princely" and favoured republicanism of the mixed representational form because it ensured liberty. But, like Patrizi, he espoused a more aristocratic form of representation through a small and close-knit group and criticized Machiavelli on this point.[62]

Guicciardini and Machiavelli both repeated the point first made by Salamonio, that the principal cause of the miseries of the Italian city-states was their excessive devotion to private wealth. They equally condemned the use of mercenary troops, as did Patrizi and Donato Giannotti, the last theorist of Florentine republicanism and an expert on the Venetian constitution. Giannoti returned to his native Florence from Venice in 1527 when the Medicis were expelled for the second time and helped organize the civic militia in unsuccessful efforts to defend the city

---

61. Guicciardini's writings are available as follows: "Considerations on the 'Discourses' of Machiavelli" in *Selected Writings*, pp. 57–124; "Dialogo e discorsi del reggimento di Firenze" and "Del modo di ordinare il governo popolare" in *Dialogo e discorsi del reggimento di Firenze*, respectively at pp. 1–172 and 218–59; "Maxims and Reflections of a Renaissance Statesman" and "History of Italy" in *History of Italy and History of Florence*.
62. Cf. Guicciardini, *Maxims*, p. 100, and *Considerations*, pp. 66, 106.

against the returning Medicis in 1529–30. He went into exile when the Medicis succeeded in the final suppression of Florentine republicanism and wrote his *Della republica fiorenta* to accompany an earlier history of Venice.[63] These late advocates of republicanism, especially Machiavelli and Giannotti, identified a third cause for the loss of their preferred form of government in the "corruption of the people."[64]

By far the most important early sixteenth-century Italian political writer, at least from the perspective of his influence on subsequent political thought, was Niccolò Machiavelli, whose treatise dedicated to Lorenzo de' Medici has earned him a unique place in the history of Western political theory. Machiavelli's *The Prince*, finished in 1513 and dedicated to Lorenzo the Magnificent in 1515, marked a definite turning point in the formulation of political ideology even though it was not specifically designed to set out a full-blown ideology; it aimed rather at little more than providing the kind of advice for rulers found in a series of political tracts going back at least as far as John of Salisbury's *Policraticus*. There is little reason to think that Machiavelli had any notion he was writing for a posterity that would divide strongly over its assessment of his work, with some condemning him as a simple- and single-minded immoralist, and others praising him for producing virtually the first work of political thought that "told it like it was" and offered serious and practical advice to those who would exercise political authority.

The novel feature of *The Prince*, and the one responsible for dividing the house, was its direct and deliberate advocacy of a set of "virtues" to be practised by a ruler that differed from those traditionally espoused by earlier political theorists. Machiavelli took direct aim at those who would advise rulers to embody and employ the standard Christian virtues governing individual behaviour and advocated that another set of values should be practised instead by anyone who would exercise political power as it should be exercised. In effect, he accepted the humanist combination of honour, glory, and fame in a ruler, the *vir virtutis*, and tailored his advice to rulers strictly in terms of the means necessary to achieve these ends in a polity. Thus, to Machiavelli, the aim of political rule was the preservation and expansion of a ruler's power rather than the more traditional aim of preserving and expanding the common

---

63. Donato Giannotti, "Della republica fiorentia," in *Opere*, 2:1–279; "Libro della republica de Viniziani," in *Opere*, 1:1–243.
64. Machiavelli, *Discourses*, 1.17 and 18.

good. Of course, it can be argued that preservation and expansion of a ruler's power is compatible with pursuit of the common good insofar as a state that does not survive and whose ruler does not achieve and maintain greatness cannot offer much to its citizens. But this was not the argument Machiavelli made in *The Prince*. Further, emphasis on a ruler's self-preservation in office carried much more the tone of advantage to the ruler than advantage to the ruled, and absence of explicit reference to the common good only served to underline this point.

Not that Machiavelli stressed this dichotomy. Indeed, he was careful, in the ambiguous style in which he presented his case, not to indicate that he had put the common good in the shade, presumably because to do so would risk collapsing the distinction between good ruler and tyrant that went back to Plato and Aristotle and constituted the touchstone of all previous medieval political theory. Arguably, however, Machiavelli does not deserve blunt condemnation as a simple immoralist who blandly and without apology insisted that the end justifies the means. Any ethical teleology of the sort advanced by both classical and Christian moral philosophers accepted, and even insisted, that the end does justify the means: what, apart from its end or purpose, can justify any action? The house divides, so to speak, on what the proper end of political authority is, and it seems clear that in *The Prince* it is the preservation and well-being of the single ruler in office.

Elsewhere Machiavelli expressed a different, slightly more comprehensive theory of polity, emphasizing the usual humanist political notion of liberty in a republican context. The *Discourses* were begun about 1514 and completed before the end of 1519. It had become clear, while he worked on them, that his efforts to curry favour with the Medicis had been stillborn, and Machiavelli now appeared as an advocate of self-government and of the earlier Florentine humanist notion of liberty as independence from external aggression and tyranny. His general attitude in the *Discourses* is hostile to monarchy and favourable towards republicanism as the best form of government because the most likely to provide for the liberty of its citizenry. The ideal of political liberty was the theme in the first three books of the *Discourses*, and Machiavelli employed as his context the standard historical account of Italian republicanism in ancient Rome seen in the early fourteenth century in Remigio de' Girolami and Ptolemy of Lucca.[65]

---

65. See *supra*, pp. 17–18.

The *Discourses* also addressed the issues of how republican ideals had been lost and how, if at all, they might be recovered. As noted earlier, Machiavelli emphasized excessive devotion to private wealth as a sign of civic decadence and singled out dependence on mercenary armies as a fatal sign of this weakness. The most important and particular form of this corruption was exclusion of the people from an active role in government, corruption being equated with "ineptitude for a free life," which in turn rested on "the inequality one finds in a city" when oligarchy functions as the political norm.[66] In explaining how such a state of affairs had come about, Machiavelli made explicit a view expressed only indirectly in *The Prince*: that the virtues needed for proper political rule and the achievement of greatness in a commonwealth are different from those espoused by Christianity. When describing the *vir virtutis* in *The Prince*, Machiavelli had emphasized the Aristotelian distinction between the virtues of an ordinary individual and those required for the exercise of public office;[67] in the *Discourses*, he openly rejected the ordinary Christian virtues of truth-telling, modesty, and humility as those needed for political authority. He even criticized Christianity for having stressed such humble values, inimical as they are to the attainment of civic greatness. While accepting that religious practices help to keep a commonwealth "good and united" and that "those princes and republics desiring to remain free from corruption above all else should maintain incorrupt the ceremonies of their religion," Machiavelli went on to assert that the "right" values of "magnanimity, bodily strength and everything that conduces to make men very bold"[68] are essential and must be stressed. And while conceding that Christianity could have performed this function, he faulted it for having emphasized the wrong values by assigning "as man's highest good humility, abnegation and contempt for mundane things," thereby espousing a way of life that made the world weak and handed it over "as a prey to the wicked."[69] Guicciardini picked up this point with alacrity.[70] The deliberate expression here of preference for the "old religion" of the Romans with its hierarchy of "manly" civic virtues and its emphasis on the use of physical force could not go unnoticed.

66. Machiavelli, *Discourses*, 1.17. Cf. Skinner, *Foundations*, 1:166.
67. Aristotle, *Politics*, 3.4.1276b11–31.
68. Machiavelli, *Discourses*, p. 278.
69. Ibid.
70. Guicciardini, *Maxims*, p. 104.

Machiavelli did not directly address the question of whether it might be possible to recover these former civic ideals, but indicated that earlier republican examples, especially the old Roman republic, should be studied as models. He placed his stress on the machinery of government, apparently assuming that there was some kind of fixed order in human behaviour that assured that what had worked in the past might be expected to do so again, an attitude criticized by Guicciardini.[71] Machiavelli identified the oligarchic element, the great council, as the appropriate locus of political authority in a republic. Unlike Patrizi and Guicciardini, he favoured a larger over a smaller one, "into whose hands it is best to place the guardianship of liberty."[72]

Machiavelli also adopted a different stance from conventional humanist political thought on the issue of "civil discord." Since Plato's criticism of democracy in *The Republic*, it had been accepted almost as a given that liberty for all citizens could be expected to lead to factional disputes and political chaos, civil tumult; the experiences of Italian city-states in the late medieval period suggested to humanist political thinkers that this was indeed a serious, if not intractable, problem. For his part, however, Machiavelli defended republican liberty in the *Discourses* on the grounds that, in this form of polity, conflicting class interests tended to cancel each other out: "All legislation favourable to liberty is brought about by the clash" between classes; hence this sort of conflict is the cement rather than the solvent of a state.[73]

It is ironic, perhaps, but not altogether surprising, that Machiavelli's reputation has been more negative than positive in Western intellectual history. It rests more on the self-interested text of *The Prince* than on what might be regarded as his more personally authentic views in support of republicanism and individual liberty in the *Discourses*. Even there, however, he favoured a form of republicanism in which ordinary citizens enjoyed only such freedom as their oligarchic rulers were prepared to grant, and this did not, in the final analysis, include their active participation in governance.

In this, of course, he differed little from earlier medieval constitutional thinkers, who were always indistinct about how individual citizens

---

71. Machiavelli, *Discourses*, Preface to 1; cf. Guicciardini, "Considerations," pp. 66, 101. Skinner notes that some modern scholars have attempted to renew this criticism of Machiavelli: *Foundations*, 1:169.
72. Machiavelli, *Discourses*, 1.5.
73. Machiavelli, *Discourses*, 1.4. Cf. Skinner, *Foundations*, 1:181.

should participate in governance even while insisting that legitimate authority had its limits—a point never expressly stated by Machiavelli. And he differed not at all from contemporary and earlier Italian humanist political writers whose emphasis on the liberty of citizens was always conditioned by their willingness to equate the purpose of political authority with civic fame. This attitude suggested that collective greatness and power, *virtù* in the sense of material and worldly magnificence rather than qualities of soul, was most obviously expressed in terms of public power and wealth. The contrast between these virtues of public greatness and the traditional Christian values of charity and humility had not been made explicit before Machiavelli and Guicciardini, but the potential to do so had existed from the beginnings of Christianity, and Marsilius of Padua had taken at least a step in this direction by asserting that law, properly understood, was grounded in coercive power.[74] Furthermore, the behaviour and lifestyle of prominent clerical members of the Church had for centuries illustrated the hypocrisy of many official exponents of the Christian way of life. The tension between a conceptually ideal society exhibiting only simple and modest virtues and one that displayed the full range of human values, including those exhibited in wealthy and sophisticated forms, was recognized by Plato, who had Glaucon respond to Socrates's first description of the perfect state in the *Republic* with the remark that such an idyllic form of pastoral existence was more like "a society for pigs." And Plato was equally perceptive when he had Socrates reply that inclusion of personal and civic greatness, wealth, and culture as social values was the cause of political aggrandizement and warfare.[75]

One of the features differentiating representatives of so-called "northern humanist"[76] political thought from their Italian confrères was their rejection of this seemingly necessary emphasis on things bellicose and

---

74. Gewirth, *The Defender of Peace*, 1.13. Cf. Monahan, *Consent, Coercion, and Limit*, p. 211 and n. 16.

75. Plato, *Republic* 373D–E. A recent, modest, but highly intriguing interpretation of More's *Utopia* connects More's ideal society and its explicit rejection of the Italian humanist model of civic glory with the original Platonic ideal republic as a simple arcadian society: Starnes, *The New Republic*.

76. Following Margaret Mann Phillips, Skinner uses the term "the northern humanists" along with "the northern Renaissance" to describe the spread of the humanist movement north of the Alps as well as into Spain and Portugal, and I have followed him on the point. Skinner, *Foundations*, 1:199, n. 2. He also expresses a carefully nuanced view showing the elements of continuity and similarity as well as those of regional and national differences between the native Italian form of humanism and its expression elsewhere: *Foundations*, 1:193–262.

military. Though by no means rejecting the use of military and coercive force in defence of political society,[77] Erasmus produced an eloquent statement against the horrors of war based on the Stoic and Christian notion that all humans are brothers and sisters. However, this statement was directed at least as much against the traditional Christian just-war theory, with its origins in St Augustine, as against his Italian fellow humanists.[78] The Erasmian view was echoed by More and Colet in England, as well as by Vives in Spain.[79] Erasmus was never prepared to accept warfare as a normal instrument of political society, any more than he countenanced the use of physical coercion to suppress what he perceived as the large-scale religious "dissent" of the Reformation.[80] Though expressed in an altogether different literary form, a similar view rejecting the Italian humanist emphasis on bearing arms in support of civic values can also be seen in Thomas More's *Utopia*: the Utopians found that bearing arms was distasteful and to be avoided wherever possible and, in contrast to the strictures of Italians like Guicciardini and Machiavelli, had no compunction about hiring others to engage in necessary military operations on their behalf. Nor was there any trace in the Utopia of aspirations to civic fame, greatness, and honour: More was particularly outspoken in repeating a criticism common to the northern humanists, that the chief defect in contemporary politics was failure to pursue the common good.[81] More also reverted to the more genuine republican position that recognized the value of involving all citizens in governing a polity. It is worth noting that the *Utopia* was much more than indirect advice to a prince or courtier; its audience was the literate public as a whole.

In general, the humanist writers north of the Alps and on the Iberian peninsula did not emphasize the two dominant features of Italian humanist political thought: the need to preserve political liberty and the

---

77. See Fernandez, "Erasmus on the Just War."

78. Desiderius Erasmus, *The Complaint of Peace*. Erasmus expressed his hatred of war in other texts as well, although the *Complaint* was one of his most popular writings. See, for example, his essay on *Dulce bellum inexpertis* in the 1515 edition of *The "Adages" of Erasmus*. Cf. Phillips, *Erasmus and the Northern Renaissance*, pp. 86–109, and Adams, *The Better Part of Valor*.

79. Colet's view on the traditional just-war theory can be found in his commentary on Paul to the Romans. Colet, *Exposition on St Paul's Epistle to the Romans*. Cf. Adams, *The Better Part of Valor*.

80. See *infra*, pp. 149–50.

81. More, "Utopia," in *Complete Works*, 4:205–07; 149; 211; 241.

danger it faced in the existence of mercenary forces. Naturally enough, this reflected different conditions of the political *status quo* in these areas: the dominance of hereditary monarchical forms of government in the north were inimical to republicanism, and the political realities in England, France, Spain, and Portugal obviated the issue of purchasing military power from "foreign" sources inasmuch as the capacity of these countries to raise national armies on their own was a function of their continuing development as nation-states. There were traces of discontinuity, then, between various national forms of humanism and their Italian primogenitor, as one would expect. At the same time, however, other broad and significant elements of continuity moved across national boundaries, and fundamental features of Italian humanism had lasting and far-reaching effects virtually everywhere else in western Europe.

One such effect was the near-universal acceptance among scholars and academics of the new humanist philological techniques and forms of historical criticism that were being applied to texts of the ancient world. One of the most radical and successful users of these methods of textual criticism was Lorenzo Valla, who applied them to the study of Roman legal texts, especially the Justinian *Code*. Through such works as his *Elegantiarum latinae linguae libri sex*, many of whose examples were taken from jurists like Ulpian, Marcus, and Modestinus, Valla's sarcastic and strident condemnations of the Latin barbarisms of medieval writers became the standard by which humanists everywhere began to reread and reinterpret authoritative texts in law, history, and literature, as well as the Christian Scriptures themselves.[82] Perhaps his most famous success was his identification of the Donation of Constantine as a forgery.[83]

A number of practising Italian jurists like Salamonio and Andrea Alciato began to accept Valla's criticisms of classical legal texts. Alciato employed humanist legal techniques in the development of a new approach to formulating a systematic legal science by completely rejecting the traditional scholastic method of textual commentary. He preferred to work on the original text itself from a knowledge of Greek and Latin literature in order to examine possibilities for textual emendation and to develop a set of legal terminology. Alciato also interested himself in the history of Roman legal offices and wrote a brief history of the mag-

---

82. Valla, "Elegantiarum latinae linguae libri sex," in *Opera omnia*, 1:1–235.
83. Valla, *Treatise of Lorenzo Valla on the Donation of Constantine*.

istracies of ancient Rome, listing civil and military dignitaries in both the eastern and western empire.[84]

The basic humanist textual methodology was transplanted to northern Europe in the early decades of the sixteenth century. The first example was *Annotationes in Pandecta* (1508), a polemic on scholastic jurisprudence written by Guillaume Budé (1467–1540) in France. Northern law schools began to incorporate legal humanism when Alciato himself took a professorship at Avignon in 1518. He moved to Bourges in 1529 to make the law school there famous for legal studies that embodied humanistic methods of criticism, which came to be known simply as the *mos docendi Gallicus*. The four most famous French jurists of the sixteenth century, Le Douaren, Doneau, Baudoin, and Cujas, all employed it.[85]

Humanist legal scholarship came also to Germany in the early sixteenth century. One example was the publication of the first printed text of Valla's *The Donation of Constantine* by Ulrich von Hutten (1488–1523), a work that impressed Luther in about 1518.[86] However, the establishment of humanist legal methodology in German law schools was attributable to Ulrich Zasius (1461–1536), who held the chair of civil law at Freibourg for more than thirty years. Like Alciato, Zasius retained some respect for the great medieval jurists such as Bartolus and cited them on important legal points. But he always emphasized his admiration for the *studia humanitatis* and practised close textual analysis from a philological perspective, paying great attention to the historical frame of reference for any legal dictum.[87] The overall consequence of this northern acceptance of humanistic legal methods was that the Code was treated as a kind of pot-pourri of legal material that had little, if any, contemporary value for sixteenth-century European polities. The result was to stimulate the search for a new scientific basis on which law could be set and encourage an historical examination of various systems of custom in an effort to discover universal features that could be seen to reflect the "sci-

---

84. See Alciato, "In tres posteriores codicis Justiniani libros annotatiunculae," in *Opera omnia*, 2:91–138; "Paradoxorum iuris civilis," in *Opera omnia*, 3:6–177. His historical treatise is "De magistratibus, civilibusque et militaribusque officiis," in *Opera omnia*, 2:495–519. The practice of identifying and defining Roman (and later) legal and political officers was, of course, longstanding and well-known in medieval writings. Cf. Isidore of Seville, *Etymologiae* and Ptolemy of Lucca, "De regimine principum" 4.26 and 28.

85. Budé, "Annotationes in Pandecta," in Budé, *Opera omnia*, 3:1–399. On the Bourges school and its representatives see Kelley, *Foundations of Modern Historical Scholarship*.

86. See Holborn, *Ulrich von Hutten*, pp. 81, 85, 129. On Luther's reaction to the Hutten text, see Fife, *The Revolt of Martin Luther*.

87. See Skinner, *Foundations*, 1:206–08.

entific" character of law. Mid-sixteenth-century efforts by French jurists and the later self-consciously scientific efforts of Bodin, Althusius, and Grotius are examples of this approach.

The next part of this work examines the political thought developed in the late medieval Church movement known as conciliarism. This will involve retracing our historical steps through the fourteenth and fifteenth centuries, with additional background commentary on earlier medieval ecclesiology. The political perspective, however, is quite different: it was in the Middle Ages that the political relationship between papal authority and other orders in the ecclesiastical polity of the Christian church, and the notions of limitation of power and consent of the governed, received their most thoroughgoing analysis.

PART TWO

# *Constitutionalism in the Church*

## 1. INTRODUCTION

ONE OF THE MOST DIFFICULT problems in presenting the history of later medieval political thought involves the organization of material. Much of the evidence can be fitted into two or more categories, even though to do so would result in repetition. Alternatively, separating the material by placing each element in only one location can produce fragmentation and make the account even more unsatisfactory. I have blended these two approaches to provide a continuous account, while keeping the element of repetition to a minimum.

Human thought, however, is expressible only through concepts and language, the intrinsic limitations of which make some form of categorization unavoidable. One category I have employed elsewhere with reference to the history of medieval political thought is "ecclesiastical,"[1] emphasizing that the Middle Ages cannot be understood without full recognition of the role played by the institutional church. It is a commonplace of medieval history that European society in that period reflected an overlapping, if not almost a fusion, of church and state. The basic medieval Christian social and political perspective was that of a social unity, christendom, organized into a complexity of related units and subsets under a transcendental principle of hierarchy and subordination whose ideological sources were both religious and philosophical. Christian monotheism, with its fundamental doctrine of a single God as a supreme transcendent being who is also the creator and divine ruler of the whole of reality, set the principle firmly. As well, the neo-Platonic

---

1. Monahan, *Consent, Coercion, and Limit.*

philosophical form in which Christianity was given intellectual expression by virtually all its early and most influential authorities gave further emphasis to the conception of reality as a hierarchy of entities and forms, all organized under, and subordinated to, an ultimate unity.[2]

Another obvious but essential point emphasized in my earlier work was the close, parallel connection between developments of political thought and organization in the two spheres of medieval society, church and state. An important aspect here was that medieval educational institutions, whose faculty and students were clerics under ecclesiastical control, supplied the pool from which both ecclesiastical and temporal ruling and administrative authorities took their advisors and bureaucratic personnel. The parallel developments and cross-over activity between church and state as regards both theory and practice is nowhere more evident than in the field of law. Many concepts brought into active use in the civil law of the Middle Ages had their origins in church law and were developed by canonists to facilitate jurisdictional practices in the Church, itself the most sophisticated and complex political structure of the time.[3]

It must be kept in mind, however, that the canonists were not interested in developing a theory of temporal polity as such, but concerned themselves exclusively with an examination of the nature and structure of the medieval institutional church. Yet thought in this area is still a form of political thought, and carry-over from one jurisdiction to the other could be expected in the medieval period, often without there being anything conscious or deliberate in the transfer. Gierke maintained in the late nineteenth century that medieval canonical thinking concerning the exercise of ecclesiastical authority owed something to secular thought and development. But it is probably truer to say that the more significant influence worked in the other direction; that innovations in secular political thought and practice from the middle of the thirteenth century to at least the seventeenth century were strongly affected by canonical thought. Certainly this can be argued with regard to

---

2. A forceful application of neo-Platonic, essentially pseudo-Dionysian structure to political thought is clear in the papal absolutism of Aegidius of Rome: *De potestate ecclesiastica*, 1.4, pp. 18–19.

3. Three important examples of the medieval contribution to secular legal theory are the notions of representation, corporation and full powers of consent. See Monahan, *Consent, Coercion, and Limit*, pp. 97–133, and for a fine presentation of recent scholarship on the first of these concepts, see Hofmann, *Repraesentation*. Cf. Zimmermann, ed., *Der Begriff der Repreasentatio im Mittelalter*. Cf. infra, pp. 66–68; 69–127 *passim*.

forms of corporate theory and practice, as well as the theory and use of representative bodies of various kinds.[4] The point here is obvious, of course; the Church was by far the most elaborate institutional structure of the medieval period and had at its disposal the very best in educated and committed personnel to formulate and implement its interests. Lines of influence and correspondence can be expected to have followed channels of interest and perceived needs when secular authorities and their advisors made use of elements developed in ecclesiastical political thinking. An early example is the appeal in 1239 to the college of cardinals by Petrus de Vinea, chancellor to the Holy Roman emperor Frederick II, for support against the pope; it shows a clear awareness of current canonical thinking on a possible procedure for setting limits to papal authority.[5] The early fourteenth-century French attack on Boniface VIII and calls for his deposition by a general church council illustrates the same thing.[6]

Later medieval secular political thought was developed to justify, among other things, the exercise of some form of sovereignty and political independence by the city-states of northern Italy in the fourteenth century. As shown in the first part of this book,[7] civilian jurists like Bartolus of Sassoferrato and Baldus de Ubaldus deliberately emphasized the principle that law should respond to and express current realities rather than attempt to align the contemporary scene with traditional forms of legislation.[8] Likewise with the canonists: Decretist and Decretalist writings clearly show agreement between both groups that canon law should reflect the current ecclesiastical situation and respond to the Church's current needs. Canonical writers had given systematic and unqualified expression to this principle for many centuries, beginning with efforts to base the Gregorian Reform on the contention that it represented a return to traditional church norms. There seems to have

---

4. See Gierke, *Das deutsche Genossenschaftrecht.* Vol. 3. *Die Staats-und Korporationslehre.* Cf. Monahan, *Consent, Coercion, and Limit,* pp. 97–133.

5. Cf. Tierney, *Foundations of the Conciliar Theory,* pp. 77–78. This work is the standard treatment of early canonical sources for conciliarism, and I have followed it largely in my account. See also Tierney, "Pope and Council."

6. The classic presentation of the dispute between Boniface and Philip the Fair is Digard, *Philippe le Bel et le Saint Siège.* Cf. Wood, ed., *Philip the Fair and Boniface VIII*; Jean Rivière, *Le problème de l'Église et de l'État.* A fine recent summary of the conflict is Strayer, *Reign of Philip the Fair.*

7. See *supra,* p. 21.

8. See *supra,* pp. 21–24.

been little hesitation to engage even in such questionable practices as forgery, the Donation of Constantine being a prime example, to justify papal interests of the day, and this must be borne in mind when assessing documents from canonical sources for a history of medieval political thought, but without discounting the historical value of these works.

The Church endured two overriding and almost overwhelming events in the fourteenth and early fifteenth centuries: the move of the papacy from Rome to Avignon in 1318—the so-called Babylonian captivity—and the subsequent scandal of the Great Schism that began in 1378 and racked the Church for forty odd years.[9] The well-known response to the Great Schism was the conciliar movement, the development and application of a theory of ecclesiastical polity that was designed to resolve the absurd and scandalous position into which church authorities had managed to place themselves. But it was a movement that would have far-reaching consequences for secular political thought as well.

As an intellectual and political movement, conciliarism was a reaction to a real and urgent problem within the late medieval church. As such, it is a paradigm of the notion that political theory develops in response to political realities from which relief is sought. It rested, however, on a theoretical foundation that was neither entirely new nor manufactured solely to meet the schism scandal; its roots can be found in earlier times. What the conciliarist advocates at the Councils of Constance and Basle achieved was, in essence, a fine tuning of standard canonical concepts in a precise formulation and its application to contemporary political conditions in the Church.[10]

This is not to imply, however, that the conciliar theory of the late fourteenth century existed earlier as a fully formed position, but only that its basic ingredients had both theoretical and practical antecedents. Conciliarism's end combination of conceptual elements was achieved only when the protracted schism in the Church's highest office needed urgent attention. The approach, at this critical juncture, involved material from two sources, theology and canon law, of which the second played the more decisive role for the simple reason that, while the schism was not unconnected with other matters, its resolution was essentially a legal matter for the institutional church and required jurisdic-

---

9. Oakley has suggested, however, that the character and harm inflicted on the Church from these conditions have sometimes been exaggerated. Oakley, "Religious and Ecclesiastical Life."

10. See *infra*, pp. 75ff.

tional or legal action. However, profound legal problems almost always involve substantive metalegal issues, since law and jurisdictional practice develop to give formal expression to matters of primary reality and importance at a more profound level of intellectual theory and discourse.

In fact, both problem and response proved relatively easy to formulate. The problem itself had two facets: the first and, in the short run, more serious stemmed from the fact that the medieval western church perceived itself to be the earthly embodiment of its divine founder, Jesus Christ, and was organized hierarchically under a single authoritative head, the pope.[11] An indisputable feature of the western Christian theory of ecclesiastical polity was that there could be only one pope and that his authority originated directly in the divine. Hence the nub of the schism difficulty was how to determine which, if any, of the current contenders for the throne of Peter was the "right one." A second feature of the problem, again essentially legal and procedural, was the need for a means of identifying the true pope and imposing this judgment on all other contenders.

To some, the issue of implementation appeared intractable on both theoretical and practical grounds. For centuries, the general understanding of papal authority and the claims made for its supremacy accepted that an incumbent pope was not accountable to any human agency: *prima sedes a nemine judicatur.* Conventional thinking had long held that only the pope could address the issue of his own legitimacy and competence.[12] But if this were so, it was unclear how the system could be made to work when several persons claimed supreme ecclesiastical jurisdiction and when no one, apparently, could exercise authority over any of them.

Yet an adequate theoretical response was no more difficult to formulate than the problem itself. An answer emerged easily enough from a combination of several generally recognized basic ingredients in the medieval notion of authority. Probably the most common feature in every such theory of polity was the notion of limit as a correlative to the concept of legitimate authority. The standard view was that exercise of power must be conditioned by its purpose; the logical entailment, often

11. Western Christendom promoted and sustained this self-image until the Reformation, but Eastern or Orthodox Christianity had always held much less strictly to the notion of an established hierarchy among the various churches making up christendom.

12. See Moynihan, *Papal Immunity and Liability,* pp. ix–x. This monograph remains the standard work on the subject. Cf. de Vooght, *Les pouvoirs du concile.*

explicitly drawn, was that failure to observe this limit required a response and correction. The theory was general and applied to all types of authority, ecclesiastical as well as temporal. Even papal power, universally acknowledged to be the supreme form of authority on earth, was understood to have limits and, in theory, to be capable of abuse, though insufficient attention may have been paid to connecting limit in the exercise of ecclesiastical authority with the notion of a monarchical papacy whose foundations were said to have been established by God Himself: "Thou art Peter, and upon this rock I will build My church."[13] It is understandable that medieval canonists and theologians might have been unenthusiastic about dealing with this thorny issue under what might be called normal conditions in church administration and government, where exercise of papal authority was always monarchical and always enveloped in the rhetorical mists associated with divine establishment. But application to the papacy of the notion of limit was precisely what was needed to resolve the actual schism at the end of the fourteenth century; accordingly, this was both the theoretical and practical ground on which conciliarists and the various papal claimants met.

The specific issue was how to deal with papal abuse of power, and this was where limit on papal power came into play. Though not of great theoretical difficulty, as already noted, the reality could be fraught with almost overwhelming practical problems. Conceptually, all that was needed to resolve the issue satisfactorily within the general theory was a mechanism to which the papal officeholder would ultimately be accountable—a legitimate instrument for holding an officeholder to account, and for dealing with him in the event that he exceeded his authority.

Earlier theoretical discussion of this matter had led to several interesting, if not immediately practical, conclusions. The problem of delineating a specific behaviour that constituted an abuse of papal power had been addressed by the canonists from the time of Gratian's *Decretum*.[14] The principle of papal immunity from ecclesiastical discipline, on the other hand, had been accepted by both popes and canonists from its first appearance in a sixth-century forgery, although it had

13. Matthew 16:18.
14. Gratian makes the critical statement that heresy constituted such an abuse: "[*papa*] *a nemine est iudicandus nisi deprehendatur a fide devius*" at D.40 c.6, attributing the principle to St Boniface.

not gone unchallenged.[15] The Decretists, commentators on Gratian's *Decretum* in the period c.1140–c.1220, had expatiated at length on heresy as the ground on which an incumbent pope could be challenged for abusing his office;[16] their examination of possible papal abuse of power had extended the grounds to include schism and a broader, more ambiguous, and therefore potentially more radical category: that of causing serious damage to the Church's well-being. Decretist thought on the matter, however, was not as a whole either systematic or uniform. Several theories appeared, often in conflict with one another, and no concerted effort was made to reach conclusions based on deductive reasoning. One principal line of thought had declared a general church council superior to the pope in matters of faith; but at the outset of the Great Schism there was no general consensus on this issue among canonists, though there was abundant material to be exploited as the need became more urgent.

There was also the narrower matter of how to deal with an authority that had no earthly superior. The suggestion that the pope would simply have to control himself, mentioned specifically by Gratian and several Decretists,[17] made little or no practical sense. The scarcely distinguishable alternative, that because the pope had no earthly superior only God could exercise authority over him, so that an errant pope must simply be "left to heaven," offered no more practicable a solution. Nor was Huguccio's cautious suggestion that a heretical pope simply ceased to be pope a practical means for dealing with the actual schism: however attractive the notion of direct, divine intervention might have seemed to

15. The forged document, *Constitutum Sylvestri*, purported to be a decree from a Roman synod of 342 presided over by Pope Sylvester and the emperor Constantine. It appeared in the *Pseudo-Isidoriana* and the *Collectio 74 titulorum*, as well as in the collections of Ivo of Chartres and Gratian. Cf. Moynihan, *Papal Immunity*, p. 25.

16. Rufinus added schism to heresy as a papal crime warranting deposition (*Summa ad Dist.* 40 c.6) in Rufinus *Die Summa Decretorum der Magister Rufinus*, ed. H. Singer, p. 96) and, along with the *Summa Parisiensis*, referred to the right of "the whole Church" (*ecclesia tota*) to judge a pope (*Summa ad Dist.* 21 c.4, p. 46; *Summa Parisiensis ad Dist.* 21 *post* c.3, p. 21. Tierney discusses further important developments by Huguccio, offering three citations (Tierney, *Foundations of Conciliar Theory*, pp. 57–64) and provides Huguccio's gloss on *nisi deprehendatur a fide devius* in an Appendix at pp. 248–50.

17. On the point that the pope stood above all human judgment see Gratian C.9 q.3 c.13; see also D.17 *post* c.6; D.18; Huguccio *Summa ad Dist.* 21 c.4. Cf. Moynihan, *Papal Immunity*, p. 142. Nonetheless, 1018; C.17 q.4 c.30. On the point that in historical instances in popes submitted to judgment they did so voluntarily see D.21 c.7; D.17 c.6 and C.2 q.72 q.2 q.7 *post* c.41; C.2 q.7 c.41.

the religious inclinations of the medieval mind, not even the most fervent believers could accept it as an automatic or even very promising solution for the current problem.[18] Aegidius of Rome, one of the strongest medieval advocates of papal monarchy, had cautioned against counting on God to act in extraordinary ways, pointing out that divine intervention was rare in human affairs, since God preferred to operate through the ordinary laws of physical and human nature.[19]

However, other avenues could be explored in the general theory of ecclesiastical polity. From the beginnings of the formal development and teaching of canon law with Gratian in the mid-twelfth century, consideration had been given to precisely how the pope came into power. The possibilities of extending this issue into an enquiry about how he might be removed had not gone unnoticed among thirteenth- and fourteenth-century Decretists and Decretalists. There was agreement on a general view of how the pope came into office: he was chosen by the cardinals and confirmed by the Church as a whole. Further, although there was a paucity of canonical legislation detailing its precise terms, the elective function of the cardinalate had been accepted in practice since the middle of the twelfth century when cardinals began to assume prominence as advisors and assistants to the successor of Peter; Cardinal Humbert had expressed the curialist view that pope and cardinals together constituted the Church. Correlatively, then, there would have been at least a measure of canonical opinion identifying the cardinals as a potential agency for controlling papal abuse of power.[20]

The concept of the Church as a whole, the other essential element mentioned in texts on papal election, was a much more ephemeral notion. Because of its relative vagueness and obvious universal extension, its employment in any theory of ecclesiastical polity seemed both necessary and valid; yet its meaning was not clear. The uncertainty of meaning in the relevant texts was twofold. First, what was meant by the Church as a whole—who or what group was so specified? And secondly, precisely what function was required of this group so that the Church could be

---

18. Huguccio *Summa ad Dist.* 21 c.4. Cf. Moynihan, *Papal Immunity*, p. 142. Nonetheless, both Lutheran and Calvinist theologians at first employed the same type of thinking in the sixteenth century, when they rejected the legitimacy of actual physical resistance to political suppression of their religious views. See *infra*, pp. 208–16 passim; 227–31.

19. Aegidius of Rome, *On Ecclesiastical Power* 3.3, p. 221.

20. See Ullman, "Cardinal Humbert." Cf. Tierney, *Foundations of Conciliar Theory*, p. 57, and note 3. But cf. Moynihan's reservation: Moynihan, *Papal Immunity*, pp. 33–36. See also Watt, "Constitutional Law of the College of Cardinals."

said to have consented to a papal election? Both questions received careful, analytical attention from thirteenth- and especially fourteenth-century canonists, thereby providing more grist for the conciliarist mill when the need arose.

Finally, there was the issue of the meaning and role of church councils in ecclesiastical governance and administration. Councils had functioned in church governance from the early centuries of the Christian era and were universally accepted as having some authority, but again, without either agreement or essential specification concerning just what was involved. The relation of a general church council to pope, cardinalate, and, indeed, the Church as a whole was another matter about which canonists could be expected to speculate and even disagree. In the event, of course, the general church council was the specific institution to which appeal would be made to resolve the schism.

As already noted, the conciliar movement involved both a theoretical and a practical appeal to a general church council as the means for exercising jurisdiction over an incumbent in the papal office. The fundamental distinction between office and officeholder had been accepted in the Church for centuries, naturally, and its particular application to the papacy is found in Gratian's examination of the possibility of an errant pope,[21] although his personal views prevented him from being a serious innovator on the subject. But the fact that his widely used and authoritative text included material on the issue and clearly signalled the need for a method to deal with papal abuse of authority made it inevitable that later canonists would take up the question.

The possibility of an incumbent pope abusing his office was simply too obvious to be overlooked by ecclesiastical lawyers seeking a comprehensive set of laws and interpretations to govern the life and well-being of the institutional church. A preferred locus for examining the problem, as mentioned, was the issue of papal election: election and deposition, along with resignation, are correlative issues. Gratian had provided material on papal election from early canons as well as authoritative statements from more recent and convenient forgeries, and all these sources made it clear that the pope came into office through election, with the Church as a whole playing a role by way of consent. Too much a product of the Gregorian Reform to think otherwise, Gratian had been careful to exclude the laity from any formal or essential function in papal elec-

21. Gratian D.40 c.6. The distinction itself is found in Leo I. Cf. Ullmann, *Law and Politics*, p. 229, and note 3.

tion and to remove any possibility of the laity, especially secular rulers, dominating the Church through procedures governing ecclesiastical officeholding. His intent set the terms of his formulation. He aimed to show that church authority and administrative practices were based on models established by the Church itself and its founder, Christ. He cited texts to show how the Church had conducted its affairs from earliest times, documents indicating that popular consent by the Christian community was an essential element in how bishops, and even the pope, came into office. It was thus unavoidable that Gratian should acknowledge some role for the Christian community as a whole in choosing its leaders: the earliest texts, even Scripture itself, made it plain that some such role of this sort had existed in the Church from the beginning.[22]

Gratian also connected papal deposition with the issue of how a pope came into office and accepted deposition as necessary should papal power be sufficiently abused. At the same time, however, he introduced the delicate qualification that the pope had no earthly superior and, therefore, could not be deposed by any human agency, temporal or ecclesiastical. The literal implication of this view was that the pope might have to depose himself, a thin, airy notion utterly bereft of either practical or procedural value. Huguccio later expressed the same view, that a pope "deposes himself" by wilfully and pertinaciously performing actions that abuse his office,"[23] and this became the basis for the much-repeated thirteenth-century position that a heretical pope deposes himself by wilfully supporting heresy. This view did little, however, to advance either theory or practice in the case of actual papal heresy or other abuse of papal authority. How does one determine when a pope is in heresy? Does he himself have to make such a declaration, or can some other ecclesiastical agency do so? If the latter, which one? Further, exactly what occurs if and when a heretical pope refuses either to acknowledge himself to be in heresy, or to step down when declared heretical by some other agency?

The case of Pope Anastasius II (November 496–November 498) was generally accepted as a notorious example of a pope advocating heresy and thus abusing his authority. Of his death, it is said in the *Liber pontificalis* that he was "struck by the divine will" for having shown diplo-

---

22. See Acts 1:23–26; 6:5; 11:2; 15:4 and 22; 1 Cor. 49:3. Cf. Schnachenburg, "Community Co-Operation in the New Testament."

23. Gratian C.24 q.1 *ante* c.1; cf. C.2 q.7 *post* c.26; 1 C.6 q.1 c.20 and C.6 q.1 *post* c.21; Huguccio *Summa ad Dist.* 21 c.4.

matic friendship to Photinus, a representative of a strong supporter of Acacianism. While the case was cited regularly in the canonical literature, it was not until shortly after Boniface VIII ascended the papal throne in 1296 that the legitimacy of papal deposition became a serious political matter. Opposition to Boniface's enthusiastic advocacy of an extreme form of papal monarchism led advisors of Philip the Fair of France to persuade their ruler to call for the pope's deposition. They took the canonically plausible view that a general church council should be convened for the purpose, thus identifying a specific instrument for effecting papal deposition. The stated grounds for deposition were that Boniface held office illegally insofar as his predecessor, the saintly but hapless Celestine V, had not resigned properly: Celestine's resignation was said to be illegal because it lacked approval from the college of cardinals. But attached to the charge that he held his pontifical position illegally was the added charge that Boniface was thereby abusing the authority of his office; added to this, for good measure, was the mischievous catch-all claim that his behaviour was irreparably damaging the Church. The dispute between Boniface and his French adversaries is noteworthy for the numerous elements of ecclesiastical political theory it brought into play: election and deposition of a pope, the role of the cardinals in these procedures, and the role and authority of a general church council in papal deposition.

The argument that a person in a position of authority cannot resign on his own, that is, without the approval of those who placed him in office, is such a simple-minded piece of legal sophistry that it is hard to take seriously; presumably even its French formulators had little faith in its intellectual rigour: the idea that people can be required to hold office against their own wishes because simple resignation is *ultra vires* makes little or no theoretical sense, and when the office at issue is the papacy, whose occupant is described as the most powerful authority on earth, the idea seems altogether ludicrous. If a pope can resign, however, he can also be deposed, assuming there is sufficient reason to do so: acceptance of the validity of resignation implies that an officeholder is not beyond all forms of human control and regulation.

The anti-Boniface forces insisted on this latter point, but without acknowledging its logical inconsistency as applied to Celestine. Also rejected, incidentally, was the conventional canonist doctrine that placed the pope beyond the jurisdiction of any earthly authority. Indeed, the king of France actually undertook a formally ecclesiastical function, an appeal to a general church council, thereby bringing into play a general principle of both polity and law, viz., that only a higher authority can exercise jurisdiction over a lower one. Philip's call for a general church council to depose Boniface implied that, in this matter at least, he possessed a higher authority than the pope, an implication for which, of course, there was ample historical precedent, if not carefully argued canonical warrant. It was further the case that the initiative in convening a general church council to deal with purely ecclesiastical matters had first been taken by a lay ruler when Constantine the Great convoked the Council of Nicaea in 314.

Theoretical justification for the actual exercise of power by a higher authority over a lower, however, needs further consideration. Conceding that authority A is superior to B does not *ipso facto* make A's action over B legitimate. Arbitrary use of authority, even higher authority, is not self-justifying, and it is arguably one of the worst forms of abuse of power; authority is legitimate only when directed to its proper purpose. Legitimate exercise of authority by a general church council in deposing a pope, then, must meet several conditions: firstly, the pope himself must be judged to be abusing his office; secondly, a general council must possess an authority higher than the pope's; and thirdly, this higher authority must be legitimately used in the act of papal deposition. General conciliar power must only be used for a legitimate purpose.

The argument for both papal resignation and deposition was basically teleological. People who were unwilling to meet their obligations of office, or those who believed they were incompetent and wished to leave office for that reason, could resign on their own authority. Similarly, those who abused their office or were incompetent could be removed by an appropriate higher authority. Conceptually, moreover, this view was clearly superior to the conventional canonical tenet that the pope was the highest single authority, which seemed implicitly to accept that an errant pope might continue in office at his own pleasure. It also had greater rational force than the conventional minor variant to papal abdication, which suggested that a pope who abused his power deposed himself *eo ipso*. While superficially attractive in that it obviated, in theory, the need to identify an authority higher than the pope, this position also embodied the unattractive problem of how to specify and address the circumstances in which a pope indirectly deposes himself: by what agencies or procedures is such a conclusion reached, and how then to deal with such an eventuality?

As well as introducing both the issue of papal deposition and the general textual context for its possible resolution, Gratian had also introduced what Tierney called "an unresolved antithesis" into the problem of papal abuse of authority.[24] A strong advocate of the Gregorian Reform emphasis on papal hegemony, Gratian had made a strong case for the pope's unique status as head of the Church and supreme authority in specific and weighty matters of doctrine and jurisdiction, without, however, associating the critical feature of the Church's indefectibility with the occupant of the papal throne. He accepted that Christ had guaranteed the Church's eternal integrity ("I am with you all days"[25]), but did not identify the papacy as the vessel of indefectibility. As with the community's role in choosing ecclesiastical leaders, the historical record and earlier authorities on this issue required a different position, and Anastasius II's case, though legendary, was on record as a notorious case of heresy admitting no defence. Accordingly, the papacy was not indefectible.[26]

Maintaining without qualification that the pope must always be obeyed and followed *tout court* was indefensible against the facts of history; the integrity Christ guaranteed to the Church could not be attributed absolutely, automatically, and in all circumstances to a reigning pope. Accordingly, the Decretists normally distinguished between the Church of Rome understood as a local geographical constituency where the pope exercised jurisdiction as bishop, and the Roman church defined as *ecclesia universa*, the universal church. Indefectibility resided in the latter, in the *universitas fidelium*.[27]

No medieval ecclesiological term requires more careful delineation than "church," particularly given that its meaning, originally imprecise, was evolving. It was often used broadly to designate the community of which the pope was supreme authority; but even in this meaning a crucial distinction was drawn between the successor of Peter as apex of ecclesiastical authority and the community over which he ruled. The pope

---

24. Tierney, *Foundations of Conciliar Theory*, p. 39.
25. Matthew 28:20.
26. Gratian's reference to the Anastasius case became a *locus classicus* for examination of the problem of papal abuse of power and indefectibility (Gratian D.19 c.9 Anastasius), as did the *Decretum* text claiming that the Church never erred: C.24 q.1 c.9. Cf. *Glossa ordinaria* on these two canons. The *Decretum* actually identified four heretical popes: Anastasius II, Marcellinus, Liberius, and Honorius, and Gratian had asserted that even Peter had fallen into error: C.2 q.7 *post* c.39. Cf. Lebreton and Zeiller, *History of the Primitive Church*, vol. 2; Tierney, *Foundations of Conciliar Theory*, pp. 47–64; Sigmund, *Nicholas of Cusa*, p. 79 and note 18.
27. See Huguccio *Summa ad Dist.* 93 c.24; 21 c.3 and 23 c.1.

was never held to embody the unfailing faith of the Church either in his person or in his office. Asserting, as Humbert had done,[28] that the Church was constituted of pope and cardinals together might seem to offer a more certain ultimate authority than that of the pope alone; but again no real identification could be made here between pope and cardinals and the Church as a whole. The distinction between office and officeholder was brought into play, and the operative term was the Church of Rome (*ecclesia Romana*). If it stood for either the Roman church or the diocese of Rome, it could arguably designate the combination of pope and cardinals; but it could also designate the universal church, the whole body of the faithful, and this alone could be the vessel of indefectibility.

Huguccio was clear on this distinction as early as the late twelfth century, and his interpretation had been widely accepted. Indeed, he had expressed an early form of conciliarist theory in his *Summa Decretorum* (1188–90), the greatest achievement of Decretist thought, when he commented on Gratian's view that the pope was not answerable to the church "unless found to be in heresy."[29] Accepting that something had to be done with a heretical pope, Huguccio placed the Church as a whole above the pope when its own welfare was at stake, and he stipulated that the cardinals had the right in such circumstances to call a general church council. He also added the category, mentioned above, of "contumacious criminal [who persists] in notorious crimes" to the grounds on which a general church council could be called to deal with an errant pope. It was Joannes Teutonicus, however, who gave this its most influential expression, not necessarily because he voiced a more extreme or clearer position than Huguccio, but because his *Glossa ordinaria* became the best known early Decretist work.[30] For canonists like Huguccio and Joannes, the promise of unfailing faith given to the church by its founder was not associated with an unerring teaching authority, the meaning normally attached nowadays to the concept of indefectibility or infallibility, but meant only that the Church as a whole would never be entirely polluted by heretical error.

The distinction between pope and the Church as a whole that was current among twelfth-century canonists prefigured a key concept of

28. See Ullmann, "Cardinal Humbert and the Ecclesia Romana."
29. Tierney has reproduced the Huguccio gloss in *Foundations of Conciliar Theory* as Appendix 1, pp. 248–50. Cf. Huguccio *Summa ad Dist.* 19 c.9.
30. Joannes Teutonicus, *Glossa ordinaria ad* C.24 q.1 c.9.

fourteenth-century conciliar thought, although the earlier canonists did not have the later frame of reference when articulating conciliar-like views. Nor did their positions develop in quite the same context as that found in someone like William of Ockham.[31] The distinction between the Roman church and the whole congregation of the faithful in matters of faith captured the essence of later conciliar thought when it stressed the Church as a whole in guiding people to salvation through true doctrine and practice; but the Decretists did not explicitly link indefectibility to an ecclesiastical entity superior to the papacy itself. They said interesting things about the functions and authority of a general church council, but they did not address directly the question of whether such a council would be superior to the pope in terms of ultimate authority and jurisdiction. This was left to the later conciliarists in their efforts to resolve the Great Schism.[32]

Gratian's *Decretum* also was ambivalent about two critical concepts dealing with the exercise of papal power. While on the one hand he connected papal authority with its purpose, a specification entailing the notion of limit, the canonical master's broad description of papal power offered grounds for ascribing to the pope the kind of absolute power often associated with the medieval church. Twelfth- and thirteenth-century glossators and commentators on the *Decretum* made no serious effort to bring these variant themes together, and thereby failed to develop any comprehensive constitutional form of ecclesiology. The notion of limit usually appeared in texts dealing with whether a pope, bishop, or other ecclesiastical authority could be deposed or censured in any way, but the Decretists were relatively uninterested in discussing how to limit papal authority constitutionally through its relationship with other agencies in the overall ecclesiological system. The rather simple view that the pope was supreme in this world and had no earthly authority over him seemed to satisfy them; they raised subtle questions about what might be done with a seriously errant pope, but appeared unwilling to press these speculations against the notion of papal supremacy.

The Decretalists, commentators on the wealth of new legislation and statements from post-Gregorian Reform popes, many of whom were themselves well trained in canon law and strong advocates of an expanding papacy, showed even less inclination to examine how papal power might be subjected to constitutional limits. However, as strong propo-

---

31. Cf. Monahan, *Consent, Coercion, and Limit*, pp. 240–53.
32. See Tierney, *Foundations of Conciliar Theory*, pp. 45–46.

nents, for the most part, of papal absolutism, they devoted considerable attention to delineating the pope's relationship to the Church as a whole by developing increasingly sophisticated notions of the Church as a corporation, and of how the pope and other ecclesiastical administrative officers, specifically the college of cardinals and the general church council, related to the universal Church, *ecclesia universa*. Ironically, it was largely from the speculations of these forceful and sophisticated advocates of papal monarchy that the comprehensive conciliar position developed. While the Decretists were often more open-minded and freewheeling when expressing the need for constitutional limit on the exercise of papal authority, it was the Decretalists, who were generally enthusiastic about extending papal absolutism in both church and state, who forged the tools employed in the later conciliarist arguments for the superiority of a general church council over the papacy. Neither Decretists nor Decretalists can be said, however, to have been anything more than forerunners of later conciliarism.

## 2. JOHN OF PARIS

In an early fourteenth century text almost certainly occasioned by the current controversy between Boniface VIII and Philip the Fair, John of Paris (c.1240–1306), a Dominican theologian teaching at the University of Paris, offered a strikingly innovative view of the nature of a general church council. His *De potestate regali et papali* (1302) provided a carefully argued examination of papal authority and its relationship with temporal powers and addressed, in its last several chapters, the issue of whether a pope could resign or be deposed.[33] In formulating a position that sided, at least on theoretical grounds, with Philip the Fair, who would, of course, have had to supply the empirical data, John presented a clear conciliarist position whose organized expression was not to be seen again until the latter decades of the century. As noted earlier, the French king's publicists had called for a general church council to depose Boniface as an heretical incumbent of the papal throne, arguing that he had pre-empted the papacy inasmuch as Celestine V's resigna-

---

33. The Quidort text in a critical Latin edition is available in *Johannis Quidort von Paris: Überkönigliche und papstliche Gewalt: text-kritische Edition mit deutscher Übersetzung*, ed. & trans. F. Bleienstien; one English translation is *John of Paris on Royal and Papal Power*, trans. Arthur P. Monahan. The relevant material on papal resignation and deposition is in chapters 22–25, pp. 118–37.

tion, which had not been approved by the college of cardinals, was illegal. They had also invoked against Boniface the vague category of notorious misconduct in office, which had been mentioned in earlier canonical literature as grounds for papal deposition.

In the event, then, nothing novel was raised against Boniface by Nogaret and Philip's other advisors in their allegations and claims for relief. Similarly, nothing in John of Paris's views on papal deposition broke new theoretical ground. His significance for future conciliarist thought rested rather on a straightforward organization of current canonical and theological principles that drew hitherto unexpressed conclusions that had implications for the relationship between pope and general church council. John's views on the papacy and its relation with the Church as a whole can be found in Hostiensis, who himself had elaborated a doctrine of the constitutional structure of the Church in terms of basic medieval corporation theory some thirty years earlier.[34]

Setting aside the Decretalist's juridical details with which he was not directly concerned, Quidort applied Hostiensis's general corporation theory to the Church. Accepting the Church as a corporation, he construed the papacy as head of a corporate entity, so that the pope thus appears as *curator* or *dispensator* rather than *dominus*. The authority of the Church as a whole, then, is not solely concentrated in the pope, but is diffused among the totality of church members who confer authority on the pope in the same way a bishop receives authority over his diocese by being elected to office through the involvement of the diocesan religious community as a whole. John simply applied to the papacy, without any special qualification, the accepted canonical doctrine on how a bishop comes into office. Application of current corporation theory to the papacy's relationship with the Church as a whole, however, drastically altered the conventional notions about papal authority.

The whole matter of how to deal with papal claims to supreme authority was moved from the arena of rhetoric to that of law. For John, the relationship between pope and Church was the same as that between any prelate and his diocesan corporation, that of a superior exercising rule over a religious community. Quidort's position is clear when he asks whether the pope is *dominus* with respect to ecclesiastical property: does

---

34. Tierney identified Hostiensis's *Lectura in quinque Decretalium Gregorianum libros* [1271], along with the *Glossa ordinaria*, as sources for Quidort's conciliarist position without giving the relevant citations. Tierney, *Foundations of Conciliar Theory*, p. 163. Cf. Tierney, "Hostiensis and Collegiality."

the pope "own" the goods of the Church? His answer was a simple no; the pope no more owns ecclesiastical property than any bishop or head of a religious community owns property under his jurisdiction. The appropriate designation for his jurisdictional function is dispenser or curator, which carries rights of control and use but not actual ownership. The owner is the corporation itself, the community of which the prelate is head; and however authoritative and supreme such headship might be, it does not entail ownership.[35]

The main ingredient in John's case for the legitimacy of papal deposition was the traditional distinction between authority of office and quality of occupant. Taken with the concepts that the corporate head has the status of dispenser rather than owner and that authority resides ultimately in the corporation itself, this distinction enabled him to express a coherent theory that included both the notion of the pope as supreme authority in the Church with no equal among other members, and the much more radical view that the community as a whole retained power to bring an errant pope to book. John forthrightly rejected the current conventional view that the pope was not accountable to anyone because there was no higher authority to call him to account, declaring simply that he could not understand what this view could mean when measured against canonical texts describing circumstances in which a pope could be tried and deposed.[36]

Fundamental to Quidort's position was the long-accepted but vague notion that papal jurisdiction was conferred by the people of the Church as a whole. He did not deny the supremacy of papal jurisdiction or status in the Church, but distinguished between status achieved and the method whereby an individual came into office: the latter occurred through human agency. And this being the case, those who put someone in office could remove him, given sufficient cause a view for which there was ample canonical warrant.[37] John also took the position that the cardinalate acted for the whole Church in a manner similar to that of nobles in a kingdom. On this point, he merely offered a justification for

---

35. For implications of this position with regard to the theory of property developed by John Locke, which show a thread of ideological continuity between medieval and modern political thought that is seldom acknowledged, see Coleman, "Dominium in Thirteenth and Fourteenth-Century Political Thought." Note, however, the cautionary note struck about Coleman's simplistic identification of the views of Quidort and Locke in Nederman, "Nature, Sin and the Origins of Society," p. 18, note 70.
36. John of Paris, *Royal and Papal Power* 25(4), p. 132.
37. Ibid.

the jurisdictional *status quo,* as might be expected of someone who neither saw himself, nor was seen by his contemporaries, as a dangerous radical. In doing so, however, he was also supporting Philip the Fair's theoretical attack on Boniface in his claim that the cardinals were an essential element in placing a pope in office.[38]

### 3. CONCILIAR THOUGHT IN THE FOURTEENTH CENTURY

Fourteenth-century canonists engaged in a number of activities that had an impact on conciliar thinking. The basic conciliarist structure and argumentation had been worked out by John of Paris, and subsequent canonist thinking provided further raw material for the final formulation when a response was required to the scandal of the Great Schism. The excessive claims and torrid rhetoric with which papal monarchism was being advanced, along with the questionable political activities and excesses of several fourteenth-century popes, quite naturally invited criticism from contemporaries. The critics fell roughly into two categories. In the first were those opposed to papal policies directed primarily against the then Holy Roman emperor Ludwig of Bavaria, whose election had been set aside by Pope John XXII largely because of papal expansionist interests in northern Italy, which produced more than a quarter-century of acrimony between *imperium* and *ecclesia* and ended only with Ludwig's death in 1347. In the second were what might be called internal ecclesiastical critics: canonists and prelates who objected to the way incumbent popes were administering the Church. Marsilius of Padua and William of Ockham were the most important members of the first group, while Joannes Monachus and Guilielmus Durantis were prominent churchmen belonging in the second.[39]

### *Joannes Monachus*

Both Joannes Monachus and Guilielmus Durantis were prominent canonists of their day, and both adopted a clear line of criticism somewhat ahead of their time against both papal theory and papal practice. A sometime advisor to Philip the Fair of France and named cardinal by

---

38. Ibid. 13, pp. 67–68. See *infra,* pp. for the use made later by the author of the *Vindiciae contra tyrannos* of the alleged parallel between the powers of both cardinals and nobles relative to a supreme ruler.

39. On Marsilius and Ockham, see Monahan, *Consent, Coercion, and Limit,* pp. 209–53; and further on Marsilius *supra,* pp. 19–21.

Celestine V, Monachus (d. 1313) was a severe critic of Boniface VIII, especially on the issue of the pope's relationship with his cardinals. He advanced the view that Boniface failed to give adequate attention to the cardinalate and contended that, inasmuch as the pope was constrained by church law, he could not legislate on his own without the advice and consent of his cardinals. Monachus rested his case on a clear statement of the legal relationship between pope and cardinals and the latter's role in exercising authority in the Church. He even held that the cardinals alone enjoyed the exercise of *plenitudo potestatis* when the papacy was vacant.[40]

As already shown, the Monachus doctrine was no more novel than the position of John of Paris. Monachus simply applied standard medieval corporation theory to the relationship between pope and cardinals, as Quidort had done, and gave the cardinalate a mandated function in church administration as an ordinary feature of papal government that had generally been conceded to them for some time. In fact the cardinalate had acquired considerable prestige over time precisely because of its increasingly active role in papal administration. For Monachus, the function of the cardinals *vis-à-vis* the pope was that of canons in a cathedral chapter towards their bishop: "The pope relates to the college of cardinals as any bishop in respect of his college [of canons]."[41] Accordingly, as Hostiensis and John of Paris had earlier maintained, there was a basis for attributing technical legal authority to the cardinals. In claiming genuine authority for the cardinals, Monachus was stipulating a limit on papal power, even though in doing so he did not envisage a cardinalate that represented the Church as a whole, at least not in a juridical sense. While mooted broadly but indistinctly by John of Paris, the concept of cardinals as representative of the *congregatio fidelium* only came to full expression among later conciliarists.

Monachus's use of standard corporation theory was quite straightforward: inasmuch as the cardinals enjoyed genuine juridical status as advisors to the pope, the pontiff could not make law without consulting them properly. And he drew a further inference, that a papal declaration made in the absence of formal consultation with the cardinalate lacked the force of law. Commenting on the Roman legal dictum *princeps legibus solutus est*, Monachus remarked that, while it could be taken in some sense as a given, the pope had more than a moral obligation to obey his

40. Joannes Monachus, *Glossa ad Sext.* 5.11.2. Cf. *infra*, p. 82.
41. Joannes Monachus, *Glossa ad Sext.* 5.3.1.

own laws. Previous popes, Monachus contended, had shown that they took seriously the need to consult the cardinals in order to make their pronouncements legally binding. He cited two instances, one involving Benedict XI and the other Boniface II, to show that papal edicts promulgated *absque consilio fratrum* were invalid. His conclusion was that "a defect in the person or necessary number of such persons renders an action useless."[42]

The substance of Monachus's gloss on the *princeps legibus solutus* dictum had appeared regularly in earlier medieval legal and political thought whenever the tendency emerged in either secular or ecclesiastical jurisdictions to use such a formula in a merely literal or rhetorical way. *Princeps legibus solutus* was a wonderfully simple declaration that seemed, on the basis of classical Roman jurisprudence, to offer justification for the exercise of arbitrary and absolute power by any ruler, prince or pope; but its literal interpretation was regularly rejected. John of Salisbury had done so as early as the twelfth century when delineating the limits of temporal power in the *Policraticus*.[43]

Monachus did the same when opposing claims to unlimited papal authority. He rejected a literal understanding of the papal claim to *plenitudo potestatis*, stipulating quite precise limitations on papal authority by subjecting the conventional and relatively unreflective notion of papal *plenitudo potestatis* to a more rigorous analysis than it had yet received. Without in any sense denying its applicability to the papacy, he construed it to show that the pope's authority, while "full," had been delegated to him by the other members of the corporate unity of which he was head. Monachus thus was able to undermine the theory of papal monarchy while continuing to use the conventional terminology of its strongest supporters.[44]

### Guilielmus Durantis

The challenge by Guilielmus Durantis (or William Durant) to papal monarchy and absolutism came from another quarter, although his case

---

42. Joannes, Monarchus, *Glossa ad Sext.* 3.7.8.
43. John of Salisbury, *Policraticus*, 4.7.527A-C; English translation: *John of Salisbury. Policraticus*, ed. and trans. Cary J. Nederman. Cf. Monahan, *Consent, Coercion, and Limit*, pp. 61–62.
44. Joannes Monachus, *Glossa ad Sext.* 5.3.1., fol. 366n2. Cited in Tierney, *Foundations of Conciliar Theory*, p. 189.

against papal claims was very similar. While Joannes Monachus had argued as a cardinal and criticized papal absolutism by claiming rights for the cardinalate, Guilielmus (d.1330), speaking as a prominent French bishop, asserted the authority of the episcopate and local churches vis-à-vis the pope, expressing views that were often original but overshadowed in his own day by the more radical speculations of Marsilius of Padua and William of Ockham. Guilielmus also appealed to the general theory of corporation insisting, like Monachus, that the pope's position was that of a bishop with respect to his cathedral chapter and that the pope was therefore subject to church law the same as anyone else: he was constrained to act only in ways approved by canonical legislation.

Basing his argument solely on texts from Gratian's *Decretum*, Durantis claimed that no pope could enact legislation contrary to existing canons unless he received approval to do so from a general church council. Listing an impressive number of canonical authorities on the point,[45] he reinforced his view by invoking the well-known Roman legal maxim, *quod omnes tangit ab omnibus approbetur*—"what touches all must be approved by all." Guilielmus made this principle the centrepiece of his case, citing an instance from Boniface VIII and employing it in a way that had widespread currency in both ecclesiastical and secular jurisdictions.[46]

Durantis thus opened a kind of second front against excessive papal claims under the rubric *plenitudo potestatis*. Where Joannes Monachus appealed to the rightful legal authority of the cardinals as a necessary element in the exercise of papal power, Guilielmus highlighted another limiting agency, the episcopacy, and he offered many *Decretum* texts that portrayed the episcopacy, like the papacy, as divinely instituted; were not the other Apostles chosen along with Peter to have charge of Christ's church? And like Monachus's emphasis on the cardinalate's role in the

---

45. He cited Gratian, D.12 c.5, 6, 16 and C.25 q.2 c.4 in *Tractatus de modo generalis concilii celebrandi* 1 Tit. 2 [Paris, 1545] pp. 4–5. A fine treatment of Durantis's political thought has just appeared: Fasolt, *Council & Hierarchy*. One notable feature of this work is the juxtaposition of Durantis's views and practices in the two political spheres, spiritual and temporal. He was one of the few medieval political theorists who exercised both pen and jurisdiction in both church and state.

46. Durantis, *Tractatus* 1 Tit. 3, pp. 10–11. For a summary of the widespread use of *quod omnes tangit* in medieval political thought see Monahan, *Consent, Coercion, and Limit*, pp. 97–111. Cf. Gaines Post, "A Roman Legal Theory of Consent," pp. 66–78; "A Romano-Canonical Maxim."

proper functioning of the papacy, Durantis's insistence on the role of the episcopate in limiting excessive papal pretensions reflected contemporary concerns. Papal centralization and concentration of power were not without opponents, and Guilielmus's criticism, however little acted upon by himself as bishop of Mende or other contemporaries in the episcopate, would have found resonance among many ecclesiastical lawyers and administrators, especially those beyond the immediate territorial and jurisdictional control of the papacy.

For Durantis, papal and episcopal authority were equally of divine origin, and his description of episcopal authority was an ingenious blend of current medieval hierarchical and corporation concepts. The Church of Rome, of which the pope is corporate head, is only one of many ecclesiastical corporations, each with its own corporate head. The corporation of the universal church, or *universitas fidelium*, has the pope as jurisdictional head, but a general church council is its supreme authority—a not uncommon notion in this period, as already shown. Yet as is so often the case in legal and political theory, the novelty of Durantis's position lay in the blending of a conventional concept, the role of a general church council, with other elements. For him, all important decisions concerning the well-being of the Church as a whole could only be made by the instrument that expressed the authority of the whole Church, a general church council. Such councils were to be convoked "whenever something is to be ordained concerning matters touching the common state of the Church or new law is to be made."[47] Again he employed the *quod omnes tangit* principle within a standard *Decretum* position, but his use of it went beyond conventional Decretist views and was invoked to deny the pope the right to legislate on his own, a position previously condemned as heretical by Joannes Teutonicus.[48]

Durantis was specific about the functioning of general church councils. They should be convened every ten years and play an ordinary constitutional role in church government and administration as regular channels for ecclesiastical taxation and legislation. He maintained further that the pope on his own could not overrule acts of previous councils, that a general council must be called to promulgate laws affecting "the common state of the church," and that adequate funding for the upkeep and operation of the papal curia should be contingent on its ob-

---

47. Durantis, *Tractactus* 3 Tit. 1, p. 163.
48. Joannes Teutonicus, *Glossa ad Dist.* 19 c.5.

serving the laws passed by general councils.[49] Where previous canonical thought had seen general councils as occasional gatherings to be called in circumstances of crisis or abnormality, Durantis gave them an ordinary and regular function.

## The Academic Canonists

In addition to the literary and sometimes directly political activities of papal critics like Monachus and Guilielmus, the more ordinary academic efforts of fourteenth-century canonists also provided material that later conciliarists would put to use in efforts to resolve the Great Schism. As might be expected, the conventional academic activity of canonical explication was mainly directed at explaining and defending the papal *status quo*, the increasingly absolutist and centralist administration of the Avignon papacy. But despite their best efforts, these church legists failed to construct a wholly satisfactory theory to underpin the extravagant claims for papal monarchy that had become commonplace at the time. The unity of the late medieval church thus rested more on tradition and practice than on an adequate theory of ecclesiastical polity. Furthermore, real tensions existed between the Church and a variety of temporal interests, as well as between various elements of administration and authority within the Church itself: papacy and cardinalate, and bishops and their rights *vis-à-vis* increasing papal financial demands and jurisdictional claims. On the secular political scene, the long-running conflict between Emperor Ludwig of Bavaria and a series of Avignon popes provided the historical backdrop for the last great enactment of the theoretical issue involving relations between church and state in the medieval period.

One problem the fourteenth-century canonists encountered in developing a comprehensive ecclesiology was the presence in Gratian's *Decretum* of so many disparate and even contradictory texts concerning the nature of the Church and the attribution of *plenitudo potestatis* to the papacy. Textual ambiguities and ambivalences had become more ob-

---

49. Durantis, *Tractatus* 3 Tit. 27 pp. 190–91. Durantis's views on the role of a general church council, specifically prepared as a "position paper" for the Council of Vienne (1311), did not receive any support at that meeting. This probably explains why Durantis offered a more politically correct version of ecclesiology in his later *Tractatus minor*, where neither his call for decennial general councils nor his prescription for controlling papal finances was repeated: see Fasolt, *Council & Hierarchy*, pp. 122, 160–66; 198–99; 242–43; esp. 302–4.

vious early in the century and succeeding decades thanks to vigorous efforts to publish compendia of canonical texts and interpretive comments. The results of this medieval academic publishing showed just how disparate current opinions were on many issues of the greatest moment, and how lacking in both historical and doctrinal uniformity were the claims on behalf of papal absolute monarchy. One critical feature that was not necessarily recognized at the time was the increasingly sophisticated effort to understand the meaning of the Church as a whole. As already noted, the term *universitas fidelium* had come into use in the late thirteenth century to designate Christianity, and this was reflected in fourteenth-century canonical glosses on the term *ecclesia*, marking the beginnings of a change in emphasis from earlier interpretations. *Ecclesia* came more and more to be identified with *universitas fidelium* and *congregatio fidelium*, whose corporatist connotations are unmistakable. The more fourteenth-century glossators were inclined to express the nature of the Church in such legalistic terms, the greater became the prospect for a similar description of the relation between pope and church, wherein the difficulties of correlating such a conception of papal authority with the current broad claims for monarchical power were not insignificant.[50]

Similarly, canonistic examination of the nature and authority of the cardinals, stimulated to a large extent by their continually expanding role and prestige, produced a careful scrutiny of relevant canons and standardization of vocabulary. Attention fastened on the role of the cardinalate in choosing a pope, and on its function when the papal throne was vacant. A correlative but more narrowly focused issue was that of the role of the cardinals in the continuity in the Church itself: if the pope were head of the Church and embodied the Church's *plenitudo potestatis*, where did the headship and fullness of power reside when the papal throne was vacant? Even though conventional canonist opinion of the day supported the strong papal-monarchy position entitling the pope to legislate on his own and against his cardinals' advice, the very fact that attention was now being directed to the precise relationship between pope and cardinals held prospects for later, more conciliar, developments.

According to the conventional view, the cardinalate had no headship role during a vacancy on the papal throne: Christ Himself was head of the Church when there was no pope. Yet vague and impracticable as this

---

50. Cf. Tierney, *Foundations of Conciliar Theory*, pp. 205–06.

position was, the question was of more than speculative interest; the papal throne had been vacant on several occasions in the late thirteenth century for months and even years. And however congenial the standard view might be towards papal monarchism in denying real authority to the cardinals in respect of the papal office, it did not sit well with another aspect of standard canonical doctrine—that divine authority in the Church needed to be continued through some earthly head or agency.

Finally, there was the problem of how to justify excepting the Church of Rome from the general corporation theory, according to which ecclesiastical administrative units were considered collective entities whose head was an administrator. Was not the Church of Rome the paradigm of an ecclesiastical collectivity; and if so, why was her structure an exception to this general model of organization? The most critical issue here was the relationship between pope and universal church, *ecclesia universa* or *ecclesia fidelium*. No one denied the theoretical need for a means of dealing with a heretical pope; indeed, it is difficult to imagine that anyone would wish to do so. There was even substantial agreement about the appropriate procedure, with the common but not universal opinion of late thirteenth-century canonists being something of an advance over earlier Decretist and Decretalist views: an errant pope had to be identified by formal allegation and afforded some kind of judicial procedure or trial. Guido de Baysio, for example, specified a general church council as the judicial body but without offering any detail on how such a council was to conduct this procedure, or even be convened.[51] Others suggested that the cardinals might convene a general council to deal with an errant pope, and there was also some inclination to broaden the grounds for action against a pope to include less serious behaviour than heresy. Various procedures for dealing with an erring pope were mentioned in the literature, then, while conventional canonical thought continued to conceive of the papacy in monarchical form.

### 4. CONCILIARISM AT THE TIME OF THE GREAT SCHISM AND BASLE

The Great Schism, with its attendant scandal, brought widespread disruption of ecclesiastical affairs in a variety of areas, doctrinal and theological as well as juridical and administrative. It could be said that the events of the schism provided an almost perfect political context within

---

51. Guido de Baysio, *In sextum decretalium commentaria* 5.2.5, fol. 114ra.

which to formulate conciliarism as a theory of ecclesiastical polity. The realities of the schism itself and the strenuous, well-intentioned, but ineffective efforts to resolve it over a period of decades led to calls for a general church council to bring the matter to resolution. In fact, all the other obvious alternatives had been tried in the first quarter-century of the schism. The various occupants of the several papal thrones had been importuned, encouraged, even pressured as strongly as possible by officials of both church and state to end the scandal by whatever means they could be persuaded to agree on; various temporal authorities, including the Holy Roman emperor and assorted European monarchs, had acted on their own initiative and had been solicited to intervene in the mess; the cardinalate, whether following the contending popes in factions or acting collectively, at least to some extent, when the contending groups could get together, had tried its hand at the job; and the general membership of the church itself had registered serious discontent with the fractured *status quo* in a variety of ways.

But four figures were dominant in formulating and advocating the conciliar position at the time of the general church councils that were convened in the early fifteenth century to resolve the schism. Two were French, Cardinal Pierre d'Ailly and Jean Gerson, both important figures at the University of Paris, a major centre of intellectual activity on both the schism and conciliarism; one was Italian, Cardinal Franciscus Zabarella; and one, Cardinal Nicholas of Cusa, was German. Political thought is largely embodied in the writings of important thinkers, and since each of these four left texts, a separate treatment and examination of their respective theories on ecclesiastical polity will be offered.

*Pierre D'Ailly*

Born in 1352 and educated in philosophy and theology at the University of Paris, d'Ailly was a prominent figure at the Councils of Pisa (1409) and Constance (1414–18), representing French ecclesiastical and temporal interests. He had adopted a moderate conciliarist position as early as 1379 in reaction to the scandal of the Great Schism that had begun the previous year. He was at the time a theological student at Paris, where two German members of the English nation, Conrad of Gelhausen and Henry of Langenstein, each took the bold step of calling for the convening of a general church council to resolve the schism at a time when Charles V of France was supporting the pope at Avignon,

Clement VII.[52] On Charles's death and the succession of a minor to the French throne in 1380, the University of Paris took a public stand favouring a conciliar solution to the schism despite the fact that the regent, Louis of Anjou, continued to favour the Avignon papacy.[53]

D'Ailly's personal career rose quite rapidly. He received his doctorate in theology in 1381 and was university chancellor at Paris by the end of the decade, from 1389 to 1395. He acquired several prominent ecclesiastical benefices in the 1390s—the bishoprics of Puy in 1395 and Cambria in 1397—and was named a cardinal in 1411. During his rise to academic and ecclesiastical prominence, d'Ailly offered public support to the *via cessionis* position favoured by France on the schism, the proposal that both papal claimants resign to enable the cardinals to choose a single pope, "getting it right" this time. Here he found himself at odds with his Parisian university colleagues, who continued to favour the conciliar solution (*via concilii*), and who viewed him as furthering his personal ambitions by taking a politically popular stand. At one point d'Ailly was even excluded from university meetings in a display of collegial displeasure at his apparent place seeking. By 1408, however, with his ecclesiastical position and stature secure, d'Ailly became convinced that the obduracy of both contenders to the papal throne was such that further effort to gain their consent to any solution was fruitless, and he came out once more in favour of the moderate conciliar position from which he never again deviated. He worked diligently and effectively at both Pisa and Constance to achieve it.

Despite his extensive involvement in the practical affairs of his university and the Church, d'Ailly produced some one hundred and seventy written works: books, treatises, letters, and sermons. Most of his writings were devoted to the schism issue, which he approached through various different literary forms, philosophical and theological works and publicist tracts. His philosophical works on the subject are few in number and for the most part brief in expression, but the theological ones are much more substantial. An early work, *Questions on the Sentences of Peter Lombard*,

---

52. Oakley, citing Ullmann, *Origins of the Great Schism*, p. 176, calls Conrad's *Epistola concordiae* of May 1380 "the first systematic exposition of the so-called conciliar theory." Oakley, *Council over Pope?*, p. 56.

53. Oakley, *Political Thought of Pierre d'Ailly*, p. 11. This work remains the standard treatment of d'Ailly's political thought, and I have followed it largely in my presentation. A fine recent presentation of the relationship between a general church council and pope in late medieval thought is Becker, *Die Appellation vom Papst an ein Allegemeines Konzil.*

is the most extensive and authoritative expression of his views. It was written during d'Ailly's academic appointment at Paris in the 1380s before he embarked on the more practical and political portion of his career.

Another early and lesser work, composed in about 1385 in connection with an internal fracas at the University of Paris, shows d'Ailly's grasp of current corporation theory. Contrary to the traditional practice at Paris, the then university chancellor, Jean Blanchard, had imposed a fee on applicants for the *licentia dociendi,* and the university corporation appointed d'Ailly to argue its objection to the imposition before the papal court. He prepared two tracts in refutation, resting his argument on the familiar corporation theory. The second contains an extended description of the university chancellor's authority, contrasting it with rectoral powers in the university as a whole and its various faculties. D'Ailly held that the authority of rectors was political but that of the chancellor was not, a distinction that led naturally to a general account of the nature of polity, *prima facie* political thought.

Proceeding in terms of the standard corporation theory, d'Ailly described the university as a political entity whose officials had authority from the members of the corporate community who placed them in office. Authority in the university is assigned to an individual by the university corporation for the purpose of "preserving and defending their political community," and rectors have authority to take action and impose such exactions as will contribute to the well-being of the community as a whole. D'Ailly's application of this view, of course, denied that the university chancellor had authority from the university corporation to exact licencing fees for his personal benefit.[54]

D'Ailly's properly conciliarist thought retains and emphasizes its basis in corporation theory. He speaks constantly of the common good or common utility of the Church when writing about the nature of the Church as a whole and employs a number of roughly interchangeable terms: public utility (of the Church), the common utility, the common good, common necessity, supreme necessity. These occur on some twenty occasions in his *Tractatus de ecclesiastica potestate.*[55] Ecclesiastical authority exists to promote the common ecclesiastical good, the criterion by which all forms of ecclesiastical jurisdictional authority and administration are measured. When a general council is assembled, then,

---

54. d'Ailly, *Tractatus II adversus cancellarium Pariensis,* in Gerson, *Opera Omnia,* edited by Louis Du Pin 1:769–70. Subsequent citations to this edition are given as Du Pin.

55. Oakley, *d'Ailly,* p. 107, note 16.

its object is to secure the welfare of all; ecclesiastical reform, if envisaged, must be directed to the utility and integrity of the whole Christian republic and not simply the particular church at Rome. Focusing on the specific procedure assigning papal election to the Roman church through the "representative" body of the cardinals, he asserted that the Roman people received their right to elect the pope for the sole purpose of serving the public utility of the whole church, and they must exercise their right in accordance with this purpose. Popes, above all, must pursue policies conducive to the common welfare, if they are to rule well.[56]

Here is another instance where views advanced for a given political purpose were neither novel nor particularly radical. D'Ailly repeated notions seen in John of Paris's *On Royal and Papal Power* and elsewhere, describing in terms of administration rather than ownership the power ecclesiastical authorities, including the pope, have over church goods. He applied corporation theory to papal authority just as canonists had applied it earlier to collegiate communities and churches where episcopal authority operated: every discrete ecclesiastical congregation has its own unity and common good, and the prelate heading a particular unity has administrative and general disposition of the community's goods solely to further its well-being. Similarly, a universal ecclesiastical unity brings all particular unities together under the administrative headship of the pope, who functions over the universal church in this fashion. The pope does not own the church's possessions; nor can he dispose of them at will or arbitrarily: papal power is limited by the need to act for the common good of the Church as a whole. D'Ailly's position reflected that of contemporary civilian jurists on the authority of temporal rulers, with one crucial difference: while the civilians made the common good an explicit basis for extending political authority beyond that normally available to a temporal ruler in virtue of his feudal status, d'Ailly's reference to the Church's common good was intended to limit, rather than extend, the pope's power.[57]

D'Ailly took his basic material from the works of earlier canonists, both Decretists and Decretalists, who had argued for some time that ecclesiastical prelates derived their jurisdictional power by way of election rather than directly from their spiritual status as ordained ministers. Conceived of as a successor to Peter on whom Christ had directly conferred leadership in the Church, the pope was normally not lumped to-

---

56. Oakley offers a number of citations on the point in *d'Ailly*, p. 108, note 18.
57. Ibid., p. 111, citing Tierney, *Foundations of Conciliar Theory*, p. 51.

gether with other prelates; but d'Ailly did just that by introducing a distinction in his description of how the pope receives power. As legitimate successor of Peter and vicar of Christ, the pope can be said to derive his authority immediately from God. But this did not mean that no human agency was involved in the process. Direct transfer of papal power to the pope immediately from God is distinct from its "ministerial" manner of transmission. When Christ placed Peter at the head of all Christians and gave him authority to establish other episcopal seats where he wished, this did not deprive the community over which he exercised jurisdiction of its natural right, "which belongs to all those over whom any authority, either secular or ecclesiastical, is placed," to elect its ruler.[58] This right, then, pertains to the whole church causally or finally and to a general council as representative of the Church, a view that enabled d'Ailly to make the pope subject to correction by a general council representing the whole church whenever he abused his office in a manner leading to the Church's destruction rather than preservation.

D'Ailly also dealt directly, and in familiar fashion, with the age-old defence of absolute rule by either king or pope through appeal to the Roman legal maxim *princeps legibus solutus*. The pope is only above laws of his own making, not "divine laws or those laws promulgated with divine authority by the universal Church."[59] He also had a clear conception of the Church's well-being, the *status ecclesiae*, and applied it directly to the schism problem. His view was that "no community is sufficiently ordered if it cannot resist its own ruin and open destruction"; the ecclesiastical polity would be badly organized indeed if it were unable to resist a pope attempting to destroy it by manifest heresy, open tyranny, or other notorious crime. D'Ailly argued that to suggest the Church could do nothing in such scandalous circumstances was tantamount to admitting that the pope had authority "not for edification but for destruction,"[60] and he listed the standard canonical categories warranting papal deposition.

The heart of d'Ailly's conciliarism thus involved specific application of medieval corporation theory to the papacy and invocation of two of its inherent principles: the notion that authority in a corporation is jurisdictional and administrative rather than that of *dominium*; and the concept

---

58. d'Ailly, *Tract. de eccl. pot.*, ed. du Pin, 2:936.
59. d'Ailly, *Tract. de mat.* reproduced in Oakley, *d'Ailly*, p. 313. Cf. *d'Ailly*, pp. 261 and 320.
60. d'Ailly, *Tract. de eccl. auct.*, ed. du Pin, 2:259.

that corporational authority is exercised in virtue of consent from its members and only for the purpose for which the community itself exists. He applied the implications of these principles to the college of cardinals and the Church as a whole as represented by a general council, naming both as instruments for exercising control over an errant pope. He thereby repeated a second position found in John of Paris, who seems to have derived it from a constitutional text in Thomas Aquinas's *Summa theologiae*: approval of a "mixed" form of government. Aquinas had spoken of the best form of temporal governance; Quidort applied the concept to the Church and identified the cardinalate as equivalent to an aristocratic element of advisors, and a general church council as the democratic element representing the Church as a whole.[61]

D'Ailly repeated John's position with certain modifications, applying the notion of mixed constitution to both temporal and ecclesiastical polities. Simplistically speaking, kingship would be the best form of governance if one could presume the absence of corruption; but it degenerates easily into tyranny because of the general weakness of humans. The best form of polity because the most practicable, then, is kingship combined with aristocracy and democracy where all elements in society have a role to play: God provided this type of polity for the Israelites, over whom one man, Moses or Joshua, for example, was pre-eminent but advised by a group of elders, the aristocratic feature, while election of the seventy-two elders from and by all the people reflected the democratic feature. Similarly, the Church would have the best form of government if, under one pope, it also had a group of advisors, the cardinals, "elected by and from every province ... cardinals who, with the pope and under him, might rule the church and temper the use of the *plenitudo potestatis*."[62]

D'Ailly made a more explicit statement on the same point when asking whether the fullness of power rested in the Roman pontiff alone. His answer raised another crucial distinction: the Church's fullness of power does not rest only in the pope, but is found in him "separably" and in the *universitas* of the Church "inseparably"; the pope may lose the *plenitudo potestatis* when, for example, he misuses his office, but it always

---

61. Ibid., pp. 946–47. Cf. Thomas Aquinas, *ST* 1–2.105.1 and *ad* 1; John of Paris, *Royal and Papal Power* 19 *ad* 35, p. 100. Advocacy of a "mixed" form of polity for the Church was repeated by Gerson: *De potestate*, cons. 8, col. 237; cons. 12, col. 248; cons. 13, col. 254, cited in Sigmund, *Nicholas of Cusa*, p. 114, note 83. It recurs later in Calvin's political thought and some examples of Huguenot resistance theory. Continuity with conciliarist theory is unmistakable here: see *infra*, pp. 225; 269; 63–64.

62. d'Ailly, *Tract. de eccl. auct.*, ed. du Pin, 2:946.

remains in the whole church. D'Ailly's other texts on *plenitudo potestatis* were not always so clear and even seemed to attribute it to the pope alone. But in the final analysis, he always maintained that it existed in the papacy' "as if in the subject receiving it and the minister exercising it," while being in the universal church as in its object, that is, in terms of the purpose to which it is ordained, and in a general council "as in the image representing and ordering it as a matter of course."[63]

D'Ailly was also explicit on the cardinals' role and share in *plenitudo potestatis*. He connected the cardinalate with the Church of Rome as regionally understood, that is, considered as the diocese over which the pope ruled as bishop. "The plenitude of power is represented in some way in the Roman church just as it is in a general council, though not equally, because it represents the universal church and acts in its place in creating ecclesiastical laws or canons."[64] The regional Roman church has this power because its head, the pope, is himself pre-eminent in the universal church, and, in promising as a condition of consecration to exercise his office "with the advice, consent, love and remembrance of the cardinals,"[65] he shares his power with them. D'Ailly even insisted that the cardinals enjoyed their authority as the inherited counterpart of the "senate" of the Apostles. As such, they are special assistants to the pope and act "in the place and name of the universal church as well as of the Roman church."[66] Their duty is to serve the pope as principal assistants, counsellors, and cooperators in ruling the universal church; this is why it is fitting for the pope to be elected by the cardinals. Earlier canonical thinkers, specifically Hostiensis and Joannes Monachus, had also asserted the authority of the cardinalate and its role in church administration, as we have seen, claiming that pope and cardinals together constituted the corporation of the church of Rome. For his part, however, d'Ailly maintained that the cardinalate derived its status from its place in the Church as a whole, the *universitas ecclesiae*. His remarks on this point lack the clarity and precision shown later by Cardinal Zabarella at the Council of Constance, but they mark an advance over John of Paris's *On Royal and Papal Power*, where d'Ailly had found them.

63. d'Ailly, *Tract. de eccl. auct.*, ed. du Pin, 2:951.
64. Ibid.
65. Ibid., 2:929–30.
66. Ibid., 2:930. The notion that there had been a senate in the early church re-emerged in Reformation ecclesiology with Calvin, and Huguenot resistance publicists extended it explicitly to the temporal order in arguing that lower magistrates had a right to resist tyranny. See *infra*, pp. 229–72, *passim*.

Popular consent is also found in the d'Ailly doctrine, linked with representation in an expression of corporation theory that had roots in the origins of medieval political thought, both Christian and Roman. But for all that, consent was one of the least developed concepts in the vocabulary of medieval political discourse and caution must be used in analysing its meaning. Virtually every political writer in the Middle Ages acknowledged that authority of any kind, both temporal and ecclesiastical, rested on consent from the community over which it was exercised, but they normally paid little attention, if any, to how consent was to be expressed. Moreover, it usually designated passive acceptance rather than active participation in an elective process.[67]

Though integral to medieval ecclesiology, consent was less significant than the claims concerning divine establishment and the principle that the divine is superior to the earthly. Accordingly, the authority of the Christian community was subordinate to that of Christ, Who had established the Church. Advocates of papal monarchy always stressed the divine source of the pope's authority, deriving it from its original grant by Christ to Peter. And while the efforts that began with the Gregorian Reform to extricate ecclesiastical offices from the control of temporal powers were never totally successful, subsequent development of a highly centralized papal authority and the activities of many popes produced a theory of papal monarchy with a high level of acceptance and practice. Later, in the heyday of the divine-right-of-kings theory, temporal rulers also claimed God as the direct source of their power, arguing that they too were subject only to God. For medieval Christians, stressing the virtually self-evident view that Christ had established the Church entailed acceptance of a hierarchical institution whose head claimed to hold authority in direct succession from St Peter and thus directly from God, and this in turn became one of the strongest arguments an occupant of the papal throne could employ to bolster claims of an absolutist kind: no earthly power, spiritual or temporal, was superior to his, and he was responsible to no other power.

It has been mentioned that this position still required that canonists wishing to develop a coherent doctrine of ecclesiastical polity admit, at least in theory, that an individual pope was subject to error and misuse of power, however diffident they might have been about specifying the point in a practical way. Hence it is ironic, though not totally unexpected,

---

67. See Monahan, *Consent, Coercion, and Limit*, pp. 97–110, and various articles in the magisterial Gaines Post collection, *Studies in Medieval Legal Thought*.

that the first formulations of a coherent theory of limited or constitutional government based on popular consent are found in canonical and theological sources, and that this development occurred as a result of the desperate need to resolve a political disaster that took an essentially spiritual form: the scandal of the Great Schism.

By the fifteenth century, the idea of the whole community as ultimate source of political authority had become something of a cliché, as is clear from the fact that conciliar thinkers of the period were able so easily to apply it to the Church. Combining the principle of popular authority with the legal concept of representation, however, was what completed a genuinely practical theory of polity for both church and state, even though, as also already noted,[68] representation did not entail its modern sense of actual popularly controlled delegation. The standard medieval understanding of representation was that of personification: the ruler, king or pope, was perceived to embody in his person the group he was said to represent, while the relationship between his person and that of any other member of society was construed in feudal terms as an essentially contractual relationship; the notion of a collective entity with rights of control or exercise over a ruler was not yet present. However, representation as personification began to be undermined as early as the thirteenth century through the developing use of representation in the legal administration of both church and state. Conducting business at a distance and dispensing a uniform system of justice controlled by a central authority, king or pope, made such a development inevitable.

A correlative notion with significant implications for the later development of democratic government was that of full powers, *plena potestas* or *plenitudo potestatis*. Originally employed in the ecclesiastical jurisdiction to guarantee that the pope or other prelate could be assured that his jurisdiction, exercised at a distance, was accepted by those to whom it was being applied, it required that those seeking adjudication of their interests either come themselves or be represented by persons having "full powers" to treat on their behalf. It also came into play in the secular sphere when a temporal ruler found it useful, and even necessary, in dealing with his subjects. In such cases agreement was *from* rather than *with* a plenipotentiary; his consent did not necessarily follow from his concurring as an equal in negotiation. Representatives of individuals or various groups of the people gave their consent necessarily; they were

---

68. *Supra*, p. 83. Cf. Monahan, *Consent, Coercion, and Limit*, pp. 119–21.

not perceived as having the right to withhold consent inasmuch as the ruler's authority entailed an obligation on subjects to accede to his views.[69]

The first and ordinary instances of this procedure in the temporal sphere occurred within a judicial rather than a law-making jurisdiction, where the temporal ruler was dispenser of justice. It was his authority that settled an issue between two private individuals—the traditional feudal perspective where even the king was a private person, and the law and juridical procedure were private rather than public. As a judge, however, the ruler did not negotiate with a litigant before him but rendered judgment alone, though often with advice from counsellors and the other party or parties "consented." The notion of the ruler as a public figure and the state as something other than the private possession of its highest authority acquired theoretical substance only over time. The first signs of these developments are found within the medieval Church, where the implications of the exercise of would-be absolute and arbitrary power by the pope, the accepted head of the collective entity, underwent careful scrutiny by theologians and legists and drew political response from those subject to his jurisdiction.

Two somewhat opposing movements emerged. Statements concerning supreme authority in the Church were always of the strongest and most forceful kind; the pope was always described as the greatest power on earth, over whom no earthly individual or agency had jurisdiction. At the same time, however, precisely because his supreme authority was spiritual and its purpose directed to heavenly and ultimate things, there was always concern that it be exercised properly. As well, and also because ecclesiastical power was spiritual in kind, it was in itself only moral and lacked the physical character of temporal coercive force. Accordingly, there would have been a greater tendency to be more critical of its use in the ordinary course of events than was the case in the temporal sphere, where opposition to a temporal ruler ordinarily could be expected to produce a "physical" response from the ruler. This spiritual/temporal dichotomy probably did not work quite as simply and naturally as this in practice; but spiritual authority was likely to come under more rigorous scrutiny than temporal authority, both because it was spiritual and thus attracted attention from those who were concerned with their eternal salvation, and because it was moral and thus did not directly entail the crudest forms of coercion.

69. See Monahan, *Consent, Coercion, and Limit*, pp. 121–26; Post, *Studies*, pp. 91–162.

In placing ultimate ecclesiastical authority in the church itself and more particularly in its members, taken as a corporation, d'Ailly gave real clarity and impetus to a procedure for resolving the schism. He also gave a clear constitutional character to his proposed solution, setting it on accepted general principles and within conventional Christian theology by employing a distinction favoured by strong advocates of papal monarchy such as Aegidius of Rome: that between the absolute and the ordinary or ordained powers of God. All authority comes from God, Who disposes of it as He wills according to His absolute power. But just as God, the first cause of things, freely chooses in virtue of His ordained power to operate through natural secondary causes, He similarly chooses to connect His bestowal of authority with purely human signs of legal disposition; hence possession of legitimate authority is manifest to us *de facto* only through some created title or sign. A particular example is papal authority expressed in terms of its relation with the Roman church and the general church council: "Immediately it is principally from God, but it is also from humans, or depends on human power in a ministerial way, for the pope attains his position through election by the cardinals, and the cardinals theirs by the authority of the pope."[70]

D'Ailly's main concern in his theory of ecclesiastical polity was to identify the community of the church as the source of authority. Although this might seem to imply that d'Ailly was mounting a call for the pope to be elected by those subject to him, he apparently accepted the current *status quo*: the cardinals choose the pope, and popular consent by the Church as a whole evidently contained the indistinct notion that the cardinalate represented the whole Church. His position nonetheless had immediate practical impact since the schism presented highly abnormal circumstances and normal procedures for choosing a pope were inade-

---

70. d'Ailly, *Tract. de eccl. auct.*, ed. du Pin, 2:938. D'Ailly appended what Oakley calls a "very awkward" qualification to the general notion of authority resting ultimately in the people when he stated that members of a community over whom authority, "either secular or ecclesiastical," is exercised can elect their ruler "unless the contrary is ordained by themselves ... or by their superior": *Tract. de eccl. auct.*, ed. du Pin, 2:936; Oakley, *d'Ailly*, p. 141, note 5. Oakley points out, however, that d'Ailly was working here directly from a position found in William of Ockham, *Dialogus* 3.2.3.6; Goldast 2:934, whose text shows, on careful reading, that the qualification does not amount to very much. Certainly it does not remove the generality of the d'Ailly view that the group over which authority is exercised always retains the right, at least in unusual circumstances, to take action to prevent its own destruction. Further, the notion simply continues the view of Thomas Aquinas that the people are one of two alternative sources of ultimate political authority: Thomas Aquinas, *ST* 1–2.90.3.

quate. D'Ailly devoted considerable attention to the role of the people in church affairs, although his main emphasis was on the essential role of popular consent in terminating papal authority rather than on its elective function in originating it. And here, like Ockham and others before him, d'Ailly used the principle *quod omnes tangit* to limit papal authority: those responsible in the first instance for bringing a ruler into office, temporal or ecclesiastical, can exercise control to guarantee proper use of his power.

D'Ailly described the various levels of papal administrative power when examining the rights of the Church as a whole to exercise control over the papacy, linking them together to show how each expressed popular consent, the linchpin in his theory. And when describing the function of the cardinalate he rose above the conventional understanding of representation, even though he sometimes used the term to connote embodiment or personification. When speaking precisely in a careful presentation of his ecclesiology, d'Ailly had in mind something much closer to the modern paradigm: representation involved delegation and even election from constituencies. He advocated that the cardinals, as representatives of the Church as a whole, be elected from all ecclesiastical provinces and even that they be chosen by the provinces themselves.[71] He was silent about an electoral mechanism, but what he had in mind certainly went beyond the notion that the cardinals "represent" only in a symbolic sense: symbols do not need to be elected to office.

D'Ailly's final position was that a general council could resolve the schism because it represented the whole Church; but again he was not precise about how representation occurred. General councils, he asserted, derive their authority from "the consent of all the faithful" as well as from the authority of Christ;[72] but he was silent on procedures by which the faithful were to express consent through their representatives at a general council. However, while apparently accepting the current assumption that general councils as traditionally organized and convoked were more or less automatically representative bodies, he did concern himself to some extent with the actual voting procedures at the Council of Constance, and here his views were anything but democratic. Council members were to be drawn from the ranks of the nobles and the learned; while no one could be excluded, d'Ailly held that the un-

---

71. d'Ailly, *Tract. de eccl. auct.*, ed. du Pin, 2:946.
72. d'Ailly, *Epistola ad regem Carolum directa*, Denifle 3:621.

learned and persons of the lowest rank need not be summoned.[73] Also, without addressing the issue of how the church community as a whole selected representatives to a general council, he emphasized that representation entailed a spectrum of council members. His views on this are found in a relatively late treatise, *Disputatio de jure suffragii quibus competat*, written in 1415 during the council at Constance. This is a particularly important text insofar as it was clearly intended to present a general theory of ecclesiastical polity rather than merely an expedient solution to the current schism.

Asking who should have a place in a general church council, d'Ailly acknowledged that the gathering at Constance was responding to an abnormal situation and thus operating without clearly established precedent; but he contended that more than bishops should participate in general councils.[74] Abbots, doctors of canon and civil law, and especially doctors of theology had a place, the latter because they have "the authority to preach and teach anywhere on earth, which is no little authority among a Christian people, and much greater than that of a single ignorant and merely titular bishop or abbot."[75] Kings, princes, or their ambassadors were entitled to be present as well and to have a voice.

Pre-eminence was to be given to persons of authority and quality, those superior in wisdom and influence who could be expected to discern and implement policy most in conformity with the common good of the Church as a whole. Something more than the collected expressions of individual members of the *universitas ecclesiae* was involved here; d'Ailly was expressing the traditional medieval conception of the common good as divined and expressed by those superior beings in a community who were best able to do so and who represented the whole seemingly by definition inasmuch as their representative status did not derive from any form of direct and universal suffrage. His doctrine was one of trusteeship and not representation as we understand it today. Nor did d'Ailly repeat here his earlier view that cardinals should be chosen from and by various geographical regions; but he did call for some kind

---

73. d'Ailly, *Oratio de officio imperatoris*, ed. du Pin, 2:921. Oakley offers other citations on the same point in *d'Ailly*, pp. 149–50 and notes. D'Ailly again seems to be following Ockham here.

74. D'Ailly here rejects his earlier position that only bishops should attend general councils: *Tractatus de materia concilii generalis*, reproduced in Oakley, *d'Ailly*, pp. 244–342. The remark concerning exclusive episcopal participation in general councils is at p. 268.

75. d'Ailly, "Disputatio 12," in Hardt, ed., *Rerum concilii oecumenici Constantiensis* 2:225–26.

of presence or representation of all Church members in general church councils and accepted the notion that council members at least were somehow responsible to the Christian community as a whole for the Church's well-being.[76]

The corresponding feature of the obligation on members to obey church authority was also a concern for d'Ailly, particularly in its negative aspects. Must the faithful obey directives of an errant ecclesiastical authority; more seriously, were they obliged to disobey in order to correct the damaged state into which an unworthy ecclesiastical official had placed them? Earlier medieval political thought had examined tyrannicide as a response to tyranny in the secular sphere. Some writers, like John of Salisbury, had explicitly sanctioned it, while others, like Aquinas, expressed cautious approval in carefully circumscribed circumstances that excluded action by a private individual. Gradual development and application of corporation theory to both secular and ecclesiastical spheres, moreover, tended to locate resistance to tyranny in the community as a whole and to produce the resistance theory later propounded by Protestant reformers in the mid-sixteenth century.

For his part, d'Ailly maintained the patristic view sanctioned by St Augustine, that tyrants could exercise legitimate authority over Christians and other subjects, and he supported his successor as chancellor at the University of Paris, Jean Gerson, in securing a formal condemnation of tyrannicide at the Council of Constance—one example of activity at Constance devoted to matters other than the schism. The formal condemnation and burning of John Hus was another. The council had been asked to condemn as heretical a treatise by the Dominican Jean Petit, which justified the 1407 assassination of the duke of Orléans. Its response was to condemn tyrannicide, but without naming either Petit or his treatise. In supporting the council's action d'Ailly gave a more severe personal judgment against the Petit position, aligning it with a view attributed to Wyclif and already judged heretical, viz., "that the multitude (*populares*) can, of its own choice, correct a delinquent lord."[77] He considered Petit's views even more worthy of condemnation than this one, but he did not condemn tyrannicide *tout court*, perhaps considering that his own doctrine on constitutional procedures available

---

76. See Oakley's point that when speaking of the role of doctors of theology at a general council d'Ailly grounds their importance in the notion that they have authority as teachers and experts in doctrine over large numbers of the faithful. Oakley, *d'Ailly*, p. 154, note 55, and *supra*, note 75.

77. d'Ailly, *Additio Cardinalis cameracensis pro sua opinione*, du Pin 5:475.

against tyrannical exercise of authority would preclude the need for more drastic action.

While d'Ailly's most complete statement on the authority of a general church council to resolve the current schism is found in the second part of his *Tractatus de materia concilii generalis*, most of which he repeated in the later *Tractatus de ecclesiastica potestate*, his most valuable comments on the issue are found among the several "useful propositions" appended to a letter sent to the cardinals assembling for the Council of Pisa in 1409. Their combination of brevity, comprehensiveness, and clarity offers a striking statement of the theoretical assumptions involved. The unity of the Church, d'Ailly said, did not necessarily originate in the unity of the pope, for the Church always remains one even if it has no pope.[78] It has the means to preserve its own unity from the natural law as well as from the authority of Christ: "Any civil body, civil community or rightly ordained polity" can naturally resist its own division and destruction, as can any natural or animate body.[79] This direct, even cryptic, emphasis on the limits of legitimate political authority and the rights of its beneficiaries to act to maintain its values against abuse of power expresses the essence of any general constitutional theory of polity. It should not be surprising, then, to find d'Ailly's political thought in the historical line of development of this form of Western political theory.

## *Jean Gerson*

The second major French churchman who played a significant role in formulating and applying the conciliar theory to a resolution of the Great Schism was Jean Gerson. Born in 1363 in Gerson-les-Barbery, from which he took his surname, he studied philosophy and theology at the University of Paris (the College of Navarre). One of his teachers was Pierre d'Ailly, who became and remained a close friend and who sponsored Gerson for the licentiate in theology in 1392, two years before he received his doctorate in the same subject.[80] Gerson succeeded d'Ailly

---

78. d'Ailly, *Propositiones utiles*. The text is printed in Martène and Durand, eds., *Veterum scriptorum et monumentorum*, 7:909–11.

79. Ibid.

80. The standard works in English on Gerson are Morrall, *Gerson and the Great Schism*, and Pascoe, *Jean Gerson, Principles of Church Reform*. See also Meyjes, *Jean Gerson*. Gerson writings are available in a fine modern edition: *Jean Gerson: Oeuvres complètes*, ed. Palémon Glorieux. I cite the earlier du Pin edition of Gerson, *Opera omnia* as P, and the Glorieux edition of Gerson, *Oeuvres complètes* as G.

as university chancellor at Paris in 1394, by which time he had acquired a reputation as a preacher and begun a close association with Philip the Bold, duke of Burgundy, as his almoner. He thus entered the political circles of the house of Burgundy through a relationship that continued until Gerson condemned the Burgundian involvement in the 1407 assassination of the duke of Orléans.

As mentioned earlier in connection with d'Ailly, the faculty at the University of Paris had generally supported the *via concilii* method of resolving the schism, but in 1394 it officially endorsed the *via cessionis*, attracting thereby an imposition of silence from the king of France. An assembly of Parisian clergy in 1395 also adopted the *via cessionis* position calling for the abdication of both popes, Boniface IX at Rome and Benedict XIII at Avignon. Gerson for his part took little or no role in the increasing tensions over both the ecclesiastical and political aspects of the continuing schism scandal, apparently preferring to follow his inclination towards a life of piety, contemplation, and scholarship, although he seems generally to have accepted the *via cessionis* position at this time. Failure to achieve agreement among and between contesting papal parties and contenders on resolution of the schism, however, caused Gerson to consider the conciliar solution, and he had turned in this direction as early as 1403. He had become a firm advocate of conciliarism by the time the Council of Pisa was convened in 1409 and, though his official university and pastoral responsibilities in Paris kept him from attending the council, he published several tracts justifying its convocation. Moreover, he was one of the most dominant conciliarists at the Council of Constance, where he also took a prominent part in the condemnation of John Hus and in the efforts to condemn tyrannicide as espoused by Jean Petit; Gerson had already publicly condemned the assassination of the duke of Orléans. Gerson never returned to Paris from Constance, although he remained nominally its university chancellor until his death. He went from Constance to Vienna and taught there briefly in 1419 before taking up residence in Lyons, where he died ten years later.

While Gerson was a strong and effective proponent of the conciliar position among French ecclesiastics and one of its most persistent supporters at the Council of Constance, where the Great Schism was finally resolved, there is little of interest for our purposes in his actual formulation of doctrine. Essentially a theologian, he expressed his conciliarist views in theological rather than political or legal terms and was primarily influenced by general hierarchical concepts derived from the Neo-platonism of the Pseudo-Dionysius.[81] He had little to say, then, about the trace elements of popular consent, representation, and election, or about specific limits to the exercise of legitimate political authority, spiritual or temporal.

Unlike d'Ailly,[82] Gerson was nothing of a populist as regards the institutions of Church government and administration, and certainly no advocate of any modern notion of functional equality among individuals in any form of polity, secular or ecclesiastic. He categorically rejected the Ockhamist view that the Church, as the means of eternal salvation and indefectible vessel of divine institution, could exist in a single person, even a woman. For him, the Church would always have bishops and priests organized in an appropriate hierarchy: its hierarchical structure was one of its essential features. While conceding that the existing ecclesiastical structure in theory could be changed, he insisted that only the Holy Spirit, not human effort, could accomplish this. And he seems to have had little time for the standard canonical defence of church rights against the pope.[83]

Responding to the standard objection that only the pope could convene a general council, however, Gerson did acknowledge that there were occasions when the Church could call such a gathering on its own initiative. His argument reflected a position already seen in d'Ailly: the Church is a perfect type of institution and as such must be able to provide for its own well-being. He invoked a number of religious authorities here in an essentially theological argument based largely on the

---

81. Pascoe provides a summary of the Gerson application of Pseudo-Dionysian hierarchical theory to the Church: Pascoe, *Jean Gerson, Principles of Church Reform*, pp. 17–48. Cf. Aegidius of Rome's similar dependence on the Pseudo-Dionysius, *supra*, p. 51, note 2.

82. The basic similarity in much of their conciliarist doctrines as well as the close personal relationship between d'Ailly and Gerson inevitably points to the influence of the former on the latter, something Gerson acknowledged in a general way by referring to himself as "disciple" of the preceding chancellor of Paris: Gerson, *Liber de vita spirituali*, P, 3:1–2; G, 3:113; cf. 2:80.

However, precise details concerning this dependency, especially in regard to Gerson's ecclesiology, are not yet fully developed, and there has been a movement in recent scholarship to reverse the conventionally accepted and *prima facie* plausible historical sequence placing Gerson as pupil and d'Ailly as master, by arguing that d'Ailly was influenced by Gerson in both mystical theology and issued of ecclesiastical reform. Oakley's seemingly sensible assessment of this issue is that while Gerson may have been less influenced by d'Ailly in his ecclesiology than traditionally has been assumed, the case for Gerson as an influence on d'Ailly remains unproven. For details on this matter, including references to the sources as well as the arguments involved, see Oakley, "Gerson and d'Ailly."

83. Sigmund, *Nicholas of Cusa*, p. 114.

Christian Scriptures, the same argument employed by d'Ailly. Unlike his academic compatriot and friend, however, Gerson took an exclusively clerical approach to the issue of church membership. He specifically declined to accept laity and even mere religious, anyone not an ordained cleric, as full-fledged members of the Church. He listed three ranks in the Church, only the first two of which, prelates and priests, possessed what he called the hierarchical power marking them as full members of the ecclesiastical polity. He considered the third rank, everyone below the rank of a male in holy orders, as strictly speaking below the salt in terms of full membership in the community of the Church.[84] He did repeat, however, the d'Ailly view also found in earlier medieval ecclesiology that the Church exhibited a mixed form of polity, with the pope as its monarchical component, the cardinals as the aristocratic, and the general council the democratic or timocratic one.[85]

He maintained that a general church council is the best forum for treating essential church business because of its collective character: it gives fullest expression to the Church's hierarchical nature and is the best instrument for exercising the church's hierarchical powers. Gerson's focus here was on the episcopacy, however, the bishops considered as successors of the Apostles, to each of whom power was given equally by Christ when He established the Church.[86] Gerson did refer to the corporate character of the Church as a whole when he asserted that heresy "touches" all Christians, a kind of back-handed reference to the principle of *quod omnes tangit*, perhaps;[87] but he did not exploit the principle for either ecclesiastical or political purposes as d'Ailly did. And he would have understood any necessary popular consent for ecclesiastical authority in the conventionally conservative meaning that all church members were represented at a general council by whoever was present.

Nor did Gerson take up the conciliar cause as a radical reformer, even though he was a strong advocate of the *via concilii* by the time of the Council of Pisa (1409) and became even more committed after that council managed only to produce a third candidate for the papal

---

84. Gerson, *De potestate ecclesiastica*, G, 6:227. Cf. *Responsio ad errores de orationibus privatis fidelium*, P, 2:654A; *Quomodo stabit regnum*, G, 7:982.

85. See *supra*, p. 81.

86. Gerson, *Ambulate dum lucem habetis*, G, 5:40.

87. Gerson also employed the *quod omnes tangit* formula directly in connection with the definition of matters of faith. Gerson, *De concilio*, P, 2:25C; G, 6:52, cited in Oakley, "Gerson and d'Ailly," p. 81, n. 45.

throne. He proved indefatigable in the conciliarist cause, particularly at the Council of Constance, where his sermon *Ambulate dum lucem habetis* roused the flagging conciliarist forces after John XXII had left the gathering without agreeing to accept its jurisdiction.

Moreover, the formal expressions of Gerson's position favouring a general council as the needed instrument for church reform also revealed his critical attitude towards current papal practices, especially those seeming to confuse temporal and spiritual spheres. Such confusion, he contended, had been introduced into the Church many centuries earlier by the Donation of Constantine. Not that Gerson was unwilling to concede to the papacy a right to temporal power in virtue of this eighth-century forgery that was still considered genuine by most Christians; nowhere did he suggest that the pope or the Church in general had no business concerning themselves with the ownership and control of temporalities. Gerson's point was that, having been granted such entitlement by Constantine, the Church had proceeded to make a mess of exercising temporal rights and had allowed church law to become "confused" by mixing legislation to deal with temporal affairs with its proper spiritual concerns. In his view, entirely too much canonical legislation and too many church concerns dealt with this secondary order of authority. This attitude enabled him to be almost as critical of the legal practice and practitioners of his day as d'Ailly, although he never spoke on the subject with anything like d'Ailly's acerbity.

Gerson maintained that the Church should employ only temporal methods in dealing with temporal interests and not impose spiritual penalties like excommunication for secular offences. More importantly, he called for a return to the proper forms of the two orders of law, divine and natural, to regulate the government and administration of church affairs. He insisted that these two orders of law took precedence over existing church legislation and were the standard by which existing canons and decisions should be measured. He also invoked the Aristotelian concept of *epikeia* (equity) as the means of measuring the value and application of existing legislation against the higher forms of divine and natural law, being quite convinced that the existing canons were not an effective means of resolving the schism.[88]

In fact, his proposal for calling a general church council rested directly on this notion of *epikeia*, which he identified with equity (*aequitas*) and used as the suggested instrument for getting round the various interminable and in some sense irrefutable objections that invoked earlier

---

88. Gerson, *De unitate ecclesiae*, G, 6:143; *De vita spirituali animae*, G, 3:189.

canons as relevant to the schism scandal.[89] Slavish acceptance of the literal statements in existing canonical legislation seemed to him to offer no practical way of addressing the current scandal. Rather than simply consulting the canons, then, one had to underline what they were intended to achieve: the ordered activity of the institutional church. To accept this as their overarching purpose meant that the canons could not be used properly when all their literal application seemed to achieve was *de facto* prevention of reform.[90]

### Franciscus Zabarella

Franciscus Zabarella brought the most scholarly and sustained formulation of conciliarism to efforts at solving the Great Schism. Born in Padua in 1360 (Tierney says c.1335), he was one of the most distinguished canonists of the late fourteenth century. He produced an enormous output of canonical literature covering the whole range of ecclesiastical law, so that his comprehensive presentation of all the essential elements of conciliar theory was set in the context of his overall doctrine. Created a cardinal by John XXII in 1411 he was a papal legate at the Council of Constance, where he died in 1417 before the council had concluded its work. His *Tractatus de schismate*, a work of pure canonical scholarship written at intervals in the period 1403–8, brought together conciliar material from the preceding two centuries and set it in his bulky commentary on the *Decretals* as a gloss on 1.6.6.; his commentary on the five books of the *Decretals* had been written slightly earlier, from 1396–1404.[91] As well as being a canonist of great reputation, then, Zabarella was a member of the college of cardinals and a major participant at the Council of Constance, and like d'Ailly, he was on record as a thoughtful and formidable conciliarist before both Pisa and Constance.

The basic structure of Zabarella's conciliarist thought was the now familiar corporation theory first applied in a coherent form to the Church as a whole by John of Paris, from whom Zabarella drew much of his doc-

---

89. Gerson, *De auferibilitate sponsi ab ecclesiae*, G, 3:301.
90. See Pascoe, *Jean Gerson*, pp. 71–79, 208.
91. Zabarella, *Super quinque libri Decretalium commentaria*. The *De schismate* is at fol. 107rb–110vb, and was also printed as a separate treatise in Schardius, *De iurisdictione, auctoritate, et praeeminentia imperiali ac potestate ecclesiastica* pp. 688–711. For Zabarella's importance as a conciliarist and a presentation of his doctrine see Tierney, *Foundations of Conciliar Theory*, pp. 220–37, and Ullmann, *Origins of the Great Schism*. I have followed the Tierney account.

trine but without explicit acknowledgment: the Italian canonist preferred to cite only canonical sources and to cast his arguments in a legal frame of reference. Inasmuch as the Great Schism could be seen as essentially a legal problem requiring a canonically justifiable solution, there was a great deal to be said for framing its resolution in these terms. Zabarella began with the flat assertion that the whole of christendom was one great corporation over which the pope presided as rector in the same way any other corporate head did: "The pope is he whom judgment and agreement by the corporation (*universitas*) choose, understanding by corporation the corporation of the whole of christendom (*totus christianitas*).[92] He proceeded to examine the essential feature of unity in the Church as a whole, an especially relevant approach to the *de facto* division in the Church caused by the schism, and went on to suggest that the existing scandal in which more than one person was claiming to occupy the ultimate institutional expression of unity, the papacy, could be construed to mean that there was a "quasi-vacancy" in that singular office, inasmuch as neither papal claimant could exercise effective authority over the whole Church—an abnormal and harmful circumstances in which, then, exercise of the authority of the Church rested in the *congregatio fidelium*: "The church has a quasi vacancy ... and when the church has [such] a vacancy, the church's universal power seems to rest in the whole Church which is the whole body of the faithful (*fidelium congregatio*)."[93]

The power of the Church as a whole, he continued, could be exercised by its "greater part" (*valentior pars*) as assembled in a general church council, and by the "greater part" of the council insofar as that body was itself a corporation whose activities were under the control of the majority of its members.[94] While Zabarella did use the Marsilian term *valentior pars*, he used it interchangeably with the terms *pars potior* and *pars idoneior*. Accordingly, not much, if anything, should be made of this echo of Marsilian language; the term *valentior pars* also appeared in William of Moerbeke's mid-thirteenth-century translation of Aristotle's *Politics*, and the concept for which it stood was a standard juridical notion.[95]

Turning to the concern about how a general council should be convoked to deal with schism or any other serious peril to the Church,

92. Zabarella, *Commentaria*, fol. 107rb, p. 688.
93. Ibid., fol. 107va, p. 688.
94. Ibid., fol. 107rb, p. 688.
95. Cf. Tierney, *Foundations of Conciliar Theory*, p. 223.

Zabarella advanced the conventional canonical view that the pope had direct responsibility here and asserted that the proper course would be for the two rival popes to convene a council by enjoining their respective followers to do so. In the event this did not happen, on the other hand, the right and responsibility devolved on the cardinals and ultimately on the Christian people as a whole, whose agent could be the emperor, while in the final analysis any means could be used to bring a general council together.[96] Evidently, Zabarella was more concerned with the notion that the full ecclesiastical authority of the whole Church rested in a general council rather than with the procedural niceties of how such a gathering might be brought together. In this, he showed a lack of imagination that was all too normal in the Middle Ages concerning the importance of procedural details in the exercise of political authority.

However, he did address the issue of how to relate the notion of papal plenitude of power with the contention that a general council was superior to a pope in the existing circumstances. Again, while echoing views seen earlier in John of Paris, Joannes Monachus, and Guilielmus Durantis, Zabarella's position was expressed with a clarity and crispness that turned his formulation into a formidable conciliar weapon: "The statement that a pope has plenitude of power should not be understood to mean that he alone possesses it, but that he has it in virtue of being head of a corporation (*universitas*) such that this power resides fundamentally (*in fundamento*) in the corporation, and in the pope as its first minister through whom the power is expressed."[97] Zabarella was always clear on the point that such power as the pope had was conferred on him by the Church as a whole and could be withdrawn in certain circumstances, since a pope was never able to exercise authority against the interests of the ecclesiastical corporation, the Church, whose proctor he was: the Church ultimately could decide whether or not papal behaviour was appropriate and had the power to depose a pope as necessary.[98]

Zabarella also applied the general corporation theory to the episcopacy, following Durantis, and to the college of cardinals, following Monachus, in drawing limits around papal authority by asserting its presence in papal episcopal peers and his fellow corporate members of the

---

96. Zabarella, *Commentaria*, fol. 108rb, p. 693.
97. Ibid., fol. 109va, p. 703.
98. Ibid., Zabarella made clear in a number of texts that a general council is superior to the pope, and he cited the *Glossa ordinaria*, sometimes construing his sources in ways that stretched their meaning well beyond their author's original intent: *Commentaria*, fol. 109rb, p. 701; *Commentaria ad* 1.6.4, fol. 104va; *ad* 3.8.15, fol. 661ra.

Roman church. For example, the pope simply could not legislate on his own on important matters without consulting the cardinals—a Monachus view also found in Huguccio two centuries earlier and repeated in the *Glossa Palatina* known to Zabarella through Guido de Baysio's *Rosarium*.[99] In attributing power to the cardinals over the pope, moreover, he did not reject or even confuse the principle that fullness of power rested originally and ultimately in the whole community of the Church, for he contended that "the college of cardinals represents the universal Church and functions as its regent."[100] It was for this reason that authority devolved directly on the cardinals when a pope proved negligent, and also passed directly to the whole church if the cardinals proved unable to act properly. He suggested specifically in the circumstances of the current schism that all cardinals should withdraw their allegiance from both popes and was prepared to have the cardinals' authority pre-empted by the "congregation of the faithful," should the cardinals fail to take such an initiative.[101] Finally, Zabarella held that any dispute between papacy and cardinalate should be referred to a general council: "I assert that [when] discord between pope and cardinals occurs ... the church, that is, the whole congregation of Catholics and principal ministers of the faith, namely, prelates who represent the entire congregation, should be called."[102] He accepted, however, that existing canon law did not afford to the cardinals a right to depose the pope on their own, although he accepted the logic of the view expressed earlier by John of Paris that such a conclusion followed from the principle that a body that can elect can also depose.[103]

### Nicholas of Cusa

One of the most prominent figures at the Council of Basle, along with the Spanish theologian and historian of the council Juan de Segovia, was Nicholas of Cusa, or Cusanus, German canonist, mystical theologian, ecclesiastical diplomat, and cardinal. Nicholas was a latecomer to the conciliar movement. One aspect of his thought and career that makes him particularly interesting was his change of position regarding the relationship between papacy and council. He formally took the papalist side on

---

99. Ibid., fol. 109rb, p. 701. Cf. *Commentaria*, fols. 108vb–109ra, pp. 698–701.
100. Ibid., fol. 107va, p. 690. Cf. also fol. 108vb, p. 698, and fol. 110vb, p. 711.
101. Ibid., fol. 109ra, p. 700.
102. Ibid., fol. 109va, p. 702.
103. Ibid., fol. 110va, p. 708.

the issue of ultimate authority in the Church shortly after the final break between Basle and Pope Eugene IV, but had become anticonciliar in attitude even before the council ended. Apparently deeply disturbed by the rapidly growing anti-papal extremism at Basle, he went over to the papal side in 1437 and was described in 1439 by Aeneas Sylvius (later Pius II) as the "Hercules of all the followers of Eugenius."[104] Eugene appointed him cardinal in late 1446, but he was elevated to the position by Eugene's successor, Nicholas V. When Aeneas became pope in 1458, Nicholas was one of his most trusted advisors. The motives and causes that led Nicholas to reverse his position can be left to his biographers and church historians, but one might recall that d'Ailly also changed views on specific proposals for settling the schism, and that his support for conciliarism came somewhat late in his career after his earlier preference for the *via cessionis* solution.

Born in 1401, Nicholas received a thorough training in canon law at the University of Padua, where he had enrolled as a young German cleric. He also became acquainted with Italian humanism in Padua and took his first steps there on the road to ecclesiastical advancement, which he was to follow for the rest of his career. A well-known bibliophile, he collected various German manuscript remains of classical texts and circulated them among the intellectual acquaintances he made in Italy, compiling a personal library that proved useful in his ecclesiastical career.

Nicholas came to the Council of Basle early in 1432 as one of three representatives of Count Ulrich von Manderscheid of Trier, who was attempting to gain the archbishopric of Trier against a papal nominee. Arguably, then, Nicholas might have arrived at Basle as an opponent of the current pope on at least one issue involving his own legal mandate. The council was already involved in a dispute with Eugene over ultimate authority, having taken its stand on the Constance doctrine of council superiority over pope. Eugene was resisting this view, as well as rejecting the council's insistence that he come himself to Basle, where he was represented at the time by an embassy headed by Giovanni Berardi, arch-

---

104. Piccolomini (Aeneas Sylvius), *De gestis* 14–15, cited in Watanabe, "Authority and Consent in Church Government," p. 221 and note 14. A fine recent study of the Council of Basle, dealing in great detail with the involvement of temporal rulers, political background, and ecclesiological and political aftermath as well as with the confrontation between Eugene IV and the conciliarists at Basle, is Stieber, *Pope Eugenius IV.* See also Oakley, *Council over Pope?* Literature on the conciliarist councils, Pisa, Constance, and Basle, is enormous, as the critical apparatus in the Steiber monograph makes clear.

bishop of Toranto. Originally, Nicholas seemed less interested in the "real action" at the council than in the narrow issue of his own brief. He left Basle shortly after his arrival and returned to Germany, rejoining the council briefly in October 1432 but apparently not attending on a regular basis until the following February. At that point, however, he became an active member of the council committee charged specifically with dealing with the pope.

Nicholas produced a major work on political theory for the council in the fall of 1433, *De concordantia catholica*, some of which had been written earlier away from Basle. The original form of the text, designated as "a pamphlet on the harmony in the Church," was an effort to demonstrate the superiority of council over pope (Books One and Two, chapters 1–7, 16–21, and 26–30 in its modern edition). The tract begins with the typically medieval issue of the best form of government and shows clearly that Nicholas intended his answer to encompass both ecclesiastical and secular forms of polity, both *regnum* and *sacerdotium*. The *De concordantia*, then, was more than a treatise on ecclesiology; it used material from both classical and Christian sources to produce a synthesis describing the proper ordering of spiritual and temporal authorities within a unified Christendom.[105]

Nicholas set out to describe and prescribe for a universal and transcendental unity and harmony reflected in reality as a whole, with the Church as just one element in the total picture, though a major one. His overarching theory of unity and order generally followed the Neoplatonic tradition seen also in d'Ailly and Gerson[106] and presented the standard corresponding doctrine of the presence of rationality throughout nature: the ancient, if not entirely clear, notion of natural law. He asserted the traditional view that reason was present in the universe in two ways: in physical nature in the form of immutable laws and structures that reflect the order and hierarchy of nature as a whole; and in human nature as the individual human's ability to exercise judgment and will and thereby discover the order of the whole universe and implement it in human action. This conception of human reason as part of the natural law led to the conclusion that consent—human agreement to and willing acceptance of what is recognized as natural—is the very

---

105. Sigmund, *Nicholas of Cusa*, p. 121. Another recent study of Cusanus's political thought is Watanabe, *Political Ideas of Nicolas of Cusa*. A modern edition of the works of Cusanus is the *Opera omnia* (Hamburg: Meiner, 1963–68).

106. Cf. *supra*, pp. 81, 92.

sign and expression of reason in human affairs. This was a metaphysical perspective with a much more prosaic focus in political thought, but not, for all that, antithetical in meaning to a theory of polity, even though it did not directly express a modern connotation.

For Nicholas, the social order could be unified in two ways: by employing an objective standard in accordance with which different functions or offices were allocated in a hierarchical manner, and through agreement by all members of society to accept the social order of which they were a part.[107] Nicholas provided an interesting blend of items from a variety of sources; the neoplatonic theology and philosophy found in early Christian writers like Augustine and Cyprian and in later medieval thinkers like Hugh of St Victor and St Bonaventure was combined with terminology reflective of fervent advocates of papal monarchy like Aegidius of Rome. He was, nonetheless, a conciliarist.

One notion Nicholas took from Cyprian's grand hierarchical description of reality and its triadic expression was that all bishops are equal in rank, a commonplace in conciliar thought validated by appeals to St Augustine and Cyprian such as had appeared already in John of Paris, d'Ailly, and Gerson. Nicholas's purpose, of course, was to accommodate the notion of pope as supreme head of the Church with the assertion that the bishop of Rome was only one among episcopal equals. In maintaining this view, he employed the distinction between the pope's sacramental and jurisdictional or administrative status: the pope had no more sacramental authority or power than any other bishop, even though he possessed the jurisdictional status of supreme administrator and judge in the Church. Nicholas here exhibited his tendency to consider both secular and ecclesiastical spheres in parallel fashion by describing the emperor in similar terms.[108]

He also employed the notion of popular consent in describing the proper exercise of both ecclesiastical and secular authority: those who are wise rule over consenting subjects. "Since all are free by nature, every rulership which restrains subjects from evil and directs their freedom to good through fear of punishment, whether through written law or in living form through a prince, can come only from the agreement and consent of the subjects. For if humans are by nature equally powerful and equally free, true and properly ordered authority of one common ruler

---

107. Sigmund, *Nicholas of Cusa*, p. 125.
108. Nicholas of Cusa, *De concordantia catholica* 3.1, p. 327.

equal in power to all the others can only be naturally constituted by their election and consent."[109]

While his material derived in large part from the canons, Nicholas went beyond the legalism of both ecclesiastical and Roman law and used the concept of natural law as his main theoretical tool. Nature had created all humans free and equal, just as it ordained that the more wise should exercise authority over others by being chosen or elected with their consent. He also offered the standard theological argument, which had so long a history in medieval political thought, that legislative authority, both secular and ecclesiastical, comes directly from God and is consented to by its subjects. "Rulership is from God through men and councils, by elective consent."[110] The formulation was largely rhetorical, of course, deriving its authority from tradition and consistency of use, and Nicholas seems not to have employed it in any more substantial way. Nor did he provide any analysis of the formula.

The question of how to implement the principle of popular consent, accordingly, was addressed by Cusanus in very conservative terms. Election of rulers in both church and state was done by the people's representatives, papal election being effected by the cardinals who represented the provinces of the Church—again, a notion seen earlier in d'Ailly and Gerson—while the emperor was chosen by the electors of the Holy Roman Empire who were said to represent units making up the empire. Going some way in pressing a literal understanding of popular consent, however, Nicholas maintained that in both cases the people transferred their right of election to representatives. And he drew the appropriately constitutional conclusion from this position, though expressing it very lamely and impractically, that the transferred right was not alienated totally, and the people retained it in some manner: "The people have transferred, that is, conceded, power to the emperor, for they have kept for themselves the power to withdraw it ... It is the common opinion of scholars that the Roman people can take the power

---

109. Ibid., 2.14, p. 161. Nicholas's assertion that all human beings are by nature free and his explicit connection between freedom and consent, while not without earlier medieval scholastic echoes, likely reflects his humanist educational background. The link between natural freedom and consent as the origin of political authority was soon to receive a prominent place in Spanish neo-scholastic political theory in virtue of a similar influence from humanist sources reinforcing the traditional scholastic theological notion of free will. See *infra*, pp. 143–44, 171–83.

110. Ibid., 2.34, p. 293.

to make laws away from the emperor, because the emperor has this power from the people."[111]

Nicholas was clear, however, on the need to insist on the people's inalienable right to consent to the legitimate exercise of authority; otherwise he would have vitiated the whole purpose of the *De concordantia catholica*, which was to justify conciliar action against the pope. He was explicit on this point when describing a general council as the appropriate body for giving authority to universal church statutes, "since, according to divine and natural law, the power to enact legislation depends on common consent."[112] Following Durantis, he asserted that laws and conciliar decrees had force only if approved by the council as a corporate entity. The same apparently went for the empire as well, although he was somewhat ambiguous on the point even when citing the principle of *quod omnes tangit*.[113] His invocation of consent reflected nothing more than tacit acceptance, and his views on the natural abilities of ordinary citizens were typically aristocratic and conservative.[114] Yet he was the only conciliarist to suggest that all church leaders should be elected for the council to indirectly represent the Church, again reflecting the corporation conception of the relation between the Church as a society and the council as a collective assembly.[115]

Nicholas's ecclesiology accepted that a general church council brought together the Church as a whole, the *congregatio fidelium*, and was thus more than an assembly of bishops, even though he made no specific provision for attendance and participation by the laity, who were in fact to be excluded except for a potential role as witnesses to decisions on dogma. They were represented by the various ranks of clergy and gave consent through that medium. His understanding of representation should be reasonably clear from these details. He also addressed the matter directly in the *De concordantia*, where he even spoke of the pope as representing the Church as a whole, but without any apparent legal connotation: the pope represents the Church "in a very confused way (*confusissime*) ... and it [the council] is always better in judgment than the

---

111. Ibid., 2.18, p. 197.
112. Sigmund cites several texts on the point from the *De concordantia catholica*: Sigmund, *Nicholas of Cusa*, p. 151, note 27.
113. Nicholas used *quod omnes tangit* when speaking of consent in the Empire: Nicholas of Cusa, *De concordantia catholica* 3, preface, p. 318.
114. Cf. Sigmund, *Nicholas of Cusa*, pp. 141–57.
115. Black, *Monarchy and Community*, p. 16.

pontiff alone who is a more uncertain representative."[116] The traditional medieval impersonationist theory of representation was in play here, rather than that of delegation; although Nicholas made use of the latter in the *De concordantia*, he did not do so when speaking of the representative character of either general council or papacy.[117]

Nicholas also addressed squarely the question of what to do in circumstances where the pope refused to call a general council himself, the old problem of how to interpret the conventional canonical view that only a pope could call a council. His response invoked the principle that "necessity knows no law" and offered a range of possibilities. In the first instance the emperor could call a general church council; the clergy would be obliged to obey such a call, even though they were normally exempt from civil law, "inasmuch as the exemption (*privilegium fori*) was established to conserve the Holy Church, and we revert to methods appropriate to the time to attain the same end."[118] Once called in this way, a council would be legitimate in that it was bringing together all the principal officers of the Church who would participate either directly or through representatives. The pope, as *rector* of the *universitas ecclesiae*, should be present, however, and the council could not legislate without him. Nicholas then addressed the obvious difficulty this posed, the problem of a pope declining to present himself. His inadequate response was that, even if the general council could not act in the pope's absence, all requisite provincial councils could meet together simultaneously and achieve the same goal. Here Nicholas seems to have ignored the possibility that a recalcitrant pope could stymie such collective action by provincial councils simply by declining to call his own Roman provincial council, thereby foreclosing the requirement that all provincial councils must meet.[119]

Elsewhere, Cusanus suggested that a general council must be very patient in its attempts to persuade a pope to attend and should await his appearance for a considerable period of time. In the final analysis, however, he held that "the council can provide for its needs and the safety

---

116. Nicholas of Cusa, *De concordantia catholica* 2.18, p. 194.

117. Ibid., 2.34, pp. 292 and 305; 2.18, pp. 199 and 205; 2.21, p. 236; 2.25, p. 245.

118. Ibid., 3.15, p. 388. Sigmund notes that earlier conciliarists also appealed to "necessity" and suggests Bartolus as the probable source for the notion in his commentary on the *Codex*: Sigmund, *Nicholas of Cusa*, p. 172.

119. Nicholas of Cusa, *De concordantia catholica* 2.13, pp. 155–60; but cf. *De auctoritate presidendi in concilio generali*, p. 32.

of the Church,"[120] an ambiguous and unhelpful statement contradicting his view that a general council could not act in the pope's absence. Nicholas was explicit, moreover, in requiring the pope's presence for one form of general council business: the pope or his representative must participate in conciliar activity involving the promulgation of Church dogma. "If the authority of the Apostolic See is absent even when the council has been properly convened, no decision can be taken on matters of faith without considering the opinion of the Roman church."[121] But Cusanus did accept forthrightly the primacy of council over pope at least in special and unusual circumstances, even though he was silent about the universalist *haec sancta* position of Constance.

Nicholas identified four criteria for the legitimacy of a general church council: it must be properly convoked; it must include all principal members of the Church or their representatives; it must be marked by free discussion and open meetings; and it must be brought to a harmonious conclusion. On this last point, he held that harmony was a sure sign of the Holy Spirit's presence at any such gathering: "When a council which has been properly and legitimately convoked and assembled with all called, freely celebrated and concluded with the common consent of all, and has in any way issued a decree concerning the salvation of the faithful we read that it has never erred; for it represents the whole Catholic church proximately, and has the consent of all the faithful through their representatives (*legati*) and rulers (*praesides*) ... a universal council coming to this kind of conclusion with consent and representation (*legatione*) of all the faithful necessarily truly and infallibly comes to such a conclusion in the presence of Christ, and with the inspiration of the Holy Spirit."[122]

Addressing the simple issue of council over pope, Nicholas was clear about a general church council's superiority, even though the pope was greater than any individual member of the Church. As minister of the whole church, the pope is himself superior to all other church members distributively (*distributive*); but the general council is superior collectively (*collective*): the universal Church assembled in council is over the pope in every respect.[123] It can depose him for reasons of negligence of

---

120. Nicholas of Cusa, *De concordantia catholica* 2.13, pp. 156–60; 2.2, pp. 98–99.

121. Ibid. 2.2, p. 99.

122. Ibid. 2.34, p. 292.

123. Here is an early foreshadowing of the later dictum in constitutional theory and Reformation resistance thought, *princeps maius singulis, minor universo*. See *infra*, pp. 112, 246.

duty (*quando inutiliter administraret*) as well as when he lapses into heresy. It can also review papal decisions: on this point Nicholas cited the Council of Chalcedon's review of Leo I's condemnation of Dioscorus as a heretic.[124] Nicholas also suggested in one place that a pope could be deposed on purely practical rather than ideological grounds (*propter utilitatem*),[125] but he conceded that popes apparently had legislated on their own in the past and the Church customarily seemed to tolerate the practice. He maintained, however, that this must have been permitted only with tacit consent from the Church. Further, while papal decrees were previously issued with the consent of the pope's annual metropolitan council and now should have at least the consent of the cardinals who stand for the whole church, laws touching the general welfare (*status*) of the whole church might only be made in a universal council, where the pope was only one member and had authority similar to, or even less than, a patriarch in a patriarchical council or archbishop in a provincial council.[126]

All of this notwithstanding, Nicholas was careful to give a full range of administrative authority to the pope as head of the Church. Special powers attached to the papal office through the divine intention of Christ, the Church's founder; as well, the pope was particularly charged with maintaining church unity. At the same time, however, when push came to shove Nicholas upheld conciliar supremacy over the pope, accepting that while the normal relationship between pope and council was one of cooperation, a general council would be supreme in the event of conflict. Moreover, exclusive authority to call a general council did not rest with the pope; the emperor could so act when necessary. Alternatively, all provincial councils could meet together, although, as already noted, the Cusan position contained a problem here. For Nicholas, the Church's structure was strictly hierarchical, with the general council at the system's apex and the pope ultimately administrative head under whom the cardinals functioned as advisors and normal representatives from all provincial sectors of the *universitas ecclesiae*. He con-

---

124. Nicholas of Cusa, *De concordantia catholica* 1.16, p. 8; 2.8, p. 130; 2.17, p. 182; 2.18, p. 197.

125. Nicholas of Cusa, *De auctoritate presidendi in concilio generali*, p. 28.

126. Nicholas of Cusa, *De concordantia catholica* 2, ch. 11–12, pp. 139–45. Sigmund points out that the prohibition on changing law affecting the *status ecclesiae* derived from the canonist tradition concerning diocesan administration, citing Tierney, *Foundations of Conciliar Thought*, *passim*: Sigmund, *Nicholas of Cusa*, p. 179, note 41.

sidered the empire to be similarly structured but did not develop this point.

5. CONCILIARISM AFTER BASLE

*Introduction*

The advocates of conciliarism lost any real chance of producing significant change in either the ecclesiology or the practices of the Church when the Council of Basle failed to "bridle" the papacy by implementing the theory of strict conciliarism. Nonetheless, the theory itself did not cease to have currency and supporters. The successors of Eugene IV moved quickly to place it beyond the pale of orthodox doctrine, using Pius II's bull *execrabilis* (1460) as their most authoritative weapon; yet conciliarism was not completely eliminated.[127] While losing its place as a significant ideological and political alternative within the Church as a whole, it remained the dominant view among theologians and canonists at the University of Paris throughout the fifteenth century and well into the sixteenth. It continued to have supporters, particularly in France where it became part of the antipapalist armoury of the French monarchy in furthering territorial ambitions in Italy in the early sixteenth century, as well as a foundation stone for later Gallican ultramontanist views in general. It also came to play an important role in both the formulation and expression of Protestant resistance theory, thereby directly entering the mainstream of modern political theory.

This was particularly the case with respect to views expressed during the early decades of the Reformation movement in Scotland, especially during the period of Catholic restoration under Mary Tudor, and even earlier for a brief period when Henry VIII still expressed strong support for the traditional Church and aspired to regularize matters by resolving the conflict between reformers and the papacy. It can also be recalled in this respect that, though no conciliarist himself, Luther at an early point in his "revolt" considered carrying his dispute with the papacy to a general church council. Some of the arguments conciliarism used to show

---

127. The now generally accepted view of the continuing nature of conciliarism after Basle rests on the efforts of a number of scholars. See Jedin, *History of the Council of Trent*, 1:1–165; Klotzner, *Kardinal Domenikus Jacobazzi*; la Brosse, *Pape et Concile*; Baumer, *Nachwirkungen des Konziliaren Gedankens* and "Die Konstanzer Dekrete 'Haec sancta' und 'Frequens' "; and Oakley, "Almain and Major," and "Conciliarism at the Fifth Lateran Council?"

that misuse of papal authority was subject to control and resistance by the Church as a whole also influenced later continental resistance theory among Calvinist publicists such as Beza and the author of the *Vindiciae*, the immediate link probably being John Ponet, whose *Short Treatise of Politic Power* (1556) has been called "the first complete doctrine of resistance formulated by a Protestant thinker on other than purely religious grounds."[128] Ponet was acquainted with at least one of John Major's writings and was himself a teacher of George Buchanan, whose *De iure regni apud Scotos*, along with Mornay's *Vindiciae*, has been described as "probably the most important of all the political works opposing absolute monarchy written in the two centuries before the appearance of Locke's *Second Treatise* ... both [being] certainly well known in England."[129] The doctrinal parallels between medieval theories of ecclesiology and temporal polity have often been consciously employed as means for weaving important strands of constitutional theory into Western political thought; but conciliarism as the most significant ecclesiological vehicle for such transmission has yet to be fully acknowledged, especially among English-speaking interpreters and historians.

Yet the conciliarist tradition was well known in England in the seventeenth century and figured prominently on both sides of the debate over the nature of the English monarch's powers before the outbreak of the Civil War, even though there was some reluctance to make use of arguments from Catholic sources. Clearly, the applicability of conciliarism as a constitutional doctrine concerning the relations of pope to Church as a whole was recognized and accepted as equally applicable to the temporal order in terms of the relationship between king and Commons or Estates General as representative of the people as a whole.[130]

---

128. Oakley, "Road from Constance to 1688." This important article contains a good account of the conciliarist views of both Major and George Buchanan and is the basis for my summary of their positions.

Buchanan's conciliarism also shows a strong reliance on non-religious arguments, historical and philosophical, evidence perhaps of Ponet's influence on his student but more likely a reflection of the fact that Buchanan was a humanist and literary figure throughout his career, not a cleric. Cf. *infra*, pp. 109–14 for Major, and pp. 121–26 for Buchanan.

129. Oakley, "Road from Constance," p. 11. The description of its influence is from Harold Laski's introduction to his edition of *A Defence Against Tyrants, the Vindiciae contra tyrannos*, pp. 46–57.

130. Oakley provides an impressive body of evidence for the fact that conciliarism was well known as a bulwark of constitutional thought in the seventeenth century. From French sources he cites Edmund Richer, *Libellus de ecclesiastica et politica potestate, Apologia pro Johanne Gersonis*, and *Vindiciae doctrinam Majoram scholae Parisiensis*; and Bossuet, *Appendix*

As mentioned, the primary locus for the continuing conciliarist tradition was the University of Paris, where a series of academic publicists extended into the sixteenth century the ecclesiology expressed by their Parisian conciliarist predecessors, Pierre d'Ailly and Jean Gerson.[131] Three names stand out in this connection: John Major (or Mair), Jacques Almain, and George Buchanan. Their careers were interwoven in a number of significant ways and bridge the period from the last decades of the fifteenth century to the end of the first half-century of the Reformation.

## John Major

John Major (1467–1500) was a Scot who taught at Glasgow, Paris, and St Andrews after receiving his formal education at the University of

---

*ad defensionem declarationis Cleri Gallicani*; from English sources, D. Owen, *Herod and Pilate Reconciled*; Robert Burhill, *De potestate regia et usurpatione papali*; Samuel Rutherford, *Lex Rex: The Law and the Prince*; John Maxwell, *Sacro-Sancta Regum Majestas*; John White, *The Way to the True Church*; William Prynne, *Soveraigne Power of Parliaments and Kingdoms*; William Bridge, *The Wounded Conscience Cured, the Weak One Strengthened and the Doubting Satisfied* and, at least in respect of limitations on papal authority, Robert Burhill, *De potestate regia*, and even James I, *A Premonition to all most mightie Monarches* and *A Remonstrance for the Right of Kings and the Independence of their Crownes on the English side of the Channel*. The relevant data are found in Oakley, "Road from Constance," 3–9. Oakley returned to the task of providing data showing the prevalence of information about and use of conciliarist thought in the polemical literature of seventeenth-century England and Scotland in "Almain and Major," pp. 684–85 and note 50.

Another interesting bit of data is Leibniz's support for conciliarism as a possible instrument for reuniting Christendom. G. Leibniz, "Observations on the Abbé St Pierre's 'Project for Perpetual Peace,'" in Riley, *Political Writings of Leibniz*, p. 180. Cf. Riley's introduction (p. 1), which states that Leibniz "vigorously defended the Conciliar movement of the fifteenth century".

131. Skinner refers to the Major doctrine as a "revival of Gerson's conciliarism": Skinner, *Foundations*, 2:117; but this surely is not literally true. Both Major and Almain stated explicitly that their conciliarist views expressed a long-held and continuing tradition at Paris and in France as a whole. See Major, "Disputatio de potestate papae," in Gerson, *Opera omnia* 2:1150, cited in Oakley, "Road from Constance," p. 16 and note 78; and Almain, "Tractatus de auctoritate ecclesiae," in Gerson, *Opera omnia* 989C–92, cited in Oakley, "Almain and Major," p. 678; see *infra*, p. 115. The largest collection of opinions favouring the authority of general church councils over pope expressed by persons at the University of Paris in the period is Boulay's *Historia universitatis Parisiensis*, vol. 4, *1300–1400*; vol. 5, *1400–1500*.

Paris.[132] The most renowned scholastic theologian at Paris in the early sixteenth century and first teacher and then colleague of Jacques Almain, he is remembered today in the English-speaking world principally as an early historian of Great Britain and teacher of the Scottish humanist and reformer George Buchanan. Another of his Scottish students was John Knox. Major produced many works in fields ranging from history to logic, ethics, metaphysics, and theology. The most important were his *History of Greater Britain* and *Commentarium in IV libris Petri Lombardi*. Like his *Commentarium in Mattheum*, these contain unsystematic elements for a theory of polity, and their relevant sections were included in Ellies Dupin's collected works of Jean Gerson (1706).[133] Beginning in 1518, two years after the Franco-papal concordat ended the conflict between Louis XII and Julius II, a portion of the *Commentarium in Mattheum* circulated separately as a conciliar tract under the title *Disputatio de auctoritate concilii supra pontificem maximum*. Like the best-known political treatise of Jacques Almain, this text may also have been part of the Sorbonnist rejection of Cajetan's defence of papal supremacy and of Julius II's reaction to the self-serving conciliarist position taken by the French monarch in agreeing to support the Council of Pisa in 1511.[134]

In keeping with his medieval theologian predecessors, Major was interested in ecclesiology rather than a theory of temporal polity and, more specifically, in the relationship between papacy and the Church as a whole. But he made it clear that his theory of ecclesiastical polity was transferable to the secular sphere and offered both principled argument and historical data for his views, the latter being the most interesting and apparently most serviceable for later Protestant resistance theorists in his native Scotland and on the Continent. Major took it as given that the historical record showed political authority in various jurisdictions of western Europe to have been limited in significant ways by ancient and customary forms: he cited precedents from the customs and legal practices in France, Scotland, and Spain. And while his principal concern was

---

132. Although brief, the best biography of Major remains that of Aeneas J. G. Mackay, "Life of the Author," in the introduction to John Major's *History of Greater Britain*, trans. Archibald Constable, pp. xxixff.; but see also Durkan, "John Major: After 400 Years," and Burns, "New Light on John Major." A Major bibliography is in Durkan, "The School of John Major: Bibliography." See also Oakley, "Road from Constance" and "Almain and Major," which examine Major's political thought both on its own and as compared with that of Buchanan and Almain.

133. Gerson, *Opera omnia*, 2.

134. Oakley, "Almain and Major," p. 682; see also note 34.

to espouse an ecclesiology asserting limits on papal power, like earlier conciliarists he did not hesitate, and arguably felt it strengthened his case, to show that comparable limitations existed in the temporal sphere. While conceding that temporal political conditions did not correspond precisely to those in the church, he argued that relevant similarities could be seen. It was his contention that guarantees for the proper exercise of authority in the Church must be as sound as those in the temporal sphere, "otherwise better provision had been made [by God] for the secular polity than for the church."[135]

Major treated directly the question of constitutional limits on authority in the context of the relationship between pope and general church council, repeating the basic views of earlier conciliarists like Gerson and d'Ailly, while also presenting a parallel discussion of limits on the power of the Scottish monarchy. For him it was inconceivable that an errant and incorrigible pope was immune from judgment and deposition, just as it was irrational to contend that a tyrant could not be deposed by his subjects. A basic principle in any theory of temporal polity was the traditional notion that the ruler was essentially a public person exercising authority for the well-being of those over whom he ruled: the ruler acts for "the common welfare of the people and not his own."[136] Similarly, in the Church, God provided the faithful with a leader to promote their spiritual welfare, "just as it is in the secular polity."[137] Accordingly, both king and pope were limited in the legitimate exercise of their authority insofar as they are administrators of power for the common good of their respective jurisdictions: "[the king] holds of his people no other right within his kingdom but as its governor."[138] The pope is head also of the Church as minister or servant of its members, so that his power is not unlimited.[139]

On the practical issue of who should, and how to, determine when a ruler, spiritual or temporal, has become tyrannical, Major offered an ar-

---

135. Major, "Disputatio de authoritate concilii," in Gerson, *Opera omnia*, 2:1139. An English translation of part of this work is "A Disputation on the Authority of a Council," ed. and trans. James Kerr Cameron, in Matthew Spinka, ed., *Advocates of Reform*, pp. 175–84.

136. Major, "Disputatio de authoritate concilii," in Gerson, *Opera omnia*, 2:1141. Major makes an interesting application of this principle, extending it to cover the religious well-being of the people, when he justifies the forceful removal (by the Spaniards) of Indian rulers in the Americas because of their toleration of idolatrous practices. See Losada, "Controversy between Supúlveda and las Casas," in *Bartolomé de las Casas in History*, p. 303.

137. Major, "Disputatio de potestate papae," in Gerson, *Opera omnia*, 2:1151.

138. Major, *History* 4.18, p. 220.

139. Major, "Disputatio de authoritate concilii," in Gerson, *Opera omnia*, 2:1142.

gument essentially embodying a maxim that was seen in many later resistance theories and stated earlier in principle by Nicholas of Cusa *apropos* of the papacy: while a king is superior to any other individual in his kingdom, he is inferior to the citizenry taken as a whole—*rex singulis major, universo minor*. Addressing the issue as it applied to the papacy, he asserted that everyone agreed the pope was superior in spiritual matters to any other individual, but there was disagreement concerning his superiority to the whole church or a general church council. Major cited the Council of Constance as maintaining a council's superiority to the pope and went on the say that the same position was held by the University of Paris (the Sorbonnists) and the whole of France: "When a universal council is assembled it is superior to the Roman pontiff."[140] The superiority of the council over pope derived from the fact that it represented the whole church and expressed its common purpose. He then applied the same reasoning to the secular sphere, arguing that, while "the king does not have his power and authority except from the kingdom which he freely rules, whereas the pope has his authority from God ... it is not true to say that God did not leave this power in the church in the same way as this political power resides among the persons in one kingdom; [for] otherwise, better provision had been made for the secular polity than for the church."[141]

Major held that temporal authority rested in popular consent and, similarly, that papal authority rested in the people of the Church as a whole even while also rooted directly in a divine ordinance. The people as a whole, then, ultimately were superior to the monarch, just as the Church as a whole was superior to the pope; hence a tyrannical and incorrigible ruler of either type could be deposed. The people could "deprive its king and his posterity of all authority, when the king's worthlessness calls for such a course, just as it had the power to appoint him king";[142] a king who "destroys the welfare of the commonwealth and is incorrigible should be deposed by the community over which he rules."[143]

---

140. Ibid., 2:1141. Cf. "Disputatio de potestate papae," in Gerson, *Opera omnia*, 2:1150.
141. Major, "Disputatio de authoritate concilii," in Gerson, *Opera omnia*, 2:1135–37.
142. Major, *History* 4.17, p. 214.
143. Major, "Disputatio de authoritate concilii," in Gerson, *Opera omnia*, 2:1135. Oakley notes that some have attributed a doctrine of tyrannicide to Major, but his own view is that this is too extreme and that the furthest Major seemed prepared to go was to permit the execution of a justly condemned tyrant by a minister of the community having full popular consent. Oakley, "Road from Constance," p. 17.

Major also addressed the issue of what instrument could act for the whole people against an errant ruler. Again, his position was unremarkable in the context of medieval conciliarism, even though it did not answer all the procedural questions so important for modern theories of representation. A general council was superior to the pope because it represented the whole church, and not only did its superiority rest in its representative character but it was also granted directly by God. A decision by the *maior pars*, the greater part, of a general council was a decision by the whole, from which there could be no appeal.[144] Similarly, though Major never explicitly addressed the issue of representation in the temporal sphere, he made clear that for him the situation was precisely comparable. The king of France had authority from "the superior part" (*praecipua pars*) of the polity;[145] the pope could demand deposition of a king only if "the greater part" consented;[146] hence "it is from the people, and most of all from the chief men and nobility who act for the common people, that kings have their institution; it belongs, therefore, to the princes, prelates and nobles to decide any ambiguity that may emerge with regard to a king."[147] In the case of his own kingdom of Scotland, he stated that the king could not be deposed "unless under a solemn consideration of the matter by the three estates."[148]

Major's theory of polity, then, was a rather straightforward and conscious restatement of the strict conciliarism of his Parisian predecessors, d'Ailly and Gerson, but without their stated interest in church reform or assignment of specific responsibilities for church administration to the college of cardinals.[149] The same conclusion obtains for the views of

144. Major, "Disputatio de authoritate concilii," in Gerson, *Opera omnia*, 2:1139.
145. Ibid.
146. Major, "Disputatio de potestate papae," in Gerson, *Opera omnia*, 2:1157.
147. Major, *History* 4.17, p. 215.
148. Ibid. 4.18, p. 219.
149. Oakley identifies three features of the conciliarism that led to Constance and Basle: the principle that a general council was superior to the pope, the desire for church reform in head and members, and the aristocratic feature of attributing a jurisdictional role to the cardinalate in the universal Church. He holds that only the first of these remained and was reflected in the sixteenth-century conciliarism of Major, Almain, and Buchanan: "Almain and Major," 686–89. His judgment is that their continuing emphasis on only the first "strict conciliarist" point showed that, by the sixteenth century, conciliarism had become "reduced in stature, from a strategic weapon of supranational range to a merely tactical device, lodged in the armoury of Gallican pretensions, and divorced, therefore, from programs of more complex provenance and more exalted purposes." "Almain and Major," p. 689.

Major's two Parisian students, Jacques Almain and George Buchanan, whose doctrines are examined below. The precise doctrinal relationships among these three sixteenth-century conciliarists is not easy to detail or document, particularly as regards Major and Almain, who were colleagues at Paris as well as teacher and pupil. It seems clear, however, that Major was at least one of the main sources for Buchanan's theory of polity, even though Buchanan never acknowledged this explicitly.[150]

## Jacques Almain

Jacques Almain (c.1480–1515) is less well-known as a conciliarist than Major, his contemporary but longer-lived associate at the University of Paris. Born at Sens, he rose to prominence in Parisian academic circles early in the sixteenth century as one of Major's most brilliant students. He studied with Major at Montaigu College under the strenuous regime of the Flemish reformer Jean Standonck and briefly taught logic and natural philosophy there before, like Erasmus, leaving Montaigu's apparently too harsh regimen. He went to Navarre, where Major also held an academic appointment, and completed his theological studies there in 1511 before taking up teaching duties alongside Major. Already the author of many philosophical and theological works, his promising academic career was cut short by a premature death only four years later.[151]

As a highly regarded Parisian academic, Almain was chosen in 1512 by his university's Faculty of Theology to reply formally to the *De comparatione auctoritatis papae et concilii*, in which the Dominican master general, Thomas de Vio, later Cardinal Cajetan, upheld Julius II's repudiation of the general council at Pisa in May 1511. The council had been convoked by several dissident cardinals with the support of Louis XII of France as part of his campaign for French territorial expansion into Italy. Louis's action gave current and practical expression to the claim that a general church council was superior to the pope and brought the whole theoretical issue, complete with French precedents going back to Philip the Fair's struggle with Boniface VIII two hundred

---

150. See Oakley, "Road from Constance," *passim* and especially 29–31. Cf. *infra*, p. 124.

151. The best treatment of Almain's life and works is Ricardo Garcia Villoslada, *La Universidad de Paris*. Cf. Oakley, "Almain and Major," p. 675, note 3; and "Conciliarism in the Sixteenth Century." The two Oakley articles present details of Almain's political thought and my account is based on them, particularly the second, which examines all three of Almain's conciliar writings. A number of Almain's writings were published together as *Aurea clarissimi et acutissimi Doctoris Theologi Magistri Jacobi Almain Senonensis Opuscula*.

years earlier, into the political arena again in a way that involved both temporal and spiritual concerns. That Julius was able to ignore the effort to depose him or bring him to heel because only a few cardinals supported the Pisan *conciliabulum*, as it came derisively to be called, should not obscure the fact that the event itself attempted to revive in the universal church an ecclesiology that had remained alive and well in French theological circles despite papal efforts to squelch it after the Council of Basle, some seventy years earlier.

Almain's reply to the Cajetan treatise was his *Tractatus de auctoritate ecclesiae et conciliorum generalium*, published in the spring of 1512. This was not his first conciliarist work; he had written *De dominio naturali, civili et ecclesiastico* a short while earlier, and it was probably because of this that he was chosen to respond to Cajetan. He expressed his theory of polity a third time in the *Expositio circa decisiones Magistri Guilielmi Occam super potestate ecclesiastica et laica*.[152] The doctrine in all three works is of a piece, but his response to Cajetan is the best known.

Like Major and earlier conciliarist thinkers, Almain presented his position as a theory of ecclesiastical polity, while accepting that the general theory held equally in the secular sphere. Examining in the first instance the nature of the Church as a whole and carefully distinguishing between ecclesiastical and political societies, he nonetheless insisted that the Church be regarded as "one of a class [of] political societies."[153] Almain made this view clear when, following John of Paris's *On Royal and Papal Power*, he listed powers ceded to the Church at its institution and identified jurisdiction in the external forum as the relevant one in regard to the exercise of authority in the Church as a whole.[154] Power of this sort has nothing to do with the internal forum of purely spiritual powers such as the administration of the sacraments, but is comparable to the exercise of temporal authority in the external forum and is subject to the natural law. Papal plenitude of power, then, is to be construed in terms of the monarchical form of polity Christ mandated for His church, according to which one person, the pope, was granted supreme authority to be exercised over every other member of the Church, to none of whom he was himself subject.[155]

---

152. All three of the Almain works are in Gerson, *Opera omnia*, 2:961–1120. Cajetan's "Tractatus primus de comparatione auctoritate papae et concilii" is in *Bibliotheca maxima pontificia*, ed. Rocaberti, vol. 19, pp. 474–76.
153. The quotation is from Figgis, *Political Thought from Gerson to Grotius*, p. 56.
154. Cf. John of Paris, *Royal and Papal Power*, 12, pp. 57–62.
155. Almain, "Expositio," in Gerson, *Opera omnia*, 2:1024B–C.

It must be recognized, however, and this for Almain was where Cajetan went wrong, that the monarchical character of the Church, like that of a temporal monarchy, does not imply that church members as a body are inferior to the single supreme head, but only that no other single individual is superior to the pope. It does not follow, therefore, that a church council cannot be superior to the pope; indeed, it is superior precisely because it represents the Church as a whole and is not merely one single individual. Nor is a secular ruler said to have supreme power in the sense of being superior to the people as a whole; rather, a secular polity is monarchical only insofar as the monarch is superior to any other individual in the kingdom because he represents the whole people who cannot ordinarily meet in assembly.[156] More simply, it is a constitutionally limited monarchy.

Almain's advocacy of the conciliarist position invoked the relevant decrees of both Constance and Basle, but derived more of its force from rational argumentation based on three points. First, he contended that ultimate power existed in the Church as a whole before being located in an individual officeholder, just as supreme temporal power resided in the people as a whole before being exercised by an individual ruler: the plenitude of ecclesiastical power that Christ admittedly gave to Peter and his successors had been conferred earlier on the Church. So much was this the case that had Christ failed after the Resurrection to designate one person as supreme pontiff, the Church, already possessing "supreme coercive ecclesiastical power," could itself have chosen a pope.[157] The power to elect a pope rested in the Church even before Peter became the first pope.[158] The fact that papal election was now conducted by the college of cardinals only indicated that this function had been delegated to them by the Church as a whole.[159] Further, the pope could not be assumed to have on his own the power to name his successor merely because the papacy exercised control over the procedure for electing a pontiff.[160]

156. Almain, "Tractatus de auctoritate ecclesiae," in Gerson, *Opera omnia*, 2:996c. Cf. 979A and "Expositio," 1074D–75C.
157. Almain, "Quaestio resumptiva ... de dominio naturali," in Gerson, ibid., 971C–72A; "Tractatus de auctoritate ecclesiae," ibid., 993B–C and "Quaestio resumptiva ... de dominio naturali," ibid., 972B; "Tractatus de auctoritate ecclesiae," ibid., 993C; "Expositio," ibid., 1019A.
158. Almain, "Tractatus de auctoritate ecclesiae," In Gerson, ibid., 993C.
159. Almain, "Expositio," in Gerson, ibid., 1017B. Cf. "Tractatus de auctoritate ecclesiae," ibid., 1000B–D.
160. Almain, "Quaestio resumptiva ... de dominio naturali," in Gerson, ibid., 973A; "Tractatus de auctoritate ecclesiae," ibid., 997B–C, 999A.

## Constitutionalism in the Church                                117

Secondly, the power residing in the Church as a whole is "greater in extension" than that of the pope, whose authority was conferred by Christ on a single individual, Peter, "as a sign and figure" representing the universal church.[161] Insofar as ultimate authority was conferred on the Church in the first instance, it was in virtue of the possession of this power by the Church as a whole that Peter or any other pope employed the power of the keys, "just as kings exercise the act of jurisdiction in place of the community."[162] And a general church council has the power of the keys "more directly than Peter does" inasmuch as *eo ipso* it represents the Church as a whole.[163] So close was Almain's identification of a general council with the Church as a whole that, when comparing papal powers with those of the Church, he was indifferent about whether he specified the Church or a general council.[164]

And, finally, Almain contended that the power residing in the Church as a whole was "greater in perfection" than that of the papacy; for it rests in the universal church in an unwavering fashion (*indeviabiliter*) such that the Church "cannot err in those things pertaining to the faith and good morals, nor can it err in passing judgment [on such matters] ... since it is always aided by the Holy Spirit, doctor of truth and infallible director."[165] Similarly, a legitimately assembled council representing the universal church cannot err in matters of faith and morals, although it can be mistaken on issues of fact; accordingly, its definite pronouncements on faith and morals cannot be retracted, although its judgments on facts are revocable.[166] Conversely, of course, it was a commonplace that popes could err publicly in matters of faith.[167]

Almain's conclusion regarding a general council's jurisdictional superiority over the papacy and its authority to impose restraints on, and even

---

161. Almain, "Tractatus de auctoritate ecclesiae," in Gerson, ibid., 990D; "Expositio," ibid., 1069B. This was the main thrust of Almain's criticism of Cajetan's defence of papal supremacy. See *infra*, p. 143.

162. Almain, "Tractatus de auctoritate ecclesiae," in Gerson, ibid., 991A. Cf. ibid., 991B–C, 996C.

163. Almain, "Expositio," in Gerson, ibid., 1069B, 1074C. See also Almain's point that the pope represents the church *remote* while a general council does so *propinquissime*: "Tractatus de auctoritate ecclesiae," ibid., 1004C.

164. Almain, "Tractatus de auctoritate ecclesiae," in Gerson, ibid., 989C. Cf. 987C.

165. Almain, "Quaestio resumptiva ... de dominio naturali," in Gerson, ibid., 972C.

166. Almain, "Expositio," in Gerson, ibid., 1072D–74A; "Tractatus de auctoritate ecclesiae," ibid., 1003B–04D. Cf. *In tertium Sententiarum lectura* D.24, q.1, in Almain, *Opuscula*, fols. 78v–79r. This text presents Almain's lengthiest examination of the respective claims to infallibility of church, general council, and pope.

167. Almain, "Tractatus de auctoritate ecclesiae," in Gerson, ibid., 1005A.

depose, an errant pontiff followed easily from these principles. Again, he drew the parallel between pope and temporal ruler regarding the limits to their authority that were rooted in the community over which they exercised power: "Just as ... the power of a *baillivus* is subject to the power of a *praepositus*," though both derive their power immediately from the king, so too the pope's power is subject to that of a general council, which can impose constraints on the exercise of his prerogatives and bind his actions to its laws and constitutions.[168] It can judge, punish, and, in certain circumstances, even depose a pope by exercising authoritative power rather than issuing a merely declarative sentence. Contrary to Gratian's view, a general council has the authority to function as "ordinary judge" not only in cases of papal heresy but in every case of notorious sin, and even in circumstances where the pope is guiltless but the general well-being of the Church is at issue.[169]

Some attention might be given to Almain's direct response to the Cajetan position, which shows his intellectual acuity when posing an early sixteenth-century version of conciliarism against its authoritative rejection. It will be recalled that the Cajetan document defending papal superiority over a general council was prompted by the political circumstances that had led Louis XII of France to join with the emperor Maximilian and some dissident French cardinals in the calling of a general council at Pisa in 1511. Louis's purpose was to bring ecclesiastical as well as political and military pressure on Pope Julius II, who had forsaken his earlier neutrality in the ongoing conflict for control of northern Italy. Julius rejected the call for a general council and enlisted Cajetan, master general of the Dominican order and perhaps the most authoritative theologian of the day, to defend his supremacy.

For his part Cajetan acknowledged a point it would have been difficult, if not impossible, to deny: that the Church as a whole or a general council had a role to play in deposing a heretical pope because a heretical pope did not cease *ipso facto* to hold office; he had to be deposed.[170]

---

168. Almain, "Expositio," in Gerson, ibid., 1072B; "Quaestio resumptiva ... de dominio naturali," ibid., 973A; "Tractatus de auctoritate ecclesiae," ibid., 1010B; "Expositio," ibid., 1965B, 1070d–72B. Cf. 1055D.

169. Almain, "Quaestio resumptiva ... de dominio naturali," in Gerson, ibid., 973B–74A; "Tractatus de auctoritate ecclesiae," ibid., 1011C–12C; "Expositio," ibid., 1067A–D, 1074C; "Tractatus de auctoritate ecclesiae," ibid., 1008D–11B, 1010C. Cf. 1009C. Here Almain repeats the sweeping grounds for papal deposition mentioned earlier by Nicholas of Cusa. Cf. *supra*, pp. 105–06.

170. Cajetan, "Tractatus primus de comparatione auctoritatis papae et concilii," in *Bibliotheca Maxima Pontificia*, 19:474–76. Cf. ibid., 478. The Cajetan position is examined

Accordingly, in arguing the superiority of pope over council, Cajetan was forced to explain how what was inferior, a general council, could exercise authority over a superior, indeed over the person acknowledged to be the supreme power in the Church. Cajetan's somewhat ingenious argument introduced a novelty into a centuries-old debate: he made a threefold distinction between the papacy itself, the person of the pope, and the two as conjoined. The papacy was established directly by God, while the person of the pope was the issue of his father; and, except in the original case of Peter, who was chosen pope directly by Christ, conjoining papal office and an individual officeholder was achieved through a human process of election. Accordingly, the power exercised when the Church or a general council deposed a pope is not superior or even equal to that of the papacy because it is directed only at the human accomplishment of conjoining papal office and officeholder. The only power superior to the pope is God Himself; "otherwise there would be two supreme powers in the church, and Christ would not have instituted a monarchical regime in it."[171]

Almain zeroed in on Cajetan's description of the Church as a divinely instituted monarchy. It began with an examination of the nature of temporal polity and the source of royal authority in a secular monarchy, showing Almain's acceptance of the parallel between temporal and spiritual spheres and his willingness to transfer inferences from one sphere directly to the other. Secular authority did not come directly and immediately from God or from the ruler himself, he noted, but from the whole community, and because the community confers authority on its ruler, it can also deprive him of it for good reason; otherwise the community would lack the ability to prevent its own ruin, something so irrational as to require no elaboration.[172]

---

in Pollet, "La doctrine de Cajetan sur l'Église." Cf. Oakley, "Almain and Major," pp. 674–81. Canonical and theological debate on papal deposition, and whether papal heresy entailed *ipso facto* deposition, began with Gratian's *Decretum*, but a consensus on the position taken by Cajetan had been reached long before this time. See *supra*, pp. 55–65, passim.

171. Cajetan, "Tractatus primus de comparatione auctoritatis papae et concilii," in *Bibliotheca Maxima Pontificia*, 19:475, col. 2.

172. Almain, "Tractatus de auctoritate ecclesiae," ch. 1, in Gerson, *Opera omnia*, 977C–79C, esp. 978C–D. Cf. "De dominio naturali," ibid., 961A–65B.

Major had employed and extended the same argument in the parallel between ecclesiastical and secular authority: unless the Church had the power to constrain papal abuse of authority it would be less perfect than a temporal polity, a position presumably irrational on two counts. Cf. *supra*, pp. 110–11.

While asserting the traditional view that the supreme ecclesiastical power owed its existence to the direct divine action of Christ's having conferred supreme papal power directly on Peter, Almain took pains to assert that "Christ conferred this power directly on the Church, i.e., if we take the Church to mean the body (*collectio*) of all the faithful, or the body of all the prelates, greater or lesser, who succeed the Apostles and disciples, or [again] the general council of the church."[173] The relative superiority of pope and council thus involved the relationship between these two instances of power conferral, it being understood that this conferral on the Church as a body meant either the power conferred on the Church as a whole excluding the pope, or that conferred on a general council as representing the whole church. Almain went on to state that Cajetan erred here and that the Church or a general council representing it was superior in jurisdiction to the pope. In receiving powers directly from Christ the pope received them only "as a sign and figure of the whole Church," so that they were conferred on the Church itself rather than on the papacy. He pointed out that the Councils of Constance and Basle had made this clear and cited texts from Augustine, Ambrose, and Jerome to show that this was by no means a new doctrine.[174] Otherwise, Almain concluded, provisions for the maintenance and well-being of the Church would have been less adequate than those for a temporal polity; he made some sport here with Cajetan's reference to the Church as an ecclesiastical monarchy.[175]

Finally, on the technical issue of who, if anyone, other than the pope could call a general council, Almain argued that, while according to divine law no one but the pope could convene a general council, this meant that no single individual could do so, but did not preclude a corporate ecclesiastical entity such as any particular church acting to provide for the well-being of the Church as a whole. He held that a particular church that had evidence of the need for a general council should so inform the remaining churches and name a location where all could come together; the other churches would have to consent to such a general gathering, not because the initiating church had any superior authority—it did not—but because to do so would conform to divine precept.[176] In a final remark that sounded a contemporary note as re-

173. Almain, "Tractatus de auctoritate ecclesiae," in Gerson, ibid., 987C.
174. Ibid., 989B–992A.
175. Ibid., 991C–D. Cf. ibid., 978D.
176. Ibid., 1012A.

gards the *conciliabulum* of Pisa, Almain asserted that the authority of the entire Church would reside in such a gathering even if some particular churches "contumaciously declined to appear."[177]

## 6. CONCILIARISM SECULARIZED: GEORGE BUCHANAN

George Buchanan (1506–82) was a pupil of John Major in Paris and spent much of his life on the continent before returning to his native Scotland in 1560. A humanist rather than a theologian or philosopher like Major, he was also a poet, linguist, essayist, dramatist, and historian best known today as the author of a reasonably systematic work in political thought, the dialogue *De iuri regni apud Scotos*, first published in 1579. This justification for the forced abdication of Mary, Queen of Scots may have been drafted for use by Scottish representatives to Elizabeth who were urging the legality of Mary's deposition in 1571, though it may have been written even earlier when the Scottish chieftains took action against Mary in 1567.[178] Ostensibly a Catholic for much of his life, Buchanan adopted the Scottish Reformed religion in 1560 and became a Protestant revolutionary writer from that time onward, although his views were not published until somewhat later. He had become acquaintained earlier on the Continent with a number of well-known reformers, and there is evidence that his Catholic orthodoxy was suspect as early as the 1540s, when he acknowledged to the Inquisition at Lisbon that he

---

177. Ibid., 1012B–C.
178. Trevor-Roper, *George Buchanan and the Ancient Scottish Constitution*, pp. 6–7 and *passim*. Trevor-Roper found an anonymous document he dates to 1571 containing in both form and substance much of the material found in Buchanan's *De iure regni apud Scotos* and *Chronicle of the Kings of Scotland*. He contends that the arguments were those employed by the Scottish representatives to Elizabeth in the late 1560s and may also have been the ones used earlier by the Scottish nobles to depose Mary: ibid., p. 14. He suggested that Buchanan might have formed his historical perspective for the *De iure regni* much earlier and begun its formal preparation by 1563: ibid., p. 15. Cf. *infra*, note 181. Oakley says the *De iure regni* was written about 1567: "Road from Constance," 10; Skinner says that Buchanan seems to have begun it in draft in 1567 but published it more than a decade later, in 1579: Skinner, *Foundations* 2:339.
There are two modern English translations of Buchanan's *De iure regni*: one by Arrowood, *George Buchanan on the Powers of the Crown in Scotland*, and the other by MacNeill. J. H. Burns has argued that both are defective: on the Arrowood translation, Burns, "Political Ideas of George Buchanan," pp. 67–68; on the MacNeill translation, the Burns review in *The Scottish Historical Review* 48 (1969): 190–91. For a critical assessment of the Trevor-Roper thesis regarding the provenance and formulations of the Buchanan position, see Barrow, *Annali della Fondazione italiana per la storia amministrativa* 4 (1967).

had taught the supremacy of council over pope.[179] His best-known works are *The Powers of the Crown of Scotland (De iuri regni apud Scotos)*, published in 1579, and his *History of Scotland*, dedicated to James VI when published in 1582. Both contain material that was prepared years before publication.[180]

The *De iure regni apud Scotos* is the more significant because the more systematic of Buchanan's two best-known works. As already noted, it was intended to legitimate the removal of Mary from the Scottish throne; but its form of argument was set in general historical terms showing the Scottish throne as traditionally elective, even though hereditary succession was clearly visible. The work is historically inaccurate but nonetheless of interest: it is a curious blend of would-be historical data and conciliar-like argumentation for limited monarchy written at a critical period in the development of Protestant resistance theory by a then-Protestant publicist who had been a Catholic and whose apparent connections with continental reformers, both before and after its preparation, suggest a link in the chain of ideological continuity for which, unfortunately, not all the evidence is yet available.

In fact, Buchanan offered a mix of material from historical sources, Scottish, medieval European, and classical history, along with specific invocation of conciliar sources such as the Council of Basle, to make the case that monarchy traditionally had been, and therefore should be, limited. He argued also that he preferred to cite "men distinguished in the school of action than men from the retirement of the schools."[181] He took the familiar position, however, that rulers are accountable to their

---

179. Trevor-Roper, *George Buchanan*, p. 2. Cf. Aiken, ed. and trans., *The Trial of George Buchanan*.

180. Trevor-Roper, *George Buchanan*, p. 15. Trevor-Roper points out that earlier Buchanan had prepared, at least in note form, much of the erroneous pre-Christian history of Scotland found in his *History*, using without acknowledgment data from Hector Boèce's *Scotorum Historia* (Paris, 1526), shortly after the Boèce work was published in Paris where Buchanan could have read it. Trevor-Roper contends further than Buchanan himself knew, or ought to have known by the time he finally prepared the *History* for publication (the early 1570s), that the Boèce account was an innocent repetition which combined large dollops of fancy with deliberate distortions of some seven hundred years of Scottish history: the Welsh antiquarian Humphrey Lhuyd had established this conclusively in a work published posthumously in 1572. Trevor-Roper also shows that, while Buchanan apparently accepted the accuracy of his own version of Scottish history until 1571, he had tried to "tidy up" his thesis after the Lhuyd publication and retained for publication in his own work stories about the "forty kings of Scotland" he should have known were mere fantasies. Trevor-Roper, *George Buchanan*, p. 29.

181. Buchanan, *Powers of the Crown*, p. 61; *De iure*, pp. 9–10.

subjects for the quality of their performance and that, accordingly, Mary could be removed by the appropriate other elements of authority in the event of misuse of power. He accepted that rulers were appointed for the common good of their subjects consistent with the natural law governing the actions of all persons, with reason the rightful guide for discovering its contents. Following the standard humanist account of the origins of human society, he repeated the notion that humans originally lived alone or in herds, "in hovels and even caves, and wandered about as lawless vagabonds without any rooted culture."[182] But he referred also to the divinely infused spark of natural law as the instrument that wrought the transition to some form of society: "God, not some orator or lawyer who brought men together, is the author of human association."[183] He went on to ring the usual changes on reason, through which humans came to realize that the means for ridding themselves of the "conflicting elements" among individuals in the state of nature was to designate someone as "physician" over the body politic, just as the physical body could be tended properly and cured of its diseases only by a medical expert: "Each has a twofold duty, to preserve health and restore it when it is impaired, [so that] the king has been set up, not to serve his own interests, but for the good of the people."[184] At this point, Buchanan gave further evidence of his humanist background, asserting that in taking his position he had been "striving exclusively for this one thing, that the Ciceronian principle, 'the public welfare is the supreme law', might be held in reverence and perfectly observed."[185]

He then addressed the issue of how, amongst individuals who are free and equal, a single person could assume authority, given the stipulation of natural law that it is "neither possible nor right for one to assume au-

182. Buchanan, *Powers of the Crown*, pp. 45–46; *De iure*, pp. 3–4.
183. Buchanan, *Powers of the Crown*, p. 48; *De iure*, p. 5. Here Buchanan claimed a fusion that is logically incompatible for those who insist on contrasting humanist and medieval scholastic political thought, the latter giving prominence to natural law in the establishment of political society. His rejection of the notion that oratory might have inspired the invention of political society is a criticism of Cicero's account of how humans came to form polities after emerging from the original state of nature: Cicero, *De inventione* 1.2.2; and *infra*, p. 123. He did, however, acknowledge Cicero directly as a source for other views of his own: *infra*, p. 123 and note 186.
184. Buchanan, *Powers of the Crown*, pp. 45–46; *De iure*, pp. 3–4.
185. Buchanan, *Powers of the Crown*, p. 73; *De iure*, p. 14. Buchanan clearly had no difficulty aligning a Ciceronian conception of the nature and origins of polity with a Christian theology of politics; nor need he have had, since as this Ciceronian view had long been a component of Christian political thought. Cf. *infra*, p. 140.

thority among their equals, [but] naturally just for the position of equals to be alike with respect to the exercise of and subjection to political authority."[186] As one might anticipate, however, Buchanan had no difficulty with the point; he simply repeated the view, often seen before, that the people themselves could assign ruling power to someone of their choice. "We cannot have a legitimate ruler unless we have elected him with the full consent of the people."[187] It followed directly that a ruler chosen by the people enjoys only limited authority, and the limit is set by the purpose for which authority is exercised—the common good—while the people retain the right to limit their obedience to just laws established by their ruler. Further, in a move that he must have known ran contrary to early Lutheran and Calvinist doctrines on obedience to temporal authority, he stated that the Pauline injunction to obey did not apply to a tyrant, but only to a true and lawfully appointed ruler, "a minister to whom God has entrusted the sword that he may punish evil-doers and support the good." John Chrysostom was cited to support this interpretation.[188]

Buchanan thus stood four-square with his teacher, Major, on the two basic principles of temporal authority: that rulers are appointed by popular election, and their task is to further the common good. Accordingly, the people themselves are above their ruler in the sense that his authority derives from them, and this is also why they can depose or otherwise regulate him when he transgresses the limits of his legitimate authority. Buchanan showed another clear difference between himself and earlier and contemporary continental resistance theorists. Unlike Beza and Mornay, he did not speak of any religious "covenant" between God's people and the divinity through which they promise to act as a godly people; he took his stand on the ground of political theory and history rather than religious commitment.[189]

Applying these general principles to the Scottish monarchy, Buchanan referred to the coronation oath as the instrument through which the

186. Buchanan, *Powers of the Crown*, p. 52; *De iure*, p. 6.
187. Buchanan, *Powers of the Crown*, p. 54; *De iure*, p. 7.
188. Buchanan, *Powers of the Crown*, p. 113; *De iure*, p. 28. Peter Martyr Vermigli made the same point, though not so bluntly, in his *Commentary on the Epistle of St Paul to the Romans*, and this raises the tantalizing question of influence. Vermigli's *Commentary* was published in an English translation in 1568, and appeared in its original Latin ten years earlier. Cf. *infra*, p. 255.
189. Skinner points out that here Buchanan anticipated Althusius, who was quite explicit that, unlike even Bodin, he kept the science of politics distinct from theology: Althusius, *Politica methodice digesta*, pp. 1–2; Skinner, *Foundations*, 2:341–42 and note 1.

people exercise a limiting effect on the ruler and the ruler commits himself to these limits. The king promises to "maintain the law in justice and goodness ... there is, then, a mutual compact between king and citizens [and, if the king breaks it, he] forfeits whatever rights belong to him under it" and may then be treated as a public enemy rightly to be destroyed by the whole people, or even by an individual. "Although it is our duty to pray for bad princes, we ought not to conclude from this that their crimes ought not to be punished."[190] On the question of how the people are to exercise control over a tyrannical ruler, Buchanan offered the standard response from medieval corporation theory: "What is sought is that the law shall be of advantage to the *maior pars* of the people, and that the *maior pars* have confidence in the person chosen." The *maior pars* of the people "may decree a law or create a ruler"; the authority to judge a king "resides with those persons in whom the people or its *maior pars* has vested it."[191] Applying these views to Scotland, Buchanan wrote that "all the estates of Scotland in public assembly gave judgment that James III was lawfully put to death."[192] Elsewhere, he noted his understanding of the specific procedure at issue: "[I] never thought the management of affairs should be left to the decision of the whole people but that, according to our custom, selected persons from all estates should join with the king in council."[193]

    190. Buchanan, *Powers of the Crown*, pp. 142–43 and 113; cf. pp. 117–18 and p. 148; *De iure*, p. 38; cf. pp. 29–30 and p. 40.
    191. Buchanan, *Powers of the Crown*, pp. 131 and 133; *De iure*, p. 34. Buchanan's position on the power of the people as a whole *vis-à-vis* their monarch repeated exactly Zabarella's view of how the *ecclesia fidelium* related to the pope in the spiritual sphere where, of course, a general Church council represented the people. See *supra*, p. 96. An interesting Catholic formulation of the theory of constitutional monarchy in traditional medieval form by a contemporary of Buchanan, the Scottish Benedictine abbot of Ratisbon (Regensburg) in Bavaria, is described in Burns, "Winzerus."
    192. Buchanan, *Powers of the Crown*, p. 125; *De iure*, p. 32.
    193. Buchanan, *Powers of the Crown*, p. 71; *De iure*, p. 13. Oakley has noted that Arrowood, Sabine and Allan all have distinguished Buchanan's position from that of Mornay in his *Vindiciae* about who can exercise popular control over a ruler, contending that Buchanan referred this to the "majority" in a community, translating Buchanan's term *maior pars* as "majority." Oakley is surely right to call this a mistaken interpretation, however, inasmuch as *maior pars*, a term of lengthy medieval provenance brought into particular prominence in political thought by Marsilius of Padua, had a qualitative as well as a quantitative connotation. See Oakley, "Road from Constance," 24–26; cf. Monahan, *Consent, Coercion, and Limit*, pp. 227–28. On the Marsilian meaning of *maior pars* see Wilks, "Corporation and Representation."

The issue of just what influences operated on Buchanan's political thought and what influence he in turn had on contemporary Reformist thought is difficult to address with any accuracy. Trevor-Roper attributes an anonymous document dating from 1571 to Buchanan on the grounds that it reflects views and language Buchanan used in the *Powers of the Crown of Scotland* and *History of Scotland*. This would place the Buchanan doctrine on constitutional and elected monarchy prior to Huguenot publicist works of the 1570s, for which it thus becomes a probable source. Without insisting that Huguenot resistance writings came directly from Buchanan texts, Trevor-Roper suggests that the texts themselves would not have been necessary: the Huguenot writers could have become familiar with the general tenor and details of Buchanan's thought through earlier contact with him on the Continent and in the general climate of intellectual exchange among reformers at the time. And he points out further the enigmatic "published in Edinburgh" that appears on the title pages of the anonymous Hotman and Mornay publications. Trevor-Roper also pointed out the 1571 document's use of arguments found in Melanchthon, notably the Trajan story and references to other "good" Roman emperors who exercised self-limiting rule, as well as references to the Calvinist doctrine of inferior magistrates. All of these items were found in later Huguenot tracts and in Vermigli before they were actually published by Buchanan. It is also the case that Buchanan's conciliarism directly reflects the position of his teacher, John Major, and that these views reappear very shortly on the Continent in the writings of Beza and Mornay, both of whom use an argument found in Major's *Commentarium in Sententiis Petri Lombardi*[194] about people coming together to form a political society in order better to provide for their needs.

This treatment of late medieval conciliarist thought after Constance and Basle has extended into the first half-century of the Reformation era. The issue raised here—of coordinating current Reformation resistance theory with Buchanan's views regarding the limits of political authority and the right to withdraw obedience from an errant ruler and even oppose him with force—can only be addressed fully in the context of

---

194. Details on these several items as part of the armoury of arguments set forth in resistance theory tracts composed by Lutheran, Calvinist and Huguenot authors can be found in Part Four. *Re* Vermigli see *supra*, note 189 and *infra*, pp. 249–56.

Reformation political thought as a whole. Hence it will be left to Part Four, where it will be possible to draw conclusions concerning the intersection of two distinguishable historical strands emerging from the late Middle Ages that have to do with popular consent and the limits of political authority. One strand reflected the traditional expression of a medieval theory that received its most comprehensive and forceful expression in conciliarism, and the other was an expression of the humanist emphasis on liberty and the importance of the human individual. In the meantime, the specifically scholastic model of medieval political thinking embodied in the great thirteenth-century philosopher-theologian Thomas Aquinas will be examined through the vehicle of Spanish neo-scholasticism in Part Three.

PART THREE

# Consent and Limit in Spanish Neo-Scholasticism

1. SPANISH SCHOLASTICISM

THE MATERIAL DEALT WITH HERE illustrates the organizational difficulties mentioned earlier: in many instances individual thinkers treated under the category of Spanish neo-scholastics could be placed equally well in other sections. Juan de Segovia, for example, has been mentioned already as a conciliarist and leading figure at the Council of Basle. Molina was Portuguese rather than Spanish. Both Cajetan and Bellarmine were Italian. Bellarmine could also be treated as a leading figure both in the post-Tridentine reaction to the Reformation and in the treatment of resistance theory, as could Suárez.[1] Juan Luis Vives, on the other hand, was not a scholastic in the strict sense of the word, but a Spanish nobleman who taught the humanities at Leuven University in the first half of the sixteenth century.

Skinner, following Gierke, has tended to present the political thinkers of the Spanish neo-scholastic school in the context of their reaction to the Reformation, particularly Lutheranism, emphasizing their repudiation of the Lutheran view of the Church and the whole concept of political life associated with the evangelical Reformation.[2] Counter-Reformation polemical activity was indeed the deliberate purpose

1. In fact Bellarmine is not treated separately at all; nor is Molina or Juan de Segovia. Although Skinner is arguably correct in describing Bellarmine's *Controversies* as "the most learned and comprehensive of the numerous Jesuit attacks on the political as well as the theological assumptions associated with the Lutheran faith" (Skinner, *Foundations*, 2:137), Bellarmine's political thought, except for his association of the people's choice of form of polity with the *ius gentium*, followed Vitoria in almost every detail. Cf. *infra*, p. 160 and note 89.

2. Skinner, *Foundations*, 2:138. Cf. Gierke, *Development of Political Theory* and *Natural Law and the Theory of Society*.

of a number of works by members of the Spanish school, such as Bellarmine's *De justificatione* and Suárez's *Defensio*, and Skinner has shown a pattern of "anti-heretical" language and argument employed by Vitoria, Bellarmine, De Soto, and Suárez, particularly as regards the Reformation insistence on "making the Church invisible."[3] Moreover, a Counter-Reformation approach strikes a resounding note in terms of historical context, illustrating a major element in Skinner's methodological assumptions concerning the essentially "fact-construed" character of political theorizing. However, it undervalues the connection between the coherent and comprehensive nature of Spanish neo-scholastic political thought and the theory of polity found in the earlier Parisian Dominican tradition from which it came. Skinner himself acknowledges "the remarkably homogeneous outlook" of Suárez's final formulation, and notes that Vitoria makes no mention of the Lutheran doctrine of the godly prince which "the Thomists clearly felt a special need to attack."[4] He also points to the disparity between Vitoria and later Spanish Thomists who criticized him concerning the source of political authority. But he does not mention that Suárez's emphasis on popular consent as the efficient cause of political authority—a feature he considers to have been consciously used in the Suárezian doctrine to contrast it with Reformation political thought—can be found in several pre-Reformation texts by Cardinal Cajetan.[5]

    3. Skinner, *Foundations* 2:138–40 and 138, n. 2. Identifying this heresy as Lutheran, de Soto traces the error of making the Church invisible back to the "Waldensians": Domingo de Soto, *Libri decem de iustitiae et iure*, fol. 18a. Cf. Bellarmine, "De conciliis," in Bellarmine, *Opera omnia*, 2:317, 344. John of Paris also referred to the Waldensians as a source of heretical error in the early fourteenth century: John of Paris, *Royal and Papal Power*, Prologue, p. 1.
    4. Skinner, *Foundations*, 2:140. This same criticism has already been levelled at Skinner. Antony Black has suggested that at least some political thinkers, among them a number of the Spanish neo-scholastics, might be presumed to have intended to speak universally even when they were writing in a counter-Reformation context, and therefore that to construe their texts in terms of the single purpose of opposing Protestant thought is to minimize their positions. He includes Skinner's treatment of Dante and Marsilius of Padua in the same criticism and delivers what might be seen as a *coup de grâce* by commenting that if all meaning in a political text is to be fact-construed in terms of conscious contemporary purpose, then any study of historical documents of this type is fruitless in terms of furthering the development of a general theory. See Black's review of Skinner's *Foundations* in *Political Studies* 28 (1980): 451–57.
    5. This is not to suggest that Suarez had no counter-Reformation intention in mind but only that, even if he did, it was not the whole, or necessarily even the main, reason for his theory of consent. On the Cajetan and Suarezian views, see *infra*, pp. 142–45 and pp. 166–83.

Skinner is undoubtedly correct to maintain that historical realities condition and mould the precise thought patterns that are presented as political theory. But the members of the Spanish neo-scholastic school may not all have been as single-mindedly motivated in their political thinking by opposition to Reformation theology and political doctrine as he implies. The basic uniformity in late neo-Thomistic political thought probably has more to do with the formidable internal consistency of the theory itself, even when expressed in a sixteenth-century historical context different from that experienced by Aquinas.

This is not to say that ideas, political or otherwise, have a transhistorical existence of their own. But even as individual thinkers give them new shape for their own purposes and in their own historical context, ideas, particularly seminal ones, frequently possess in themselves a certain solidity and resistance to change. Their presence and use in a given text is often at least as well explained from within the general intellectual tradition they are part of as by reference to more immediate historical events. Works by Vitoria, Bellarmine, and Suárez on the relations between church and pope, for example, owe something of their purpose and meaning to the political realities and thought of the Reformation; but as is clearly the case with Cajetan, they probably owe more to the general character of the Roman Catholic church itself, which of course was also affected by its own Counter-Reformation thought and activity.

A straightforward approach that identifies purpose with the title of a text seems indicated, for example, for Vitoria's *Relectio de Indis*, where the historical context, the conquest and exploitation of native peoples in Central and South America, is specifically Spanish. The issue of slavery had become a focus of considerable economic, social, and, ultimately, ethical concern for Spanish and Portuguese moralists and political theorists, as well as for those in the Spanish Netherlands, when the two Iberian nations, particularly Portugal, got involved in the slave trade and in colonial rivalry with other European nations.[6] It might be recalled in this connection that Molina was Portuguese and held a prominent academic appointment in his homeland. Both Suárez and Molina sanctioned slavery by invoking a noble-sounding theory of individual rights: the "Aethopians," or African blacks, were said to be free like all other

---

6. Tuck, *Natural Rights*, p. 54.

human beings, a status that entitled them to sell themselves into slavery if they chose to do so.[7]

One of the most important issues addressed by the Spanish neo-scholastics was the nature of law, more particularly the law of nature, or natural law. The term "law of nature" has had a tremendously complex history in both philosophy and law, Roman and canonical, as well as in Christian theology. Classical Roman jurists used it in arguing that humans do not have property rights over another or over material goods; property rights in anything derive from mutual agreement. Further, Ulpian held that "everyone was born free under the law of nature,"[8] while Hermogenianus asserted that "wars, separate nations, the origin of kingdoms, private property (*dominia distincta*), the division of land, grouping of houses, commerce" came about through the *ius gentium*[9]—everything was held and used in common in the state of nature. Christian theologians and lawyers had always expressed the same view, as cited by Gratian from Isidore of Seville: "The *ius naturale* is common to all nations; it is what is received everywhere by natural instinct, not by any convention. It includes the union of men and women, the begetting and education of children, common possession of all things, and freedom for everyone."[10]

The meaning of "natural" for a human being and the question of what constituted the state of nature were closely examined by Spanish neo-scholastic thinkers beginning with Vitoria, who raised the problem in an enquiry concerning the legitimacy of the Spanish conquest of the

---

7. Luis de Molina, *De iustitia et iure*, 1:162–63, cited in Tuck, ibid., note 51. Slavery, even at the level of theory, had always been a problem for Christian thinkers, principally because of St Paul's implicit sanction of it: Col. 3:22ff., 4:1; Eph. 6:5–9, and St Augustine and St Ambrose's general acceptance of the political legitimacy of the Roman Empire, within which slavery was an accepted legality. See Vitoria, *De Indis*, 3.17.

8. Ulpian, *Digest* 1.1.14. Thomas Aquinas combined the notions of one individual not having property rights over another with personal freedom when he asserted that "in the state of innocence no person was master over another as slave": *ST* 1.96.4. But cf. later comments on the need for care regarding the distinction between "state of innocence" and "state of nature" among Christian political writers; *infra*, p. 133 and note 15.

9. *Digest* 1.1.5.

10. Isidore, *Etymologia* 5.4; cited in Gratian 1.1.7. Cf. Tuck, *Natural Rights*, p. 18, notes 26 and 27. New Testament texts could also be cited to show that early Christian communities held material goods in common: Acts 3:44–45, 4:32; and, of course, the formal holding of all goods in common was a standard feature of Christian religious orders and communities.

Americas. While he would have been aware that contemporary Reformation political thinking discounted, where it did not simply ignore, the natural law and state-of-nature thinking conventionally associated with Aristotle's *Politics* and the Thomist tradition, he had a more direct and urgent issue on which to focus his critical acumen. The depredations of the conquistadores in the early sixteenth century had raised in an immediate and poignant way the issue of human dignity and personal and jurisdictional rights: were the "Indians" of America human; and if so, was it morally permissible to conquer and enslave them?

Because of the specific intellectual and literary context in which later Spanish scholastics raised these questions, they were treated virtually as an extended commentary on the introductory chapters of Aristotle's *Politics*. Medieval Christian thinkers had found in this classical and authoritative, if largely undeveloped, text the distinction between free and servile and had encountered for the first time the question of what it means to be human posed in philosophical terms. They had also found there the assertion that humans are naturally social. The long and continuing history of the consideration of the state of nature in modern Western political thought, the distinction between social and political, and the issue of how humans came to form political societies began with William of Moerbeke's translation of the *Politics* from Greek into Latin around 1250. This is not to say, however, that only Aristotelian elements can be found in medieval and later political thinkers in the Western tradition, even on these specific points. Christian theology in general, as well as Stoicism, also contributed significantly to the political thinking in our tradition. The blending of these sources began in the late thirteenth century and continues, without having yet produced either a comprehensive or fully acceptable doctrine of polity. Again, the development of Western political thought must be traced from medieval origins. When Hobbes offered a mid-seventeenth-century description of the state of nature, he was working within a centuries-old intellectual tradition that had already paid considerable attention to the concept. While the Hobbesian view does not conform completely with earlier ones on which he depended, like those of Marsilius of Padua, Jean Bodin, Althusius, and Grotius, he was not uninfluenced by them.[11]

Historically, Aristotle's concept of the human state of nature and his apparently straightforward assertion that humans are by nature social appear in a different and more functional formulation in the Stoic tradi-

---

11. See Tuck, *Natural Rights, passim.*

tion. Late medieval thinkers blended both Aristotelian and Stoic perspectives into a view that was also significantly influenced by the Christian theological doctrine of Original Sin. For Christians human nature was necessarily wounded and distorted in every member of the human race by Adam and Eve's first transgression of God's (divine) law in the Garden of Eden. For the Christian thinker, only two people had actually existed or could have existed in the pure state of an Aristotelian human nature, that is, in the purely natural state in which God created them, and they did so for only the first period of their lives. Adam and Eve alone had exercised natural human existence in the manner provided by God's original act of creation.

The Christian doctrine of Original Sin, of course, was not originally expressed in Aristotelian philosophical terminology. Thomas Aquinas was the first to systematically formulate Christian thought in a specifically Aristotelian conceptual structure. For centuries before, the doctrine of Original Sin had been construed without explicit reference to "human nature" or "state of nature." Previous Christian thinkers customarily used "state of innocence" to designate the pre-lapsarian condition of the first parents. The first authoritative use of the term was by St Augustine,[12] and it remained current well after Aristotle made his overwhelming impact on Christian thought in the thirteenth century. Thomas Aquinas employed it exclusively when discussing the condition of Adam and Eve before their expulsion from the Garden of Eden,[13] as did Ptolemy of Lucca in the early fourteenth century[14] and subsequent Christian theologians, including late medieval scholastics of the Spanish school.[15]

---

12. Augustine, *City of God* 4.16.

13. See Thomas Aquinas, *ST* 1.95.3 and the balance of his treatment of Adam and Eve in the Garden: 1.96–99, *passim*. For an example of the complexities of Aquinas's theological examination of the effects of Original Sin on the descendants of Adam see Eschmann, "Thomistic Social Philosophy."

14. Ptolemy of Lucca, *Governance of Rulers* 2.9.

15. Caution must be exercised, however, when reading Spanish neo-scholastic texts that refer to the state of innocence since there is sometimes a tendency to elide the two stages of human existence, the pre-lapsarian and the pre-political. Cf. Vitoria, "De potestate ecclesiae prior" 1:46; Castrillo, *De republica*, p. 59. The term "state of innocence" always appears in its technical meaning in theological texts examining the nature of Original Sin, as, for example, in commentaries on Aquinas's *Summa theologiae* at the relevant locations: *v.g.* on *ST* 1.95–99. Suárez was more careful than some of his Spanish predecessors when speaking about the pre-political stages of human existence: the "eliding" term he normally used was "the nature of things" rather than "state of nature" or "state of innocence". Cf.

The issue, however, is whether medieval and later Christian thinkers in the neo-scholastic tradition who also employed the Aristotelian philosophy of nature construed Adam and Eve's original state of innocence as synonymous with Aristotle's natural state of human nature. Were Adam and Eve before the Fall in the state of nature as Aristotle would have understood the term; and if so, how should they be described *after* the Fall? This aspect of medieval Christian theology has yet to receive adequate investigation, though it is crucial in late medieval political thought as the source for the modern notion of state of nature. In fact, later Christian theologians in the Thomistic tradition did not normally designate Adam and Eve's condition of innocence before the Fall as the Aristotelian state of nature; they used the latter term to describe the human condition after the Fall but before the formal establishment of political society.[16]

---

Suárez, *De legibus* 3.2.3. Suárez speaks of the "state of innocence" in its strictly theological sense in texts like his commentary on the work of creation, "De opere sex dierum," where Wilenius notes what he calls "some peculiar chapters" dealing with what the political and economic organization of humankind would have been like without the commission of the Original Sin. While perhaps peculiar to a modern commentator, such issues would have been perfectly ordinary for a Christian theologian like Suárez. See Wilenius, *Social and Political Theory of Francisco Suárez*, p. 77, note 5.

16. When speaking of humans living in the state of nature prior to forming political societies, then—and this was a standard feature of medieval historical and political as well as theological works—Christian writers would have understood individuals to have been in a post-lapsarian state of "fallen" human nature. See Isidore of Seville, *Etymologia* 5.4, cited in Gratian 1.1.7; Hugh of St Victor, *On the Sacraments* 1.11.1. One of the fullest formulations of this view in medieval political texts is that by Aegidius of Rome: "In the beginning by law [i.e., natural law] there is no such thing as private property; anyone could claim an object as their own in the absence of convention, or agreement among persons about what was theirs. Such a convention and agreement for partitioning and developing the world obtained in the case of the sons of Adam ... As the population increased ... it became necessary for agreements and conventions to be extended more broadly ... none was able to appropriate for themself except by mutual agreement and convention with others ... Still later men began to exercise dominion over the earth and become kings, and laws were formulated both to continue this and add other arrangements." Aegidius of Rome, *On Ecclesiastical Power* 2.12, pp. 146–47.

That Aegidius did not draw a hard and fast distinction between the state of nature and the existence of polities, however, is evident when he speaks of there being kingdoms in the law of nature: "*in lege naturae, ubi fuerunt regna gentilium*": ibid. 1.5; 2.5, pp. 22 and 80. Aegidius's view was that some kingdoms existed among non-Israelites before the Jewish people established a monarchy of their own and, more generally, that some humans existed in a pre-political style in early times in the post-lapsarian state of nature, while others at the same time were formed into polities. Following the Old Testament history of the Israelites, he maintained that kings existed among "the Gentiles" before there was a

A number of later Spanish neo-scholastics maintained that human beings moved into political communities from an original state of nature where they had enjoyed the condition of freedom and independence because of a rational perception that the state of nature had imperfections and disadvantages that needed to be overcome; they willingly gave up personal freedom for these other benefits. Thus, the question posed by John Locke—why should humans enjoying the benefits of freedom and independence give these up to form a political society that would restrict their freedom—received a plausible answer from Christian thinkers whose conception of the state of nature was post-lapsarian, so that every individual therein was a victim of the baneful effects of Original Sin. To the extent that one can assume Locke was a believing Christian who accepted the traditional doctrine of Original Sin, his question appears more rhetorical than some interpreters have perceived. Moreover, the notion made much of by the Spanish neo-scholastics, that political societies originated in groups of individuals consenting or "contracting" to live under a given ruler, the concept of political society in some sense originating in agreement among a group of individuals, can be found as early as the early fourteenth century in Aegidius of Rome and John of Paris: "They live civilly and in community according to the promptings of a natural inclination which is from God. Accordingly, they choose different types of rulers to oversee the well-being of their communities to correspond with the diversity of these communities."[17]

Life within the limiting structures of a political society is preferable to a free and independent existence in the state of nature, because a political community offers the means to avoid and overcome the harmful effects of Original Sin. While appearing superficially as another version of St Augustine's view of political society as a consequence of fallen human nature, this doctrine has a much more affirmative thrust. Governmental authority is not merely something to be suffered and accepted as a corrective; it has a positive function to further and perfect human

---

Jewish monarchy, citing Augustine and Peter Comestor in support of this Standard view. See *infra*, p. 140 and note 31.

A good example of the need to be cautious in understanding what the neo-scholastics meant by what is natural for humans, what we might call the "state of (human) nature," is Suarez's use of the term "the nature of things" rather than "the state of nature" when referring to what is natural for humans. He uses this term with reference to both pre- and post-lapsarian phases of human history. See *infra*, p. 176.

17. John of Paris, *Royal and Papal Power*, 3:14. On Aegidius of Rome, see *supra*, note 16.

well-being.[18] While it is not "natural" in a purely philosophical and Aristotelian meaning, it comes as close to this meaning as any Christian thinker, for whom no Aristotelian "natural" human beings any longer exist, could get. A post-lapsarian Christian state of nature is not a purely philosophical state; it is not quite what Aristotle had in mind when he spoke of human nature as naturally social. Juan Luis Vives encapsulates these nuances when he delineates the late medieval doctrine by identifying three stages in human history: the original and perfect pre-lapsarian state of nature; the post-lapsarian state of nature before political societies came into being; and the period when polities or states did and do exist.[19]

The political doctrine of Spanish neo-Thomists also emphasized a distinction found, but not explicated, in Aquinas's *On Kingship* between humans as naturally social and naturally political.[20] Skinner is right to note that at least some of them employed this distinction as a criticism of the Reformation theory concerning the direct divine origin of political authority.[21] They maintained that humans are social by nature, but not political by nature in the sense of being necessarily determined to live together under some form of polity. Though inclined by nature to form political societies, humans actually did so only as a result of agreement and consent among free individuals. It has been seen that the notion that polities, at least kingdoms, came into existence only as the result of human convention and agreement was common in the late thirteenth century; what is new here is the distinction between social and

18. Augustine accepted that human nature was social, but his doctrine emphasized the selfish and anti-social effects of Original Sin: "There is nothing so social by nature, so unsocial by its corruption, as this [human] race": Augustine, *City of God* 12.27. Suárez expressed the Spanish neo-scholastic view best when he asserted that "in the nature of things," humans were naturally social in the sense that they needed to live and benefited from living together, even in the state of innocence. In this idyllic "natural" state, however, there was no dominion or political jurisdiction of any one individual over another: Suárez, *De legibus* 3.2.3. Political society and its essential feature of coercion derive from the agreement of individuals to live under a ruler. See *infra*, p. 179.

19. See *infra*, p. 147. Skinner notes that Suárez, among others, identified the state of nature with the post-lapsarian condition of Adam and Eve: Skinner, *Foundations*, 2:155. Not all modern commentators are careful to distinguish between the states of innocence and fallen nature, however. Wilenius speaks of directive, but not coercive, power operating in the "state of innocence": Wilenius, *Social and Political Theory of Francisco Suárez*, p. 77.

20. Thomas Aquinas, *On Kingship* 1.1.4. Aquinas made the verbal distinction between social and political in several texts. See also *ST* 1–2.72.4 and *In Perihermenias* 1.2; the Aristotelian formula held that a human is a political animal.

21. Skinner, *Foundations*, 2:148–68.

political deliberately employed to reinforce the conventional or consenting character of the formation of a polity.

Consistent with the distinction between social and political is a further distinction marking the transition from the social to the political condition: that between social and political contract. Its purpose was to preserve the natural character of human society, while at the same time accommodating the notion that political society came about by way of consent (contract) among rational human beings: free persons agree or consent to establish a government, and they also agree to submit themselves to the authority of a ruler. The consenting agreement among a group of humans establishing a political society and handing over governing authority to a ruler is a "political" contract. Accordingly, political society originates directly from the consent of free individuals to hand over political authority to, and be governed by, a specific ruler.

Such a ruler, then, holds political authority from the people at least in the first instance, and in virtue of their having consented to allocate it to him. The two interpretations offered by medieval canonical and civilian legists concerning the implications of popular consent as the basis for political authority now reappear, but in a context of increased sophistication that collapses the earlier distinction into retention of power in the people. On the one hand, popular consent is seen to entail an absolute transfer of authority such that the people forfeit any power of recall unless it is specifically provided for in the original political contract. Suárez held this view, for example, as did Hobbes though in a more forthright and less sophisticated way.[22] On the other hand, the people are said to delegate authority to a ruler in such a way that they remain capable of withdrawing it in certain conditions. This was the view of Vitoria and Mariana and, later, John Locke.[23] The second interpretation, it must be stressed, operated under the general principle that a tyrant *ipso facto* violated his agreement with the people and thereby freed them from the obligation of obedience. All the Spanish neo-scholastics subscribed to this view, including Suárez, who held that subjects could not opt out of political obligations "on their own," but agreed that a tyrant's actions dissolved the original political contract.[24] The "social" contract, on the other hand, was something that occurred before the

22. Cf. *supra*, p. 27; and *infra*, p. 180.
23. For Vitoria and Mariana see *infra*, pp. 154 and 163; Locke, *Second Treatise of Government*, 18, 202.
24. See *infra*, p. 180.

agreement that produced an actual polity; it appeared at the origin of political society itself as the act by which, following the promptings of rational human nature, humans decided to move out of their postlapsarian condition as free and independent entities living in the natural world. Their motive for doing so was recognition of the imperfections, difficulties, and evils besetting their independent existence because of the effects of Original Sin.

The two types of contract together constituted a kind of lock-step procedure. The first, the social contract, signalled agreement among free and consenting individuals to come together in a society, which their human nature rationally inclined them to do, while the second, the political contract, specified mutual agreement concerning who should exercise political authority. The complexity of the twofold stage of contract was a response to the gap created by the earlier distinction between humans as naturally free and naturally social. As naturally free, individuals can come together only through their own consent; they are not determined by their nature to be members of a political society as fire is determined to rise or stones and other heavy objects to fall.[25] Their nature, however, *inclines* human individuals to join together, and the inclination is given rational expression when individuals freely enter into the original social contract. The doctrine at this point has difficulty avoiding at least the appearance of trying to "have it both ways," a difficulty that afflicts certain modern thinkers in their efforts to account for how humans can be called free when they are determined by the laws of the physical universe.[26]

The origins of the double-contract theory, it should be clear, were basically medieval, even though it was not spelled out clearly before the sixteenth century. The concept that power originated in contractual agreement was so commonly accepted in late medieval thought as having come from feudal and Roman law—the primary model in the latter instance being the relationship between emperor and citizen—that it virtually excluded any other interpretation of human social relationships.[27] The notion of social contract, moreover, was intended to explain rather than deny the natural character of a political community; hence the modern dichotomy between natural and conventional did not operate. The political contract was seen as both natural and conven-

---

25. Cf. Aristotle, *Physics* 2.1, 192b5–193b22.
26. Cf. Schlick, *Problems of Ethics*, ch. 7.
27. Jarlot, "Les idées politiques de Suárez," p. 72.

tional, the latter in the sense that agreement by free consent was a necessary condition for establishing a polity. The social contract assumed and accounted for the necessity of juridical organization in a political society as a response to "fallen" human nature, a kind of juridical condition of every human individual resulting from Original Sin.[28] As noted earlier, the Christian conception of human existence after the Fall precluded the possibility of human individuals ever living in a state of "pure" Aristotelian nature. Interpreting Hobbes and Locke within this late medieval frame of reference makes their notions of state of nature and social contract more intelligible than they appear to be in many modern interpretations.

For all that, neither the social contract nor its political counterpart was considered fully constitutive of political authority as such. The essential element in the doctrine was delegation of authority, initially from each individual to the community or society as a whole, and secondly from the society as a whole to a specified political ruler. As one modern interpreter has expressed it, what is involved, "using a modern formula, is an act of adhesion, consented to on the grounds of natural necessity, and a formal determination [i.e., a giving of formal or specific determination] of this necessity."[29] The political contract, then, does not create authority *eo ipso*; the traditional Christian view that all authority comes ultimately from God was still universal and beyond question. In the language of the Aristotelian doctrine of causality, God is the primary efficient cause of political authority and the *respublica* the material cause. The people function as a secondary efficient cause of the polity that has been brought into being and give it its formal cause through their second act of consent that establishes the "form" through which political authority functions, monarchy, republic, etc., while the final cause or purpose, of course, is the common good.[30]

Another strand of thought concerning the original human state of nature entered Spanish neo-scholastic thought from neo-Stoicism by way of Italian humanism. Apparent here was an effort to fuse humanistic political theory with Aristotelian and Christian doctrinal threads concerning the human condition, and the result gave an historical dimension to a basically Aristotelian philosophical doctrine. Derived almost exclusively

---

28. See Eschmann, "Thomistic Social Philosophy," *passim*.

29. Jarlot, "Idées politiques de Suárez," p. 79. What is at issue here, of course, is what is "necessary" as regards the nature or essence of what it means to be human, *not* the necessary determinism or descriptive necessary laws of the physical universe.

30. Ibid., p. 80.

from Aristotle, Aquinas's conception of society, of humans as both social and political, was organic and lacked any explicit historical dimension until a conscious effort was made by later neo-Thomists to accommodate the Aristotelian theory of polity to notions about the origins of human society emphasized by the humanists from classical sources. An historical dimension did exist, however, in some medieval accounts of the formation of political societies, reflecting the Old Testament story of the Jewish people from their origins in the Garden of Eden onwards. Aegidius of Rome, who followed Peter Comestor and Hugh of St Victor, exemplifies this perspective.[31]

Aeneas Sylvius Piccolomini, a well-recognized and prominently placed Italian humanist and historian who later turned ecclesiastic and ultimately became pope (Pius II), spoke in his *De ortu et authoritate imperii romani* (1446) of humans coming together as a result of rational decision making after having lived like wild beasts following their expulsion from the Garden of Eden.[32] For Aeneas, human beings passed historically through a prepolitical phase before forming polities and establishing governmental forms of authority.[33] The notion that humans originally lived like beasts in an independent, free type of existence was common to classical texts, of course, beginning with Hesiod's *Works and Days*.[34] It is found as well in Cicero's *De inventione*[35] and, most importantly, in Seneca, Epistle 90.[36] It was in regular use in the late thirteenth century, but without the explicit reference to "wild beasts."[37] These classical sources struck an historical note that easily aligned with the loose

---

31. Aegidius of Rome, *On Ecclesiastical Power* 2.12, pp. 146–47; Peter Comestor "Historia scholastica," PL 198; Hugh of St Victor, *On the Sacraments* 1.11.1. The origins of this historical frame of reference were various Old Testament texts noted by St Augustine, who spoke of Cain as the first to establish an individual kingdom before the Flood and Nimrod as the first to have done so after, citing Gen. 10: Augustine, *City of God* 15.8 and 16.4. Cf. Suárez, *De Legibus* 3.2.5.

32. Piccolomini (Aeneas Sylvius), "De ortu et auctoritate imperii Romani" 1:391. Aeneas also published a chatty account of the Council of Basle, which he had attended: Piccolomini, *De gestis Concilii Basiliensis*.

33. Lewy calls this first phase "presocial," a term I consider mistaken: Lewy, *Constitutionalism and Statecraft*, p. 39. The point is to distinguish political from social; the social phase came first, and was followed by the political. Cf. *infra*, note 145 *re* Skinner's designation of this first phase as "pre-political."

34. Hesiod, *Works and Days* 1.145–264; 303–30.

35. Cicero, *De inventione* 1.2.2.

36. Seneca, "Epistle 90," pp. 396–99.

37. See Aegidius of Rome, *On Ecclesiastical Power*, 2, 12, pp. 145–46. Cf. *supra*, note 16.

Old Testament account of human history after Adam and Eve's expulsion from the Garden seen in Aegidius of Rome, for example, and Aeneas grafted them onto the standard medieval account of human social origins.

A certain blurring of the specific characteristics of pre-political human beings occurs, however, when the two accounts are blended. Aeneas provides a Christian account of post-lapsarian humans suffering from the adverse consequences of the Fall, while the classical account following Hesiod, Cicero, and Seneca speaks of purely natural human beings who are not "damaged": they are at least potentially perfect and in their original state display no distortion of their nature. The Ciceronian account had greater influence on the Italian humanists because it extolled rhetoric and eloquence, even though it was well known throughout the Middle Ages. It emphasized the brutish character of the natural human condition, which was not, however, a negative feature resulting from sinful human behaviour but a perfectible lack to be overcome through the use of human reason.[38] To "live like beasts," then, was to live gently in communal harmony and the immediate enjoyment of the best and simplest of human pleasures, a condition that did not include possession of private property. The Senecan description was the more fulsome, making clear that the state of nature was a "golden age." This notion was given its most compelling modern expression by Rousseau, whose writings also exhibit the ambiguity between the perfection of the state of nature and the value to humans of living in society.[39]

The revival of Thomism began in the early sixteenth century at the Dominican college of St Jacques attached to the University of Paris, where both Thomas Aquinas and Albert the Great had studied and taught. Pierre Crockaert, a French intellectual trained in the *via moderna* of Ockhamite nominalism, had became disenchanted with this approach to Christian theology in the early years of the century and had turned to Thomism. He joined the Dominican order and began to teach theology at St Jacques in 1509, using the *Summa theologiae* of Aquinas rather than Peter Lombard's *Sentences* as the basic text. Three years later he published the first of what was to become a virtually unending series of commentaries on Aquinas's most famous work; his collaborator was a Spanish pupil, Francisco de Vitoria.

---

38. See Tuck, *Natural Rights*, pp. 33–34. On the influence of Ciceronian social and political thought in general on medieval writers see *supra*, p. 8, note 4.
39. Rousseau, *Social Contract, passim*.

Political conditions on mainland Spain as well as events overseas gave impetus to, and provided a context for, the political thought of Spanish theologians like Vitoria and his successors. The most significant political event in early sixteenth century Spain was the unsuccessful effort made by the Santa Junta General de Reino of Castile to arrogate to itself the role of royal council and enforce a conciliarist or corporatist view of the relations between the Spanish king and itself as a public body. It regarded itself as a representative group for the sovereign community of Castile and therefore able to transfer authority from the people to specific rulers in an expression of the people's consent to be governed. On 20 October 1520, it drafted a formal series of petitions and grievances embodying these views, demanding that its deputies be elected, paid, and controlled by the nineteen cities traditionally represented in the Cortes, and that it be convened regularly in total independence of the king in order to exercise political authority.[40] The *Comunero* or *Comunidades* movement spearheading this effort at corporatist representative government pushed its campaign to the point where the Spanish king, Charles, who was also Holy Roman emperor, took the field against it and crushed it at the Battle of Villalar on 23 April 1521.[41] All subsequent Salamancan political thinking was at least in some sense a function of these historical events.[42]

## 2. CARDINAL CAJETAN (TOMMASO DE VIO)

Cardinal Cajetan (1468–1534) was a major figure in the rehabilitation of Thomism in the late fifteenth and early sixteenth centuries. An Italian Dominican educated at the order's college in Rome, he taught there for his entire professional career and produced an extensive corpus of works designed to promote and reflect the thought of his great thirteenth-century Dominican predecessor, Thomas Aquinas. His writings on law and the origins of political society are of interest to the history of late medieval political thought, the second being particularly significant in that they contained views that were not found explicitly in Aquinas and that influenced later neo-scholastic formulations. Cajetan's

---

40. See Perez, *Révolution des Communidades de Castile*. The relevant documents are in Danvilay Collado, *Communidades des Castilla*. See Fernandez-Santamaria, *State, War and Peace*, pp. 17–18.

41. Charles was a very busy monarch at this time: he also was engaged in his capacity as Holy Roman Emperor in the 1521 Diet of Worm's efforts to come to grips with the spread of Lutheranism in his German principalities: see *infra*, p. 208.

42. Fernandez-Santamaria, *State, War and Peace*, p. 23.

*Commentarium in summa theologiae sancti Thomae Aquinatis* and *De auctoritate papae et concilio* are his most important writings for my purposes. The latter was written at papal request to defend papal absolutism against fresh expressions of conciliarist thought from the French monarchy and the University of Paris; as noted earlier in connection with the examination of Jacques Almain, it has a certain interest in these terms, even though its position is neither unique nor very novel.[43]

Cajetan's views on the origins of political authority in both works warrant study. While he tended simply to repeat the Thomistic theory of law and expressed himself in very conservative terms on the status of the pope *vis-à-vis* a general church council, he was much more explicit in attributing authority to the people in establishing political rule. Arguably, he was interested in stressing the distinctive character of papal authority as an authority settled on an individual directly by God, with the Church as a whole precluded from the causal sequence. But his emphasis on the causal role of the people in establishing temporal authority not only expressed a conventional contrast between the ways ecclesiastical and temporal forms of authority were created but provided a specific statement on the origins of temporal polities that would be reiterated and developed by the Spanish neo-scholastics, especially Suárez.

Cajetan argued that the people have a right, derived from natural law, to choose their form of government and those to whom they consign political authority: "It pertains to the people according to natural law to decide whether their future polity will be democratic (*populare*), aristocratic (*optimatum*) or monarchical (*regale*)."[44] Domingo de Soto (1495–1560), a pupil and successor of Francisco de Vitoria at Salamanca, followed Cajetan closely in declaring that the people choose their rulers; he stated explicitly that, while God is its source by way of the natural law, the people are the bearer of political authority.[45] De Soto also stated that the choice of a ruler involved a majority decision of the people in a public gathering (*publicus eis conventus*).[46] Cajetan maintained further that the community's act of choosing precedes whichever

---

43. See *supra*, pp. 114–20.
44. Cajetan, in *ST* 2–2.50.1 *ad* 3.
45. De Soto, *De iustitia et iure* 1.1.q.1, a.3. Cf. q.6, a.4, cited in Bowe, *Origin of Political Authority*, p. 37. This work is a fine, brief treatment of late neo-scholastic political thought, with accurate information on sources for the range of views among the Spanish school and a clear expression of the distinction between the "translation" and the "designation" theory options of the Catholic tradition. Cf. *infra*, note 52. Suárez expressed the same position in a more carefully formulated fashion: see *infra*, pp. 177–79.
46. De Soto, *De iustitia et iure* 1.4, q.4, a.2.

of the three basic forms of polity the people select: "The choice of a form of polity is not part of the polity but precedes any form of polity."[47] Accordingly, he did not attribute democracy to the state of nature or natural law; it is a form of polity, while the state of nature exhibited no polity of any kind.

Accepting that monarchy is ordinarily the chosen form of government, Cajetan repeated the traditional medieval corporational notion that the king is the people's representative insofar as the community has committed the common good to him; otherwise he would be a tyrant. A temporal ruler, then, does not hold office directly from God, as the pope does, even though he is *de facto* God's minister; he is God's minister only as the people's representative. "Kings are not said to be God's proximate and immediate ministers; rather they are the people's representative (*vice multitudinis gerens*) while undoubtedly being God's ministers; they are said to be representative immediately of the people, not God."[48] And: "[The nature of authority] is found differently in king and pope; for a king's power exists by natural law first in the people, and derives to the king from them."[49]

Another traditional notion follows from this, that the people who choose a king can depose him for tyrannical behaviour. Their right to do so, however, derives from his behaviour, not from the fact that the people chose him. Only in a democracy do the people have a continual right to change those who exercise authority over them, because there the people's representative is only an administrator, even though he may appear to be a monarch.[50] The prepolitical condition of the community before the people choose a specific form of polity is not a democracy, however, because it is not a polity at all. Nor is a king simply an administrator: "[A king] does not derive from a democratic form of polity (*regimen populare*) ... nor is he their [the people's] administrator (*vices*)."[51] Cajetan's position is that, while the people as a whole have the power to create the form of polity in which they consent to live, their "natural"

47. Cajetan, in *ST* 2–2.50.1 *ad* 3.
48. Cajetan, *De comparatione auctoritatis papae et concilii*, tr. 2 par. 2 c.9. Note the categorical rejection of any theory of the divine right of kings, a position Suárez will reiterate later in an explicit interchange with James I of England: see *infra*, p. 181.
49. Ibid. As mentioned earlier, Cajetan's argument here was designed as a defence of papal absolutism. See *supra*, pp. 143, 114.
50. Cajetan, *De comparatione*, tr.2, p. 2, c.3.
51. Cajetan, in *ST* 2–2.50. 1 *ad* 3. Cf. *De comparatione*, pp. 562–64. See Suárez's contrasting view on this point, *infra*, p. 179.

condition before they so choose does not exhibit one form of polity rather than any other; that is, the natural state of humans is not democratic.[52]

### 3. ALONZO DE CASTRILLO

One of the first Spanish political writers of the period, the Trinitarian monk Alonzo de Castrillo, also addressed the issue of how political society came into being in his treatise *Tractado de republica* (1521), published the same year as Charles's victory over the *Comuneros* at Villalar. He held that humans were solitary in the beginning, although naturally social insofar as God had supplied them with reason; he followed Aristotle in connecting the social nature of humans with rationality. He went on to say, however, citing the standard Old Testament references to Nimrod and other early tyrants,[53] that in practice the earliest political societies formed by individuals were themselves evil. Political authority as currently exercised, then, results from the need to compensate for the reality of sin and will remain until the second coming of Christ.

Castrillo thus repeated the traditional Augustinian account of the origins of political society as a consequence of and response to the sinful condition of humankind. But, following the Thomistic tradition, he

---

52. See McCoy, "Origin of Political Authority." In this important article McCoy applies to Cajetan, Bellarmine, and Suárez a distinction prominent in so-called Catholic political thought: viz., the distinction between "transmission" and "designation" theories of the origin of political authority. According to the former, (T), the whole people are the immediate or principal cause of political authority, and the corollary is drawn that one form of government, direct democracy, is thus somehow a natural institution that precedes any other form established by the free choice of those willing to enter into a political society. On the other hand, the latter, (D), considers God to be the immediate cause of political authority in whomever the people designate to exercise it, with the people acting only as secondary efficient or instrumental cause to name the person or persons who will rule, the corollary here being that the people as a whole do not constitute any form of political entity in their original or natural condition.

McCoy shows that Thomas Aquinas held (T) but without drawing the corollary; he says it is found in the Church Fathers, although he gives no references. He accuses Suárez of drawing the corollary regarding the natural character of direct democracy and maintains that Bellarmine took the more traditional and appropriate stance of denying that any specific form of polity can be discovered in the state of nature, making it clear that the multitude as a body politic is not a form of government. Bellarmine, "De membris ecclesiae" 3.6, in *Politia opera omnia* 3:10–12. Cf. Bowe, *Origin of Political Authority* and *supra*, note 45. For Suárez on this point see *infra*, p. 179.

53. Castrillo, *Tratado de republica*, pp. 66, 45–49. Cf. *supra*, p. 140, n31.

grafted an Aristotelian branch onto this Augustinian trunk by making reference to natural law as a sanction for society, while at the same time distinguishing sharply between the social and political. Like Vives after him, Castrillo thought society was a necessity commanded by God and sanctioned by natural law, but "political" society was not; it was a reasonable rather than a "natural" condition for human beings in the *de facto* state of degenerate human nature. Faced with the reality of evil, the only reasonable course for humans to follow was to "obey the monarch to avoid greater evils."[54] This is the antithesis of the view expressed by his French contemporary, Claude de Seyssel, in *La monarchie de France* (1515). Seyssel accepted the standard Aristotelian view that political authority is natural and argued that monarchy is the best form of governance.[55]

As already noted, the Castilian Junta had argued that a ruler's power derived by way of transfer from the people and, accordingly, reverted to the people when misused. Charles's acceptance of the foreign Roman imperial crown was deemed to have constituted such misuse. Rather than siding directly with the Junta, however, Castrillo chose middle ground. He was satisfied to retain the monarchy as a given, but wished the ruler to act properly. A cautious royalist, he argued that monarchy was better than chaos. He also emphasized that citizenship involved more than mere membership in a political community; what he seems to have had in mind was an Aristotelian activity requirement for citizenship.[56]

### 4. JUAN LUIS VIVES

The great Spanish humanist Juan Luis Vives (1492–1540) agreed with Castrillo and St Augustine that the existing political scene and political societies in general were the result of a reaction to the presence of sin; but otherwise he formulated a rather unique theory of polity reflecting his humanist inclinations and the general influence of Erasmus. Describing the original state of human nature as perfect, he followed

---

54. Ibid., pp. 59 and *passim*.
55. Seyssel is discussed *infra*, pp. 259; 261.
56. Fernandez-Santamaria, *State, War and Peace*, p. 26. Fernandez-Santamaria comments that, with the defeat inflicted by Charles on the *comunero* movement in 1521, "a monarchy which had been universally understood as contractual now became largely absolute"; he disagrees with J. Russell Major's claim that the Renaissance concept of monarchy as basically constitutional was applicable to Spain after 1519: to France, perhaps, he says, but not to Spain. Ibid., p. 33 and note 57.

Aeneas Sylvius in identifying it with the classical golden age and went on to distinguish sharply between the social and political. Although not specific on the point, Vives seems to have been speaking of the early postlapsarian condition of the immediate offspring of the first parents, in which case his humanist predilection for speaking of this as a golden age is implicitly at odds with the Christian doctrine of the effects of Original Sin. He stated in *De concordia et discordia in humano genere* (1529) that human nature was created social inasmuch as individuals were born to live together in a single universal society: "In the beginning nature created a union among humans which was broken later by malice."[57]

The original society, however, was not a polity. After humans had destroyed the perfection of the natural order, they formed various artificial groupings, the best and greatest of which was "the city" (*civitas*). These human-made institutions are imperfect, however, and do not begin to approach the perfection of the original human condition. Rather, they produce further divisions and fragmentation among humans, thereby leading humankind farther from its original natural state of perfection. The state, then, is not something natural but the result of "differences imbedded in humankind by the guilt of the old Adam."[58] But while useful in protecting humans from one another's depravity, polities also inhibit a return to human nature's proper condition. Actually, he asserted, the state is no longer necessary, having lost its *raison d'être* along with all other purely human institutions once Christianity provided for a return to the incomparable unity of the original golden age through its message of love and peace. God had presented the Christian religion as the means for fallen humans to return to their true natural state, and to a pure social order ordained by nature.[59] For Vives, the eclipse of political society occurred with the first coming of Christ, not, as Castrillo maintained, with the second.

5. FRANCISCO DE VITORIA

Francisco de Vitoria (1483–1546) was born in Burgos and entered the Dominican order in his home town in 1504. Going to Paris to study at the College of St Jacques in 1506, he remained there for nearly eighteen years, first as a student and then as a teacher of theology. In Paris he was

---

57. Vives, "De concordia et discordia in humano genere," in *Opera omnia*, 5:388.
58. Ibid.
59. Ibid., p. 201. Cf. Fernandez-Santamaria, *State, War and Peace*, pp. 53–54.

exposed to the last advocates of Gerson's theology and the humanism of the day, including the first works in its juridical form, as well as to the revived Thomism of his teacher, Crockaert.[60] Returning to Spain in 1523, he taught at Valladolid and three years later became professor of theology at the University of Salamanca, where he spent the remaining twenty years of his life. Publishing nothing directly himself, he is known through a series of *relectiones* (or *relationes*), transcriptions prepared by former students of his public lectures on topics of current interest, and through an extensive commentary, prepared in the same way, on the *Secunda secundae* of Thomas Aquinas. The entire set of *relectiones* was published in 1557, appearing in a modern edition in 1933–36. Two of them are recognized as important texts in the history of international law:[61] *De Indis recenter invenitur relectio prior*, delivered as a formal public lecture in January 1538, and *De Indis sive de iure belli Hispanorum in barbaros relectio superior*, delivered as a lecture on 18 June 1539.

As one might expect, the Thomism of sixteenth- and seventeenth-century Spain was dominated by members of the regular clergy, Dominicans and Jesuits, and its impact on and contribution to political thought at the time reflected two historical events of momentous importance. The first, particularly, if not exclusively, Spanish in impact, was the exploration and conquest of the Americas; the other, of more uni-

60. Tuck, *Natural Rights*, p. 46. Hernandez, following the judgment of a seventeenth-century Dominican historian, has placed the date of Vitoria's birth as 1483: Truyol Serra, *Conception de la paix chez Vitoria*, addenda between pp. 274 and 275.

61. The *corpus* of Vitoria's *relectiones* is published as Francisco de Vitoria, *Relecciones teologicas*, ed. Luis G. Alonso Getino. More recent editions of individual *relectiones* in Latin with a Spanish translation are *Relectio de Indis, o Libertad de los indios*, ed. and trans. L. Perena and J. M. Perez Prendes; *Relectio de iure belli*, ed. L. Perena et al.; and *Releccion "De dominio,"* ed. and trans. Jaime Brufau Prats. An English translation of the first two of these *relectiones*, along with an earlier Latin text, is in *De Indis et de iure belli relectiones*, ed. Ernest Nys, trans. John Pawley Bate. The lecture on civil power is also available in English: "Relectio Concerning Civil Power," trans. G. L. Williams, in James Brown Scott, ed., *The Spanish Origins of International Law*, vol. 1, *Francisco de Vitoria and his Law of Nations*, Appendix C. A recent selection of Vitoria texts in English has been published: Vitoria, *Political Writings*, ed. Anthony Pagden and Jeremy Lawrence. I cite the relevant English translations and the *De potestate ecclesiae* text from the Getino edition of the *Relecciones teologicas*, vol. 2, pp. 1–168.

*Re* the dates for these public lectures, see Beltran de Heredia's edition of Vitoria's Thomistic commentary, *Comentarios a la Secunda secundae de Santa Tomas*, 5 vols., Salamanca, 1932–35, cited in Fernadez-Santamaria, *State, War and Peace*, p. 63, note 5. Another example of the topicality of Vitoria's *relectiones* is his *On Marriage*, delivered formally on 25 January 1531 from classroom material presented in the period 1528–30. Its text deals direclty with the divorce of Henry VIII.

versal European interest and essentially, though by no means exclusively, theological, was the Protestant Reformation. The latter occupied the attention of all Catholic theologians and churchmen of the period while the former, though of much less concern for the Church, related more directly to political theory.

Vitoria addressed the issue of the American discoveries and conquests twice in formal lectures at Salamanca, as his published *relectiones* attest, and he was the first to apply traditional scholastic teaching on the nature of temporal polity to what was a new and unique situation for European intellectuals. Though failing to eliminate or even significantly mitigate the tragic effects of Spanish conquest on the indigenous population of Central and South America, his and others' publicly expressed views at least showed a determination not to allow the depredations of the burgeoning Spanish-American empire to go unchallenged intellectually.

Indeed, the greater part of consciously formulated Spanish political thought in the first half of the sixteenth century was concerned with issues raised by the situation in the American Indies, specifically with whether or how to justify the transformation of the mother country into an empire through acquisition of new lands and the conquest of alien peoples. Though overseas territorial expansion and the subjugation of foreign populations were relatively novel features on the European geopolitical scene, their novelty did not induce any significant change in the current neo-scholastic paradigm of political thought; it was apparently expected to accommodate an examination of Spanish imperialism under the doctrine of just war: the notion that defence of national interests could extend as necessary to the destruction of an aggressor by occupation and seizure of enemy territory and subjugation of its people.[62] That this approach could be seen as an appropriate frame of reference for ex-

---

62. A fine summary of the conceptual elements in the traditional medieval just-war theory, which had its origins in the writings of St Augustine, is Barnes, "The Just War"; the relevant Augustinian texts are cited at p. 771, note 3 and p. 772, note 8, and other authoritative medieval sources at p. 772, note 4. For a more extensive treatment see Russell, *Just War in the Middle Ages*.

Vitoria's use of the traditional medieval conceptions of just war and how to deal with "infidel" peoples is interestingly discussed in Muldoon, *Popes, Lawyers and Infidels*. Muldoon traces the main outlines of this position back to the mid-thirteenth century canonical writings and diplomatic activities of Innocent IV, and maintains that the Spanish neo-scholastic critics of the Spanish conquest of the Americas owe more to medieval canonical sources than to scholastic theology: he treats Vitoria at pp. 143–50. An interesting recent application of the Spanish neo-scholastic notions of just war and sovereignty to the "discovery" activities in North America is Dickason, "Old World Laws". Cf. Dickason, *Myth of the Savage*, and Green and Dickason, *Law of Nations and the New World*.

amining, much less justifying, the morality of events in the Americas in the early sixteenth century must seem fatuous today, and probably did so at the time for all but the most enthusiastic apologist for Spanish imperialism; the military initiative, after all, had been Spanish, and to portray conquistador activity as self-defence against attacking Indians was simply nonsense.

More elaborate justification was needed. And while Vitoria and others did employ the just-war theory in their examination of the Spanish presence in the Americas, they blended it with loftier elements. In general the focus fell on two other aspects of traditional scholastic political and moral theory: first, the possibility of describing the Indians as naturally servile in the Aristotelian sense, so as to judge them unfit to exercise political authority in their own right and therefore appropriate objects for subjugation by naturally superior European states; and second, the attribution of political responsibilities to Spain for the spiritual interests and well-being of the Indians through conversion to Christianity. Vitoria found no value in the former, but was prepared to consider the latter as at least theoretical ground for Spanish-American expansionism.

The most outspoken critic of the Spanish conquest of the Indians was Vitoria's fellow Dominican, Bartolomé de Las Casas (1474–1566). He had travelled as a cleric and missionary to the New World in 1502 with an early Spanish colonizing group and at first accepted and assisted in the brutal suppression of the native population. But, ultimately revolted by the harshness of Spanish depredations, he entered the Dominican order and became an outspoken advocate of the Indians' cause for more than thirty years, returning from the Indies to Spain in 1547, where he continued to speak out against Spanish imperialist practices.[63] The chief spokesman for Spanish imperial expansionism at the expense of the native Americans was Juan Gines de Sepúlveda, an erudite and prominent Italian-educated Spanish humanist. In the climax to a continuous and increasingly acrimonious argument over the Spanish conquests that began in the 1530s, Las Casas and Sepúlveda publicly confronted each other in 1550–51 as contending advocates at a meeting of theologians con-

63. See Hanke, *The Spanish Struggle for Justice.* Cf. by the same author, *All Mankind is One* and Friede and Keen, eds., *Bartolomé de las Casas in History.* This latter collection of essays contains a good biography of las Casas: Fernandez, "Fray Bartolomé de las Casas," and an updated bibliography compiled by Raymond Marcus, pp. 603–17. Cf. Hanke and Fernandez, *Bartolomé de Las Casas, Bibliografia crítica.* Fernandez's most extensive treatment of las Casas is *Bartolomé de Las Casas,* 2 vols. (Seville: Escuela de Estudios Hispano, 1953, 1960).

vened at Valladolid by Charles V to advise him and the Council of the Indies on the morality of subjugating the Indies.[64]

As already noted, Vitoria applied traditional Thomistic notions of polity to the Spanish conquests and seems to have experienced no difficulty in doing so. Appealing in the first instance to the natural law as common to all humans, he accepted the notion of a common human nature across diversity in political communities and cultures, and he referred to a *ius communicationis* shared in by Europeans and Indians alike, in virtue of which they could understand and appreciate their common humanity, and to the *ius gentium* as somehow rationally and universally based.[65]

For Vitoria, the world contained a number of absolutely equal states, their collective range and extent limited only by the size of the world itself. Fundamental to his political thinking, however, was an acceptance of territorial conquest as an essential feature of a polity and one of the traditional grounds for creating a polity: legitimate political authority could be acquired by conquest insofar as God permitted it. This represented a naïve and inadequate effort to blend the Augustinian conception of political authority as a providential though perhaps divinely punitive response to human sinfulness with the acceptance, even advocacy, in Roman law of the right of Romans to conquer other peoples. The best that medieval political and moral theorists had been able to do with this almost open-ended invitation to military aggression was to connect it with the notion of communal self-defence. Vitoria followed this tradition, becoming somewhat innovative when taking into account the novelty of an actual encounter with "barbarians" who were heathens, that is, non-Christian.

Emphasizing that a state has religious responsibilities, he held that a Christian polity could make war on barbarians (*barbari*) in certain circumstances, to assist their eternal salvation by providing for and supporting their conversion to Christianity. Employing an academic form appropriate to a professional theologian, he outlined principles and

---

64. On Las Casas see Losada, *Fray Bartolomé de las Casas*, and Hanke, *All Mankind Is One*; on Sepúlveda see Losada, *Juan Ginés de Sepúlveda*. Fernandez-Santamaria provides a box score for the theologian judges at the 1550–51 debate in *State, War and Peace*, pp. 167–68. Cf. Hanke, *Aristotle and the American Indians*. A Spanish edition of political writings by Sepúlveda is *Tratados politicos de J. Ginés de Sepúlveda*, trans. A. Losada. Relevant Las Casas texts are published by the same author: Losada, "'Los Tesoros de Peru' y 'La Apologia contra Sepulveda,' obras ineditas de Fr. Bartolomé de las Casas," *Boletin de la Real Academia de la Historia* 132 [1953]: 269–333.

65. See Fernandez-Santamaria, *State, War and Peace*, p. 61.

ideological criteria for assessing political and military activities against territories and peoples that do not come directly under a state's own jurisdiction. The moral legitimacy of Christian states making war on nonbelievers had been articulated in the late eleventh century, of course, when the papacy began to sponsor the crusading movement against nonbelievers inhabiting territory Christians considered peculiarly their own, and the current sixteenth-century threat to eastern Europe from "the Turks" represented a roughly comparable political situation; but Vitoria was the first European political thinker to extend the argument to other continents.

His political theory began with the assertion that the natural law guarantees freedom to all individuals. "By natural law no man is king over other men; by natural law all men are born free." And: "By natural law mankind is free save for paternal and marital dominion ... therefore no one by natural law has dominion over the whole world [this against the concept of a universal imperialism]."[66] Political society, he continued, was formed some time after humans began to occupy the earth and came about from practical necessity. Vitoria may seem here to reflect humanist theory on the origins of political society and its view that humans lived originally in a completely prepolitical condition; but he was simply repeating Castrillo and Vives. And inasmuch as he always stressed the natural-law basis for humans being political, he rejected the view that political society came about by convention or agreement among the constituent parties, thereby differing from humanist political thought as well as from Cajetan.[67] Later Spanish neo-Thomists gave similar emphasis to natural law, while also accepting the humanist emphasis, shared by Cajetan, on popular consent as the immediate cause of political society. That they did so, reviving the traditional medieval concept of consent, may reflect their reaction to Reformation political thought, which originally rejected a direct role for the people in establishing polities; they were willing to follow Cajetan in not speaking only of God as their cause.

66. Vitoria, *On the Indians* 2, p. 131.
67. He did distinguish in one text between what is founded on nature and what is founded on law, and put political society in the latter category: "Although [civil power] may take its rise in nature and so may be said to be based in natural law ... humans being political animals, it is not founded on nature but on law." Vitoria, *De Indis*, p. 131. He was quite explicit, nonetheless, in rejecting the view that human consent caused civil authority: "Cities and republics did not have their fount and origin in human invention but sprang, as it were, from nature which produced this way of protecting and preserving mortals ... the same purpose and necessity underlies the existence of public powers." Vitoria, *Concerning Civil Power*, pp. 75–76.

For his part, however, Vitoria does not appear to have been concerned in Spain in the 1530s with directly countering Protestant political thought, although elsewhere he did show his familiarity with the Catholic rejection of Luther's doctrine of the Church.[68]

For Vitoria, humans came together in political society because of the promptings of the natural law, whereas for the humanists, polities were formed by human agreement—by convention not nature. Humanism emphasized positive law and legal forms about which humans could be said to agree, the *ius gentium* and *ius civile* rather than the *ius naturale*, and followed Ulpian's view of natural law as something shared by humans and other animals.[69] Ironically, the disagreement between Vitoria and later Spanish Thomists, all of whom stressed the natural character of political society, and the humanists who stressed convention and agreement was largely semantic, for both groups stressed reason as the ground of governmental authority. The neo-scholastics maintained that the natural law is present in all humans insofar as they can use reason: reason is what prompts individuals to form political societies. The humanists also stressed reason as the instrument leading humans to agree among themselves about the value of founding polities; they spoke of such agreements as conventions among free individuals rather than as consequences determined by human nature. It is a pity that a conception of natural law different from Ulpian's could not have been agreed upon. In fact, Thomas Aquinas had favoured a non-Ulpian definition that restricted natural law to humans and attached directly to rationality, although he also repeated the Ulpian formula; but it was Cajetan who connected the prepolitical state of nature and natural law with popular choice a century before Suárez returned to this issue.[70]

Vitoria accepted Castrillo's view that political authority could not be dispensed with in the present circumstances of human existence, and insisted further that it could not be eliminated even where individuals agreed to do so. An aggregation of power occurs in a polity (*respublica*) whether the citizens as a whole like it or not: political authority and public power are grounded somehow in the natural law itself.[71] This is because the state's purpose is the protection and well-being of those living

68. Vitoria, *De potestate ecclesiae*, p. 132.
69. Ulpian, *Digest* 1.1.1.3. Cf. Tuck, *Natural Rights*, p. 34.
70. Vitoria, *Concerning Civil Power*, p. 72. See Thomas Aquinas, *ST* 1–2.91.2 and *ad* 2. Cf. Crowe, "St Thomas and Ulpian's Natural Law." For Suárez see *infra*, p. 178.
71. "... constituta est enim in republica, omnibus etiam civibus invitis, potestas reipsum ministrandi." Vitoria, *Concerning Civil Power*, p. 72. Fernandez-Santamaria speaks of "a seri-

in fellowship within it, who cede their natural right of self-defence to political authority and authorize the state to regulate them in return for the protection, well-being, and justice provided by the state. The state must have sufficient authority to fulfil its purpose; it must be able to defend its citizens against external aggressors, as well as punish its own subjects when they transgress its laws. The legitimate coercive authority of a state thus faces in two directions, so to speak, internal and external: it possesses the power to control its citizens and to make legitimate war on other states.

Vitoria distinguished between power (*potestas*) and authority (*auctoritas*) when describing the transition from pre-political to political society. Power inheres in a community of individuals; it becomes authority when transferred to a temporal ruler. It really inheres in each individual in the state of nature in their right to defend themselves and punish evildoers; but it exists in an indeterminate and inconvenient fashion in a simple community of individuals. Accordingly, power must be handed over to someone to whom the community gives authority to administer it.[72] Vitoria makes the point here, repeated by Bellarmine and Suárez, that state power to punish wrong-doers by death, capital punishment, must accrue to a political ruler from the people as a whole inasmuch as no specific individual has such a right in the state of nature. Because an individual's right of self-defence in the state of nature is inalienable, however, the community's transfer of power to a ruler in the form of authority to exercise this right on behalf of the many cannot be unqualified.[73] Furthermore, the people as a whole do not create or cause their

---

ous impasse," but one he resolves easily enough, between Vitoria's insistence on natural law as the basis for political society, and Vitorian texts distinguishing between the state of nature and the formation of political societies. He is right to reject any contradiction between these various expressions of Vitoria's views, and right also to relate the difficulty in interpretation to Vitoria's acceptance of an antediluvian period when some human beings did not live in political societies. Accepting the Scripture-based account of humankind after the Fall and before the Flood, however, poses a serious difficulty only if one construes the natural character of political society to mean a necessarily determined condition for all human beings at all times, and this is not what Vitoria or any neo-scholastic would have understood by the "naturalness" of a polity. Fernandez-Santamaria, *State, War and Peace*, pp. 66–68.

72. "Haec potestas per ipsum multitudinis exercerci non potest (non enim commode posset leges condere atque edicta proponere, lites dirimere et transgressores punire), necesse est ergo ut potestatis administratio alicui aut aliquibus commendaret, qui huiusmodi curam gererent." Vitoria, *Concerning Civil Power*, p. 186.

73. Ibid., p. 191.

ruler's power, even though they commit the power they possess to a particular person; rather, they specify the ruler as the instrument through which power that comes ultimately from God is to be exercised.[74]

Vitoria accepted monarchy as fully consonant with both divine and natural law, but he did not consider it the only legitimate form of polity. The people (*populus*) create a king by giving him original authority to defend them, and the donation, once made, is revocable only when used tyrannically. Yet royal power is always less than that of the people considered as a whole. Even though a king has full authority to make law and do whatever is necessary to exercise his authority, he is an administrator rather than a lord. He has only the *dominium* of jurisdiction, not ownership, over his territory; and he is bound by the law. Vitoria also acknowledged that different states with different religious practices could all be perfect or legitimate polities and that any state can defend itself against external depredation with no obligation to preserve the integrity of any other state to its own detriment.[75]

The first of Vitoria's *relectiones* devoted to the Spanish-American situation contains a systematic examination of Spanish hegemony in the Americas, and the second treats the issue from the perspective of just-war theory. *De Indis* lays out grounds for legitimating a Spanish presence elsewhere than in its own territory by presenting a theory of polity that ascribes explicit religious responsibilities to temporal authorities; *De iure belli* offers a general theoretical justification for the Spanish presence in the Americas through the just-war theory. These texts by no means offered a blanket justification of the Spanish activities in the Americas, however, and there is evidence that the Spanish authorities took Vitoria's views as an indictment of their policies and behaviour.[76]

The theological and religious character of Vitoria's views in *De Indis* and the ultimate theoretical basis they present for possible legitimation

74. Ibid., p. 189.
75. Vitoria, *De potestate ecclesiae*, p. 72. Cf. Fernandez-Santamaria, *State, War and Peace*, pp. 75–76, and notes 31 and 32.
76. Muñoz notes that the emperor Charles objected to Vitoria's public statements on the Indians in a letter addressed to his religious superior at Salamanca, 10 November 1539. This would have been only a few months after Vitoria's second *relectio* on the Indians. Muñoz, *Vitoria and the Conquest of America*, p. 19. McGrade also asserts that Vitoria, among other Spanish neo-scholastics, "attacked ... the Spanish conquests in the Americas and the seizure of Indian possessions ... in his lectures on *The Recently Discovered Indies*." A. S. McGrade, "State of Nature and Origin of the State," p. 763.

of the Spanish presence in the Americas are immediately revealed in the author's description of his lecture as essentially a commentary on the Scriptural text "Teach all nations, baptizing them in the name of the Father, Son and Holy Spirit,"[77] a text, he says, that "raises the question whether the children of unbelievers may be baptized against the wishes of their parents." He then sets the historical context: "The whole of the controversy and discussion was started on account of the aborigines of the New World, commonly called Indians, who came into the power of the Spaniards forty years ago, not having been previously known to our world."[78] He divides the work into three sections (or questions) that consider by what right these Indian natives came under Spanish sway, the illegitimate claims of those who pretend to ownership of the New World, and the rights by which barbarians came under Spanish jurisdiction insofar as the (Spanish) sovereigns or the Church obtained rights in matters spiritual and religious.

The first considers the natural rights of the Indians themselves. Vitoria argues that unbelief does not prevent people from being true owners or having political jurisdiction over their own territories.[79] Nor can the barbarians (*barbari*) be barred from territorial jurisdiction because of unsound mind; they are not mentally inferior, having the use of reason according to their own fashion. The second section identifies seven spurious claims for Spanish entitlement to the territory of the American aborigines: 1) the emperor is "lord of the world." Vitoria rejected this because, even if the statement were true, which it is not, Charles still could not seize Indian property because his entitlement would involve only jurisdiction and not property ownership. 2) To the claim that the pope has full jurisdiction *in temporalia* over the whole world and presumably, then, could assign jurisdiction over the Americas to the Spanish ruler, Vitoria responds that the pope has no such authority. 3) As regards any claim based on discovery, he noted simply that any (European) discoverer of the Americas could not be the first owner inasmuch as the territory was owned already by the Indians. 4) To a claim

77. Matthew 28:19.
78. Vitoria, *De Indis*, 1:2.
79. The position that non-adherence to the Christian religion was no deterrent to legitimate property holding and exercise of political jurisdiction was clearly articulated by Innocent IV in a discussion of papal-infidel relations in a commentary on the decretal *Quod super his* of his predecessor, Innocent III: X.3.34.8. Cf. Muldoon. *Popes, Lawyers and Infidels*, pp. 6–15, and "'Extra ecclesiam non est imperium?' The Canonists and Secular Power," at 572–75.

based on the Indians' refusal to accept Christianity although advised and adjured to do so, Vitoria replied that their ignorance could be considered invincible, and use of force to produce Christian belief is never legitimate. 5) He also rejected on the same grounds any claim based on the Indians' sinful behaviour. 6) The claim that the Indians chose voluntarily to be conquered he rejected as contrary to fact, as he also rejected the claim 7) that God delivered the Indians into Spanish jurisdiction from some special divine judgment of condemnation for their abominations. Vitoria noted that he could not identify anyone holding this last view; he termed it contrary to common law and Scripture and therefore in need of support from extraordinary evidence such as miracles, of which he had seen none.[80]

The third section advances seven possibly legitimate grounds, or "lawful titles," on which the barbarians might be brought under Spanish jurisdiction, the first of which is "natural society and fellowship." Vitoria mentioned seven subpoints here, none going directly to the issue of political jurisdiction, although the last three are suggestive in this connection: 1) the Spanish had a right to travel and sojourn in foreign lands; 2) they might lawfully trade with the Indians; 3) they could "communicate and participate" in goods common to both citizens and strangers in a foreign land; 4) the children of Spaniards born in a foreign land could become citizens of that land and thereby gain entitlement to property ownership and jurisdiction over persons in that state; 5) Spaniards could defend the above rights by force, after trying by reason to have them accepted; 6) Spaniards could defend themselves against the use of force against them, to the extent of seizing cities and reducing them to subjection; 7) Spaniards could make war on hostile aborigines after doing their best not to interfere with the aborigines' peace and well-being and might enforce all the rights of war.

The six remaining "lawful titles" related directly to the legitimacy of Spanish hegemony over the American Indians: (2) "Christians had a right to preach and declare the Gospel in barbarian lands," from which Vitoria concluded that the pope might entrust such a task to the Spaniards. (3) The Spaniards could act to protect native converts to Christianity from being forcibly returned to idolatry. (4) For reasonable cause the pope could give a Christian sovereign the right to depose an unbelieving ruler, a large part of whose Indian population had converted to Christianity. (5) The Spaniards could intervene to remove tyr-

---

80. Vitoria, *De Indis*, 2, *passim.*

anny from the Indian people even without papal authority; Vitoria mentioned here the sacrifice of innocent people and the killing of innocents for cannibalistic purposes as grounds for such intervention. (6) Spain could exercise jurisdiction if the Indians themselves had voluntarily accepted Spanish rule. And finally, (7) the Spanish might have a claim resting on their support for "the cause of allies and friends."[81]

Arguably, Vitoria's acceptance of any Spanish entitlement to political jurisdiction over the Indians under the first title of "natural society and fellowship" reduces to the Spaniards having the right to defend themselves against "hostile aborigines", as provided for in the fifth, sixth, and seventh subpoints. This, however, would require labelling the Indians as attackers and the Spanish as defenders. Similarly, the applicability of the other six theoretically lawful titles would rest on the facts of the case. Accordingly, even accepting that the Spanish had a right, even a duty, to preach Christianity to the Indians, the pope had not entrusted this task specifically to Spain (title 2), nor had he formally delegated to Spain the deposition of an unbelieving ruler, for any reason (4). Nor had the Indians voluntarily accepted Spanish jurisdiction (6), nor did Spain have any treaty with the Indians as "allies and friends," for the sake of which she could legitimately intervene politically (7).

The remaining two entitlements, Spain's right to protect Christian Indians from forcible return to idolatry (3) and her right to intervene against the tyranny of sacrificing innocent Indians and killing for cannibalistic purposes (5), were the only grounds on which the "facts of the case" might sustain a Spanish claim for full political authority in the Indies. In the final analysis, then, Vitoria did provide a theoretical basis for Spain's burgeoning empire, but it was expressed in terms of Spain's Christian missionary obligations to the indigenous Indian population. He accepted the theoretical legitimacy of some form of Spanish jurisdiction on the grounds of Spain's right and duty to bring Christianity to barbarian peoples, and her consequent right and duty to defend Christian barbarians against pagan political authorities, even by force of arms. But the whole thrust of his position in both *relectiones* on the Indians was to qualify and limit such rights. He spoke of what "might be" titles of legitimacy for Spanish authority in the Americas and conceded that "the seizure and occupation of those lands of the barbarians whom we style Indians can best, it seems, be defended under the law of war."[82] But

---

81. Ibid., 3.
82. Vitoria, *De iure belli*, 1, p. 165.

while asserting that "I personally have no doubt that the Spaniards were bound to employ force and arms to continue their work there," he added, "I fear measures were adopted in excess of what is allowed by human and divine law."[83]

Vitoria thus accepted the logic of his theological position concerning the use of political force to promote religious ideals. Yet he was unhappy with the realities of Spanish American policy and unwilling to accept political or economic justification for current Spanish imperialism. His final statement on the subject makes this clear when he advanced and responded to the notion of Spanish self-interest:

Now it seems to follow from all this discussion that, if there be no force in any of the titles which have been put forward, so that the native Indians neither gave cause for just war nor wished for Spanish rulers, etc., all the travel to, and trade with, those parts should be stopped, to the great loss of the Spaniards and also to the grave hurt of the royal treasury (a thing intolerable). My first answer to this is: There would be no obligation to stop trade for, as already said, there are many commodities of which the natives have a superfluity and which the Spaniards could acquire by barter. Also there are many commodities which the natives treat as ownerless or as common to all who like to take them, and the Portuguese, to their own great profit, have a big trade with similar people without reducing them to subjection. Secondly, there would probably be no diminution in the amount of royalties, for a tax might quite fairly be placed on the gold and silver which would be brought away from the Indians, as much as a fifth or even more, according to quality, and it would be well-earned, inasmuch as the maritime discovery was made by our sovereign and it is under his authority that trade is carried on in safety.[84]

His ultimate conclusion, withal, returns to an uneasy acceptance of a Spanish right to exercise some form of jurisdiction on behalf of Indians who are Christian: "It is evident, now that there are already so many na-

---

83. Vitoria *De Indis*, 3.12, p. 158.
84. Ibid., 3.18, pp. 161–62. Losada argues, not conclusively I feel, in "Controversy between Sepúlveda and Las Casas," that las Casas had the more successful criticism of current Spanish policy on war against the indigenous peoples of Central and South America." He also offers an interesting contemporary assessment of Vitoria's ultimate justification of war against the Indians for religious reasons, arguing that Vitoria's invocation of the appropriate principles held, in the instant case in the Americas, only on Vitoria's assumptions concerning the actual facts; he held further that Sepúlveda considered the facts assumed by Vitoria to be true, while las Casas himself, on the basis of personal experience in the Americas, rejected them as false. Losada, ibid., pp. 304–5.

tive converts, that it would be neither expedient nor lawful for our sovereign to wash his hands entirely of the administration of the lands in question."[85] The Spanish government, it might be noted, never argued in Vitorian terms to justify its sixteenth-century expansionism; nor did any Spanish missionaries to the Indians ever suggest that Spanish political hegemony was required to fulfil their religious purpose, or that this was the only or even the major purpose for which Spanish authorities exercised political jurisdiction in the Indies.

Another aspect of Vitoria's political thought is worth mentioning because it is clear only by implication in the thought of his mentor, Thomas Aquinas. This is his view that the papacy had absolutely no claims by virtue of its spiritual authority to the direct exercise of power over temporal rulers. For Vitoria, "the temporal commonwealth is perfect and complete in itself, and therefore not subject to anything outside itself; otherwise it would not be complete."[86] On the separateness and distinctiveness of spiritual and temporal spheres, he claimed that, "even if no spiritual power at all existed, there would still be an order in the temporal commonwealth."[87] His comment regarding papal claims to the contrary was blunt: "[that] the pope possesses direct temporal authority and jurisdiction in the whole world [is] indubitably and manifestly false ... [it is] offered merely as a piece of flattery and adulation to the pope ... temporal power does not depend in the least on the pope ... civil authority in no way is directly subject [to him]."[88] Bellarmine and Suárez took the same position, citing Vitoria on the subject.[89]

85. Losada, ibid.
86. Vitoria, *De potestate ecclesiae*, p. 67.
87. Ibid., p. 71.
88. Ibid., pp. 65–66.

89. Skinner comments that Vitoria's view enabled Spanish neo-scholastics to elide the Ockhamist insistence on the separateness of *imperium* and *sacerdotium* with the Thomist theory of polity and achieve a kind of sycretism between Thomism and Ockhamism. Skinner, *Foundations*, 2:175. The more likely interpretation, however, is that Vitoria and other Spanish Thomists did not take their cue from Ockham but from John of Paris, whose doctrine on the distinctiveness and integrity of spiritual and temporal spheres appeared before Ockham's texts on church/state relations, and was part of the Dominican/University of Paris theological tradition. Further, it had none of the negative features of Ockham's sometimes strident anti-papal writings. Quidort also formulated the very distinction between direct and indirect exercise of spiritual authority in the temporal sphere that later Spanish Thomists employed. See John of Paris, *Royal and Papal Power* 12 and 13, pp. 56–70.

## 6. JUAN DE MARIANA

Perhaps the best-known late sixteenth century Spanish political writer was Juan de Mariana, who became notorious in his own day because of his doctrine of tyrannicide. Born in 1534, he entered the Jesuit order at the age of eighteen and taught in both Rome and Paris as a young man. One of his pupils in Rome was Robert Bellarmine, and he was in Paris during the St Bartholomew's Day Massacre (1572). He returned to Spain in 1574 to teach at the University of Toledo and remained there until his death in 1622. Mariana published a number of academic works in both history and political thought. The most extensive of these was a history of Spain published in Latin in 1592 and translated in expanded form into Spanish by Mariana himself in 1601. His prominence rested on the fact that his views on tyrannicide were named by Huguenot magistrates after the assassination of Henry III by a young French Dominican, Jacques Clement, in 1589 and publicly represented as a fundamental teaching of Catholic theology especially promoted by the Jesuits. His most significant treatise on political thought was *De rege et regis institutione* (1599). It was from this that his views on tyrannicide had been excerpted, and the work was publicly burned in Paris in 1610 by order of the French parlement.[90] Something more than an ordinary scholastic treatise in the traditional "mirror for princes" form, the well-written *De rege* was presented as advice to Philip II of Spain, although its dedication was to Philip III, who succeeded to the Spanish throne just as the work was completed. One of its principal points of interest relates to what Mariana says about the origins of political society and his stress on popular consent and the feature of limit on legitimate political authority, a notion also reflected in his views on tyrannicide.

While not particularly original, Mariana's position shows the general continuity of doctrine among Spanish neo-scholastics. He began *De rege* by setting the framework within which his political thought developed. Chapter 1, entitled "Man by nature social," offered what had by then become the standard Spanish neo-scholastic description of the origins of human society. In the beginning humans lived independently, unfettered by any ruling authority except the instincts of nature, which encompassed an innate impulse to form family groupings and offer

---

90. The standard account in English of Mariana's political doctrine is Lewy, *Constitutionalism and Statecraft*; biographical details on Mariana are at pp. 7–27. Cf. Laures, *Political Economy of Juan de Mariana*.

honour to the eldest family member as superior.[91] Mariana followed Aeneas Sylvius and Vives here without, however, making direct reference to the expulsion of Adam and Eve from the Garden of Eden. He even suggested that humans in this state gambolled in virtue, implying the past existence of a kind of golden age. On its face, this idea appears to be a straight repetition of the classical and purely philosophical Stoic view of the naturally good, though primitive, original state of humans, a view later expressed so dramatically by Rousseau in the first lines of the *Social Contract*. Such an interpretation is not very plausible, however, for a Christian theologian thoroughly familiar with the doctrines of St Paul and St Augustine regarding the human condition after commission of the Original Sin. Mariana's golden age would have been post-lapsarian. He speaks of humans in this original state as living without political organization or positive law, following the law of nature and concerned only with supplying food for themselves and their families. Nature provided for their few and simple needs, and people lived together in innocence and honesty, without guile; fraud and lying, along with ambition, were unknown. All lived in peace and equality, holding material goods in common and free of social obligations because no one was wealthier than anyone else. Clearly, something more than Adam and Eve was being described here.[92]

Without addressing the arguable lack of consistency between this somewhat idyllic description and his next remarks, Mariana considered that the prepolitical state of nature lasted for only a short period of time and that individuals in it were subject to needs and perils, to overcome which they agreed to form a political community. Their need to defend themselves was a prime motivation in this respect. Individuals combined by agreement for mutual assistance to eliminate the unpleasant features of a virtual state of war among free individuals.[93] Sounding more and more like an early Thomas Hobbes, he asserted that individual people

91. Mariana, *De rege* 1.1, pp. 12–16.
92. Ibid., pp. 12–13.
93. Lewy states that Mariana follows Thomas Aquinas here, citing Aquinas's *On Kingship* 1.1. It should be noted, however, that while the Thomistic text speaks of the inability of individual humans to provide for their own needs it makes no reference to a need for protection against aggression by others. Lewy also comments that Mariana offered no explanation for the transformation of the golden age into one where human aggression was a serious problem. The explanation, as just noted, probably involved the distinction between pre- and post-lapsarian conditions of human existence, although Mariana's positive comments concerning the golden age seem to belie the point. See Lewy, *Constitutionalism and Statecraft*, pp. 43–44.

agreed to form a political society and entered into a contract to establish a governmental form of monarchy.[94] He also specifically distinguished between the contract by which a society comes into being (*pactum societatis*) and that by which individuals, having consented to form a political society, agree further to establish and obey a specific ruler (*pactum subjectionis*).[95]

Thus monarchy, as well as any other form of polity entered into by a group of freely consenting individuals, is the result of human decision making. The exercise of royal power has its beginning when individuals, having consented to come together for protection, choose one man to rule them because of his perceived uprightness and prudence.[96] Though not explicit on the point in *De rege*, Mariana made clear in his *Historia de rebus Hispaniae* that those who establish a monarchy retain the right to transform it into another form of polity or even disestablish it: "Kingships can be changed through the consent of people [insofar as] what originated in the people's will can be transferred to others if the circumstances require it."[97] Mariana also reported as an historical fact that succession to the Spanish monarchy rested on popular consent, not heredity.[98]

Following Aquinas again, Mariana opted for a limited monarchy, but added a feature that explicitly reflected the sixteenth-century Spanish scene: extensive powers were reserved for the Cortès.[99] Individuals consenting to come together for mutual protection chose one man to rule them and opted for a mixed constitutional monarchy that Mariana termed "an aristocracy and hereditary monarchy."[100] Once more, the origins of his position were clearly Thomistic, reflecting the tradition that began with Aquinas's interpretation of the Israelite monarchy described in Samuel, the Old Testament text employed earlier by John of Salisbury

---

94. Mariana, *De rege* 1.1, p. 112.

95. Ibid. Suárez repeated this distinction: see *infra*, p. 179. Lewy also notes that this doctrine was condemned as heretical by the Church of England in 1604: *Constitutionalism and Statecraft*, p. 46, note 45.

96. Mariana, *De rege* 1.2, p. 115.

97. Mariana, *Historia de rebus Hispaniae* 19.15, p. 910; cited in Lewy, *Constitutionalism and Statecraft*, p. 45, note 41.

98. "The place of deceased kings was filled not through hereditary right but the will of the multitude." Mariana, *Historia de rebus Hispaniae* 19.15, in Lewy, ibid.

99. Mariana, *De rege* 1.8, p. 161. Cf. Lewy, *Constitutionalism and Statecraft*, pp. 51 and 57–58.

100. Mariana, *De rege* 1.2, pp. 124–27.

in the *Policraticus*.¹⁰¹ According to Mariana, the people unquestionably choose their ruler. He was less clear, however, about how the people came to possess the power they transfer to a ruler, although an obvious and probably correct inference is that he considered them to possess it in virtue of having somehow been granted it directly by God. He was equally unspecific about whether the people retained any political power after transferring it to the ruler, although his position seems clear. Asserting that "royal power, wherever legitimate, takes its form from its citizens, by whose grant the first kings in every state were raised to the throne," he added that "the people cannot give a king greater power than they have in themselves."¹⁰²

He did not mean by this, however, that the ultimate source of political authority was the people themselves. For Mariana as for any Christian thinker of the period, Catholic or Protestant, God was the ultimate source of all power.¹⁰³ Suárez later made explicit what Mariana probably had in mind here: the people received their power directly from God and were free to dispose of it as they chose.¹⁰⁴ Mariana contended that the question whether the community can alienate its authority completely to a ruler was not crucial. Perhaps dissembling a bit, he stated that the issue is unimportant "provided one concedes that the community (*respublica*) would act unwisely if it surrendered, and that a prince would be rash to accept power which would make the people slaves rather than free, and would cause a principate constituted for the public good to degenerate into tyranny."¹⁰⁵

---

101. Ibid., pp. 121 and 124–27; Thomas Aquinas *ST* 1–2.105.1 and *ad* 1; John of Salisbury, *Policraticus* 5.6. 548D–49A. Salisbury identified the Israelite monarchy as the model for a proper polity; Aquinas applied the Aristotelian concept of the mixed type of polity, although he did not use the notion of "mixed" in quite the same way as Aristotle did. On this latter point see Blythe, "Mixed Constitution."

102. Mariana, *De rege* 1.8, pp. 156, 160. An ambiguity remains as to whether Mariana accepted that the people could change forms of government "at their pleasure," so to speak, or whether their rights in this respect were circumscribed by the terms of transfer of authority to a ruler. His view likely was that later expressed clearly by Suárez, viz., that the people had the power to control the exercise of tyranny on the part of the ruler but that they were not free to change the rulers or forms of rulership to which they had consented unless the conferred authority was being abused. Suárez, *De legibus* 3, 4.6. Cf. Laures, *Political Economy of Mariana*, p. 43; Lewy, *Constitutionalism and Statecraft*, p. 45 and note 41.

103. Aquinas, whom all Spanish neo-scholastics followed, was explicit on this point, and the notion goes back in an unbroken line to St Paul. Thomas Aquinas *In 2 Sent.* 44.2.2.

104. Mariana, *De rege* 1.1, p. 14, and "De morte et immortalitate," in *Tractatus VII* 2.9, p. 405. Cf. Suárez, *De legibus* 3.3.1–2 and 3–4.

105. Mariana, *De rege* 1.8, p. 160.

He went on to make the factual point that the current authority of the community was greater than the king's in several regions of Spain, where a division of powers existed between king and the community of the whole people. In these jurisdictions, he said, the king had authority to carry on war, dispense justice, and appoint leaders and magistrates, while the people were responsible for levying taxes, abrogating laws, and determining the royal succession; the king must submit "whenever the community as a whole, or men of the first rank selected from all orders of society and responsible for the undertaking of public functions, come together in one place and reach a common decision."[106] His final statement on the matter was, "This is the main point: I prefer that the power of restraining the prince rest in the commonwealth (*respublica*) ... although this is not at present the case in Castile; it is in Aragon."[107] The power of the community, especially to levy taxes, he reserved for the Cortès, which he apparently considered " representative" of the people as a whole in the traditional medieval connotation of that term. He did say at one point that the king can tax; but this would have been understood to mean only with the people's consent, as was the case in Spain.[108]

Mariana thus reflected in a clear, even graphic, manner the traditional medieval view that no ruler possessed unlimited and arbitrary power, while the authority of any political community as a whole, the commonwealth, must be greater than that of the ruler it chose insofar as the ruler received his power from the community. Further, a ruler must respect the rights of his subjects and obey the laws of the land. He acknowledged that minor princes in the temporal sphere and bishops in the Church could rule absolutely, that is, without reference to authoritative representative bodies, but this was so only because a higher power existed to correct them. And he asked rhetorically, "Who can correct the king if the power of the commonwealth is completely subordinated to him?"[109]

Mariana began, but did not pursue, the possible parallel between temporal and ecclesiastical authority: he commented that some wise men have considered papal power also to be subject to the Church as a whole as represented by a general church council, but declined to state whether he agreed. The remark is suggestive, however, given the renewal

---

106. Ibid., pp. 157 and 159.
107. Ibid., p. 161.
108. Ibid., 1.5, p. 137.
109. Ibid., 1.8, p. 160.

of papal monarchism as the dominant ecclesiology at the time, roughly half a century after the Council of Basle had dissolved in confusion.

There was also Mariana's lengthy consideration of tyrannicide. It was probably the attention he paid to the topic rather than any particularly radical views that accounts for the notoriety of his doctrine. He did not offer significantly stronger support for this extreme form of resistance to tyranny than that found in other scholastic and neo-scholastic texts. He began with the standard distinction between tyrants who establish their tyranny by seizing power, where the tyranny then rested on the absence of consent from the people over whom control was being exercised, and rulers who become tyrants after coming legitimately into office. The distinction itself came into the civil law through *De tyrannia*, written by Bartolus of Sassoferrato, who could have taken it from Aquinas; it was also used by Bartolus's contemporary, Coluccio Salutati (1331–1406), in his *Tractatus de tyranno* and became standard in the literature. It is carried in the Spanish civil code, *Las Siete Partidas*, completed in 1265 and promulgated in 1348.[110]

Mariana's readers would have been struck, however, by his mention of specific incidents in Spanish history to illustrate a political community's right to remove a tyrant, particularly his inclusion of a summary account of Henry III's assassination and praise for the young French Dominican who carried it out. Accordingly, though his typically scholastic examination of the issue offered a highly qualified justification for killing a tyrant, his own application of the theory to earlier and contemporary historical events not unexpectedly aroused strong feelings against him.

## 7. FRANCESCO SUÁREZ

The most comprehensive political thinker among late Spanish scholastics was the Jesuit Thomist Francesco Suárez (1548–1617). Along with his fellow Jesuit Luis de Molina (1535–1600), he was in the first rank of philosophers and theologians in the immediate post-Reformation era and carried the official banner of the Catholic Counter-Reformation with considerable distinction. Like Molina and two other notable sixteenth-century Spanish neo-Thomists, Francesco de Toledo and Gregorio de Valencia, Suárez began his studies at the University of

---

110. For the distinction in Aquinas see *In 2 Sent.* 44.2.2; for Bartolus see "De tyranno"; for Salutati, *Tractatus de tyrannis*, see English translation by Ephraim Emerton, in *Humanism and Tyranny*, pp. 70–116; Scott, trans. *Las Siete Partidas* 2.1.10, pp. 274–75.

Salamanca, the seat of Vitoria's long tenure and of an impressive group of Vitorian disciples. Suárez taught for some years at the Jesuit college in Rome before being named to the chair of theology at Coimbra in 1593, winning the post over Molina, and he remained there for the rest of his career. A mature and recognized scholar even before his appointment to Coimbra, he was encouraged by both papal and Jesuit authorities to develop and publish what became a corpus of some thirty volumes, an important portion of which was devoted to political and legal philosophy.

In 1596 Suárez gave a series of lectures on the concept of law. They were published in 1612 under the title *Tractatus de legibus et de legislatore* (*On Laws*) and are a major source for his views on the nature of law and polity. A second important work on political thought, also published in 1612, was his *Defensio fidei catholicae et apostolicae adversus anglicanae sectae errores* (*Defence of the Catholic Faith*), specifically commissioned by the papacy to refute James I's *Apology* in defence of the English oath of allegiance. Suárez's *De legibus* and *Defensio* together constitute the clearest statement of the comprehensive position developed by Spanish neo-Thomist political thinkers in the course of the sixteenth century. What makes Suárezian political thought interesting and significant for modern democratic political theory is that, while remaining a particularly graphic example of the retention of medieval conceptual baggage and conclusions, it also expresses views that have led to Suárez being called "the first modern democrat."[111]

As one might expect, he began his lengthy treatise on law and the divine legislator by considering the nature of law and its various types, roughly following the treatise on law in Aquinas's *Summa theologiae*. What emerges are several positions that occupy a prominent place in his overall theory of polity, views on the natural law and the state of nature, the origins and purpose of political society, the function of popular consent and the limits of political authority, tyrannicide, and the relations be-

---

111. Fichter, *Man of Spain. Francis Suárez*, p. 306. Similar encomiums have been assigned other Jesuits of the late Thomist group: Bellarmine for having revealed "the true sources of democracy" in Rager, *Political Philosophy of Bellarmine*, p. 129, and the Jesuits as a whole for "inventing" the concept of the social contract and first exploring its implications for a theory of justice in Jarlot, "Les idées politiques de Suárez," 98, and Figgis, *Political Thought from Gerson to Grotius*, pp. 201–3. Skinner is inclined to agree with all these designations. Skinner, *Foundations*, 2:174–75.

A fine recent study in English of Suárez's political thought is Wilenius's *Social and Political Theory of Suárez*. See also Jarlot, "Les idées politiques de Suárez," 64–107.

tween spiritual and temporal authority, which involve as well those between pope and council. All are dealt with specifically and at length, with Suárez's customary care.

His definition of law as "a common precept, just, stable and adequately promulgated" was not as tightly worded as that of Aquinas, but followed the Thomistic pattern of offering a general definition subsequently broken down into different species or types.[112] Suárez followed the Thomistic text directly in differentiating the various types of law—eternal, natural, human or positive, and divine—although it has been suggested that, to some extent, he fractures the direct link Aquinas maintained between natural and positive law.[113] However, an effort to distinguish Suárez from Aquinas on this point seems a bit forced and stems from construing the notion of deduction in too formal a fashion. Aquinas did hold that humans can come to rational conclusions about how to relate to one another and thereby formulate rules, positive or human laws, that govern behaviour in political society. Indeed, his view that positive laws had to correspond to the natural law rested on this base. His link between the two forms of law, however, was rationality and, following Aristotle, Aquinas did not construe deduction in terms of purely formal logical analysis, but accepted it as a description of forms of argument containing contingent material. In these terms, even materially different conclusions in positive law could be "deduced" from the natural law. Deduction considered as an exclusively formal process was not what Aquinas had in mind when he spoke of deducing conclusions from principles of the natural law.

Failure to recognize the real meaning of the medieval view connecting natural and positive law has often led to sterile criticism of natural-law theory for its failure to acknowledge the existence of differing, even conflicting, systems of positive law. This variety is alleged as evidence that there cannot be a universal positive law corresponding to a univocal and morally absolute natural law. Thomas Aquinas and other medieval natural-law theorists did accept variation in the legitimate but different systems of positive law, conceding variables in geography, climate, etc., as well as, though less explicitly, those rooted in history, culture, and so-

---

112. Suárez, *De legibus* 1.12.5. Cf. Thomas Aquinas, *ST* 1–2.90.4.

113. Wilenius contends that Suárez did not repeat Aquinas's insistence that one can deduce the specifics of positive law from the principles of the natural law, and thereby loosens the bond between natural and positive law, but I am not convinced of Suarez's deviation here: Wilenius, *Social and Political Theory of Suárez*, pp. 52–53.

cial values.[114] The diverse systems nonetheless would all have rationality in common, that is, a rational connection between the content of a given human-made law and the law of nature. The meaning of rationality here was not spelled out; nor could it be with full deductive specification both because and although something more than content is involved. This does not make the content of law a meaningless issue or deny its primary importance; it indicates rather the acceptance of a certain fluidity in content—which may be what many empirically oriented social scientists and investigators in "human studies" take as evidence for their faulty conclusion that the norms of law and morality are relative or subjective across the range of human experience and history. The importance attached by medieval legal theorists to the binding character of custom reflects this attitude.[115]

Suárez picked up the Thomistic element missing from his own general definition when he asserted that law is made by an agent that possesses coercive power: coercion is an essential feature of public, that is, community, power; the efficient cause of law is the common power to coerce.[116] He used the Marsilian term coercion (*coactio*) rather than the term authority (*auctoritas*) found in Aquinas,[117] indicating the widespread tendency at this time, even among neo-scholastics who rejected Marsilius's political theory because it subordinated the Church to temporal polity, to emphasize the feature of law Marsilius had made its only essential property.[118]

Distinguishing among the basic kinds of law, Suárez asserted that law was an imposition of order on humans as a community, with natural law

---

114. Cf. Thomas Aquinas, *ST* 1–2.95.3; 97 *ad* 2; John of Paris, *Royal and Papal Power* 3, p. 14; Dante, *De monarchia* 1.14; Englebert of Admont, *De ortu, progressu et fine Romani imperii* 16. See Monahan, "Demise of Natural Law."

115. Cf. the arguments made by Bartolus and Baldus to justify the independent status of the Italian city-states, *supra*, pp. 21–22; 24–28.

116. Suárez, *De legibus* 1.8.1–2.

117. Thomas Aquinas, *ST* 1–2.90.3; Marsilius of Padua, *Defensor pacis* 1.10.4.

118. Some have suggested that this is too harsh an indictment of Marsilius as a legal positivist, while others have complimented his modernity on the same point, a fine example of the distinction between a vessel being half full and half empty. For the former view see Lewis, "'Positivism' of Marsiglio of Padua"; for the latter, Gewirth, *Marsilius of Padua* 1: *Marsilius of Padua and Medieval Political Philosophy*. Others, notably Thomas Gilby, have argued that the element of coercion is not present in the Thomistic concept of law—that for Aquinas, law rests on reason, not power. I suspect, however, that "power to enforce a law" [=coercion?] is present in Aquinas's fourth essential of any law: authority. Cf. Gilby, *Political Thought of Thomas Aquinas* and *Principality and Polity, passim*.

applying to humankind as a whole.[119] The end or purpose of law is the common good, which he divided into two types, both, it seems, primarily related to material or physical things. One form, things common to all members of society and not the property of any individual, are "immediate" common goods, for example common pastures or public administrative offices.[120] The second type, "mediately" common goods, are the property of individuals in the first instance and are thus "immediately private" ; but they are common in a mediate or indirect sense inasmuch as public authority has a certain higher right even over its citizens' private goods, when the common or public need requires. Immediate private goods can also be called "mediately common" insofar as the entire community benefits in some sense from the private enjoyment of a good privately held and properly used so as not to cause injury or harm to anyone else.[121] The Suárezian distinction anticipated that between public and private goods in modern economic and social theory.

Like all adherents of the natural-law tradition, Suárez rejected any incompatibility between positive and natural law: "Law is just in its content."[122] But it must also be just in form; that is, it must satisfy a number of formal conditions. Here Suárez introduced the conventional distinction among three types of justice, legal, commutative, and distributive, all of which it is the function of positive law to maintain. Legal justice is maintained by having the law aim at the common good and safeguard the well-being of the community as a whole; commutative justice operates insofar as lawgivers are authorized to command only their own subjects; and distributive justice requires that legal burdens fall proportionately on citizens such that all are obligated according to their proper position in the polity.[123] The law must also be stable as regards both ruler and subject; it must remain in force across a succession of incumbents in office and remain an obligation on all subjects, regardless of their wishes, unless and until abrogated. Finally, it must be promulgated adequately, although this does not mean that it has to be written.[124] Suárez devoted considerable attention to custom as unwritten

---

119. Suárez, *De legibus* 1.6.8 and 1.8.1.
120. Ibid. 1.7.7. A contemporary Suárezian likely would list other material commodities, such as pure air and water, belonging to no one individual and for which public authority has a responsibility on behalf of all.
121. Suárez, *De legibus* 1.7.7. Cf. 1.7.8 and 3.34.20.
122. Ibid. 1.9.2.
123. Ibid. 1.9.13 and 16.
124. Ibid. 1.10.7, 1.11.9.

law: Book Seven of *De legibus* is the earliest comprehensive treatment of this important feature in medieval legal theory.

Custom (*consuetudo*) has two meanings: something actual, that is, a certain frequency of identical actions or behaviour; and something legal that denotes an obligation, entailing sanctions, to act in a certain way because of past repetition of similar action.[125] Suárez went on to specify three conditions under which custom in its first meaning acquires its second, acquires the force of positive law. To begin with, the custom must initially be introduced by a "perfect" community; the activity must exist in the political society as a whole and not simply be the behaviour of certain individuals or groups.[126] In this connection two further stipulations were made. First, the fact that a given behaviour is the custom of the prince or ruler is not enough to transform it into law, *pace* the *Basilicon* of James VI of Scotland (soon to become James I of England), written in 1612. Of course, Suárez would not have been familiar with James's work when he first presented *De legibus* as lectures, even though he came to know the *Basilicon* well enough later: he cited the *Digest* on the point.[127] Second, the majority in a perfect community *is* sufficient to turn a custom into law, and Suárez held that women and persons under twenty-five could be numbered in the total.[128]

The second condition for transforming a custom into law is the voluntariness with which the act is performed by the people concerned. Suárez insisted that a custom, to become an actual law, must reflect popular willingness or consent in the people themselves. Behaviour that is compelled cannot be the basis for a custom becoming law; it must be free in the sense that external compulsion is absent. Thirdly, to become legal a custom must meet all the essential criteria in the original definition of law, the principal one being coercive sanction, and Suárez provided considerable detail about the grounds on which legitimate coercive authority rests.[129]

He did the same when examining popular consent. A custom acquires the force of law only when agreed to by the agency with the requisite authority to give consent. The agency will differ in different forms of polity.

---

125. Ibid. 1.11.9.
126. Ibid. 7.9.3.
127. *Digest* 1.3.32, cited at Suárez, *De legibus* 7.9.3.
128. Suárez, *De legibus* 7.9.14. He argued that "I cannot find any basis in law or justification in reason to exclude either of these groups." He was not clear, however, how old one had to be to be counted.
129. Ibid. 7.9.14, 7.12.1.

In a democracy, the people never transfer their original rightful legislative power to any specific person or persons; hence majority consent in observing a custom is required and constitutes a sufficient basis for transforming custom into law: consent by a majority of the people is identical with the legal authority of the community itself.[130] In an aristocratic form of polity, on the other hand, the people have transferred their natural legislative authority to a "senate," which can then, given a majority of its members, legislate custom into law. The king performs the same function in a monarchy, where the essential ingredient of consent that transforms custom into law exists in two ways. The sovereign can legalize a custom by personal consent (*consensus personalis*) either by expressly declaring it law himself, or by recognizing it tacitly by not expressly forbidding it. Alternatively, he can enact legislation to give a custom full legal consent (*consensus legalis seu juridicus*); this presumably would entail formal advice and obtaining consent of whatever type from the monarchy. Suárez made clear that the required popular consent can be tacit in every form of polity.[131]

He also maintained that custom can abrogate written law, with different forms of abrogation corresponding to the different forms of polity; custom automatically abrogates contrary written law in a democracy, for example.[132] Suárez was categorical, then, about how to determine the validity of written law in a democracy: a statute ceases to be a law when a majority of the population ceases to obey it. Presumably, he would have had direct rather than representative democracy in mind, but it is interesting to speculate on what his views might have been concerning the validity of democratic government by referendum. Of course, he always insisted that natural law places limits on the legitimacy of positive law in every polity, and the same limits would apply to legalized custom.

Customary law was important for Suárez, then, in that it displayed some retention of popular authority in aristocracies and monarchies as well as in democracies, and for this reason it is an important locus for his views on popular consent. He suggested, for example, that a sovereign ought to permit the abrogation of law by custom even in circumstances where monarchical authority does not require him to do so.[133] And his invocation of the equal rights of individual citizens, both men and

---

130. Ibid. 7.13.1.
131. Ibid. 7.13.6.
132. Ibid. 7.18.3.
133. Ibid. 7.18.3–6 and 14.

women, in establishing customs and converting them into law was quite striking. Citing Julianus from the *Digest*, he asks rhetorically, "What difference does it make whether the people declare their will by a vote or by facts and deeds?"[134] His notion of custom was not the expression of a *volkgeist*, however; neither was it an essential part of the natural law strictly speaking, because it was not fully and necessarily deducible from it.

Suárez's conception of the natural law afforded a significant role to consent in the origins of political society as it developed from the state of nature after the Fall. He generally followed the theory found in texts from Aquinas to the earlier members of the Spanish neo-Thomist school like Vitoria and Mariana, but introduced a distinction between positive and negative aspects of the natural law. Its positive features specify proper behaviour for rational human beings and enjoin forms of action requiring compliance by all human individuals in all societies. Reflecting essential features of human nature, they express basic normative rules for all human behaviour; comprising principles and rules for right conduct, they assert necessary and immutable truths about humans.

Negative aspects of the natural law, on the other hand, relate to the historical character of human nature. They have existed since the beginning of human existence, but do not enjoin conformity from all human individuals in all historical contexts. They are descriptive of how humans actually lived in the original state of nature before and for at least a short while after the Fall; at best they are recommendations for how humans are to live generally. They entail no obligation on all humans, but are somehow morally neutral as regards human behaviour and involve features of human life that may be changed.[135] Individuals living in given historical circumstances may or may not conform to the negative features of natural law; as free and rational beings they can choose or not

---

134. Ibid. 7.14.8, citing the *Digest* 1.3.32.1. Wilenius is unnecessarily fulsome in his assessment of the Suarezian position: "When Suárez gives all citizens, both men and women, prince and subjects, an equal vote in the introduction of customary law, he seems to be approaching the democratic idea of universal and equal suffrage." Wilenius, *Social and Political Theory of Suárez*, p. 83. But there is no real notion of "vote" or "suffrage" in Suárez here.

135. Suárez, *De legibus* 2.14.18; cf. 2.18.2. The distinction did not originate with Suarez, however; it can be found as early as the twelfth century in the canonist Rufinus, *Summa decretorum* D.1. *Dictum Gratiani ad* c.1; cited in McGrade, "State of Nature and Origin of the State," p. 760.

choose to do so. The negative features are always valid, but do not always bind.[136]

Suárez's purpose in distinguishing between positive and negative aspects of the natural law seems clear from the examples he gives of the latter, which relate generally to what he calls "rights to a thing" (*ius, iura*) and involve property ownership (*dominium*).[137] He applied the distinction to two forms of property: an individual's ownership of material goods (private property), and ownership over one's own person (liberty and its antithesis, slavery). He maintained that natural law as reflected in the historical origins of human existence, the actual dispensation in the original state of nature, provided for common ownership of material goods, while later and current practice accepted a system of private ownership.[138] Similarly, the independence of all individuals in the state of nature has given way to a more or less absolutist form of monarchy,[139] and the original condition of freedom has been supplanted at least for some individuals by slavery: humans today live in subjection to the laws of political institutions, and existing positive law sanctions slavery as a social institution.[140]

Suárez used the distinction between the two aspects of natural law to explain and justify features of his own society that were absent from or rejected by traditional classical and Christian descriptions of the state of nature. He was thus able to go beyond conclusions reached by earlier natural-law theorists. As regards private property, for example, Aquinas accepted its legitimacy even while repeating the conventional classical and Christian view that, in the beginning, all things were common. But Aquinas argued for private ownership in terms of practical necessity and made no reference to the creation of political society by an act of consent or contract. Suárez's emphasis on popular consent at the outset of political society certainly fleshed out the Thomist position in a way that was generally consistent with Aquinas's basic thinking and improved it

---

136. Suárez, *De legibus* 2.14.15. Suárez asked specifically whether it was right to interpret negative natural law in such a way as to maintain that slavery (*servitus*) rather than liberty and private ownership (*divisio rerum*) rather than community of goods (*communitas*) were part of the natural law. Suárez, *De legibus* 2.14.15.

137. Ibid. 2.14.16, 2.18.2.

138. Suárez, *Defensio* 3.2.14.

139. Ibid. 3.2.5. Omitting the rhetorical tone, Suárez's point anticipates Rousseau's classic statement: "Man was born free, and everywhere he is in chains." Rousseau, *Social Contract*, 1:1.

140. Suárez, *Defensio* 5.7.10.

considerably by highlighting a fundamental concept that Aquinas accepted but underused. Christianity had always stressed the individual's capacity for free choice in decision making and the entailed moral responsibility before God, and a typical medieval connotation of "free" designated the legal status of townspersons and others who did not fall under feudal obligations to a lord. Thus, freemen could decide for themselves how to organize their legal arrangements. But no earlier thinker had so explicitly connected the moral status of freedom among human beings with the political and legal notion of consent found universally in medieval political thought. Suárez presumably took his cue in this from the humanist emphasis on freedom and independent judgment, an influence he would have encountered in several earlier Spanish neo-scholastics. His position also set him explicitly at odds with the general Reformation theory concerning authority as instituted directly by God.

Further, Suárez also gave coherent form to the distinction in Spanish neo-scholastic natural-law theory between the naturalness of society and the varieties of forms of polity—the distinction between humans as naturally social and naturally political, according to which humans are naturally social as a function of the natural law but become members of an actual political society by voluntary rational decision. This position derived from Aeneas Sylvius by way of Vives, Cajetan, de Soto, and Vitoria, and Suárez took it a step further: individuals could consent to form a community with conditions of social existence that were different from those experienced in the state of nature because their humanity does not enjoin on them all the actual conditions of the original state. Natural law immediately "inclines" individuals to conform only to its immutably necessary positive features;[141] but no such obligation operates for its negative aspects. The positive/negative distinction among natural-law features applied to two specific issues, common versus private ownership, and freedom versus slavery, and Suárez held that moral insistence on the latter over the former in both cases was "contrary to common understanding (*contra communem sententiam*)."[142]

One can only speculate on why Suárez accepted both private property and slavery, especially the latter. Individual ownership of property would have been much less controversial at the time than slavery, if it was an issue at all. It had been analysed thoroughly since at least the late thir-

141. Suárez, *De legibus* 2.7.3.
142. Ibid. 2.14.15.

teenth century when changing economic and social conditions signalled the emergence of capitalism, and the intensity of arguments over the Franciscan concept of poverty had given impetus to explorations of the meaning of ownership (*dominium*) and right (*ius*). Private property had never been considered incompatible with Christian doctrine except, perhaps, in the wilder speculations that espoused the views of the Franciscan spiritualists. The moral legitimacy of slavery, however, was a different matter. Suárez sanctioned it by drawing logical entailments from his notion of *ius* and *dominium*. Arguing that free individuals have rights (*iura*) to their own property, including rights to their own body and its activities, he concluded that individuals could dispose of themselves completely to someone else. And he applied the same reasoning to his account of how individuals alienated their rights of self-rule in two of the three standard forms of polity: the people lost all rights of direct control over those to whom they agreed to hand over power in aristocracies and monarchies.[143] Individuals in the state of nature, who possessed in their being the harmful consequences of Original Sin and were not yet formed into a political society, enjoyed the qualities of freedom and independence both before and after commission of the Original Sin. By nature social, they were not yet organized into any form of polity; this came later as a result of voluntary agreement when individuals consented to give up their freedom and independence for rule by a power they chose, after judging that an organized political community would provide greater well-being and protection than an independent existence in the state of nature in which they were subject to mistreatment and evil at the hands of others, all of whom suffered from the perverting effects of the Fall.[144]

In the state of nature, then, human individuals were inclined in two ways to form political societies. Firstly, they were already naturally social and lived together in family groupings that provided some mutual procreative and nurturing values to individuals within small units. Secondly, the adults at least possessed a functioning natural faculty of reason and thus could make reasoned judgments on how best to provide for their own welfare. Suárez was careful, however, not to assert that naturally free and independent individuals themselves created the power to form a po-

---

143. Ibid. 3.4.6.
144. Molina held the same view, and referred explicitly to "our loss of innocence" as the reason why individuals ignored much of natural morality and were uncertain regarding other facts of nature to which in theory their natural rational faculties gave them access. Luis de Molina, *De iustitia et iure*, p. 1705. Cf. F. B. Costello, *Political Philosophy of Molina.*

litical society; he remained sensitive to the biblical and Pauline doctrine that all power comes from God, and he was cautious not to reject this basic feature of all Christian political thought which served as the keystone of original Lutheran and Calvinist theories of politics. At the same time he would have considered the reformers' views on the nature of the Church to be heretical and their pessimistic notions about the inability of individuals suffering the effects of Original Sin to behave in a naturally virtuous way overblown.

He also defended traditional medieval Christian ecclesiology with its emphasis on an ordained clergy and ecclesiastical hierarchy, and he offered an account of human historical development that attributed to individuals a natural capacity to perceive and pursue virtues such as justice and to organize themselves in at least general congruity with the divine plan. They were, in other words, not so much completely helpless in this world as irremediably lost and sinful. Of course, Christianity had always taught that religious salvation was a gift of God and unattainable solely through natural human efforts. But a critical issue dividing Reformation and Roman Catholic theology in the sixteenth century was whether individual human beings could contribute anything towards their supernatural end: whether faith alone was enough, or whether faith *and* good works were required for people to affect their supernatural end. The latter Catholic view also favoured a more natural account of political life, in which the Aristotelian concept of efficient causality set it in contrast to early Reformation thought: God is the primary, but not the only, efficient cause of political authority; humans also perform a secondary efficient causal role here.

Suárez maintained that the power to form political societies existed originally in God, who transferred it to individuals when they came together in a genuine group by following their individual inclinations and agreed voluntarily to form a polity. The God-given power to form a polity, then, lay with the community rather than with any one individual or even with the group of them considered as an aggregate. Suárez was careful to distinguish between the community as a whole, which he spoke of as "a mystical body," and a simple collection of individuals; this is the form he gave to the medieval corporation theory, and it can be seen later in Rousseau's distinction between the general will and the will of all.[145] Once possessed of this power, the community could transfer it

---

145. Suárez, *Defensio* 3.2.7. On the point that the community as a whole is a "mystical body," see *Defensio*, vol. 1, p. 165, in Naples [1872], 2 vol. edition: Skinner, *Foundations*,

by further agreement among themselves to whomever they accepted to have as ruler over them.[146] Suárez was well aware of the challenge he posed at this point to conventional Reformation political thought, and he drew a clear contrast between it and the "divine right of kings" stand of James of England, against whom he wrote at such length in the *Defensio*. His emphasis on consent in the formation of political society reaffirmed the Aristotelian-Thomist view that the social and politicial nature of human beings is rooted in and given expression through the faculty of reasoning. This, in turn, highlighted consent as the appropriate rational act by which humans entered into and expressed political arrangements and gave renewed and forceful expression to a notion that, as shown, had a long history in Western political thought in both the temporal and ecclesiastical spheres.[147]

Suárez placed consent at the beginning of political rule and located it in the people, the community as a whole: the people choose those to whom they give the authority to rule over them. Thus, princes and kings received their authority directly from the people, not directly from God. Suárez specifically rejected a literal acceptance of texts from St Paul and St Augustine, among others, according to which all power, both temporal and spiritual, comes directly from God.[148] God is the first and direct cause of all power, but ordinarily confers it on an agent. He is the immediate cause of power in the agent on whom He confers it, but the agent

---

2:165. See also the important article by Sommerville, "From Suárez to Filmer," esp. p. 528. Sommerville takes issue with Skinner for calling the community of individuals that designates the seat of political authority "pre-political"; he points out quite properly that, since the community's consent is the efficient cause of the authority it transfers to given persons, the community has the power to make the transfer and must, then, already be a political rather than a "pre-political" entity. Sommerville, "From Suárez to filmer," pp. 531–32. Skinner is right, of course, in indicating that this community of individuals is prior to any specific form of polity it might act to form.

Skinner is also misleading when he states that Suárez's notion of *universitas* "represented a considerable advance on the accounts offered by the earlier Dominican theorists of the process by which a legitimate commonwealth comes into being" (Skinner, *Foundations*, 2:166). While he is correct in showing that Suárez speaks more formally and comprehensively on the point than Vitoria and de Soto, he ignores the fact that the Dominican, John of Paris, had employed precisely this corporation concept (*universitas*) in the early fourteenth century, and there is every reason to believe that Quidort's position had been part of the Parisian Dominican theory of polity since that time. Cf. *supra*, p. 66.

146. Suárez, *De legibus* 3.2.3, and especially *Defensio* 3.2.5.
147. See *supra*, pp. 50–68 *passim*.
148. Suárez, *Defensio* 3.2.5 and 3.2 *passim*.

has the ability and right to confer it on others. Moreover, God confers power on an agent in two ways: either by imbedding the power in the agent's specific nature, or by bestowing on him a special divine gift whereby he becomes a channel or instrument through which divine power is transmitted. In the second case the power remains divine and is not possessed by its agent, merely conveyed. God transferred civil power directly to the people as a community (*respublica*) whose nature is that of a "mystical body" composed of all its members; this body possesses the power and functions as a natural agent in conferring it on its chosen rulers. The classic example of God conferring power as a special gift, on the other hand, was the papal power conferred on Peter and his successors. The human agency employed here, the college of cardinals, acts only as a channel through which the divine power is transferred; the cardinals do not possess it in their own right or nature.[149]

Insofar as human nature is inherently social, the ability of human beings to come together in some form is as old as humankind itself and existed in Adam and Eve in their state of innocence before the Fall. In this original state, however, and at least for a certain period after the Fall, this authority rested only on a "directive" basis and lacked the essential feature of political authority: coercion.[150] Coercion came into being only when the people consented to establish a political society. Receiving power to do so directly from God, they formed a polity of a specific type and gave authority and coercive power to a chosen ruler.[151]

Suárez conceded the possibility that democracy, as the type of polity in which all citizens have an equal share in power, might best reflect the natural tendency for humans to unite in political society. Addressing the issue of why, historically, the political societies formed by human beings had not been democracies, Suárez fell back on his distinction between positive and negative aspects of the natural law and, again stressing free choice and consent, argued that individuals are not naturally determined or required to establish democracies, even though to do so would produce a polity whose basic feature reflected human life in the state of

---

149. In making this distinction Suárez employs the by-now classical medieval theological distinction between the ordinary and absolute powers of God. Suárez, *Defensio* 3.2.2. He treats at some length the issue of how the people come to have power to designate the form of polity they agree to: *Defensio* 3.2 *in toto*. His application of the distinction between the positive and negative aspects of the natural law to this agreeing process or contract is at 3.2.7.
150. Suárez, *De legibus* 3.1.12. Cf. *De legibus* 3.3.19.
151. Ibid. 3.2.4.

nature: the equal right of each individual to rule could be set aside by human decision because it is only a negative feature of the state of nature. Individuals as a group may agree, then, to adopt some other political form than democracy; they may even be forced by rational recognition of their circumstances to eliminate this feature of their natural state when they form political communities.[152]

Accepting monarchy as the general norm, Suárez asserted that subjects have a standard obligation to obey laws established by the ruler, in whose hands coercive power rests. He was even prepared to accept an absolute form of monarchy in some circumstances, arguably on the ground that people who consent to this form are bound by their decision. Correspondingly, however, he insisted on the two-way character of an agreement between ruler and ruled.[153] No secular ruler has a "divine right" to rule, because kingly rule is the product of an agreement binding the monarch to the community with which the agreement was made. Further, the subjects can sever the agreement if its terms permit. Suárez's views on the origins of temporal authority and the existence of a contract between people and ruler paralleled Huguenot resistance theory, although his sources would not have been Huguenot texts, but earlier scholastic ones from which the Huguenot publicists themselves had borrowed.

He did not, however, explicitly concede a general right of the people to break their agreement. Subjects of a polity could change its specific terms only when their right to do so was spelled out in the original agreement; and this would have applied only in democracies, where the putative founding agreement left authority in the people. In the final analysis, nonetheless, Suárez held common cause with Protestant polit-

152. Suárez, *Defensio* 3.4.1. On the point that individual communities may adopt nondemocratic forms of polity, see *Defensio* 3.2.9. Sommerville's interpretation shows Suárez's relatively minimal interest in democracy as the best or only legitimate form of government. Sommerville, "Suarez to Filmer," p. 528. Both Cajetan and Bellarmine were also explicit on the notion that democracy was not part of the natural law inasmuch as the state of nature was pre-political in the Skinnerian sense mentioned above in note 145, i.e., that the people had not yet chosen any specific form of polity. In making this point Bellarmine was the first neo-scholastic to assert that the determination of form of polity was related to the *ius gentium* rather than natural law, because it involved the people as a whole rather than any single individual. Bellarmine, *De membris ecclesiae*, reproduced in *De controversiis Christianae fidei*, 2 vols. (Milan, 1858), pp. 41–42; cited in Bowe, *Origin of Political Authority*, p. 40 and note 34. This reference to the *ius gentium*, however, also was common enough in the humanist tradition.

153. Suárez, *Defensio* 6.6.11.

ical publicists on the general notion of the legitimacy of resistance to temporal authority. It cannot be precluded simply because the ruler never agreed to yield authority under any circumstances; a subject's obligation to obey always functioned under the basic medieval political principle that obedience followed on legitimacy of office holding and dissolved under serious and persistent tyrannical behaviour. Suárez made this clear in his doctrine on resistance and tyrannicide when he argued that a tyrannical ruler in effect breaks his contract with the people. The same point was made by Huguenot publicists, as will be seen later.

Suárez also expressed the medieval theory of limited government within the general framework of corporation doctrine in the *Defensio*, written as a direct response to James I of England, who had the work burned in 1613. Again emphasizing the contractual character of human political society, Suárez rejected the divine-right-of-kings theory and stressed the role of the people in a temporal polity. He also rejected the alternative Pauline/Augustinian insistence on the obligation to obey political thinkers that had been given renewed and even strident expression by the early Reformers, particularly Luther and his close associates. Suárez reaffirmed, moreover, the medieval theory that limitations on the exercise of royal authority stem from the natural law and thus are nonnegotiable. He repeated this notion in his critique of the personal views of the reigning king of England.[154]

Correspondingly, and again fully aware of its contemporary implications, Suárez spelled out a general theory of revolution and tyrannicide in Book Six of the *Defensio*, as well as in the posthumously published *De fide, spe et caritate*. The argument is familiar, going back to Aquinas and Bartolus. Tyrants come in two forms: those who seize power illegally (*tyrannus in titulo*), and those who turn tyrant in office (*tyrannus in regimine*). The former can be killed by any member of a polity, even a foreigner, when the people's well-being cannot be defended otherwise. This type of tyrant directly violates the people's common good, the purpose for which political power is exercised; hence whatever is necessary to defend the common good is permissible. The same argument applies to a tyrant violating his legitimately acquired office by persistently acting against the common good. As a legitimate reaction to specific tyrannical behaviour, however, tyrannicide must be understood as being directed against what is "actually the commonwealth," rather than against

154. Ibid. 3.3.11, 6.6.11.

the ruler himself or the legitimate basis on which he had come into office.¹⁵⁵

To the question who decides whether the behaviour of a ruler is tyrannical, Suárez answered, the people. He went on to state, however, that such a decision was to be taken at "a public and common council," but he did not specify the makeup of such a gathering or how it was to be convened. He also maintained that the pope could depose a tyrant if the common good of the Church required it, but again offered no procedural details for papal action. Once deposed either by the appropriate council in a temporal jurisdiction or by the pope, a tyrant could be opposed by anyone employing any method.¹⁵⁶ This acceptance of tyrannicide as expressed by a Spanish Jesuit in a work explicitly commissioned by the papacy appeared only two years after Mariana's published views on the same subject were publicly burned by Protestant authorities in Paris.

As already indicated, in reasoning that popular consent is the true and original basis for political authority, Suárez placed strong emphasis on freedom as a natural characteristic of human beings in the original state of nature. "In the nature of things, all humans are born free; consequently, no individual has political jurisdiction over another. There is no reason why, in the nature of things, power of this type should be attributed to one person over another, rather than the other way about ... the only dominion (*dominium*) granted to humans in the natural law is that over material things and lower creatures."¹⁵⁷ A leading interpreter of Suárezian political thought has attributed a positive notion of freedom to this doctrine, a positive natural quality inherent in both individuals and the political societies they found by their own agreement.¹⁵⁸ Ironically, however, Suárez went on to designate freedom as a negative feature of the state of nature and natural law and hence negotiable. He declined to make it a necessary feature of all human political societies because, apparently, he wanted a theory that would accommodate to both the contemporary *status quo* and human history in general as he understood it. He accepted that monarchy was and had been the near-universal historical form of polity and that slavery had always been

---

155. Ibid. 6.4.13.
156. Ibid. 6.4.15–16.
157. Suárez, *De legibus* 3.2.3; *Defensio* 3.2.7. Cf. Sommerville, "Suárez to filmer," p. 528 and note 6.
158. Wilenius, *Social and Political Theory of Suárez*, p. 105.

legitimized in the law and accepted by Christian authorities. Whether he was simply unwilling to reverse the historical record and conventional Christian theology on the acceptance of slavery or because he was making at least a semiconscious effort to justify Spain's behaviour in the Americas, Suárez argued that freedom was a natural human characteristic but could be self-liquidated by personal choice: humans could legitimately choose to enslave themselves.[159] Thus began a theoretical debate on whether slavery is natural that continued in English-speaking circles into the mid-nineteenth century when John Stuart Mill gave it careful liberal examination, and it still echoes in the more strident contemporary exponents of natural rights and pure libertarian doctrine.

For his part, Suárez was still not finished with his emphasis on freedom as a natural human quality. He drew further entailments often spoken of today in terms of human rights: individuals can maintain and preserve their own life; they have a right to life and well-being; they can preserve their good name and reputation and have a right to honour and respect; an individual male has the right to take a wife; an unmarried woman has the right to her own freedom.[160] With one exception, however, these rights were alienable as negative features in human nature; they could be waived by any individual freely agreeing to do so. The right to life is the only exception. A gift from God, it is a positive human feature and cannot be relinquished even by an individual consenting to do so.[161]

---

159. Tuck has argued that Suárez extended the right of individuals to choose slavery to whole communities: *Natural Rights*, pp. 56–57. But Sommerville has shown that this misinterprets the Suárezian position: Suárez agreed that a community could cede its civil authority, but did not accept that it could give itself into slavery. Sommerville, "Suárez to Filmer," pp. 533–34. Hobbes argued that an individual could not alienate his own life without addressing directly the issue of whether he could alienate his own body as property into slavery. Hobbes, "Leviathan," in Molesworth, ed., *English Works*, 3:120, pp. 127–28. John Locke, for his part, held that "a man, not having the power of his own life, cannot, by compact, or his own consent, enslave himself to any one, nor put himself under the absolute, arbitrary power of another, to take away his life as he pleases." Locke, *Second Treatise of Government*, 4.23.

160. Suárez, "De opere sex dierum," *Opera omnia* 15.8.4.2, 15.8.4.10; *De legibus* 2.23.2; "De opere sex dierum," *Opera omnia* 15.1.1.14.

161. Suárez, "De opere sex dierum," *Opera omnia* 15.8.4.2. One might note how Locke, following in the same neo-scholastic and theological tradition as Suárez on this point, produced a view on the inalienability of human life consistent with other aspects of his doctrine, while Hobbes, opting for a "scientific" formulation, encountered difficulties of consistency when he also attempted to insist that an individual could defend his own life against the laws of the state. See Locke, *Second Treatise of Government*, 4.23; Hobbes, *Leviathan*, 2.21.

The state, however, has a rightful claim to the lives of its citizens in defence of the common good—citizens are obliged to defend their political community even at the cost of their lives.[162]

Suárez marked the highpoint of extensive and relatively sophisticated political theorizing among the Spanish neo-scholastics, a level not exceeded or, in most cases, even matched among later seventeenth-century Catholic thinkers. The historical and ideological dimensions of this enquiry focus next on the most disruptive feature in western European society in the sixteenth century and for some time to come: the Protestant Reformation.

---

162. Suárez, *Opuscula theologica* 6.4.6.

PART FOUR

# Emerging Rights as a Basis for Resisting Authority: Reformation Political Thought

## 1. INTRODUCTION

The fracturing of the unity of western Christendom in the early sixteenth century by the several distinguishable threads of the Reformation movement brought significant and lasting changes to the political and social map of western Europe, as well as to its theology, religious practices, and ecclesiastical institutions. That this monumental upheaval in the doctrine, structure, and institutions of the Christian church was to have a large-scale effect on the political thought of the period and on the subsequent history of Western political institutions, both secular and ecclesiastical, goes without saying.

The reasons behind the fracturing of western ecclesiastical unity into Roman Catholicism and the various branches of Protestantism are both too simple and too complex to require extensive presentation in a history of political thought. They fall roughly into two categories, theological and institutional, and these can be used as a frame of reference in describing Reformation influence on political thinking. As befitted religious reformers committed to the rejection both of specific religious doctrines and the institutional organization and behaviour of the Christian church in western Europe in the sixteenth century, men like Martin Luther, John Calvin, and England's Henry VIII criticized both current Christian theological doctrine and ecclesiastical practice. Dissatisfaction with the theological content and practice of the institutional church had been widespread in Europe throughout the fifteenth century, from the scandal of the Great Schism in the early years to the continuing and intensifying criticism of the widespread abuses of ecclesiastical authority, which, after the failure of the conciliar movement, remained unfinished business.

This last was the more immediate focus of the reformers' zeal. So intensive did their criticism become that excommunication was accepted, if not actually courted, in their assaults on the "unreformed" church. But their criticism extended to doctrinal theology as well, and the more substantive elements in the reformers' positions indeed were doctrinal or theological. Reformation political thought came in the first instance from these views. As with Christian political thought in general and earlier medieval theories of polity in particular, political thinking in the various groups of Protestant reformers rested on an essentially theological structure and various religious doctrines, most specifically a conception of the nature of God and His relationship with human beings, and the precise character of Christ's role in providing eternal salvation for individual human beings, who exist in a state of fallen nature as a result of Adam and Eve's commission of the Original Sin.

This does not mean that factual circumstances and concrete historical conditions played no part in the development of Reformation political thinking; such factors must always be taken into account. One of the most striking examples of this was Luther's volte-face concerning the legitimacy of active resistance against a persecuting secular ruler. Nevertheless, justification and rationalization in the political thought of the reformers always remained religious, and failure to appreciate this would seriously distort our understanding of their thought. A further useful division in Reformation political thinking that accommodates its three main currents—Lutheranism, Calvinism, and Anglicanism—will show that each made its own contribution, just as each was conditioned in its own way by the particular circumstances of its development.

One of the most remarkable features of the Reformation was the speed and extent of its spread over a large portion of western Europe. Historical hindsight marks its formal beginnings with the nailing of Luther's Ninety-five Theses on the church door of Wittenberg Castle in 1517. By the end of the century it had spread across much of northern and western Europe, producing in both political and social terms the most significant changes since the collapse of the Roman Empire in the fifth century. In less than a hundred years, Reformation theology, along with its political and social doctrines, had become officially recognized by secular rulers in Germany, England, and the Scandinavian countries and had been adopted by a large portion of the population and leading citizens in France and Holland. It was the moving force behind the tragic wars of religion in late sixteenth-century France and the equally tragic and seemingly interminable wars of the Spanish succession and the struggle for independence in the Benelux area. Finally, although the political ideology in play here owed more to late medieval and traditional Catholic formulations than to Reformation thought, it served at least as the original stimulus for the first wave of modern political revolutions in Holland, France, and England.

The fundamental ground chosen by Luther for rejecting traditional sixteenth-century Christian theological doctrine and its institutionalization through the Roman papacy involved a desire to return to what he considered a purer conception of the nature of God and His relationship with human beings through the redemptive actions of Jesus Christ. At stake was a conception of humankind after the Fall and a consequent conception of the nature and function of the Church in the religious task of salvation. When Luther challenged the behaviour and claims of the papacy, he recognized that his challenge entailed a rejection of the institutional church's self-image and role in the economy of Christian salvation. Quite simply, he would deny to the Church the role it claimed for itself and had assumed with increasing institutional centralization over the preceding centuries. At least in terms of doctrinal coherence and cogency, the success of his challenge depended on developing an alternative to the current ecclesiology favoured by the papacy and institutional church as a whole. This, in turn, required an alternative description of human beings in the state of fallen nature and of their personal relationship with God through Christ as Saviour.

In developing a Reformist theology, however, Luther was not working from a completely blank slate to produce a new doctrine *ex nihilo*; various threads had existed for some time in the Christian intellectual tradition from which new theological cloth could be manufactured. And one of the obvious explanations for the remarkable speed of Lutheranism in attracting followers was its founder's ability to blend into his new theological formulation attitudes and specific positions that already had widespread familiarity and acceptance. The most fundamental of the Lutheran theological concepts was the insufficiency of human nature in its post-lapsarian condition, insufficiency as regards even the possibility of achieving religious salvation through merely human or natural resources, or of such resources being able to make any contribution to this essential task.

The notion that human nature and behaviour were in themselves totally inadequate to the task of bridging the infinite gap between divine creator and limited human existence had always been an essential element in Christian doctrine, even without the additional view of human nature as further damaged by the effects of Original Sin. Luther was at one here with the whole of earlier orthodox Christian doctrine: salvation could not be achieved through human effort alone; eternal life in the presence of God, the destiny for which God had created human beings, was attainable only because God alone freely offered it to individual humans, who were completely unworthy of such largesse and themselves incapable of doing anything that could make them worthy. What was new in the Lutheran view was the heavy and seemingly unqualified emphasis placed on the radical character of human insufficiency with regard to the attainment of religious salvation and eternal life. Literally nothing any person could do was of the slightest value for achieving the purpose God had ordained for humankind. The gap between God and human beings was not only infinite and unbridgeable from the human side; it was not even possible for humans on their own either to understand or to appreciate their situation, or to make any purely human progress towards their proper goal. Human beings were incapable of knowing the divine mind or of coming to understand God's plan for them; nor could they do anything on their own to move along the road God had laid out for them. God's will as regards human salvation moved in totally incomprehensible ways; hence the only proper description of the human condition as perceived by humans themselves was of a completely helpless and hopeless lot. Humans saw themselves as commanded by God to seek an eternal goal beyond their powers and completely incomprehensible in terms of both its accessibility and its intelligibility.

The notion that humans could not understand the divine mind, that the ways of God were unknown and unknowable, did not come into being with Luther, of course. Nor was the concept of the divine will as unfathomable and hence, in some respect, as seemingly arbitrary in its behaviour when perceived from the limited and limiting perspectives of human intelligence.[1] It was the emphasis Luther gave these notions, however, that struck radical sparks and ignited the reformation in theology. He construed these basic Christian theological concepts to exclude any functional role in the religious economy of salvation for either individual or institutional structure, including the Church. Salvation was

---

1. Literature on the forerunners of the Lutheran "revolt" and the reformers' dependence on earlier Christian theology and discontent with the medieval institutional Church is extensive. See Iserloh, *The Theses Were Not Posted*; Dickens, *Reformation and Society*; Ozment, *Reformation in the Cities*; Oberman, *Harvest of Medieval Theology* and *Forerunners of the Reformation*.

achieved by God alone; He provided saving grace to an individual whose sole access to this gift was by way of a comprehensive act of faith: no mediation from any other source was possible or necessary. No place existed in the divine plan of salvation, then, for an institutional church, a priestly hierarchy or a clerical class. The Church was not even an institution but merely a grouping of individual believers, a *congregatio fidelium*. Each individual believer was equal to every other, each a priest in the sense that no real distinction existed between clerical and lay estates: a special category of Christian priests did not exist. Luther's concept of the "priesthood of the laity" captured the original purpose of Christianity as the true religion; the historical manifestation of a hierarchical institution that was organized and directed by a self-appointed superior category of clergy headed, in turn, by a pope who claimed absolute ecclesiastical authority over all Christians was simply a monstrous, even wilfully evil, appendage to authentic Christianity never envisaged by its founder.

The Lutheran conception of human nature as irremediably damaged by the effects of Original Sin was only a stark and in some sense rhetorical re-expression of the Augustinian view of human nature after the Fall, when its normal bent was towards things fleshly and material so that it required rigid control and divine aid to ensure that its higher, more spiritual aspects might function properly; left to their own devices, human beings were little more than cesspools of vice and corruption. This grossly oversimplified notion of the human condition had predominated in Christian theology for many centuries. But beginning in the late thirteenth century, it had gradually come to be supplanted by an alternative theory that was essentially Aristotelian in formulation. Aristotelianized Christian theology took the view that the human soul and body were natural, mutually reinforcing elements, rather than antithetical, and that rationality was the peculiarly human perfection. By using reason, humans could know themselves and their place in the divine scheme of things and even come to understand something of God's nature, at least by way of indirect, negative, or analogical knowledge, and also decide freely how best to live so that they would stay on the path to eternal fulfillment.

This is not to say that the Aristotelian view of human nature could have been received into Christian thought in its complete and exclusively philosophical integrity. Aristotelianism as a philosophy contained no doctrine of Original Sin; nor did it explicitly accommodate the notion of the harmful consequences for the entire human race of the Fall.

A tension always existed within Christian thought formulated in an Aristotelian frame of reference between certain Aristotelian views and the accepted contents of Christian revelation. The doctrine of Original Sin and its consequences on all humankind was a striking case in point, but by no means the only one; there were also the doctrines of creation, eternal salvation, and personal immortality. From the beginning of Aristotle's extensive impact on Christian thought in the thirteenth century, when much of the Aristotelian philosophical corpus and a significant portion of commentaries on it from Greek and Arabic sources came into the West, Christian religious authorities had felt sufficiently apprehensive about the potentially heretical character of Aristotle's thought to subject his writings to both censorship and ecclesiastical condemnation. Not even Thomas Aquinas, the most talented and enthusiastic Aristotelianizer among medieval Christian theologians, escaped censure on this score, though he was canonized by the Church less than fifty years after his death. In the final analysis, however, Aristotelianization of much of the traditional formulation of Christian theology took place before and despite the widespread condemnation imposed simultaneously at Paris and Oxford in 1277.[2]

The condemnations produced a substantial anti-Aristotelian backlash, the consequences of which yielded material that enjoyed considerable currency and ultimately influenced Luther's and other reformers' theology in identifiable ways. Two major thrusts are discernible among the more conservative theologians of the late thirteenth and early fourteenth centuries, who apprehended that adoption of an Aristotelian mode of thought could lead to unorthodox formulations of Christian doctrine. One was a de-emphasis on the presumed natural abilities of human reason to arrive at truth. Aristotle had emphasized the role of human understanding and came to be designated by medieval thinkers as "the Philosopher"; yet he espoused doctrines that were at odds with the revealed truths of the Christian religion. So much, then, for the vaunted abilities of reason to conform with the truths of the Christian faith; for example, the coordination of faith and reason could not be achieved in the optimistic manner described by Thomas Aquinas.[3] Nor was there warrant for accepting that the human intellect could demonstrate God's existence or identify His essential attributes; scepticism was

---

2. See Gilson, *Christian Philosophy in the Middle Ages*, pp. 402–10.
3. Thomas Aquinas *Summa contra gentiles* 1.1–8.

a much more realistic posture concerning the limits of certainty in the operation of the human mind.[4]

Closely related to this was a second area of reaction against Aristotelian views about the operations of natural objects, including human beings. Aristotle's natural philosophy gave a particular thrust to the doctrine of natural law, according to which human beings possessed a specific nature of their own that was characterized by rationality and permitted them to situate themselves *vis-à-vis* the universe as a whole. In virtue of their ability to understand the things of nature and the interrelationship or pattern in the universe as a whole, humans could make their own behaviour conform to the overall pattern. It was through reason that human beings discovered the truth of things and acquired insight, or moral knowledge, concerning their own proper behaviour. Thomas Aquinas's brilliant synthesis of this aspect of Aristotelian ethical thought and the traditional Christian concept of divine law produced a theory of law that combined Aristotelian and Christian notions in a form that still survives in the Catholic Christian intellectual tradition.

The possibility that knowledge of nature and God and of natural and divine laws could be accessible to human reason came under question in the aftermath of the late thirteenth century ecclesiastical condemnations of heresies allegedly found in Aristotle. And while the Aristotelian form of scholasticism continued to dominate in major university centres such as Paris and Oxford, new currents of philosophical and theological thought were also established, and much of the pre-condemnation scholastic *via antiqua*, as it was known in the fourteenth century, came under increasing challenge from the *via moderna*, whose principal spokesman was William of Ockham.[5]

A number of *via moderna* attitudes foreshadowed Lutheran doctrines that became foundation stones for Reformation theology. Evolved specifically in reaction to the Aristotelian/Thomist emphasis on the abili-

---

4. Cf. Gilson, *Christian Philosophy in the Middle Ages*, pp. 438; 464–65; 470; 498; 528; and Leff, "The Fourteenth Century." The Gilson interpretation of the late Middle Ages as characterized by scepticism regarding the natural ability of the human reason, voluntarism, and a general intellectual decline has been challenged recently by several varying interpretations. See Ozment, *Reformation in the Cities*, pp. 2–5.

5. The thought of William of Ockham has undergone considerable revisionist interpretation in the last quarter-century, chiefly as the result of the pioneering work of Philotheus Boehner. See Boehner, *Collected Articles on Ockham*. On Ockham's nominalism as a forerunner to Lutheran theology see Oberman, *Harvest of Medieval Theology*; "From Ockham to Luther"; "Shape of Late Medieval Thought."

ties of human reason and its natural correspondence with religious faith, the new intellectual fashion stressed the dichotomy, or implied contradiction, between faith and reason. A series of distinguished followers of the new learning taught at Paris during the fourteenth century, including Robert Holcot, Gregory of Rimini, Pierre d'Ailly, and Jean Gerson, the last two of whom, as shown earlier, were prominent in the conciliar movement.[6] A fresh flowering of *via moderna* criticism directed at late scholastic retention of Aristotelianism also occurred in the late 1400s, again at Paris, when John Major, mentioned before as a late conciliarist,[7] and Gabriel Biel (1410–95) stimulated a brilliantly effective revival of Ockhamist thought and style and won a host of followers. This late fifteenth century revival of Ockhamism, as already mentioned, was followed shortly in Paris by a new wave of neo-scholasticism that led to the flowering of Spanish neo-scholasticism in the sixteenth century.

Gabriel Biel was the link between *via moderna* theological thought and Lutheranism. Interrupting a successful academic career in Paris to join the Brethren of the Common Life, Biel later taught at the newly established University of Tübingen just a generation before Luther studied theology. Luther was formally exposed to the *via moderna* during his own university studies from 1501–5 at Erfurt, where he was taught by two Biel disciples, Jodorus Trutveller and Arnold von Usinger.[8] On several theological issues, one being how humans understand God, Biel and his followers took a position strikingly similar to Lutheran Reformation theology. This can be seen, for example, in *Eternal Predestination and its Execution in Time* by Johann von Staupitz (1468–1524), who was taught at Tübingen by several disciples of Biel from 1497–1500. The treatise depicts an omnipotent God whose will is essentially inscrutable and whose activity in this world is constant but apparently arbitrary, at least in the sense that it is inscrutable to humans. God is "of infinite power and majesty [but] His wisdom is unfathomable ... knowledge fails and scientific proof is out of the question as regards understanding his ways."[9]

Von Staupitz also enquired into the efficacy of human behaviour in the economy of personal salvation and rendered a totally negative judgment: "Man's nature is incapable of knowing or wishing or doing good."

6. Cf. *supra*, pp. 76–94.
7. *Supra*, pp. 109–14.
8. Oberman, *Harvest of Medieval Theology*, pp. 9–19.
9. Staupitz, *Eternal Predestination*, pp. 177–78.

A person is saved "due to grace and not nature: let no one pride themself that they are enrolled among the faithful from any of their own merits; and let no one claim for nature what properly belongs to grace."[10] Biel had made similarly clear statements.[11] Both Biel and von Staupitz remained orthodox, however, and differed sharply from Luther regarding the limited value of human freedom in attaining salvation. As already noted, traditional Christian theology had always accepted that salvation could be effected ultimately only by divine action, but it also stressed freedom as a characteristic of genuine human behaviour, enabling individuals to participate in the process of eternal salvation by choosing freely to conform to God's will. Luther, on the other hand, held that humans were incapable of doing anything that would make them worthy of eternal life.[12]

The immediate context for Luther's revolt was directed at longstanding abuses in the institutional church, of which the sale of indulgences was a particularly blatant example. The vices of simony and nepotism in ecclesiastical administration, the generally worldly activities and outlook of the Church hierarchy—especially the papacy and curial establishment in Rome—the sexual behaviour of so many avowedly celibate clergy, and the widespread ignorance of Church doctrine and orthodox practice among the pastoral clergy had also been widely and volubly criticized for many decades. The need for serious and sustained reform of both clerical life and education and papal administrative and financial practices had been on the Church's own agenda for more than a century, going back as far as efforts to resolve the Great Schism. General church councils at Constance and Basle had both intended to engage in church reform, but the extended disputes between pope and conciliar forces at these councils left insufficient time and energy to address what in many ways was the more mortal disease from which the institutional church was suffering at the time. The ultimate defeat of the conciliar party at Basle and the return of practical ecclesiastical hegemony to the papacy led, for the most part, to a return to curial business as usual; but the level of criticism directed at continuing abuses in the Church rose steadily.

10 Ibid., p. 178.
11. Biel, "Circumcision of the Lord," in Oberman, ed., *Forerunners of the Reformation*, pp. 167–70.
12. See Vignaux, *Justification et prédestination au XIV$^e$ siècle*; "On Luther and Ockham," pp. 107–18.

One source of criticism was quattrocento humanism, which displayed the same sort of disaffection expressed later in Luther and the other reformers. Many distinguished humanists were strongly attracted to Luther's cause as soon as he launched his 1517 attack on indulgences. In Germany, especially, but also in France,[13] a number of prominent intellectuals gave public support to Luther's call for reform. Among these were Willibald Pirkheimer and Jacob Wimpfeling, two leading humanists, and Crotus Rubianus, rector of Luther's university at Erfurt, who even gave an official reception when Luther passed through Erfurt in 1520 on his way to the Diet of Worms. These three men all ultimately remained in or returned to the traditional church, but their initial endorsement of Luther's criticisms of church behaviour showed the level of support he had won. Some prominent humanists, particularly in Germany, also joined Luther in breaking decisively with the Church of Rome. The most important was Philippe Melanchthon (1496–1540), who had come under Luther's influence at Wittenberg, where he was appointed to the chair of Greek language and literature, and immediately converted to the Reformed religion in 1518. Several prominent humanists in the Scandinavian countries and England did the same.

Luther, of course, denounced the early sixteenth century church for more than the behaviour of its clerical hierarchy and the money-grubbing practices of the papacy. He mounted an assault on the hierarchical structure of the Church itself, and on the doctrine of papal supremacy and ecclesiastical monarchy that had reasserted itself with increased vigour after the eclipse of the conciliar movement. On these issues too he found many supporters both inside and outside the Church, especially among members of the hierarchy and in university centres, and among the laity, particularly those in positions of secular temporal authority. To give this a context,[14] it is necessary to bear in mind the conciliarist conception of the pope as administrator, essentially, of the ultimate ecclesiastical corporation and hence simply a representative of the whole Christian people, the *congregatio* or *corporatio fidelium*, through whose consent he comes originally into office, and the continuation of this current of legal and theological thought into the second half of the fifteenth century after Basle, particularly at the University of Paris with Major and Buchanan.

13. Skinner, *Foundations*, 2:30.
14. Cf. *supra*, Part Three, *passim*. It should also be recalled that Luther appealed twice to the possibility of a general council resolving his differences with the papacy, first in 1518 and again in 1520, though neither came to anything.

## 2. MARTIN LUTHER

As a "reformed" Christianity, Lutheranism formulated a political theory almost as quickly as it did a theology. Only a few years after its founder nailed his theses to the Wittenberg church door, treatises containing political thought were published by Luther himself as well as several of his principal followers, specifically Melanchthon and Eberlin von Gunsburg.[15] In 1521 Eberlin produced *The Fifteen Confederates*, a tract in German treating the relations between the Reformed religion and political authorities, and Melanchthon published an important treatise on "worldly authority" as the final section of his *Common Topics in Theology* in the same year.[16] Similar Reformation political writings appeared shortly thereafter in England, where William Tyndale and Robert Barnes, both of whom had studied in Wittenberg in the early 1520s and become converts to Lutheranism, published tracts presenting their newly acquired theological views. Tyndale's major work, *The Obedience of a Christian Man*, appeared in 1528,[17] while Barnes published several important political tracts in 1529, among them *What the Church Is* and *Men's Constitutions*.[18] Luther's own early political writings include the explicitly political tract *Temporal Authority: to what Extent It Should Be Obeyed* (1523) and an earlier, more theological work containing explicit social and political implications, the *Address to the Christian Nobility of the German Nation* (1520). A later ecclesiological work, *On the Councils of the Church* (1539), also contained political material.

The fundamental expression of Lutheran political thought came from Luther himself, and is found in the first instance in his theological writings. The works of his followers, particularly those produced during the first decade of the Reformed religion, were in many respects simply glosses on Luther's original texts. As noted earlier, when Luther took his formal stand against the existing church, its hierarchy, and institutions, he produced a theology that offered different conceptions of the human condition in this world and the individual's relation to God as regards religious salvation, and a different notion of the Church and its place in this world. The effect, particularly of the Lutheran notions of the

---

15. Melanchthon is treated separately, *infra*, pp. 211; 214–15.
16. Cf. *infra*, p. 250.
17. Tyndale, *Obedience of a Christian Man*, pp. 127–344.
18. Barnes, *What the Church is and Who be Thereof*, pp. 37–52; *Men's Constitutions not grounded in Scripture*, pp. 81–93.

Church and of Christianity itself, was a complete rejection of the hierarchical and institutional structures of medieval Christianity and out-of-hand denial of the legitimacy of the traditional notions of clergy as enjoying a special status, and of the Church as a mediating entity between God and individual Christians. The centuries-old conception of *sacerdotium* as an institutional reality established by Christ as a necessary mediating device between God and human beings was dismissed.

Luther viewed the Church as a simple *congregatio fidelium*, with no essential hierarchical structure or institutional juridical authority. For him the word *ecclesia*, habitually used in Christian texts to designate the early church, meant simply a congregation or gathering of the faithful; it bore none of the connotations that tended to justify the historical development of a large-scale institution with pretensions to universal juridical authority over the lives of all believers. Similarly, the word *presbyter* connoted only an elder in the Christian community, not a special class of Christians whose superior status was the basis for claiming immunity from all forms of temporal jurisdiction, developing a distinct and comprehensive set of laws, and establishing a visible and distinct jurisdiction side by side with ordinary political societies while claiming universal jurisdiction over them. For Luther, quite simply, the institutional church and its clergy, with their separate and superior status and hierarchical structure, were a travesty on Christ's original intent to provide the means of salvation for individual human beings.

The profound implications of this Reformed theology for political theory were expressed directly by the reformers themselves. Luther denied that the institutional church had any Scriptural warrant for its existence; neither had the papacy nor other curial aspects of the Roman church. The whole intricate structure of claims behind the traditional notion of *sacerdotium* was, as far as Luther was concerned, a perversion of Christ's divine plan for salvation, and should be eliminated. Claims by the institutional church for independent and superior status *vis-à-vis* political authority were false. As members of political society Christians had only the same rights as every other citizen, Christian believer or not. The proper view of how Christians were to act in temporal society was to be found in the Scriptures—the only source for correct teaching on any subject—and primarily in the texts of St Paul. All authority, including political authority, comes from God, and Christians must be subject to this authority. Other Scriptural authorities such as 1 Peter 2 and the Fourth Commandment, which was always construed as applying to all forms of authority,[19] were invoked to reinforce this view. Luther referred constantly to Paul's injunction at the beginning of chapter 13 of the Epistle to the Romans that Christians submit themselves to the higher powers and treat all such powers as ordained by God, thereby making this text the single most important authority in Reformation political thought.[20]

From its earliest formulation, Lutheran political thought marked a return to the simple early church views expressed so authoritatively in the Augustinian interpretation of the relevant Pauline texts. Luther saw himself as a political thinker of significant stature: "No other teacher has written so nobly or so usefully about temporal government since the time of the Apostles, unless it be St Augustine."[21] By this he meant that his political thought was a deliberate offshoot of his return to the Christian Scriptures and flowed expressly from his theology and ethical teachings. His first specifically political tract, *Secular Authority: to What Extent it Should be Obeyed* (1523), set out many of the principles that dominated his political thinking throughout the 1520s. A fundamental feature was his teaching concerning the two states or spheres of authority (*zwei-reiche* or *zwei-regimente*), the basic frame of reference for his theory of polity as a whole. Christians had a moral obligation to obey their political superiors; disobedience was sinful and active resistance utterly forbidden. The reformers generally elaborated on this injunction by maintaining that worldly authority was simply one aspect of the order God imposed on His creation. For example, Melanchthon began his account of temporal authority in *Common Topics in Theology* by noting the

---

19. Cargill Thompson, *Political Thought of Luther*, p. 94. This manuscript was published posthumously from notes made by Cargill Thompson before his untimely death. See also his *Studies in the Reformation*.

20. "Luther's influence helped to make this the most cited of all texts on the foundations of political life throughout the age of the Reformation, and it furnishes the basis for the whole of his argument in the tract on *Temporal Authority* [1523]. The text here begins with an insistence that "we must provide a sound basis for the civil law" and goes on to identify this basis as the Pauline injunction, "Let every soul be subject to the governing authority, for there is no authority except from God." Skinner, *Foundations*, 2:15–16. The citation from Luther is Martin Luther, "Temporal Authority," trans. Schindel, in *Luther's Works*, ed. Lehmann and Pelikan, 45:85. Cf. Melanchthon, "Commentarii in epistolam Pauli ad Romanos," in Melanchthoñ, *Opera omnia*, 15:326–27; cf. also Barnes, at the beginning of *Men's Constitutions*, and Tyndale, at the beginning of *Obedience of a Christian Man*.

21. Luther, *On the War against the Turks*, cited in Cargill Thompson, *Political Thought of Luther*, p. 1.

"order and works" decreed for the protection and maintenance of this life;"[22] Tyndale opened *The Obedience of a Christian Man* by praising the order of God's creation and compared the obedience subjects owe their rulers with the obedience God enjoins on children towards parents, wives towards husbands, and servants towards their masters.[23] Similar Lutheran writings offer the same fundamental conclusion: existing political systems must be accepted as part of God's providential plan for the world.

This theory of temporal polity clearly inclined, at least by logical implication, towards "divine right of kingship" claims and support for absolute monarchy, though Luther was explicit on neither position. He never articulated a divine right theory; nor did he expressly favour monarchy over other forms of government. Like so many other Christian theologians, Luther was not interested in formulating political theory as such, and he produced a political doctrine only as a logical extension of his theology and ecclesiology. That is, while recognizing the need to formulate something in the way of political thought as a response to the political consequences of his Reform movement, he cast this response, particularly in the early phase between 1517 and about 1530, in the form of conclusions that flow from a literal acceptance of the Christian Scriptures. The result was some form of political theory, to be sure, but not one at all attuned to the conceptual problems integral to that subject, and much less to the political realities that Luther and his followers soon confronted.

Luther and his followers, along with other reformers, were not unaware of certain obvious implications and difficulties of a literal insistence on a Scripture-based obligation for Christians to obey political authority. Nonetheless, his views on the nature of political society and its authority developed from his wish to excoriate the contemporary institutional church as a juridical institution, and to leave no place for claims by the Church to exercise jurisdiction in the temporal sphere. As always, when moved by his own perception of the scandals and illegitimacy of current church doctrine and behaviour, Luther tended to express his Reformist position in strident and immoderate terms. If there was no place in the temporal world for a "visible" church, if the whole notion of a "visible" ecclesiastical jurisdiction was anti-Christian and the work of the Devil, then the whole of the temporal sphere, including the com-

---

22. Melanchthon, *Melanchthon on Christian Doctrine*, pp. 323–24.
23. Tyndale, *Obedience of a Christian Man*, pp. 168–73.

plete regulation of the Church itself and individual Christians as subjects, fell under the jurisdiction of existing temporal powers. Without acknowledging it, and perhaps without being consciously aware of it, Luther adopted a general principle urged two centuries earlier by Marsilius of Padua concerning the role of temporal power over both church and clergy. Few temporal rulers of the Reformation era were long in urging precisely this view themselves.

Again, however, Luther accepted certain implications of his view of political authority as part of God's providential plan: what if the ruler were a tyrant; what if Christian subjects were obliged by political authority to act in ways inconsistent with, or contrary, to their Christian beliefs? Here Luther and his followers again returned to the early Christian position, specifically that of St Augustine. It must be accepted that tyrants could and did exist; but it must also be accepted that tyrants derive their authority from God, at least in the sense that God allows them to exercise jurisdiction. Accordingly, the authority even of tyrants obliges all subjects generally to obedience, although Christians are neither obliged nor even permitted to engage in behaviour that is clearly contrary to God's law and the tenets of the Christian religion. Christians commanded by political authority to engage in this kind of activity must refuse to obey, but must accept the consequences of doing so with Christian resignation and humility.

Though obliged to disobey a ruler who would require behaviour contrary to the law of God, under no circumstances were Christians to offer active resistance to temporal authority, even that of a tyrant: to do so would vitiate the principle that all authority is from God and constitute an evil committed against God Himself. The contrast between the duty of disobedience and that of non-resistance to tyranny was clearly expressed in the central section of Luther's early tract on *Temporal Authority* (1523). If a ruler commands a subject to do evil, the subject must refuse: "It is not fitting for Lucifer to sit beside God." If consequently, however, the disobedient subject has "your [*sic*] property seized on account of this and [is punished] for such disobedience ... [you must submit passively and] thank God you are worthy to suffer for the sake of the Divine word. [We must never] sanction [tyranny], or lift a little finger to conform, or obey ... [nonetheless, tyranny] is not to be resisted but endured."[24]

Luther's early followers such as Melanchthon, Barnes, and Tyndale

---

24. Luther, "Temporal Authority," trans. Schindel, in *Luther's Works*, ed. Lehmann and Pelikan, 45:112.

expressed the same doctrine. After asserting the Pauline view that all authority comes from God, the first question for each of them was what the subject's obligation to obey entailed. They all gave the same decisive answer as Luther. For Melanchthon, "a member of Christ [should not use] the authority of government [without realizing that to do so involves] works that are against God ... Obedience is necessary ... disobedience hurts the conscience ... and God condemns it."[25] For Barnes, in *Men's Constitutions*: "We must be obedient to this power in all things that pertain to the ministration of this present life and of the commonwealth ... [not only] for avoiding punishment [but also] for conscience's sake, for this is the will of God."[26] If a ruler "tyrannically makes any command contrary to right and law [all a Christian may do is] only flee or else obey the thing that is commanded you ... in no case may you resist with sword and hand."[27] Tyndale makes the same point, insisting with St Paul that to fight one's superiors is equivalent to fighting God; he illustrates his conclusions by referring to Biblical incidents where resistance to authority was always evil and never legitimate.[28]

There has been considerable scholarly controversy, recently, over the meaning of Luther's basic *zwei-reiche* view; but it seems basically Augustinian in origin and reflects the "two-cities" motif of Augustine's *City of God*, a formulation not without conflicting interpretations of its own.[29] Luther followed the two-cities model explicitly and carefully, distinguishing with Augustine between the states (cities) of God and the Devil, and he constantly employed this language to describe the interweaving of the two. Ambiguities similar to those found in *City of God* are the result, along with difficulties that stem from a sometimes oversimplified identification of the city of the Devil with temporal polity. He even speaks of it being the Devil's task to confuse the two states and sometimes identifies the papacy as the agency in this diabolical task.[30]

Luther's basic theme here was the Gospel text "My kingdom is not of this world," from which it follows that there are two radically dissimilar "kingdoms." But in fact, since one designates political society or the state, the two kingdoms could be said to differ even in kind. God estab-

---

25. Melanchthon, *Melanchthon on Christian Doctrine*, p. 334.
26. Barnes, *Men's Constitutions*, p. 81.
27. Ibid., pp. 81–82.
28. Tyndale, *Obedience of a Christian Man*, pp. 175–78.
29. On the various interpretations of the Augustinian "two cities" concept see Gilson, *Les métamorphoses de la cité de Dieu*; English translation in "Introduction" to St Augustine, *City of God*. On Luther's doctrine see Cargill Thompson, "The 'Two Kingdoms' ".
30. Cargill Thompson, *Political Thought of Luther*, p. 48.

lished two realms for humans to inhabit, each corresponding to one of the two aspects of human nature: a spiritual order where individual human beings enjoy a relationship solely with God, the realm or sphere of salvation; and a material or worldly order, the natural realm of political society, in which life is lived according to the flesh and people do not exist on their own but enjoy relations with others. Further, God established two forms of government in this world to correspond to the two states: a spiritual government relating to the order of salvation, and a temporal order to deal with material things, each of these two states or kingdoms (*reichs, regiments*) being the antithesis of the other.

For Luther, the relationship between the two kingdoms was parallel rather than hierarchical, echoing the relation between *regnum* and *sacerdotium* in traditional medieval thought. The Lutheran conception of the two kingdoms placed the temporal on roughly the same plane as the spiritual *vis-à-vis* the divine: the temporal was not subordinated to the spiritual. John of Paris had also held that one sphere was not subordinate to the other; but for him this meant that the temporal did not receive its authority from God by way of the spiritual: each received authority directly from God.[31] Quidort, however, explicitly maintained the superiority of the spiritual over the temporal. Luther did as well, of course, but this was obscured by the particular emphasis he and his followers placed on the notion that the authority of political rulers came directly from God, and by his categorical rejection of separate ecclesiastical juridical authority and of the Church's institutional reality. However, one should not draw too sharp a distinction between Lutheran ecclesiology and medieval conceptions of the relation of church and state. For the reformers had the same problem on this point as all Christian thinkers: how to balance the view that the spiritual and temporal spheres are distinct with the contention, integral to Christianity and other religions with a doctrine of eternal salvation, that the order of the spiritual is superior to the material or temporal. Simply to insist that the two are distinct, as Luther did, does not really address the basic problem in political theory. The issue is not distinctness so much as the relationship between the two spheres. Straightforward repetition of the view that they are not the same tends to obscure and suppress the crucial issue of the precise nature of their relationship.

Luther pursued the contrast between the two parallel spheres or "regiments" by applying a standard medieval ethical and canonical distinction between internal and external forums (*forum internum, forum*

---

31. John of Paris, *Royal and Papal Power* 5, p. 20.

*externum*), although he would have been unlikely to acknowledge that he was borrowing from ecclesiastical legalists, whom he considered to be a particularly baneful class of clerical charlatans. Righteousness is interior in the spiritual "regiment" and exterior in the temporal sphere; in the latter, it is a righteousness of action or physical behaviour whose purpose is external peace, the absence of physical conflict among human beings. This sort of peace requires conformity or obedience to a given rule of behaviour that specifically enjoins humans from performing evil acts: evil action fractures peace in the external forum of political society.

God has provided for the external form of righteousness through the institution of political authority, with its requisite sword for enforcing obedience through physical coercion. Luther was again using concepts and language that were thoroughly familiar to medieval theorists of polity: the temporal state has the sword of physical coercion at its disposal, while the spiritual polity has only instruments of spiritual coercion applicable to the internal forum. Applying the age-old two-swords motif, Luther asserted that both were established by God, but were independent of one another. Further, human behaviour in the external, political sphere achieves righteousness through the use of reason, temporal righteousness being largely synonymous with the precepts of the natural law implanted in the hearts of all. Following Augustine, Luther conceded the existence of natural law "in the hearts of humans"; but also like Augustine, he was not sanguine about the ability of individuals who were morally disoriented by the effects of Original Sin to act rationally on their own. Coercive power is an essential feature of political authority because the majority of individuals, even the majority of Christian believers, are not true Christians and will not behave in a manner consistent with true righteousness unless compelled to do so: human beings in general must be compelled to avoid sin. Temporal coercive power, the essence of political authority, exists "to prevent men from tearing one another to pieces like wild beasts."[32] The thought is originally Marsilian, while the language is a vivid anticipation of Hobbes.[33]

Temporal authority, however, is not authorized to coerce the spiritual individual; it has no powers of spiritual coercion at its disposal, nor is it entitled to employ temporal coercive authority to lay down laws in matters of religion. Nonetheless, like Calvin, Luther had no compunction about assigning responsibility for establishing and protecting the "true"

32. Cargill Thompson, *Political Thought of Luther*, p. 47.
33. Marsilius of Padua, *Defensor pacis*, 1.10.4; cf. Thomas Hobbes, *Leviathan*, 1.13.

religion to temporal authority, even though he did not directly address the issue of how to correlate this view with his insistence that political rulers operated only in the "external forum." This is not to say that he could not have done so. Secular authority extended only to physical life and property;[34] its behaviour was limited by the rules of reason and the natural law, and the criteria for identifying tyranny in the exercise of political power were the same for Luther as for all other Christian political thinkers. He also contended that rulers were bound, for the most part, to follow the laws and customs of their own territories.[35] His acceptance of the natural law, however, was more limited than that found in traditional medieval and contemporary Spanish neo-scholastic political thought and was clearly related to his doctrine of the two "kingdoms." The temporal sphere is governed by the natural law and reason, reinforced in a practical and necessary way by the divine law found in the Scriptures, and especially in the Decalogue. Again, the theory is familiar: the natural law is the universal moral code imposed by God on all human beings; it is present in the hearts of individuals and accessible by the exercise of reason. But because reason is imperfect in the majority of people, God has spelled out his law in Scripture.

As already noted, the Christian's obligation is to obey legitimate political authority as instituted by God. The divinity exercises jurisdiction through temporal rulers, who are thus, in a sense, gods as well: their rule is divine.[36] Luther could be fulsome about the implied legitimacy of any action by a temporal ruler, seeming to sanction any behaviour on the part of king or prince. This attitude explains his unqualified opposition, before 1530, to any theory of resistance to temporal authority. He was well aware, however, of the tendency to tyranny and sin among persons exercising power of any kind and was not at all confident that it could be avoided. For all his insistence on citizens' obligations to obedience, Luther was no real admirer of rulers as a group; he maintained that, in practice, leaders of political societies were usually "consummate fools" and the worst scoundrels on earth.[37] He also stressed the traditional Christian and classical Greek view of the legitimate exercise of authority, that its purpose was to serve the good of the whole society and not merely that of the ruler. He set the same limitations on the legitimate ex-

34. Cargill Thompson, *Political Thought of Luther*, p. 97.
35. Ibid., p. 69.
36. Ibid., p. 64.
37. Luther, *Temporal Authority*, pp. 106, 113.

ercise of political power as all earlier and later Christian thinkers: kings and princes may not act contrary either to the natural law or God's law as expressed in the Scriptures. He persisted, nonetheless, in the Augustinian notion that tyranny is a providential response to the sinfulness of subjects and identified only one limit on a subject's obligation to submit to injustice: Christians were obliged to disobey a law that would treat someone else unjustly, but they must suffer injustice towards themselves in patience.[38] Soldiers, for example, were not permitted to participate in an unjust war, although they were advised to follow orders where the justice or otherwise of a situation was unclear.[39]

Luther also repeated the late medieval view that coercion did not exist among human beings before the Fall, but came into being later when humans actually established political societies as they became more numerous and immorality more commonplace. He referred in this connection to Noah and the Flood, while also undoubtedly accepting the earlier view that a division of the earth's territory into at least the forerunners of separate political divisions and kingdoms had occurred among the sons of Adam.[40] He also considered all forms of polity to be God-given and made no choice among them as to which was best. Thus, he showed no particular preference for monarchy, although he accepted it as the conventional form throughout history. Luther never displayed any serious interest in political forms as such, probably because, for him, faults in a political society were caused by the sinfulness of individuals, not by political institutions themselves. In the final analysis, tyranny was to be left to God.[41]

38. Ibid., p. 112.
39. Luther, *Whether Soldiers, Too, Can be Saved*, passim. Cf. Cargill Thompson, *Political Thought of Luther*, p. 98.
40. Cargill Thompson, ibid., p. 67.
41. Clearly, then, Luther agreed substantially with many of the elements in contemporary neo-scholastic political thought: though monarchy was the *de facto* norm and historically favoured form of polity, it enjoyed no a priori superiority over other forms; rulers were to be obeyed but themselves had moral obligations to rule in ways consistent with the laws of God and nature. But because Luther and other continental reformers insisted at the beginning of their Reform political ideology that temporal power came directly from God, they were unable to give meaningful expression to the need for a means whereby a tyrannical ruler could be held to his obligations. The centuries-old concept of popular consent served Catholic political writers at least as a hook on which a general theory of the people's right to oppose tyranny could be hung, but because the concept of some form of political power vested in the people was seemingly antithetical to the Protestant view of the direct link between God and temporal ruler, it came only later into Reformation political thought.

Some of Luther's strongest statements of political doctrine are made in the context of his views on resistance to established authority. Initially, he was unequivocal in rejecting any possible ground for resistance to temporal authority: rebellion was the worst of social sins. His writings in direct response to the violent and ill-fated Peasant Revolt that broke out in Germany in 1524 contain shocking statements of disregard for ordinary human values and dignity. *Against the Robbing and Murdering Hordes of Peasants* (1525) was little more than an overwrought tirade against the rebels who had just won a short-run series of military clashes with government forces in Thuringia and were ravaging the countryside of southern Germany. Again, Luther took a simple stand on the Pauline command that "all persons must be subject to the governing authorities" and roundly condemned the peasants for ignoring this injunction: "[they] are now deliberately and violently breaking this oath of obedience [and this constitutes] a terrible and horrible sin [such that all] have abundantly merited death [and have already] forfeited body and soul."[42] Arguably, Luther was seriously concerned at the time lest his Reformed religion be linked with, or, worse yet, seen as a cause for, the disturbances taking place among the oppressed peasant population, and he appears to have been apoplectic in his desire to dissociate his doctrine from any support for armed revolt. Unquestionably, this attitude fuelled his strident criticism of the uprising. There had already been serious dissension among Lutheran reformers themselves on both theological and political issues, and some reformers who had come out with Luther against the established church had already broken with him because of his apparent willingness to support the political *status quo* by offering explicit theological support to political rulers of the day.

The emergence of several radical sects and variations on the Reform doctrine, Williams's "radical Reformation,"[43] were causing Luther and his supporters real concern, as other reformers quickly made new and more strident claims against the old religion. In 1521–22, quarrels broke out between orthodox Lutherans and the followers of Andreas Carstadt in Wittenberg, whom Luther derisively termed the Zwickau prophets. In 1521, Gabriel Zwilling, earlier one of Luther's close disciples, performed a more radical form of communion service at Christmas

---

42. Luther, "Against the Robbing and Murdering Hordes of Peasants," pp. 49–50.

43. G. H. Williams, *Radical Reformation*. Other important works on the more radical forms of Protestantism emerging at the time are Clasen, *Anabaptism*, and Rott and Verheus, eds., *Anabaptistes et dissidents*.

and shortly thereafter began an active campaign of iconoclasm. A radical evangelical group under Conrad Grebel emerged in Zurich as early as 1523 to challenge the city's Lutheran community, which was headed by Huldrich Zwingli, who himself had significant differences with Luther. Nicolas Storch and Thomas Müntzer attacked Lutheranism for being insufficiently Reformist: the latter produced a violently anti-Lutheran *Protestation* in 1524, and his *Sermons before the Princes*, written in the same year, attempted to enlist secular authority in support of a more radical Reformed religion; almost immediately Müntzer himself joined the peasant uprising.[44] Luther had reason, then, to feel more than a little embattled, given the swiftness and complexity of Reform developments more radical than his own, many of which aimed directly at social and political as well as religious changes.

Nonetheless, Luther's opposition to resistance against political authority probably owed more to his theological convictions than to immediate concerns about ecclesiastical or secular politics. His unqualified emphasis on the duty of nonresistance rested ultimately on the basic theological view that the entire existing social and political order directly reflected the divine will. In his 1525 tract *Whether Soldiers also can be Saved*, Luther insisted that the people must willingly "suffer everything that can happen [rather than] fight against your lord and tyrant." He argued the point first in practical terms: "It is easy to change a government, but difficult to get a better one; and there is danger that you will not." But in the final analysis, he claimed simply that established political authority rests "in the will and hand of God [hence] those who resist their rulers resist the ordinance of God."[45]

Recent scholarship has now established in some detail that Luther came to reject his early stand against the right of Christians to resist political authority. This change came about slowly during a ten-year period that began in 1530, with the abandonment by some of his immediate disciples, notably Melanchthon, of the original passive position. The principal factor in this change, not unnaturally, was the perceived need to respond to new political realities: the theory had to be adjusted, even radically revised, to accommodate new political circumstances. The issue of right to resistance has great significance for the general history of sixteenth-century political thought and its impact on later centuries. Contemporary debate on the subject led to the Calvinist doctrine of the

---

44. Skinner, *Foundations*, 2:75–76.
45. Luther, *Whether Soldiers, Too, Can be Saved*, pp. 112–13, 126.

right of lower magistrates—political and judicial officials—to resist their superiors, and ultimately to the notion that the people themselves, even as individuals, are entitled to resist tyranny. Resistance theory became, in the hands of Protestant reformers, what the doctrine of tyrannicide was in Catholic Counter-Reformation thought: the most dynamic extension of the general principle that political authority, when it exceeds the limits set by its purpose, can be opposed by those over whom it is exercised.

Ironically, Catholic and Protestant publicists at the time criticized one another's theoretical efforts to apply a principle they both accepted and did so without taking the trouble to acknowledge the ideological ground they held in common. Catholic Counter-Reformation writers like Suárez, Bellarmine, and Mariana continued to publish a carefully qualified case for tyrannicide—notwithstanding certain superficially clear but extremely oversimplified authoritative ecclesiastical condemnations of the act—while consistently excoriating Reformation thinkers for legitimizing resistance to established authority and thereby preaching sedition.[46] For their part, Protestant political writers roundly condemned Catholic publicists for advocating tyrannicide. Each criticized the other for promoting what they identified as the same basic error, that advocacy of direct action against existing political powers violated the injunction on Christians to obey political authority because it comes from God. Neither side seemed able to admit that the doctrines they condemned, Protestant resistance theory on the one hand and Catholic acceptance of tyrannicide on the other, both rested logically on a more general principle accepted by each: that there are limits to the legitimate exercise of even God-given authority and that, accordingly, an adequate political theory must incorporate and justify some practical procedure for responding to circumstances where the limit is exceeded.

A comprehensive theory of polity must provide its victims with a means of dealing with tyrannical excess. Of course, disagreement about the propriety of specific means of response is possible and even, practically speaking, inevitable. Resistance as armed and violent revolt against authority may be too radical to be morally defensible in every case, while a lesser form of resistance remains legitimate; similarly with tyrannicide, in its literal meaning of the violent taking of ruler's life by direct action. But the view that legitimate authority is intrinsically limited and that the people over whom it is exercised must therefore possess some means of

---

46. On the traditional justification for tyrannicide as expressed by sixteenth-century Spanish neo-scholastics, see *supra*, p. 166; 181–82.

reacting when its limits are exceeded entails the realization that an appropriate form of reaction must be specified in any acceptable political theory. Had Protestant and Catholic critics in the Counter-Reformation era been more interested in examining the conceptual structure and internal mechanisms of the others' political theories than in trying to score theological points against each other by citing general principles in largely rhetorical fashion, they might have seen how fundamentally similar their views were.

As already noted, Luther's original rejection of any active form of resistance to political authority led him to admonish the German peasantry for their revolt in 1525 by asserting that a Christian's duty was always to obey political superiors unless ordered to act contrary to the divine or natural law. In the latter circumstances, they were obliged to disobey and accept the consequences, but in no case were they to act directly against authority. He was equally explicit in applying this doctrine to individual princes and rulers who owed allegiance to the Holy Roman emperor: they had absolutely no rights of resistance.[47] This straightforward pacifist position had urgent practical significance for Luther and his followers. The very existence of Lutheranism as a Reformed religion was to be tested in the current context of the Holy Roman Empire, wherein Luther had sought protection under the elector John of Saxony. John himself was legally subject to the emperor Charles V, who in 1521 at the Diet of Worms had announced his intention of forcibly returning his Lutheran subjects to the unity of the Church. Hence the question of whether Luther's temporal protector had a right to resist his Catholic emperor's move to suppress the Lutheran "heresy" had an immediate and pressing context. In flatly rejecting resistance, Luther accepted two principles as basic to his general theology. Firstly, only spiritual means could be employed to address a spiritual problem—presumably, religious persecution as something essentially spiritual could only be opposed by a spiritual response such as prayer (and martyrdom?). Secondly, God would never allow religious tyranny to triumph. Allied with this second attitude was the notion that a Christian who used physical force to protect religious interests might lack faith in God.[48]

Luther made his first explicit response to the question of what a prince could do to protect members of the Reformed religion in the tract on *Secular Authority* (1523). Accepting that a ruler might defend his

---

47. Cargill Thompson, "Luther and Right of Resistance," p. 6.
48. Ibid., p. 13.

people if attacked by another prince whose intention was to suppress Lutheranism, he specifically denied that any prince had so much as a hypothetical right to resist such an attack from the emperor. Arguably, Luther's position was not so much a universal rejection of the use of arms to support the "true" religion—he clearly sanctioned force on grounds of self-defence—as a narrower claim that a ruler exercising political authority under *de iure* imperial jurisdiction could not act against that jurisdiction without violating his legal and moral obligations to obey. Hence his subsequent views on the legitimacy of resisting imperial efforts to suppress Protestantism represent less of a change of mind than might at first be thought. Luther repeated his opposition to a German prince's resisting the emperor in *Whether Soldiers also can be Saved*: it is always wrong for an inferior to take up arms against superiors, even if tyrants break oaths and contracts: only God can punish in these circumstances.[49]

The practical issue of defending Lutheran regions and their inhabitants against possible imperial Catholic military action did not disappear, of course. On 27 January 1530 his princely protector consulted Luther, along with Justus Jonas, Johann Begenhagen, and Melanchthon, on the precise question of whether the emperor might be resisted were he to attack the reformers while an appeal to a general church council was pending. An imperial move to suppress the Lutherans seemed imminent, since the emperor was apparently intent on applying the earlier resolution adopted at Worms. Luther's reply on his own and his colleagues' behalf was a long, carefully worded letter of 6 March 1530 that itemized answers to a series of specific issues. To the question whether the emperor could be resisted on the grounds that his behaviour violated the imperial oath of office, Luther answered no: Christians must accept tyrannical behaviour and take its consequences. To the argument that resistance could be justified by an appeal to the natural-law maxim *vis vi repellere licet* (it is licit to repel force with force), his reply again was negative: if the maxim held at all as public law, it only permitted hostilities between equals, and the emperor represented superior authority. He also rejected the argument that resistance was permissible pending appeal to a general church council and conceded only that the emperor might be deposed with the unanimous consent of the electors and estate.[50]

49. See ibid., pp. 13 and 15.
50. Ibid., pp. 21–23.

Seven months later, however, Luther signalled a change in position. The Catholic majority at the Augsburg diet held in mid-1530 had rejected the Augsburg Confession drawn up by Melanchthon in a last ditch effort to stave off an imperial military campaign, and had passed a resolution demanding that all Lutherans return to unity with Rome. The prospects of imperial military action now looked even more ominous. Again, the Lutheran divines were asked for their views on a specifically formulated set of issues, the formulation this time being the product of agreement at another, directly political, level. In attempting to promote a defensive alliance against the emperor among the German Protestant princes, Philip of Hesse had written to John of Saxony requesting his participation in a Protestant League against the emperor, and John had received an argument justifying resistance to imperial authority developed by his legal experts, chief among whom was his chancellor, Gregory Brück. This was an ingenious restatement of the feudal and particularist theory of empire employed by the electors to remove Emperor Wenzel in 1400. It made a case for resistance while also upholding the principle, insisted upon by Luther and other reformers, that all political power comes from God. The Pauline doctrine of obedience was construed to mean that all territorial sovereigns, hence all the princes and electors in the empire, possessed their authority directly from God rather than the emperor. Each of these sovereigns, it was then argued, had specific duties and obligations, any efforts to jeopardize which must be opposed by the territorial sovereign concerned. Since the general obligation on all rulers was to maintain the well-being and salvation of their immediate subjects, it followed clearly that the princes had a right to resist if and when the emperor interfered with their sovereign rights or their responsibilities to their own subjects, for by so doing the emperor violated the special obligations he accepted as a condition of his election.[51]

Luther's response to the particularities of this Hessian position appeared in what is known as the Torgau Declaration of October 1530. Philip of Hesse had sought the advice of a group of jurists and Lutheran theologians meeting at the Palace of Torgau from October 25–28 on a memorandum containing the Brück document's alleged grounds for re-

---

51. Brück, "Iudici procedenti iniuste an licitum sit resistere," pp. 3–6. At least in the sense that it went to the question of imperial legitimacy, the argument contained something of the notion of resistance considered earlier in terms of whether the emperor could be resisted for having violated his oath of office. Luther and his colleagues, it will be remembered, had rejected this argument only a few months earlier.

sisting the emperor. At the conclusion of this conference Luther issued a formal statement, written in his own hand and signed by Melanchthon, Jonas, Spalatin, and himself, withdrawing earlier opposition to armed resistance. Though the change in intellectual position between the Torgau statement and previous Lutheran texts may appear slight, it represented a crucial turning point in the development of Lutheran political thought, and its practical implications were significant in both the short and the long term. In effect, Luther and his fellow theologians withdrew their opposition to the use of force in resisting the emperor and conceded the right of inferior rulers (the princes) to act against him. They did so by announcing they would offer no theological argument against what seemed to have legal justification within the jurisdiction of the empire itself. The Torgau position turned on the argument that the emperor would be exceeding his own legal authority were he to act while a general church council was pending—ironically, one of the arguments explicitly rejected by Luther only a few months earlier. But the crucial aspect of Torgau was not that Luther and his fellow theologians agreed with the argument as made, but simply that they acknowledged that legal authorities had found it cogent and declared that they would not, as theologians, employ Scriptural arguments against it.[52] Here, seemingly, was a dramatic illustration of the two-regiments concept pressing its "never the twain shall meet" implication lest Lutheran political authorities be seen as violating their religious leader's formal interpretation of Christian Scripture, while simultaneously exposing the rational inadequacy, if not incoherence, of the excessive simplicity of that aspect of Lutheran political thought.

In the next few years, Luther and his followers went even further and accepted constitutional grounds on which the electors and princes of the empire could resist the emperor. By 1536, the natural-law argument used by Melanchthon as early as 1532 to justify the use of force to repel force in self-defence became part of the general Lutheran political doctrine,[53] and the Torgau position was completely superceded. In 1539, Luther again directly addressed the resistance issue in two documents that contained his most important personal statements on the subject. The first was a letter of 8 February to Johann Ludiche, and the second

52. Cargill Thompson, "Luther and Right of Resistance," p. 27.
53. Melanchthon, "Letter to Heinrich von Einseidel, July 8, 1532," in Melanchthon, *Opera omnia*, ed. C. G. Breschneider, vol. 2, n. 1066, col. 603–4. Cf. Skinner, *Foundations*, 2:202–3.

a set of theses prepared in April-May 1539 for the year's *Zirkulardisputation*. A new argument was used in both instances to justify armed resistance to the emperor, one not found at all in the 1536 theological opinion, much less in the earlier Torgau Declaration. It accepted a position developed by the propagandists of the Schmalkaldic League, that the emperor could be resisted on the grounds that he was an agent of the pope, *miles papae*. In taking over this argument, however, Luther added a new twist that changed its original legal character into a religious formulation of formidable rhetorical power: the pope was the anti-Christ of the Apocalypse.[54]

Having in a sense capitulated to the political and legal authorities of the German Lutheran princes in 1530, Luther began shortly thereafter to show signs of an actual acceptance of their arguments. Along with other Lutheran theologians, he also began to develop the private-law argument, formulated by Brück, of an individual's right to repel force with force. His 1531 reply to an accusation by Lazarus Spengler that he had "recanted his former opinion that resistance to the Emperor was wrong" reiterated Luther's acceptance of the view that imperial law itself legitimated resistance to the emperor in certain circumstances. Luther admitted in the same reply that he had not been impressed by the invocation of the dictum that force might always be repelled by force, but he did concede to "what the law commands," viz., that it would be legitimate "to resist [the emperor] by force."[55]

A short time later, in April 1531, Luther published his *Warning to My Dear German People*, which offered an even stronger acceptance of the private-law argument. His position was that Catholic authorities who would use force against Protestant believers could not be considered legitimate rulers. They would be acting unlawfully when using such unjust force, for "their plans are built exclusively on force and their cause relies on the power of the fist." The Catholic authorities, then, would be the real rebels, assassins, and traitors for refusing to submit to government and law, and "much closer to the name and quality which is termed rebellion" than the Protestants whom they so accuse.[56] Accordingly, "if war breaks out [Luther] will not reprove those who decide to resist these murderers and bloody papists ... [but will] accept such action and let it pass as self-defence."[57] Similar statements were expressed informally in

---

54. Cargill Thompson, "Luther and Right of Resistance," p. 38.
55. Skinner, *Foundations*, 2:201, citing Preserved Smith, *Life and Letters of Luther*, p. 217.
56. Luther, *Warning*, pp. 12, 16, 20.
57. Ibid., p. 19.

*Table Talk*: a magistrate who exceeds the bounds of his office automatically reduces himself to the status of an errant private citizen.[58] Leaving aside Luther's customary rhetoric, this was precisely the same argument used by civilian medieval jurists like Panormitanus when articulating the right of opposition to a tyrant, and by the medieval canonists and theologians who were trying to limit the powers of an errant pope or bishop. It was also found in the Spanish neo-scholastic delineation of the legitimacy of tyrannicide.[59] In 1539, Luther again cited the civil-law doctrine of the legitimacy of self-defence when replying in the affirmative to the question whether the emperor could be resisted on behalf of the Gospel.[60]

The first prominent Lutheran theologian to assert the constitutional theory of resistance seems to have been Andreas Osiander, the probable author of a letter addressed in 1529 to the city of Nuremberg in an attempt to have it join Philip of Hesse's proposed defensive alliance against the emperor. The letter accepted that the Pauline injunction in Romans 13 raised a serious objection to the alliance proposal, but went on to argue in the same vein as Philip's Hessian jurists: Paul meant his principle to apply only to magistrates who ruled justly, not to sinful magistrates. More significantly, the powers Paul said were "ordained of God" included "inferior" political rulers like princes and other local (municipal) authorities, as well as the emperor. Accordingly, lesser temporal rulers also had responsibilities to act, even against a higher authority (such as the emperor) that failed in its duties; they, too, were "no less ordained of God" to maintain good and godly government.[61]

Martin Bucer provided the main Lutheran expression of the constitutional argument for resistance, in his *Explication of the Four Gospels* and *Commentaries on the Book of Judges*. The first of these, published in 1527, advanced the constitutional view without reference to the right of resistance. The relevant passage appeared in the 1530 edition of the *Explication* and subsequently in the *Commentaries*, published in 1554. Bucer held that the Pauline injunction concerning the obligation to obey, while applying absolutely, fell only on private individuals as ordinary citizens: "Do not resist evil ... whatever harm is done ... never offer any resistance [is a rule that applies] in the case of private individuals."[62]

---

58. Skinner, *Foundations*, 2:202.
59. Cf. *supra*, pp. 166; 181–82.
60. Luther, "Colloquies," in *Colloquia, Meditationes, Consolationes*, 1:363–64.
61. Osiander, "Brief," 2:83–85; 85: cited in Skinner, *Foundations*, 2:204–5.
62. Bucer, *In sacra quattuor evangelica enarrationes perpetuae*, fol. 54a.

Persons in public office, on the other hand, had a quite different responsibility. He rejected categorically the position that God has "transformed all power [within a single kingdom] to a single man" and used Old Testament examples to show that "God always disperses power to many people," and specifically to sets of lower magistrates (*magistratus inferiores*), all of whom possess authority (*merum imperium*) and so can use the *ius gladii* on their own behalf.[63]

Further, validly authorized secular powers, all of which hold their authority "of God," each have specifically assigned tasks in the divine order of things. It is the prime duty of a Christian prince and magistrate to "study to live and rule according to the will of God in all things ... in order to preserve the people of God from evil and defend their safety and goods."[64] Except that he placed much greater emphasis on the need for Christian rulers to strengthen and defend the "true" religion, Bucer reflected the same view as the Hessian jurists; he was especially insistent that lower magistrates have this responsibility if and when a superior fails to implement it, except that again he placed greater emphasis on the need for Christian rulers to strengthen and defend the "true" religion. This is an echo, though not a very resonant one, of the more radical attitude, expressed by certain reformers in 1523 and 1524 and later by Calvin and Knox, that political leaders had a moral obligation to establish the Reformed religion in their territories.

As already noted, Melanchthon also came around to supporting resistance to imperial authority, accepting the legitimacy of the use of force in self-defence while continuing, in his *Commentaries on the Epistle of St Paul to the Romans* (1532), to uphold the unqualified character of the Pauline injunction. Later, in his 1539 treatise *The Office of the Prince (Officium principiis)*, he went so far as to assert that the Roman civil code (the *Digest*) accepted the private killing of a public official by a husband or father who found the official in bed with his wife or daughter, and he extended this to the parallel case of subjects defending themselves against a tyrannical ruler.[65] This treatise was the earliest expression of Melanchthon's changing view.

A more comprehensive statement of Melanchthon's support for resistance is found in the 1542 second edition of his *Prolegomena to Cicero's Treatise on Moral Obligation*, published originally in 1530. A new section

63. Ibid., fol. 54a–b; cf. *Commentarii in librum Judicum*, p. 488.
64. Bucer, *Enarrationes*, fols. 54b–55a.
65. Melanchthon, "Philosophiae moralis epitome," In Melanchthon, *Opera omnia*, 16:105.

on the office of magistrate examined the relationship between a political ruler and the Church, and considerable emphasis was placed on the view that private law affords the ordinary citizen a right to resist a tyrannical magistrate. Melanchthon remained aware, however, of the danger of seeming to afford to ordinary subjects too many rights to reject authority, and he maintained that "the dictum that it is permissible to repel force with force ... [applies always and only] to powers which have been ordained ... [so that] it is never permissible [for private individuals] to engage in acts of sedition."[66] Traditional medieval accounts of tyrannicide from John of Salisbury to Thomas Aquinas and later had always made the same distinction between private citizen and officeholder and restricted the legitimacy of tyrannicide to the latter, as did the Spanish neo-scholastics,[67] and the question whether individual citizens could be seen in any circumstances to have legitimate political authority to act in the public good against a tyrant remained open for Melanchthon, as it had for the medieval and scholastic writers.

Melanchthon was quite explicit, however, in his view that there were legitimate grounds for resistance and seems in at least one instance to concede this right to individuals. He implicitly invoked the natural-law concept of the instinct for self-preservation implanted by God, whereby individuals are moved to repel unjust violence: "natural knowledge ... the testimony God has given us for discriminating between justice and injustice ... Nature allows force to be repelled by force (*vis vi repellere natura concedit*) ... in any case of manifest injury which is both atrocious and notorious ... and if a magistrate fails in his office or begins to behave criminally, it must be lawful to repel this force [with] whatever help one can call on, or even with one's own hands."[68]

In this one instance at least, Lutheran political thought had come to terms with the legitimacy of resistance even before the Torgau Declaration of 1530. And while Luther's final personal doctrine showed a significant change over his pre-1530 views, some of his followers had been moving in this direction even before their leader's official turn-around. His own final doctrine showed a fusion of three arguments. The first, found more in the joint statements of the Lutheran divines than in Luther's personal writings, stressed that Christian magistrates have a duty to uphold true religion and suppress idolatry. The second was the

66. Melanchthon, "Prolegomena in de Officiis Ciceronis," in Melanchthon, *Opera omnia*, 16:573–74.
67. Cf. *supra*, pp. 181–82.
68. Melanchthon, ibid.

constitutional argument that the imperial electors and princes were not merely subordinates of the emperor but enjoyed some association with him in governing and hence had certain rights they could and must defend. The third justified resistance in the event that an emperor attacked the Protestant religion because he would be acting thus merely for the pope. As already shown, a combination of the first two views developed in secular legal circles under the encouragement of Philip of Hesse and expressed what became the standard mid-sixteenth-century Protestant resistance theory, the clearest expression of which was the Magdeburg Declaration of 1550. Calvin, Beza, and the English Marian exiles all put roughly the same argument later in the century, as did a number of Huguenot publicists. It has often been said that the doctrine originated with Calvin and the Genevan reformers in the 1560s. However, Calvinists were advocating it in the 1550s, and its original formulation lay with Lutheran thinkers in the 1530s and 1540s, and even earlier with the legal advisers of German Reformist princes. Luther ultimately accepted the general formulation and gave it his own anti-papal rhetorical twist.

Lutheran authorities, both spiritual and temporal, theologians and secular princes, gave strongest expression to their resistance doctrine after the outbreak of the Schmalkaldic War in 1546. They stressed the constitutional argument for resistance by lower magistrates while continuing to employ the private-law position developed by Brück and his associates in 1530. The former was obviously the more applicable and plausible in the face of imminent military action by the emperor. The most important restatement of the Lutheran position was the *Confession and Apology of the Pastors and Other Ministers of the Church at Magdeburg*, published in Latin and German by the pastors of that city on 13 April 1550, after Magdeburg had come under imperial siege for its armed resistance to the emperor Charles. The *Confession* also made use of the private-law argument, thus giving it, along with the so-called constitutional argument, an authoritative and cogent formulation in a document that was important, particularly as a public statement, in the transmission of Reformist resistance theory.[69]

69. The *Confession* was the only text to which John Knox made reference in his disputation with Lethington at the General Assembly of the Scottish Church in June, 1564: Ridley, *John Knox*, p. 437. Du Hames requested a copy of the *Confession* from Count Louis of Nassau, younger brother of the Prince of Orange, for use by the Huguenots in the Netherlands in 1566. Du Hames, "Letter to Count Louis of Nassau (February, 1566)," in *Archives ou correspondance inédite de la maison d'Orange-Nassau*, 2:34–38; cited in Skinner, *Foundations*, 2:210. Cf. pp. 207–10 and 217–19.

## 3. JOHN CALVIN

As a fundamental and early feature of the Reformation movement in sixteenth-century western Europe, Calvinism had a somewhat different impact than Lutheranism on both the contemporary sociopolitical landscape and the political thought of the period. Historians of Western political thought, even in recent work, have tended to approach this model of the Reformed religion almost exclusively in terms of its contribution to resistance theory. But this does not quite give the whole picture. It was Luther, not Calvin, who first threw down a fundamental challenge to the political *status quo*, rejecting both the practice and ideological foundations—theological, ecclesiological, and political—of the late medieval church and erecting an alternative theology and political ideology in their stead.

Reformist resistance theory offered a parallel case. It was developed initially by Lutheran political writers, as were a number of fundamental and general tenets of the Reformist theological dispensation such as the doctrine of salvation by faith alone; emphasis on the direct relationship between Christ the Saviour-God and individual Christians; corresponding notions of the Christian church as a simple *congregatio fidelium* and of believing Christians as their own *presbyters* (the priesthood of the faithful); and the correlative rejection both of the institutional church and papacy and of the notion that the clergy enjoyed a special status in temporal polities. Except for the doctrine of the priesthood of all believers, a position Calvin did not explicitly support,[70] these views were held commonly by Calvin and Luther. While first formulated in Luther's Reformist doctrine, they constituted the fundamental structure of Calvinist as well as Lutheran theology, and their theological formulation had certain implications for political theory, there was little difference between the basic outlines of Calvinist and Lutheran political thought.

An obvious example is the close similarity in early Lutheran and Calvinist writings on the obligations of Christian subjects towards political authority. Both streams were explicit and forceful in employing Romans 13 to stress the need for subjects to obey their political rulers, even tyrants. Both argued the need to give precedence to the laws of God

---

70. See Hopfl, *Christian Polity of Calvin*, pp. 35–36. Cf. pp. 59 and 252, n. 80. The Hopfl monograph is the best recent study of Calvin's political thought; it is particularly good in providing an analysis of the changing character of Calvin's political theory as it responded to the realities of his time. Cf. Hancock, *Calvin and Foundations of Modern Politics*.

and nature over positive human legislation, and, in their early teachings, both upheld an absolute proscription against active resistance to laws imposed by temporal authority: Christian subjects were not to obey laws that conflicted with divine and natural law, but they were obliged to suffer the consequences of disobedience with due Christian humility, accepting that even tyrants have a place in the divine plan as a form of punishment for the sinful. A resistance theory did soon replace the original pacifism among both Lutheran and Calvinist writers, but again, Calvinism followed rather than led. The obvious explanation for this was that the practical need for the Reformed religion to defend itself politically and militarily was first perceived by the Lutherans, and a little later by Calvin's followers in France. Calvinist advocacy of armed resistance had acquired a certain notoriety by the second half of the sixteenth century, but it came slightly later than and was influenced to some extent by the preceding Lutheran formulation, especially the Magdeburg Confession. There was also a general similarity between Lutheran and Calvinist thought on the relationship between church and state: the Church had no special juridical status in political society, and the primary responsibility for both the moral and material well-being of Christians, as well as for maintaining the "true" religion, lay with the "godly" civil ruler.

Calvin, however, did make a considerable contribution in his own right to the development of political thought and practice, especially the latter, as regards basic structure and operating procedure in a functioning temporal polity. While not primarily interested in political theory as such, his training both as a lawyer and a theologian motivated him to direct his reforming zeal in Geneva far more to the actual political and social implementation of the Reformed religion than Luther had done in Germany; Luther was first and foremost a theologian and purely religious reformer. But from inclination and opportunity alike, Calvin was able, in Geneva, to examine and implement his conception of the temporal functioning of a Christian community. Luther was often explicit about how political rulers should carry out their responsibilities and exercise relations with the Church; but largely because of the circumstances in which he found himself, he was satisfied to leave the implementation in the political sphere of his two-regiments doctrine to the German princes and nobles. Calvin, on the other hand, along with other Genevan Reform leaders, took an active role in constructing a political system and policies in Protestant Geneva, as did Zwingli in Zurich, and it is this intervention that largely accounts for the influence of the Calvinist Reformation on the history of political thought.

An essential feature of Calvin's sixteenth-century Geneva was its city-state character, which had developed over the medieval period from a type of polity familiar in the early Swiss cantons, a kind of direct democracy. Like many other medieval city-states, however, it had evolved quickly into a city-state type of aristocracy after throwing off domination by the dukes of Savoy while retaining a strictly technical status under the Holy Roman emperor, and its control rested in the hands of an oligarchy composed of merchants and nobles. In the late fifteenth century it was a kind of semi-ecclesiastical polity whose ultimate political and ecclesiastical authority rested in the hands of the local bishop, with temporal episcopal rule exercised for the most part through an appointed council to which the leading citizens would have had at least informal and advisory input. Neither an imperial free city nor a separate canton in the Helvetic Confederation, Geneva was of no great consequence at the beginning of the sixteenth century. Its autonomy was by no means traditional or well-established, resting as it did on the not entirely benign protection of Bern, which had aspired for some time to reduce Geneva to dependency status as a buffer between itself and Savoy territories. Its independence and political integrity were to undergo further development with the coming of the Reformation.

"Civic Protestantism" arose in the first half of the sixteenth century when a number of German, Swiss, and Scandinavian civic communities enjoying some form of political independence became caught up in the energy and religious changes of the Reformation. This was a form of government by representative councils roughly reflecting the civic counterpart of representative assemblies and institutions that had been common in many larger European jurisdictions during the fourteenth and fifteenth centuries. The ruling councils adopted a form of the Reformed religion and imposed it in various ways on their citizens and community members. Principal among the municipal jurisdictions opting for the Reformed religion were Zurich under Zwingli in the early 1520s, followed in very short order by Strasbourg under Bucer and Geneva under Calvin. The structure and character of Geneva, which became the model for many later Protestant communities, were largely the work of Calvin himself, whose legal training and experience provided a solid base for his interest in these matters, and whose dominant personality and singleness of purpose compelled the Genevan city fathers to adopt his policies while insisting that control of the Church lay with them, rather than that the church ministers controlled secular affairs.[71]

Calvin seems to have been the principal framer of three basic sets of Genevan law: the *Ecclesiastical Ordinances*, adopted on 20 November 1541, in which the Genevan reformer "asked that the church be set in order";[72] the *Edict of Light* (i.e., of justice) of 12 November 1542; and the *Ordinances on Offices and Officers* of 28 January 1543.[73] Taken together, these documents codified Geneva's form of representative government in a way that proved both durable and influential. Although the ecclesiology set out in the *Ecclesiastical Ordinances* provided a limited role for representative elements, the *Ordinances on Offices* established a city-state that offered a really central role to representative institutions. Consistent with the general Reformation approach to ecclesiastical deinstitutionalization that located the Church directly under secular control, these representative bodies exercised ultimate authority over Church institutions as well as over the whole range of civic affairs. In simple terms, Calvin's proposals for Geneva embodies the theological and ecclesiological contents of his earlier doctrinal formulations found in the first two editions of the *Institution of Religion* (1536 and 1539) and applied them directly to the republican city-state structure of contemporary Geneva, complete with the considerable institutional detail specified in the ecclesiology spelled out in the 1543 edition of the *Institution*.[74]

---

71. It must not be assumed, however, that Calvin always dominated Genevan political authority, particularly in the early years of his ministry there. Though he rapidly achieved prominence as a Reformist authority and preacher—he arrived in Geneva in August 1536 at the age of twenty-seven and had become the city's leading Reformation spokesman in little more than a year—he did not succeed immediately in having the city authorities adopt his ecclesiastico-political views. In 1538 a direct confrontation between Genevan magistrates and religious ministers led by Calvin and Guillaume Farel, another early Genevan reformer, prompted the temporal authorities to prohibit preaching by Geneva's more outspoken Reformist ministers. This was followed quickly by the ministers' refusal to administer communion and their ignoring the prohibition on preaching, which led in turn to the summary dismissal of Calvin and Farel along with one other intransigent minister, Courrault, from their publicly supported religious charges. Calvin retired to Strasbourg at Bucer's invitation and returned to Geneva in 1541 with clear popular approval; at this time he presented his ecclesiastical ordinances to the Genevan city council for approval. He continued in later years to have detractors in Genevan conciliar ruling circles.

72. See Hopfl, *Christian Polity of Calvin*, p. 79 and p. 256, n. 9.

73. Kingdon, "John Calvin's Contribution to Representative Government," p. 185.

74. Without being able to specify the precise details, Hopfl suggests that Calvin must have profited greatly from his sojourn in Strasbourg with Bucer, who "was regarded as perhaps the most efficient ecclesiastical organizer in Europe." Hopfl, *Christian Polity of Calvin*,

As already noted, the representative institutions and the Genevan political practices to which Calvin applied his theory had their general origins in medieval times and had existed, at least in skeleton form, for several centuries. They had achieved some specification in Geneva as part of the extension of episcopal jurisdiction into the secular sphere; but the responsibilities of the conciliar structure had remained largely symbolic rather than directly functional, as was often the case in late medieval jurisdictions where some form of representative assembly or council developed from either regional or national councils of king's advisors, or from the vestiges of primitive forms of direct democracy in city-states. In Geneva, as elsewhere, effective legal authority had remained with the titular head of state; the bishop of Geneva and his Savoyard allies exercised ultimate authority over foreign policy, coinage, and the major areas of law and the administration of justice until the Catholic bishop, Pierre de la Baume, left in 1533, signalling the triumph of the Reformation in the city.[75] The coming of the Reformation gave greater emphasis to the *de facto* exercise of republican administration in the city through an elected magistracy and conciliar structure that had been in place for some time, and through which the conventional sixteenth-century amalgam of political independence, religious orthodoxy, and regulation of public and personal morality was expressed.[76]

The ordinances drafted by Calvin and adopted by the Genevan secular authorities under his direction in the early 1540s consolidated the

---

p. 89. Hopfl prefers the term "Institution" to designate Calvin's principal theological treatise rather than the more commonly used English term "Institutes," and I have followed him on this point. Cf. Hopfl, *Christian Polity of Calvin*, pp. 20–23.

75. It was Farel who had successfully preached and promoted the Reformation in Geneva after performing a similar service in Bern. The Mass was suppressed in Geneva by decree of the Council of Two Hundred in August 1535, and after troops from Bern occupied Geneva as part of their military operations against Savoy, its citizens celebrated what seemed to be their definitive liberation from external political authorities by meeting in a General Council on 21 May 1536 to declare their formal adhesion to the Reformed religion and swear that "in close union and unanimously we all want to live according to the holy law of the Gospel and the Word of God as it has been announced to us, and we wish to abandon all Masses and other ceremonies and papal abuses, images and idols." Domergue, *Jean Calvin*, 2:147–48.

76. Detailed descriptions of Geneva in Calvin's day can be found in Monter's *Studies in Genevan Government* and *Calvin's Geneva*; Kingdon, *Geneva and the Wars of Religion*; Fulpius, *Institutions politiques de Genève*; and cf. Hopfl, *Christian Polity of Calvin*, pp. 129–38.

Reformist character of Geneva's ecclesiastical and political arrangements. They spelled out the details of political organization in a reasonably clear and comprehensive fashion, with one signal omission: there was no precise line of demarcation between the temporal and ecclesiastical spheres. The imprecision on this point seems to have allowed the magistracy to assume that it wielded ultimate authority on all public matters, as indeed it would have maintained; the magistracy, after all, possessed and exercised the right to appoint religious ministers. It was in any case a position emphasized by the dominant anti-Romanism of both the Calvinist and Lutheran brands of the Reformed religion. At the same time, however, the influence wielded over Genevan law makers and magistracy by the Reformist clergy, particularly by Calvin himself, guaranteed the functioning of a kind of practical theocracy.

Under the new laws, Geneva's city council, which was elected, had ultimate authority over all aspects of municipal affairs. Several levels of elected councils were organized in a hierarchical form, and the whole conciliar structure was concentric, interdependent, and cross-regulating. At the apex was an elected executive council of some twenty-five members and four "syndics." Known as the "narrow" or "small" council or simply the "council," it met several times a week under the joint direction of the four syndics and conducted the ordinary business of the city. Below it was a relic of the fifteenth century, a council of sixty that met occasionally at the behest of the small council to deal with specific issues, commonly those having to do with external affairs and foreign policy; but the council of sixty does not seem to have been active in Calvin's time. A larger body known as the council of two hundred also met occasionally when summoned by the small council and enjoyed a status comparable to that of the council of sixty. It was first established in Geneva in 1527, in imitation of a similar body in Bern, as a more viable alternative to a council of all citizens. Among its specific responsibilities were those concerned with the electoral process. At the base of the conciliar hierarchy was a general council made up of all male Genevan property holders. It met annually to elect the syndics from a list of eight drawn up by the outgoing syndics, the small council, the council of two hundred, and other officers of city government, and to ratify legislation approved by the various other councils in the preceding twelve months. The four chief executive officers, the syndics, were elected annually to a twelve-month term, as were members of all three councils. Only citizens of Geneva were eligible for election to the small council and city offices, and only native-born bourgeousie were considered to be citizens. In consequence, both office holding and the franchise were quite restrictive.[77]

For the most part, Calvin seems to have incorporated existing features of Genevan practice into his municipal system of governance. But in doing so he gave particular emphasis to several characteristics rarely found in other political jurisdictions of the period. The vast majority of Christian religious communities at the time, as well as the institutional church, embraced the representative features of medieval corporation theory in procedures for placing individuals in authority. But none exhibited anything like the limits on Genevan political and ecclesiastical office holding inspired by Calvin. Calvin stressed collegial rule in ecclesiastical and civic community alike and made no provision for a leadership position in his conception of the Church. Nor were there ecclesiastical officers in the original Calvinist church of Geneva. While Calvin himself, as leader of its pastors, was *de facto* head of the Genevan church, he made no ecclesiological provision for any pre-eminent institutional position. On his death Calvin was succeeded by Theodore Beza, who was subsequently elected sixteen consecutive times to fill the position of chief pastor, his tenure being extended in each instance for one year at a time. And the position of moderator was put on a monthly basis when Beza relinquished the leadership of the pastors in 1580. Similarly in the secular sphere: while the *Ordinances on Offices* did provide for civil leadership of at least a titular type with one syndic designated annually as leader, the primacy was little if anything more than symbolic. The position itself lasted for only a year and was held by the syndic that had seniority of service on the small council. The executive body as a whole exercised effective control over the city.[78]

A second crucial concept inserted by Calvin into the regulations for church and state governance in Geneva was accountability for officeholders. This notion soon became part of Reformist resistance theory: lower magistrates had a duty to defend ordinary citizens against the tyranny of rulers, especially against religious oppression, and were accountable for how they met this responsibility. All elected members of both church and civic structures had to show themselves competent according to specific standards. Further, civic offices were usually filled by election and for only one year, and the election procedures were often very complex. Moreover, individuals were required to serve if elected.[79]

77. Kingdon, "John Calvin's Contribution," p. 189.
78. Ibid., pp. 191–92.
79. Ibid., p. 193.

The political and constitutional realities of Calvinist Geneva were widely noticed during Calvin's lifetime. Calvin himself became well known in his own day as a religious and civic reformer, and he was regularly consulted on both theological and sociopolitical matters, just as Bucer, from whom Calvin seems to have learned much, had been in Strasbourg. Geneva also became a haven for both continental, and English and Scottish Reform clergy and believers when Catholic forces began to make serious moves to suppress Protestantism and persecute its adherents, especially in France and England. Calvin came to be associated with the republican model of civil government he had established in Geneva, a model that was dominated by legally elected representative institutions, but that also ceded considerable indirect authority to the clergy. Geneva thus was seen as a working model of Reformation governance. As noted earlier, it was this, rather than any carefully articulated political theory, that was Calvin's chief contribution to the development of politics. The Reformed religion had been accepted by local governing authorities elsewhere, but Reform leaders looked to Geneva for inspiration. What they found there was radically different from the form of polity exercised elsewhere in western Europe at the time: a civic government dominated by representative councils controlled by the principles of collegial leadership and accountability. Many reacted negatively, at the time, to this Genevan political model because of its contrast with the more common and conventional notion of one-person rule in all human institutions from the family to the state. Yet the Genevan polity offered an alternative that would have an immense impact on later political groupings, as well as on political thought.

Even so, Calvin's own commitment to any specific form of polity, particularly representative democracy, should not be overstated. The various editions of the *Institution* repeated the view that had been adopted by Christian theologians from the time Aristotle's *Politics* had appeared in the West—that no single form of government is superior to any other: "This question permits of no absolute solution ... for the nature of the discussion depends on circumstances."[80] However, Calvin did indicate something of a personal preference for a mixed form of aristocracy modelled, as one would expect, on the Israelite polity prior to the reign of kings. "The form which [in itself] (*in se*) greatly surpasses the others is aristocracy, either pure or modified by popular government."[81] Nor did

80. Calvin, *Institution* (1536 ed.) 4.20.8.
81. Calvin, *Institution* (1543 ed.) 4.20.8.

he attribute any real sovereignty to the people: the only source of sovereign power was God, Who granted it to whomever He pleased.[82] He did allot a role to the people in controlling and agreeing to the exercise of political authority in both church and state—the traditional *quod omnes tangit* concept—though he did not identify it as such;[83] nor did he implement it in Geneva. In general, and consistent with his tendency to consider government in church and state in parallel terms, Calvin favored collegiality in the exercise of authority.

While the Genevan reformer did not explicitly attribute sovereignty to the people, he did accept that the exercise of authority should be construed in terms of benefit to the people as a whole. It is in the expression of this traditional principle that Calvin located his obliquely stated resistance theory. His views concerning the legitimacy of using armed force to resist efforts to suppress the Reformed religion show that, originally, he appeared unready to offer opposition, theoretical or practical, to the prospects of Catholic military action aimed at suppressing the Reformation. As noted earlier, a firm resistance position was available by 1546 from Lutheran sources, both legal and theological, preceding the Magdeburg Confession by four years and dating back as far as 1530, when actual war broke out between the imperial forces of Charles V and Protestant troops mobilized by the Schmalkaldic League of German princes. In contrast, the only major Calvinist statement on resistance at the time was the section on civil government at the end of his *Institution*, published first in 1536. The text did not offer any substantial grounds for the right to defend against political authority, but it did contain the seeds from which a resistance theory could be developed.

An adequate resistance argument must be grounded on the contention that authority *de facto* has ceased somehow to be legitimate, since this is the only contention with sufficient intellectual energy to counter the moral injunction that authority must always be obeyed. One can either deny the universality of the injunction (thus depriving it of logical, moral, and legal value[84]), or concede the truth of the universal statement but deny that a given instance falls within its purview.

---

82. Kingdon, "John Calvin's Contribution," p. 198.
83. Hopfl, *Christian Polity of Calvin*, p. 125.
84. Legal statements of this kind would be considered valid by legal positivists of the Austinian type, of which there are actually few adherents today even though many legal theorists still insist on calling themselves positivists, on the ground that the coercive authority of the state provides the only sufficient basis for legal validity.

Though Calvin's *Institution* seems to accept the simple universality of the Pauline injunction to obey all forms of political authority, he did note several exceptions to the general principle of obedience. The first was the traditional one that a Christian subject's duty to God transcends any obligation to secular authority: "In that obedience we exhibit as due to the authority of rulers, we must always make this exception, in fact to observe it as primary, that such obedience is never to lead us away from obedience to Him to whose will all kings' desires ought to be subject."[85] A second exception, which appeared in every edition of the *Institution* after 1539, was that if the people "implore the Lord's help," God may sometimes respond by raising up "open avengers from among His servants [providing them] with His command to punish the wicked government and deliver His people, oppressed in unjust ways, from miserable calamity."[86] The Old Testament style of this comment was presumably intended to compensate for its lack of specificity or coherence when juxtaposed to the Pauline injunction.

In addition to these standard Christian theological reservations on a subject's obligation to obey secular authority, Calvin placed two other qualifications on the general rule of obedience, the first of which made reference to lesser public officials and their duty to protect citizens. Some analysts have made much of this portion of Calvin's text, maintaining erroneously that it appeared only in later editions, not in the 1536 original, and finding in it the basis for later Calvinist resistance theory of the "ephoral" type. In fact the first (1536) edition contains the whole discussion on magistrates and remains unaltered in subsequent editions. Calvin did make an alteration, however, in the definitive 1559 Latin edition of the *Institution*, in a section dealing with the obligation of obedience, and there is evidence that he had begun by this time to alter his doctrine of purely passive resistance, although his text is never clear and unequivocal on the subject.[87]

---

85. Calvin, *Institution* 4.20.32, p. 1520. Page references for the *Institution* are to the McNeill/Battles English translation of the definitive 1559 Latin edition. This translation is listed in the bibliography as *Institutes*.

86. Ibid., 4.20.30, p. 1517.

87. "This never prompts him to state a clear and unequivocal theory of revolution, but it certainly results in a tendency, as Filmer shrewdly observed in *Patriarcha*, for Calvin to 'look asquint' at the possibility of active resistance to lawful magistrates (p. 54)." Skinner, *Foundations*, 2:192.

Probably even more than this can be said to show that Calvin supported, or at least countenanced, armed resistance against Catholic political authority over his co-religionists, even

The portion of the *Institution* that offered Calvin's narrowly drawn rejection of armed resistance to civil authority was first written within a few years of the radical Anabaptist social experiments in anarchism and their efforts to eliminate any form of political authority. It is worth noting that, like Luther, Calvin was totally opposed to this type of radical interpretation of the Christian Scriptures and more than a little anxious to condemn such experiments out of hand. The possibility that the Reformation movement might take on such a wild and woolly form, especially during the period of peasant revolt in southern Germany and possible civil discord in some of the independent city-states, received no encouragement from Luther or Calvin. Like Luther's diatribe *Against the Robbing and Murdering Horde of Peasants*, Calvin's *Institution* condemns those "insane and barbarous men [who] furiously strive to overturn this divinely established order," and Calvin roundly condemned the "outrageous barbarity ... of those fanatics" in a defence of the necessary and godly character of secular authority, citing the traditional position of Romans 13.1.[88]

The *Institution* also examines the nature of law and the function of magistrates as persons exercising lawful authority in political society. The general conclusion was that "the first duty of subjects towards their magistrates [is] to think most honorably of their [magisterial] office," and further, that subjects ought not only to be obedient, but also should avoid gratuitous political activity, being careful not to "intrude in public affairs, or pointlessly invade the magistrate's office."[89] The main thrust

---

though the consciously definitive formulation of his theology in the *Institution* provides no clear evidence on the point. Hopfl points out that Calvin was scrupulous in offering a solid Scriptural basis for his theological views—Paul's epistle to the Romans was critical here—while at the same time not being particularly concerned with working out the specific determinations of his general principles in the actual circumstances of his own day. As well, he must have been fully aware of the political and military actions of the French Huguenots in the late 1550s, and of Beza's involvement even to the point of joining a military campaign. It is almost inconceivable that Calvin would not have spoken out against this "resistance" by his French co-religionists had he considered it morally indefensible. On the contrary, he permitted recruitment of preachers from Geneva to serve the many Huguenot communities and regions springing up in southern France and claiming *de facto* independence from the French monarchy's jurisdiction over them. Calvin's silence in failing to condemn this Huguenot resistance seems much louder than his silence in not approving it in the *Institution*. See Hopfl, *Christian Polity of Calvin*, pp. 209–17.

88. Calvin, *Institution*, 4.20.1, p. 1485; 4.20.3–4, pp. 1488–89.
89. Ibid., 4.20.22–23, pp. 1510–11.

of Calvin's message was clear: "Let no man deceive himself here. For since the magistrate cannot be resisted without God being resisted at the same time, even though it seems that an unarmed magistrate can be despised with impunity, still God is armed to avenge mightily this contempt towards Himself."[90] While Calvin obviously had "lower" magistrates in mind in that someone holding ultimate political authority would not be "unarmed," the principle remains the same for all levels of authority.

Calvin also raised explicitly the question whether his injunction concerning obedience applied to magistrates who carried out their responsibilities inadequately; his answer was that it does. "We are subject not only to the authority of princes who perform their offices to us uprightly and faithfully as they ought, but also to the authority of all who, by whatever means, have got control of affairs, even though they perform not a whit of the prince's office ... A very wicked man utterly unworthy of all honor [must be held in] the same reverence and respect by his subjects [as] ... the best of kings if he were given to them ... [even if] we are cruelly tormented by a savage prince [or] vexed for piety's sake by one who is impious and sacrilegious [we are] not allowed to resist."[91] The fervour with which Calvin accepted what he saw as the clear Gospel message enunciated by St Paul led him to reject even the traditional medieval distinction between a tyrant who seizes power unjustly and one who holds office legitimately but exercises it tyrannically. For the Genevan reformer, both are to be obeyed without apparent qualification: Christians must obey "the authority of all who, by whatever means, have got control of affairs."[92]

As indicated already, this was not Calvin's final word on the resistance issue. The definitive 1559 edition of his *Institution* contains an arresting addition of little more than a few lines that indicates, however ambiguously, that adherents to the Reformed religion might have a right to defend themselves against efforts to suppress them. Calvin added a final chapter in this edition to the last section on temporal authority, presumably with malice aforethought, given the current situation. He inserted in this new material what seems to be an equivocally worded allusion to the private-law theory of resistance. Without referring explicitly to the notion that a ruler exceeding his authority is *ipso facto* reduced to the sta-

---

90. Ibid., 4.20.23, p. 1511.
91. Ibid., 4.20.25–31, variously pp. 1512–18.
92. Ibid., 4.20.25, p. 1512.

cated that a ruler who behaves in this fashion exceeds his authority and thus ceases to qualify as a genuine magistrate. He illustrated his position with a citation from the Old Testament. According to Calvin, when Daniel "denies [sic] that he has committed any offence against the king for refusing to obey the king's impious edict," he was justified in his stand, because "the king had exceeded his limits, and had not merely been a wrongdoer against men but, in lifting up his horns against God, had himself abrogated his own power."[93]

Furthermore, in a passage strategically placed on the last page of this new chapter, he offered his famous comments on the nature of "ephoral" responsibilities.[94] Extremely brief, oblique, and conditional in form and tone, Calvin's text does not explicitly assert that the ephoral powers to which he refers actually exist in any contemporary European state; Beza was much less circumspect in his 1554 tract *De haereticis*,[95] in which he made explicit reference to the Magdeburg authorities. Nor did Calvin argue that lower magisterial authorities had a clear duty to oppose tyranny where they found it. But what he did say is worth noting; his mention of ephoral magistrates makes it clear that, while he accepted that they are ordained of God for their public role, he considered them somehow elected by, and responsible to, the people. Referring to them as "popular magistrates" (*populares magistrati*), he called them appointed (*constituti*) rather than ordained (*ordinati*) and declared that it was their responsibility "to moderate the power of kings." They were said to possess the right "to withstand the fierce licentiousness of kings" since failure to do so would involve them in "an act of nefarious perfidy ... [conniving at] a fraudulent betrayal of the liberty of the people."[96]

Calvin cites examples from secular history to confirm this assessment: the Spartan ephors themselves, the tribunes of the *plebs* among the Romans, and the demarchs of the Athenians, all of whom Calvin would have known were annually elected officials. And, significantly, the text extends the concept of ephoral authority at least conditionally to the modern world, repeating a point made earlier by Zwingli: "There may

---

93. Ibid., 4.20.32, p. 1520.
94. Ibid., 4.20.31, p. 1519. Skinner considers the standard English translations of this passage "misleading" and for this reason offers his own, and gives references to the 1559 Latin edition of the *Institution*. He also makes the telling point that Calvin never refers to "lower" magistrates but uses the term "popular" (*magistratus populares*). Cf. Skinner, *Foundations*, 2:232.
95. Beza, *De haereticis*, p. 133; cf. infra, p. 241.
96. Calvin, *Institution*, 4.20.31, p. 1519.

be [sic] magistrates appointed at the present time to moderate the power of kings, [and if so] the three estates of each kingdom when they are gathered together [may be examples]."[97] Since Calvin was well aware of the elective nature of such assemblies, it is not at all implausible that the cautious, legally scrupulous leader of the Genevan Reformed church was making reasonably clear that he considered the power to resist tyranny in his own day rested in magistrates who were chosen by the people to represent them in contemporary forms of popular assemblies, and who remained responsible for the protection of the people's well-being.[98] If this definitive Calvinistic theological text was intended, however indirectly, to legitimate resistance to Catholic political authorities through the obligation of "ephoral" magistrates to defend the "true" religion of Protestant subjects, it is ironic that the proferred justification would have had greater immediate applicability for Lutheran believers in Germany than for Calvin's Huguenot coreligionists in France, though Calvinists in the Spanish provinces of the Low Countries might have found something serviceable here. But this is not to say that Calvin was unprepared to support Huguenot activities in France.[99]

Although his remarks in the 1559 edition of the *Institution* are enigmatic, and although it is not clear that the right to "oppose" given to lower magistrates extends to actual resistance as well as to disobedience, Calvin had earlier begun to show signs of modifying the simple Pauline position on disobedience. In the *Commentary on the Acts of the Apostles*, published first between 1552 and 1554, he commented directly on the injunction that "it is better to obey God than man." He maintained that every type of ruler with a godly office to perform has power from God, so that "if a king or prince or magistrate conducts himself in such a way as to diminish the honor and right of God, they become nothing more than an ordinary man (*non nisi homo est*).[100] To this he later added the significant point that "it is in fact possible to claim that we are not violating the authority of the king [where] our religion compels us to resist (*resistere*) tyrannical edicts which forbid us to give Christ and God the honor and worship which is Their due."[101]

---

97. Ibid. Cf. Zwingli, "Der Hirt,' in Zwingli, *Samtliche Werke*, 3:27–33.
98. Cf. Skinner, *Foundations*, 2:233.
99. See *supra*, note 87.
100. Calvin, "Commentarium in Acta Apostolorum," in Calvin, *Opera ... omnia*, 48:109.
101. Ibid., p. 398. This text seems to address directly the issue of resistance, even though it is possible to construe Calvin's *resistere* in the weaker meaning of "disobey."

More significant because totally lacking in ambiguity is a reflection of the private-law argument that occurs in Calvin's *Readings on the Prophet Daniel*, published first in 1561. As in the 1559 edition of the *Institution*, Calvin exonerates Daniel from any wrongdoing for failing to obey Darius's command to worship a pagan idol: Daniel "committed no sin [since] in any case where our rulers rise up against God [they] abdicate their worldly power."[102] Discussing the same passage in his *Sermons sur les huit derniers chapitres du Livre de Daniel* (1563), he repeated that Daniel "committed no sin when he disobeyed the king [because] when princes claim that God is not to be served and honored ... they are no longer worthy to be counted as princes ... when they raise themselves up against God ... it is necessary for them in turn to be laid low."[103] There is still no explicit acceptance of the legitimate use of armed force for resistance; but given the situation in the Spanish colonies of the Netherlands at the time, as well as in France, not to speak of statements by Lutherans and other Calvinist leaders at the time, there is little doubt about the meaning and intent of these words.

On other fronts, however, Calvin reiterated the need for subjects to maintain loyalty and obedience to their lawful rulers, a striking example being his attitude towards the increasingly radical position John Knox was taking towards the political establishment in Scotland and England. Educated in theology under John Major at St Andrews in the 1530s, Knox was ordained a Catholic priest in 1536, but converted to Protestantism in 1543 after coming under the influence of Thomas Gwilliam, former prior of the Black Friars monastery at Inverness. Two years later, he became an energetic exponent of the Scottish model of Calvinism as an associate of George Wishart.[104] Scottish reformers had almost succeeded in establishing a Calvinist form of Protestantism in Scotland in the 1540s when Henry VIII's brand of Reformed religion was in the ascendant in England and an English victory over Scottish national forces at Solway Moss in 1542 had deprived the established Catholic church in Scotland of solid political support. The Catholic archbishop of Glasgow-Edinburgh, Cardinal Beaton, had been forced

---

102. Calvin, "Praelectiones in Danielem Prophetam," in Calvin, *Opera ... omnia*, 40:25–26.
103. Calvin, "Sermons sur les huit derniers chapitres du livre de Daniel," in Calvin, *Opera ... omnia*, 41:415.
104. The standard biography of Knox is Ridley, *John Knox*. Details of Knox's education and early ecclesiastical and professional life are at pp. 1–44.

out of office and imprisoned in 1543; the Scottish parliament had approved the circulation of vernacular bibles in the same year, and a number of Reformist preachers such as Wishart and Gwilliam began to attract large crowds to their sermons.[105]

However, the succession of Mary Tudor to the English throne introduced a serious Catholic reaction to the Reformed religion in both England and Scotland, and the Catholic church quickly regained ascendancy in both jurisdictions. French naval forces supporting the Scottish Catholic position laid seige to St Andrews in 1547 and captured some of the strongest defenders of Scottish Protestantism, including John Knox, and took them off as galley slaves. Back on home soil a few years later, Knox had begun in earnest to examine possible grounds for defending himself and his religion with the same weapon the Catholics had employed—armed force. But the persecution of Protestants in England and Scotland under Mary forced him to flee in early 1554 to the Continent, where he consulted Calvin and Heinrich Bullinger on the appropriateness of resistance to English political authority. To Bullinger, Zwingli's successor in Zurich, he put the specific question "whether obedience is to be rendered to a magistrate who enforces idolatry and condemns true religion?" And to Calvin: Could an "idolatrous sovereign" be lawfully resisted by the nobility or other lesser magistrates?[106]

Both Bullinger and Calvin replied in the negative, Calvin confirming to Bullinger by letter that he had informed "the Scot" that active resistance in the circumstances was not legitimate. For his part, Bullinger told Knox that "godly persons" must avoid "any rash attempt" at resistance, making certain that they "attempt nothing contrary to the laws of God."[107] In a later communication to the court of Queen Elizabeth,

---

105. On the Reformation in Scotland see G. Donaldson, *Scottish Reformation*; Renwick, *Story of the Scottish Reformation*.

106. Knox, "Certain Questions Concerning Obedience to lawful Magistrates," in *Works*, 4:225. That Knox couched his query in terms of "lesser magistrates" might suggest that he was aware of Calvin's position on "ephors" even before the 1559 edition of the *Institution* appeared, but it is much more likely that he was familiar with this terminology from the Magdeburg Confession or other Lutheran sources. Given the same date for publication of Beza's tract *On Heretics*, 1554, Knox probably would not have been familiar with it inasmuch as his communications with Bullinger and Calvin were in February and March of that year. Cf. *infra*, note 107 on the dating. It might also be recalled that the Calvin terminology was "popular magistrates."

107. Ibid., p. 226. Ridley reports that Knox probably visited Calvin and Bullinger in February and March 1554, shortly after he fled from England to France. Ridley, *John Knox*,

Calvin assured the English Crown that he dissociated himself from the radical views of Knox, who by this time had delivered himself of some strong statements on the obligation of public authority to support his brand of the Reformed religion against the "idolatrous" behaviour of the English queen, Mary.[108] Presumably, Calvin meant that a general theory of justification for resistance does not automatically imply its direct application to every set of political circumstances; as already noted, he did admit a legitimate role for inferior magistrates in controlling the tyrannical activities of princes and kings in his enigmatic remarks on the role of the ephors in the last chapter of the *Institution*.

The earliest reference to the "ephoral," or lower magisterial, level of political authority found among Reformation thinkers seems to be in a vernacular sermon, *Der Hirt (The Pastor)*, delivered by Zwingli in Zurich

---

p. 545. He also gives references for the letter Bullinger sent to Calvin concerning his answer to Knox's questions, dated Zurich, 26 March 1554, and Calvin's letter to Viret dated 23 February 1554, noting that he had seen Knox in Geneva and that the Scot was travelling to Zurich via Lausanne: ibid.

108. Skinner notes that this information is found in Knox, *Works*, at 4:356–57. Skinner, *Foundations*, 2:217. By this later date (1559) Knox had published *The First Blast of the Trumpet Against the Monstrous Regiment of Women* from his haven with Calvin in Geneva, a work of far-reaching circulation that earned him a contemporary reputation as a revolutionary firebrand.

This reputation was well deserved. In *The First Blast* and the three tracts he published in the summer of 1558 Knox expressed clearly and forcefully a full doctrine of revolution against Mary. In his *Faithful Admonition made unto ... England* he challenged directly the doctrine of Christian obedience by calling on the nobility to revolt against Mary; in his letter to the nobility and parliament of Scotland he put the view that anyone supporting an idolatrous ruler even passively was an "apostate of God"; and in his letter to Mary of Lorraine, the Queen Regent, he asserted that if the nobility and commonalty of Scotland followed their leaders into moral inequity, they would be punished as Pharaoh's army had been punished by drowning in the Red Sea, and that they, including individual citizens, had a moral obligation to "put idolaters to death" insofar as Moses' commandment in Deuteronomy to slay the idolater was directed to the whole people as well as the nobles. The whole population would be responsible if idolatry were not punished. "Letter to the Commonalty of Scotland," in *Works*, 4:523–38, esp. pp. 527–28, 533–36. Cf. Ridley, *John Knox*, pp. 265–85, esp. pp. 273–76.

Goodman also argued concurrently in *How Superior Powers ought to be Obeyed*, published in Geneva on 1 January 1558, that it was the duty of all classes to rise up against an idolatrous sovereign. Ridley, *John Knox*, p. 281. As well, the Geneva Bible published in 1560, the most important piece of radical Protestant propaganda circulating in England and Scotland in the sixteenth century, explicitly instructed its readers that they had a duty to resist wicked rulers and kill idolaters. Ridley, *John Knox*, p. 288.

at a meeting of Reform pastors in 1523 and published the next year.[109] Zwingli seems to stress that all ministerial authority comes directly from God and is to be used to "defend the people." He cited Old Testament examples of priests being charged with this responsibility, but he also referred to instances where civil magistrates who undoubtedly held elective positions possessed "the power to check their rulers," and he specifically mentioned "the ephors in Sparta and the tribunes in Rome."[110] Zwingli went on to draw an explicit contemporary parallel by suggesting that magistrates in existing communities might also possess powers that, while not strictly speaking ephoral, give them the responsibility to "uphold the interests of the people."[111] Calvin's statement in the *Institution* was much more telling: Calvin drew no explicit parallel between ephors and popularly elected magistrates and asserted that inferior magistrates were "placed over us as guardians by the ordinance of God," but, as already noted, he also referred to them as "popular" (*populares magistrati*) and appointed (*constituti*) rather than ordained (*ordinati*). Moreover, Calvin was explicit about their having genuine authority, even though he drew no direct inference from this to the legitimacy of their resisting higher authority.

Calvin's overall political doctrine was consciously formalized in the *Institution of the Christian Religion*, an essentially theological tractate that set down in comprehensive and carefully edited terms the authoritative doctrine of the founder of Genevan Protestantism.[112] It was in essence a blend of concepts that were fundamental to ecclesiology and secular political theory alike: law, church, and state. Beginning with the set of theological and ecclesiological principles common to all early sixteenth century reformers, Calvin took direct aim at the centuries-old doctrine of the institutional Christian church by stressing three fundamental

---

109. Chenevière points out that Luther and Melanchthon, as well as Zwingli, also mentioned ephor resistance before Calvin's reference in the *Institution*, and cites Bohatec to the effect that reference to lower magistrates in a theory of resistance appeared in Marsilius of Padua, Leopold of Bebenburg, and Comenius. Bohatec gives no citations for these remarks, however, and his reference to the Marsilian notion of *sanior pars* does not seem to make his point. Chenevière, *La pensée politique de Calvin*, p. 332 and note 21; Bohatec, *Calvins Lehre von Staat und Kirche*, p. 108 and note 277.

110. Zwingli, "Der Hirt," in Zwingli, *Samtliche Werke*, vol. 3, p. 36.

111. Ibid.

112. Hopfl, however, shows with considerable ingenuity the limitations of the *Institution* as a formal theological text, and the corresponding need to measure its statments on polity against other Calvinist writings as well as the Genevan reformer's personal activities. Hopfl, *Christian Polity of Calvin*, passim.

tenets of Reformation theology: the idea of an exclusively personal relationship between God and the individual Christian, through the divine gift of salvation and the individual's believing response; the concept of the Church as a simple *congregatio fidelium*, with no juridical status or authority in the temporal world nor any clergy of superior status to other believers in the political sphere; and the corresponding view that temporal authority was the direct gift of God and an integral portion of his providence that obliged obedience from all subjects.

However, while staking out clear and solid ground for the exercise of political authority, Calvin was no more an advocate of absolute authority in the state than Luther or, indeed, any other Christian political thinker; such a position would have been inconsistent with basic Christian theological and religious convictions. For Calvin, the laws of God and nature always took precedence over human legislation or legislators, and however much he counselled and insisted on the Christian obligation of obedience to authority, he never advised the godly to do anything other than follow God's law whenever it conflicted with that of the state, and to suffer the consequences of civil disobedience with Christian humility. This primary insistence on general obedience to political authority caused difficulty for Reformation political thought, not because the reformers were unaware of, or failed to note limits to, the legitimacy of such authority, or failed to accept a corresponding limitation on the subject's obligation to obey: as seen in Calvin's halting efforts to formulate a resistance theory, for example, the difficulties stemmed more from failure to realize the conceptual issue of accommodating two notions that everyone accepted, viz., the legitimacy of temporal authority itself, and the necessary implications of the limits to this legitimacy. But Reformation political thinkers were not the first to fail in this area; their medieval predecessors had done the same, and the explanation was likely the same in each case. As theologians and religious thinkers, they were concerned only indirectly with political thinking in its own right. Lawyers, canonists, and civilians alike had failed to develop a coherent and comprehensive political ideology. However, early Lutheran and Calvinist reformers seemed to have greater problems in articulating a coherent theory of limit because of their insistence on a direct return to Christian Scriptural authority—where they ran head-on into Romans 13—and their rejection of the medieval institutional church, which led them to insist, again taking their stand on Romans 13, that power, including temporal power, comes directly from God.

Another feature of Calvin's political thought also reflected a basic and common aspect of Reformation thinking. Like Luther and other Reformist contemporaries, he had a far less optimistic view of the human condition than traditional medieval scholastic theologians and, correspondingly, a different conception of the abilities of human beings to understand and employ the natural law in ordinary affairs. The original and later sixteenth century forms of Thomism and scholasticism had based their notion of law on reason and defined law in terms of the rational, but Calvin and other reformers were not prepared simply to accept this. Their view rested more on *via moderna* scepticism concerning the ability of natural human reason to perceive essential and absolute truth, a scepticism grounded ultimately on rejection of Aristotle's conception of the universe and optimistic belief in the capacity of the human intellect to attain truth. Calvin and other reformers intensified the general epistemological *via moderna* scepticism by re-emphasizing the pessimistic Augustinian perception of the baneful effects of Original Sin on human nature in general and human reason in particular.

For Calvin, human reason corrupted by Original Sin was seemingly incapable of grasping reality or recognizing within it the place of human beings and their obligations to act in certain ways. Calvin seems to have extended this limited view of the capability of human reason to its natural condition, that is, before Adam and Eve transgressed in the Garden of Eden. Certainly he considered that the now corrupt nature of human reason rendered it incapable of judging how best to act in accordance with God's laws. Proper determination of moral and religious judgments required that individuals receive direction and guidance from the Christian Scriptures, which, as divinely inspired texts, constituted the only sure source of information about how humans were to achieve their proper end, eternal salvation. On its own, human reason could acquire only experimental knowledge of the empirical world, which led at best to universal knowledge of material bodies and played no useful role in the development of either moral knowledge in an individual or a general science of ethics or politics.[113] Disorganized by the effects of Original Sin, and directed only to empirical knowledge of the things of this world, human reason is not even capable of "perfect" science concerning the nature of the material world and what is real within it. Individuals may possess some ability to think about material things and entertain moral concepts such as honesty and truthfulness, but they lack

---

113. Chenevière, *Pensée politique de Calvin*, p. 31.

the natural ability to give specific content to laws that must follow from such basic notions.[114]

For Calvin, then, law in both ecclesiastical and secular contexts has an essentially theological component. Because human reason suffers from the distorting conditions of sin, which subject it to errors and false starts, human beings are incapable of achieving through natural rational judgement the insight into their own social conditions that would enable them to give specific and appropriate content to laws. An infusion from Scriptural sources is required to provide them with the necessary insight.[115] Human beings have intelligence and a natural inclination to make law, but this ability is fundamentally incomplete, if not distorted without assistance from the Christian Scriptures, mediated by experience. Calvin's notion of law was amplified by his conception of conscience, which he considered to be the means whereby an individual grasps the general tenets of natural law. However, this was done in a manner different from rational formulation: the process involved "sentiment" rather than rational specification. Natural law, then, was not meaningful for the individual as a form of knowledge contributing to proper human behaviour and hence not really functional as an integral element in human nature: individuals get the merest glimpse of it and perceive it only vaguely. Natural law is not something intrinsic to human nature and given expression through the natural exercise of human rationality; it is a law imposed by God on His creatures from "without."[116]

Calvin did not always distinguish clearly in the *Institution* between reason and conscience, although it is clear that the natural law is what conscience perceives, not conscience itself: conscience provides individuals with a subjective version of justice, i.e., the natural law. But this subjective version is radically incomplete; it is not genuine knowledge because conscience is an imperfect knowing instrument and expresses itself only in the production of "sentiment," an indistinct, confused, inadequately specified form of knowledge. Directed only confusedly to the real nature of the human being, this sentiment is too vague to be useful even to the individual who experiences it. It must be made specific to be functional, and specification can only be achieved by knowing the divine will concerning what human beings are required to do. This knowledge of God's will is found in the Word of God, the Christian Scriptures.

114. Ibid., pp. 53–54. Cf. Calvin, *Institution*, 2.2.12–13, pp. 270–73.
115. Calvin, ibid., 2.2.13, pp. 271–73; 2.2.25, pp. 284–86.
116. Ibid., 2.2.17, pp. 276–77.

In the final analysis, Calvin used his definition of law to validate the standard Reformation description of polity derived from St Augustine: law is a practical necessity whose justification involves further reference to the human condition after the Fall. For Calvin, as for Luther, political society is a necessity because of the sinful condition of human beings.[117] He repeated, however, the conventional humanist and Spanish neo-scholastic position that humans lived freely and without restraint in the original state of nature, and that the constraints of political society were necessary only after the Fall as a response to the corrupting effects of Original Sin.[118]

As already noted, Calvin's advocacy of the value of political society and positive legislation was not unconditional. Political authority and legislation must always be consistent with the higher orders of divine and natural law, and, as shown, Calvin's tendency was to conflate the contents of natural law with Scripture itself by construing natural law as something "external" to clear human perception. Consistent with this conception of natural law, he defined the limits of legitimate authority without directly invoking the natural law, a quite different approach to the concept of limit than that found in traditional medieval political thought. Calvin appealed directly to the Christian Scriptures to validate his general theory of political authority and then added a curious historical twist by referring to "ephors."

His view of the need for political authority was consciously directed against Anabaptist anarchism, among other things, and rested on a straightforward appeal to Scriptural texts. He used the same basis for the view that lawful authority in the hands of civil magistrates is limited, emphasizing biblical teaching concerning the duties of magistrates. Magistrates, further, derive their authority directly from God, not the people: *Non est in arbitrio populi constituere principes.*[119] For Calvin, the ruler has a purely moral responsibility *vis-à-vis* the citizenry in terms of

---

117. Calvin, "Sermon 3 sur Daniel 5," in *Joannis Calvini opera ... omnia*, vol. 41, col. 348; cf. Calvin "Appendices quinti praecepti ex Exodi 21:17," in *Joannis Calvini opera ... omnia*, vol. 24, col. 606; Calvin, "Homilia 38, in 1 Samuelem 11," in *Joannis Calvini opera ... omnia*, vol. 29, col. 660.

118. Calvin, "Sermon 101 sur Deuteronomy 16," in *Joannis Calvini opera ... omnia*, vol. 27, cols. 412 and 409; Calvin, "Deuxième sermon sur Deuteronomy 17:5," in *Joannis Calvini opera ... omnia*, vol. 27, col. 447.

119. Calvin, "Institutio," p. 1116. While noting this, Skinner rejects the view held by both Baron and Chenevière that Calvin here does nothing more than repeat Bucer's theory of inferior magistrates by pointing out that Calvin spoke of these magistrates as *populares*. Skinner, *Foundations*, 2:232.

providing for their needs, even in democracies. Accordingly, only God has the right to act against a magistrate; the people do not: to resist a magistrate is to resist God.[120] Laws must always be obeyed unless they go against the cult of the true God.[121] Even at the height of the persecution of Huguenots, Calvin advised the Huguenot communities in France to leave the punishment of tyrants to God: "Revolt [against the true religion] will not go unpunished."[122] The people, however, could be helped through the responsible actions of the "lower" magistrates, whose duty it was to assist them in this way.

#### 4. THEODORE BEZA

Another leading reformer who made a significant contribution to political thought in the second half of the sixteenth century was Theodore Beza, or de Bèze (1519–1605). Educated in the French humanism of his day, he had a profound religious experience after a near-fatal illness in 1548 and became a follower of Calvin. By the early 1560s he had become one of Calvin's closest associates as well as the leader of the Reformed religion in France. He led the Huguenot delegation to the conference called at Poissy in 1561 by Catherine de Medici in a futile attempt to resolve the Catholic/Protestant differences in France and accompanied Condé and Coligny during the first religious war in 1562–63, among other things writing their Huguenot manifestos. On Calvin's death in 1564, Beza succeeded him as moderator of the group of pastors in Geneva, a position he held until his resignation in 1580. After a long period of chronic ill health, he died in 1605.[123]

Like his mentor and predecessor in high clerical office in Geneva, Beza did not formulate a comprehensive theory of polity. But he did take certain positions that are important for this survey. In particular, his views on the right of Protestants to offer armed resistance to their Catholic persecutors advanced resistance theory beyond anything found in the writings of Calvin himself while Calvin was still alive. Beza's views on resistance also set out a general statement on the nature and origins of political authority that placed him in a direct line from medieval to modern political theory, in terms of his balanced use of the concept of

---

120. Calvin, *Institution*, 4.20.23, p. 1511.
121. Ibid., 4.20.32, p. 1520.
122. Calvin, *Lettres françaises de Calvin*, 2:91ff.
123. The standard biography on Beza in still Geisendorf, *Théodore de Bèze*.

limit in the exercise of political power and clear, if incomplete, articulation of the essential element of popular consent.

Though his theology and political thought were not the most original, Beza occupied a position in the Genevan church that gave his views more than ordinary prominence and authority. His first expressly political work was the polemical tract *De haereticis a civile magistratu puniendis*, written in 1554 to defend Calvin's decision to have Servetus burned at the stake. Beza argued a position generally accepted at the time among both Reformers and Catholics, viz., that civil authority had direct responsibility for the religious orthodoxy and moral uprightness of its subjects, hence the right, acting on the advice of religious leaders, to put dangerous heretics to death for the sake of the common good of the godly community. In describing the nature of civil government and its basic functions, Beza began with a notion that, while not novel to political thought at the time, was not ordinarily employed in Lutheran or Calvinist political writing: that civil governments are established by social consent.[124] Reference to popular consent as the origin of polity was at odds with the customary Reformation doctrine that all authority comes directly from God and normally appeared in Catholic political writings by persons like Vitoria and Mariana. Just where Beza came across the notion is not clear. It had been a fundamental feature of humanist political thought for nearly a century or more, and this may explain how it entered Spanish neo-scholasticism with Vitoria, although it had a lengthy provenance in medieval scholastic political thought going back at least to Thomas Aquinas, a tradition with which Vitoria was thoroughly familiar. Beza may have picked it up from these sources. Both he and Calvin were educated in circles that would have given them access to humanist thought.[125]

Beza argued that magistrates came into office through public consent of the citizenry and thus were custodians of the peace and tranquillity for which political society exists. Reference to peace and tranquillity as the purpose of a polity was also part of standard Catholic political thinking, although its Platonic and Aristotelian origins and the Augustinian doctrine of the "peace of order" made it a feature common to virtually all

---

124. Kingdon, "First Expression of Beza's Political Ideas," 89. Cf. Kingdon, "Les idées politiques de Bèze," pp. 566–69.

125. Beza may also have taken it from Catholic sources. See Skinner's excellent summary of the incorporation by Calvinist publicists of Catholic ideas and arguments from the natural law, private law, and conciliar traditions: Skinner, *Foundations*, 2:232.

Western political writing. In fact, Beza's position on popular consent as the basis of a republican form of polity corresponded directly to actual conditions in Calvinist Geneva—in terms of the historical traditions of The Genevan city-state itself and, more particularly, the legal regimen developed by Calvin—and, to a large extent, other cities in Western Europe at the time.[126] He extended his view that authority rested in popular consent to civil legislation, again simply pointing to the actual situation in Geneva: popular consent was essential for the enactment of law. He went on to say, however, that popular control over lawmaking and law enforcement should be under the superintendency of God's church; indeed, a principal church function was to provide essential and authoritative input on such matters to magistrates, a kind of quality control for the nature and functioning of the city's legal system.[127] Justification of Servetus's execution for heresy followed directly from this argument.

The legitimacy of resistance was raised when Beza asked what was to be done if princes or other political authorities combatted the reign of Christ, and he listed a series of graduated responses. In the first instance, the persecuted church should pray and attempt to reform itself, recognizing that its members were being punished by God for their sinfulness through the imposition of tyrannical measures. But, if it is possible (*quam possibile*) for lesser magistrates to maintain the pure religion of God, as occurred at Magdeburg, "when, then, several princes abuse their office, whoever still feels it necessary to refuse to use the Christian magistrates offered by God against excessive violence whether of the unfaithful or of heretics, I charge deprives the church of God of a most useful and, as often as it pleases the Lord, a necessary defence."[128] Reference to the Magdeburg Confession shows a clear doctrinal connection between Lutheran and Calvinist resistance theory at this point, as well as Beza's willingness to draw a parallel between Magdeburg and Geneva—while Magdeburg remained technically a fiefdom of its local Catholic bishop, it had exercised self-proclaimed independence under a town-council type of jurisdiction since its formal acceptance of the Reformation. Beza, then, was directly influenced by the Magdeburg Confession, itself a clear and careful distillation of Lutheran thought developed over a twenty-year period (1530–50).

126. Cf. *supra*, pp. 219–23.
127. Beza, *De haereticis*, p. 26.
128. Ibid., p. 133.

Beza may also have been familiar with these earlier Lutheran views, although it is difficult to be sure. Certainly he would have known Calvin's reference to magistrates in the *Institution*; Calvin was more precise in consigning genuine political authority to inferior magistrates than Beza was in the *De haereticis*. But the Beza text expressed its main point on the right of resistance clearly, while Calvin's did not, even in the 1559 edition. Beza may also have been influenced here as in other matters by Martin Bucer: the second edition of Bucer's *In evangelium Matthei enarrationes* (1530) offered an account of the origins and nature of political authority in city-states very similar to Beza's.[129] Beza in turn may have influenced John Ponet, whose *Short Treatise of Politic Power* published in 1556 contains a strong defence of resistance and material similar to the Magdeburg statement. More likely Beza influenced John Knox and Christopher Goodman, and perhaps even Calvin himself, and his work was certainly used by the French Calvinists after 1560. As already mentioned, Beza actively assisted several French Huguenot groups to engage in revolt in the 1560s—unsuccessfully, as it turned out.

Beza made a second statement on the legitimacy of resistance to political authority in *Du droit des magistrats sur leurs sujets* (1574), published two years after the St Bartholomew's Day Massacre.[130] Though purporting to be a reprint of the anonymously published Lutheran political tract issued at Magdeburg in 1550, it was widely attributed to Beza at the time and was immediately and widely circulated; it was printed at least ten times in French between 1574 and 1581 and far oftener than that well into the seventeenth century, in a Latin translation that appeared first in 1576.[131] *Du droit* reflected the general concerns and line of argument in other Calvinist tracts of the time and repeated Beza's earlier position on the rights and responsibilities of inferior magistrates to act against higher authorities who persecute the Church of God. It was clearly sim-

---

129. Kingdon, "Beza's Political Ideas," p. 95. It should also be recalled that Calvin showed at least the probability of having been influenced by Bucer in his own ecclesiastico-political thought as a result of their relationship in Strasbourg; and the notion that Beza's tract on heretics could have appeared when it did without both consultation and approval from Calvin stretches credulity. Cf. *supra*, p. 224.

130. The work was published anonymously in French in 1574, probably at Heidelberg, as a revised and expanded version of the Magdeburg Confession, and published again in 1576 in a Latin translation by Beza himself. An abridged English translation is in Franklin, ed., *Constitutionalism and Resistance*, pp. 101–35. Whenever possible, citations to this Beza text are to the Franklin translation, designated as F when necessary.

131. On the publishing history of Beza's *Du droit* see van Schelven, "Beza's *De Iure Magistratum in Subditos*". Cf. Skinner, *Foundations*, 2:304 and note 3.

ilar to Hotman's *Francogallia*, which had appeared in Geneva in 1573 shortly before *Du droit*. In fact, there is evidence that Beza consulted with Hotman and borrowed from him directly.[132] Hotman had fled from France to Geneva in October 1572 after narrowly escaping the extension of the St Bartholomew's Day holocaust to Bourges.

Published in the immediate aftermath of the anti-Huguenot bloodletting in various urban centres in France—a time when the situation for Protestants in France and the Netherlands had gone well beyond the merely critical—Beza's basic argument was that there are times when resistance to government is justifiable and even necessary. Like earlier Calvinists, he located the right to resist in the offices of the lower magistrates, specific institutions in the general structure of government. His argument was essentially constitutional: the various elements of political jurisdiction all possess functional and limited authority consonant with their own duties and responsibilities, and each is required to perform such duties, especially when failure at a higher level is apparent. The principal institutions in this connection are the Estates General in France or their equivalent in other European countries, such as the Parliament in England and the Spanish Cortès, in that these are the deliberative or consultative bodies composed of representatives of every influential class in their respective countries.[133] *Du droit* is much more specific than the earlier Beza text: if the "Estates" are unable for any reason to exercise their proper function, inferior magistrates such as provincial governors, elected municipal councils, or other authorities governing at a local level must take up the task.[134]

Beza's *Du droit* is one of the most important of the Calvinist resistance tracts, moving in a variety of directions in terms of the continuity of conceptual pattern and political theory. It marked a definite shift in form of argumentation and even style towards the natural-law doctrine and scholastic model—a novel development among Protestant publicists that was repeated almost concurrently by Mornay.[135] Beza's new approach was

---

132. See Giesey, "When and Why Hotman Wrote the *Francogallia*," p. 582 and note. Cf. Giesey and Salmon, "Editors' Introduction" to François Hotman, *Francogallia*, pp. 1–134. Cf. Skinner, *Foundations*, 2:304.
133. Beza, *Rights of Magistrates*, 6, pp. 118–19.
134. Kingdon, "Beza's Political Ideas," p. 29.
135. Skinner speaks of it as a "representative treatment" of the contemporary Calvinist attitude towards tyrannicide, and examines it almost in tandem with Mornay as a kind of constitutionalist document, pointing out that both Beza and Mornay move the form of Huguenot resistance theory onto rational grounds. Skinner, *Foundations*, 2:321.

quite deliberate and conscious; he said explicitly that the remedy for tyranny "is to be found in human institutions" and proceeded to formulate the more rational scholastic doctrine on the origins and nature of political societies, rather than repeat the earlier Protestant emphasis on God as the providential source of political authority.[136]

Beza forthrightly rejected the view that humans are naturally subservient according to the father/son model, rejecting in advance, so to speak, the political patriarchalism of Filmer that occasioned John Locke's version of social-contract theory; he substituted the earlier scholastic view that liberty is a natural condition for all human beings. Individuals are not created for their rulers: it is self-evident that "peoples do not come from rulers," and that they establish rulers to better regulate their affairs.[137] Beza attributed the origin of political societies to a natural cause. Individuals come together and agree among themselves to form such an entity and thereby circumscribe their natural liberty. They do so in pursuit of some value perceived in a communal arrangement: the better regulation of their own affairs, their general well-being. A short while later, Mornay did not hesitate to express the same point in terms of the preservation of individual rights.[138]

Thus, the purpose of, or final cause for, establishing a polity is the welfare of the people concerned, the common good; its efficient cause is agreement by those concerned: the general consent, freely expressed, of the citizens involved. Beza was so convinced of this that he coupled the notion of consent with the traditional view that human liberty is itself limited only by the laws of God and nature. Authority in a polity derives from the agreement of consenting parties; but "if a people knowingly, and in complete freedom, has consented to something that is in itself manifestly irreligious and contrary to the law of nature, the obligation is invalid."[139] For Beza, an act of "free and lawful consent" is always needed for the creation of any "legitimate rulers,"[140] a point subsequently reit-

---

136. Beza, *Rights of Magistrates*, p. 103. Cf. Skinner, *Foundations*, 2:326.

137. Beza, *Rights of Magistrates*, p. 104.

138. Mornay, *Vindiciae*, F, p. 162. Cf. S, pp. 139, 158. The *Vindiciae* text cited here is the abridged English translation by Franklin in his *Constitutionalism and Resistance* (F) and the 1579 Latin text (S): see *infra*, p. 260 and note 185. Skinner draws a direct link between this argument and that found in John Major's *In quartum Sententiarum questiones utilissimae*. Skinner, *Foundations*, 2:327. Cf. *supra*, p. 112. We are here at what seems to be an intersection of strands of argument concerning the limits of legitimate political authority coming from scholastic and conciliar (Catholic) sources, with a resistance theory expressed by Protestant reformers.

139. Beza, *Rights of Magistrates*, 6, p. 124.

140. Ibid., 5, p. 107.

erated by all leading Huguenot theorists. Beza then proceeded to list the various offices and levels of magisterial authority, all of which derived their legitimacy from the same general source and in the same way: "dukes, marquises, counts, viscounts, barons, chatelains, the elected officers of towns"; he took his long account of the powers of these inferior magistrates directly from Hotman's *Francogallia* and ended with the claim that "the Estates of the country" have a right of "sovereign governance" assigned to them by the whole body of the people.[141]

However, not every citizen was included in the whole body of the people. As a collectivity that actually assigned or delegated authority to political rulers, the people was not the sum of every individual citizen, but only those whom the people as a whole consented to have as their representatives: the lower magistrates below the ruler to whom the people have delegated power. A further implication was that this delegation of authority deprived individual citizens of any right to exercise power on their own initiative; denial of the right of resistance or exercise of political power to an individual was again reinforced. While the people as a whole and, in some sense, individual citizens as parts of the whole community never forfeit their basic and ultimate right of sovereignty, they give up the right to employ it directly when they consent to be represented by magistrates who exercise this authority on their behalf. The right to hold a ruler to his promises to fulfill the purpose for which he holds the highest political office lies with the magistrates who hold the people's power in their hands. The hedge against anarchism real or imagined—the age-old bugaboo of political theorists and the particular bane of Reformation exegetes of Romans 13.1 and Augustinian politico-theological texts—thus remains in place.

The relationship between ruler and people through the intermediary magistrates is essentially contractual: a pact (*pactus*) exists between king and people. As Beza explained, "Wherever law and equity [have] prevailed, no nation has ever created nor accepted kings except upon definite conditions ... [which involve] a mutual oath between king and people."[142] He did not spell out what these conditions might be, nor did he give details about how the people actually delegated their original au-

---

141. Ibid., 6, pp. 110, 123.
142. Ibid., p. 114. The reference here to a mutual oath between king and people is also made much of in other Huguenot resistance tracts. Cf. *infra*, pp. 241, 257–59, 261. It picks up an element from the Magdeburg Confession that had been developed in earlier Lutheran legal circles (*supra*, p. 216). The notion of connecting the limits of political authority with the coronation oath sworn before the people is, of course, very medieval. Cf. the position of Hotman, *infra*, p. 259 and Mornay, *infra*, p. 261.

thority to their representatives; Mornay was much more explicit on the issue of the mutual responsibilities of ruler and peoples' representatives.[143] But what Beza and later Calvinist publicists did was to spell out a view reflecting earlier scholastic political thought that had been articulated in canon and civil law traditions as far back as the late thirteenth and early fourteenth centuries and culminated in the conciliar thought of the late fourteenth and early fifteenth centuries.[144]

One critical feature of Beza's position, something else with which Mornay agreed, was the status given lower magistrates as delegates of the people and representative of popular authority: they were servants of the people, not of the rulers; they were responsible to the people who created them and not to the king whom they created. As Beza put it in a clear statement on the popular basis for sovereignty, they hold office "properly speaking, not of the sovereign but of the sovereignty ... when the sovereign magistrate dies, they nonetheless remain in office, just as the sovereignty itself remains intact."[145] He coupled this with a categorical rejection of the notion that the ruler is above the law. Consistent with the thesis that the ruler is a minister or administrator to the polity as a whole, Beza insisted that the king was not really sovereign in the literal sense of the term. His view on the dictum *princeps a legibus solutus est* was that "there is not a single law to which the ruler is not bound in the conduct of his government, since he has sworn to be the protector and preserver of them all. [To say that the ruler] is not subject to the laws [is] the false maxim of detestable flatterers, not of a subject loyal to his prince."[146] As Mornay was to put it in the scholastic jargon characteristic of the whole argument, the king was *minor universo* though *maior singulis*.[147]

---

143. See *infra*, p. 262.
144. "The Huguenots are ... in complete agreement with the most radical of their scholastic predecessors about the character of the commonwealth ... [their] main conclusion ... [is] a theory of popular sovereignty ... which forms the core of their constitutionalism, and their most celebrated argument—their defence of resistance ... merely an implication." Skinner, *Foundations*, 2:332, citing Franklin, "Constitutionalism in the Sixteenth Century." Mornay presents the clearest example of this formulation.
145. Beza, *Rights of Magistrates*, p. 111.
146. Ibid., p. 113. Here Beza's comment about applying the formula to a temporal ruler ("the false maxim of detestable flatterers") is virtually the same as that used by Vitoria to deny its literal application to the pope: "merely a piece of flattery and adultation." Cf. *supra*, p. 160.
147. Mornay, *Vindiciae*, F, p. 162. Again the connection with Spanish neo-scholastic political thought is inescapable. Cf. *supra*, pp. 112, 143, 155, 177–81.

As well as forthrightly advocating resistance by inferior magistrates, Beza also carefully examined the possible legitimacy of tyrannicide—again, not a feature of earlier Reformation political tracts. The notion of tyrannicide as a weapon against political injustice had a long history in Christian political thought, of course, and had undergone a certain amount of analytic scrutiny in the Middle Ages; but thus far it had no proponents among Reformation political writers. The explanation, at least in the 1520s and 1530s, seems to have been that to a large extent, the continental reformers were supported, if not actually promoted, by the political authorities in regions where the Reformation actually occurred. Except where imperial authorities opposed the Lutheran Reform but without, for the moment, giving their opposition tangible expression, there was little immediate need for the reformers to address the fearful question of how to deal with physical force being used to suppress their Reformed religion. There was, too, the overwhelming desire among both Lutherans and Calvinists in the 1520s to dissociate themselves from the political anarchy and bloodshed of the peasant uprisings, as well as from the theological anarchism of the Anabaptists and other radical Protestant groups. Further, the standard Reformation doctrine that all political authority, even that of tyrants, was divinely ordained offered no obvious ground for a theory of tyrannicide. It continued to get marginal play in Catholic political thinking, however, and emerged again with some fanfare, as earlier shown, among Spanish neo-scholastics in the late sixteenth century.[148] But it served no purpose in Reformation political thought until the flurry of Protestant publicist tracts was produced after the St Bartholomew's Day bloodshed.

It is difficult find any reference to tyrannicide among Protestant publicists, especially in the spate of Huguenot texts that emerged in the latter decades of the sixteenth century, even though anti-Huguenot activities in France allegedly sponsored by the French royal household gave force to the idea. However, Beza's was not the only treatment of the subject at the time: Mornay's *Vindiciae* has a section on tyrannicide, and a far more outspoken statement appeared in the anonymous *Discours politiques* (1574). Though found in Reformation political thought after St Bartholomew's Day, its expression in these sources still seems singularly Catholic, even medieval scholastic, and legalist in formulation. Beza's main concern was to locate the legitimacy of resistance at some level of specific juridical authority and deny it to individual subjects or

---

148. See *supra*, pp. 166; 181–82.

the people as a whole. The problem of distinguishing between legitimate resistance and total anarchy, ordinary citizens' entitlement to disobey any law they judged contrary to divine or natural law, had already proven insoluble for earlier Reformation thinkers, which is largely why it took so long to articulate any Protestant resistance theory at all.

Both Melanchthon and Bucer, for example, repeated the traditional doctrine that Christians were obliged to follow the laws of God and nature where these conflicted with temporal legislation; but they were careful to dissociate themselves from views that might seem to legitimate mere disobedience. Even after various forms of resistance theory had begun to circulate in Lutheran and Calvinist circles in mid-century, particularly after the 1550 Magdeburg Confession, there was considerable uneasiness about the possible equation of simple resistance with the conceptually different, and more ominous, notion of total revolution against existing authority. This concern stemmed to a large extent from the implications of a strand of the resistance argument developed by the legal advisors of Philip of Hesse and based on the Roman private-law concept of individual self-defence: the use of force to repel force. Reference to the *vi vim repellere licet* dictum by Ponet and Goodman in England and by the anonymous continental author of the *Defence civile et militaire* had, as early as the late 1550s, raised the alarm of anarchism,[149] the only counter being the by-then conventional resistance-theory feature that an individual might be authorized directly by God to resist. By the mid-1570s, however, these concerns had come to be seen as a prohibition of tyrannicide except under hopelessly impractical conditions. The anonymous *Discours politiques*, for example, heaped scorn on the "so-called theologians and preachers [who teach that] a special revelation from God" is needed to justify the killing of a tyrant; its author went on to assert that he could find "nothing solid in any of their arguments [to substantiate] their total prohibition of this means" of freeing people from oppression.[150]

Beza began his treatment of tyrannicide with the traditional medieval legal distinction between a tyrant who simply usurps power and one who begins to practise tyranny after coming into office legitimately. Someone who has "by force and fraud ... usurped a power which is not theirs by law [has no rights to rule; accordingly] every private citizen [can] exert

---

149. Skinner, *Foundations*, 2:320.
150. "Discours politiques des diverses puissances établies de Dieu au monde," in [Simon Goulart] *Mémoires de l'état de France sous Charles neuvième*, 3:293a.

all their strength to defend the legitimate institutions of their country [against someone] whose authority is not legitimate."[151] In circumstances where a "sovereign magistrate" who is otherwise legitimate acts tyrannically, the situation is different. Here resistance is permitted, but only to someone with a "vocation" for the deed, such as a magistrate or other representative of the people. No ordinary citizen can lay claim to this authority since the people are never "authorized" to take the law into their own hands.[152] An individual citizen, and even the people as a whole, has only "penitence and patience joined with prayers" as a remedy for tyranny; anything else would be bound to attract "the danger of God's curse."[153] Tyrannicide was thus legitimized as a specific form of resistance, but its execution was restricted to persons holding some form of public office. The author of the *Discours politiques* may have had Beza's text in mind when he excoriated the impractical views of "some theologians" on tyrannicide.

Its printing and translation record indicates that Beza's *Du droit* enjoyed wide circulation during the last quarter of the sixteenth century and on into the next, and it can be presumed to have been instrumental in strengthening the Huguenot position in France and the Netherlands. It would have been of immediate use to the French Huguenots who controlled many cities in France at the time, and who desperately needed to take a defensive military stance after the St Bartholomew's Day massacre; the work itself, written presumably in response to this tragedy, was evidence of Beza's involvement in post-massacre Huguenot political activity.[154]

### 5. PETER MARTYR VERMIGLI

Another reformer who expressed views on the legitimacy of armed resistance to political authority in defence of the "true" religion was Peter Martyr Vermigli. Born in England in 1520, he had converted to the Reformed religion at an early age and, on the accession of Mary in 1553, was forced to leave England; he fled to the Continent where he remained until his death in 1562.[155] Calvinist in religion, he established

---

151. Beza, *Rights of Magistrates*, pp. 105, 107.
152. Ibid., pp. 102, 129.
153. Ibid., p. 129.
154. Kingdon, "Reactions to the St Bartholomew's Day Massacre," p. 29.
155. See Marvin Walter Anderson, *Peter Martyr* and "Royal Idolatry."

himself in Strasbourg where he taught theology from 1553, but he maintained close contact with Calvin and his followers in Geneva. As with Beza, his political ideas were not particularly original, nor was the doctrine that emerged from them complete. But his ideas are of interest because they serve to fill in details and illustrate the specifics of Calvinist political thinking in the period 1550–65.

Vermigli's views on the nature of polity are found principally in his commentaries on the Old Testament, particularly the *Book of Judges* and the *Commentaries on Paul's Epistle to the Romans*. The former is the more significant and, if Kingdon's dating for it is correct, represents one of earliest explicit Reformist formulations of an unequivocal resistance theory. Apparently based on the lectures Vermigli gave at Strasbourg in the period 1553–56, its contents suggest that, as a public statement of resistance doctrine, it was roughly contemporaneous with Beza's *De haereticis* (1554), and there is some suggestion that Vermigli may have been influenced by Beza.[156] The lectures were not published until 1561, however, when they appeared in a compilation of Vermigli's writings that followed what had become an accepted format for presenting the views of various Lutheran and Calvinist divines, the so-called "Common Places" (*loci communes*). These were tracts offering commentaries on a standard set of Scriptural texts to provide a synthesis of Reformation theology. They were, in effect, manuals of theology and important vehicles for the transmission of sixteenth- and seventeenth-century Reformation doctrine.

The *loci communes* format had been adopted first by Melanchthon as early as 1521, when he published a Latin commentary on what he considered the most significant of the Old and New Testament texts on which the Reformed religion was based. Examination of these *loci communes*, particularly with reference to such Scriptural texts as the Book of Judges and Paul's Epistle to the Romans, is a useful way to discover Reformation political thought, since the reformers' commentaries on these relevant scriptural sources contain the basics of their political thinking. Melanchthon's early political views, for example, can be found in the penultimate section of his *loci communes*, where he describes both ecclesiastical and secular magistrates. And the 1553 Geneva edition contained a considerably expanded analysis of secular government treated as a separate topic, as well as an expansion into several chapters of his earlier

---

156. Skinner, *Foundations*, 2:213.

treatment of the nature of the Church.[157] Calvin's *Institution* was cast in the same format, with the entire fourth and last book devoted to an examination of the "human" institutions through which God works. The definitive 1559 Latin edition has nineteen chapters in Book Four, and its last section on "secular" government contains the statements examined earlier on ephoral authority and Calvin's cryptic defence of political resistance to tyranny.[158]

Because they were used for centuries in the seminaries for the education and educational formation of Lutheran and Calvinist clergy, these manuals of Protestant theology probably did more to spread Reformation political thought than the publicist tracts, even though the latter have become the main objects of historical research on the subject.[159] Vermigli's was the most important among the later *loci communes* manuals, and its analysis of the nature of political authority covers eight (or nine) chapters, thirteen to twenty (or twenty-one) sections in Part Four.[160] At least fourteen editions were published between 1576 and 1656 in various European centres, three of them in London, and it was a basic Calvinist reference work in the late sixteenth and early seventeenth centuries. Vermigli's complete commentaries on the Scriptures, which also contained statements excerpted in the *loci communes*,[161] would also have been published in many editions. The longer of his two political analyses appears in an extended commentary on Judges 19 entitled *De magistratu*, in which the nature of political authority is defined with some precision and Catholic arguments for legitimizing temporal powers in the hands of the clergy categorically rejected.[162] A notable feature of Vermigli's text is its great clarity; another is that he applied Aristotle's *Politics* and the classical Platonic/Aristotelian classification of

---

157. Kingdon, "Political Thought of Vermigli," p. 123.
158. Cf. *supra*, pp. 229–30.
159. Kingdon, "Political Thought of Vermigli," p. 122. Kingdon offers article 45 from Beza's *loci communes*, entitled "Confessions of Christian Faith," as an example of this judgment. The article itself, entitled "On the obedience due to magistrates" in the revised 1560 version of the *loci*, was published in French as a separate tract under the same title fourteen years later. Kingdon has published the 1560 tract as an appendix to his edition of the 1574 text, in *The Political Thought of Peter Martyr Vermigli*.
160. Kingdon, "Political Thought of Vermigli," p. 123.
161. Ibid., p. 124. Kingdon says that Vermigli's *Commentaries on Judges* was published only in 1561, though he dates their delivery as lectures as early as 1553–56; Skinner says that Vermigli's *Commentary on Paul to the Romans* was published in 1558, and the one on Judges in 1561. Skinner, *Foundations*, 2:213.
162. Kingdon, "Political Thought of Vermigli," p. 125.

the six basic types of polity to both ecclesiastical and temporal models much as Thomas Aquinas, John of Paris, and other medieval scholastics had done—an approach not found in any earlier Reformation political writer.

Vermigli argued that the Church's institutional structure conforms to the classical mixed form of polity, incorporating the best features of the three basic models: God is the monarch as supreme legislator (when this mixed form of polity was related to the Church among medieval thinkers, of course, the monarchical function was attributed to the pope[163]); the bishops, elders, doctors, and other persons of ecclesiastical rank are the aristocracy chosen by merit rather than wealth, birth, or favour; and the people are the democratic element in that specific important decisions such as excommunication are "referred" to them.[164] The same pattern of analysis is applied to the secular polity, in which the structure continues to be Aristotelian while the content is based largely on Scripture and the Church Fathers, with occasional reference to both Roman and canon law and infrequent reference to contemporary political practice.[165] In discussing the right of resistance, Vermigli alluded several times to the Holy Roman Empire and argued from current constitutional arrangements rather than Scripture: "By what law do inferior princes resist either the emperor or kings or else [other?] public wealths [commonwealths], when they defend the sincere religion and true faith? I answer by the law of the Empire, or by the law of the king, or by the law of the public wealth. For they are chosen of emperors, kings and public wealths as helpers to rule, whereby justice may more and more flourish. And therefore were they ordained (*ordinati*) according to the office committed to them, rightly, justly, and godly to govern the public wealth. Wherefore they do according to their duty, when in the cause of religion they resist the higher power."[166]

Arguing against the Anabaptists, Vermigli maintained that magistrates, like leaders of the Church, derive their authority from God and thus have all the powers normally claimed by existing political authorities. Like

---

163. Cf. John of Paris, *Royal and Papal Power* 19, ad 35, p. 101; and Monahan, *Consent, Coercion, and Limit*, pp. 201–3.

164. Vermigli, *Loci communes* 5.9. Cited in Kingdon, "Political Thought of Vermigli," p. 127.

165. Vermigli, *Loci communes* 13.2. Cited in Kingdon, "Political Thought of Vermigli," p. 128–29.

166. Vermigli, Scholium on Judges 1:36. See also his widely circulated argument in favor of resistance at *Loci communes* 21.13. Cited in Kingdon, "Political Thought of Vermigli," p. 130.

Calvin and others, he deferred the issue of resistance to the very end of his consideration of secular authority and examined it in terms of tyranny. Accepting the legitimacy of all basic models of governance—monarchy, aristocracy, and democracy—he asked about citizens' obligations under a tyranny in any of the three. Acknowledging the traditional distinction between tyranny as simple seizure of power and tyranny as practised by an otherwise legitimate ruler, Vermigli was not comfortable with the traditional medieval view that the first could be resisted by anyone and seemed to reject tyrannicide in both cases, apparently on the ground that a tyrant held genuine authority regardless of how he may have come into office.[167]

Vermigli made one critical exception to the obligation to obey genuine though tyrannical authority: the case of tyranny exercised over the "true" religion. Invoking the traditional directive that Christians must obey the laws of God over those of humans, he maintained that every Protestant was obliged to disobey an order to engage in false worship; he extended this obligation further in the case of magistrates, who were forbidden even to resign in such circumstances and were required to use all their powers to frustrate tyrannical laws. He advocated passive acceptance on the part of Christian subjects in the first instance, but did not ultimately reject active resistance. Vermigli was unwilling to trust God to defend the Reformation without human help, and like many other Protestant leaders at this critical time, he held that inferior magistrates were entitled to lead resistance against a tyrannical government that was engaged in the direct suppression of the Reformed religion.[168]

He cited as examples of legitimate resistance by inferior magistrates (1) the ancient Romans, who sometimes forced an elected consul to leave office; (2) the Danes of his own day, who had deposed and imprisoned their king; and (3) the English, who, according to Polydore Vergil, sometimes forced kings to account for misspent monies. Vermigli's argument here was developed further in a scholium on Judges 1:36, published separately as a pamphlet in English while he was still in Strasbourg.[169] Here Vermigli appealed ultimately to Roman law, employing a traditional argument that implied the existence of a contract

---

167. Vermigli, Scholium on Genesis 34, in *Loci communes* 21.19. Cited in Kingdon, "Political Thought of Vermigli," p. 133.

168. See Vermigli, *Commentaries on Romans* 13:1–4, a position refined and developed in the scholium on Judges 3 in *Loci communes* 4.20.12–13. Cited in Kingdon, "Political Thought of Vermigli," p. 134.

169. Vermigli, Scholium on Judges 3, in *Loci communes* 4.20.12–13. Cf. Kingdon, "Political Thought of Vermigli," p. 134, and Anderson, *Peter Martyr*, pp. 349ff.

between ruler and people, the *lex digna*: "The Emperor testifieth in the *Code*, that his mind is not that any of his decrees should take place in judgment against right, but that they ought to be made void and of no force if that peradventure they be known to decline from justice." And he repeated from Trajan the nostrum "If I rule justly, use it [the sword] on my side; but if I rule unjustly, use it against me," justifying the use of the sword in defence of what is just even in circumstances where such use is against the emperor himself.[170] These invocations of the *lex digna* and the Trajan dictum would be repeated again and again by Protestant resistance theorists in the late sixteenth century—Beza used both of them, for example—and by using them, Vermigli placed himself squarely in the main stream of Protestant theory, even though he was not the originator of some of its principal arguments.

Vermigli's position on resistance was basically Lutheran and less radical than those of his fellow exiles from England or Calvin's more militant followers in France. Although the channels through which he absorbed Lutheran political thought are not clearly known, his heavy reliance on Romans 13 was reminiscent of Luther, and he reflected Melanchthon in his extensive use of Aristotle.[171] He began by endorsing the Pauline assertion that the powers that be are "ordained of God," but inserted two corrections to this general interpretation. Firstly, he says that "some cavil in vain that they should do no reverence to inferior magistrates [because they] think it sufficient if they be subject to the higher powers, as to emperors and kings [failing to realize that Paul's text] comprehends all manner of power [including] such as have the charge of cities or are appointed governors of provinces."[172] Secondly, and more radically, Vermigli asserted that St Paul intended his injunction to apply only to those powers that exercised authority properly. Here he was making the traditional distinction between office and officeholder that went back in Christian thought at least as far as Leo the Great, and that canonists had invoked to justify action against an errant ecclesiastical authority, bishop or pope.[173]

Vermigli held that, while God was directly responsible for creating the

---

170. Vermigli, Scholium on Judges 1:36, in *Loci communes*. Cited in Kingdon, ed., "Political Thought of Vermigli," p. 135.

171. Kingdon, ed., ibid., p. 137. Kingdon suggests that Johann Sleidan, who taught at Strasbourg in the period 1553–56, may have been a channel of Aristotelian influence.

172. Vermigli, *Commentaries ... upon the Epistles of St Paul to the Romans*, trans. H. B. (London: 1568): fol. 429A.

173. Vermigli, *Commentaries on Romans*, fol. 427B; 430B. Cf. *supra*, p. 55.

authority of an office, He could not be held accountable for any abuse of office by its occupant. By applying this distinction to the Pauline text, Vermigli made a clear break from the simple Reformation interpretation of St Paul and Augustine, according to which God ordained even tyrants as part of His providential plan to show the sinful character of subjects who were their victims. His position appears all the more startling when contrasted with other comments in the same *Commentary on Romans*: "In kingdoms many things are done ... unjustly ... laws are perverted [so that] many think it cannot be that such powers are from God. [But] it is not enough [to say] God does not do these things, but only permits them. [He often] executes his just judgment [through evil rulers and] therein commits no offence [providing] tyrants to afflict the people [for] their grievous acts."[174] It is clear, nonetheless, that Vermigli adjusted the Pauline doctrine espoused by early Lutherans and Calvinists alike in a way that Catholic writers had done centuries earlier and then interpreted it to permit resistance to tyrannical oppression. Individual citizens were not allowed to engage in active opposition to tyranny, but it did not follow "that superior powers cannot be put down by inferior magistrates." All magistrates possess certain "ordained" powers to fulfil a specific responsibility, and even the highest authorities can be "constrained" by lower ones "if they transgress the ends and limits of the power which they have received."[175] Vermigli made no direct reference to the notion of ephors or inferior magistrates; nor did he give straightforward expression to the so-called private-law argument by which citizens were entitled to act against a ruler who had broken his contract with them by transgressing the limits of his legitimate authority. But he did

---

174. Vermigli, *Commentaries on Romans*, fol. 427B. Cf. *Commentary on Judges*, fol. 256B and *Commentaries on Romans*, fol. 426A. Skinner finds Martyr's position incoherent in argument and confused at this point insofar as he seems to be both denying and affirming resistance to political authority. I suspect it would not have seemed so to his contemporaries, who would not have been as likely as a modern reader to take literally the strictures about the illegitimacy of any resistance to tyranny against the "true" religion. It is true that the *Commentary on Judges* text is later than that on Romans, leading Skinner to say that Vermigli "reverts" to the position that "the present state of things [as] instituted by God ... ought not to be altered without him." *Commentary on Judges*, fol. 149B; Skinner, *Foundations*, 2:216. But he did say both things in the *Commentaries on Romans*. Skinner is quite right, however, to point out that Ponet and Goodman, and to a certain extent even Knox, were much more forthright and lucid than Vermigli in advancing the private-law argument to justify resistance on the grounds that rulers who exceed their authority can be opposed. Skinner, *Foundations*, 2:221–24.

175. Vermigli, *Commentaries on Romans*, fol. 430B.

move away from the simple Protestant position that all the depredations of a tyrant must be suffered patiently by Christian believers.

## 6. FRANÇOIS HOTMAN: THE FRANCOGALLIA

As much for the circumstances of its publication and circulation as for its contents, one of the most important documents in the history of Reformation political thought was the publicist tract posing as a history of France known as the *Francogallia*. The work of a French Huguenot humanist and teacher of law, François Hotman, it appeared very shortly after the St Bartholomew's Day massacre, responding to the event with an indirect critique of the contemporary French monarchy. Published in Latin in three distinct editions, the first in 1573 and the last in 1586, it provided an historical basis for an alternative political structure. It was the first in a series of classic texts setting out a full-fledged revolutionary Huguenot political theory.

Hotman had published an earlier work on the history of law in France, the *Anti-Tribonian*, a self-indulgent effort excoriating the harmful effects of importations from Roman law, both civil and canon, into the French legal system. An early convert to the Calvinist religion in France, he was a well-known advocate of the Huguenot cause and barely escaped the massacre of Huguenots at Bourges after the Paris mass murders in late 1572; he fled to Geneva, never to return to France. Hotman had apparently begun the *Francogallia* before his escape from France and pushed it rapidly to a conclusion from his haven in Geneva, where it was published in July 1573. He consulted on its contents with Theodore Beza, it seems, and there are marked similarities between it and Beza's *Du droit des magistrats*, published about a year later.[176]

Nothing shows more clearly the pro-Huguenot purpose behind the *Francogallia* than Hotman's thoroughgoing efforts to revise and re-edit his text, not once, but twice in the space of less than fifteen years, adding material from recently published sources for French history as well as a mass of legal documentation. He even significantly modified the nature and form of his argument. The original version contained little more than half of the final text, the second edition about three-quarters, and the balance of material was added to the last.[177] The second edition (1576) contained more than fifteen new historical and legal sources that

---

176. Cf. *supra*, p. 243. See Giesey, "When and Why Hotman Wrote the *Francogallia*."
177. Giesey and Salmon, "Editors' Introduction," p. 52.

had been published after 1567 in Latin, French, and English, all of them directly relevant to the political and legal history of Western Europe. The final edition contains more than eight hundred references to some 158 separate authorities, and it is largely in this edition that the Roman legal sources Hotman uses can be found.[178]

The *Francogallia* was generally recognized from its first appearance as an *oeuvre d'occasion* in support of the Huguenot communities in France, even though it portrayed itself as an objective history of France.[179] A spate of histories of the French people had been produced in the period 1560–80, all using basically the same sources and emphasizing similar themes, specifically the origins of the French people prior to and during the Roman imperial era and the character of the French monarchy and its relationship to the people as a whole. While Hotman's work made no direct reference to the unprecedented number of current histories in French, he almost certainly would have consulted them; the similarity of approach shows the currency of many views found in the *Fracogallia* and affords an opportunity for a comparative assessment of Hotman as an historian of the time. He seems in general to have been as competent as most of his peers, although at times he deliberately distorted the data on which he worked. And one or two of his contemporaries, such as François de Belleforest in his *Chroniques et Annales de France* (1573), showed greater critical acumen in their use of source material.[180] In reading the *Francogallia*, however, it is essential to keep its *parti pris* purpose and character clearly in mind.

Hotman's history portrayed the French monarchy as owing its existence and character to the people as a whole, by whom it had been established, hence from whom it derived authority in such a way that its powers were limited by the terms agreed to by the subjects themselves. This constituted a new approach in defending the Huguenot cause and a different form of advocacy than it had earlier received. Prior to the grisly events of late 1572, the Protestant cause had been urged on the ground that its adherents were opposing Catholic forces who were themselves rebelling against the proper function of the monarchy, viz., to support the rights of and offer protection to the Huguenots as loyal citizens;

---

178. Ibid., p. 57.
179. Franklin is of the view that Hotman's work was more than a *livre de circonstance* and "one (the second) part of an ambitious scholarly enterprise" to assist the codification of French law begun under the French chancellor, Michel l'Hôpital. Franklin, *Constitutionalism and Resistance*, p. 49.
180. Giesey and Salmon, "Editors' Introduction," p. 50.

but after the St Bartholomew's Day massacre this posture was abandoned. What was needed now was a justification for resisting the monarchy itself, and this meant pressing a twofold argument: on the one hand, a doctrine that could justify Huguenot resistance on grounds of conscience, a case made to persuade members of the Reformed religion about the legitimacy of resisting lawful authority; and on the other, a constitutional appeal to the other side showing that persecution of large numbers of citizens exceeded the legitimate limits of political authority.

Hotman's *Francogallia* was the first Huguenot tract to mould the kind of constitutional argument urged by French Protestants in the late 1550s and 1560s into a more revolutionary doctrine. He himself had been a leading exponent of the moderate position in the 1560s, but the appalling events of 1572 induced a more revolutionary stance. When he began to draft the *Francogallia* in the 1560s, Hotman's original intention seems to have been simply to expand the historical frame of reference of his earlier *Anti-Tribonian* into a full historical justification for a popular constitution in France. By 1573, however, he had realized the possibilities and advantages of presenting something more than a putatively accurate account of the historical record. What was needed at this time was an historically based account that offered a political argument for a modern state that reflected the original arrangements made by the French people for their own polity whose essential feature was popular consent. Hotman was prepared to doctor the historical record to achieve this purpose; he wanted the original French constitution as described in the *Francogallia* to be taken as normative for the present and future French state. In fact it was soon widely appealed to as a political model, in Holland and England as well as France, and it played a central role in the attack on the English monarchy during the reign of the ill-fated Charles I.[181]

A glance at the text of the *Francogallia* shows the Hotman methodology. Chapter 6 begins with Tacitus's celebrated statement that the Germans chose their king *ex nobilitate* and their military leaders *ex virtute* rather than by hereditary succession and goes on to observe that similar practices existed in present day Germany, Scandinavia, and Poland.[182]

---

181. Skinner, *Foundations*, 2:311. Cf. Pocock, *Ancient Constitution and Feudal Law*, pp. 30–55.

182. Tacitus, *Germania* 7, cited in Hotman, *Francogallia* 6, p. 221, as are the contemporary elective practices. The page references to the *Francogallia* are to the fine English translation by J. H. M. Salmon, edited by Ralph E. Giesey.

The core of Hotman's position is reflected in the titles to chapters 10 and 11 of the 1573 edition (chapters 13 and 14 in the 1586 edition): *De regis maiestate et annuo gentis Francogallicis conventu, placito, curia, parliamenti* ("The royal majesty and the annual assembly of the Francogallican people, also known as the Placitum, Curia and Parlementum"); and *De sacrosancta publica concilii auctoritate et quibus de rebus in eo agere* ("The sacred authority of the public council and what was done there").

Hotman's general case followed lines similar to those of other constitutional writers of the 1560s such as Beza and Peter Martyr Vermigli: the crown (higher authorities) must be controlled and limited by *la police*, that is, by what we would call some form of constitutional structure surrounding the monarchy and circumscribing its authority. He referred in this connection to the *Leges imperii* and devoted an entire chapter in the 1586 edition to "Laws established to restrict kings." What he had in mind particularly was a notion found originally in Seyssel's *La monarchie de France*: that the French monarchy was regulated by customs and established feudal practices such as the coronation oath sworn by the monarchy as a contract with the people. Hotman quoted Seyssel directly in the 1586 edition of the *Francogallia*, describing "the institutions and practices of the kingdom sanctioned throughout many ages and confirmed by longstanding custom."[183]

The most important limits and checks on the monarchy come from religion and justice as exercised through popular assemblies and juridical bodies. The emphasis here was placed forcefully on the estates general as the instrument for guaranteeing the conformity between legislative activity and religion and justice. However, Hotman was contemptuous of the French parlements in this connection, dismissing them on historical grounds as a late interventionist instrument invented by the Capetian kings to ensure that a kept group of royalist appointees was always available to approve the monarch's personal wishes. According to him, even the term *parlementum* had been usurped by the French juridical entity currently so designated; originally, it had referred to the assembly of the three Estates, "a solemn and public council" convened at least once a year under the ancient constitution and possessing the authority "to deliberate on the general welfare ... [It was thus] something sacrosanct ...

---

183. Hotman, *Francogallia*, p. 473. His tripartite enumeration of the types of checks and limits on the French monarchy, *la police*, *la religion*, *la justice*, also repeats the Seyssel text, *Monarchie*.

over a vast period of time."[184] In a separate chapter inserted in the 1586 edition, Hotman did acknowledge the function of the Parlement of Paris in ensuring that "neither the king's laws nor his edicts [are accepted] unless they have been examined ... [and] approved by its judges."[185] But otherwise he was simply dismissive of parlement as the legal council for approving legislation, and hostile in general to the notion that any instrument of a legal or juridical type could guarantee the general welfare of the people. His preference for estates general over parlement was reflected later to some extent in Bodin's *Method*.[186]

### 7. MORNAY: THE VINDICIAE CONTRA TYRANNOS

One of the most comprehensive of the Huguenot political works of the 1570s, certainly the most influential if not the most radical in content, was the *Vindiciae contra tyrannos*, published anonymously in Geneva in 1579 (the title page names Edinburgh as the place of publication) but now generally, though not universally, attributed to Philippe du Plessis Mornay (1544–1633). Mornay may also have written an anonymous *Exhortation à la paix* (1570), a plea to the French government to recognize the Huguenots as the only way to prevent further civil chaos in France.[187] The *Vindiciae* contains the fullest summary of the major arguments developed by the Huguenot publicists in the wake of the St Bartholomew's Day massacres.

The text is extensive—some 165 pages in its original Latin edition— and provides a careful, systematic, even brilliant summary of a theory of civil governance based on the primary rights of the people to exercise control over, and limit, the authority of a supreme ruler through chosen representatives. It is divided into four parts, or questions, that make its purpose clear. Part One asks whether subjects are bound and ought to obey princes, if these command what is against the law of God; Part Two, whether it is lawful to resist a prince who infringes the law of God or ruins the Church? By whom, how and the extent to which it [resistance]

---

184. Hotman, *Francogallia*, pp. 323, 397. Cf. pp. 499–500.

185. For the reasons why Hotman inserted this additional chapter in his 1586 edition of the text, see Franklin, *Constitutionalism and Resistance*, pp. 28–29.

186. Cf. *infra*, p. 262.

187. Skinner, *Foundations*, 2:253. Cf. Patry, *Philippe du Plessis-Mornay*. I am satisfied that Franklin has settled the issue of whether Mornay was the author of the *Vindiciae*. Franklin, *Constitutionalism and Resistance*, pp. 138–40. See his references to bibliography on this long-running controversy at p. 139, note 1 and p. 208, notes 2–7.

is lawful; Part Three, whether it is lawful to resist a prince who oppresses or ruins a public state, and how far such resistance may be extended? By whom, how and by what right it is permitted; and Part Four, whether neighbour princes or states may be, or are, bound by law to give aid to the subjects of princes afflicted for the cause of true religion or oppressed by manifest tyranny. The primary ground on which the legitimacy for resistance is set, at least in terms of the sequence of elements considered, is defence of the "true" religion. Defence against tyranny, a more general and more exclusively political value, comes second. In other words, the work was pitched as a whole towards Huguenot supporters, offering them as a first line of defence the argument that they had a right to resist efforts to suppress their religion. The stress was on the defensive character of the policy being advocated, even though that policy aimed at justifying a direct attack on the French monarchy.

Mornay followed the Hotman line in emphasizing the coronation oath as the popular base limiting the French monarchy by a form of contract. Hotman himself took the position from Seyssel's *Monarchie*, although the *Vindiciae* frames it in doctrinal terms rather than the historical terms employed by Seyssel. Mornay first describes how the monarchy originated, asserting that, although "in certain regimes the right of free elections almost seems no longer to exist ... in all properly constituted kingdoms the practice still remains inviolate [so that] even those who seem today to come to the throne by succession must first be inaugurated by the people."[188] He later applied the concept directly to France, introducing the Hotman historical judgment and reference to the coronation oath: "It is commonly thought that pure succession obtains [but history shows that] when a king of France is inaugurated [the bishops] ask all the people present if it is their pleasure to have the designee as king ... [there is] a statement in the coronation formula that the people have elected him."[189]

The *Vindiciae* also employed the notion that lower magistrates exercised legitimate political authority. Like other later Huguenot theorists, Mornay alluded to the traditionally authoritative dispute between Azo and Lothair about whether an official other than the king had genuine authority; he opted for the Bartolist position favouring Azo's view that magistrates might also exercise *imperium*, the power of the sword.[190]

188. Mornay, *Vindiciae*, F, pp. 160, 161.
189. Ibid., p. 183.
190. *Re* Bartolus of Sassoferrato, cf. *supra*, p. 22.

Raising the question who can exercise the *ius gladii* when analysing the relationship between people and ruler, he distinguished between "officers of the kingdom" and "officers of the king" and asserted that, while the latter were merely the king's personal servants bound only to obey the king, the former were "associates in the royal power ... [and] all of them are bound, just like the king, to look after the welfare of the commonwealth," with the king as "president" among this group.[191]

The *Vindiciae* carefully presented the argument that checks against unlimited royal authority existed in representative bodies in the French government structure. Again, this material is in the section dealing with relations between people and king (Part One), where Mornay addresses this critical issue more fully than any other Huguenot writer. He identified the parlement of France, not the estates general as Hotman had done, as "judge between the king and the people, and especially between the king and particular individuals." If the king presumed to act against an individual "in contravention of the law, it is the right and duty of parlement to see that justice is done. If the monarch "passes any edict or decision in his private council, or if a war is to be declared or peace is to be made," agreement by the parlement is necessary in every case. Parlement thus is given a central place in the French polity: "every thing relating to the commonwealth has to be entered in the record of its [parlement's] acts," and nothing is to be considered lawful, "ratified," until parlement has given formal approval.[192] Mornay's claims for the rights of a popular representative body, it should be noted, were comprehensive: all, not just some, royal decisions, including declarations of war and decisions involving the exercise of judicial discretion— matters accorded to the royal prerogative by other, less thoroughgoing, constitutionalists—fall under the jurisdiction of the parlement.[193]

Ironically, Mornay's formulation of popular sovereignty was far more legalistic than Hotman's, though it was Hotman rather than Mornay whose personal background and experience were concentrated in the law. But Hotman was virulently opposed to the contemporary French legal establishment, particularly as embodied in the parlement of Paris; he regularly heaped scorn on the parlement as a warren of placemakers and royal flunkies, and his judgment on the harmful effects of the importation of Roman civil and canon law into the French constitutional system was no less caustic. For these reasons, Hotman opted for the es-

191. Mornay, *Vindiciae*, F, pp. 161–62.
192. Ibid., p. 165.
193. Cf. *supra*, p. 165.

tates general as the bastion of popular sovereignty, making his case in historical rather than legal terms. In fact good legal and historical arguments could also have been used to show that parlement was the legal protector of basic citizens' rights, both individual and collective, in France, as Mornay maintained, precisely the kind of claims made regularly and forcefully, if unsuccessfully, in the parlement itself throughout the 1550s and 1560s.

The same emphasis on a legal approach to his constitutionalist position can be seen in Mornay's use of the "ephors" argument, which had become standard, to legitimate resistance activity. His view that lower magistrates had genuine authority in their own right as representatives of the people again exhibited the clarity of his thought. Magisterial authority was not said to come directly from God or in any sense to be related exclusively to protection of the "true" religion. Rather, the magistrates, no less than members of regular collective representative bodies, parlements or estates general, were constituted by the people and thus possessed the same ephoral powers to put bridle and reins on kings. Mornay repeatedly used the "bridle and reins on the ruler" motif, a standard formula in medieval scholastic constitutionalist thought, to describe the function of lesser magistrates and mentioned the monthly oaths sworn between the kings of Sparta and their ephors. The officers of the kingdom in France were examples of ephoral authorities to whom "the people give the administration" of the kingdom no less than to the king and his estates.[194] If the king "breaks his oath [or] wrecks the commonwealth," these lower magistrates have "an even greater obligation [towards the kingdom] since, like the ephors, they were established primarily for this purpose."[195] Mornay even asserted at one point the historically accurate judgment that in a sense, the Spartan ephors were "more powerful" than Spartan kings.[196]

In another respect the *Vindiciae* showed an advance over Hotman's and earlier Reformation efforts to defend Protestant religious rights against political suppression. This was the use of an argument Beza employed in *Du droit*, from which Mornay must have taken it: the neoscholastic notion that liberty was a natural condition of human beings before the formation of political society. With Beza, Mornay moved completely away from the simple Reformation view that political society in all its forms is a function of divine providence instituted directly by God. By

194. Mornay, *Vindiciae*, F, pp. 181, 194.
195. Ibid., p. 194.
196. Mornay, *Vindiciae*, S, p. 102.

adopting the natural-law approach that described human beings as naturally free individuals who form political societies through some form of mutual agreement, Beza and Mornay offered a far more rational theory of politics. At this point Huguenot political thought ceased to be a simple extension of reformer theology and, with the inclusion of material found in neo-scholastic political writing, became a more rational form of discourse.

The origins of this development were medieval in the first instance. Their roots lay in traditional natural-law theory and Aristotelian political thought. In contrast, the general humanist tendency to reject natural law in favour of a more positivist emphasis on authority as derived from the element of coercion had tended to downplay emphasis on human nature, without altogether removing it from consideration.[197] In this connection, it is possible to overstate the contrast between the Reformist theory of polity—allegedly based, at least in its early expression, on biblical texts and a theological doctrine of innate human sinfulness that requires the providential intervention of divinely instituted coercive temporal authority—and the Catholic, which retained the traditional medieval Aristotelian natural-law theory in law and politics. In particular, the concept of consent needs careful delineation in the contexts of late medieval philosophical and political theory and fifteenth- and sixteenth-century humanist thought, specifically with regard to the emphasis it received in Reformist publicist tracts in the 1570s and beyond. The element of consent, relating to the prior notion of liberty as a natural human condition in the state of nature, was a fundamental feature of the natural-law position; hence crediting humanism with a positivist attitude and implying that its rejection of natural law was an unmixed blessing, a turning away from darkness towards the light, is a serious oversimplification of the historical record, as well as a blunder in the formulation of an adequate theory of politics.

There had been several harbingers of the effort to take over, or at least employ, natural-law arguments in support of the reformers' position, even before Beza defended the execution of Servetus with the notion of social consent.[198] Ponet had noted in his *Short Treatise* (1556) that political rulers derived their authority originally "of the people,"[199] and

197. See *supra*, p. 169 and n118.
198. See *supra*, pp. 240–41.
199. John Ponet, "A Short Treatise of Political Power," reprinted in Hudson, *John Ponet*, p. 107.

Goodman had used the language of natural rights in his *Superior Powers* (1560) to assert that "men may lawfully claim [liberty] as their own possession [and] if they suffer this right to be taken from them," they allow themselves to be robbed, as would be the case if a ruler were to take their property.[200] But Mornay put the argument squarely where these earlier texts only hinted at the point at issue, and he did so in a way that was hard to reconcile with accompanying detail concerning the basic Reformist view that all powers are ordained directly by God.[201] When discussing tyranny, for example, he did not hesitate to state views taken directly from the medieval scholastic tradition, or to refer directly to Aquinas, Bartolus, Baldus de Ubaldus, and codifiers of the Roman law.[202] However, while coupling the more natural consent theory of the scholastics with the Reformation ephoral doctrine to demonstrate how royal authority should be limited in both theory and practice, Mornay followed Beza in retaining and developing the providential conception of inferior magistrates as ordained by God to protect the religious rights of the followers of the "true" religion. The result was a doctrine of two types of covenant and a corresponding double basis for legitimate resistance to tyranny: the covenant between God and humans, and that between ruler and people.[203]

Consistent with his primary interest in the legitimate defence of Huguenot religious interests, Mornay first examined the covenant between God and temporal authorities, making a significant distinction between God's covenant with the king as supreme authority in a polity (treated in Part One) and that between God and lesser public authorities (Part Two). His basic view of the relationship "between God and king" was that "all kings are ministers ordained by God to govern justly and rule on His behalf [with a convenant] regularly concluded between the king and God [according to which the king agrees to ensure that his laws] are not in conflict with God's law."[204] The agreement between God and inferior magistrates, on the other hand, rested on "a covenant between God and the people." Here Mornay repeated a view found earlier in Bucer, that God considered it "dangerous to entrust [supreme re-

---

200. Goodman, *How Superior Powers ought to be Obeyed of their Subjects*, pp. 149–60.
201. Skinner, *Foundations*, 2:321.
202. Ibid. and note 1.
203. Mornay, *Vindiciae*, F, pp. 142–51. Skinner's view is that the two covenants are "barely compatible" with one another. Skinner, *Foundations*, 2:325.
204. Mornay, ibid., p. 146; S, p. 73.

sponsibility] to a single, all too human individual," and decided accordingly to appoint "magistrates below the king" as a further means to this end.[205] The essential conclusion, then, was that God had an agreement with both king and lesser magistrates as joint "promissory parties," the latter "jointly obligated" to preserve a commonwealth founded on God's laws and to maintain therein his temple and church.[206] What might be called a third covenant, that between ruler and people, was set out in Part Three as the typically scholastic contract between king and people through their representatives, and it provided the framework for examining the legitimacy of opposition to a tyrant, including possible deposition.

From the several forms of covenant he outlined, Mornay offered a dual basis for resistance to political tyranny by members of the "true" religion. On the one hand, they could argue that a tyrant failed to meet his covenanted obligations to God to protect his church and fulfil his duty to serve the people by following God's laws, in which case the duties of similarly convenanting lesser magistrates came into play, and they were obliged to correct the ruler's failures. Alternatively, or concurrently, the ruler could be said to have broken his essential commitment to the people through their representatives and could therefore be resisted to the point of deposition. Skinner contends that these two arguments are really incompatible, apparently on the ground that the first is theological and the second political; hence they originate from "different and incompatible views about the origins and purpose of the commonwealth.[207] The two arguments are obviously different, one stressing what might be called a religious duty of lower magistrates to act against a ruler suppressing the "true" religion he has covenanted with God to uphold, while the other is political in the sense that it invokes a ruler's natural obligation to serve his people's good. Yet the difference is really only in the form of argument. Arguments are not incompatible simply because one is religious or theological and the other philosophical unless one holds that philosophy and religion are inherently contradictory or incompatible with one another.[208]

205. Mornay, *Vindiciae*, F, pp. 146–48.
206. Ibid., p. 147.
207. Skinner, *Foundations*, 2:325.
208. Skinner does, however, concede the obvious connection between a right and a duty in connection with the same issue, and notes that after 1572 emphasis on the religious duties of ephors to oppose tyranny diminished greatly, along with the so-called providentialist argument itself. Skinner, *Foundations*, 2:328.

As well as stressing the natural covenant between ruler and people in Part Three, Mornay regularly employed the natural-law and humanist view that human beings were both free and equal in the state of nature: "No one is born a king, and no one is king by nature [for] a king cannot rule without a people, while a people can rule itself without a king ... Clearly beyond all doubt," the people must have lived originally without rulers or even positive laws, and these came about as a result of the people agreeing to accept them.[209] Humans are "free by nature, born to hate servitude and desirous of commanding rather than yielding obedience"; this freedom is "a [somehow inalienable] privilege of nature.[210] Humans yield their natural condition of liberty and consent to enter into political society because "they expect some very considerable profit to arise out of agreeing in this way to submit to the commands of others."[211] Further, kings should remember that "it is due to the people, and for the sake of the people's welfare, that they exercise power ... they must not say, as they often do, that they hold their sword by the ordination of God, unless they also say that it was the people who first placed it in their hands."[212]

Mornay also made it clear that he was not discussing the common good of a political community as some kind of merely collective or corporatist value: what he had in mind was the preservation of individual rights. Again he unhesitatingly employed material not previously found in reformer publicist sources; his discussion of right exactly followed the position found in Gerson and his Conciliar followers, particularly John Major in his *Questiones in Sententiis Petri Lombardi*.[213] The people's welfare entails their "rights and privileges [never being] given up [to] the unbridled liberty of their kings." Mornay illustrated what he meant here by referring to the material possessions of individual citizens: a polity protects the right to retain the possessions its individual citizens had before entering into political society. Political society comes into being and exists to preserve these original rights and to provide its citizens with greater security therein. Mornay thus anticipated Locke's formulation that political society came into existence "when the concepts of *meum* and *tuum* first entered the world," and differences began to arise within

---

209. Mornay, *Vindiciae*, F, p. 160.
210. Mornay, *Vindiciae*, S, p. 107.
211. Ibid.
212. Ibid., p. 79. Here is just as strong a rejection of the theory of the divine right of kings as that stated several decades later by Suárez: cf. *supra*, p. 181.
213. Skinner, *Foundations*, 2:327. Cf. *supra*, p. 110.

the body of the people over the question of ownership of material goods.[214] Of course, the notion that a political authority, even the pope in the case of an ecclesiastical polity, has no ownership rights over the goods of the individual members of his community was not new; John of Paris had articulated it in the early fourteenth century.[215] Nor was the idea that individuals in the state of nature acquired some form of property rights over the material goods they brought into their possession.[216] But the emphasis Mornay gave these notions was striking; he stated explicitly that the principal reason for establishing political society must have been to provide greater protection for property, and to prevent "devastation of the territories or any other such material calamities."[217]

In common with Locke a century later, the author of the *Vindiciae* had more in mind than property rights to material goods. His position on the nature of property was that of traditional medieval scholasticism, later expressed in Locke's *Second Treatise*, that the property rights of each individual in the state of nature included moral as well as physical and material features; they included the specifically human characteristics of freedom and equality, life and liberty, that each individual is able to dispose of consistent with the laws of God and nature. Mornay concluded his discussion of the "right of the people" by asserting that no action by a lawful government "must ever detract in any way from the right of the people's liberty ... [the principal aim of government] must always be to act as the guardian of the liberty and security of the people."[218]

Further, just as the final cause or purpose of political society is the public welfare expressed as the rights and possessions of its citizens, the efficient cause—the action bringing a polity into existence—is the consent of the people, popular consent. At the beginning of Part Two, Mornay gave an elaborate account of how governments come into existence and how magistrates are placed in office. The cause is common consent: "Kings are created by the people,"[219] and a specific role is assigned to the individuals who actually engage in this process, the magistrates who function as representatives of the people, "those who represent the people's majesty [who place the monarch in office] come

    214. The general notion, however, is very old and had extensive expression in the Middle Ages. Cf. *supra*, p. 134 n16.
    215. See *supra*, p. 65.
    216. See *supra*, p. 134 n16.
    217. Mornay, *Vindiciae*, S, p. 109.
    218. Mornay, *Vindiciae*, F, p. 168.
    219. Ibid., p. 158.

together with the sceptre and crown."[220] And Mornay illustrated what he meant by giving a detailed account of how Saul became the first king of Israel as described in the Old Testament: he was selected by God but also had to be established by the general consent of the people.

An explicit distinction was made here between choosing and establishing, the former being the act of God in identifying the ruler and the latter an essential function performed by the people. The act of establishing had two parts: first, the people "acclaimed" the ruler and subsequently expressed their approval by formal vote showing majority acceptance. Mornay thus took literally the procedure, rather informally expressed in Samuel, whereby the Israelites, with the reluctant approval of their God, came to have a king "like other nations."[221] Notable here is the insistence on majority support from the people for the successful candidate, although of course the elected person would already have been chosen by God directly. Given the infinite superiority of divine judgment and the chronologically prior nature of His act of choosing, it is not clear whether or how there could have been any discontinuity between God's and the people's choice. And as far as one can tell, majority popular consent would have been expressed by the people's representatives, themselves selected by lot from the various segments of the community as a whole, originally the tribes of Israel.

One thing that is clear from Mornay's description of the people's role in giving consent to the choice of ruler is that popular consent was expressed through chosen representatives, rather than through any procedure permitting individuals to register their judgment directly. The people as a whole were perceived as having delegated authority to lesser magistrates, who thus became the appropriate persons through whom the community exercised its collective judgment. How things ought to go in a country like France was addressed directly: "Good government depends on a degree of order that cannot be maintained" if large numbers of individuals are all given a direct activity to perform. Similarly, many "affairs of state ... cannot be communicated publicly [to the whole people] without danger to the common interest." Accordingly, the sovereign rights and privileges held originally by all the people were now to be exercised by their "elected officers of the kingdom, on their behalf

---

220. Ibid., p. 160.
221. 1 Sam:10; Mornay, *Vindiciae*, F, p. 159. The notion that the manner in which God appointed a king for the Israelites was the "right way to do it" was centuries old, going back at least as far as John of Salisbury. Cf. Monahan, *Consent, Coercion, and Limit*, pp. 65–66.

and in their best interests."²²² The argument for representative over direct democracy seems pragmatic rather than ideological, however, and Mornay was not precise about how various individuals and classes came to represent the people.

Along with Beza, Mornay listed certain categories of persons in the community as lesser magistrates in virtue of their social rank and *eo ipso*, presumably, their being popular representatives. These "officers of the kingdom" were of two types: local and seigneurial magistrates. Among these groups Mornay paid particular attention to "elected officers of the towns," insisting that "each town forming part of the kingdom [must be accepted as having] individually and expressly sworn" to act for the people as a whole.²²³ Many French towns, particularly in the southern part of the country, had become Huguenot enclaves at the time, so attribution to them of legitimate public authority was a crucial element in the *Vindiciae* case. The other officers of the kingdom were the persons chosen to sit in the assemblies of the three Estates, the parlement "and other such assemblies as the German diet"; Mornay assigned to such bodies ultimate responsibility for ensuring that "no harm is suffered by the commonwealth or by the church."²²⁴

It is clear from all this that for Mornay, as for Beza, "the people" with whom the monarch was said to have contractual relations limiting his authority were the lesser magistrates who were popular representatives, "those who receive authority from the people, that is, the magistrates below the king who have been elected by the people," and not directly the citizenry as a whole.²²⁵ The people as a whole exercised only indirect authority over the ruler; the specific compact enjoining the monarch with respect to what he was entitled to do was between himself and the body of lesser magistrates, and only the latter had the right to hold the ruler to his contract, since they were "the authorities that have the power of the people in them."²²⁶ Once more, any anarchical possibilities that might accrue from individual citizens having a right to resist were covered off.

Details of the covenant between ruler and lesser magistrates are presented in Part Three of the *Vindiciae* under the general rubric of cove-

---

222. Mornay, *Vindiciae*, F, p. 150.
223. Ibid., p. 152.
224. Ibid., p. 150.
225. Ibid., p. 149. Cf. S, p. 120.
226. Mornay, *Vindiciae*, F, p. 154.

nant between ruler and people. As with Beza, the *lex regia* was invoked to bind the king to his commitment to maintain the public welfare. The form of the argument was explicitly political and constitutional rather than religious or theological: this covenant was not between God and any human being but between political ruler and people. Mornay's account was more thorough than that found in Beza or any other reformer publicist of the time and appears in a separate section entitled "The covenant or compact between the king and the people."[227] The *Vindiciae's* author again unmistakably underlined popular sovereignty as essential and distinguished between the types of commitment sworn by the two parties: the king swears an "absolute" commitment to fulfil his side of the bargain, while the commitment of the people's representatives is "conditional." When, having agreed among themselves to establish a political society, "the people made the king," they required him to swear an absolute oath "to preserve the people's welfare"; in return, the people's representatives agreed that "they would faithfully obey, as long as his commands were just."[228] The contract thus achieved embodied a "mutual obligation" between monarch and magistrates that "cannot be superceded by any other compact or violated in the name of any other right ... [the force of the contract is such that] a king who breaks it wilfully may properly be called a 'tyrant,' while a people that breaks it may properly be called 'seditious.'"[229]

In making clear that the purpose of political authority is the public welfare—the traditional scholastic notion of the common good—and that naturally free individuals consent to live under political authority only to achieve this goal—another notion taken directly from scholastic sources—Mornay used a series of analogies from feudal times and employed the same vocabulary found in contemporary and earlier scholastic circles. Originally the people were free and not subject to any political authority; hence they must consent to be governed only under conditions that serve their own welfare and purposes. Moreover, they remain "the true proprietor" of the polity in which they have consented to live and retain "supreme dominion" over it in the same way the owner of a fiefdom remains its proprietor even though he delegates its actual administration to someone else.[230] The people "remain in the position of

227. Ibid., p. 180.
228. Ibid., pp. 180–81.
229. Ibid., p. 185.
230. Ibid., pp. 162, 191.

owner" of their original sovereignty and merely delegate it to the monarch, "in order that he may exercise it for the public good."[231] The ruler, then, is not above the people: "the whole people is greater than the king and is above him."[232] Mornay concluded that, once it is clear that the people never alienate their sovereignty but merely delegate the right to exercise it to their king, "it can hardly be thought strange if we insist that the people must be more powerful (*notior*) than the king."[233]

Just as the king is essentially an administrator for the people, really their servant, so also are the lesser magistrates. They are "servants not of the king, but of the kingdom ... [they] receive their authority from the people in public council, and cannot be removed unless that body consents."[234] Moreover, the fact that the ruler exercises essentially only administrative authority means that ultimately he does not stand above the law. Mornay held that the monarch was not really sovereign in any literal sense of the term but "a kind of minister to the commonwealth";[235] his status is that of agent for the people, servant of the commonwealth (*servus reipublicae*), guardian (*custos*), administrator (*minister*), "merely the supervisor and executor of the laws,"[236] the people themselves being "the true proprietor" of the commonwealth.[237] Accordingly, the notion of the ruler as *solutus de legibus* makes no sense at all: it is "completely ridiculous for kings to regard it as a disgrace to be subject to the law [because this rejects the essential fact that] kings receive their laws from the people [who remain] owners [of the commonwealth]."[238] While Beza had made the same point, Mornay expressed it in the traditional scholastic terminology; the ruler is *minor universo*, but *maior singulis*: "the entire people is above the king when taken as a body," although all individual citizens and even magistrates are "below the monarch as individuals."[239]

---

231. Mornay, *Vindiciae*, S, p. 86.
232. Mornay, *Vindiciae*, F, p. 190.
233. Mornay, *Vindiciae*, S, p. 88.
234. Mornay, *Vindiciae*, F, pp. 161–62.
235. Ibid., p. 161.
236. Mornay, *Vindiciae*, S, pp. 86, 114, 125.
237. Mornay, *Vindiciae*, F, p. 191.
238. Mornay, *Vindiciae*, S, pp. 86, 115, 119.
239. Mornay, *Vindiciae*, F, p. 162.

## 8. RICHARD HOOKER

In many ways, the most idiosyncratic of the early sixteenth century Reformation movements was the one that took place in England under Henry VIII. Its underlying causes were the same as those that prompted the almost instantaneous emergence of full-fledged Reformer groups in many European countries and regions as soon as Luther posted his theses on the Wittenberg church door: widespread and deep anxiety among church leaders, especially theologians and intellectuals, about the deeply entrenched worldliness and ignorance of the lower clergy; increasingly trenchant criticism, even mockery, among humanists and other writers of the same vices; resentment at papal efforts to increase income through ever more burdensome levies, the large-scale practice of simony, and the sale of indulgences; the growing restiveness of political authorities, especially those at a distance from Rome, at the efforts of pope and curia to press claims of papal monarchy; and so on. However, the English broke with Rome only in 1532, after Henry failed to persuade Pope Clement VII to grant an annulment of his marriage to Catherine of Aragon. While the papacy did not rule against the annulment until 1534, the formal break with the Holy See began in 1531 when the clergy of the Canterbury Convocation accepted the English monarch as "supreme head of the church and clergy in England," and it was virtually complete by the following year.

Because of its historical background and pattern, the political thought emanating from the English Reformation, like the general event itself, was distinctly different from that seen on the Continent, where there was a certain sameness to Reformation thinking as a whole. Early English and Scottish response to the Reformation on the Continent was significant. Many members of the clergy and the academic and humanist communities, as well as government authorities and the people themselves, responded enthusiastically to the Reformed religion in the 1520s, even before Henry made his formal break with the Roman church. But as with continental developments, the English Reformation was ultimately viable because of the support it received from existing political authority.

The initial reaction of the English monarch to the Reformed religion was cautious, if not altogether negative. Henry, who fancied himself something of a theologian, actually defended the traditional religion against certain Lutheran theological tenets in his *Assertio septem sacramentorum*, thereby earning for himself the papal title "defender of the faith," an epithet that clung throughout his later advocacy of a Reformed religion to become part of the litany of English monarchical designations. This brought the English Crown into an uneasy negative relationship with the more flamboyant teachers of the Reformed religion in England, who were urging the English political establishment to accept the Reformation in England, and even impose it on the country.[240] It was not until the reign of Elizabeth that a version of the Reformed religion achieved permanence as the established religion in England.

The political thought of Richard Hooker has proved something of a difficulty, if not an embarrassment, for many modern writers on the history of English political theory, for no other reason than that it is in some ways anachronistic. Hooker's great work, *The Laws of Ecclesiastical Polity*, is not political theory at all in the normal secular meaning of that term: it does not present a doctrine of temporal polity. It could arguably be ignored in a history of political thought, or at least not be taken seriously in terms of the influence it has had on later political theory. Yet, in a manner quite unlike other Reform and medieval theologians, Hooker did advance an explicit theory of polity that made temporal authority *eo ipso* the ultimate authority even in the Church, a kind of Marsilianism in reverse. For where the argument in the *Defensor pacis* depicted the institutional church as a department of state in order to relegate things ecclesiastical to their proper level in political society and eliminate clerical claims to the exercise of political authority, Hooker's deliberate intent was to attribute at least some of the spiritual functions of religion to the temporal ruler in order to guarantee them the highest level of importance.

*The Laws of Ecclesiastical Polity*, the first major work on political thought in English, contains the core of Hooker's political thought. Its first five books, were published in the period 1593–97; the balance, including the very important Book Eight, was published posthumously in 1648 and 1661–62, in the middle of the next century.[241] While the *Laws* is in many ways the most extended single work of Reformation political

---

240. Cf. Tjernagel, *Henry VIII and the Lutherans*.
241. On the complicated and somewhat contentious issue of the publication history of the *Laws* text, see Houk's edition of *Hooker's Ecclesiastical Polity: Book VIII*, where the authenticity of the posthumous books is argued. Cf. Sisson, *Judicious Marriage of Mr Hooker*; Novarr, *The Making of Walton's "Lives."* An authoritative recent article on the subject by the editor of the critical edition of the works of Hooker is Hill, "Evolution of Hooker's *Law of Ecclesiastical Polity*," expecially pp. 117–58. Cf. Eccleshall, *Order and Reason in Politics*, pp. 126–50.

thought and ranks, at least in size, with the massive scholastic efforts of Cajetan and Suárez, it is not an *ex professo* statement of Hooker's views on the nature of temporal polity, nor is it a comprehensive theory of the nature of the Church. However, it does provide a wealth of information about Hooker's theory of polity, even though its direct purpose was something else.

Hooker did not set out to describe the nature of political society; even his examination of what he termed "ecclesiastical polity" did not lead him to treat this subject in all its essential aspects. He did not, for example, directly address the issue of resistance to the political suppression of religious views, because this was not part of the brief be gave himself: his purpose in the *Laws* was very specific and quite narrow in scope. To ignore this is to risk distorting his position, as a number of interpreters have done in various contradictory readings of Hooker, some of which even include the quite unfounded charge of inconsistency.[242]

Consistent with the historical context in which it was produced, the primary aim of Hooker's *Laws* was to justify the Church of England's constitution against criticism from Puritan Reformers, and to address the main issue separating the two protagonists—the legitimacy of the hierarchical structure of the Reformed English church. The English model of the Reformed religion, Anglicanism, retained an episcopal and general hierarchical structure similar to that of the medieval church, including the full panoply of church (canonical) law but substituting, so to speak, the English monarch for the pope as *apex ecclesiae*. As the historical record makes clear, and as the contents of the *Laws* abundantly illustrate, Hooker professedly subscribed to the laws and constitutions of the Church of England as set down by the government of his day and fully accepted both the English monarch and the doctrine of royal supremacy over the Church. The *Laws*, then, was an apologia for the *status quo religionis et rerum politicarum* in late sixteenth century Elizabethan England.

This does not, however, make it valueless as an exercise in political theory, incomplete and *parti pris* though it is. A systematic effort by an extremely astute and experienced Anglican thinker of the late sixteenth century, Hooker's work reflects deep knowledge of both the theological and philosophical heritage of the Middle Ages on which so much of his

---

242. As one commentator has put it, "The logical structure of Hooker's argument and theory was more consistent than some recent critics accept." Cargill Thompson, "Philosopher of the Politic Society," pp. 12–13.

religious creed and basic intellectual attitudes depend. Because of his prose style, he came to be known as "the judicious Hooker,"[243] a title that led to a false image of him as a disinterested analyst of the contemporary politico-theological scene. Hooker's real intention was to put the best case possible for Anglicanism against a potentially serious threat to the established Church of England from the radical Calvinism of the English Puritans and Scottish Presbyterians. Just how right he was to see both a religious and a political threat to the English establishment from these quarters would become clear with the outbreak of the Civil War some fifty years later.[244]

The general style and structure of the *Laws* show that Hooker, like many of his contemporaries, was thoroughly familiar with the scholastics of his day, and his own use of this intellectual frame of reference was not accidental. The treatise begins with generalities and proceeds to specifics; the parts of greatest significance for a theory of polity are Book One, where Hooker gives a general definition and classification of the types of law and describes the origin of society; and Book Eight, which outlines the specific character of the temporal polity of England and offers a defence of both the royal supremacy over the Church and the royal power of *dominium*.

Hooker's essentially juridical rather than philosophical or theological approach is evident in the title of his work and the placement of his theory of law at the beginning. Suárez's contemporary works on *Law* show a similar approach, although neither Hooker nor Suárez, it seems, could have exercised any direct influence on the other.[245] As already

---

243. Locke, *Second Treatise*, 2:13. McGrade has noted that "it would be interesting to explore the growth of Hooker's reputation (and the reasons for it) which we can trace in the epithets applied to him by his contemporaries, such as 'judicious,' 'godly,' 'humble,' 'venerable,' 'reverend' "; and he records Marvel's wish that Samuel Parker "had rather imitated the incomparable modesty and candour of reverend Mr Hooker in all his writings." Marvel, *The Rehearsal Transposed*, ed. D. I. B. Smith, p. 303; McGrade, "Introduction," p. 59, note 11.

244. A good summary of the historical context in which Hooker composed his *Laws* is in the McGrade "Introduction" to Richard Hooker, *Of the Laws of Ecclesiastical Polity: An Abridged Edition*. Cf. Eccleshall, "Richard Hooker's Synthesis."

245. Suárez's *De legibus* was given as a series of lectures in 1596, and was published at Coimbra in 1612. There is no evidence, and it is most unlikely, that Hooker's work was available in Spain at the time, nor even that Suárez could read English, and it is similarly unlikely that the Suárez lectures could have found their way to England before Hooker produced the *Laws*. Of course, the 1612 Latin text of Suárez's *De Legibus* as well as his rebuttal to the *Defensiones* of James I's views were known in England.

suggested, Hooker's purpose in framing a general conception of law and listing its basic types was to make the case that ecclesiastical law falls equally on all members of the Church, Puritans as well as others. His basic contention was that there are many forms of law, just as there are many forms of activity; each form is specific to a given mode of action, and the various modes and forms exhibit an order or pattern such that each part fits with all the others. The Anglican form of ecclesiastical law, he contended, was appropriate to the proper activities of the ecclesiastical polity in England. Following the broad outline of the original Thomistic formulation, Hooker's notion of law in its most general character made more of the modern distinction between its descriptive and prescriptive forms than did Aquinas, or even Marsilius of Padua and his followers, who tended to emphasize law in its prescriptive form by insisting that its formal essential constituent was coercion.[246] He divided eternal law into two categories: that "which with Himself [God] He purposed Himself in all His works to observe [and] that which with Himself He hath set down as expedient to be kept by all His creatures, according to the several conditions wherewith He hath endued them."[247] The first category, in simple terms, is the intelligible plan of creation in the divine mind, while the second exhibits the element of coercion, and Hooker was clear that his distinction went beyond the meaning of " 'law eternal' [used by] the learned for the most part," linking the latter view with the second of his categories.[248]

246. Hooker, *Laws*, 1.1–2. Cf. 1.3.1. Hooker cited Aquinas, *ST* 1–2.93.4–6 in the latter text. Cf. Marsilius of Padua, *Defensor pacis* 1.10.4.
247. Hooker, *Laws*, 1.3.1.
248. Ibid. McGrade says that Hooker differs from Aquinas at this point because, while Aquinas spoke of the eternal law as a method by which God "instructs" humans, one of the essential features of his definition of law is the element of coercive authority, and this places Aquinas among Hooker's group of "the learned for the most part." McGrade, "Introduction," p. 19. For McGrade, Hooker's notion of the eternal law is "nonauthoritative" and "simply the intelligible plan—the thought of God." Ibid.
So sharp a distinction between Aquinas and Hooker may not be appropriate, however. Hooker was more coherent than Aquinas in his distinction between eternal law as descriptive and prescriptive, and McGrade's point that Hooker's position has not been adequately noticed is well taken. But Aquinas did refer to the divine plan for the whole of creation as the eternal law: "the divine reason's conception of things": *ST* 1–2.91.1; and, following Augustine, as "the supreme exemplar of ... the things made by His [God's] art": *ST* 1–2.93 *sed contra* and *resp.*, while also agreeing with the Hooker view, of course, that God has no superior. There may be a more (or less) subtle shift in emphasis between Hooker and Aquinas on coercive force as an essential in law, especially as this relates to Hooker's polemical purpose, but I suspect that Aquinas could take refuge in the notoriously slippery

Following his own emphasis on the intelligibility feature of eternal law, Hooker emphasized the intelligibile or rational aspect of other forms of law as well and moved from this to an emphasis on consent as a fundamental feature of human law and political society. One must be a bit cautious about the character and emphasis in Hooker's position here, however, for the general thrust of his argument seems to move from the assertion or implication of rationality to the presumption, or at least advocacy, of consent, rather than the other way around. Hooker knew well enough what he was about in defending the political *status quo* of Tudor England and was seemingly quite content with the contemporary forms in which popular consent was expressed. His handling of the element of coercion as essential to law has been termed somewhat ambiguous because of his stress on law's rationality, and because he downplayed the issue and at times seemed not to regard it as central.[249] However, he did emphasize its value in connection with human or positive law. The difficulties modern legal positivists have experienced in trying to ground this meaning of law by exclusive reference to coercive authority may testify to the shrewdness of Hooker's general move away from this feature.[250]

While Hooker's conception of the natural law followed the general Thomistic and scholastic model, it did not differ significantly from that held by other leading Reform thinkers, all of whom, like Catholic political theorists of the time, also subscribed to a doctrine of natural law, though perhaps not always as emphatically and consistently as their Counter-Reformation counterparts. Too sharp a distinction should not be drawn, then, between Catholic and Reform writers on their acceptance or rejection of the natural-law tradition.[251] Their differences in this area were a matter of degree and emphasis, particularly with regard to

---

notion of analogy in order to insist that the eternal law as an intelligible divine exemplar is law, even though lacking the feature of coercion in the primary sense in which he defined law. McGrade is also quite right to point out the clear contrast between Hooker's position and the legal positivism of his contemporary, Bodin: ibid.

249. McGrade, "Introduction," p. 19.

250. "It is easy enough to accuse him [Hooker] once again of evasion here, but the philosophical difficulties which have been increasingly found in modern theories of legitimacy suggest that the principles underlying earlier political theory may deserve re-examining." McGrade, "Introduction," p. 20.

251. Cargill Thompson, "Philosopher of the Politic Society," pp. 29–30. Skinner is much more inclined to contrast Catholic and Protestant writers on their use of natural-law theory.

the accessibility and intelligibility to human individuals of the content of the natural law.

Here Hooker was much more closely aligned with the Catholic or scholastic conception. For him reason was God's greatest gift to human beings, giving them the capacity to understand God's plan for reality as a whole and situate themselves within it. His world view was essentially affirmative, and he maintained that human beings found themselves in a basically positive state wherein they were able to see their place in God's providential plan and what this entailed in terms of their own behaviour. Law, then, was essentially a kind of reinforcement of this basic attitude, a guide and an assistance. Hooker was thus much more in tune with the Aristotelian/Thomistic conception of human reason and law than with the Augustinian, even though he acknowledged that humans were far from perfect. His position was quite unlike that of the Lutheran and Calvinist reformers, who tended to see natural human beings as wallowing in sin and perverted in their judgments, or of Hobbes, for whom law and the structures of government were necessary to correct the strife-torn conditions of the state of nature.

As already noted, consent was a fundamental feature of Hooker's theory of law, and on this score he proceeded well beyond the explicit doctrine of Thomas Aquinas. For Hooker, laws derive their authority from the consent of the people who are to be governed by them.[252] The idea was not new or unique, of course; if was a fundamental feature of much current Protestant resistance thinking as developed from the constitutionalist theory of political authority formulated centuries earlier by canonists and *via moderna* theologians in connection with the conciliar movement and general efforts to exercise limits on papal authority.[253] Thus, while expressing no explicit position on resistance himself, Hooker can be considered to have been familiar with the general arguments in its favour and the constitutional theory it embodied. Further, too, the notion of popular consent as an ultimate basis for political authority and law had been part of English political and legal traditions for centuries.[254]

Hooker's views on the integral and essential nature of popular consent as the basis for political authority are found in Book One of the

252. Hooker, *Laws*, 1.10.8.
253. Cf. *supra*, p. 268.
254. The standard reference to medieval England in this connection is to the thirteenth-century legist, Henry Bracton. Cf. Monahan, *Consent, Coercion, and Limit*, p. 136; cf. also pp. 96–111.

*Laws*, where he examines the nature of political society and its origins. He returned to the same material in Book Eight. His basic theory of society and government repeated Aquinas's effort to reconcile the Aristotelian conception of the natural character of society with the Augustinian view that government and coercive temporal authority were essentially providential compensations for the negative effects of the Fall. The same general function of reconciling these two disparate, if not incompatible, accounts of political society had existed for Christian political thinkers since Aristotle's *Politics* had come into the ambit of Western medieval thought in the mid-thirteenth century, and the late medieval and sixteenth-century Spanish neo-scholastic tradition had been grappling with it ever since. But what make Hooker's efforts of particular interest was that he was attempting the reconciliation from the reformer side of the Reformation divide, after earlier Reformation political thinkers had almost unanimously laid aside Aristotelian concepts and begun to emphasize the Augustinian thesis.

For Hooker, society and government were necessary for two reasons: firstly, human beings have a natural need to live in society; and secondly, government is a necessary consequence of fallen human nature. In making the latter point, Hooker placed considerable strain on the Aristotelian aspect of his position. Consciously, one assumes, he employed the scholastic distinction seen earlier between the social and political aspects of the coming together of human beings—a distinction exploited precisely to blend the Aristotelian doctrine of humankind as naturally social with the Augustinian explanation of coercive political authority as a function of Original Sin. Another essential feature of Hooker's formulation taken from late scholastic doctrine is fully consistent with the use of this distinction, namely, that the origin of any actual political society requires consent among the individual people concerned, all of whom, being rational and free in the conditions of nature after the Fall, must come together and decide to form a polity if one is to exist. This emphasis on consent as the origin of political society was the most important feature of Hooker's theory of polity, as it was in Hotman's and Mornay's Huguenot resistance tracts, and for Mariana, Cajetan, and Suárez in their Spanish neo-scholastic treatises; it certainly carried him beyond the purely Aristotelian account of political society, as indeed was the case for the Spanish neo-scholastics. For Hooker, what took humans from their original condition of individual liberty to membership in political society was an application of their rationality to the circumstances of their lives as individuals; this brought them to see that the conditions of strife caused by the Fall could be overcome by a willingness to subject themselves to some form of government.[255]

Hooker offered a slightly different approach to the same position in his account in Book Eight of the three ways human beings can be brought under subjection to political authority. This material correlates to Book One in that the earlier account offered a general and roughly historical account of the origins of political society, while the later material gave a more logically systematic account of the ways subjection can occur. Hooker identified three such ways, all legitimate in the eyes of God because all divinely sanctioned. He began by distinguishing between rulers who receive their authority directly from God, and those who receive their power from the people, and made a further subdivision within the former. The basic distinction is the traditional medieval one found in Aquinas and going back at least to John of Salisbury,[256] but Hooker probably employed it in direct response to the Reformation view that all rulers held their authority directly from God.

The first way a ruler holds power directly from God is by force: groups of individuals can be brought under political authority through conquest, divine providence so disposing. As Hooker asserted, God does give victory in war, and he referred further to the *ius gentium* as validating this mode of subjection.[257] Secondly, God himself can specially appoint political authority over a people; Hooker cited here the traditional example of the Israelites, whose monarchs held power "immediately from God, by mere right."[258] Thirdly, rulers hold legitimate authority if it is bestowed on them by human discretion, when individuals are left free by God to make their own choice of who shall govern them. England was an example of such a polity.[259] As already noted, Hooker considered each of these methods legitimate. God accepts any and all of them; hence those who rule in any of these ways can be said to derive their authority from God. As for consent, Hooker accepted hereditary succession as legitimate within this category, thereby rejecting categorically the position of Mornay in the *Vindiciae*, and Hotman as well, probably knowingly: "Which strange, untrue, and unnatural conceites, set abroad by seedsmen of rebellion, only to animate unquiet spirits, and to feed them

---

255. Hooker, *Laws*, 1.10.4.
256. Thomas Aquinas, "De regimine" 1.6.49–50; 2 *Sent.* 44.2.2, *solutio*; *ST* 1–2.97.3 *ad* 3; John of Salisbury, *Policraticus* 5.6.
257. "It is God Who giveth victory in the day of war." Hooker, *Laws*, 8.2.5.
258. Ibid.
259. Ibid., 8.2.7.

with a possibility of aspiring unto thrones and sceptres, if they can win the hearts of the people, what hereditary title soever any other before them may have, I say, these unjust and insolent positions I would not mention, were it not thereby to make the countenance of truth more orient."[260]

Hooker was equally clear, however, that the nature and extent of a ruler's authority are circumscribed by the way the ruler came into office:

> In power of dominion, all kings have not an equal latitude ... kings by lawful conquest set their own terms; kings appointed directly by God have the power God assigns ... Touching kings which were first instituted by agreement and composition made with them over whom they reign, how far their power may lawfully extend, the articles of the compact between them must shew: not the articles only of compact at the first day beginning, which for the most part are either clean worn out of knowledge, or else known unto very few, but whatsoever hath been after in free and voluntary manner condescended unto, whether by express consent, whereof positive laws are witnesses, or else by silent allowances famously notified through custom reaching beyond the memory of man.[261]

He was reasonably relaxed, then, in terms of the actual requirements for consenting agreement on the nature of political authority: specific limitations on public authority can vary according to the manner in which that authority came into being. Further, the nature of the consent itself can vary in the beginning from express to tacit, just as it can throughout the life of a polity. The terms of agreement themselves may change over time; so, too, will the character of laws in a polity differ, from positive laws that are the result of explicit legislation, to laws of custom that bind "by silent allowance." It seems, further, that in the original compact between people and ruler, Hooker may have imagined the ruler as negotiating the terms of his authority on his own behalf, rather than simply agreeing to accept the conditions agreed to by the community as a whole. If so, this is a more benevolent attitude towards the sovereign than what either Hotman or Mornay had in mind, and also more consistent with actual practice in England and the continental kingdoms of the day. The Hooker text is not unambiguous on the point, however: "Composition made with them [i.e., the rulers themselves?] over whom

---

260. Ibid., 8.2.8. There can be no doubt that Hooker knew exactly what Calvinist (Knoxian, Presbyterian, and Puritan) views he was rejecting here.
261. Ibid., 8.2.11.

they reign, how far their power may lawfully extend, the articles of the compact between them must shew."²⁶²

Accepting, then, that the specifics of limited political authority are a matter of agreement and not something deduced from the natural law or any other such source, Hooker proceeded to deal with the situation in England as an instant case of historical fact. The power of the English monarch, he maintained, is limited by law, the law of the land, in both positive and customary forms. He suggested, moreover, that limitations on royal authority are expressed more in terms of what the ruler is allowed to do than by express prohibitions: limitations on the Crown's legislative power is mainly negative, one of veto.²⁶³

Consistent with the foregoing, Hooker was prepared to embrace even the possibility of an absolute monarchy: whatever was agreed to would stand. And again, like Molina and Suárez and later English political thinkers like Selden, he expressed a rather simple, straightforward natural-rights position: free agents can willingly give up whatever they choose. Presumably, however, limitations from the higher law could be invoked to rule out tyranny, although Hooker did not say so. Moreover, power handed over by the people to a ruler has been alienated. Hooker was clear on this point; government once established was to all intents and purposes irrevocably conveyed to the ruler.²⁶⁴ This would have been an essential element in his case against the Puritan position, his whole aim being to show that all forms of the law, with those of the ecclesiastical polity most relevant for his purpose, applied to all citizens without qualification. His brief would have been weakened had he conceded the possibility of revoking the political compact, which accordingly must be said to be beyond the people's power of revision. Nor did Hooker address the question of any popular right of deposition as a correlative of the right to establish public authority.

The fact that there is no theory of deposition or resistance in the *Laws* is perfectly intelligible in terms of the work's purpose. But it has been used to dissociate Hooker's general position from social-contract theory, on the grounds that his doctrine of consent was always stated tentatively because he accepted consent as tacit rather than active, and that his overall position lacked the theological overtones of late sixteenth and early

---

262. Ibid.
263. Ibid., 8.6.8 and 13.
264. Cargill Thompson, "Philosopher of the Politic Society," p. 39.

seventeenth century social-contract statements advocating the rights of resistance and popular sovereignty: in a word, that Hooker's interest in the social compact was philosophical, not political.[265] But leaving aside the possibility that the doctrine might have had both these interests, philosophical and political, in view, it seems unlikely that Hooker was urging only the former, for two reasons: first, current social-contract theory on the origin of political society did not insist on a positive act of consent as a necessary condition for founding a polity—nor did Hobbes or Locke; and second, Hooker's purpose in publishing the *Laws* was just as political as that of other Reformation political writers, involving different ideology, perhaps, but nonetheless *parti pris*. Intellectually and practically, however, he had far more sympathy for a compliant attitude towards the exercise of monarchical power than other Reformation publicists, except for Luther himself in his early writings, although this too is probably more explicable on prudential than philosophical grounds.

Hooker's political theory, on the other hand, should not be confused with the far more liberal social contractarianism of John Locke. This error is made often enough, but it has more to do with Locke's careful references to Hooker as a way of providing respectability to his own otherwise quite antithetical views, a not uncommon practice among other late seventeenth and eighteenth century Whig authors. Locke and Hooker differed on two essential points: (1) Hooker had taken from the late scholastic tradition (as found, for example, in Suárez and argued more deductively by the Spanish neo-scholastics) the view that the original condition of individuals in the state of nature permitted them to opt even for absolute monarchy, which in itself was not considered contrary to the natural law;[266] this was not Locke's position; and (2) Hooker did not articulate a theory of individual rights as being inalienable because rooted in the state of nature, whereas Locke did.[267]

---

265. Ibid., pp. 40–41.
266. "The case of man's nature standing therefore, as it doth, some kind of regiment the Law of Nature doth require; yet the kinds thereof being many, Nature tieth not to any one, but leaveth the choice as a thing arbitrary." Hooker, *Laws*, 1.10.5. "It seemeth almost out of doubt and controversy, that every independent multitude, before any certain form of regiment is established, hath, under God, supreme authority, full dominion over itself, even as a man not tied with the bond of subjection as yet unto any other, hath over himself the like power. God creating mankind did endue it naturally with full power to guide itself, in what kinds of societies soever it should choose to live." Hooker, *Laws*, 8.2.5. Of course, Hooker's own preference was for the form of limited monarchy in the England of his day. For Locke, see *Second Treatise*, 11.135–42.
267. Cf. d'Entrèves, *Medieval Contribution to Political Thought*, pp. 81–102.

It has been suggested, too, that Hooker's conception of the social compact between ruler and ruled was less legalistic and not, strictly speaking, enforceable, in contrast with the position of Buchanan, from whom the Anglican divine seems to have taken much of his notion concerning the origins of political society.[268] In this he would have been repeating the standard, but not universal, medieval view of the compact between ruler and ruled.[269] A point of difference to be noted between Hooker and his putative source, Buchanan, however, concerned whether the king was above the law. Buchanan was explicitly negative on this issue while Hooker was not; he took the view that, while the king should rule consistent with the laws of his own jurisdiction, in the final analysis nothing more than moral suasion operated here.[270] Cargill Thompson made this distinction between the two on the grounds that Hooker accepted all forms of polity, including absolute monarchy, as legitimate since none is *eo ipso* contrary to the natural law.[271] But Hooker might be shown greater sympathy here. Certainly, he was of the view that rulers were bound by the terms of their compact with the people; in which case, could it not be said that in this sense kings were subject to the law?

Hooker made it clear that his own preferred form of government was the limited monarchy of the England of his day, where the English monarch operated under a version of the rule of law but without much in the way of actual limitation. Hooker seems to have seen the other organs of the English polity, parliament in particular, as largely consultative. He also accepted the distinction between ordinary and absolute royal power, a distinction made much of later by James I in his role as political publicist as well as ruler, which did little to endear him to the many critics of the divine right of kings in his realm. The monarch was possessed of both kinds of power, ruling in a manner totally consistent with the laws of the land in virtue of his ordinary powers, but possessed of the authority to set aside his own laws and function entirely on his own through

---

268. Cargill Thompson pointed out that, while Hooker never referred to Buchanan by name, he must have known the latter's *De iure regni* as one of the most famous political pamphlets of the time, and that "many of the distinctive features of Hooker's theory are also to be found in Buchanan's dialogue, and the argument of [*Laws*] 1.10.1–5 in particular appears at times to follow Buchanan very closely." "Hooker as Political Thinker," pp. 42 and 44.
269. Cf. *supra*, p. 143.
270. Hooker, *Laws*, 8.2.12.
271. Cargill Thompson, "Philosopher of the Politic Society," pp. 44–45.

his absolute powers.[272] There was never any question about the legitimacy of exercising royal authority for purely selfish interests, of course: such behaviour was always classified as tyrannical. But the difficulty of determining when the exercise of absolute power was legitimate and when merely a function of self-interest was never resolved.

This distinction has an interesting history in political theory. Oakley has shown that it had achieved significant status in voluntarist theology as early as the last quarter of the thirteenth century, when the issue of divine omnipotence and its expression and definition as a fundamental tenet of Christian theology arose.[273] Omnipotence was clearly a divine property; but what exactly did this mean? Were there some things that not even God could do, or were there literally no limits to God's capacity for action? One consequence of the impact of Aristotelian philosophy on medieval Christian theology was the tendency to Aristotelianized descriptions of the Christian God and his relations with creation as a whole, and human beings in particular. Emphasis on the Aristotelian notions of intelligence and rational structure as reflected in the universe had produced a Christian theology that described God as a supreme intelligence that created the universe and saw to its operation in terms of a divine plan, the eternal law, designing a place for everything, and with everything functioning as it should, consistent with this supremely intelligible scheme.

This emphasis on the rational character of the universe, structured throughout by laws expressing the divine plan conceived by the divine intelligence, had given rise in conservative theological circles to the question whether Aristotelian philosophical presuppositions and conclusions were, or could be made, compatible with the Christian religion. Was it really possible to construe the truth about God as revealed in Christian Scripture in Aristotelian philosophical paradigms? Critical to this issue was the description of God's nature, concerning which one of the specific touchstones was the issue of divine omnipotence. Christians held their God to be all-powerful; but how to express that revealed truth in an Aristotelian frame of reference? The Aristotelian prime mover was a pure intelligence; hence one could describe the Christian God as the supreme intelligence. But how does one relate the Aristotelian concept of supreme intelligence to the notion of divine omnipotence? Aristotle, it must be recalled, maintained that the universe was necessary and eternal

---

272. Hooker, *Laws*, 2.17.
273. See Oakley, *Omnipotence, Covenant, and Order*.

and that the prime mover moved by way of final causality; his account of reality contained neither the concept of creation nor that of voluntary, divine, efficient causality.

The anti-Aristotelian backlash in the last three decades of the thirteenth century involved a reaction against descriptions of the Christian God as an Aristotelian intelligence and a switch in emphasis to the voluntary character of divine action that stressed the divine will and God's omnipotence. It is ironic, in a way, that this anti-Aristotelian focus continued to use the thought structure and language of the Philosopher, even while eschewing certain seemingly Aristotelian conclusions: the only acts God could not perform were those clearly involving a logical contradiction. Even granting His omnipotence, God could not square a circle or make a triangle with more or fewer than three sides, and so on. Logical impossibilities aside—in which case divine omnipotence was not at stake at all—there was nothing God could not do, including setting aside the laws of nature.

Of course, even Christian theologians like Thomas Aquinas with an Aristotelian turn of mind agreed basically with this position: to do otherwise would cast a shadow on divine omnipotence. But another theological distinction was invoked to preserve the Aristotelian description of the divine nature: that between God's ordinary and absolute power. Employing the former, God maintained an activity consistent with the nature of his creatures and the natural law. God could act outside or contrary to natural and physical laws, however, and perform miracles in virtue of his absolute power; but He did so rarely and only for special providential reasons. God could cause the sun to rise in the west and set in the east, or not rise at all on a given day, for example, or eliminate the burning effect of fire on human flesh as He did for the children in Nebuchadnezzar's fiery furnace. But He did not act in this "absolute" fashion unless moved to perform a miracle, for such behaviour would reflect negatively on the rational structure of His own creation, and thus on His own perfection as Creator.

Use of the ordinary/absolute distinction, however, was not good enough for the critics of Aristotelianized Christian theology. Their stress on divine omnipotence entailed also an insistence on the limited knowledge of human beings concerning what God can and will do. Leaving open the issue of what God "could but would not do," they preferred not to stipulate that divine ordinary power was "necessary" in the Aristotelian sense of scientifically certain. The consequence was a sceptical attitude towards human certainty concerning even natural events, and an emphasis on the inscrutable character of both divine and natural acts in terms of their accessibility to human rational judgment. Not surprisingly, this attitude found its way quickly into medieval ecclesiological thought, where parallels between divine and papal authority had been standard paradigms for bolstering the pretensions of papal monarchy. Aegidius of Rome applied the ordinary/absolute distinction in claims for papal *plena potestas*, describing the pope as having two types of power of jurisdictions: ordinary, where the pope followed God's example in agreeing to be regulated by the normal laws and customs governing temporal and ecclesiological jurisdictions and the relation between them; and absolute, by which he had the authority, as supreme ruler on earth, to set aside existing legislation and act on his own in a way that brooked no limitation from human authority.[274] The same claim was made later for temporal rulers holding monarchical office: ordinarily, they were pleased to act consistently with the laws of the land; but strictly speaking, they also had an absolute power that entitled them to act on their own like a kind of "god on earth." Hooker attributed just such power to the English monarch of his day, and it should come as no surprise that James I expressed the same view and specifically invoked the ordinary/absolute distinction in doing so.[275]

Hooker also flatly conceded a royal veto over Parliament, something he may well have taken from Bodin, whose doctrine he was familiar with and cited at least once.[276] In the final analysis, he had a conventional Tudor conception of the authority and role of the monarchy and an equally orthodox view on the inadmissability of rebellion under any circumstances, though he did not pay careful attention to this latter issue. One unorthodox feature of his political thought *vis-à-vis* the contemporary English scene was his insistence that the royal "power of dominion" derived originally from popular conveyance, "conveyance from the peo-

---

274. Cf. *supra*, pp. 27–28.

275. "The king, through his supreme power, may do great things and sundry himself, both appertaining unto peace and war, both at home, by commandment and by commerce with states abroad, because so much the law doth permit. Some things on the other side, the king alone hath no power to do without consent of the lords and commons assembled in parliament." Hooker, *Laws*, 2.17. On James's views concerning these two forms of royal power, see Oakley, *Omnipotence, Covenant, and Order*, pp. 95–118.

276. Cargill Thompson noted that Hooker cites Bodin's *De republica* in a fragment Keble printed as an appendix to *Laws* 8, "Supposed Fragment of a Sermon on Civil Disobedience, hitherto printed as part of the Eighth Book," Hooker, *Works*, 3:457–58. Cargill Thompson, "Philosopher of the Politic Society," p. 74, note 69.

ple."²⁷⁷ Hooker sounds here like Buchanan and Mornay, with both of whom he would have been familiar, as earlier shown. In practice, however, he elided popular consent with the orthodox view of monarchy accepted in the English common law and, unlike Buchanan and Mornay, accepted hereditary succession without stressing the election of monarchs, even though he did mention popular acclamation as a feature of the royal coronation.²⁷⁸

Hooker's final view on the English monarchy, arguably the most interesting and perhaps the most idiosyncratic, located ultimate ecclesiastical as well as temporal authority in the Crown. His position thus far, stressing the *de facto* consensual character of English political society and the correspondingly limited character of royal authority, does not seem well designed to accommodate this last claim as part of his argument against the Puritans in England, or indeed against any of the less radical forms of Reformation thought. However attractive a limited temporal authority might be to an adherent of the Reformed religion as a safeguard against tyrannical oppression of his religious rights, and however consoling to hear that the people themselves are the source of a ruler's authority, transferring it to him through their own consent, neither point justifies the attribution of ultimate ecclesiastical authority to a temporal ruler. Hooker's position was, in fact, the antithesis of the Reformation doctrine of the separation of church and state, although one must be careful about the meaning of this doctrine in the late sixteenth and early seventeenth centuries: the separation described by the reformers lacked anything of the modern implication that temporal government must have nothing to do with regulating the religious behaviour of its citizens. While accepting that religious and moral matters were the prerogative of the clergy, Reform theologians considered themselves entitled to direct political authorities in the implementation of spiritual judgments.

Reformation political thought aimed in the first instance at removing the institutional church from every facet of political and legal jurisdiction and denied it any political status "in the world": it was, precisely, spiritual not temporal; it was "not of this world." The more obvious implications of such a view are easy to grasp, but the full logical implica-

277. Hooker, *Laws*, 8.2.9.
278. On the acceptability of hereditary succession see Hooker, ibid. On the point that popular acclamation is part of the coronation process but does not constitute an act of investiture from the spiritual power, see ibid., 2.8–10.

tions by no means so. The notion itself can seem both clear and attractive long after the point where it has degenerated to little more than a slogan or rhetorical flourish. It seems evident that the Church is a purely spiritual community, with its members under the jurisdiction of temporal rulers whose legitimate, God-given authority requires obedience in the material and visible sphere. But is this to say that secular authorities have *no* authority over the religious or spiritual activities of their citizens, whatever "spiritual activity" might mean? Conversely, does it mean that religious leaders should exercise *no* authority or influence in determining purely temporal policies, whatever a "purely temporal issue" might be? Further, can the state presume to operate in the moral, not to say the religious, sphere as regards the behaviour of its citizens? In rejecting the institutional and juridical character of the medieval Christian church, did the reformers intend to subsume these aspects of the Church into the temporal sphere; and if so, how? Had they fully thought out these knotty issues? The history of the Reformed church in the first century of its existence showed that, like the opposing Catholic forces in this particularly tragic period of early modern European history, the reformers expected temporal powers to employ political and physical (coercive) means to advance and maintain the "true" religion.

Hooker, for his part, simply reflected what was still the nearly universal attitude found on both sides of the Reformation theological divide. He assumed that a primary function of political authority was to advance true religion and the argument he directed at his Puritan opponents involved persuading them that the established Church of England was the "true" church for all subjects of the English Crown and that, consequently, all citizens were obliged to obey the laws of their polity, ecclesiastical as well as secular.

Given the nature of his case and its slender alignment with any of the more standard theories in Reformation political thought, it is difficult from this distance to see how Hooker could have hoped to win Puritans to his Anglican conception of the "true" religion. Nonetheless, it is his conception of the theological and ecclesiological role for the monarchy that makes his position interesting, interesting because different, and different because uniquely English, deliberately formulated to describe and justify the Reformation church as it developed officially in England.

Hooker accepted that secular authorities had an obligation to promote religion and based his judgment on the same argument from Aristotle's *Ethics* employed by medieval scholastic political thinkers. Aristotle had held that the function and purpose of political society was to promote the "good" life of its citizens and that this involved more than material well-being, arguing cogently that human happiness does not consist in material goods, sensual pleasures, wealth, or the like.[279] Further, as everyone in western Europe who had read Aristotle in the preceding three and a half centuries knew perfectly well, he considered politics to be a branch of ethics. Hooker argued quite plausibly, following the standard medieval mode of commentary on Aristotelian political thought, that the purpose of political society and the particular province of its ruler was to serve its citizens' well-being, which included their ultimate happiness, eternal salvation.[280] While there was no doctrine of eternal happiness in Aristotle's text—it is even questionable whether he taught a doctrine of personal immortality—the notion of human happiness fulfilled in another world was a gloss on Aristotle consistently supplied by any number of medieval Christian theologians anxious to "baptize" the Philosopher and provide a more effective rational gloss on the Christian doctrine of eternal salvation.

Hooker simply re-employed a traditional medieval doctrine to insert Christian salvationist content into the Aristotelian social purpose of perfecting human life and thereby defined his own conception of political society as an essentially religious institution, a church,[281] while accepting at least by implication the reverse notion that the Church is a political society in some other guise. So much for the insistence on the separation of church and state. Not unnaturally, then, the ruler plays a fundamental ecclesiastical and "clerical" role: his office is at once the fulcrum of political power and the apex of spiritual and temporal authority, because one of its essential responsibilities is concern for the salvation of the individual souls of his subjects.[282]

Moreover, it is important to note another traditional medieval feature Hooker incorporated into his theory of royal supremacy over both state and church, a notion quite antithetical to previous Anglican views on the

---

279. Aristotle, *Nicomachean Ethics* 1.4–5.
280. Hooker, *Laws*, 8.1.4.
281. Ibid., 1.2.
282. The notion that the English monarch was head of the English church and that every English subject was a member of that church had been expressed by Stephen Gardiner in his *De vera obedientia* (1535), and Cargill Thompson pointed out that Whitgift also employed it before Hooker to refute the Puritan claim that church and commonwealth were different. Gardiner, *Obedience in Church and State*, pp. 92–97; Whitgift, *Works*, 1:21–22, cited in Cargill Thompson, "Philosopher of the Politic Society," p. 59 and note 80.

role of the monarch in the English polity. Where earlier advocates of the royal supremacy such as Stephen Gardiner had assumed or accepted that the basis of royal authority in all its forms was divine—the basic Reformation view on the origin of political authority—Hooker repeated the corporation view that temporal authority derived from the people and drew the logical conclusion that a ruler's right to exercise ultimate ecclesiastical, as well as temporal, power rested in the consent of the people. He appended the further consequence that the ultimate authority to legislate for the external government of the Church belonged not to the king alone or even the clergy alone, but to the whole body of the Church, including the laity, viz., parliament together with convocation. He thus repeated, with the addition of appropriate English detail, a conciliarist doctrine expressed by John of Paris in the early fourteenth century.[283]

Nor did Hooker hesitate to bolster his ecclesiology by making explicit reference to the claims of papal monarchists, who advocated the pope's superiority over temporal powers as well as over ecclesiastical authorities subordinate to them. He perceived clearly that his own view in a way resembled that of the late medieval conciliarists and maintained that the Church had erred in rejecting their conception of church councils as superior to popes; he cited "Friar de Soto" as evidence in support of the conciliarist position he compared with his own.[284] Hooker advocated a conciliarist form of temporal authority that also included ecclesiastical affairs within its mandate, thus establishing a *via media* between what he considered the excessive monarchism of Catholic ecclesiology, and the radical tendencies of Puritanism in stressing the distinction between the spiritual and temporal spheres as measured by their unwillingness to accept the royal supremacy. His argument in this latter connection amounted to the following: the distinction between spiritual and temporal need not be expressed in separate authorities for each sphere when a body politic is sufficiently Christian; independence of the two spheres was not needed in the actual circumstances of the England of his day. The traditional medieval view of the pope as apex, with his *plena potestas*

---

283. "As for supreme power in ecclesiastical affairs the work of God doth no where appoint that all kings should have it, neither that any should not have it, for which cause it seemeth to stand altogether by human right, that unto Christian kings there is such donation given." Hooker, *Laws*, 8.2.5. On the role and responsibility of Convocation and Parliament in the Church, see Hooker, *Laws*, 8.6. Cf. John of Paris, *Royal and Papal Power*, 12; 14 *ad* 5; 19 *ad* 35; *supra*, p. 67.

284. Hooker, *Laws*, 8.6.2.

seeming to subsume all temporal power into itself, was thus turned upside down, so to speak; for Hooker, the apex of all authority in England was the monarch, whose temporal authority subsumed all spiritual authority within itself.

Hooker was the last of the important Reformation theologians and activists whose writings expressed what might be called first-generation Protestant political thought, which itself was to be repeated by subsequent proponents of the varying Reformist traditions, Lutheran, Calvinist (Prebyterian in Scotland and Puritan in England), and Anglican. An obviously distinguishable variant in the political thinking that follows continental Reformation views marks the beginning of modern "scientific" political science, which will be examined in a sequel to this volume covering the historical period of the seventeenth and eighteenth centuries.

# *Conclusion*

Despite the length of this manuscript, the addition of some kind of conclusion is necessary to ensure the object is not obscured by the details of so thick a slice of the history of Western political thought. As already noted, the material cannot readily be organized into a simple assessment of, or perspective on, the meaning or value of what I have called core concepts in political thinking, even though consent and limit were both successfully appealed to in resolving the scandal of the Great Schism and were transferred directly to the temporal sphere in a relatively coherent theory of resistance to the reimposition of traditional medieval western Christianity on adherents of the new "reformed" religion.

On the other hand, the notion of coercion continued to make ideological mischief when viewed simplistically in Marsilian terms as the only essential (and therefore uniquely legitimate) feature of positive law, or in the naively literal theological terms of Paul's Epistle to the Romans 13, which required simple submission to tyranny. As shown, such interpretations were a source of anguish for early Protestant Reformist political thinkers, Lutheran and Calvinist alike, especially the implication that all political authority, even tyranny, should be accepted as a divine providential dispensation.

In the period under study, there is no such thing as linear development of an increasingly superior and comprehensive theory of polity. Yet one could argue that the ingredients for a more rational theoretical mix were becoming better recognized and more widely employed as the harsh realities of heavy bloodshed in conflicts that amounted to civil wars tore at the fabric of developing nation-states, especially France and, in the next century, England. Accordingly, so long as the thesis is not urged too strongly or pressed too hard, it is possible to maintain that some progress was made in articulating political thought during this period, at least to the extent that there was a deepening awareness of the validity and value of certain elements in basic political discourse.

Those who assert the straightforward principle that obligations entail rights might also want to argue that the traditional medieval emphasis on the need for those who exercise political authority to respect the limits of power as defined by the common good entails *eo ipso* certain essential rights for citizens, as does the ordinary meaning of popular consent. Certainly the point is well taken in purely conceptual terms; yet it must also be pointed out that medieval political thinkers perceived such rights largely, if not exclusively, in a corporatist context that afforded little positive recognition to members of a political community as individuals. Nor was there any clear expression at the time of the contemporary notion of personal rights.

In the Middle Ages, for the most part, the integrity of individual human beings and their freedom to exercise personal judgment untrammelled by physical coercion from the political community was rarely, if ever, recognized, much less articulated, even when individual judgments on personal matters, especially those involving religious commitment, were considered inviolable. Both theologians and canonists, it is true, traditionally rejected forced religious conversion as inimical to personal dignity and the nature of Christianity; nor did they hesitate to link this prohibition to the natural law and apply it directly to both individual property holding and the exercise of political authority: non-Christians, it was agreed, possessed full rights in natural law to the ownership of property and the exercise of political jurisdiction.

Withal, however, the thorniest problem in medieval political theory remained: how to explain that human individuals somehow transcended the state because of their status as spiritual persons who were concurrently subject to political authority. Given the authoritative Christian Gospel advice "to render to Caesar the things that are Caesar's, and to God the things that are God's," the main failure here was the inability to explain how human beings could exist in different communal spheres, one temporal and the other spiritual, and, in particular, the inability to map the interface between them. The Gospel injunction first found practical, if negative, expression during the Roman imperial persecutions, when refusal to submit to laws and policies that Christians found to be incompatible with their religious beliefs produced an age of martyrs. Augustine's later "two cities" conceit, coupled with his view that the legitimacy of temporal authority was grounded in a divine providential plan that accommodated even tyrannical coercion as a necessary part, did little to clarify the original religious insight or make its acceptance easy; the basic church/state distinction was acknowleged, but its meaning was only loosely explored. Moreover, the attribution to a political ruler of providential powers directed towards the eternal salvation of subjects implied a denial of the distinction. And to complicate conceptual matters still further, there had been a centuries-long development of the vague and often confused notion of Christendom, wherein the delineation between what was God's and what was Caesar's became even more mysterious.

In the general ambiance of political thought in this period, nonetheless, a fuller and more conscious theoretical meaning was given to the notion of popular consent, which came to be extended to individuals, or at least to individuals as members of minority groups when their religious convictions and practice were at variance with the majority in their own political community. When, for example, no actual consent was given and no reasonable assumption could be made that the Huguenot subjects of the French Crown would again accept Roman Catholicism as the mandated religion of their country; or that the English model of Reformed Christianity in either its Arminian or neo-Christian form could be accepted by Scottish Presbyterians or English Puritans, much less Mary's efforts to restore Catholicism, the argument was made—and came ultimately to be accepted among serious political thinkers, however indistinctly or grudgingly—that the absence of consent did not legitimate forceful imposition of an official state religion. Indeed, it was considered that any such imposition would constitute an overt act of tyranny against (some of) the citizenry.

This is not to say that this view was explicitly accepted by given political authorities in every instance, or necessarily even in one. But my agenda has had to do with political theory, not practice. And if the arguments and claims were not always expressed in the language of rights (though occasionally they were, as when Mornay's *Vindiciae* followed John Major), the identification of critical items still moved in this direction. Of course, not all participants in the ongoing political dialogue entered with equal enthusiasm into this "deeper analysis" of the key concepts involved. Even as late sixteenth century writers of Huguenot political tracts were expressing the traditional concept of popular consent and spelling out its implications for the religious rights of individuals, others, like Bodin, were employing the new "scientific" language of sovereignty to deny individual subjects any rights in a political society on the grounds that there can be only one locus of sovereign power. Ironically, as a sequel study will show, the Bodinian notion of sovereignty performed the same function for his doctrine as the requirement of uniformity of religious belief did in earlier theories of polity: to ensure political unity and stability. In both cases such intellectually shallow perspectives tended to undervalue the concept of limit for the legitimate exercise of political authority, as the more recent and increasingly arrid dispute between legal positivists and natural-law theorists conclusively shows.

Not surprisingly, perhaps, none of the thinkers I have examined actually rejected the concept of limit; neither Luther nor Calvin did even when preaching the absolute necessity of obedience to temporal authority that came "directly from God." A sympathetic examination of these political thinkers shows that, in the final analysis, they all agree that political authority must be denied the right to act in certain ways against the citizenry: there are limits within which the exercise of political power can legitimately be restrained. Failure to accept this makes a nonsense of political theory, just as failure to implement it leads to the unjust denial of what a writer like Mornay was actually calling individual rights (*iura*) by the end of the period under study.

In modern-day talk, rights are often construed as features or possessions of individuals, things that somehow belong to human beings. In fact, as shown, the terms rights (*iura*) and ownership (*dominium*) enjoyed currency in the Middle Ages with reference to the generally accepted notion of an individual's legitimate relationship to material goods, and to the exercise of political and legal authority. Neither term was unambiguously defined at the time, however, or for several centuries to come. Suárez, for example, following in the neo-scholastic tradition, was still speaking of *ius* in the early seventeenth century as having a tripartite meaning: it could be used as a synonym for *lex*, as well as for *dominium* and *quasi-dominium*.

These ambiguities have led to problems in interpreting the relevant medieval documents, many of which are still relatively inaccessible because of the nature and language of the sources, the dearth of modern critical editions, conscious and unconscious presuppositions regarding the set of the medieval mind, and so on. Efforts have been made to apply modern conceptual tools to this material: the distinction between subjective and objective (public) rights has been applied to *ius* (Villey, Tuck, Skinner), as well as that between natural and conventional (contractual) rights (Tuck). But any insight gained by this exercise has been attended by difficulties. Similarly, the medieval concept of *dominium* has been examined both in terms of the modern notion of personal ownership of property (Coleman and Nederman), and as a forerunner to the modern concept of sovereignty. But again, not surprisingly, careful analysis has shown that medieval texts resist interpretation by means of a contemporary glossary of terms.

This is why I have simply presented the views of various late medieval and early modern political writers in an appropriate historical context: the story in itself is worth telling. In the end, perhaps, all one can say about the critical notions of *ius* and *dominium* is that they developed at different times in this period in seemingly opposite directions and that, consequently, a comprehensive history of these terms as they have come into modern usage from the Middle Ages remains to be written. Yet by the beginning of the seventeenth century, both were being applied by significant political thinkers, as well as by supporters of political policies, to such intangibles as the right to practise one's religion free and independent of state authority, the right to agree on who could exercise political authority and depose a ruler, and the right to dispose of one's own freedom along with other "property" rights. This last view, seemingly antithetical to rational implications in the first two, bespoke a radical theory of natural rights that illustrated once more the volatile ambiguity in basic "pure concepts of the political understanding."

The rights at issue were three in number: (1) the general right to resist political authority judged to be tyrannical: procedural details concerning how such judgment might legitimately be made remained, however, surrounded by a fog of conceptual ambiguity and sometimes even apparent contradiction; (2) a citizen's right freely to practise a form of religion other than that approved by current political authority: ambiguity is also found here, concerning whether the relevant concern was with group or individual dissent, the argumentation on offer being clearer about the former than the latter; and (3) an individual's right to property, initially material possessions but extended by deductive reasoning to include jurisdiction over one's physical person. Details of the various theories examined show that in some cases, especially in those most carefully argued on purely rational grounds among both advocates of the traditional medieval theory of polity (Suárez) and proponents of modern humanist theories rejecting the traditional notion of natural law as controlling the legitimacy of positive law (John Selden is a good example from the English early seventeenth century), excessive advocacy of property rights seemed somehow to make the first two redundant. The ideological contradiction between these various facets of developing rights theory remained for later modern political thinkers to address and seems with us still, as the ongoing and seemingly unending project to formulate a comprehensive theory of both positive and negative rights shows.

# Bibliography

Aarsleff, Hans. "The State of Nature and the Nature of Man in Locke." In *John Locke: Problems and Perspectives*, edited by John Yolton, pp. 99–136. Cambridge: Cambridge University Press, 1969.
Abray, Lorna Jane. *The People's Reformation: Magistrates, Clergy, and Commons in Strasbourg, 1500–1598*. Ithaca: Cornell University Press, 1985.
Adams, Robert P. *The Better Part of Valor: More, Erasmus, Colet and Vives on Humanism, War, and Peace, 1496–1535*. Seattle: University of Washington Press, 1962.
Aegidius of Rome. *De potestate ecclesiastica*. Edited by Richard Scholz. Leipzig: Böhlau, 1929. Reprint. Aalen: Scientia Verlag, 1961.
– *De regimine principum*. Rome, 1556. Reprint. Frankfurt: Minerva, 1968.
– *On Ecclesiastical Power by Giles of Rome*. Translated by Arthur P. Monahan. Lewiston: Edwin Mellen Press, 1990.
Agrippa, Heinrich Cornelius. *Of the Vanity and Uncertainty of the Arts and Sciences*. Edited by Catherine M. Dunn. Berkeley: University of California Press, 1974.
Aiken, James M., ed. and trans. *The Trial of George Buchanan before the Lisbon Inquisition, including the Text of Buchanan's Defences*. Edinburgh and London: Oliver and Boyd, 1939.
d'Ailly, Pierre. "Disputatio 12." in *Rerum concilii oecumenici Constantiensis*, edited by H. von der Hardt, vol. 2, pp. 225–26. Leipzig, 1697.
– "Epistola ad regem Carolum directa." In *Chartularium universitatis Parisiensis*, edited by H. Denifle and E. Chatelain, vol. 1, p. 621. Paris: Delalain, 1889–97.
– "Oratio de officio imperatoris." In Jean Gerson. *Opera omnia*, edited by Louis du Pin, vol. 2, pp. 912–24. Antwerp, 1706.
– "Propositions utiles." in *Veterum scriptorum ... amplissima collectio*, edited by E. Martène and V. Durand, vol. 7, cols. 909–11. Paris, 1733. Translated by Francis Oakley as "The Propositiones Utiles of Pierre d'Ailly: An Epitome of Conciliar Theory." *Church History* 29 (1960) 398–403.

- *Quaestiones super I, III et IV Sententiarum.* Lyons, 1500.
- "Tractatus de ecclesiae ... auctoritate." In Jean Gerson, *Opera omnia,* edited by Louis du Pin, vol. 2, pp. 905–60. Antwerp, 1706.
- "Tractatus de materia concilii generalis." In Francis Oakley. *The Political Thought of Pierre d'Ailly.* New Haven: Yale University Press, 1964.

Alberigo, Guiseppe. *Cardinalato e collegiata: Studi sull' eccleziologia tra l'XI e il XIV secolo.* Florence: Vallechi, 1969.
- *Chiesa conciliare. Identita e significato del conciliarismo.* Brescia: Paideia, 1981.
- *Election and Consensus in the Church.* New York: Herder and Herder, 1972.
- "Il movimento conciliare (XIV-XV sec.) nella ricerca storica recente." *Studi Medievali,* 3d series, no. 19 (1978): 913–50.

Alberigo, Guiseppe, et al., eds. *Conciliorum Oecumenicorum Decreta.* 3d ed. Bologna: Herder, 1973.

Alberti, Leon Battista. *The Family in Renaissance Florence. A Translation of I libri della famiglia.* Translated by Renée New Watkins. Columbia: University of South Carolina Press, 1969.
- "The Family." In *The Albertis of Florence: Leon Battista Alberti's* Della famiglia, edited by Guido A. Guarino. Lewisburg: Bucknell University Press, 1971.
- "Three Dialogues." In *Renaissance Philosophy.* Vol. 1, *The Italian Philosophers.* Translated and edited by Arturo B. Fallico and Herman Shapiro, pp. 28–40. New York: Random House, 1967.

*Album Helen Maud Cam. Studies Presented to the International Commission for the History of Representative and Parliamentary Institutions.* 2 vols. Louvain: Béatrice Nauwalaerts, 1960.

Alciato, Andrea. "In tres posteriores codicis Justiniani libros annotatiunculae." In Andrea Alciato. *Opera omnia,* vol. 2, pp. 91–138. Basle, 1557.
- "De magistratibus, civilibusque et militaribusque officiis." In Andrea Alciato. *Opera omnia,* vol. 2, pp. 495–519. Basle, 1557.
- *Opera omnia.* Basle, 1557.
- "Paradoxorum iuris civilis." In Andrea Alciato. *Opera omnia,* vol. 3, pp. 6–17. Basle, 1557.
- "Parergon iuris." In Andrea Alciato. *Opera omnia,* vol. 2, pp. 173–494. Basle, 1557.

Allen, C. K. *Law in the Making.* 7th ed. Oxford: Clarendon Press, 1964.

Allen, John William. *A History of Political Thought in the Sixteenth Century.* Rev. ed. London: Methuen, 1957.

Allen, William. *A True, Sincere and Modest Defense of English Catholics that Suffer for their Faith.* Rouen, 1584. Reprinted in *English Recusant Literature* 68 (1971). Also in *Transition and Revolution ...,* edited by Robert M. Kingdon. Minneapolis: University of Minnesota Press, 1974. And in *The Execution of Justice in England,* edited by William Cecil Burghley. Ithaca: Cornell University Press, 1965.

Allison, A. F. "The Latin Life and Writings of Joseph Geswell, S. J. (1556–1623)." *English Recusant History* 15 (1979): 79–144.

Almain, Jacques. *Aurea clarissimi et acutissimi Doctoris Theologi Magistri Jacobi Almain Senonensis Opuscula.* Paris, 1518.

- *De dominio naturali, civili et ecclesiastico.* In Jean Gerson. *Opera omnia,* edited by Louis du Pin, vol. 2, pp. 971–76. Antwerp, 1706.
- "Expositio, circa decisiones magistri Guillielmi Occam, super potestate summi pontifici." Reprinted as "De potestate ecclesiastica et laica" in Jean Gerson. *Opera omnia,* edited by Louis du Pin, vol. 2, pp. 1013–1120. Antwerp, 1706.
- "Libellus de auctoritate ecclesiae." In Jean Gerson. *Opera omnia,* edited by Louis du Pin, vol. 2, pp. 976–1012. Antwerp, 1706.
- "Quaestio resumptiva, de dominio naturali, civili et ecclesiastico." In Jean Gerson. *Opera omnia,* edited by Louis du Pin, vol. 2, pp. 961–76. Antwerp, 1706.
- "Tractatus de auctoritate ecclesiae." In Jean Gerson. *Opera omnia,* edited by Louis du Pin, vol. 2, pp. 925–60. Antwerp, 1706.

Allmand, C. T., ed. *War, Literature and Politics in the Late Middle Ages.* Liverpool: Liverpool University Press, 1976.

Almasy, Rudolph. "The Purpose of Richard Hooker's Polemic." *Journal of the History of Ideas* 39 (1978): 251–70.

Althaus, P. *The Theology of Martin Luther.* Translated by Robert C. Schultz. Philadelphia: Fortress Press, 1966.

Althusius, Johannes. *Politica methodice digesta.* Edited by Carl J. Friedrich. Cambridge, MA: Harvard University Press, 1932. Reprint. New York: Arno, 1979.

- *The Politics of Johannes Althusius. An Abridged Translation of the Third Edition of Politica Methodice Digesta.* Translated and edited by Frederick S. Carney. London: Eyre and Spottiswoode, 1965.
- *Politica methodice digesta.* 3d ed. Herborn, 1614. Reprint. Aalen: Scientia Verlag, 1967.

Altschul, Michael. "Kingship, Government, and Politics in the Middle Ages: Some Recent Studies." *Medievalia et Humanistica,* n.s. 2 (1971): 133–52.

Alvarez Gendin, S. *Doctrinas politicas de Vitoria y Suárez.* Oviedo: Imprente La Cruz, 1950.

Ames, William. *The Marrow of Sacred Divinity.* London, 1642. Reprint. Edited by John W. Eusden. Boston: Pilgrim Press, 1968.

[Amsdorff, Nicolas von.] *Confessio et apologia pastorum et reliquorum ministrorum ecclesiae Magdeburgensis.* Magdeburg, 1550.

Anderson, Marvin Walter. *Peter Martyr: A Reformer in Exile (1542–1562). A Chronology of Biblical Writings in England and Europe.* Nieuwkoop: de Graff, 1975.

- "Rhetoric and Reality: Peter Martyr and the English Reformation." *Sixteenth Century Journal* 19 (1988): 451–69.
- "Royal Idolatry: Peter Martyr and the Reformed Tradition." *Archive for Reformation History* 69 (1978): 157–201.

Anderson, Perry. *Lineages of the Absolutist State.* London: New Left Books, 1974.

- *Passage from Antiquity to Feudalism.* London: New Left Books, 1974.

Andres Marcos, T. *Los imperialismos de Juan Gines de Sepúlveda en su Democrates alter.* Madrid: Instituto de Estudios Politicos, 1947.

Andresen, C. "Geschichte der abendlandischen Konzile des Mittelalters." In *Die ökumenischer Konzile de Christenheit*, edited by H. J. Margull, pp. 75–200. Stuttgart: W. Kolhammer, 1961.
Angemeier, H. "Das Reich and der Konziliarismus." *Historische Zeitschrift* 192 (1961): 529–83.
Anglo, Sydney. *Machiavelli: A Dissection*. London: Gollanz, 1969.
Antholz, Heinz Werner. *Die politische Wirksamkeit des Joannes Althusius in Emden.* Aurich: Verlag Ostfriesische Landschaft, 1955.
Appleby, Joyce Oldham. *Economic Thought and Ideology in Seventeenth Century England*. Princeton: Princeton University Press, 1978.
Arendt, Hannah. *The Life of the Mind: Willing*. New York: Harcourt Brace Jovanovich, 1978.
Arendt, Paul. Die Predigten des Konstanzer Konzils; Ein Beitrag zur Predigt- und Kirchengeschichte des ausgehenden Mittelalters. Freiburg-im-Breisgau: Herder, 1933.
Aristotle. *Nicomachean Ethics*. Translated by David Ross, revised by J.L. Ackrill and J.O. Urmson. Oxford: Oxford University Press, 1980.
- *Physics*. Translated by Hippocrates G. Apostle. Grinnell, 10: Peripatetic Press, 1980.
- *Politicorum Libri Octo*. Translated by William of Moerbeke. Edited by F. Susemihl. Leipzig: 1872.
Armstrong, R. Z. *Primary and Secondary Precepts in Thomistic Natural Law Teaching.* The Hague: Martinus Nijhoff, 1966.
Arnaud, Jean-Jacques. *Les Origines doctrinales du Code Civil français*. Paris: Librairie générale de droit et de jurisprudence, 1969.
Arnisaeus, Henning. *De auctoritate principis in populum semper inviolabili*. Strasbourg, 1635.
Arnold, M. S., T. A. Green, S. A. Scully, and S. D. White, eds. *On Laws and Customs in England: Essays in Honor of Samuel E. Thorne.* Chapel Hill: University of North Carolina Press, 1981.
Arquillière, H.-X. *L'Augustinisme politique: Essai sur la formation des théories politiques du Moyen Âge*. 2d ed. Paris: J. Vrin, 1955.
Arrowood, Charles F. ed. *George Buchanan on the Powers of the Crown in Scotland.* Austin, TX: University of Texas Press, 1949.
Ashcraft, Richard. "Hobbes's Natural Man. A Study in Ideology Formation." *Journal of Politics* 33–34 (1971): 1076–1117.
- "Locke's State of Nature: Historical Fact or Moral Fiction?" *American Political Science Review* 62 (1968): 898–915.
- "On the Problem of Methodology and the Nature of Political Theory." *Political Theory* 39 (1975): 5–25.
- "Political Theory and Practical Action: A Reconsideration of Hobbes's State of Nature." In *Hobbes Studies*, edited by Martin A. Bertman, vol. 1, pp. 63–88. Assen: Van Gorcum, 1988.
- *Revolutionary Politics and Locke's Two Treatises of Government*. Princeton: Princeton University Press, 1987.

– "The Two Treatises and the Exclusion Crisis: The Problem of Lockean Political Theory as Bourgeois Ideology." In *John Locke: Papers Read at a Clark Library Seminar*, 10 December, 1979, pp. 25–114. Los Angeles: William Andrews Clark Memorial Library, University of California, 1980.
Ashley, Kathleen M. "Divine Power in the Chester Cycle and Late Medieval Thought." *Journal of the History of Ideas* 39 (1978): 387–404.
Association internationale Vitoria-Suárez. *Vitoria et Suárez: contribution des théologiens au droit international.* Paris: A. Pedone, 1939.
Association of American Law Schools, ed., comp. *Select Essays in Anglo-American Legal History, III.* Boston: Little, Brown, 1909.
Aston, Margaret. "Lollards and the Reformation: Survival or Revival?" *History* 49 (1964): 149–170.
Atiya, Aziz S. *The Crusade in the Later Middle Ages.* London: Methuen, 1938. Reprint. New York: Kraus, 1965.
Aubenas, Roger, and Robert Ricard. *Histoire de l'Église.* Vol. 15, *L'Église et la Renaissance (1449–1527).* Paris: Bloud & Gay, 1951.
Augustine. *The City of God.* Translated by Demetrius B. Zema and Gerald G. Walsh. 3 vols. New York: Fathers of the Church, 1950–54.
Aylmer, G. E. "The Meaning and Definition of Property in Seventeenth Century England." *Past and Present* 86 (1980): 87–97.
Aylmer, G. E., ed. *The Interregnum: The Quest for Settlement.* London: Macmillan, 1972.
Bacon, Francis. "A View of the Differences in Question betwixt the King's Bench and the Council in the Marches." In *The Letters and Life of Francis Bacon*, edited by James Spedding, vol. 3, pp. 368–89.
Bailyn, Bernard. "The Challenge of Modern Historiography." *American Historical Review* 87 (1982): 1–24.
– *The Ideological Origins of the American Revolution.* Cambridge, MA: Harvard University Press, 1967.
Bainton, Roland H. *Concerning Heretics: An Anonymous Work Attributed to Sebastian Castellio.* New York: Columbia University Press, 1935.
– "The *Querela pacis* of Erasmus, Classical and Christian Sources." *Archiv für Reformationgeschichte* 42 (1951): 32–48.
– *The Reformation of the Sixteenth Century.* Boston: Beacon Press, 1953.
– *Studies on the Reformation.* Boston: Beacon Press, 1964.
Bak, Janos, ed. *The German Peasant War of 1525.* London: Cass, 1976.
Baker, Derek, ed. *Church, Society and Politics.* Oxford: Oxford University Press, 1975.
– *Religious Motivation: Biographical and Sociological Problems for the Church Historian.* Oxford: Oxford University Press, 1978.
Baldus de Ubaldis. *Commentaria ad IV Institutionum libros.* Pavia, 1489.
– *Commentaria super I-V libris Codicis.* Lyon, 1498.
– *Lectura in VI-IX libros Codicis.* Lyon, 1498.
Bale, John. *The Acts of English Votaries.* Wesel [London], 1546.
Ball, Terence. "Contradiction and Critique in Political Theory." In *What Should*

*Political Theory Be Now?*, edited by John S. Nelson, pp. 127–68. Albany: State University of New York Press, 1983.
Ball, Terence, James Farr, and Russell L. Hanson, eds. *Political Innovation and Conceptual Change*. Cambridge: Cambridge University Press, 1989.
Balon, Joseph. "La 'ratio,' fondement et justification du droit avant Gratien." *Studia Gratiana* 9 (1966): 11–26.
Baluzius, Stephanus. *Vitae paparum Avenionensium*. New ed. G. Mollat. 4 vols. Paris: Letouzey et Ane, 1914.
Baluzius, Stephanus, and J. D. Mansi. *Miscellanea*. 4 vols. Lucca, 1761–64.
Bandman, E., ed. *Bioethics and Human Rights: A Reader for Health Professionals*. Boston: Little, Brown, 1978.
Bañez, Domingo. *Decisiones de iure et iustitia*. Douai, 1615.
Barcia Trelles, Camilo. "Francesco Suárez (1548–1617)." *Académie de droit international: recueil des cours* 43 (1933): 385–553.
Barclay, William. *The Kingdom and the Regal Power: Against Buchanan, Brutus, Boucher and the other Monarchomachs*. Translated by George Albert Moore. Chevy Chase: Country Dollar Press, 1954.
– *De potestate papae*. Menston: Scholar Press, 1973.
– *De regno et regali potestate adversus Buchananum, Brutus, Boucherium, et reliquos monarchomachos, libri sex*. Paris: 1600.
Barker, Ernest. "A Huguenot Theory of Politics—The 'Vindiciae contra tyrannos.'" *Proceedings of the Huguenot Society of London* 14, no. 39 (1930): 37–61.
– *The Social Contract*. Oxford: Oxford University Press, 1947.
Barlowe, William. *Dialogue concerning the Lutheran Factions*. Edited by John Robert Lunn. London: Ellis and Keene, 1897.
Barnes, Jonathan. "The Just War." In *The Cambridge History of Later Medieval Philosophy* ..., edited by Normand Kretzman et al., pp. 771–84. Cambridge: Cambridge University Press, 1982.
Barnes, Robert. *A Supplication ... unto ... King Henry VIII*. London, 1534.
– *The Reformation Essays of Dr Robert Barnes*. Edited by Neelak S. Tjernagel. London: Corcordia Publishing House, 1963.
– "That Men's Constitutions, which are not grounded in Scripture bind not the conscience of Man." In Robert Barnes. *The Reformation Essays* ..., edited by Neelak S. Tjernagel, pp. 81–93. London: Concordia Publishing House, 1963.
– "What the Church is, and Who be Thereof." In Robert Barnes. *The Reformation Essays* ..., edited by Neelak S. Tjernagel, pp. 37–52. London: Concordia Publishing House, 1963.
Baron, Hans. "Calvinist Republicanism and its Historical Roots." *Church History* 8 (1939): 30–42.
– "Cicero and the Roman Civic Spirit in the Middle Ages and Early Renaissance." *Bulletin of the John Rylands Library* 22 (1938): 72–97.
– *The Crisis of the Early Italian Renaissance: Civic Humanism and Republican Liberty*

*in an Age of Classicism and Tyranny.* 2 vols. Princeton: Princeton University Press, 1955. 2d ed. 2 vols. in 1. 1966.
- "Franciscan Poverty and Civic Wealth as Factors in the Rise of Humanistic Thought." *Speculum* 13 (1938) : 1–37.
- *From Petrarch to Leonardo Bruni. Studies in Humanistic and Political Literature.* Chicago: University of Chicago Press, 1968.
- *Humanistic and Political Literature in Florence and Venice at the Beginning of the Quattrocento: Studies in Criticism and Chronology.* Cambridge, MA: Harvard University Press, 1955.
- "Leonardo Bruni: 'Professional Rhetorician' or 'Civic Humanist'?" *Past and Present* 36 (1967): 21–37.
- "Machiavelli: The Republican Citizen and the Author of 'The Prince.'" *English Historical Review* 76 (1961): 217–53.
- "Religion and Politics in the German Imperial Cities during the Reformation." *English Historical Review* 52 (1937): 405–27; 614–33.
- "A Struggle for Liberty in the Renaissance: Florence, Venice and Milan in the Early Quattrocento." *American Historical Review* 68 (1953): 265–89; 544–70.

Baron, Salo Wittinger. *A Social and Religious History of the Jews.* Vol. 9, *Under Church and Empire.* 2d ed. New York: Columbia University Press, 1965.

Barraclough, Geoffrey. *The Medieval Papacy.* New York: Harcourt, Brace and World, 1968.
- *Papal Provisions: Aspects of Church History, Constitutional, Legal, and Administrative in the Late Middle Ages.* Oxford: Basil Blackwell, 1935.

Barrère, Joseph. "Observations sur quelques ouvrages politiques anonymes du XIVe siècle." *Revue d'histoire de la France* 21 (1914): 375–86.

Barrow, C.W.S. *Annali della Fondazione italiana per la storia amministrativa* 4 (1967).

Barth, Wilhelm. *Die Luthersache (Causa Lutheri) 1517–1524*: Die Anfange der Reformation als Frage von Politik und Recht. Lubeck, Hamburg: Matthiesen Verlag, 1970.

*Bartolo da Sassoferrato – Studi e Documenti per il VI Centenario.* 2 vols. Milan: Guiffrè, 1962.

Bartolus of Sassoferrato. "De Guelphis et Gebellinis." In *Humanism and Tyranny* ..., edited by Ephraim Emerton, pp. 273–84. Cambridge, MA: Harvard University Press, 1925. Also in Diego Quaglioni. *Politica e diritto* ... Florence: L. S. Olschki, 1983.
- "De regimine civitatis." In Diego Quaglioni. *Politica e diritto* ... Florence: L. S. Olschki, 1983.
- *Opera Omnia.* 12 vols. Basle, 1588.
- "De tyrannia." In *Humanism and Tyranny* ..., edited by Ephraim Emerton, pp. 126–54. Cambridge, MA: Harvard University Press, 1925. Also in Diego Quaglioni. *Politica e diritto* ... Florence: L. S. Olschki, 1983.

Barton, John L. "Roman Law in England." In Société d'histoire des droits de l'antiquité. *Ius Romanum Medii Aevi.* Pars V, 13.a. Milan: Guiffrè, 1971.

Bataillon, Marcel. *Érasme et l'Espagne: Recherches sur l'histoire spirituelle du XVI$^e$ siècle.* Paris: E. Droz, 1937.
– *Études sur Bartolomé de Las Casas.* Paris: Centre de recherches de l'Institut d'études hispaniques, 1965.
Battaglia, Felice. "Societa civile ed autorita nel pensiero di Francesco Suárez." *Rivista Internazionale di Filosofia del Diritto* 27, series 3 (1950): 213–34.
Batz, William G. "The Historical Anthropology of John Locke." *Journal of the History of Ideas* 35 (1974): 663–70.
Baudry, Leon. *Lexique Philosophique de Guillaume d'Ockham. Études des notions fondamentales.* Paris: Lethielleux, 1958.
– *La Querelle des futurs contingents. (Louvain, 1465–75).* Paris: J. Vrin, 1950.
Bauer, Roger. "Sacrum imperium et imperium germanicum chez Nicholas du Cues." *Archives d'Histoire doctrinale et littéraire du Moyen Âge* 21 (1954): 207–40.
Baumer, Franklin L. "Christopher St German: the Political Philosophy of a Tudor Lawyer." *American Historical Review* 42 (1937): 631–51.
– *The Early Tudor Theory of Kingship.* New Haven: Yale University Press, 1940.
Baumer, Franklin L., ed. *Main Currents of Western Thought. Readings in Western European Intellectual History from the Middle Ages to the Present.* New York: Alfred A. Knopf, 1954.
Baumer, Remigius. "Die Bedeutung des Konstanzer Konziles für die Geschichte der Kirche." *Annuarium Historiae Conciliorum* 4 (1972): 26–45.
– "Die Erforschung des Konziliarismus." In *Die Entwicklung des Konziliarismus ...,* edited by Remigius Baumer, pp. 3–56. Darmstadt: Wissenschaftliche Buchgesellschaft, 1977.
– "Eugen IV, und der Plan eines 'Dritten Konzils' zur Beilegung des Basler Schismas." In *Reformata Reformanda; Festgabe für Hubert Jedin zum 17. Juni 1965.*
– "Die Interpretation und Verbindlichkeit der Konstanzer Dekreter." *Theologisch-praktische Quartalsschrift* 116 (1968): 44–53.
– "Die Konstanzer Dekrete 'Haec sancta' und 'Frequens' im Urteil katholischer Kontroverstheologen des 16. Jahrhunderts." In *Von Konstanz nach Trient ...,* edited by Remigius Baumer, pp. 547–74. Munich, Paderborn, and Vienna: Schoningh, 1972.
– *Nachwirkungen des konziliaren Gedankens in der Theologie und Kanonistik des frühen 16. Jahrhunderts.* Münster: Aschendorff, 1971.
– "Die Reformkonzilien des 15. Jahrdunderts in der neuren Forschung." *Annuarium historiae conciliorum* 1 (1969): 153–64.
– "Die Stellungahme Eugens IV. zum Konstanzer Superioritätdekret in der Bulle 'Etsi non dubitemus.'" In *Das Konzil von Konstanz ...,* edited by A. Franzen and W. Müller, pp. 337–56. Freiburg: Herder, 1964.
Baumer, Remigius, ed. *Die Entwicklung des Konziliarismus: Werden und Nachwirken der konziliaren Idee.* Darmstadt: Wissenschaftliche Buchgesellschaft, 1977.
– *Von Konstanz nach Trient: Beitrage zur Geschichte der Kirche von der Reformkonzilien bis zum Tridentinum.* Munich, Paderborn, and Vienna: Schoningh, 1972.
– *Das Konstanzer Konzil.* Darmstadt: Wissenschaltliche Buchgesellschaft, 1977.

Baumgartner, Frederic J. *Radical Reactionaries: the Political Thought of the French Catholic League.* Geneva: Droz, 1976.
Baumgold, Deborah. *Hobbes's Political Theory.* Cambridge: Cambridge University Press, 1988.
Baur, Jurgen. *Gott, Recht und weltliches Regiment im Werke Calvins.* Bonn: H. Bouvier, 1965.
Baxter, James H. "Four 'New' Medieval Scottish Authors." *Scottish Historical Review* 25 (1928): 90–97.
Bayer, H. "Zur Soziologie des mittelalterlichen Individualisierungs prozesses: Ein Beitrag zu einer wirklichkeitsbezungen Geistsgeschichte." *Archiv für Kulturgeschichte* 58 (1976): 115–73.
Bayley, C. C. "Pivotal Concepts in the Political Philosophy of William of Ockham." *Journal of the History of Ideas* 10: (1949): 199–218.
– *War and Society in Renaissance Florence; The De militia of Leonardo Bruni.* Toronto: University of Toronto Press, 1961.
Baynes, Kenneth, James Bohman, and Thomas McCarthy, eds. *After Philosophy: End or Transformation?* Cambridge, MA: MIT Press, 1987.
Beame, E. M. "The Limits of Toleration in Sixteenth Century France." *Studies in the Renaissance* 13 (1966): 230–65.
Beck, Hans-George. "From the High Middle Ages to the Eve of the Reformation." Translated by Anselm Biggs. Vol. 4 of Hans-George Beck et al. *Handbook of Church History.* New York: Herder and Herder, 1970.
– "'Protestation,' 'Protest': Funktion und Funktionswandel eines rechtlichen Instruments." *Zeitschrift für historische Forschung* 5 (1978) 385–412.
Beck, Hans-George et al. *Handbook of Church History.* 10 vols. New York: Herder and Herder, 1970.
Becker, Hans-Jurgen. *Die Appellation vom Papst an ein allgemeines Konzil: historische Entwicklung und kanonistische Diskussion im späten Mittelalter und in der frühen Neuzeit.* Cologne and Vienna: Böhlau, 1988.
Becker, Marvin. *Medieval Italy, Constraints and Creativity.* Bloomington: Indiana University Press, 1981.
– "Some Aspects of Oligarchical, Dictatorial and Popular Signorie in Florence, 1282–1382." *Comparative Studies in Society and History* 2 (1960): 421–39.
– "Florentine 'Libertas': Political Independents and 'Nova Cives,' 1372–1378." *Traditio* 18 (1962): 393–407.
Bedouelle, G. *Lefèvre d'Étaples et l'Intelligence des Écritures.* Geneva: Droz, 1975.
Beer, S. "The Rule of the Wise and the Holy: Hierarchy in the Thomistic System." *Political Theory* 14 (1985): 391–422.
Beik, William. *Absolutism and Society in Seventeenth Century France. State Power and Provincial Aristocracy in Languedoc.* Cambridge: Cambridge University Press, 1985.
Bekinsau, John. *De supremo et absoluto regis imperio.* London: 1546.
Belch, Stanislaus F. *Paulus Vladimiri and His Doctrine Concerning International Law and Politics.* 2 vols. The Hague: Mouton, 1965.

Bell, Susan G. "Johann Eberlin von Günsburg's *Worlfaria*: The First Protestant Utopia." *Church History* 36 (1967): 122–39.
Bellarmine, Robert. "De conciliis." In *Roberti Bellarmini Opera Omnia*, edited by Justin Fèvre, vol. 1, pp. 187–407. Paris: Vives, 1870–74. Reissue. Frankfurt am Main: Minerva, 1965.
- "De Justificatione." In *Roberti Bellarmini Opera Omnia*, edited by Justin Fèvre, vol. 6, pp. 149–386. Paris: Vives, 1870–74. Reissue. Frankfurt am Main: Minerva, 1965.
- *De laicis or The Treatise on Civil Government*. Translated by Kathleen E. Murphy. New York: Fordham University Press, 1928.
- "De membris ecclesiae." In *Roberti Bellarmini Opera Omnia*, edited by Justin Fèvre, vol. 2, pp. 409–633; vol. 3, pp. 5–48. Paris: Vives, 1870–74. Reissue. Frankfurt am Main: Minerva, 1965.
- *Opera*. Edited by S. Tromp. 9 vols. Rome: Gregorian University, 1942–50.
- *Roberti Bellarmini Opera Omnia*. Edited by Justin Fèvre. 12 vols. Paris: Vives 1870–74. Reissue. Frankfurt am Main: Minerva, 1965.
- *Tractatus de potestate summi ponticis in rebus temporalibus adversus G. Barclaium*. Rome: Zannetti, 1950.
- *The Power of the Pope in Temporal Affairs, against William Barclay*. Translated and edited by George Albert Moore. 2d ed. Chevy Chase: Country Dollar Press, 1950.
- "De Summo Pontifice." In Robert Bellarmine. *Politiani Opera Omnia*, edited by Justin Fèvre, vol. 1, pp. 449–615; vol. 2, pp. 5–167. Reissue. Frankfurt am Main: Minerva, 1965.
- *Extracts from Politics and Government by the Supreme Pontiff*. Translated and edited by George Albert Moore. Chevy Chase: Country Dollar Press, 1951.
- "De Verbo Dei." In Robert Bellarmine. *Politiani Opera Omnia*, edited by Justin Fèvre, vol. 1, pp. 65–231. Reissue. Frankfurt am Main: Minerva, 1965.
Beltran de Heredia, Vicente. "Un precursor del Maestro Vitoria, el P. Matias de Paz, O.P., y su tratado 'De Dominio Regnum Hispaniae super Indos.'" *La ciencia Tomista* 40 (1929): 173–90.
Bender, Harold S. *Conrad Grebel, 1498–1526, The Founder of the Swiss Brethren Sometimes called Anabaptists*. Scottdale: Herald Press, 1971.
Bendix, Reinhard. *Kings or People: Power and the Mandate to Rule*. Berkeley: University of California Press, 1978.
Benert, Richard R. "Lutheran Resistance Theory and the Imperial Constitution." *Il Pensiero Politico* 6 (1973): 17–36. Reprint. *Lutheran Quarterly* 2 (1988): 187–207.
Bense, W. F. "Paris Theologians on War and Peace, 1521–1529." *Church History* 41 (1972): 168–85.
Benson, Robert. "Medieval Canonistic Origins of the Debate on the Lawfulness of the Spanish Conquest." In *First Images of America ...*, edited by Fredi Chiapelli, vol. 1, pp. 327–34. Los Angeles: University of California Press, 1976.

Bentley, J. H. *Politics and Culture in Renaissance Naples.* Princeton: Princeton University Press, 1987.
Bergendoff, Conrad. *Olaus Petri and the Ecclesiastical Transformation in Sweden.* New York: Columbia University Press, 1928.
Berkhofer, Robert F. Jr. *The White Man's Indian: Images of the American Indian from Columbus to the Present.* New York: Alfred A. Knopf, 1978.
Berlin, Isaiah. "Does Political Theory Still Exist?" In *Philosophy, Politics and Society,* edited by Peter Laslett and W. G. Runciman, series 3, vol. 2, pp. 1–33. Oxford: Basil Blackwell, 1967.
Berljak, Matya. *Il Diritto naturale e il suo rapport con la divinita in Uga Grozio.* Rome: Gregorian University, 1978.
Berman, Harold J. "Conscience and the Law, the Lutheran Reformation and the Western Legal Tradition." *Journal of Law and Religion* 5 (1987): 177–202.
– *The Interaction of Law and Religion.* Nashville: Abingdon Press, 1974.
Berner, S. "Florentine Political Thought in the Late Cinquescento." *Il Pensiero Politico* 3 (1970): 177–99.
Bernstein, Alan E. *Pierre d'Ailly and the Blanchard Affair.* Leiden: E.J. Brill, 1978.
Bertman, Martin A. *The Natural and the Artifacted Good.* Bern: Lang, 1981.
– "Semantics and Political Theory in Hobbes." In Bertman, *Hobbes Studies,* edited by Martin A. Bertman, vol. 1, pp. 134–62. Assen: Van Gorcum, 1988.
Bertman, Martin A., ed. *Hobbes Studies.* 2 vols. Assen: Van Gorcum, 1988, 1989.
Bethel, Slingsby. *The Present Interest of England Stated.* London, 1671.
Betti, Emilio. *Teoria generale della interpretazione.* Milan: Guiffrè, 1953.
Beza, Theodore. *Concerning the Rights of Rulers over their Subjects and the Duty of Subjects towards their Rulers.* Translated by Henri-Louis Gonin. Edited by A. H. Murray. Cape Town: H.A.V.M., 1956.
– *Du droit des magistrats.* Edited by Robert M. Kingdon. Geneva: Droz, 1971.
– *Du droit des magistrats sur leurs subiets, 1574* Edited by M. Marabuto. Saint Julien-L'Ars: Imprimerie monastique, 1968.
– *De haereticis a civili magistratu puniendis.* Geneva, 1554.
– *De iure magistratuum.* Edited by Klaus Sturm. Neukirchen-Vluyn: Neukirckener Verlag, 1965.
– *Icones.* Geneva, 1580.
– "The Rights of Magistrates over their Subjects." In *Constitutionalism and Resistance ...,* edited by Julian H. Franklin, pp. 103–35. New York: Pegasus, 1969.
– Théodore de Bèze. *Cours sur les Épîtres aux Romains et aux Hébreux.* Edited by Pierre Fraenkel and Luc Perrotet. Geneva: Droz, 1988.
– *Les Vrais portraits des hommes illustres.* Geneva, 1581. (French translation of *Icones.*)
Bianchi, Lorenza. *Tradizione Libertina e Critica Historia.* Milan: Franco Angeli, 1988.
Biechler, J. E. "Nicholas of Cusa and the End of the Conciliar Movement: A Humanist Crisis of Identity." *Church History* 44 (1975) 5–21.

Biel, Gabriel. "The Circumcision of the Lord." Translated by Paul L. Nylus. In *Forerunners of the Reformation* ..., edited by Heiko Oberman and translated by Paul L. Nylus, pp. 165–74. London: Butterworth, 1967.
— *Defensorium obedientiae apostolicae et aliae documentae.* Edited and translated by H. A. Oberman, D. E. Zerfoss, and W.J. Courtenay. Cambridge, MA: Harvard University Press, Belknap Press, 1968.
Bieler, André. *La pensée économique et sociale de Calvin.* Geneva: Librairie de l'université, 1959.
Bilderback, Loy. "Proctorial Representation and the Conciliar Support at the Council of Basle." *Annuarium Historiae Conciliorum* 1 (1969): 140–52.
Binder, Karl. "Der 'Tractatus de Ecclesiae' Johannus von Ragusa und die Verhandlungen des Konzils von Basel mit den Husiten." *Angelicum* 28 (1951): 30–54.
— *Wesen und Eigenschaften der Kirche bei Kardinal J. de Torquemada, O.P.* Innsbruck: Verlagsonstalt Tyrolia, 1955.
Binkoff, S. T., J. Hurstfield, and C. H. Williams. *Elizabethan Government and Society. Essays Presented to Sir John Neale.* London: Athlone Press, 1961.
Binz, L. *Vie religieuse et réforme ecclésiastique dans le diocèse de Génève pendant le Grand Schisme.* Geneva 17: Droz, 1973.
Birk, E., ed. *Monumenta conciliorum generalium seculi decimi quinti.* 4 vols. Reprint. Vienna: Typis C.R. Officinae typographicae aulae et status, 1977.
Bisson, Thomas N. "The General Assemblies of Philip the Fair: Their Character Reconsidered." *Studia Gratiana* 15 (1972): 537–64.
— "The Problem of Feudal Monarchy: Aragon, Catalonia, and France." *Speculum* 53 (1978): 460–78.
Bitton, Davis. *The French Nobility in Crisis, 1560–1640.* Stanford: Stanford University Press, 1969.
Black, Antony J. *Council and Commune. The Conciliar Movement and the Fifteenth Century.* London: Burns & Oates, 1979.
— *Guilds and Civil Society in European Political Thought from the Twelfth Century to the Present.* London: Methuen, 1984.
— "Heimericus de Campo: The Council and History." *Annuarium Historiae Conciliorum* 1 (1970): 78–96.
— *Monarchy and Community: Political Ideas in the Later Conciliar Controversy, 1430–1450.* Cambridge: Cambridge University Press, 1970.
— "The Political Ideas of Conciliarism and Papalism, 1430–1450." *Journal of Ecclesiastical History* 20 (1969): 45–65.
— *Political Thought in Europe, 1250–1450.* Cambridge: Cambridge University Press, 1992.
— "The Realistic Ecclesiology of Heimerich van de Valve." In *Facultas S. Theologia Lovanensis, 1432–1797: Bijdragen tot haar geschiednis*, edited by Edmond J. M. van Eijl, pp. 273–91. Louvain: Presse universitaire, 1977.
— "Skinner on the Foundations of Modern Political Thought." *Political Studies* 28 (1980): 451–57.

- "Society and the Individual from the Middle Ages to Rousseau: Philosophy, Jurisprudence and Constitutional Theory." *History of Political Thought* 1 (1980): 145–66.
- "The Universities and the Council of Basle: Ecclesiology and Tactics." *Annuarium Historia Conciliorum* 6 (1974): 341–51.
- "What was Conciliarism? Conciliar Theory in Historical Perspective." In *Authority and Power* ... , edited by Brian Tierney and Peter Linehan, pp. 213–24. Cambridge: Cambridge University Press, 1980.

Blakney, R. B. *Meister Eckhart: A Modern Translation.* New York and London: Harper & Bros, 1941.

Bleznick, Donald W. "Spanish Reaction to Machiavelli in the Sixteenth and Seventeenth Centuries." *Journal of the History of Ideas* 19 (1958): 542–50.

Blickle, Peter. *The Revolution of 1525: The German Peasants' War from a New Perspective.* Translated by Thomas A. Brady, Jr and H. C. Erik Midelford. London: Johns Hopkins University Press, 1981.

Bliemetzrieder, F. P. *Literanische Polemik zu Beginn des grossen abendlandischen Schismas.* Vienna: Tempsky, 1910.

Bloch, M. *Les rois thaumaturges: Études sur le caractère surnaturel attribué à la puissance royale, particulièrement en France et en Angleterre.* Rev. ed. Paris: A. Colin, 1983.

Bloch, R. Howard. *Medieval French Literature and the Law.* Berkeley: University of California Press, 1978.

Blythe, James M. *Ideal Government and the Mixed Constitution in the Middle Ages.* Princeton: Princeton University Press, 1992.

- "The Mixed Constitution and the Distinction Between Regal and Political Power in the Work of Thomas Aquinas." *Journal of the History of Ideas* 47 (1986): 547–65.

Boas, George. *Essays on Primitivism and Related Ideas in the Middle Ages.* Baltimore: Johns Hopkins Press, 1948.

Bodin, Jean. *De republica libri sex.* Ursellis, 1601.

- *The Six Books of A Commonwealth.* Translated by Richard Knolles and edited by Kenneth D. McRae. Cambridge, MA: Harvard University Press, 1962.

Boehmer, Heinrich. *The Road to Reformation.* Translated by J. W. Doberstein and T. G. Tappert. Philadelphia: Muhlenberg Press, 1946.

Boehner, Philotheus. *Collected Articles on Ockham.* Edited by E. M. Buytaert. St Bonaventure: Franciscan Institute Publications, 1958.

Bohannan, Paul. *Justice and Judgment among the Tiv.* London: Oxford University Press, 1957.

Bohatec, Josef. *Budé und Calvin: Studien zur Gedankenwelt des französischen Frühhumanismus.* Graz: H. Böhlaus, 1950.

- *Calvins Lehre von Staat und Kirche mit besonderer Berucksichtigung des Organismusgedankens.* Breslau: M. & H. Marcus, 1937. Reprint. Aalen: Scientia Verlag, 1961.

Bohnenstadt, Elizabeth. *Kirche und Reich im Schriften des Nikolaus von Cues.* Heidelberg: C. Winter, 1939.
Boisset, Jean. *Érasme et Luther: Libre ou self arbitre?* Paris: Presses universitaires de France, 1962.
– *Sagesse et sainteté dans la pensée de Jean Calvin: essai sur l'humanisme du réformateur français.* Paris: Presses universitaires de France, 1959.
Bonadeo, Alfredo. *Corruption, Conflict, and Power in the Works and Times of Niccolo Machiavelli.* Berkeley: University of California Press, 1973.
Bonet, Honoré. *The Tree of Battles of Honoré Bonet. An English Version with Introduction.* Translated by E. W. Coopland. Cambridge, MA: Harvard University Press, 1949.
Boniface VIII. "*Clericos laicos.*" In *Quellen zur Geschichte des Papstums ...*, edited by Carl Murbt and Kurt Aland, vol. 1, pp. 457–58. Tübingem: N.P., 1967.
– "Unam sanctam." In *Quellen zur Geschichte des Papstums ...*, edited by Carl Murbt and Kurt Aland, vol. 1, pp. 458–60. Tübingen: N.P., 1967.
Bonini, Cissie R. "Lutheran Influences in the Early English Reformation: Richard Morison Re-Examined." *Archiv für Reformationgeschichte* 64 (1973): 206–24.
Bonolis, Guido. *Questioni di diritto internazionale in alcuni consigli inediti di Baldo degli Ubaldi.* Pisa: N.P., 1908.
Bontemps, C., L. P. Raymond, and J. P. Brancourt, eds. *Le Prince dans la France des XVI$^e$ et XVII$^e$ siècles.* Paris: Presses universitaires de France, 1965.
Boockmann, H. "Zur politischen Geschichte des Konstanzer Konzils." *Zeitschrift für Kirchengeschichte* 85 (1974): 45–63.
Borah, Woodrow. *Justice by Insurance.* Berkeley and Los Angeles: University of California Press, 1983.
Borchert, Ernst. *Der Einfluss des Nominalismus auf die Christologie der Spätscholastik.* Münster i. W: Aschendorff, 1946.
Bornet, René. *La réforme protestante du culte à Strasbourg au XVI siècle (1523–1598): Approche sociologique et interprétation théologique.* Leiden: E. J. Brill, 1981.
Bornkamm, Heinrich. *Luther's World of Thought.* Translated by Marten H. Bertram. St Louis: Concordia Publishing House, 1958.
Bossuet, Jacques Benigne. *Politique tirée des propres paroles de l'Écriture.* Edited by Jacques Le Brun. Geneva: Droz, 1967.
Botero, Giovanni. *Ragion di Stato.* Edited by Luigi Firpo. Turin: Unione tipografico-editrice torinese, 1949.
– *The Reason of State.* Translated by P. J. and D. P. Waley. New Haven: Yale University Press, 1956.
Botte, B., et al. *Le Concile et les Conciles. Contribution à l'histoire de la vie conciliare de l'église.* Ed. Oliver Rousseau. Paris: Chevetogne, 1960.
[Boucher, Jean.] *De iusta Henricii tertii abdicatione e francorum regno.* Paris, 1589.
Boulay, César Egasse du [Bulaeus]. *Historia universitatis Parisiensis.* Vol. 4. *1300–1400.* Vol. 5. *1400–1500.* Paris, 1668–70. Reprint. Frankfurt am Main: Minerva, 1966.

Bourret, E. *De l'origine du pouvoir d'après S. Thomas et Suárez.* Paris, 1857.
Boussard, Jacques. *Le Gouvernement de Henri II, Plantaganet.* Paris: Librairie d'Argence, 1956.
Bouwsma, William J. *Concordia mundi: The Career and Thought of Guillaume Pastel (1510–1581).* Cambridge, MA: Harvard University Press, 1957.
- "From History of Ideas to History of Meaning." *Journal of Interdisciplinary History* 12 (1981): 279–89.
- "Gallicanism and the Nature of Christendom." In *Renaissance Studies in Honor of Hans Baron,* edited by A. Moldo and J. A. Tedeschi, pp. 811–30. De Kalb: Northwestern University Press, 1971.
- *John Calvin: a Sixteenth-Century Portrait.* Oxford: Oxford University Press, 1988.
- *Venice and the Defence of Republican Liberty.* Berkeley: University of California Press, 1968.
Bowe, Gabriel. *The Origin of Political Authority: an Essay in Catholic Political Philosophy.* Dublin: Clonmore and Reynolds, 1955.
Bowles, Paul. "The Origin of Property and the Development of Scottish Historical Science." *Journal of the History of Ideas* 46 (1985): 197–209.
Bowsky, William M. "The Medieval Commune and Internal Violence: Police Power and Public Safety in Siena, 1287–1355." *American Historical Review* 73 (1967): 1–17.
Bowsky, William M., ed. *Studies in Medieval and Renaissance History.* Lincoln: University of Nebraska Press, 1964.
Boyance, Pierre. *Études sur l'Humanisme Cicéronien.* Brussels: Latomus, 1970.
Boyer, Charles. *Calvin et Luther: Accords et différences.* Rome: Gregorian University, 1973.
Boyle, Leonard E. "The *Oculus Sacerdotium* and Some Other Works of William of Pagula." *Transactions of the Royal Historical Society,* 5th series, vol. 5 (1955): 81–110.
Boyle, Robert. *The Works of the Honourable Robert Boyle.* Edited by Thomas Birch. 6 vols. London, 1772.
Bracton, Henri de. *De Legibus et Consuetudinibus Angliae. Bracton on the Laws and Customs of England.* Edited by Samuel Thorne. Cambridge: Harvard University Press, 1977.
Bradshaw, Brendon. "Transalpine Humanism." In *The Cambridge History of Medieval Political Thought ...* , edited by James H. Burns, pp. 95–131. Cambridge: Cambridge University Press, 1991.
Brady, Thomas A. *Ruling Class, Regime and Reformation at Strasbourg 1520–1555,* Leiden: E.J. Brill, 1978.
- *Turning Swiss: Cities and Empire, 1450–1550.* Cambridge: Cambridge University Press, 1985.
Brandmüller, Walter. *Das Konzil von Pavia-Siena, 1423–1424.* 2 vols. Münster: Aschendorff, 1968–74.
- *Papst und Konzil im Grossen Schisma (1378–1431).* Paderborn: Schoningh, 1990.

Branki, Karl. *The Emperor Charles v: the Growth and Destiny of a Man and of a World-Empire.* Translated by C. V. Wedgewood. London: Jonathan Cape, 1939.
Brant, Sebastian. *The Ship of Fools.* Translated by Alexander Barclay. Amsterdam: Theatrum Orbis Terrarum, 1970.
Brants, V. "Les théories politiques dans les écrits de L. Lessius (1554–1623)." *Revue Néo-Scolastique de Philosophie* 10 (1912): 42–85.
Braudel, Fernand. *The Mediterranean and the Mediterranean World in the Age of Philip II.* Translated by Sian Reynold. 2 vols. London: Collins, 1972–73.
Braun, Dietrich. "Luther über die Grenzen des Staates 1523." *Archiv für Reformationgeschichte* 78 (1978): 61–80.
Breen, Quirinus. *Christianity and Humanism: Studies in the History of Ideas.* Green Rapids: W.B. Eerdmans, 1968.
– *John Calvin: a Study in French Humanism.* Hamden: Archon Books, 1968.
Brewer, John S., ed. *Letters and Papers Foreign and Domestic, of the Reign of Henry VIII.* Revised by R. H. Brodie, 22 vols. London: H.M. Stationery Office, 1920–32.
Bridges, John. *A Defence of the Government Established in the Church of England for Ecclesiastical Matters ... Answering also to the arguments of Bodinus ...* 2 vols. London, 1587.
Briggs, William D. "Sidney's Political Ideas." *Studies in Philology* 29 (1932): 534–42.
Brimo, Albert. *Les grands courants de la philosophie du droit et de l'état.* 3d ed. Paris: Éditions A. Pedone, 1978.
Broadhead, Philip, ed. *Studies in the Reformation.* Brighton: Harvester, 1984.
Brock, P. *The Political and Social Doctrines of the Unity of Czech Brethren in the Fifteenth and Early Sixteenth Centuries.* The Hague: Mouton, 1957.
Brodie, D. M. "Introduction." In Edmund Dudley. *The Tree of Commonwealth,* edited by D. M. Brodie, pp. 1–17. Cambridge: Cambridge University Press, 1948.
Brodrick, James. *The Life and Work of Blessed Robert Francis Cardinal Bellarmine, S.J., 1542–1621.* 2 vols. London: Faber and Faber, 1928.
– *Robert Bellarmine: Saint and Scholar.* London: Burns and Oates, 1961.
Bromley, J. S., and E. H. Kossman, eds. *Britain and the Netherlands.* London: Chatto and Windus, 1962.
Brooke, C. N. L., D. E. Luscombe, C. H. Martin, and Dorothy Owen. *Church and Government in the Middle Ages. Essays Presented to C.R. Cheney on His Seventieth Birthday.* Cambridge: Cambridge University Press, 1976.
Brosse, Olivier de la. *Le Pape et le Concile: La comparaison de leurs pouvoirs à la veille de la Réforme.* Paris: Gregorian University Press, 1965.
Brown, A. M. "Platonism in Fifteenth Century Florence and its Contribution to Early Modern Political Thought." *Journal of Modern History* 58 (1986): 383–413.
Brown, D. C. *Pastor and Laity in the Theology of Jean Gerson.* Cambridge: Cambridge University Press, 1987.

Brown, E. A. R. "Reform and Resistance to Royal Authority in Fourteenth Century France: The Leagues of 1314–1315." *Parliaments, Estates and Representation* 1 (1981): 109–37.
Brown, Frieda S. *Religious and Political Conservatism in the Essais of Montaigne.* Geneva: Droz, 1963.
Brown, K. S., ed. *Hobbes Studies.* Oxford: Basil Blackwell, 1965.
Brown, Norman O. *Love's Body.* New York: Vintage, 1968.
Brown, Stuart M. "The Taylor Thesis: Some Objections." In *Hobbes Studies*, edited by K. S. Brown, pp. 57–71. Oxford: Basil Blackwell, 1965.
Bruce, F. F. *The English Bible: A History of Translations.* Rev. ed. London: Oliphants, 1970.
Brück, Gregory. "Iudici procedenti iniuste an licitum sit resistere." In Heinz Scheible. *Das Widerstandrecht ...* , pp. 63–66. Gutersloh: G. Mohn, 1969.
Brucker, Gene A. *Florentine Politics and Society 1343–1378.* Princeton: Princeton University Press, 1962.
– *Renaissance Florence.* New York: Wiley, 1969.
– *The Society of Renaissance Florence. A Documentary Study.* New York: Harper and Row, 1971.
Brundage, James A. *Medieval Canon Law and the Crusader.* Madison: University of Wisconsin Press, 1969.
Bruni, Leonardo. *Dialogues.* In *Prosatori Latini del quattrocento*, edited by Eugenio Garin, p. 44–99. Milan: R. Ricciardi, 1952.
– "De militia." In C. C. Bayley. *War and Society in Renaissance Florence ...* , pp. 360–97. Toronto: University of Toronto Press, 1961.
– "Historiarum Florentini populi." Edited by Emilio Santini. In *Rerum Italicarum Scriptores*, edited by Ludovico Muratori. Vol. 19. Bologna, 1926.
– "Laudatio Florentinae urbis." In Hans Baron. *From Petrarch to Leonardo Bruni ...* , pp. 217–63. Chicago: University of Chicago Press, 1968.
Brutus, Junius. *Vindiciae contra tyrannos; a Defence of Liberty against Tyrants. Or, of the lawfull power of the prince over the people, and the people over the prince. Being a treatise written in Latin and French by Junius Brutus, and translated out of both into English.* London: Matthew Simmons and Robert Ibbitson, 1648.
Bucer, Martin. *Commentarii in librum Judicum.* Geneva, 1554.
– *In sacra quattuor evangelica enarrationes perpetuae.* Geneva, 1553.
– *Opera omnia.* Edited by François Wendel et al. 15 vols. Paris: Presses universitaires de France, 1955.
Buchanan, George. *Buchanani opera omnia.* Edited by T. Ruddiman. 2 vols. Edinburgh, 1715.
– *A Chronicle of the Kings of Scotland from Fergus the First to James the Sixth.* Edinburgh: 1830. Reprint. New York: AMS Press, 1973.
– *De iure regni apud Scotos.* Edinburgh, 1579. Reprint. Theatrum Orbis Terrarum, 1969.
– *The Powers of the Crown in Scotland.* Translated by Charles Flinn Arrowood. Austin, TX: University of Texas Press, 1949.

- *The Tyrannous Reign of Mary Stewart.* Translated and edited by W. A. Gatherer. Edinburgh: Edinburgh University Press, 1958.
Budé, Guillaume. "Annotationes in Pandectas." In Guillaume Budé. *Opera omnia,* vol. 1, pp. 1–399. Basle, 1557. Reprint. Farnborough: Gregg Press, 1966.
- *De l'institution du prince.* Paris, 1547. Reprint. Farnborough: Gregg Press, 1966.
- "L'institution du prince." In *Le Prince dans la France des XVI$^e$ et XVI$^e$ siècles,* edited by C. Bontemps, L. P. Raymond, and J. P. Brancourt, pp. 77–143. Paris: Presses universitaires de France, 1965.
- *Opera omnia.* 45 vols. Basle, 1557. Reprint. Farnborough: Gregg Press, 1966.
Bueno de Mesquita, D. M. "The Place of Despotism in Italian Politics." In *Europe in the Later Middle Ages,* edited by J. R. Hale et al., pp. 301–31. Evanston: Northeastern University Press, 1965.
Bugenhagen, Johann. "Brief [to the Elector John of Saxony, September, 1529]." In Heinz Scheible. *Das Widerstandsrecht ... ,* pp. 25–29. Gutersloh: G. Mohn, 1969.
Buisson, Ludwig. *Potestas und Caritas; die papstliche Gewalt in Spätsmittelalter.* 2d ed. Cologne: Böhlau, 1982.
Bull, George. "What Did Locke Borrow from Hooker?" *Thought* 7 (1932): 122–35.
Buonaccorso da Montemagra. "A Declamation of Nobleness." Translated by John Tiptoft. In Rosamund J. Mitchell. *John Tiptoft (1427–1470),* Appendix 1, pp. 213–41. London: Longmans, 1938.
Buranelli, Vincent. "The Historical and Political Thought of Boulainvilliers." *Journal of the History of Ideas* 18 (1957): 475–94.
Burckhardt, J. *The Civilization of the Renaissance in Italy.* Translated by S. G. C. Middlemore. New York: New American Library, 1961.
Burdick, F. M. "Contributions of the Law Merchant to the Common Law." In *Select Essays in Anglo-American Legal History, III,* compiled and edited by a committee of the Association of American Law Schools, pp. 34–50. Boston: Little, Brown, 1909.
Burghley, William Cecil, ed. *The Execution of Justice in England.* Ithaca: Cornell University Press, 1965.
Burns, James H. "The Conciliarist Tradition in Scotland." *Scottish Historical Review* 42 (1963) 17: 89–104.
- "*Jus gladii* and *jurisdictio*: Jacques Almain and John Locke." *Historical Journal* 26 (1983) 369–74.
- "John Ireland and 'The Meroure of Wyssdome.'" *Innes Review* 6 (1955): 77–98.
- "Knox and Bullinger." *Scottish Historical Review* 34 (1955): 90–91.
- "New Light on John Major." *Innes Review* 5 (1954): 83–100.
- "Politia regalis et optima: The Political Ideas of John Mair." *History of Political Thought* 2 (1981): 31–61.
- "The Political Ideas of George Buchanan." *Scottish Historical Review* 30 (1951): 60–68.

- "The Political Ideas of the Scottish Reformation." *Aberdeen University Review* 36 (1956) 251–68.
- Review of Duncan H. MacNeill, *George Buchanan on the Powers of the Crown in Scotland* (Glasgow: Glasgow University Press, 1964), in *The Scottish Historical Review* 48 (1969): 190–91.
- "Scholasticism: Survival and Revival." In *The Cambridge History of Medieval Political Thought, 1450–1700*, edited by James H. Burns, pp. 132–55. Cambridge: Cambridge University Press, 1991.
- *Scottish Churchmen and the Council of Basle*. Glasgow: Burns, 1962.
- "Sovereignty and Constitutional Law in Bodin." *Political Studies* 7 (1959): 174–77.
- "Winzerus: a Forgotten Political Writer." *Journal of the History of Ideas* 21 (1960): 124–30.

Burns, James H., ed. *The Cambridge History of Medieval Political Thought 1450–1700*. Cambridge: Cambridge University Press, 1991.

Bush, Douglas. *The Renaissance and English Humanism*. Toronto: University of Toronto Press, 1939.

Caenegem, R. C. von. *The Birth of the English Common Law*. 2d ed. Cambridge: Cambridge University Press, 1989.
- *Royal Writs in England from the Conquest to Glanvil*. London: B. Quaritch, 1959.

Caesarea Academica Scientarium Vindobonensis, eds. *Monumenta conciliorum generalium seculi decimi quinti*. 4 vols. Vienna, 1857–1935.

Caillet, L. *La Papauté d'Avignon et l'église de France*. Paris: Presses universitaires de France, 1975.

Cajetan, Tommasso de Vio. *Summa totius theologiae d. Thomae Aquinatis ... cum commentariis r.d.d. Thomae de Vio Cajetan ...* Rome: Julius Accoltus, 1571.
- "Tractatus primus de comparatione auctoritate papae et concilii." In Juan Thomas Rocaberti, ed. *Biblioteca maxima pontificia*. Vol. 19, pp. 474–76.

Calasso, F. *I Glossatori e la teoria della sovranita: studio di diritto comune publico*. 3d ed. Milan: Guiffrè, 1957.

Calvin, John. *Calvin's New Testament Commentaries*. Edited by D. W. Torrance and T. F. Torrance. 12 vols. Grand Rapids: Eerdmans, 1959.
- *Calvin's Tracts and Treatises*. 3 vols. Edinburgh: Calvin Translation Society, 1844. Reprint. T. F. Torrance, ed. Grand Rapids: Eerdmans, 1958.
- *Commentaries on the Old Testament*. 30 vols. Edinburgh: Calvin Translation Society, 1845–55.
- "Commentarius in Acta Apostolorum." In John Calvin. *Ioannis Calvini opera ... omnia*, edited by Wilhelm Baum et al., vol. 48, pp. 1–574. Brunswick, 1863–1900.
- *Commentary on Seneca's "De clementia."* Edited and translated by F. L. Battles and A. M. Hugo. Leiden: E.J. Brill, 1969.
- *Concerning the Eternal Predestination of God*. Translated by J. K. S. Reid. London: James Clarke, 1961.

- "Homilia in Primum Librum Samuelis." In John Calvin. *Ioannis Calvini opera ... omnia*, edited by Wilhelm Baum et al., vol 29, pp. 232–738; vol. 30, pp. 1–734. Brunswick, 1863–1900.
- *Institutes of the Christian Religion*. Edited by J. T. McNeill. Translated by F. L. Battles. 2 vols. Philadelphia: Westminster, 1960.
- "Institutio christianae religionis (1559 ed.)." In John Calvin. *Ioannis Calvini opera ... omnia*, edited by Wilhelm Baum et al., vol. 2, pp. 1–1118. Brunswick, 1863–1900.
- *Institutio christianae religionis*, Basle: T. Platterus & B. Lasius, 1536.
- *Institution de la religion chrestienne*. Edited by T. Pannier. Paris: Belles Lettres, 1961.
- *Ioannis Calvini opera quae supersunt omnia*. Edited by Wilhelm Baum et al. 59 vols. Brunswick, 1863–1900.
- *Joannis Calvini opera selecta*. Edited by Peter Barth and W. Niesel. 5 vols. Munich: C. Kaiser, 1926–36.
- *Letters of John Calvin*. Edited by Jules Bonnet. 4 vols. Philadelphia: Presbyterian Board of Publications, 1858.
- *Lettres françaises de Jean Calvin*. Edited by Jules Bonnet. 2 vols. Paris, 1854.
- "On Civil Government [*Institutio christianae Religionis*, Book IV, chapter 20]." Translated by Harro Hopfl. In *Luther and Calvin on Civil Government*, edited by Harro Hapfl, pp. 47–86. Cambridge: Cambridge University Press, 1991.
- "Praelectiones in Danielem Prophetiam." In John Calvin. *Ioannis Calvini opera ... omnia*, edited by Wilhelm Baum et al., vol. 40, pp. 517–722; vol. 41, pp. 1–304. Brunswick, 1863–1900.
- "Sermons sur les huit derniers chapitres du Livre de Daniel." In John Calvin. *Ioannis Calvini opera ... omnia*, edited by Wilhelm Baum et al., vol. 41, pp. 305–688; vol. 42, pp. 1–176. Brunswick, 1863–1900.
- *Theological Treatises*. Translated by J. K. S. Reid. Philadelphia: Westminster, 1954.
- *Tracts and Treatises on the Reformation of the Church*. Translated by Henry Beveridge and edited by Thomas F. Torrance. 3 vols. Edinburgh and London: Oliver and Boyd, 1958.
- "Trois sermons sur l'histoire de Melchisedec." In John Calvin. *Ioannis Calvini opera ... omnia*, edited by Wilhelm Baum et al., vol. 23, pp. 641–82. Brunswick, 1863–1900.

Campbell, William E. *More's Utopia and his Social Teaching*. London: Eyre & Spottiswoode, 1930.

Canning, Joseph P. "The Corporation in the Political Thought of the Italian Jurists of the Thirteenth and Fourteenth Centuries." *History of Political Thought* 1 (1980): 9–32.

- "A Fourteenth-Century Contribution to the Theory of Citizenship in the Thought of Baldus de Ubaldis." In *Authority and Power ...* , edited by Brian Tierney and Peter Linehan, pp. 197–212. Cambridge: Cambridge University Press, 1980.

- "Ideas of the State of Thirteenth and Fourteenth-Century Commentators on the Roman Law." *Transactions of the Royal Historical Society*, 5th series, vol. 33 (1983): 1–27.
- *The Political Thought of Baldus de Ubaldis*. Cambridge: Cambridge University Press, 1987.
Cantor, Norman F. *Medieval History: the Life and Death of a Civilization*. New York: Macmillan, 1963.
Cappelletti, Mauro, and Joseph M. Perillo. *Civil Procedure in Italy*. The Hague: M. Nijhoff, 1965.
Caprariis, Vittorio di. *Francesco Guicciardini. Dalla politica alla storia.* Bari: Laterza, 1950.
- *Propaganda e pensiero politico in Francia durante le guerre di religione.* Naples: Edizioni scientifiche italiane, 1959.
Carafa, Diomede. *Dello Optime cortesano.* Edited by G. Paparelli. Salerno: Beta, 1971.
- "De regentis et boni principis officiis." In Johann A. Fabricius. *Bibliotheca latina mediae et infimae aetatis*, vol. 6, pp. 645–64. Florence, 1858.
Cardasia, Guillaume. "Machiavel et Jean Bodin." *Bibliothèque d'humanisme et renaissance* 3 (1943): 129–67.
Cargill Thompson, W. D. J. "Luther and the Right of Resistance to the Emperor." In *Church, Society and Politics*, edited by Derek Baker, pp. 159–202. Oxford: Oxford University Press, 1975. Reprinted in *Studies in the Reformation*, edited by Philip Broadhead, pp. 1–41. Brighton: Harvester, 1984.
- "The Philosopher of the 'Politic Society': Richard Hooker as a Political Thinker." In *Studies in Richard Hooker* ... , edited by William Speed Hill, pp. 3–76. Cleveland: Case Western Reserve University Press, 1972. Reprint in *Studies in the Reformation*, edited by Philip Broadhead, pp. 131–91. Brighton: Harvester, 1984.
- *The Political Thought of Martin Luther*. Edited by Philip Broadhead. Brighton: Harvester, 1984.
- "The Problem of Luther's 'Tower Experience' and Its Place in His Intellectual Development." In *Religious Motivation* ... , edited by Derek Baker, pp. 187–211. Oxford: Oxford University Press, 1978. Reprint in *Studies in the Reformation*, edited by Philip Broadhead, pp. 60–80. Brighton: Harvester, 1984.
- "Seeing the Reformation in Medieval Perspective." *Journal of Ecclesiastical History* 25 (1974): 297–308.
- "The Sources of Hooker's Knowledge of Marsilius of Padua." *Journal of Ecclesiastical History* 25 (1974): 75–81.
- *Studies in the Reformation: Luther to Hooker*. Edited by C. W. Dugmore. London: Athlone Press, 1980.
- "The 'Two Kingdoms' and the 'Two Regiments': Some Problems of Luther's Zwei-Reiche-Lehre." *Journal of Theological Studies* 20 (1969) 164–85. Reprint in *Studies in the Reformation*, edited by Philip Broadhead, pp. 42–59. Brighton: Harvester, 1984.

Carlson, Edger. "Luther's Conception of Government." *Church History* 15 (1946): 257–70.
Carlyle, R. W., and A. J. Carlyle. *A History of Mediaeval Political Theory in the West.* 6 vols. Edinburgh and London: Blackwood, 1903–36.
Carmichael, D. J. C., "The Right of Nature in Leviathan." *Canadian Journal of Philosophy* 18 (1988): 257–70.
Caroti, S., ed. "Quaestio contra divinatores horoscopios de Nicole Oresme." *Archives d'Histoire doctrinale et littéraire du Moyen Âge* 43 (1976): 201–310.
Carrerras, L. *La doctrina del Padre Suárez sobre et origen del poder civil.* In *Conmemoración tercentenario de Suárez,* pp. 181–96. Barcelona, 1923.
Carro, Venancio D. *Los colaboradores de Francisco de Vitoria: Domingo de Soto y el derecho de gentes.* Madrid: B. del Amo, 1930.
– "Las controversias de Indios y las ideas teolo-jurídicas medievales que las preparan y explican." *Anuario de la Associación Francisco de Vitoria* 8 (1947–48): 13–53.
– *Domingo de Soto y su doctrina jurídica.* Madrid: Hijos E. Minuesa, 1943.
– "The Spanish Theological-Juridical Renaissance and the Ideology of Bartolomé de las Casas." In *Bartolomé de las Casas in History ...* , edited by Juan Friede and Benjamin Keen, pp. 237–77. De Kalb: Northern Illinois University Press, 1971.
Carsten, Francis Ludwig. *Princes and Parliaments in Germany from the Fifteenth to the Eighteenth Centuries.* Oxford: Clarendon Press, 1959.
Carter, Charles H., ed. *From the Renaissance to the Counter-Reformation. Essays in Honor of Garrett Mattingly.* New York: Random House, 1965.
Caspari, Fritz. *Humanism and the Social Order in Tudor England.* New York: Teachers College Press, 1954.
Cassirer, Ernst. *The Myth of the State.* New Haven: Yale University Press, 1946.
Cassirer, Ernst, Paul Oskar Kristeller, and John Herman Randall, eds. *The Renaissance Philosophy of Man.* Chicago: University of Chicago Press, 1948.
Castellio, Sebastian. *Advice to a Desolate France.* Edited by Marius F. Valkhoff. Translated by Wouter Valkhoff. Shepherdstown: Patmos Press, 1975.
– *Conseil à la France désolée.* Edited by Marius F. Valkhoff. Geneva: Ambilly-Annemasse, 1967.
– *Concerning Heretics: Whether they are to be Persecuted and how they are to be Treated.* Translated by Roland H. Bainton. New York: Columbia University Press, 1935.
Castiglione, B. *The Book of the Courtier.* Translated by C. S. Singleton. Garden City: Doubleday, 1959.
Castrillo, Alonzo de. *Tratado de republica.* Madrid. Instituto de Estudios Politicos, 1958.
Catlin, G. E. G. *A History of the Political Philosophers.* London: Allen & Unwin, 1950.
Catto, Jeremy. "Ideas and Experience in the Political Thought of Aquinas." *Past and Present* 71 (1976): 3–21.
*Certain Queries Upon the dissolving of the Late Parliament.* London, 1650.

Chabod, Federico. *Machiavelli and the Renaissance*. Translated by David Moore. London: Bowes and Bowes, 1958.
- "Was There a Renaissance State?" In *Development of the Modern State*, edited by Heinz Lubasz, pp. 26–42. New York: Macmillan, 1964.

Chadwick, H. *The Early Church*. Harmondsworth: Penguin, 1967.

Chamberlain, John. *The Letters of John Chamberlain*. Edited by N. E. McClure. 2 vols. Philadelphia: The American Philosophical Society, 1939.

Chambers, R. W. *Thomas More*. London, Toronto: Jonathan Cape, 1935.

Chaney, William A. *The Cult of Kingship in Anglo-Saxon England*. Berkeley and Los Angeles: University of California Press, 1970.

Chanteur, Janine. "L'idée de Loi Naturelle dans la République de Jean Bodin." In Denzer, *Jean Bodin*, pp. 195–212.

Charron, Jean Daniel. *The "Wisdom" of Pierre Charron: An Original and Orthodox Code of Morality*. Chapel Hill: University of North Carolina Press, 1961.

Charron, Pierre. *De la sagesse, trois livres par Pierre Charron, Parisien, chanoine théologal et chantre de l'église de Codom*. Paris, 1601.
- *Of Wisdom: Three Books*. Translated by George Stanhope. 3d ed. 3 vols. London, 1729.

Chasseneuz, Barthelemy de. *Catalogus gloriae mundi*. Lyon, 1529.
- *Consuetudines ducatus Burgundiae*. Geneva, 1616.

Chenevière, Marc-Édouard. *La pensée politique de Calvin*. Geneva: Editions Labor, 1937. Reprint. 1970.

Cheney, C. R. *The Papacy and England, 12th–14th Centuries*. London: Variorum, 1982.

Cheney, C. R., and Mary G. Cheney, eds. *The Letters of Pope Innocent III (1198–1216) concerning England and Wales. A Calendar with an Appendix of Texts*. Oxford: Clarendon Press, 1967.

Chester, Allan G. *Hugh Latimer: Apostle to the English*. Philadelphia: University of Pennsylvania Press, 1954.

Chevel, Albert. *La pensée de Machiavel en France*. Paris: L'Artisan du Livre, 1935.

Cheyette, F. "La Justice et le pouvoir royal à la fin du Moyen Âge français." *Revue historique du droit français et étranger* 40 (1962): 373–94.

Cheyette, F. ed. *Lordship and Community in Medieval Europe*. New York: Holt, Rinehart and Winston, 1968.

Chiapelli, Fredi, ed. *First Images of America: The Impact of the New World on the Old*. 2 vols. Los Angeles: University of California Press, 1976.

Chrimes, S. B. *English Constitutional Ideas in the Fifteenth Century*. Cambridge: Cambridge University Press, 1936.
- *Henri VII*. London: Eyre, Methuen, 1972.

Chrisman, Miriam U. *Lay Culture, Learned Culture: Books and Social Change in Strasbourg*. New Haven: Yale University Press, 1982.
- *Strasbourg and the Reform*. New Haven: Yale University Press, 1967.

*Christianissimus Christiandus or, Reasons for the Reduction of France to a more Christian State in Europe*. London, 1673.

Christiansen, G. *Cesarini, the Conciliar Cardinal: The Basel Years, 1431–1438.* St Otilien: Eos-Verlag, 1979.
Chroust, A. H. "Hugo Grotius and the Scholastic Natural Law Tradition." *The New Scholasticism* 17 (1943): 14–29.
Chroust, A. H., and J. A. Corbett. "The Fifteenth Century Review of Politics of Laurentius of Arezzo." *Mediaeval Studies* 11 (1949): 62–76.
Church, F. C. *The Italian Reformers, 1534–1564.* New York: Columbia University Press, 1932.
Church, R. W. "Introduction." In Richard Hooker. *Of the Laws of Ecclesiastical Polity, Bk 1.* Oxford: Clarendon Press, 1882.
Church, William F. *Constitutional Thought in Sixteenth-Century France. A Study in the Evolution of Ideas.* Cambridge, MA: Harvard University Press, 1941.
– *English Constitutional Ideas in the Fifteenth Century.* Cambridge: Cambridge University Press, 1936.
Cicero, Marcus Tullius. *De inventione.* Translated by H. M. Hubbell. Cambridge, MA: Harvard University Press, 1949.
– *De re publica, de legibus.* Translated by Clinton Walker Keyes. Cambridge, MA: Harvard University Press, 1928. Reprint. 1977.
*The Civil Law.* Translated and edited by S. P. Scott. 17 vols in 7. Cincinnati: Central Trust Company, 1932.
Clancy, Thomas H. *Papist Pamphleteers: The Allen-Persons Party and the Political Thought of the Counter-Reformation in England 1572–1615.* Chicago: Loyola University Press, 1964.
Clark, David W. "William of Ockham on Right Reason." *Speculum* 48 (1973): 13–36.
Clark, J. C. D. *English Society: 1688–1832.* Cambridge: Cambridge University Press, 1985.
Clark, Peter, ed. *The European Crisis of the 1590s: Essays in Comparative History.* London, Boston: George Allan & Unwin, 1985.
Clarke, M. V. *The Medieval City-State: An Essay on Tyranny and Federation in the Late Middle Ages.* London: Methuen, 1926.
Clasen, Claus-Peter. *Anabaptism: A Social History, 1525–1618.* Ithaca: Cornell University Press, 1972.
– "Medieval Heresies in the Reformation." *Church History* 32 (1963): 392–414.
Clebsch, William A. *England's Earliest Protestants, 1520–1535.* New Haven: Yale University Press, 1964.
Clichtove, Josse. "De regis officio opusculum." In Josse Clichstove. *Opuscula.* Paris, 1526.
– "De vera nobilitate." In Josse Clichstove. *Opuscula.* Paris, 1526.
– *Opuscula.* Paris, 1526.
Cliffe, J. T. *The Puritan Gentry: The Great Puritan Families of Early Stuart England.* London: Routledge & Kegan Paul, 1984.
Cobban, A. *The Medieval Universities: Their Development and Structure.* London: Methuen, 1974.

Cochrane, E. "Machiavelli: 1940–1960." *Journal of Modern History* 33 (1961): 113–36.
Cochrane, E., and J. Kirschner, eds. *The Renaissance*. Chicago: University of Chicago Press, 1986.
Cohen, Sande. "Structuralism and the Writing of Intellectual History." *History and Theory* 17 (1978): 175–206.
Coing, H., ed. *Handbuch der Quellen und Literatur der neueren europäischer Privatrechtgeschichte, 1: Mittelalter [1100–1500 – Die Gelehrten Rechte und die Gesetzgebung; 2: Neure Zeit, 1500–1800*. Munich: Beck, 1973, 1977.
Coke, [Sir] Edward. *The Fourth Part of the Institute of the Laws of England*. London, 1797.
Coleman, Janet. "*Dominium* in Thirteenth and Fourteenth-Century Political Thought and Its Seventeenth-Century Heirs: John of Paris and Locke." *Political Studies* 33 (1985): 73–100.
- *English Literature in History, 1350–1400: Medieval Readers and Writers*. London: Hutchison, 1981.
- "Medieval Discussions of Property: *Ratio* and *Dominium* according to John of Paris and Marsilius of Padua." *History of Political Thought* 4 (1983): 209–28.
- "Property and Poverty." In *The Cambridge History of Medieval Political Thought*, edited by James H. Burns, pp. 607–48. Cambridge: Cambridge University Press, 1991.
- "The Two Jurisdictions: Theological and Legal Justification of Church Property in the Thirteenth Century." *Studies in Church History* 24 (1987): 75–110.
Colet, John *An Exposition of St Paul's Epistle to the Romans*. Translated and edited by J. H. Lupton. London, 1873. Reprint. Ridgewood: Gregg Press, 1965.
- *Opuscula quaedam theologica*. Translated by J. H. Lupton. Ridgewood: Gregg Press, 1966.
Colish, Marcia L. *The Stoic Tradition from Antiquity to the Early Middle Ages*. 2 vols. Leiden: E. J. Brill, 1985.
Collange, Jean François. "Droit à la résistance et réformation." *Revue d'Histoire et de Philosophie religieuse* 65 (1985): 245–55.
*La Collégialité épiscopale. Histoire et théologie de l'Unam Sanctam*. Vol. 52. Paris: Éditions du Cerf, 1965.
Collier, Thomas. *A Doctrinal Discourse of Self-Denial*. London, 1691.
Collini, Stefan, Donald Winch, and John Barrow. *That Noble Science of Politics: A Study in Nineteenth-Century Intellect*. Cambridge: Cambridge University Press, 1983.
Collinson, Patrick. *Archbishop Grindwal, 1519–1583*. Berkeley: University of California Press, 1979.
- *The Elizabethan Puritan Movement*. Berkeley and Los Angeles: University of California Press, 1967.
- *The Religion of Protestants*. Oxford: Oxford University Press, 1982.
Colomer, Eusebio. *Nikolaus von Kues und Raimond Llull, aus Handschriften der Kueser Bibliothek*. Berlin: De Gruyter, 1961.

Coltman, Irene. *Private Men and Public Causes: Philosophy and Politics in the English Civil War*. London: Faber and Faber, 1962.
Colville, A., ed. *Le Traité de la Ruine de l'Église de Nicolas de Clamanges*. Paris: E. Droz, 1936.
Combes, André. *Jean Gerson, commentateur dionysien. Les Notulae super quaedam verba Dionysii de Caelesti Hierarchia*. Paris: J. Vrin, 1940.
— *La théologie mystique de Gerson*. 2 vols. Paris: J. Vrin, 1963–65.
Combes, André, ed. *Joannis Charlerii de Gerson: De mystica theologia*. Lucaci: Thesauri Mundi, 1958.
Combes, Gustave. *La Doctrine politique de saint Augustin*. Paris: Les Petits-fils de Plon et Naurrit, 1927.
Commynes, Philippe de. *Mémoires*. Edited by Joseph Calmette. 3 vols. Paris: H. Champion, 1925.
— *The Mémoires of Philippe de Commeyne*. Translated by Isabel Cazeaux. Edited by Samuel Kinser. Columbia: University of South Carolina Press, 1949.
Compagni, Dino. *The Chronicle*. Translated by Else C. M. Benecke and A. G. Ferrers Howell. London: J. M. Dent, 1906.
— *Cronica*. Edited by Gino Luzzato. Turin: Guilio Einaudi, 1968.
— *The Compleat Politician ... wherein the Principles of Policy are laid Open to the View of All*. London, 1656.
Composta, Dario. "La 'moralis facultas' nella filosofia guirdica di F. Suárez." *Salesianum* 3 (1956):476–97; 4 (1957): 3–33.
Condé, Louis I de Bourbon, Prince de. "Déclaration faite par Monsieur le prince de Condé." In Condé, Louis I de Bourbon, Prince de. *Mémoires de Condé*, vol. 3, pp. 22–35. London, La Haye, 1743.
— *Mémoires de Condé*. 6 vols. London, La Haye, 1743.
Condren, Conal. "Democracy in the *Defensor pacis*: On the English Language Tradition of Marsilian Interpretation." *Il Pensiero Politico* 13 (1980): 304–38.
— "Marsilius of Padua's Argument from Authority: A Survey of Its Significance in the *Defensor pacis*." *Political Theory* 5 (1977): 205–18.
— *The Status and Appraisal of Classic Texts. An Essay on Political Theory, Its Inheritance and the History of Ideas*. Princeton: Princeton University Press, 1985.
Congar, Yves. "The Historical Development of Authority in the Church: Points for Christian Reflection." In *Problems of Authority* ..., edited by John M. Todd, pp. 119–36. London and Baltimore: Helicon, 1962.
— *Droits anciens et structures ecclésiales*. London: Variorum, 1982.
— *Die Lehre vom der Kirche; von Abendlandischen Schisma bis zur Gegenwart*. In *Handbuch der Dogmengeschichte*, edited by Michael Schmauss et al., band 3, facs. 3. Freiburg-im-Breisgau: Herder, 1971.
— "Notes sur le destin de l'idée de collégialité épiscopale en Occident au moyen âge (VII$^e$-XV$^e$ siècles)." In *La Collégialité épiscopale. Histoire et théologie de l'Unam sanctam*. Vol. 52, pp. 99–129. Paris: Éditions du Cerf, 1965.
— "Status Ecclesiae." *Studia Gratiana* 15 (1972): 1–31.

- *Vraie et fausse réforme dans l'Église.* 2d ed. Paris: J. Vrin, 1968.
Conmemoración tercentenario de Suárez. Barcelona: N.P., 1932.
Connolly, J. L. *John Gerson, Reformer and Mystic.* Leuven: Nauwalaerts, 1928.
Connolly, William E. *The Terms of Political Discourse.* 2d ed. Princeton: Princeton University Press, 1983.
Conring, E. *Kirche und Staat nach der Lehre der niederlandischen Calvinisten in der ersten Halfte der 17 Jahrhunderts.* Neukirchen-Vluyn: Neukirckener Verlag, 1965.
Contarini, Gasparo. "The Commonwealth and Government of Venice." Translated by Lewes Lewkenor. London, 1599. Reprint. Amsterdam: Theatrum Orbis Terrarum, 1969.
Coolidge, John S. *The Pauline Renaissance in England: Puritanism and the Bible.* Oxford: Oxford University Press, 1970.
Coopland, E. W., ed. and trans. *The Tree of Battles of Honoré Bonet, an English Version with Introduction.* Cambridge, MA: Harvard University Press, 1949.
Coquille, Guy. *Histoire du pape et du duché de Nivernois.* Paris, 1612.
- *Institution au droit des François.* Paris, 1630.
Cortese, E. *La norma guiridica: spunti teorici nel diritto comune classico.* 2 vols. Milan: Guiffrè, 1964.
Costa, P. *Iurisdictio: semantica del potere politico nella publicistica medievale, 1100–1433.* Milan: Guiffrè, 1969.
Costello, Frank B. *The Political Philosophy of Luis de Molina, S.J. (1535–1600).* Rome: Institutum Historicum S.I., 1974.
Costello, William T. *The Scholastic Curriculum of Early Seventeenth-Century Cambridge.* Cambridge, MA: Harvard University Press, 1958.
*Courants religieux et humanisme à la fin du XV$^e$ et au début du XVI$^e$ siècle.* Paris: Presses universitaires de France, 1959.
Courtenay, William J. "Covenant and Causality in Pierre d'Ailly." *Speculum* 46 (1971): 94–119.
- "Late Medieval Nominalism Revisited." *Journal of the History of Ideas* 44 (1983): 159–64.
- "Nominalism and Late Medieval Religion." In *The Pursuit of Holiness ...* , edited by Charles E. Trinkaus and Heiko Oberman, pp. 26–59. Leiden: E. J. Brill, 1972.
- "Nominalism and Late Medieval Thought: A Bibliographical Essay." *Theological Studies* 33 (1972): 716–34.
Couvreur, G. *Les Pauvres ont-ils des droits?* Rome: Gregorian University, 1961.
Cowell, James. *A Law Dictionary or Interpreter of Words and Terms Used either in the Common or Statute Laws.* London, 1727.
Carig, F. Edward. "The Geneva Bible as a Political Document." *The Pacific Historical Review* 7 (1938): 40–49.
Cranz, F. E. *An Essay on the Development of Luther's Thought on Justice, Law and Society.* Cambridge, MA: Harvard University Press, 1959.

Crescini, A. *Le origine del metodo analitico: il Cinquecento.* Rome: Del Bianco, 1965.
Cross, Claire. *Church and People, 1450–1660: The Triumph of the Laity in the English Church.* Atlantic Highlands: Humanities Press, 1976.
Crowder, C. M. D. "Constance Acta in English Libraries." In *Das Konzil von Konstanz ...* , edited by A. Franzen and W. Müller, pp. 477–517. Freiburg: Herder, 1964.
– "Politics and the Councils of the Fifteenth Century." *The Canadian Catholic Historical Association* 36 (1969): 41–55.
Crowder, C. M. D., ed. *Unity, Heresy and Reform, 1378–1460: The Conciliar Response to the Great Schism.* London: Edward Arnold, 1977.
Crowe, Michael Bertram. *The Changing Profile of the Natural Law.* The Hague: Martinus Nijhoff, 1972.
– "St Thomas and Ulpian's Natural Law." In *St Thomas Aquinos 1274–1974: Commemorative Studies,* pp. 261–82. Toronto: Pontifical Institute of Mediaeval Studies, 1974.
Crowley, Robert. *Select Works.* Edited by J. M. Cowper. London, 1872.
– "The Voice of the Last Trumpet." In Robert Crowley. *Select Works,* edited by J. M. Cowper, pp. 53–104. London, 1872.
– "The Way to Wealth." In Robert Crowley. *Select Works,* edited by J. M. Cowper, pp. 53–104. London, 1872.
Cudworth, Ralph. *The True Intellectual System of the Universe.* Translated by John Harrison. 3 vols. London, 1845.
Cuming, G. J., and Derek Baker, eds. *Councils and Assemblies.* London: Cambridge University Press, 1971.
Cumming, R. D. *Human Nature and History: A Study of the Development of Liberal Political Thought.* 2 vols. Chicago: University of Chicago Press, 1969.
Curcio, C. "La politica di Baldo." *Rivista internazionale di filosofia del diritto* 17 (1937): 113–39.
Curtis, Mark H. *Oxford and Cambridge in Transition 1558–1642.* Oxford: Oxford University Press, 1959.
Dabin, J. "Droit subjectif et subjectivisme juridique." *Archives de philosophie du droit* 9 (1964) 17–35.
D'Addio, Mario. *L'Idea del contratto sociale dai sofisti alla riforma e il de Principato di Mario Salomonio.* Milan: Guiffrè, 1954.
Daegens, J. "Humanisme et évangélisme chez Lefèvre d'Étaples." In *Courants religieux et humanisme ...,* pp. 121–34.
Daly, James. *Cosmic Harmony and Political Thinking in Early Stuart England.* Transactions of the American Philosophical Society, n.s. 79, pt. 7. Philadelphia: American Philosophical Society, 1979.
– "The Idea of Absolute Monarchy in Seventeenth Century England." *Historical Journal* 21 (1978): 227–50.
– *Sir Robert Filmer and English Political Thought.* Toronto: University of Toronto Press, 1979.

Daly, Lowrie J. "Medieval and Renaissance Commentaries on the Politics of Aristotle." *Duquesne Review* 13 (1968): 41–55.
- *The Political Theory of John Wyclif.* Chicago: Loyola University Press, 1962.
- "Wyclif's Political Theory: A Century of Study." *Medievalia et Humanistica* 4 (1973): 177–87.
Damiata, M. *Guglielmo d'Ockham: Poverta e potere.* 2 vols. Florence: Studi francescani, 1978–79.
Daniel, Norman. *Islam and the West: The Making of an Image.* Edinburgh: Edinburgh University Press, 1960.
Daniel-Rops, H. *The Protestant Reformation.* Translated by Audrey Butler. London: Dent, 1961.
Danner, D. G. "Anthony Gilby: Puritan in Exile: a Biographical Approach." *Church History* 40 (1971): 412–22.
Dante Alighieri, *Monarchia.* Edited by P. E. Ricci. Milan: Mondadori, 1965.
Danvilay Collado, M. *Historia crítica y documentada de las Comunidades de Castilla.* 6 vols. Madrid, 1897.
David, M. *La Souveraineté et les limites juridiques du pouvoir monarchique du IX$^e$ au XV$^e$ siècle.* Paris: Librairie Dallez, 1954.
Davies, E. T. *The Political Ideas of Richard Hooker.* London: Society for the Promotion of Christian Knowledge, 1946.
Davies, Sir John. *The Question concerning Impositions, Tonnage, Poundage ... fully stated and argued from Reason, Law and Policy.* London, 1656.
Davis, Charles T. *Dante and the Idea of Rome.* Oxford: Oxford University Press, 1958.
- "An Early Florentine Political Theorist: Fra Remigio De' Girolami." *Proceedings of the American Philosophical Society* 104 (1960): 666–76.
- "Remigio de' Girolami and Dante: A Comparison of Their Conceptions of Peace." *Studi Danteschi* 36 (1959): 105–36.
Davis, H. W. C., ed. *Essays in History Presented to Reginald Law Poole.* Oxford: Clarendon Press, 1927.
Davis, J. C. "Utopianism." In *The Cambridge History of Medieval Political Thought ...*, edited by James H. Burns, pp. 329–44. Cambridge: Cambridge University Press, 1991.
Davis, John F. *Heresy and Reformation in the South East of England, 1520–1559.* Atlantic Highlands: Humanities Press, 1983.
Dawson, Christopher. *Mission to Asia.* Toronto: University of Toronto Press, 1980.
Dawson, John P. *The Oracles of the Law.* Ann Arbor: University of Michigan Press, 1968.
"Déclaration des causes qui ont mené ceux de la religion à reprendre les armes pour leur conservation." In [Simon Goulart.] *Mémoires de l'état de France sous Charles neufième,* 2d ed., vol. 3, pp. 38a–42b. Middelburg (Geneva), 1578.
Defourney, Maurice. "L'idée de l'État d'après Aristote." *Analecta Gregoriana* 10 (1935): 98–113.

Delaruelle, E., E.-R. Labande, and P. Ourliac. *L'église au temps du Grand Schisme et de la crise conciliaire (1378–1449)*. In *Histoire de l'église* ... edited by Augustin Fliche and Victor Martin, Paris: Bloud & Gay, 1962.
Delormeau, Charles E. *Sebastian Castellion. Apôtre de la Tolérance et de la Liberté de Conscience*. Neufchâtel: H. Messeiller, 1964.
Delzell, Charles F., ed. *The Future of History*. Nashville: Vanderbilt University Press, 1977.
*The Demeanour of a Good Subject in Order to Acquiring and Establishing Peace*. London, 1681.
Demongeot, Marcel. *Le meilleur régime politique selon Saint Thomas*. Paris: A. Blot, 1928.
Denifle, H. and E. Chatelain, eds. *Chartularium universitatis Parisiensis*. 4 vols. Paris: Delalain, 1889–97.
Dennert, Jurgen, ed. *Beza, Brutus, Hotman: calvinistische Monarchomachen*. Cologne: Wesdeutscher Verlag, 1968.
Dent, C. M. *Protestant Reformers in Elizabethan Oxford*. Oxford University Press, 1983.
Denton, Jeffrey. *Robert Winchelsey and the Crown, 1294–1313: A Study in the Defense of Ecclesiastical Liberty*. Cambridge: Cambridge University Press, 1980.
– "Walter Reynolds and Ecclesiastical Politics 1313–1316: A Postscript to 'Councils and Synods, II.'" In C. N. L. Brooke et al. *Church and Government* ..., pp. 247–74. Cambridge: Cambridge University Press, 1976.
D'Entrèves, Allesando Passerin. *The Medieval Contribution to Political Thought: Thomas Aquinas, Marsilius of Padua, Richard Hooker*. Oxford: Oxford University Press, 1939.
– *Riccardo Hooker: contributo alla teoria e alla storice del diritto naturale*. Rome: Presso L'istituto guirdico della R. Universita, 1932.
Denzler, Georg. "Zwischen Konziliarismus und Papalismus; Die Stellung des Papstes im Verstandnis der Konzilien von Konstanz (1414–1418) und Basel (1431–1437)." In *Das Papstum* ... , edited by Georg Denzler, pp. 53–72. Regensburg: F. Pustet, 1974.
Denzler, Georg. ed. *Das Papstum in der Diskussion*. Regensburg: F. Pustet, 1974.
Denzler, von Horst, ed. *Jean Bodin. Proceedings of the International Conference on Bodin in Munich*. Munich: Beck, 1973.
Dérathe, R. *Jean-Jacques Rousseau et la science politique de son temps*. Paris: Presses universitaires de France, 1950.
Dewar, Mary. *Sir Thomas Smith. A Tudor Intellectual in Office*. London: Athlone Press, 1964.
– "The Authorship of the 'Discourse of the Commonweal.'" *Economic History Review* 19 (1966): 388–400.
Dhondt, J. "Les assemblées d'États en Belgique avant 1795." *Anciens pays et assemblées d'États* 33 (1965): 195–260.
Diamond, A. S. *Primitive Law Past and Present*. London: Methuen, 1971.

Dickason, Ruth. *The Myth of the Savage and the Beginning of French Colonialism in the Americas.* Edmonton: University of Alberta Press, 1984.
- "Old World Laws, New World Peoples and the Conceptions of Sovereignty." In *Essays on the History of North American Discovery and Exploration,* edited by David B. Quinn. Arlington: University of Texas Press, 1988.

Dickens, A. G. *The Counter Reformation.* London: Thames and Hudson, 1968.
- *The English Reformation.* London: B.T. Batsford, 1964.
- *The German Nation and Martin Luther.* London: Edward Arnold, 1974.
- *Lollards and Protestants in the Diocese of York, 1509–1558.* London: Oxford University Press, 1959.
- *Martin Luther and the Reformation.* London: English Universities Press, 1967.
- *Reformation and Society in Sixteenth-Century Europe.* London: Thames and Hudson, 1966.
- "The Reformation in England." In *The Reformation Crisis,* edited by Joel Hurstfield, pp. 44–57. London: Edward Arnold, 1965.
- *Thomas Cromwell and the English Reformation.* London: English Universities Press, 1959.

Diet of Roncaglia. "Curia Roncagliae." Edited by Ludwig Weiland. In *Monumenta Germaniae Historica: Constitutiones,* vol. 1, pp. 244–59. Hanover: Hahnian, 1963.

Dietrich of Niem. "De modis uniendi ac reformandi ecclesiam." In H. Heimpel. *Dietrich von Niem über Union und Reform der Kirche, 1410.* Leipzig and Berlin: Teubner, 1933.
- *Theodorici a Niem: Historiarum sui temporis libre III.* Strasbourg, 1609.
- "Ways of Uniting and Reforming the Church, 1410." Edited and translated by James Kerr Cameron. In *Advocates of Reform ...,* edited by M. Spinka, pp. 149–74. London: Student Christian Movement Press, 1953.

Digard, G. A. L. *Philippe le Bel et le Saint Siège de 1285 à 1304.* 2 vols. Paris: Sirey, 1936.

Dillenberger, John. *God Hidden and Revealed: The Interpretation of Luther's* deus abscondita *and Its Significance for Religious Thought.* Philadelphia: University of Pennsylvania Press, 1953.

"Discours politiques des diverses puissances établies de Dieu au monde." In [Simon Goulart.] *Mémoires de l'état de France sous Charles neufième,* 2d ed., vol. 3, pp. 203b–296a. Middelburg (Geneva), 1578.

Doderidge, Sir John. "Treatise on the King's Prerogative." Harleian MS 5220. British Museum, London.

Dodge, G. H. *The Political Thought of the Huguenots of the Dispersion, with Special Reference to the Thought and Influence of Pierre Jurieu.* New York: Columbia University Press, 1947.

Dolan, John P. *History of the Reformation, A Conciliatory Assessment of Opposite Views.* New York: Desclée, 1965.

Domergue, Emile. *Jean Calvin: les hommes et les choses de son temps.* 7 vols. Lausanne: G. Bridel et cie., 1899–1927.

Donaldson, Gordon. *The Scottish Reformation*. Cambridge: Cambridge University Press, 1960.
Donaldson, Peter Samuel, ed. and trans. *A Machiavellian Treatise by Stephen Gardiner*. Cambridge: Cambridge University Press, 1975.
Dondaines, A. "Aux origines de Valdeisme. Une profession de foi de Valdes." *Archivum Fratrum Praedicatorum* 16 (1946): 215ff.
Donkin, R. A. "The Growth and Distribution of the Cistercian Order in Medieval Europe." *Studia Monastica* 9 (1967): 275–86.
Donnelly, Jack. *The Concept of Human Rights*. New York: St Martin's Press, 1985.
– "How are Rights and Duties Correlative?" *Journal of Value Inquiry* 16 (1982): 287–94.
– "Human Rights as Natural Rights." *Human Rights Quarterly* 4 (1982): 391–405.
– "Natural Law and Natural Right in Aquinas' Political Thought." *Western Political Quarterly* 3 (1980): 520–25.
Donnelly, John Patrick. *Calvinism and Scholasticism in Vermigli's Doctrine of Man and Grace*. Leiden: E.J. Brill, 1976.
– "The Social and Ethical Thought of Peter Martyr Vermigli." In McLelland, *Peter Martyr and Italian Reform*, pp. 107–19.
Doucet, Roger. *Les Institutions de la France au $xvi^e$ Siècle*. 2 vols. Paris: A. and J. Picard, 1948.
Dowdall, H. C. "The Word 'State.'" *Law Quarterly Review* 39 (1923): 98–125.
Doyle, Phyllis. "The Contemporary Background of Hobbes' State of Nature." *Economica* (1927): 336–55.
Dreano, M. *La Religion de Montaigne*. 2d ed. Paris: A.-G. Nizet, 1969.
Dreitzel, H. *Protestantischer Aristotelismus und absoluter Staat: die 'Politica' des H. Arnisaeus*. Wiesbaden: F. Steiner, 1970.
Drescher, Seymour, David Sabean, and Alan Sharlin, eds. *Political Symbolism in Modern Europe: Essays in Honor of George L. Mosse*. New Brunswick: Transaction, 1982.
Drew, Katherine Fisher, Land Floyd Seyward Lear, *Perspectives in Medieval History*. Chicago: University of Chicago Press, 1963.
Duby, Georges. *Rural Economy and Country Life in the Medieval West*. Translated by Cynthia Postan. London: Edward Arnold, 1968.
Dudley, Edmund. *The Tree of Commonwealth*. Edited by D. M. Brodie. Cambridge: Cambridge University Press, 1948.
Du Fail, Noel. *Propos Rustiques*. Edited by Louis-Raymond Lefèvre. Paris: Éditions Brossard, 1928.
Duff, P. W. *Personality in Roman Private Law*. Cambridge: Cambridge University Press, 1938.
Duggan, Lawrence G. "The Unresponsiveness of the Late Medieval Church: A Reconsideration." *The Sixteenth Century Journal* 9 (1978): 3–26.
Duhamel, P. Albert. "The Medievalism of More's *Utopia*." In *Essential Articles for*

*the Study of Thomas More*, edited by R. S. Sylvester and E. P. Morc'Hador, pp. 158–73. Hamden: Archon Books, 1977.
- "The Oxford Lectures of John Colet." *Journal of the History of Ideas* 14 (1953): 493–510.
Duke, John A. *History of the Church of Scotland in the Reformation*. Edinburgh, London: Oliver and Boyd, 1937.
Du Moulin, Charles. "De legibus et privilegii regni Franciae." In Charles Du Moulin. *Opera omnia*, vol. 2, pp. 539–50. Paris, 1681.
- *Opera omnia*. 5 vols. Paris, 1681.
- "Prima pars commentariorum in consuetudines Parisienses." In Charles Du Moulin. *Opera omnia*, 5 vols, vol. 1, pp. 1–665. Paris, 1681.
Dunkley, E. H. *The Reformation in Denmark*. London: Society for the Promotion of Christian Knowledge, 1948.
Dunbabin, J. "The Reception and Interpretation of Aristotle's Politics." In *The Cambridge History of Later Medieval Philosophy* ... , edited by Norman Kretzmann et al., pp. 723–37. Cambridge: Cambridge University Press, 1982.
Dunn, John. "Consent in the Political Theory of John Locke." *Historical Journal* 10 (1967): 153–82.
- "The Identity of the History of Ideas." In *Philosophy, Politics and Society*, edited by P. Laslett, W. G. Runciman, and Quentin Skinner, 4: 158–93. Oxford: Blackwell, 1972.
- *Political Obligation in its Historical Context*. Cambridge: Cambridge University Press, 1980.
- *The Political Thought of John Locke*. Cambridge: Cambridge University Press, 1969.
- *Rethinking Modern Political Theory: Essays 1979–83*. Cambridge: Cambridge Universal Press, 1985.
- "Practising History and Social Science on 'Realist' Assumptions." In *Action and Interpretation*, edited by Christopher Hookway and Philip Pettit, pp. 145–74. Cambridge: Cambridge University Press, 1978.
- "Social Theory, Social Understanding, and Political Action." In John Dunn. *Rethinking Modern Political Theory* ... , pp. 119–38. Cambridge: Cambridge University Press, 1985.
Dupont-Ferrier, Gustave. *Études sur les institutions financières de la France à la fin du moyen âge*. Paris: Firmin-Didot, 1930.
Dupuy, P. *Histoire du différend d'entre le pape Boniface VIII, et Philippe le Bel*. Paris, 1655.
Durkan, John. "John Major: After 400 Years." *Innes Review* 1 (1950): 131–39.
- "The School of John Major: Bibliography." *Innes Review* 1 (1950): 140–57.
Du Vair, Guillaume. *A Buckler against Adversity*. Translated by Andrew Court. London, 1622.
- *The Moral Philosophy of the Stoics*. Translated by Thomas James. Edited by Rudolf Kirk. New Brunswick, NJ: Rutgers University Press, 1951.

Dvornik, F. *The Photian Schism: History and Legend.* London: Cambridge University Press, 1970.
Dwyer, J., R. Mason, and A. Murdoch, eds. *New Perspective on the Politics and Culture of Early Modern Scotland.* Edinburgh: John Donald, 1982.
Dyck, C. J., ed. *A Legacy of Faith: The Heritage of Menno Simons.* Newton: Faith and Life Press, 1962.
Ebeneter, A. "Luther und das Konzil." *Zeitschrift für katholische Theologie* 84 (1962): 1–48.
Ebert, Kurt. *Festschrift Nikolaus Grass.* 2 vols. Innsbruck: Universitätsverlag Wagner, 1986.
Eccleshall, Robert. *Order and Reason in Politics: Theories of Absolute and Limited Monarchy in Early Modern England.* Oxford: Oxford University Press, 1978.
– "Richard Hooker's Synthesis and the Problem of Allegiance." *Journal of the History of Ideas* 37 (1976): 111–24.
Eckhardt, Karl August, ed. *Sachsenspiegel V: Landrecht in hochdeutscher Übertragung.* Hanover: Hahnische Buchhandlung, 1967.
Eckstein, Alexander. *Zur Finanzlage Felix V, und des Basler Konzils.* Berlin, 1912. Reprint. Aalen: Scientia Verlag, 1973.
"Edict of the States General of the United Netherlands [26th July, 1581]." In *Texts Concerning the Revolt of the Netherlands*, edited by E. H. Kossman and A. F. Mellink, pp. 216–28. Cambridge: Cambridge University Press, 1974.
Edwards, Mark U. *Luther and the False Brethren.* Stanford: Stanford University Press, 1975.
Egenter, Richard. "Die soziale Leitidee im 'Tractatus de bono communi' des Fr. Remigius von Florenz." *Scholastik* 9 (1934): 79–92.
Eire, Carlos. *War against the Idols: The Reform of Worship from Erasmus to Calvin.* Cambridge: Cambridge University Press, 1986.
Eliot, Sir John. *De iure maiestatis.* Edited by A. B. Grosard. 2 vols. London, 1882.
Ellinger, W. *Luthers politisches Denken und Handeln.* Berlin: Evangelische Verlagsanstalt, 1952.
Elliott, J. H. *Europe Divided, 1559–1598.* London: Collins, 1968.
– *Imperial Spain, 1469–1716.* London: E. Arnold, 1963.
– "Revolution and Continuity in Early Modern Europe." *Past and Present* 42 (1969): 35–56.
Elliott, William Y. *The Pragmatic Revolt in Politics.* New York: Macmillan, 1928.
Elm, Kospar, ed. *Stellung und Wirkamseit der Bettelorden in der städtischen Geselschaft.* Berlin: Duncker & Humblot, 1981.
Elton, G. R. *The Body of the Whole Realm: Parliament and Representation in Medieval and Tudor England.* Charlottesville: University of South Carolina Press, 1969.
– "'The Commons' Supplication of 1532: Parliamentary Manoeuvres in the Reign of Henry VIII." *English Historical Review* 66 (1951): 507–34.
– "The Evolution of a Reformation Statute." *English Historical Review* 64 (1949): 174–97.

- *Policy and Police: The Enforcement of the Reformation in the Age of Thomas Cromwell.* Cambridge: Cambridge University Press, 1972.
- "The Political Creed of Thomas Cromwell." *Transactions of the Royal Historical Society* 6 (1956): 69–92.
- *Reform and Renewal: Thomas Cromwell and the Commonweal.* Cambridge: Cambridge University Press, 1973.
- "Reform by Statute: Thomas Starkey's *Dialogue* and Thomas Cromwell's Policy." *Proceedings of the British Academy* 54 (1968): 165–88.
- *Reformation Europe, 1517–1559.* London: Harper and Row, 1963.
- *Renaissance and Reformation, 1300–1648.* New York: Macmillan, 1963.
- "Thomas More, Councillor (1517–1529)." In *St Thomas More ...* , edited by R. S. Sylvester, pp. 85–122. New Haven: Yale University Press, 1972.
- *The Tudor Constitution: Documents and Commentary.* Cambridge: Cambridge University Press, 1960.
- *The Tudor Revolution in Government.* Cambridge: Cambridge University Press, 1953.

Elyot, Sir Thomas. *The Book Named the Governor.* Edited by S. E. Lehmberg. London: Dutton, 1962.

Elze, R. *Papste, Kaiser, Könige und die mittelalterliche Herrschafts-symbolik.* London: Variorum, 1982.

Emerton, Ephraim, ed. *Humanism and Tyranny. Studies in the Italian Trecento.* Cambridge, MA: Harvard University Press, 1925.

Emerton, Ephraim, ed. and trans. *The Correspondence of Pope Gregory VII: Selected Letters from the Registrum.* New York: Columbia University Press, 1932. Reprint. New York: Norton, 1969.

*Enea Silvio Piccolomini – Papa Pio II: Attidel Convergno per il Quinto Centenario della Morte e altri Scritti.* Siena: Ed. Domenico Maffei, 1968.

- *De gestis concilio Basiliensis commentariorum libri II.* Edited and translated by Denys Hay and W. K. Smith. Oxford: Oxford University Press, 1967.

Englebert of Admont. "De ortu, progresso et fine regnorum, et praecipue regni seu imperii Romani." Vol. 25, pp. 362–78. In *Maxima bibliotheca veterum patrum*, edited by Marguerin de la Bigne. 27 vols. Lyons, 1668.

Erasmus, Desiderius. "The Adages." In Margaret Mann Phillips. *The "Adages" of Erasmus: A Study with Translations.* Cambridge: Cambridge University Press, 1964.
- *The Complaint of Peace.* Translated and edited by Alexander Grieve. Chicago and London: Open Court, 1917.
- "De libero arbitrio diatrive seu colatio." In *Luther and Erasmus ...* , edited by E. Gordon Rupp and A. N. Marlow, pp. 35–97. Philadelphia: Westminster Press, 1969.
- *The Education of a Christian Prince.* Translated and edited by Lester K. Born. New York: Octagon, 1965.
- *Essai sur le libre arbitre.* Translated by Pierre Mesnard. Algiers: Éditions Robert et Réné Choix, 1945.

- *Institutio christiani principis*. Edited by O. Herding. In Eramus, *Opera omnia*, 4.1, pp. 95–219. Amsterdam: North Holland, 1974.
- "On the Freedom of the Will." In *Luther and Erasmus* ... , edited by E. Gordon Rupp and A. N. Marlow, pp. 35–97. Philadelphia: Westminster Press, 1969.
- *Opera omnia*. Amsterdam: North Holland, 1969–.
- *The Praise of Folly*. Translated and edited by Hoyt H. Hudson. Princeton: Princeton University Press, 1941.

Erdmann, Carl. *The Origin of the Idea of Crusade*. Princeton: Princeton University Press, 1977.

Erikson, Erik H. *Young Man Luther: A Study in Psychoanalysis and History*. London: Faber and Faber, 1958.

Erlanger, Philippe. *St Bartholomew's Night: The Massacre of St Bartholomew*. Translated by Patrick O'Brian. London: Weidenfeld, 1960.

Eschmann, I. T. "Thomistic Social Philosophy and the Theology of Original Sin." *Mediaeval Studies* 9 (1947): 19–55.

Fabian, Ekkehart. *Die entstehung der Schmalkaldischen Bundes und seiner Verfassung 1524/29–1531/35: Brück, Phillip von Hessen und Jakob Sturm*. 2d ed. Tübingen: Osiandersche Buchhandlung, 1962.

Fabricius, Johann A. *Bibliotheca latina mediae et infimae aetatis*. 6 vols. Florence, 1858.

Fairfield, Leslie P. *John Bale, Mythmaker for the English Reformation*. West Lafayette: Indiana University Press, 1976.

Fallico, Arthur B., and Herman Shapiro, eds. *Renaissance Philosophy*. 2 vols. New York: Random House, 1969.

Farr, James. "'So Vile and Miserable an Estate.' The Problem of Slavery in Locke's Political Thought." *Political Theory* 14 (1986): 263–89.

Fasolt, C. "At the Crossroads of Law and Politics: William Durant the Younger's 'Treatise on Councils.'" *Bulletin of Medieval Canon Law*, n.s. 18 (1988): 43–53.
- *Council and Hierarchy: the Political Thought of William Durant the Younger*. Cambridge: Cambridge University Press, 1991.
- "A New View of William Durant the Younger's 'Tractatus de modo generalis concilii celebrandi.'" *Traditio* 37 (1981): 291–324.
- "Die Rezeption der Traktate Wilhelm Durantis d. J. im späten Mittelalter und der frühen Neuzeit." In *Das Publikum politischer Theorie* ... , edited by Jurgen Miethke. Munich: Schriften des Historischen Kollegs, 1992.

Fast, Heinold. *Profiles of Radical Reformers*. Scottdale: Herald Press, 1982.

Faulkner, Robert K. "Reason and Revelation in Hooker's Ethics." *American Political Science Review* 59 (1965): 680–90.
- *Richard Hooker and the Politics of a Christian England*. Berkeley: University of California Press, 1981.

Favier, Jean. *Les Finances pontificales à l'époque du grand Schisme d'Occident*. Paris: E. de Boccard, 1966.

Feenstra, Robert. *Le droit savant au moyen âge et sa vulgarisation. Études d'histoire du droit*. London: Variorum, 1986.
- "Ouvrages du droit romain dans les catalogues des anciens Pays-Bas septen-

trionaux, XIII-XVI^e siècle." *Tijdschrift voor rechtsgeschiedenis* 28 (1960): 439–530.
- *Philip of Leyden and his Treatise* De cura reipublicae et sorte principantis. Glasgow: Glasgow University Publications, 1970.
Fell, A. *Origins of Legislative Sovereignty and the Legislative State.* Vol. 1. London: Athenaeum, 1983.
Femia, Joseph V. "An Historicist Critique of 'Revisionist' Methods for Studying the History of Ideas." *History and Theory* 20 (1981): 112–34.
Fenlon, Dermot. *Heresy and Obedience in Tridentine Italy: Cardinal Pole and the Counter Reformation.* Cambridge: Cambridge University Press, 1972.
Fernandez-Santamaria, J. A. "Erasmus on the Just War." *Journal of the History of Ideas* 34 (1973): 209–25.
- "Juan Gines de Sepúlveda on the Nature of the American Indians." *The Americas* 31 (1975): 434–51.
- "Reason of State and Statecraft in Spain, 1595–1640." *Journal of the History of Ideas* 41 (1980): 355–79.
- *Reason of State and Statecraft in Spanish Political Thought 1595–1640.* Lanham: University Press of America, 1983.
- *The State, War and Peace: Spanish Political Thought in the Renaissance, 1516–1559.* Cambridge: Cambridge University Press, 1977.
Fernandez de Valesco, Recaredo. *Referencios y transcripsiónes para la historia de la litteratura politica en Espana.* Madrid: Editorial Reus, 1925.
Ferrater Mora, José. "Suárez and Modern Philosophy." *Journal of the History of Ideas* 14 (1953): 528–47.
Ferreti, Ferreto de. "De Scaligeorum origine." In Ferreto de Ferreti. *Le Opere,* edited by Carlo Cippella, vol. 3, pp. 1–100. Rome: Istituto Storio Italiano, 1908–20.
- *Le Opere.* Edited by Carlo Cippella. 3 vols. Rome: Istituto Storio Italiano, 1908–20.
Fichet, Guillaume. *Épître adressée à Robert Gaguin, Le 1er janvier 1472.* Edited by Leopold Delisle. Paris, 1889.
Fichter, Joseph H. *Man of Spain. Francis Suárez.* New York: Macmillan, 1940.
Ficino, Marsilio. "Introductio ad commentationes in Platoni." In Marsilio Ficino. *Opera omnia,* edited by M. Sancipriano, vol. 2, pp. 116–18. Turin: Bottega d'Erasmo, 1959.
- *Opera omnia.* Edited by M. Sancipriano. 2 vols. Turin: Bottega d'Erasmo, 1959.
Fife, Robert H. *The Revolt of Martin Luther.* New York: Columbia University Press, 1957.
Figgis, J. N. *The Divine Right of Kings.* 2nd ed. Cambridge: Cambridge University Press, 1914.
- *Political Thought from Gerson to Grotius, 1414–1625.* New York: Harper Torchbooks, 1960.
- "Political Thought in the Sixteenth Century." In *The Cambridge Modern History,* edited by A. W. Ward et al., vol. 3, pp. 736–69. Cambridge: Cambridge University Press, 1902–12. Reprint. 1969.

Filastre. "Diary of the Council of Constance." Translated by Louise Ropes Loomis. In *The Council of Constance* ... , edited by John H. Mundy and K. M. Woody, pp. 227–29. New York: Columbia University Press, 1961.

Filmer, Sir Robert. *Patriarcha and Other Political Works.* Edited by Peter Laslett. Oxford: Basil Blackwell, 1949.

Fink, Karl August. "Zur Beurteilung des Grossen Abendlandischen Schismas." *Zeitschrift für Kirchensgeschichte* 73 (1962): 335–43.

Fink, Karl August. "An Historical Note on the Constitution of the Church." In *Structures of the Church's Presence*, edited by Jiménez Urresti, pp. 13–25. New York: Herder and Herder, 1970.

– "Die konziliare Idee im späten Mittelalter." In *Die Welt zur Zeit des Konstanzen Konzils*, edited by Theodore Mayer, pp. 119–34. Constance: J. Thorbeke, 1965.

– "Papstum und Kirchenreform nach dem Grossen Schisma." *Theologische Quartalschrift* 126 (1946): 110–22.

Finke, H., ed. *Acta Concilii Constanciensis.* 4 vols. Münster: Regensbergsche Buchhandlung, 1896–1928.

Firpo, L., ed. *Storia delle idee politiche economiche e sociali.* 6 vols. Turin: Unione tipografico-editrice torinese, 1973.

Fish, Simon. *A Supplication for the Beggars.* Edited by Frederick J. Furnival. London, 1871.

Fish, Stanley. *Is There a Text in This Class? The Authority of Interpretive Communities.* Cambridge, MA: Harvard University Press, 1980.

Fisher, Craig B. "The Pisan Clergy and an Awakening of Historical Interest in a Medieval Commune." *Studies in Medieval and Renaissance History* 3 (1966): 143–219.

Fisk, Milton. "The Human-Nature Argument." *Social Praxis* 5 (1978): 343–61.

Fleisher, Martin, ed. *Machiavelli and the Nature of Political Thought.* New York: Athenaeum, 1972.

– *Radical Reform and Political Persuasion in the Life and Writings of Thomas More.* Geneva: Droz, 1972.

Fleury, Jean. "Le conciliarisme des canonistes du concile de Bâle d'après le Panormitain." In *Mélanges Roger Secrétan.* Montreux: Faculty of Law, University of Lausanne, 1964.

Fliche, Augustin, and Victor Martin, eds. *Histoire de l'église depuis ses origines jusqu'à nos jours.* Paris: Bloud & Gay, 1934–.

Flick, Alexander C. *The Decline of the Medieval Church.* 2 vols. London: Kegan Paul, Trench, Trabner, 1930.

Folgado, A. "Los tratados *De legibus* y *De iustitia et iures* en los autores espanoles del siglo XVI y primera mitad de XVII." *La Cuidad de Dios* 172 (1959): 275–302.

Folz, Robert. "Les assemblées d'états dans les principautés allemandes (fin XIIIe-début XVIe siècles)." *Anciens Pays et Assemblées d'États* 36 (1965): 163–91.

Ford, Franklin. *Robe and Sword: The Regrouping of the French Aristocracy after Louis XIV.* Cambridge, MA: Harvard University Press, 1953.
Forset, Edward. *A Comparative Discourse of the Bodies Natural and Politique.* London, 1606.
Forster, Robert, and J. P. Greene, eds. *Preconditions of Revolution in Early Modern Europe.* Baltimore: Johns Hopkins University Press, 1970.
Fortescue, Sir John. *The Praise of the Laws of England.* Translated and edited by S. B. Chrimes. Cambridge: Cambridge University Press, 1942.
Fournier, Marcel, ed. *Les États et privilèges des universités françaises depuis leur fondation jusqu'en 1789.* 4 vols. Paris: L. Larose et Forcil, 1890–94.
Fournier, Paul, and Gabriel le Bras. *Histoires des collections canoniques en occident depuis les Fausses Décrétales jusqu'au Décret de Gratien.* Paris: Recueil Sirey, 1932.
Foxe, John. *The Acts and Monuments.* Edited by Stephen R. Cattley. 8 vols. London, 1837–47.
Foxe, Edward. *De vera differentia regiae potestatis et ecclesiasticae, et quae sit veritas ac virtus utriusque.* London, 1538.
— *The True Difference Between the Regal Power and the Ecclesiastical Power.* Translated by Henry, Lord Stafford. London, 1548.
Frame, Donald M. *Montaigne: A Biography.* New York: Harcourt, Brace & World, 1965.
François de Belleforest. *Les Chroniques et Annales de France dez l'origine des Françoys et leur venues es Gaules.* Paris, 1573.
Frank, Isnard Wilhelm. *Der antikonziliaristische Dominikaner Leonhard Huntpichler; Ein Beitrag zum Konziliarismus der Wiener Universität im 15 Jahrhundert.* Vienna: Verlag der Osterreichischen 17 Akademie der wissenschaften, 1976.
Frank, Joseph. *The Levellers: A History of the Writings of Three Seventeenth-Century Social Democrats: John Lilburne, Richard Overton, and William Walwyn.* Cambridge: Cambridge University Press, 1965.
Franciscus Zabarella. *Super quinque libris Decretalium commentaria.* Venice: 1602.
— "Tractatus de Schismate" In *De iurisdictione, auctoritate, et praeeminentia imperialiac potestate ecclesiastica,* edited by S. Schardius. Basle, 1566.
Franklin, Julian H. "Constitutionalism in the Sixteenth Century: The Protestant Monarchomachs." In *Political Thought and Social Change,* edited by Lewis W. Spitz, pp. 117–32. New York: Atherton Press, 1967.
Franklin, Julian H., ed. *Constitutionalism and Resistance in the Sixteenth Century.* New York: Pegasus, 1969.
Franzen, A., and W. Müller, eds. *Das Konzil von Konstanz: Beitrage zu seiner Geschichte und Theologie.* Freiburg: Herder, 1964.
Franzen, August. "The Council of Constance: Present State of the Problem." In *Church History; Historical Problems of Church Renewal.* Vol. 7, *Concilium: Theology in the Age of Renewal,* pp. 29–68. Glen Rock: Paulist Press, 1965.
Freegard, William J. "Roman Law and Resistance Theory: A Study of Question Three of the *Vindiciae contra Tyrannos.*" Ph.D. diss., University of Iowa, 1971.

Freshfield, Edwin H. *A Manual of Roman Law: The Ecloga.* Cambridge, MA: Harvard University Press, 1926.
Friedburg, Aemilius, ed. *Corpus iuris canonici.* 2 vols. Leipzig, 1879. Reprint. Graz: Akademischen Druk-u Verlagsanstall, 1959.
Friede, Juan, and Benjamin Keen, eds. *Bartolomé de las Casas in History: Towards an Understanding of the Man and His Work.* De Kalb: Northern Illinois University Press, 1971.
Friedenthal, Richard. *Luther: His Life and Times.* Translated by John Nowell. New York: Harcourt Brace Jovanovich, 1970.
Friedrich, Carl J. *The Age of the Baroque.* New York: Harper & Row, 1952.
– *Constitutional Reasons of State. The Survival of the Constitutional Order.* Providence: Brown University Press, 1954.
– *Transcendent Justice/The Religious Dimension of Constitutionalism.* Durham: Duke University Press, 1964.
Fromherz, Uta. *Johannes von Segovia als Geschichtsachreiber des Konzils von Basel.* Basle: Helving and Lichtenhohn, 1960.
Fryde, E. B., and E. Miller, eds. *Historical Studies of the English Parliament.* 2 vols. Cambridge: Cambridge University Press, 1970.
Fuller, Lon L. *The Morality of Law.* 2d ed. New Haven: Yale University Press, 1964.
Fulpius, L. *Les Institutions politiques de Genève.* Geneva: Institut national génèvois, 1965.
Fumaroli, M. *L'Âge de l'éloquence: Rhétorique et "res literaria" de la renaissance au seuil de l'époque classique.* Geneva: Droz, 1980.
Furcha, E. J., ed. *Huldrich Zwingli, 1484–1531: A Legacy of Radical Reform.* Montreal: Faculty of Religious Studies, McGill University, 1985.
Gaius. *Institutes.* J. Reinarch. Paris: Belles Lettres, 1950.
Gallet, Leon. "La monarchie française d'après Claude de Seyssel." *Revue historique de droit français et étranger,* 4ème série 23 (1944): 1–34.
Ganoczy, Alexandre. *Calvin, Théologien de l'Église et du Ministère.* Paris: Éditions du Cerf, 1964.
– "Jean Major, Exégète gallican." *Recherches de science religieuse* 56 (1968): 457–95.
– *Le Jeune Calvin: génèse et évolution de sa vocation réformatrice.* Wiesbaden: F. Steiner, 1966.
Gansfort, Johann Wessel. "Letter in Reply to Hoeck." Translated in part by Paul L. Nyhus. In *Forerunners of the Reformation* ... , edited by Heiko Oberman, pp. 89–120. London: Butterworth, 1967.
Ganshof, F. L. *The Imperial Coronation of Charlemagne.* Glasgow: University of Glasgow, 1971.
Gardiner, Stephen. *A Discourse on the Coming of the English and Normans to Britain.* Edited and translated by Peter Samuel Donaldson as *A Machiavellian Treatise by Stephen Gardiner.* Cambridge: Cambridge University Press, 1975.
– "The Oration of True Obedience – Answer to Bucer." In *Obedience in Church*

*and State: Three Political Tracts*, edited by Pierre Janelle, pp. 67–171. Cambridge: Cambridge University Press, 1930.
Garin, Eugenio. *Italian Humanism: Philosophy and Civic Life in the Renaissance.* Translated by Peter Munz. Oxford: Basil Blackwell, 1965.
Garin, Eugenio, ed. *Prosatori Latini del quattrocento.* Milan: R. Ricciardi, 1952.
Garrett, Christina. *The Marian Exiles. A Study in the Origins of Elizabethan Puritanism.* Cambridge: Cambridge University Press, 1938.
Garrett, J. L. "The Nature of the Church According to the Radical Continental Reformation." *Mennonite Quarterly Review* 32 (1958): 111–27.
Gatherer, W. A. *The Tyrannous Reign of Mary Stewart.* Edinburgh: Edinburgh University Press, 1958.
Gaudentius, Augustus, ed. *Bibliotheca juridica medii aevi.* 3 vols. Bologna: Angelus Gandolphus, 1888–1901.
Gauthier, David. *The Logic of Leviathan.* Oxford: Clarendon Press, 1969.
Geerkin, J. "Machiavelli Studies since 1969." *Journal of the History of Ideas* 37 (1976): 351–68.
Geisendorf, Paul F. *Théodore de Bèze.* Geneva: Droz, 1949.
*Geneva Bible. A Facsimile of the 1560 Edition.* Introduction by Lloyd E. Berry. Madison: University of Wisconsin Press, 1969.
Gentili, Alberico. *De iure belli libri tres.* Oxford: Clarendon Press, 1933.
– *Hispanicae advocationis libri duo.* Translated by Frank Frost Abbot. New York: Oxford University Press, 1921.
– *Regales disputationes tres.* London, 1605.
Gentillet, Innocent. *A Discourse upon the Means of Wel Governing and Maintaining in Good Peace a Kingdome, or other Principalitie ... against Nicholas Machiavell the Florentine.* Translated by Simon Patricke. London, 1602. Reprint. Amsterdam: Theatrum Orbis Terrarum, 1969.
– *Anti-Machiavel.* Edited by C. Edward Rathi. Geneva: Droz, 1968.
– *Discours contre Machiavel.* Edited by A. D'Andrea and P. D. Stewart. Florence: Casalini libri, 1974.
– *Discours sur les moyens de bien gouverner ... contra Nicolas Machiavel Florentin.* Paris, 1576.
George, Richard T. de *The Nature and Limits of Authority.* Wichita: University of Kansas Press, 1985.
Germino, Dante. *Modern Western Political Thought: Machiavelli to Marx.* Chicago: University of Chicago Press, 1972.
Gerrish, B. A. *Grace and Reason: a Study in the Theology of Luther.* Oxford: Oxford University Press, 1962.
Gerrish, B. A., ed. *Reformatio Perennis: Essays on Calvin and the Reformation in Honor of Ford Lewis Battle.* Pittsburgh: Pickwick, 1981.
Gerson, Jean. "On the Unity of the Church." Translated and edited by James K. Cameron. In *Advocates of Reform ...*, edited by M. Spinka, pp. 140–48. London: Student Christian Movement Press, 1953.

- *Opera omnia*. Edited by Louis du Pin. 5 vols. Antwerp, 1706.
- *Oeuvres complètes*. Edited by Palémon Glorieux. 10 vols. Paris: Desclée, 1960–73.
- "X considerationes principibus et dominis utilissimae." in Jean Gerson. *Opera omnia*, edited by Louis du Pin, vol. 4, pp. 622–25. Antwerp, 1706.
- "De potestate ecclesiastica." In Jean Gerson. *Oeuvres complètes*, edited by Palémon Glorieux, vol. 6, pp. 210–50. Paris: Desclée, 1960–73.
- "Ad reformationem contra simoniam." In Gerson, *Oeuvres complètes*, edited by Palémon Glorieux, vol. 6, pp. 179–81. Paris: Desclée, 1960–73.
- *Selections from A Deo exivit, Contra curiositatem studentium and De mystica theologia speculativa*. Edited and translated by E. Ozment. Leiden: E. J. Brill, 1969.
- "Tractatus de simonia." In Jean Gerson. *Oeuvres complètes*, edited by Palémon Glorieux, vol. 6, pp. 167–74. Paris: Desclée, 1960–73.

Gewirth, Alan. *Marsiluis of Padua: The Defender of Peace*. Vol. 1, *Marsilius of Padua and Medieval Political Philosophy*. Vol. 2, *Defensor pacis*. New York: Columbia University Press, 1951, 1956.
- "Philosophy and Political Thought in the Fourteenth Century." In *The Forward Movement of the Fourteenth Century*, edited by F. L. Utley, pp. 125–64. Columbus: Ohio State University Press, 1966.

Geyl, Pieter. *The Revolt of the Netherlands 1555–1609*. 2d ed. London: E. Benn, 1958.

Giannotti, Donato. "Della republica fiorentina." In Donato Giannotti. *Opere*, edited by G. Rosini, vol. 2, pp. 1–269. Pisa, 1819.
- "Libro della republica de Viniziani." In Donato Giannotti. *Opere*, edited by G. Rosini, vol. 1, pp. 1–243. Pisa, 1819.
- *Opere*. Edited by G. Rosini. 3 vols. Pisa, 1819.

Gierke, Otto von. *Das Deutsche Genossenschaftrecht*. Vol. 3, *Die Staats- und Korporationslebre*. 4 vols. Berlin: Weidermann, 1868–1913.
- *The Development of Political Theory*. Translated by Bernard Freyd. New York: W.W. Norton, 1939.
- *Natural Law and the Theory of Society, 1500 to 1800*. Translated by Ernest Barker. 2 vols. Cambridge: Cambridge University Press, 1934.
- *Political Theories of the Middle Ages*. Translated by F. M. Maitland. Cambridge: Cambridge University Press, 1900.

Giesey, Ralph E. *If Not, Not: The Oath of the Aragonese and the Legendary Laws of Sobrarbe*. Princeton: Princeton University Press, 1968.
- *The Juristic Basis of Dynastic Right to the French Throne*. Transactions of the American Philosophy Society, n.s., vol. 51, no. 5. Philadelphia: American Philosophical Society, 1961.
- "Models of Rulership in French Royal Ceremonial." In *Rites of Power...*, edited by Sean Wilentz, p. 41–58. Philadelphia: University of Pennsylvania Press, 1985.
- "The Monarchomach Triumvers: Hotman, Beza and Mornay." *Bibliothèque d'Humanisme et Renaissance* 32 (1970): 41–76.

- "Quod omnes tangit – a Post Scriptum." *Studia Gratiana* 15 (1972): 319–32.
- *The Royal Funeral Ceremony in Renaissance France.* Geneva: Droz, 1960.
- "When and Why Hotman Wrote the *Francogallia*." *Bibliothèque d'Humanisme et Renaissance* 29 (1967): 583–611.

Giesey, Ralph E., and J. H. M. Salmon, eds. "Editors' Introduction" to François Hotman. *Francogallia*, translated by J. H. M. Salmon, pp. 1–134. Cambridge: Cambridge University Press, 1972.

Gilbert, Allan H. *Machiavelli's Prince and its Forerunners.* Durham: Duke University Press, 1938.

Gilbert, Felix. "The Humanist Concept of the Prince and The Prince of Machiavelli." *Journal of Modern History* 11 (1939): 449–83.
- "Bernardo Rucellai and the Orti Oricellari: a Study on the Origin of Modern Political Thought." *Journal of the Warburg and Courtauld Institutes* 12 (1949): 101–31.
- "Florentine Political Assumptions in the Period of Savonarola and Soderini." *Journal of the Warburg and Courtauld Institutes* 20 (1957): 187–214.
- *Machiavelli and Guicciardini. Politics and History in Sixteenth-century Florence.* Princeton: Princeton University Press, 1965.
- "Machiavelli in Modern Historical Scholarship." In *Machiavelli nel V Centenario della nascita.* Pp. 155–71. Bologna: M. Boni, 1973. Italian version, pp. 219–29.
- "The Venetian Constitution in Florentine Political Thought." In *Florentine Studies ...* , edited by Nicolai Rubenstein, pp. 463–500. London: Faber and Faber, 1968.

Gilbert, Felix, and Stephen R. Graubard, eds. *Historical Studies Today.* New York: W.W. Norton, 1972.

Gilbert, Neal W. "The Concept of the Will in Early Latin Philosophy." *Journal of the History of Philosophy* 1 (1963): 17–35.
- *Renaissance Concepts of Method.* New York: Columbia University Press, 1960.

Gilby, Thomas. The Political Thought of Thomas Aquinas. Chicago: University of Chicago Press, 1958.
- *Principality and Polity: Aquinas and the Rise of State Theory in the West.* London: Longmans, Green, 1958.

Gilchrist, John T. *The Church and Economic Activity in the Middle Ages.* New York: St Martin's Press, 1969.

Gilissen, John. "Les États-Généraux des pays de par deça (1464–1632)." In *Anciens pays et assemblées d'États* 33: 261–321. Louvain: Béatrice Nauwalaerts, 1965.

Gill, Joseph. *Constance et Bâle-Florence.* Paris: Ed. de l'Orante, 1965.
- *The Council of Florence.* Cambridge: Cambridge University Press, 1959.
- "Il decreto *Haec sancta synodus* del concilio di Constanza." *Revista di storia della chiesa in Italia* 12 (1967): 123–30.
- "The Fifth Session of the Council of Constance." *Heythrop Journal* 5 (1964): 131–43.
- *Personalities of the Council of Florence.* New York: Barnes & Noble, 1964.

- "The Representation of the *Universitas Fidelium* in the Councils of the Conciliar Period." In *Councils and Assemblies*, edited by G. J. Cuming and Derek Baker, pp. 177–95. London: Cambridge University Press, 1971.
Gillet, Pierre. *La personnalité juridique en droit ecclésiastique spécialement chez les Décrétistes et les Décrétalistes et dans le Code du droit canonique.* Malines: W. Godenne, 1927.
Gilmont, J.-F. *Jean Crespin: Un éditeur réformé du XVI<sup>e</sup> siècle.* Geneva: Droz, 1981.
Gilmore, Grant. *The Death of Contract.* Columbus: Ohio State University Press, 1974.
Gilmore, Myron P. *Argument from Roman Law in Political Thought, 1200–1600.* Cambridge, MA: Harvard University Press, 1941.
- "Authority and Property in the Seventeenth Century: The First Edition of the *Traité des Seigneuries* of Charles Loyseau." *Harvard Library Bulletin* 5 (1950): 258–65.
- "Freedom and Determinism in Renaissance Historians." *Studies in the Renaissance* 3 (1956): 49–60.
- *Humanists and Jurists. Six Studies in the Renaissance.* Cambridge, MA: Harvard University Press, 1963.
- "Myth and Reality in Venetian Political Theory." In *Renaissance Venice*, edited by J. R. Hale, pp. 431–44. London: Faber and Faber, 1973.
- *The World of Humanism, 1453–1517.* New York: Harper & Row, 1952.
Gilson, Etienne. *History of Christian Philosophy in the Middle Ages.* New York: Random House, 1955.
Giocarinis, Kimon. "Speculation on the Origins of Lordship: Francesco Suárez in his *De legibus*." *Studia Gratiana* 15 (1972): 333–61.
Girard, Bernard de, seigneur du Haillan. *De l'état et succès des affaires de France.* Paris, 1571.
Glorieux, Palémon. "Autour de la liste des oeuvres de Gerson." *Recherches de théologie ancienne et médiévale* 25 (1956): 88–113.
Gluckman, Max. *Custom and Conflict in Africa.* Oxford: Basil Blackwell, 1955.
Goertz, Hans Jurgen. *Die Taufer: Geschichte und Deutung.* Munich: Beck, 1980.
Gogan, Brian. *The Common Corps of Christendom: Ecclesiological Themes in the Writings of Sir Thomas More.* Leiden: E. J. Brill, 1982.
Goldast, Melchior, ed. *Monarchia s. Romani imperii sive tractatus de iurisdictione imperiali seu regia, et pontifica seu sacerdotali.* 3 vols. Frankfurt, 1614. Reprint. Graz: Akademische Cruk-u Verlagsanstadt, 1960.
Golding, M. "The Concept of Rights: A Historical Sketch." In *Bioethics and Human Rights ...* , edited by E. Bandman, pp. 44–49. Boston: Little, Brown, 1978.
Gomez Camacho, Francisco. "Luis de Molina y la metodologie de la ley natural." *Miscelanea Comillas* 43 (1985): 155–94.
"The Golden Bull of the Emperor Charles IV." In *Select Historical Documents of the Middle Ages*, edited by Ernest F. Henderson, pp. 220–61. London: G. Bell and Sons, 1905.
Gonnet, Giovanni. *Enchiridion fontium Valdensium. Recueil critique des sources concer-*

nant les Vaudois au moyen âge, du III$^e$ concile de Latran au Synode de Chafran, 1179–1532. Edited by Giovanni Gonnet et al. Torre Pellice: Libreria editrice claudiana, 1958– .
— Il Valdismo medievale. Turin: Arti grafiche "L'Alpina," 1942.
Gooch, G. P. *English Democratic Ideas in the Seventeenth Century*. 2d ed. Cambridge: Cambridge University Press, 1967.
Goodman, Christopher. *How Superior Powers ought to be Obeyed of their Subjects, and wherein they may lawfully by God's Worde be Disobeyed and Resisted*. Geneva, 1558. Reprint. New York: Columbia University Press, 1938.
Gordon, Donald James, ed. *Fritz Saxl, 1890–1948: A Volume of Memorial Essays from His Friends in England*. London: T. Nelson, 1957.
Gough, J. W. *Fundamental Law in English Constitutional History*. Oxford: Clarendon Press, 1961.
[Goulart, Simon.] *Mémoires de l'état de France sous Charles neufième*. 2d ed. 3 vols. Middelburg [Geneva]: 1578.
Grafton, Anthony, and Lisa Jardine. *From Humanism to the Humanities: Education and the Liberal Arts in Fifteenth- and Sixteenth-century Europe*. Cambridge, MA: Harvard University Press, 1986.
Graham, Keith. "How do Illocutionary Descriptions Explain?" *Ratio* 22 (1981): 124–35.
Grandval, Marcus de. *The Best Form of Ecclesiastical and Civil Political Society*. Paris, 1512.
Gratian. *Concordantia discordantium canonicum (Decretum)*. Edited by E. Friedberg. Vol. 1, *Corpus iuris canonici*. Leipzig, 1879. Reprint. Graz: Akademische Druck-u. Verlagsanstalt, 1959.
Grause, F., ed. *Mentalitäten im Mittelalter: Methodische und inhaltliche Probleme*. Sigmaringen: J. Thorbecke, 1987.
Gray, John R. "The Political Theory of John Knox." *Church History* 8 (1939): 132–47.
Greaves, Richard L. *Society and Religion in Elizabethan England*. Minneapolis: University of Minnesota Press, 1981.
Grebel, Conrad. "Letters to Thomas Müntzer." In *Spiritual and Anabaptist Writers*, edited by George Hunston Williams, pp. 73–85. London: SCM Press, 1957.
Green, Louis. *Chronicle into History. An Essay on the Interpretation of History in Florentine Fourteenth-Century Chronicles*. Cambridge: Cambridge University Press, 1972.
Green, L. C. *Essays on the Modern Law of War*. Dobbs Ferry: Transnational, 1985.
Green, L. C., and Ruth Dickason. *The Law of Nations and the New World*. Edmonton: University of Alberta Press, 1989.
Green, O. H. *Spain and the Western Tradition. The Castilian Mind in Literature, from El Cid to Calderon*. 4 vols. Madison: University of Wisconsin Press, 1963–66.
Green, Robert W. *Protestantism and Capitalism: The Weber Thesis and its Critics*. Boston: Heath, 1959.

Green, T. H. *Lectures on the Principles of Political Obligation.* London: Longmans, 1941.
Green, Vivian. *Renaissance and Reformation.* 2d ed. London: Edward Arnold, 1964.
Greenleaf, W. H. "Filmer's Patriarchal History." *Historical Journal* 9 (1960): 157–71.
- "James I and the Divine Right of Kings." *Political Studies* 5 (1957): 36–48.
- *Order, Empiricism and Politics: Two Traditions of English Political Thought, 1500–1700.* London: Oxford University Press, 1964.
- "The Thomasian Tradition and the Theory of Absolute Monarchy." *English Historical Review* 79 (1964): 747–60.
Gregorovius, Ferdinand. *A History of the City of Rome in the Middle Ages.* Translated by Annie Hamilton. 8 vols. London: 1909–12. Reprint. New York: Schocken Books, 1967.
Gregory VII. *The Correspondence of Pope Gregory VII: Selected Letters from the Registrum.* Edited and translated by Ephraim Emerton. New York: Columbia University Press, 1932. Reprint. New York: Norton, 1969.
Grendler, Paul F. "Pierre Charron. Precursor to Hobbes." *Review of Politics* 25 (1963): 212–24.
Grice, O. R. *The Grounds of Moral Judgment.* Cambridge: Cambridge University Press, 1967.
Griffiths, Gordon. "Democratic Ideas in the Revolt of the Netherlands." *Archiv für Reformationgeschichte* 50 (1959): 50–63.
- "Grievances and Demands of the Craft Guilds of Cologne." In *Manifestations of Discontent in Germany*, edited by Gerald Strauss, pp. 138–43. Bloomington: Indiana University Press, 1953
- *Representative Government in Western Europe in the Sixteenth Century.* Oxford: Clarendon Press, 1968.
- "Representative Institutions in the Spanish Empire in the Sixteenth Century: The Low Countries." *The Americas* 12 (1956): 234–45.
- "The Revolutionary Character of the Revolt of the Netherlands." *Comparative Studies in Society and History* 29 (1960): 452–72.
Grimm, Harold J. "Luther's Conception of Territorial and National Loyalty." *Church History* 17 (1948): 79–94.
- *The Reformation Era, 1500–1650.* New York: Macmillan, 1954.
Gringore, Pierre. *La Sottie du prince des Sots.* Edited by P. A. Jannini. Milan: Cisalpino. 1957.
Grislis, Egil, and W. Speed Hill. "Richard Hooker: An Annotated Bibliography." In *Studies in Richard Hooker* ... , edited by William Speed Hill, pp. 279–320. Cleveland: Case Western Reserve University Press, 1972.
Gritsch, Eric W. *Reformer without a Church: The Life and Thought of Thomas Muentzer, 1488(?)–1525.* Philadelphia: Fortress Press, 1967.
Grossi, Paolo, ed. *La Seconda Scolastica.* Milan: Guiffrè, 1973.
Grotius, Hugo. *De jure belli ac pacis libri tres.* Edited by B. J. A. DeKanter-van Hettinger Tromp. Leiden: E.J. Brill, 1939.

- *De iure belli ac pacis libri tres*. 3 vols. Translated by Francis W. Kelsey. Oxford: Clarendon Press, 1925. Orig. ed. 1913.
Grover, Robinson A. "The Legal Origins of Thomas Hobbes's Doctrine of Contract." *Journal of the History of Philosophy* 18 (1989): 177–94.
Grundmann, Herbert. *Bibliographie zur Ketzergeschichte des Mittelalters (1900–1966)*. Rome: Edizioni di storia e letteratura, 1967.
- *Ketzergeschichte des Mittelalters*. Gottingen: Vanderhoeck & Ruprecht, 1966.
Guénée, Bernard. *Entre l'église et l'état: Quatre vies des prélats français à la fin du Moyen Âge, XII$^e$-XV$^e$ siècle*. Paris: Gallimard, 1987.
- *States and Rulers in Later Medieval Europe*. Translated by J. Vale. Oxford: Oxford University Press, 1985.
Guevara, Antonio de. *The Diall of Princes*. Translated by Thomas North. Amsterdam: Theatrum Orbis Terrarum, 1968.
Guicciardini, Francesco. "Considerations on the 'Discourses' of Machiavelli on the first Decade of T. Livy." In Francesco Guicciardini. *Selected Writings*, edited by Cecil Grayson and translated by Margaret Grayson, pp. 57–124. London: Oxford University Press, 1965.
- *Dialogo e discorsi del reggimento di Firenze*. Edited by Roberto Palmarocchi. Bari: G. Laterza & figli, 1932.
- "Dialogo del reggimento di Firenze." In Francesco Guicciardini. *Dialogo e discorsi ...*, edited by Roberto Palmarocchi, pp. 1–72. Bari: G. Laterza & figli, 1932.
- "Del modo di ordinare il governo popolare." In Francesco Guicciardini. *Dialogo e discorsi ...* , edited by Roberto Palmarocchi, pp. 218–59. Bari: G. Laterza & figli, 1932.
- *The History of Italy*. Translated by Sidney Alexander. New York: Macmillan, 1969.
- *Maxims and Reflections of a Renaissance Statesman*. Translated by Mario Domandi. New York: Harper and Row, 1965.
- *Selected Writings*. Edited by Cecil Grayson and translated by Margaret Grayson. London: Oxford University Press, 1965.
Guido de Baysio. *In sextum Decretalium commentaria*. Venice, 1577.
Guilielmus Durantis. *Tractatus de modo generalis concilii celebrandi*. Paris, 1545.
Guillaume de Pierre Godin. *The Theory of Papal Monarchy in the Fourteenth Century: Tractatus de causa immediata ecclesiasticae potestatis*. Edited by William D. McCready. Toronto: Pontifical Institute of Mediaeval Studies, 1982.
Guizard, L. *L'Oeuvre canonique de Guillaume Durand*. Montpellier: Imprimerie de la presse, 1956.
Gundersheimer, Werner L. *The Life and Works of Louis Le Roy*. Geneva: Droz, 1966.
- *Ferrara: The Style of Renaissance Despotism*. Princeton, NJ: Princeton University Press, 1973.
Gunn, John A. W. "'Interest Will Not Lie:' A Seventeenth-Century Political Maxim." *Journal of the History of Ideas* 29 (1968): 551–64.

- *Politics and the Public Interest in the Seventeenth Century.* London: Routledge & Kegan Paul, 1969.
Gunnell, John G. *Political Theory: Tradition and Interpretation.* Cambridge, MA: Harvard University Press, 1979.
Gwatkin, H. M., et al., eds. *The Cambridge Medieval History.* 8 vols. Cambridge: Cambridge University Press, 1936–49.
Hagerstrom, Axel. *Recht, Pflicht und bindende Kraft der Vertrages nach romischer und naturrechtlicher Anschauung.* Uppsala: Almquist & Wikel, 1965.
Haidacher, Anton, and Hans E. Mayer, eds. *Festschrift Karl Pivec.* Innsbruck: N.P., 1966.
Haigh, Christopher, ed. *The English Reformation Revised.* Cambridge: Cambridge University Press, 1987.
Haines, R. M. *Archbishop John Stratford: Political Revolutionary and Champion of the Liberties of the English Church, ca. 1275/80–1348.* Toronto: Pontifical Institute of Mediaeval Studies, 1986.
- *The Church and Politics in Fourteenth-Century England: The Career of Adam Orleton.* Cambridge: Cambridge University Press, 1978.
Hale, J. R. *Machiavelli and Renaissance Italy.* London: E.U.P., 1961.
- *War and Society in Renaissance Europe, 1450–1620.* New York: Fontana Press, 1985.
Hale, J. R., ed. *Renaissance Venice.* London: Faber & Faber, 1973.
Hale, J. R., J. R. L. Highfield, and B. Smalley, eds. *Europe in the Late Middle Ages.* Evanston: Northeastern University Press, 1965.
Halkin, Leon-E. "La 'Devotio moderna' et les origines de la Réforme aux Pays-Bas." In *Courants religieux et humanisme,* pp. 45–52.
Hall, B. "John Calvin, the Jurisconsults and the Jus Civile." *Studies in Church History* 3 (1966): 202–16.
Hall, G. D. G., ed. and trans. *The Treatise on the Laws and Customs of the Realm of England Called Glanvil.* London: Nelson, 1963.
Haller, J. *Papstum und Kirchenreform. Vier Kaputel zur Geschichte des ausgehenden Mittelalters.* Berlin: Weidmann, 1903.
- "Introduction." In *Concilium Basiliense ...* , edited by J. Haller, pp. 20–53. Basle: R. Reich, 1896–1936. Reprint. Nendeln: Kraus, 1971.
Haller, J., ed. *Concilium Basiliense. Studien und quellen zur Geschichte des Konzils von Basel, herausgegeben mit unterstutzung der historischen und antiquarischen Gesellschaft von Basel.* 8 vols. Basle: R. Reich, 1896–1936. Reprint. Nendeln: Kraus, 1971.
Haller, William. *Foxe's Book of Martyrs and the Elect Nation.* London: Jonathan Cape, 1963.
Hamilton, Bernice. *Political Thought in Sixteenth Century Spain. A Study of the Political Ideas of Victoria, De Soto, Suárez, and Molina.* Oxford: Clarendon Press, 1963.
Hamm, Berndt. *Promissio, Pactum, Ordinatio: Freiheit und Selbstbindung, Gottes in der scholastischen Gnatenlehre.* Tübingen: Mohr, 1977.

- *Zwinglis Reformation der Freiheit*. Neukirchen-Vluyn: Neukirchener Verlag, 1988.
Hampton, Jean. *Hobbes and the Social Contract Tradition*. Cambridge: Cambridge University Press, 1986.
Hamscher, Albert N. "The Conseil Privé and the Parlements in the Age of Louis XIV." *Transactions of the American Philosophical Society* 77, no. 2. Philadelphia: American Philosophical Society, 1987.
- *The Parlement of Paris after the Fronde, 1653–1673*. Pittsburgh: University of Pittsburgh Press, 1976.
Hancock, Ralph C. *Calvin and the Foundations of Modern Politics*. Ithaca, NY: Cornell University Press, 1989.
Hanke, L. *All Mankind is One*. De Kalb: Northeastern University Press, 1974.
- *Aristotle and the American Indians. A Study in Race Prejudice in the Modern World*. London: Hollis and Carter, 1959.
- "More Heat and Some Light on the Spanish Struggle for Justice in the Conquest of America." *Hispanic American Historical Review* 44 (1964): 293–340.
- *The Spanish Struggle for Justice in the Conquest of America*. Philadelphia: University of Pennsylvania Press, 1949.
Hanke, L., and Manuel Giménez Fernandez. *Bartolomé de las Casas, 1474–1566. Bibliografía crítica y cuerpo de materiales para el estudio de sa vita, escritos, actuación y polémicas que suscitaron durante cuatro siglos*. Santiago de Chile: Fondo Histórico y Bibliógrafo José Toribio Medina, 1954.
Hanley, Sarah. "Constitutional Discourse in France 1527–1549." In *Politics and Culture ...* , edited by Phyllis Mack and Margaret C. Jacob, pp. 153–68. Cambridge: Cambridge University Press, 1987.
- "Constitutional Ideology in France: Legend, Ritual and Discourse in the *Lit de Justice Assembly, 1527–1641*." In *Rites of Power ...* , edited by Sean Wilentz, pp. 65–106. Philadelphia: University of Pennsylvania Press, 1985.
- *"The "lit de Justice" of the Kings of France: Constitutional Ideology in Legend, Ritual, and Discourse*. Princeton: Princeton University Press, 1983.
Hannaford, I. "Machiavelli's Concept of Virtù in *The Prince* and *The Discourses* Reconsidered." *Political Studies* 20 (1972): 185–89.
Hanson, Donald W. *From Kingdom to Commonwealth: The Development of Civic Consciousness in English Political Thought*. Cambridge: Cambridge University Press, 1970.
Harding, Alan. "Political Liberty in the Middle Ages." *Speculum* 55 (1980): 423–43.
- "The Reflection of Thirteenth Century Legal Growth in St Thomas's Writings." In *Aquinas and the Problems of His Time*, edited by L. Verbeke and D. Verhelst, pp. 18–37. The Hague: Martinus Nijhoff, 1976.
Hardt, H. von der, ed. *Rerum concilii oecumenici Constantiensis*. 6 vols. Leipzig, 1697.
Haren, Michael. *Medieval Thought*. New York: St Martin's Press, 1985.

Harrington, James. *The Political Works of James Harrington*. Edited by J. G. A. Pocock. Cambridge: Cambridge University Press, 1977.

Harris, G. L. "A Revolution in Tudor History? Medieval Government and Statecraft." *Past and Present* 25 (1963): 8–39.

Harris, Jesse W. *John Bale: a Study in the Minor Literature of the Reformation*. Urbana: University of Northern Illinois Press, 1940.

Hart, H. L. A. *The Concept of Law*. Oxford: Clarendon Press, 1960.

Hartung, Fritz. *Deutsche Verfassungeschichte vom 15. Jahrhundert bis zur Gegenevart*. Stuttgart: K. F. Koehler, 1964.

Harvey, M. "Two 'Questiones' on the Great Schism by Nicholas Fakenham, O.F.M." *Archivum Franciscanum Historicum* 70 (1977): 97–127.

Haubst, Rudolf. "Wort und Leitidee der 'repraesentatio' bei Nikolaus von Kues." In *Der Begriff der Repraesentatio ...* , edited by Albert Zimmermann, pp. 139–62. Berlin: De Gruyter, 1971.

Hauck, K., and H. Mordek, eds. *Geschichtsschreibung und geistigen Leben im Mittelalter: Festschrift für Heinz Lowe zum 65, Geburstag*. Cologne: Böhlau, 1978.

Haugaard, William P. *Elizabeth and the English Reformation*. Cambridge: Cambridge University Press, 1968.

Hawkins, Richard. *A Discourse of the National Excellencie of England*. London, 1657.

Hay, Denys. *The Church in Italy in the Fifteenth Century*. Cambridge: Cambridge University Press, 1977.

– *The Italian Renaissance in its Historical Background*. Cambridge: Cambridge University Press, 1961.

– "The Early Renaissance in England." In *From the Renaissance to the Counter-Reformation ...* , edited by Charles H. Carter, pp. 95–112. New York: Random House, 1965.

– "A Note on More and the General Council." *Moreana* 15 (1967): 249–51.

Hazeltine, H. D. "Roman and Canon Law in the Middle Ages." In *The Cambridge Medieval History*, edited by H. M. Gwatkin et al., vol. 5, pp. 697–746. Cambridge: Cambridge University Press, 1936–49.

Headley, John M. "The Reformation in Historical Thought." *Journal of the History of Ideas* 48 (1987): 521–32.

Hefele, C. J. *Histoire des Conciles d'après les documents originaux*. Translated and edited by H. Leclercg. Paris: Letouzay et Ané, 1907–

Heimpel, H. *Dietrich von Niem: Dialog über Union und Reform der Kirche, 1410*. Leipzig and Berlin: Teubner, 1933.

Heitz, Gerhard, A. Laube, M. Steinmetz, and G. Vogler, eds. *Der Bauer im Klassen kampf*. Berlin: Akademie Verlag, 1975.

Heller, Henry. *The Conquest of Poverty: The Calvinist Revolt in Sixteenth-Century France*. Leiden: E. J. Brill, 1986.

Helmholz, R. H. *Roman Canon Law in Reformation England*. Cambridge: Cambridge University Press, 1990.

Helmrath, J. *Das Basler Konzil, 1431–1449*. Cologne: Böhlau, 1987.

Helps, Sir Arthur. *The Spanish Conquest in America and its Relation to the History of Slavery and to the Government of the Colonies.* 4 vols. Reprint. New York: AMS Press, 1966.
Helton, Tinsley, ed. *The Renaissance.* Madison: University of Wisconsin Press, 1961.
Henderson, Ernest F., trans. and ed. *Select Historical Documents of the Middle Ages.* London: G. Bell & Sons, 1905.
Hendrix, Scott H. "In Quest of the *Vera Ecclesia.* The Crises of Late Medieval Ecclesiology." *Viator* 7 (1976): 347–78.
Henkin, Alice, ed. *Human Dignity: The Internationalization of Human Rights.* New York: Aspen Institute for Humanistic Studies, 1979.
Henneman, J. B. "The Black Death and Royal Taxation in France 1347–1351." *Speculum* 43 (1968): 407–12.
– "Financing the Hundred Years' War." *Speculum* 42 (1967): 280–92.
Henry of Ghent. "The Absolute and Ordained Powers of the Pope." Edited by John Marrone. *Mediaeval Studies* 36 (1974): 7–27.
Henry of Langenstein. "Epistola concilii pacis." In Jean Gerson. *Opera omnia,* edited by Louis du Pin, vol. 2, pp. 835–40. Antwerp, 1706.
Herbert, Edward. *De religione laici.* London, 1645.
Hering, H. "De iure subjectivo sumpto apud sanctam Thomam." *Angelicum* 16 (1939): 295–97.
Heritier, Jean. *Catherine de Medici.* Translated by Charlotte Haldane. London: George Allen & Unwin, 1963.
Herlihy, David *Medieval and Renaissance Pistoia.* New Haven: Yale University Press, 1967.
– *Pisa in the Early Renaissance: A Study of Urban Growth.* New Haven: Yale University Press, 1958.
Hernandez, Ramon. *Un español en la O.N.U. Francisco de Vitoria.* Madrid: Biblioteca de autores cristianos, 1977.
Herschberger, Guy. *The Recovery of the Anabaptist Vision.* Scottdale: Herald Press, 1957.
Hesiod. *Works and Days.* Edited by M. L. West, Oxford: Clarendon Press, 1978.
Hess, Andrew C. "The Moriscos: An Ottoman Fifth Column in Sixteenth-Century Spain." *American Historical Review* 74 (1968): 1–25.
Heuston, R. F. V. *Essays in Constitutional Law.* 2d ed. London: Stevens, 1964.
Hesselburg, Arthur K. *A Comparative Study of the Political Theories of Ludovicus Molina, S.J., and John Milton.* Washington: Catholic University of America Press, 1952.
Hexter, J. H. "Claude de Seyssel and Normal Politics in the Age of Machiavelli." In *Art, Science and History in the Renaissance,* edited by Charles S. Singleton, pp. 389–415. Baltimore: Johns Hopkins University Press, 1967.
– "Il principe and lo stato." *Studies in the Renaissance* 4 (1957): 113–38.
– *More's Utopia: The Biography of an Idea.* Princeton: Princeton University Press, 1952.

- "Thomas More: on the Margins of Modernity." *Journal of British Studies* 1 (1961): 20–37.
- *The Vision of Politics on the Eve of the Reformation: More, Machiavelli and Seyssel.* New York: Basic Books, 1973.

Heymann, Frederick G. "The Hussite Revolution and the German Peasants' War." *Medievalia et Humanistica*, n.s. 1 (1970): 141–59.
- "John Rokycana: Church Reformer between Hus and Luther." *Church History* 28 (1959): 240–80.
- *John Zizka and the Hussite Revolution.* Princeton: Princeton University Press, 1955.

Heywood, John. *Gentleness and Nobility.* Edited by Kenneth W. Cameron. Raleigh: Thistle Press, 1941.

Heywood, John, ed. *Radical Tendencies in the Reformation: Divergent Perspectives.* St Louis: Sixteenth Century Journal Publishers, 1988.

Hildebrandt, Franz. *Melanchthon: Alien or Ally?* Cambridge: Cambridge University Press, 1946.

Hill, Christopher. *Anti-Christ in Seventeenth-Century England.* Oxford: Oxford University Press, 1971.
- "A Comment." In Paul Sweezy *et al. The Transition from Feudalism to Capitalism.* London: NLB, 1976. Pp. 118–21.
- *Intellectual Origins of the English Revolution.* Oxford: Clarendon Press, 1965.
- "The Many-Headed Monster in Late Tudor and Early Stuart Political Thinking." In *From the Renaissance to the Counter-Reformation* ... , edited by Charles H. Carter, pp. 296–324. New York: Random House, 1965.
- *Puritanism and Revolution.* London: Secker and Warburg, 1958.

Hill, William Speed, ed. *Studies in Richard Hooker. Essays Preliminary to an Edition of his Works.* Cleveland: Case Western Reserve University Press, 1972.
- "The Evolution of Hooker's *Laws of Ecclesiastical Polity.*" In *Studies in Richard Hooker* ... , edited by William Speed Hill, pp. 117–58. Cleveland: Case Western Reserve University Press, 1972.

Hillerbrand, Hans J. "The Anabaptist View of the State." *Mennonite Quarterly Review* 32 (1958): 83–100.
- *Christendom Divided. The Protestant Reformation.* London: Hutchison, 1971.
- *The World of the Reformation.* New York: Charles Scribner's Sons, 1973.

Hillerbrand, Hans J., ed. *The Protestant Reformation.* London: Macmillan, 1968.
- *Radical Tendencies in the Reformation: Divergent Perspectives.* St Louis: Sixteenth Century Journal Publishers, 1988.

Hillers, Delbert R. *Covenant: The History of a Biblical Idea.* Baltimore: Johns Hopkins University Press, 1969.

Hilton, Rodney, ed. *The Transition from Feudalism to Capitalism.* Atlantic Heights: Humanities Press, 1976.

Hinsley, F. H. *Sovereignty.* 2d ed. Cambridge: Cambridge University Press, 1986.

Hinton, R. W. K. "English Constitutional Theories from Sir John Fortescue to Sir John Eliot." *English Historical Review* 75 (1960): 410–25.

Hintze, Otto. *Gesammelte Abhandlungen.* Vol. 1, *Staat und Verfassung.* Edited by Gernard Oestreich. Gottingen: Vandenhoeck and Ruprecht, 1962.
Hirschman, Albert O. *The Passions and the Interests.* Princeton: Princeton University Press, 1977.
Hirst, Kerek. *The Representative of the People? Voters and Voting in England under the Early Stuarts.* Cambridge: Cambridge University Press, 1975.
Hobbes, Thomas. *A Dialogue between a Philosopher and a Student of the Common Law of England.* Edited by Joseph Cropsey. Chicago: University of Chicago Press, 1971.
- *The English Works.* Edited by Sir William Molesworth. 11 vols. London, 1839–45. Reprint. Aalen: Scientia Verlag, 1962.
- *Leviathan.* Edited by C. B. MacPherson. Harmondsworth: Penguin Books, 1968.
Hodgen, Margaret T. *Early Anthropology in the Sixteenth and Seventeenth Centuries.* Philadelphia: University of Pennsylvania Press, 1964.
Hodl, G. "Zur Reichpolitik des Basler Konzils. Bischof Johannes Schele von Lubeck (1420–1439)." *Mitteilungen des Instituts für oesterriechische Geschichtforschung* 75 (1967): 46–65.
Hofmann, Herbert. *Kardinalat und kuriale Politik in der ersten Hälfte des 14. Jahrhunderts.* Leipzig: C. Nieft, 1935.
- *Repraesentation; Studien zur Wort-und Begreffgeschichte von der Antike bis ins 19. Jahrhundert.* Schriften zur Verfassungsgeschichte 22. Berlin: Duncker & Humblot, 1974.
Hofmann, Karl. *Der Dictatus Papae Gregors VII.* Paderborn: Ferdinand Schoningh, 1933.
Hoffmann, Manfred. "Martin Luther: Resistance to Secular Authority." *Journal of the Interdenominational Theological Centre* 12 (1985): 35–49.
Hogrefe, Pearl. "The Life of Christopher St German." *Review of English Studies* 13 (1937): 398–404.
- *The Sir Thomas More Circle.* Urbana: Northeastern University Press, 1959.
Holborn, Hajo. *Ulrich von Hutten and the German Reformation.* New Haven: Yale University Press, 1934.
Holdsworth, William S. *A History of English Law.* 18 vols. 7th ed. London: Methuen, 1956–65.
Hollis, Martin: *Models of Man.* Cambridge: Cambridge University Press, 1977.
- "Say It with Flowers." *Supplementary Proceedings of the Aristotelian Society* 52 (1978): 43–57.
Holmes, George. *The Florentine Enlightenment, 1400–1450.* London: Weidenfeld & Nicolson, 1969.
- "The Emergence of an Urban Ideology at Florence." *Transactions of the Royal Historical Society* 23 (1973): 111–34.
Holthofer, E. "Die Literatur zum gemeinen und partikularen Recht in Italien, Frankreich, Spanien und Portugal." In *Handbuch der Quellen und Literatur ...*, edited by H. Coing, pp. 103–499. Munich: Beck, 1973, 1977.

Holton, Rodney H. *Bond Men Made Free. Medieval Peasant Movements and the English Rising of 1391.* London: Temple Smith, 1973.
Holton, Rodney H., ed. *The Transition from Feudalism to Capitalism.* New York: St Martin's Press, 1985.
Hooker, Richard. *The Folger Library Edition of the Works of Richard Hooker.* Edited by William Speed Hill, 3 vols. Cambridge, MA: Harvard University Press, Belknap Press, 1977–81.
– *Hooker's Ecclesiastical Polity: Book VIII.* Edited by Raymond Aaron Houk. New York: Columbia University Press, 1931.
– "Of the Laws of Ecclesiastical Polity." In Richard Hooker. *The Works.* Edited by John Keble. 7th ed. Revised by R. W. Church and F. Paget. 3 vols. Oxford: Clarendon Press, 1888.
– *Of the Laws of Ecclesiastical Polity: An Abridged Edition.* Edited by A. S. McGrade and Brian Vickers. London: Sidgwick and Jackson, 1975.
– *The Works.* Edited by John Keble. 7th ed. Revised by R. W. Church and F. Paget. 3 vols. Oxford: Clarendon Press, 1888.
Hookway, Christopher, and Philip Pettit, eds. *Action and Interpretation.* Cambridge: Cambridge University Press, 1978.
Hopfl, Harro. *The Christian Polity of John Calvin.* Cambridge: Cambridge University Press, 1982.
– "Fundamental Law and the Constitution in Sixteenth-Century France." In *Die Rolle der Juristen ...* , edited by Roman Schnurr, pp. 327–56. Berlin: Duncker & Humblot, 1986.
Hopfl, Harro, ed. *Luther and Calvin on Secular Authority,* Cambridge, Cambridge University Press, 1991.
Horn, N. *Aequitas in den Lehren des Baldus.* Cologne: Graz, 1968.
– "Die legistische Literatur der Kommentatoren und der Ausbreitung des gelehrten Rechts." In *Handbuch der Quellen und Literatur ...* , edited by H. Coing, pp. 261–364. Munich: Beck, 1973, 1977.
– "Philosophie in der Jurisprudenz der Kommentatorem: Baldus philosophus." *Ius commune* 1 (1967): 104–49.
Hornick, Henry. "Three Interpretations of the French Renaissance." *Studies in the Renaissance* 7 (1960): 43–66.
Horst, V. "Grenzen der papstlichen Autorität: konziliare Elemente in der Ekklesiologie des Johan Torquemada." *Freiburger Zeitschrift für Philosophie und Theologie* 19 (1972): 361–88.
Hostiensis. *Lectura in Quinque Decretalium Gregorianarum Libros.* Paris, 1512.
Hotman, François. "L'Antitribonian." In *Opuscules françoises des Hotman.* Pp. 1–112. Paris, 1616.
– *Francogallia.* Edited by Ralph E. Giesey and translated by J. H. M. Salmon. Cambridge: Cambridge University Press, 1972.
– *Francogallia, libellus statum veteris Reipublicae Galliae, tum deinde a Francis occupatae, describens.* 2d ed. Cologne, 1574.

- *De legibus populi romani liber.* Basle, 1557.
- *Opuscules françoises des Hotman.* Paris, 1616.

Howell, Wilbur S. *Logic and Rhetoric in England, 1500–1700.* New York: Russell and Russell, 1961.

Hsia, R. Po-Chia. *Society and Religion in Münster, 1535–1618.* New Haven: Yale University Press, 1984.

Hsia, R. Po-Chia, ed. *The German People and The Reformation.* Ithaca, NY: Cornell University Press, 1988.

Hudson, Stephen D. "Right Reason and Mortal Gods." *Monist* 66 (1983): 134–45.

Hudson, Winthrop S. *John Ponet (1516–1556): Advocate of Limited Monarchy.* Chicago: University of Chicago Press, 1942.

Hugh of St Victor. *On the Sacraments of the Christian Faith.* Translated by Roy J. Deferrari. Cambridge, MA: Mediaeval Academy of America, 1951.

Hughes, Philip. *The Reformation in England.* 3 vols. New York: Macmillan, 1954–56.

Huguccio. "Nisi deprehendetur a fide devius." In Brian Tierney. *Foundations of the Conciliar Theory ... ,* pp. 248–50. Cambridge: Cambridge University Press, 1955.

- *Summa ad Distinctiones.* Ms. 72. Pembroke College, Cambridge.

Huizinga, J. *Erasmus of Rotterdam.* Translated by F. Hopman. London: Phaidon Publishers, 1952.

Hull, James. *The Unmasking of the Politic Atheist.* London, 1602.

Humphrey, Lawrence. *The Nobles, or Of Nobility.* Amsterdam: Theatrum Orbis Terrarum, 1973.

Huppert, George. *The Idea of Perfect History: Historical Erudition and Historical Philosophy in Renaissance France.* Urbana: Northeastern University Press, 1970.

Hurstfield, Joel. "The Framework of Crisis." In *The Reformation Crisis,* edited by Joel Hurstfield, pp. 1–7. London: Edward Arnold, 1965.

- "The Search for Compromise in England and France." In *The Reformation Crisis,* edited by Joel Hurstfield, pp. 95–106. London: Edward Arnold, 1965.

Hurstfield, Joel, ed. *The Reformation Crisis.* London: Edward Arnold, 1965.

Hus, John. *The Church.* Translated by D. Schaff. New York: Scribner's, 1915. Reprint. Westport, CN: Greenwood Press, 1974.

- *The Letters of John Hus.* Translated by M. Spinka. Manchester: Manchester University Press, 1972.
- *Tractatus de ecclesia.* Edited by S. Harrison Thompson. Boulder: University of Colorado Press, 1956.

Hutten, Ulrich von. "Trias Romana Dialogus." In Ulrich von Hutten. *Opera omnia,* edited by Ernest Munch, vol. 3, pp. 425–506. Berlin, Leipzig, 1820–5.

- "Letters of Obscure Men." Translated by Francis E. Stokes. In Ulrich von Hutten. *On the Eve of the Reformation Letters of Obscure Men.* New York: Harper and Row, 1964.

- *Opera omnia*. Edited by Ernest Munch. 5 vols. Berlin, Leipzig, 1820–25.
Hyde, J. K. *Padua in the Age of Dante*. Manchester: Manchester University Press, 1966.
- "Italian Social Chronicles in the Middle Ages." *Bulletin of the John Rylands Library* 49 (1966–67): 107–32.
- *Society and Politics in Medieval Italy: The Evolution of the Civil Life, 1000–1350*. London: Macmillan, 1973.
Hyma, Albert. *The Christian Renaissance: A History of the "Devotio Moderna."* 2d ed. Hamden: Archon Books, 1965.
- "The Continental Origins of English Humanism." *Huntingdon Library Quarterly* 4 (1940–41): 1–25.
Iggers, George G., and Harold T. Parker, eds. *International Handbook of Historical Studies: Contemporary Research and Theory*. Westport, CN: Greenwood Press, 1979.
Innocent III. "On the Misery of Man." In *Two Views of Man*, edited and translated by Bernard Murchland, pp. 1–60. New York: F. Unger, 1966.
Iserloh, Erwin. *The Theses Were Not Posted: Luther between Reform and Reformation*. Boston: Beacon Press, 1968.
Iserloh, Erwin, ed. *Reformata Reformanda: Festgabe für Hubert Jedin zum 17. Juni 1965*. Vol. 1, pp. 87–128. Münster: Aschendorff, 1965.
Iserloh, Erwin, Joseph Glazik, and Hubert Jedin, eds. *Reformation and Counter-Reformation*. Translated by Anselm Biggs and Peter W. Becker. New York: Seabury Press, 1980.
Isidore of Seville, *Etymologiae*. Edited by W. M. Lindsay. 2 vols. Oxford: Clarendon Press, 1910.
Izbicki, T. M. "'Clericos Laicos' and the Canonists." In *Popes, Teachers and Canon Law ...*, edited by Ross Sweeney and Anthony Chodorow, pp. 179–90. Ithaca: Cornell University Press, 1989.
- *Protector of the Faith: Cardinal Johannes de Turrecremata and the Defence of the Institutional Church*. Washington: Catholic University of America Press, 1981.
Jackson, Richard A. "Elective Kingship and *Consensus Populi* in Sixteenth-Century France." *Journal of Modern History* 44 (1962): 155–71.
- "Peers of France and Princes of the Blood." *French Historical Studies* 7 (1971): 27–46.
- "The Sleeping King." *Bibliothèque d'humanisme et renaissance* 31 (1969): 525–51.
Jacob, E. F. *Archbishop Henry Chichele*. London: Nelson, 1967.
- "The Conciliar Movement in Recent Study." *Bulletin of the John Rylands Library* 14 (1958): 26–53. Reprint in E. F. Jacob. *Essays in Later Medieval History*, pp. 98–123. Manchester: Manchester University Press, 1968.
- "Dietrich of Niem: His Place in the Conciliar Movement." Reprint from *Bulletin of the John Rylands Library* 19 (1935). Manchester: Manchester University Press, 1935.
- *Essays in Later Medieval History*. Manchester: Manchester University Press, 1968.

- "Reflections upon the Study of the General Councils in the Fifteenth Century." *Ecclesiastical History Society: Studies in Church History* 1 (1964): 80–97.
- *Robert Boyle and the English Revolution: A Study in Social and Intellectual Change.* New York: B. Franklin, 1977.
Jacob, E. F., ed. *Italian Renaissance Studies: A Tribute to the Late Cecilia M. Ady.* London: Faber & Faber, 1960.
James I. (of England). *The Basilicon Doron of King James VI.* Edited by James Craigie. 2 vols. Edinburgh: W. Blackwood and Sons, 1944, 1950.
- *The Political Works of James I.* Edited by Charles H. McIlwain. Cambridge, MA: Harvard University Press, 1918.
- *Triplici modo, triplec cuneus. (Apology for the Oath of Obedience).* In James I. *The Political Works ...* , edited by Charles H. McIlwain, pp. 71–109. Cambridge, MA: Harvard University Press, 1918.
Janelle, Pierre, ed. *Obedience in Church and State.* Cambridge: Cambridge University Press, 1930.
Jannsen, Peter L. "Political Thought as Traditional Action: The Cricital Response to Skinner and Pocock." *History and Theory* 24 (1985): 115–46.
Janton, Pierre. *John Knox (ca. 1513–1572): l'homme et l'oeuvre.* Paris: Didier, 1967.
Jarlot, Georges. "Les idées politiques de Suárez et le pouvoir absolu." *Archives de Philosophie* 18 (1949): 64–107.
Jayne, Sears. *John Colet and Marsilius Ficino.* Oxford: Oxford University Press, 1963.
Jedin, Hubert. *Bischöfliches Konzil oder Kirchenparlement? Ein Beitrag zur Ekklesiologie der Konzilien von Konstanz und Basel.* 2d ed. Basel, Stuttgart: Helbing & Lichtenhaln, 1965.
- *Ecumenical Councils of the Catholic Church: An Historical Outline.* Translated by E. Graf. Edinburgh: Nelson, 1960.
- *Geschichte des Konzils von Trient.* Vol. 1, *Der Kampf um das Konzil.* 2d ed. Freiburg: Herder, 1951.
- "Giovanni Gozzadini, ein Konziliarist am Hofe Julius II." In *Kirche des Glaubes* ... , edited by Hubert Jedin, vol. 2, pp. 17–24. Freiburg: Herder, 1966.
- *A History of the Council of Trent.* Volume 1, *The Struggle for the Council.* Translated by Ernest Graf. Edinburgh: Nelson, 1957.
- *Kleine Konziliengeschichte.* 7th ed. Freiburg: Herder, 1969.
Jedin, Hubert, ed. *Handbook of Church History.* Vol. 4, *From the High Middle Ages to the Eve of the Reformation.* New York: Herder and Herder, 1970.
- *Kirche des Glaubes. Kirche der Geschichte: Ausgewahlte Aufsatze und Vortrage.* Freiburg: Herder, 1966.
Jewel, John. *Apology of the Church of England.* Edited by J. E. Booby. Ithaca: Cornell University Press, 1963.
Jewell, Helen M. *English Local Administration in the Middle Ages.* New York: Barnes and Noble, 1972.
Jiménez Urresti, Teodoro, ed, *Structures of the Church.* New York: Herder and Herder, 1970.

Joannes Monarchus. *Glossa aurea super sexto Decretalium libro.* Paris, 1535.
Joannes Teutonicus. "Glossa Ordinaria in Decretum." In *Decretum Gratiani ... una cum glossis.* Paris, 1601.
Johannes Althusius. *Politica Methodi Digesta.* Edited by Carl Joachim Friedrich. Cambridge, MA: Harvard University Press, 1932.
Johannes Andreae. *In tertium Decretalium librum Novella Commentaria.* Venice, 1605.
*John Locke: Papers Read at a Clark Library Seminar. 10 December 1977.* Los Angeles: William Andrews Clark Memorial Library, University of California; 1980.
Johannis Quidort von Paris. *Überkönegliche, und papstliche Gewalt: text-kritische Edition mit deutscher Übersetzung.* Edited and translated by F. Bleienstien. Stuttgart: Ernst Verlag, 1969.
John of Legnano. *De Bello, de represaliis et de Duello.* Edited by Thomas E. Holland. Oxford: Oxford University Press, 1917.
*John of Paris on Royal and Papal Power.* Translated by Arthur P. Monahan. New York: Columbia University Press, 1973.
John of Salisbury. *Policraticus.* Edited and translated by Cary J. Nederman. Cambridge: Cambridge University Press, 1990.
John of Segovia. *Historia gestorum generalis synodi Basiliensis.* Edited by E. Birk. In *Monumenta conciliorum generalium*, edited by Cavesarea Academica Scientarium Vindobonensis, vols. 2–4. Vienna, 1857–1935.
– "Tractatus super praesidencia in concilio Basiliensi." In Pascal Ladner. "Johannes von Segovia Stellung zur Prasidentenfrage des Basler Konzils." *Zeitschrift für Schwizerische Kirchengeschichte* 62 (1968): 1–113.
John of Viterbo. "Liber de regimine principum." Edited by C. Salvemini. In *Bibliotheca juridica medii aevi*, edited by Augustus Gaudentius, vol. 3, pp. 215–80. Bologna: A. Gandolphi, 1888–1901.
Johns, Christa T. *Luthers Konzilsidee in ihrer historischen Bedingtheit und ihrem Neuansatz.* Berlin: Topelmann, 1966.
Johnson, Harold J., ed. *The Medieval Tradition of Natural Law.* Kalamazoo: Medieval Institute Publications, 1987.
Johnson, James T. *Ideology, Reason and the Limitation of War: Religion and Secular Concepts, 1200–1740.* Princeton: Princeton University Press, 1975.
Johnson, Thomas. *A Plea for Free-Mens Liberties ...* London, 1965.
Johnston, David. *The Rhetoric of Leviathan: Thomas Hobbes and the Politics of Cultural Transformation.* Princeton, NJ: Princeton University Press, 1986.
Jones, Leonard C. *Simon Goulart, 1543–1628.* Geneva: Georg & Cie, 1917.
Jones, P. J. "Communes and Despots: The City State in Late Medieval Italy." *Transactions of the Royal Historical Society* 15 (1965): 71–96.
– *The Malatesta of Rimini and The Papal State.* Cambridge: Cambridge University Press, 1974.
Jones, Whitney R. D. *The Tudor Commonwealth, 1529–1559.* London: Athlone Press, 1970.

Jonghe, Eugeen de. "Locke and Hooker on the Finding of the Law." *Review of Metaphysics* 42 (1988): 301–25.
Joolwicz, H. F., and B. Nicholson. *Historical Introduction to the Study of Roman Law.* 3d ed. Cambridge: Cambridge University Press, 1972.
Jordan, W. K. *Edward VI.* Vol. 1, *The Young King.* Vol. 2, *The Threshold of Power.* London: Allen & Unwin, 1970.
Jouan des Longrais, Frederic. *Henry II and His Justiciars: Had They a Political Plan in Their Reforms about Seisin?* Limoges: Imprimerie Bontemps, 1962.
Joynson, James Turner. *Ideology, Reason, and the Limitation of War: Religious and Secular Concepts, 1200–1740.* Princeton: Princeton University Press, 1975.
Juan de Torquemada. *Summa de ecclesia.* Rome, 1489.
Judson, Margaret Atwood. *The Crisis of the Constitution: An Essay in Constitutional and Political Thought in England 1623–1645.* New Brunswick NJ: Rutgers University Press, 1949.
Juneau, Hubert. "La pensée politique de Rabelais." *Travaux d'humanisme et renaissance* 7 (1953): 15–35.
Junghans, Helman. *Ockham im Lichte der neuren Forschung.* Berlin: Lutherisches Verlaghaus, 1968.
Kamen, Henry. *The Rise of Toleration.* New York: McGraw Hill, 1967.
Kamenka, Eugene, and R S. Neale, eds. *Feudalism, Capitalism and Beyond.* New York: St Martin's Press, 1975.
Kaminsky, Howard. "Cession, Subtraction, Deposition: Simon de Cramaud's Formulation of the French Solution to the Schism." *Studia Gratiana* 15 (1972): 293–317.
– *A History of the Hussite Revolution.* Berkeley: University of California Press, 1967.
– *Simon de Cramaud and the Great Schism.* New Brunswick NJ: Rutgers University Press, 1983.
Kammen, Michael, ed. *The Past before Us: Contemporary Historical Writing in the United States.* Ithaca: Cornell University Press, 1980.
Kantorowicz, Ernst H. *The King's Two Bodies: A Study in Medieval Political Theology.* Princeton: Princeton University Press, 1957.
Karant-Nunn, Susan C. *Zwickaw in Transition, 1500–1547: The Reformation as an Agent of Change.* Columbus: Ohio State University Press, 1987.
Kaspar, Oldrich. "A Great Polemic concerning the Position of the Native American and the Reflection of this Polemic in Sixteenth- to Seventeenth-century Bohemia." *Archiv Orientalni* 53 (1985): 206–11.
Kasper, Franz. *Das subjektive Recht – Begriffsbildung und Bedeutungsmiehrheit.* Freiburg: C.F. Müller, 1967.
Kaufman, Peter Iver. *Redeeming Politics.* Princeton: Princeton University Press, 1990.
Kavka, Gregory S. *Hobbesian Moral and Political Theory.* Princeton, NJ: Princeton University Press, 1986.
Kaye, Françoise. *Charron et Montaigne: du plagiat à l'originalité.* Ottawa: University of Ottawa Press, 1982.

Kearney, Hugh. *Scholars and Gentlemen: Universities and Society in Pre-Industrial Britain, 1500–1700*. London: Faber and Faber, 1979.
Keen, Benjamin. "The Black Legend Revisited: Assumptions and Reality." *Hispanic American Historical Review* 49 (1969): 703–19.
Keen, M. A. *The Laws of War in the Late Middle Ages*. London: Routledge and Kegan Paul, 1965.
– "The Political Thought of the Fourteenth-Century Civilians." In *Trends in Medieval Political Thought*, edited by Beryl Smalley, pp. 105–26. Oxford: Oxford University Press, 1965.
Keifer, Howard E., and Milton Kennedy, eds. *Ethics and Social Justice*. Albany: State University of New York Press, 1970.
– "Civil Science in the Renaissance: Jurisprudence in the French Manner." *History of European Ideas* 2 (1981): 261–76. Reprint in Donald R. Kelley. *History, Law and the Human Sciences ...* . London: Variorum, 1984.
– "Civil Science in the Renaissance: Jurisprudence Italian Style." *Historical Journal* 22 (1979): 277–94. Reprint in Donald R. Kelley. *History, Law and the Human Sciences ...* . London: Variorum, 1984.
Kelley, Donald R. "Civil Science in the Renaissance: The Problem of Interpretation." In *The Languages of Political Theory ...* , edited by Anthony Pagden, pp. 57–78. Cambridge: Cambridge University Press, 1987.
– *The Foundations of Modern Historical Scholarship: Language, Law and History in the French Renaissance*. New York: Columbia University Press, 1970.
– *François Hotman: a Revolutionary's Ordeal*. Princeton: Princeton University Press, 1973.
– *History, Law and the Human Sciences: Medieval and Renaissance Perspectives*. London: Variorum, 1984.
– "Horizons of Intellectual History: Retrospect, Circumspect, Prospect." *Journal of the History of Ideas* 48 (1987): 143–69.
– "Legal Humanism and the Sense of History." *Studies in the Renaissance* 13 (1966): 184–99.
– "Murd'rous Machiavel in France: A Post-Mortem." *Political Science Quarterly* 85 (1970): 545–59.
– Review of Quentin Skinner. *The Foundations of Modern Political Thought*. Cambridge: Cambridge University Press, 1978. In *Journal of the History of Ideas* 40 (1979): 663–73.
– "Vera Philosophia: The Philosophical Significance of Renaissance Jurisprudence." *Journal of the History of Philosophy* 14 (1976): 267–79.
Kellison, Matthew. *The Right and Iurisdiction of the Prelate and the Prince*. 2d ed. Douai, 1621. Reissue. Ilkley and London: Scholar Press, 1974.
Kelly, Amy. *Eleanor of Aquitaine and the Four Kings*. Cambridge, MA: Harvard University Press, 1950.
Kendall, R. T. *Calvin and English Calvinism to 1649*. Oxford: Oxford University Press, 1979.

Kennedy, Leonard A. *Peter of Ailly and the Harvest of Fourteenth-Century Philosophy.* Lewiston: Edwin Mellen Press, 1988.
Kennedy, Leonard A., ed. *Renaissance Philosophy.* The Hague: Mouton, 1973.
Kennett, Basil, trans. *Of the Laws of Nature and Nations of Samuel von Pufendorff.* London, 1710.
Kenreedy, Duncan. "Form and Substance in Private Law Adjudication." *Harvard Law Review* 89 (1976): 1685–1778.
Keohane, Nannerl O. "Claude de Seyssel and Sixteenth-Century Constitutionalism in France." In *Constitutionalism*, edited by J. Roland Pennock and John W. Chapman, pp. 47–83. New York: New York University Press, 1986.
– *Philosophy and the State in France. The Renaissance to the Enlightenment.* Princeton: Princeton University Press, 1980.
Kern, Fritz. *Gottesgadentum und Widerstandsrecht im früheren Mittelalter: Zur Entwicklungseschichte der Monarchie.* Leipzig: K. F. Koehler, 1915.
Kidd, B. J. *The Counter-Reformation.* London: Society for the Promotion of Christian Knowledge, 1933.
King, Preston, and B. C. Parekh, eds. *Politics and Experience. Essays Presented to Professor Michael Oakshott on the Occasion of His Retirement.* Cambridge: Cambridge University Press, 1968.
Kingdon, Robert M. "Calvinism and Democracy: Some Political Implications of Debates on French Reformed Church Government, 1562–1572. *American Historical Review* 69 (1964): 393–401. Reprinted in Robert M. Kingdon. *Church and Society in Reformation Europe.* London: Variorum, 1985.
– *Church and Society in Reformation Europe.* London: Variorum, 1985.
– "The First Expression of Theodore Beza's Political Ideas." *Archiv für Reformationgeschichte*, 46 (1955): 88–99.
– "The Function of Law in the Political Thought of Peter Martyr Vermigli." In *Reformatio Perennis ... ,* edited by B. A. Gerrish, pp.159–72. Pittsburgh: Pickwick, 1981. Reprinted in Robert M. Kingdon. *Church and Society in Reformation Europe.* London: Variorum, 1985.
– *Geneva and the Coming of the Wars of Religion in France 1555–1563.* Geneva: Droz, 1956.
– *Geneva and the Consolidation of the French Protestant Movement, 1564–1572: A Contribution to the History of Congregationalism, Presbyterianism, and Calvinist Resistance Theory.* Geneva: Droz, 1967.
– "Les idées politiques de Bèze d'après son Traité de l'autorité du magistrat en la punition des hérétiques." *Bibliothèque d'humanisme et renaissance* 22 (1960): 566–69.
– "John Calvin's Contribution to Representative Government." In *Politics and Culture ... ,* edited by Phyllis Mack and Margaret C. Jacob, pp. 183–98. Cambridge: Cambridge University Press, 1987.
– "The Political Resistance of the Calvinists in France and the Low Countries."

*Church History* 27 (1958): 220–33. Reprinted in Robert M. Kingdon. *Church and Society in Reformation Europe.* London: Variorum, 1985.
- "The Political Thought of Peter Martyr Vermigli." In *Peter Martyr Vermigli,* edited by Joseph C. McLelland, pp. 121–39. Waterloo: Wilfred Laurier University Press, 1980. Reprinted in Robert M. Kingdon. *Church and Society in Reformation Europe.* London: Variorum, 1985.
- *The Political Thought of Peter Martyr Vermigli. Selected Texts and Commentary.* Geneva: Droz, 1980.
- "Reactions to the St Bartholomew's Day Massacre in Geneva and Rome." In *Massacre of St Bartholomew* ... , edited by Alfred Soman, pp. 25–49. The Hague: Martinus Nijhoff, 1975. Reprinted in Robert M. Kingdon. *Church and Society in Reformation Europe.* London: Variorum, 1985.
- "William Allen's Use of Protestant Political Argument." In *From the Renaissance to the Counter-Reformation* ... , edited by Charles H. Carter, pp. 1964–78. New York: Random House, 1965. Reprinted in Robert M. Kingdon. *Church and Society in Reformation Europe.* London: Variorum, 1985.

Kingdon, Robert M., ed. *Transition and Revolution: Problems and Issues of European Renaissance and Reformation History.* Minneapolis: University of Minnesota Press, 1974.

Kirshner, Julius. "'Ars imitatur naturam': A Consilium of Baldus on Naturalization in Florence." *Viator* 5 (1974): 289–311.
- "'Civitas sibi faciat civem': Bartolus of Sassoferrato's Doctrine of the Making of a Citizen." *Speculum* 48 (1973): 694–713.
- "Paolo di Castro on *Lives ex Privilegio*: A Controversy over the Legal Qualifications for Public Office in Early Fifteenth-Century Florence." In *Renaissance Studies* ... , edited by A. Moldo and J. A. Tedeschi, pp. 227–64. De Kalb: Northwestern University Press, 1971.

Kirsch, Guido. *Consilia: Eine Bibliographie der juristischen Konziliensammlungen.* Basle: Helbing & Lichtenhalm, 1970.
- *Enea Silvio Piccolomini und die Jurisprudenz.* Basle: Helbing & Lichtenhalm, 1967.
- *Erasmus und die Jurisprudenz seiner Zeit: Studien zum humanistischen Rechtsdenken.* Basle: Helbing and Lichtenhalm, 1960.
- *Gestalten und Probleme aus Humanismus und Jurisprudenz.* Berlin: De Gruyter, 1969.
- "Humanistic Jurisprudence." *Studies in the Renaissance* 8 (1961): 71–87.

Kittelson, James M. "The Confessional Age: The Late Reformation in Germany." In *Reformation Europe* ... , edited by Steven E. Ozment, pp. 361–81. St Louis: Center for Reformation Research, 1982.

Klaaren, Eugene M. *Religious Origins of Modern Science. Belief in Creation in Seventeenth-Century Thought.* Grand Rapids: Eerdmans, 1977.

Klaasen, Walter. *Anabaptism: Neither Catholic nor Protestant.* Waterloo: Wilfrid Laurier Press, 1973.
- *Michael Gaismair: Revolutionary and Reformer.* Leiden: E. J. Brill, 1970.

Klaasen, Walter, ed. *Profiles of Radical Reformers*. Kitchener: Herald Press, 1982.
Kleffens, E. N. van. *Hispanic Law until the End of the Middle Ages*. Edinburgh: Edinburgh University Press, 1969.
Klein, Herbert S. *Slavery in the Americas*. Chicago: University of Chicago Press, 1967.
Klein, Jurgen. *Radicales Denken in England: Neuzeit: Studien zur Geistes und Sozialgeschichte*. Frankfurt am Main: Lang, 1984.
Kliger, S. *The Goths in England, a Study in Seventeenth and Eighteenth Century Thought*. Cambridge, MA: Harvard University Press, 1952.
Klotzner, Josef. *Kardinal Dominikus Jacobazzi und sein Konzilswerk: Ein Beitrage zur Geschichte der konziliaren Idee*. Rome: Gregorian University Press, 1948.
Knight, W. S. M. *The Life and Writings of Hugo Grotius*. London: Sweet & Maxwell, 1925.
Knowler, William, ed. *The Earl of Stratford's Letters and Dispatches*. London, 1739.
Knowles, David. *The Evolution of Medieval Thought*. Baltimore: Helicon Press, 1962.
Knowles, David, and Dmitri Obolensky. *The Christian Centuries*. Vol. 3, *The Middle Ages*. New York: McGraw Hill, 1968.
Knox, John. "The Appellation from the Sentence Pronounced by the Bishops and Clergy." In John Knox. *The Works of John Knox*, edited by David Laing, vol. 4, pp. 460–520. Edinburgh: Wodrow Society Publications, 1846–48.
– "Certain Questions Concerning Obedience to Lawful Magistrates." In John Knox. *The Works of John Knox*, edited by David Laing, vol. 3, pp. 217–226. Edinburgh: Wodrow Society Publications, 1896–48.
– *A Faithfull Admonition made unto ... England*. Kalykou [= Zurich?], 1554.
– "The First Blast of the Trumpet Against the Monstrous Regiment of Women." In John Knox. *The Works of John Knox*, edited by David Laing, vol. 4, pp. 349–420. Edinburgh, Wodrow Society Publications, 1846–48.
– *The History of the Reformation in Scotland*. Edited by William Croft Dickinson. 2 vols. London: Thomas Nelson & Sons, 1949.
– "A Letter Addressed to the Community of Scotland." In John Knox. *The Works of John Knox*, edited by David Laing, vol. 4, pp. 521–38. Edinburgh: Wodrow Society Publications, 1846–48.
– *The Works of John Knox*. Edited by David Laing. 6 vols. Edinburgh: Wodrow Society Publications, 1846–48.
Kochler, G. *Juan de Mariana als politisher danker. Ein Beitrag zum spanischen Anti-Absolutismus in sechzehnten Jahrhundert*. Leipzig: Haag-Drugulin, 1938.
Koenigsberger, Helmut G. "*Dominium Regale* or *Dominium Politicum et Regale*: Monarchies and Parliaments in Early Modern Europe." *Theory and Society* 5 (1978): 191–217.
– *Estates and Revolution: Essays in Early Modern European History*. Ithaca: Cornell University Press, 1971.
– "The Italian Parliaments from their Origins to the End of the Eighteenth

Century." *Journal of Italian History* 1 (1978): 18–49. Reprint in Helmut G. Koenigsberger. *Politicians and Virtuosi* ... , pp. 27–61. London: Hambledon, 1986.
- "The Organization of Revolutionary Parties in France and the Netherlands during the Sixteenth Century." *Journal of Modern History* 27 (1955): 335–51.
- *Politicians and Virtuosi: Essays in Early Modern History*. London: Hambledon, 1986.
- "The Powers of Deputies in Sixteenth-Century Assemblies." In *Album Helen Maud Cam* ... , vol. 2, pp. 211–43.
- "Why did the States General of the Netherlands become Revolutionary in the Sixteenth Century." In Helmut G. Koenisberger. *Politicians and Virtuosi* ... , pp. 63–76. London: Hambledon, 1986.

Koenigsburger, Helmut G., ed. *Republiken und Republikanismus im Europa der frühen Neuzeit*. Munich: R. Oldenbourg, 1988.

Kogel, Renée. *Pierre Charron*. Geneva: Droz, 1972.

Köhler, Walther. *Zurcher Ehegericht und Genfer Konsistorium*. 2 vols. Leipzig: M. Heinsius Nachfolger, 1932–42.

Kolmel, Wilhelm. "Das Naturrecht bei Wilhelm Ockham." *Franziskanische Studien* 35 (1953): 39–85.
- *Wilhelm Ockham und seine kirchenpolitischen Schriften*. Essen: Hubert Wingen, 1942.

Kontos, Alkis. "Success and Knowledge in Machiavelli." In *The Political Calculus* ... , edited by Anthony J. Parel, pp. 83–100. Toronto: University of Toronto Press, 1972.

Korolec, J. B. "La philosophie de la liberté de Jean Buridan." *Studia Medievistyczne* 15 (1974): 109–52.

Koschaker, Paul. *Europa und das romische Recht*. Munich and Berlin: C.H. Beck, 1953.

Kossman, E. H. "The Development of Dutch Political Theory in the Seventeenth Century." In *Britain and the Netherlands*, edited by J. S. Bromley and E. H. Kossman, vol. 1, pp. 91–110. London: Chatto and Windus, 1962.

Kossman, E. H., and A. F. Mellink, eds. *Texts Concerning the Revolt of The Netherlands*. Cambridge: Cambridge University Press, 1974.

Kostler, R. "Consuetudo legitime praescripta. Ein Beitrag zur Lehre vom Geivohnheitsrecht und vom Privileg." *Zeitschrift der Savigny Stiftung für Rechtsgeschichte* 39. Kan. Abt. 8 (1918): 154–94.

Krahn, Cornelius. *Dutch Anabaptism: Origin, Spread, Life, and Thought, 1450–1600*. 2d ed. Scottdale: Herald Press, 1964.
- "Menno Simon's Concept of the Church." In *A Legacy of Faith* ... , edited by C. J. Dyck, pp. 17–30. Newton: Faith and Life Press, 1962.

Kramer, Werner, "Die ekklesiologische Auseinandersetzung um die wahre repraesentation auf dem Basler Konzil." In *Der Begriff der Repraesentatio* ... , edited by Albert Zimmerman, pp. 202–37. Berlin: De Gruyter, 1971.

- *Konsens und Rezeption: Verfassungsprincipien der Kirche im Basler Konziliarismus.* Münster: Aschendorff, 1980.
Krause, O. W. *Naturrechtler des sechzehnten Jahrhunderts: ihre bedeutung für die Entwicklungelnes naturlichen Privatrechts.* Frankfurt: Lang, 1982.
Kreider, Robert. "The Anabaptists and the Civil Authorities of Strasbourg, 1525–1555." *Church History* 24 (1955): 91–118.
Kreitzer, Donald J. "Problems of the Origin of Political Authority." *Philosophical Studies* (Maynooth) 10 (1960): 190–203.
Kretzmann, Normand, Anthony Kenny, and Jan Pitborn, eds. *The Cambridge History of Later Medieval Philosophy: From the Rediscovery of Aristotle to the Disintegration of Scholasticism: 1100–1600.* Cambridge: Cambridge University Press, 1982.
Kristeller, Paul. *Renaissance Thought.* 2 vols. New York: Harper and Row, 1961, 1965.
- "The Scholastic Background of Marsilio Ficino." *Traditio* 2 (1944): 257–318.
- *Studies in Renaissance Thought and Letters.* Rome: Edizioni distoria e letteratura, 1956.
- "Studies on Renaissance Humanism during the Last Twenty Years." *Studies in the Renaissance* 9 (1962): 7–30.
- "The European Diffusion of Italian Humanism." *Italica* 39 (1962): 1–20.
- *Renaissance Thought: The Classic, Scholastic and Humanistic Strains.* Rev. ed. New York: Harper, 1961.
- *Renaissance Thought II: Papers on Humanism and the Arts.* New York: Harper and Row, 1965.
Kroon, Marijn de. *Studien zu Martin Bucers Obrigkeitsverstandnis: Evangelisches Ethos und politisches Engagement.* Gütersloh: Mohn, 1984.
Kubolic, J. "Jean de Raguse: Son importance pour l'ecclésiologie du XV$^e$ siècle." *Revue des sciences religieuses* 41 (1967): 150–67.
Kuehn, Thomas. Review of Joseph P. Canning. *The Political Thought of Baldus de Ubaldis.* Cambridge: Cambridge University Press, 1987. In *Renaissance Quarterly* 41 (1988): 470–73.
Kuenning, Paul P. "Luther and Müntzer: Contrasting Theologies in regard to Secular Authority within the Context of the German Peasant Uprising." *Journal of Church and State* 29 (1987): 305–21.
Kunkel, Wolfgang. *An Introduction to Roman Legal and Constitutional Law.* Translated by J. M. Kelley. 2d ed. Oxford: Clarendon Press, 1973.
Kurz, H. *Volkssouveranität und Staatssouveranität.* Darmstadt: Wissenschaftliche Buchgesellschaft, 1970.
- *Volkssouveranität und Volksrepräsentation.* Cologne: Graz, 1963.
Kuttner, Stephan. "Cardinals: The History of a Canonical Concept." *Traditio* 3 (1945): 129–214.
- "Some Considerations on the Role of Secular Law and Institutions in the History of Canon Law." In *Scritti di sociologiae politico in honore di Luigi Sturzo.* Bologna: N. Zanichelli, 1953–54.

- "Urban II and the Doctrine of Interpretation: A Turning Point?" *Studia Gratiana* 15 (1972): 53–85.
Kyer, C. I. "The Legation of Cardinal Latinus and William Duranti's 'Speculum legatorum.'" *Bulletin of Medieval Canon Law* 10 (1980): 56–62.
Kyle, Richard G. "The Church-State Patterns in the Thought of John Knox." *Journal of Church and State* 30 (1988): 71–87.
La Brosse, Olivier de. *Le Pape et le concile. La comparaison de leurs pouvoirs à la veille de la Réforme.* Paris: Éditions du Cerf, 1965.
La Capra, Dominick. "Rethinking Intellectual History and Reading Texts." *History and Theory* 17 (1978): 245–76.
- *Rethinking Intellectual History: Texts, Contexts, Language.* Ithaca: Cornell University Press, 1983.
La Capra, Dominick, and Steven L. Kaplan, eds. *Modern European Intellectual History.* Ithaca: Cornell University Press, 1982.
Lachance, Louis. *L'Humanisme politique de Saint Thomas d'Aquin. Individu et état.* Montreal: Institut d'études médiévales, 1965.
Ladner, Gerhart B. "Aspects of Medieval Thought on Church and State." *Review of Politics* 9 (1947): 403–22.
- *The Idea of Reform: Its Impact on Christian Thought and Action in the Age of the Fathers.* Cambridge, MA: Harvard University Press, 1959.
Ladner, Pascal. "Johannes von Segovias Stellung zur Präsidentenfrage des Basler Konzils." *Zeitschrift für Schweizerische Kirchengeschichte* 62 (1968): 1–113.
Lagarde, Georges de. *La Naissance de l'esprit laïque au déclin du moyen âge.* 6 vols. 2d ed. Paris: Presses universitaires de France, 1948–56.
- *Recherches sur l'esprit politique de la réforme.* Paris: A. Picard, 1926.
- "Les Théories représentatives du XIV$^e$-XV$^e$ siècles et l'Église." In *Studies Presented to the International Committee for the Study of Representative and Parliamentary Institutions.* Vol. 18, pp. 63–76. Louvain: Nauwalaerts, 1958.
Lambarde, William. *Archeion or, a Discourse upon the High Courts of Justice in England.* Edited by Charles H. McIlwain and Paul L. Ward. Cambridge, MA: Harvard University Press, 1957.
Lambert, Gustave. *Histoire des guerres de religion en Provence 1530–1598.* 2 vols. Toulon, 1870. Reprint. Nyons: Chantemerle, 1972.
Lambert, Malcolm. *Franciscan Poverty: The Doctrine of the Absolute Poverty of Christ and the Apostles in the Franciscan Order, 1210–1323.* London: Society for the Promotion of Christian Knowledge, 1961.
- *Medieval Heresy: Popular Movements from Bogomil to Hus.* New York: Holmes and Meier, 1977.
Lamirande, E. *Church, State and Toleration. An Intriguing Change of Mind in Saint Augustine.* Villanova: Augustinian Institute, Villanova University, 1974.
Landeen, William M. "Gabriel Biel and the Brethren of the Common Life in Germany." *Church History* 20 (1951): 23–36.
Langmuir, Gavin I. *"Per commune consilium regni* in Magna Carta." *Studia Gratiana* 15 (1972): 465–85.

La Noue, François de. *Discours politique et militaire.* Edited by F. E. Sutcliffe. Geneva: Droz, 1967.
La Perrière, Guillaume de. *The Mirror of Policy.* London, 1598.
Larner, John. *Culture and Society in Italy, 1290–1420.* London: Batsford, 1971.
— *The Lords of Romagna; Romagnol Society and the Origins of The Signorie.* London: Macmillan, 1965.
Las Casas, Bartolomé de. *Apologia.* Translated by Angelo Losada. Madrid: Real Academia de la Historia, 1975.
— *In Defence of the Indians.* Translated and edited by Stafford Poole. De Kalb: Northeastern University Press, 1974.
— "De regia potestate o dereche de autodeterminacion." Edited by L. Perena, J. M. Perez-Prendas, V. Abril, and J. Azcarraga. Madrid: Consejo Superior de Investigaciónes Científicas, 1969.
— *A Selection of His Writings.* Translated and edited by George Sanderlin. New York: Alfred A. Knopf, 1971.
— *A Short Account of the Destruction of the Indies.* Edited and translated by Nigel Griffin. Harmondsworth: Penguin Books, 1992.
— "'Los Tesoros del Peru' y 'La Apologia contra Sepúlveda,' obras ineditas de Fr. Bartolomé de las Casas." *Boletin de la Real Academia de la Historia* 132 [1953] 269–333.
Laski, Harold J. "Political Theory in the Later Middle Ages." In *The Cambridge Medieval History* ... , edited by M. W. Gwatkin et al., vol. 8, ch. 20. Cambridge: Cambridge University Press, 1936–49.
Laski, Harold J., ed. *A Defence of Liberty against Tyrants: a Translation of the Vindiciae contra tyrannos by Junius Brutus.* London: G. Bell and Sons, 1924.
Laslett, Peter, ed. *John Locke's Treatises on Civil Government.* 2d ed. Cambridge: Cambridge University Press, 1967.
Laslett, Peter, and W. G. Runciman, eds. *Philosophy, Politics and Society.* Series 3. Oxford: Basil Blackwell, 1967.
Laslett, Peter, W. G. Runciman, and Quentin Skinner, eds. *Philosophy, Politics and Society.* Series 4. Oxford: Oxford University Press, 1972.
Latimer, Hugh. *The Works of Hugh Latimer.* Edited by G. E. Corrie. Cambridge: Cambridge University Press, 1844.
Latini, Brunetto. *Li Livres dou Trésor.* Edited by Francis J. Carmody. Berkeley: University of California Press, 1948.
Laugel, Auguste. *Henry de Rohan: son Rôle Politique et Militaire sous Louis XIII, 1579–1638.* Paris: Firmin-Didot, 1889.
Laures, John. *The Political Economy of Juan de Mariana.* New York: Fordham University Press, 1928.
Lawson, F. H. *The Roman Law Reader.* Dobbs Ferry: Oceana Publications, 1969.
Lawson, George. *An Examination of the Political Part of Mr Hobbs his Leviathan.* London, 1657.
— *Politica sacra et civilis.* 2d ed. London, 1689.

Lebovics, Herman. "The Uses of America in Locke's *Second Treatise of Government*." *Journal of the History of Ideas* 47 (1986): 567–81.
Lebreton, J., and J. Zeiller. *History of the Primitive Church*. Translated by Ernest C. Messenger. Vol. 2. London: Burns Oates & Washbourne, 1942–48.
Le Bras, Gabriel. *Institutions ecclésiastiques de la chrétienté médiévale*. Paris: J. Vrin, 1959–64.
Le Bras, Gabriel. *L'Âge classique: source et théorie du droit, 1140–1378*. Paris: Sirey, 1965.
Lecler, J. *Le Pape ou le concile? Une interrogation de l'église médiévale*. Lyon: Le Chalet, 1973.
– *Toleration and the Reformation*. Translated by T. L. Westow. 2 vols. London: Longmans, 1960.
Leclercq, Jean. "L'Idée de la Royauté du Christ pendant le grand schisme et la crise conciliare." *Archives d'histoire doctrinale et littéraire du Moyen Âge* 17 (1949): 249–65.
Lefebvre, C. "L'Enseignement de Nicolas de Tudeschis et l'autorité pontificale." *Ephemerides Iuris Canonici* 14 (1958): 312–39.
Leff, Gordon. "The Apostolic Ideal in Later Medieval Ecclesiology." *Journal of Theological Studies*, n.s. 18 (1967): 58–82.
– *The Dissolution of the Medieval Outlook: An Essay on the Intellectual and Spiritual Changes in the Fourteenth Century*. New York: Harper & Row, 1976.
– "The Fourteenth Century and the Decline of Scholasticism." *Past and Present* 9 (1956): 30–39.
– *Heresy in the Later Middle Ages: The Relation of Heterodoxy to Dissent 1250-c.1450*. 2 vols. Manchester: Manchester University Press, 1967.
Lehane, Brendan. *The Quest of Three Abbots*. New York: Viking Press, 1968.
Lehmberg, Stanford E. "English Humanists, the Reformation and the Problem of Counsel." *Archiv für Reformationgeschichte* 52 (1961): 74–60.
– "Introduction." In Sir Thomas Elyot. *The Book Named the Governor*, edited by S. E. Lehmberg. London: Dent, 1962.
– *The Reformation Parliament, 1529–1536*. Cambridge: Cambridge University Press, 1970.
– *Sir Thomas Elyot, Tudor Humanist*. Austin: University of Texas Press, 1960.
Lejeune, J. "De Godefroid de Fontaines à la paix de Fexhe (1316)" *Annuaire d'Histoire Liègeoise* 6 (1958–62): 1215–61.
Lemaire, André. *Les lois fondamentales de la monarchie française*. Paris: A. Fontemoing, 1907.
Lenfant, R. *Histoire du concile de Constance*. Rev. ed. 2 vols. Amsterdam, 1727.
Lentze, Hans, and Inge Gampl, eds. *Speculum iuris et ecclesiarum. Festschrift für Willibald M. Plochl zum 60 Geburtstag*. Vienna: Herder, 1967.
Le Patourel, John. "The King and the Princes in Fourteenth-Century France." In *Europe in the Late Middle Ages*, edited by J. R. Hale et al., pp. 155–83. Evanston: Northeastern University Press, 1965.

Lerner, Robert E. *The Age of Adversity. The Fourteenth Century.* Ithaca: Cornell University Press, 1968.
- *The Heresy of the Free Spirit in the Later Middle Ages.* Berkeley, Los Angeles, and London: University of California Press, 1972.
Lessius, Leonardus. *De iustitia et iure.* Antwerp, 1612.
Lever, Thomas. *Sermons, 1550.* Edited by Edward Arber. London, 1870.
Levi, A. H. T., ed. *Humanism in France at the End of the Middle Ages and in the Early Renaissance.* Manchester: Manchester University Press, 1970.
Lévi-Strauss, Claude. *The Elementary Structures of Kinship.* Translated by J. H. Bell and J. R. Von Sturmer. Edited by R. Needham. Boston: Beacon Press, 1969.
- *Structural Anthropology.* Translated by C. Jacobson and B. Schoepf. Garden City: Doubleday, 1963.
Levy, Ernst. "Reflections on the First Reception of Roman Law in Germanic States." *Gesammelte Schriften* 1 (1963): 201–09.
- "Vulgarization of Roman Law in the Early Middle Ages." *Gesemmalte Schriften* 1 (1963): 220–47.
- *West Roman Vulgar Law.* Philadelphia: University of Pennsylvania Press, 1951.
Levy, Fritz J. *Tudor Historical Thought.* San Marino: Huntingdon Library, 1967.
Levy, J.-Philippe. *Le Droit Romain en Anjou, Bretagne, Poitou: (d'après les coutumiers).* Milan: Guiffrè, 1976.
Lewis, Ewart. "King above Law? 'Quod Principi Placuit' in Bracton." *Speculum* 39 (1964): 240–69.
- "Natural Law and Expediency in Medieval Political Theory." *Ethics* 50 (1939–40): 144–63.
- "The 'Positivism' of Marsiglio of Padua." *Speculum* 38 (1963): 541–82.
Lewis, John D., and Oscar Jaszi. *Against the Tyrant.* Glencoe: Free Press, 1957.
Lewis, P. S. "The Failure of the French Medieval Estates." In *The Recovery of France ...* , edited by P. S. Lewis and translated by G. F. Martin, pp. 294–311. New York: Harper and Row, 1972.
- *Later Medieval France: The Polity.* London: Macmillan, 1968.
Lewis, P. S., ed. *The Recovery of France in the Fifteenth Century.* Translated by G. F. Martin. New York: Harper and Row, 1972.
Lewis, R. W. B. *The American Adam. The Drama of Innocence and Novelty in the Nineteenth Century.* Chicago: University of Chicago Press, 1955.
Lewy, Guenter. *Constitutionalism and Statecraft during the Golden Age of Spain: A Study of the Political Philosophy of Juan de Mariana, S.J.* Geneva: Droz, 1960.
- *Religion and Revolution.* New York: Oxford University Press, 1974.
Leyser, K. L. "The Polemics of the Papal Revolution." In *Trends in Medieval Political Thought,* edited by Beryl Smalley, pp. 42–64. Oxford: Oxford University Press, 1965.
l'Hôpital, Michel de. "Harangue de Michel l'Hôpital, chancelier de France, à l'assemblée d'états généraux à Ste. Germaine-en-Laye (January, 1562)." In

Michel de l'Hôpital. *Oeuvres complètes* ... , edited by P. J. S. Dufey, vol. 1, pp. 441–58. Paris: A. Boulland, 1824–25.
- "Harangue du chancelier l'Hôpital au commencement du Parlement (12 November, 1561)." In Michel de l'Hôpital. *Oeuvres complètes* ... , edited by P. J. S. Dufey, vol. 2, pp. 9–19. Paris: A. Boulland, 1824–25.
- "Harangue du chancelier l'Hôpital au commencement du Parlement (12 November, 1563)." In Michel de l'Hôpital. *Oeuvres complètes* ... , edited by P. J. S. Dufey, vol. 2, pp. 85–97. Paris: A. Boulland, 1824–25.
- "Harangue faite au commencement de la siège d'états généraux à Orléans (13 December, 1560)." In Michel de l'Hôpital. *Oeuvres complètes* ... , edited by P. J. S. Dufey, vol. 1, pp. 375–411. Paris: A. Boulland, 1824–25.
- "Harangue faite au Parlement de Paris sur les Édicts concernant la religion (28 June, 1561)." In Michel de l'Hôpital. *Oeuvres complètes* ... , edited by P. J. S. Dufey, vol. 1, pp. 418–34. Paris: A. Boulland, 1824–25.
- *Oeuvres complètes de Michel L'Hospital.* Edited by P. J. S. Dufey. 3 vols. Paris: A. Boulland, 1824–25.
Lilburne, John. *The Charters of London or the Second Part of London's Liberty in Chains Discovered.* London, 1646.
Limentani, U. "Dante's Political Thought." In *The Mind of Dante*, edited by U. Limentani, pp. 113–37. Cambridge: Cambridge University Press, 1965.
Limentani, U., ed. *The Mind of Dante.* Cambridge: Cambridge University Press, 1965.
Linder, Robert D. *The Political Ideas of Pierre Viret.* Geneva: Droz, 1964.
Lipsius, Justus. *De constantia libri duo qui alloquium praecipue continentur in publicis malis.* Oxford, 1663.
- *Politicorum, sive Civilis Doctrinae libri sex.* Leiden, 1589.
- *Six Books of Politiks or Civil Doctrine.* Translated by William Jones. London, 1594. Amsterdam: Theatrum Orbis Terrarum, 1970.
- *Two Books of Constancie.* Translated by John Stradling. Edited by Rudolf Kirk. New Brunswick, NJ: Rutgers University Press, 1939.
Littell, F. H. *The Anabaptist View of the Church.* Boston: Beacon Press, 1952. Rev. as *The Origins of Sectarian Protestantism.* New York: Macmillan, 1965.
Little, David. *Religion, Order and Law. A Study in Pre-Revolutionary England.* Oxford: Basil Blackwell, 1970.
Little, Lester K. "The Size and Governance of Medieval Communities." *Studia Gratiana* 15 (1972): 377–97.
Lloyd, Howell A. "The Political Thought of Charles Loyseau (1564–1627)." *European Studies Review* 11 (1981): 53–82.
- *The State, France and the Sixteenth Century.* London: George Allen & Unwin, 1983.
Loades, D. M. *The Oxford Martyrs.* London: Batsford, 1970.
Locher, Gottfried W. *Zwingli's Thought: New Perspectives.* Leiden: E. J. Brill, 1981.
- *Die zwinglische Reformation im Rahmen der europäischen Kirchengeschichte.* Gottingen: Vandenhoeck & Ruprecht, 1979.

Locke, John. *Essays on the Law of Nature*. Edited and translated by W. von Leyden. Oxford: Clarendon Press, 1958.
- *Two Treatises of Government*. Edited by Peter Laslett. 2d ed. Cambridge: Cambridge University Press, 1967.
- *Two Treatises of Government*. Edited by Richard Ashcraft. London: George Allen & Unwin, 1987.
Lockyer, Andrew. "'Traditions' as Context in the History of Political Thought." *Political Studies* 27 (1979): 201–17.
Lohff, Wenzel, and Lewis W. Spitz, eds. *Widerspruch, Dialog und Einigung. Studien zur Konkordienformel der Lutherischen Reformation*. Stuttgart: Calwer Verlag, 1977.
London School of Economics. *Government and Opposition*. London: Weidenfeld and Nicolson, 1965.
Long, A. A., ed. *Problems in Stoicism*. London: Athlone Press, 1971.
Loomis, Louise R., trans. *The Council of Constance; The Unification of the Church*. Edited by John H. Mundy and Kennerly M. Woody. New York: Columbia University Press, 1961.
Lopez, Robert S. *The Commercial Revolution of the Middle Ages: 950–1350*. Englewood Cliffs: Prentice Hall, 1971.
Lopez, Robert S., and Raymond, Irving W., eds. *Medieval Trade in the Mediterranean World: Illustrative Documents with Introductions and Notes*. New York: Columbia University Press, 1955.
Lortz, Joseph. *The Reformation in Germany*. Translated by Ronald Walls. 2 vols. London: Darton, Longman & Todd, 1968.
Losada, Angelo. "The Controversy between Sepúlveda and Las Casas in the Junta of Valladolid." In *Bartolomé de las Casas in History ...* , edited by Juan Friede and Benjamin Keen, pp. 279–306. De Kalb: Northern Illinois University Press, 1971.
- *Fray Bartolomé de Las Casas*. Madrid: Editorial Tecnos, 1970.
- *Juan Gines de Sepúlveda a travers de su Epistolario y neuvos documentos*. Madrid: Consejo Superior de Investigaciónes Científicas, 1949.
- "Los Tesoros de Peru," y "La Apologia contra Sepúlveda," obras ineditas de Fr. Bartolomé de las Casas." *Boletin de la Réal Academia de la Hiztoria* 132 (1953): 269–333.
Lossky, Vladimir. *The Mystical Theology of the Eastern Church*. London: J. Clarke, 1957.
Lousse, Émile. *La Société de l'ancien régime: Organisation et représentation corporatives*. Vol. 1. Louvain: Bibliothèque de l'Université, 1943.
Lovejoy, Arthur, and George Boas, eds. *Primitivism and Related Ideas in Antiquity*. Baltimore: Johns Hopkins University Press, 1935.
Lowers, James K. *Mirrors for Rebels: A Study of Polemical Literature Relating to the Northern Rebellion, 1569*. Berkeley and Los Angeles: University of California Press, 1953.
Lubac, Henri de. *Corpus Mysticum: L'Euchariste et l'Église au Moyen Âge*. 2d ed. Paris: Aubier, 1944.

Lubasz, Heinz, ed. *The Development of the Modern State.* New York: Macmillan, 1964.
Luciani, V. *Francesco Guicciardini and His European Reputation.* New York: Vanni, 1936.
Lucrezi, F. *Leges super principem: la 'monarchia constituzionale' di Vespasiano.* Naples: E. Jovene, 1982.
Lunt, William E. *Financial Relations of the Papacy with England, 1327–1534.* Cambridge, MA: Harvard University Press, 1962.
Luscombe, D. E. "The State of Nature and the Origin of the State." In *The Cambridge History of Later Medieval Philosophy* ... , edited by Norman Kretzmann et al., pp. 757–70. Cambridge: Cambridge University Press, 1982.
Luther, Martin. "Admonition to Peace." Translated by Charles M. Jacobs. In *Luther's Works,* edited by Helmut Lehmann and Jaroslav Pelikan, vol. 46, pp. 3–43. Philadelphia: Fortress Press, 1955–65.
– "Against the Robbing and Murdering Hordes of Peasants." Translated by Charles M. Jacobs. In *Luther's Works,* edited by Helmut Lehmann and Jaroslav Pelikan, vol. 46, pp. 45–55. Philadelphia: Fortress Press, 1955–65.
– "Appellatio F. Martini Luther ad Concilium." In Martin Luther. *D. Martin Luthers Werke* ... , vol. 7, pp. 75–82. Weimar: Böhlau, 1883–97.
– "The Bondage of the Will." Translated by Philip S. Watson and Benjamin Drewery." In *Luther's Works,* edited by Helmut Lehmann and Jaroslav Pelikan, vol. 33, pp. 3–295. Philadelphia: Fortress Press, 1955–65.
– *Colloquia, Meditationes, Consolationes* ... Edited by H. E. Bindweil. 3 vols. Halle: Lemgovia & Detmoldia, 1863–66.
"Concerning the Answer of the Goat in Leipzig." Edited by Eric W. Gritsch. In *Luther's Works,* edited by Helmut Lehmann and Jaroslav Pelikan, vol. 39, pp. 117–35. Philadelphia: Fortress Press, 1955–65.
– *D. Martin Luthers Werke Kritische Gesamtausgabe.* Weimar: Böhlau, 1883–97.
– "Dr Martin Luther's Warning to his Dear German People." Translated by Martin H. Bertram. In *Luther's Works,* edited by Helmut Lehmann and Jaroslav Pelikan, vol. 47, pp. 11–55. Philadelphia: Fortress Press, 1955–65.
– "The Freedom of a Christian." Translated by W. A. Lambert. In *Luther's Works,* edited by Helmut Lehmann and Jaroslav Pelikan, vol. 31, pp. 327–77. Philadelphia: Fortress Press, 1955–65.
– "The Judgment of Martin Luther on Monastic Vows." Translated by James Atkinson. In *Luther's Works,* edited by Helmut Lehmann and Jaroslav Pelikan, vol. 44, pp. 243–400. Philadelphia: Fortress Press, 1955–65.
– "Letter ... in Opposition to the Fanatic Spirit." Translated by Conrad Bergendorff. In *Luther's Works,* edited by Helmut Lehmann and Jaroslav Pelikan, vol. 40, pp. 61–71. Philadelphia: Fortress Press, 1955–65.
– "Letters." Translated and edited by Gottfried G. Krodel. In *Luther's Works,* edited by Helmut Lehmann and Jaroslav Pelikan, vols. 48–50. Philadelphia: Fortress Press, 1955–65.
– "Luther: On Secular Authority: how far does the Obedience owed it extend?"

Translated by Harro Hopfl. In *Luther and Calvin ...* , edited by Harro Hopfl, pp. 3–43. Cambridge: Cambridge University Press, 1991.
- *Luther's Works*. Edited by Helmut Lehmann and Jaroslav Pelikan. 53 vols. Philadelphia: Fortress Press, 1955–65.
- "Ninety-Five Theses." Translated by Charles M. Jacobs. In *Luther's Works*, edited by Helmut Lehmann and Jaroslav Pelikan, vol. 31, pp. 17–33. Philadelphia: Fortress Press, 1955–65.
- "On the Councils and the Church." Translated by Charles M. Jacobs. In *Luther's Works*, edited by Helmut Lehmann and Jaroslav Pelikan, vol. 41, pp. 3–178. Philadelphia: Fortress Press, 1955–65.
- "Preface to the Complete Edition of a German Theology." Translated by Harold J. Grimm. In *Luther's Works*, edited by Helmut Lehmann and Jaroslav Pelikan, vol. 31, pp. 71–76. Philadelphia: Fortress Press, 1955–65.
- "Preface to the Complete Edition of Luther's Latin Writings." Translated by Lewis W Spitz. In *Luther's Works*, edited by Helmut Lehmann and Jaroslav Pelikan, vol. 34, pp. 323–38. Philadelphia: Fortress Press, 1960.
- "A Sincere Admonition ... to All Christians to Guard against Insurrection and Rebellion." Translated by W. A. Lambert. In *Luther's Works*, edited by Helmut Lehmann and Jaroslav Pelikan, vol. 45, pp. 51–74. Philadelphia: Fortress Press, 1955–65.
- "Table Talk." Translated by Theodore G. Tappert. In *Luther's Works*, edited by Helmut Lehmann and Jaroslav Pelikan, vol. 54, pp. 171–200. Philadelphia: Fortress Press, 1955–65.
- "Temporal Authority: to what Extent it Should be Obeyed." Translated by J. J. Schindel. [1523.] In *Luther's Works*, edited by Helmut Lehmann and Jaroslav Pelikan, vol. 45, pp. 75–129. Philadelphia: Fortress Press, 1955–65.
- "To the Christian Nobility of the German Nation." Translated by Charles M. Jacobs. In *Luther's Works*, edited by Helmut Lehmann and Jaroslav Pelikan, vol. 44, pp. 115–217. Philadelphia: Fortress Press, 1955–65.
- "Two Kinds of Righteousness." Translated by Lowell J. Satre. In *Luther's Works*, edited by Helmut Lehmann and Jaroslav Pelikan, vol. 31, pp. 293–306: Philadelphia: Fortress Press, 1955–65.
- "Whether Soldiers, Too, Can be Saved." Translated by Charles M. Jacobs. In *Luther's Works*, edited by Helmut Lehmann and Jaroslav Pelikan, vol. 46, pp. 87–137. Philadelphia: Fortress Press, 1955–65.

Lytle, G. F., ed. *Reform and Authority in the Medieval and Reformation Church.* Washington: Catholic University of America Press, 1981.

MacCormack, John R. *Revolutionary Politics in the Long Parliament.* Cambridge, MA: Harvard University Press, 1973.

Macdonald, Margaret. *The Language of Political Theory.* Oxford: Oxford University Press, 1955.

MacFarlane, Alan. *The Origins of English Individualism.* Oxford: Basil Blackwell, 1978.

Machiavelli, Niccolo. *The Chief Works and Others.* Translated and edited by Alan Gilbert. 2 vols. Durham: Duke University Press, 1965.
- *The Discourses.* Translated by Leslie J. Walker and edited by Bernard Crick. Baltimore: Penguin, 1970.
- "The History of Florence." In Machiavelli, *The Chief Works* ... , translated and edited by Alan Gilbert, vol. 2, pp. 566–726. Durham: Duke University Press, 1965.
- *The Letters of Machiavelli: A Selection of His Letters.* Translated and edited by Alan Gilbert. New York: Capricorn Books, 1961.
- *The Prince.* Translated by George Bull. Baltimore: Penguin, 1961.
- *Machiavelli nel Ve centenario della nascita.* Bologna: Massimiliano boni editore, 1973.

MacIver, R. M., ed. *Conflict of Loyalties.* New York: Harper and Brothers, 1952.

Mack, Phyllis, and Margaret C. Jacob, eds. *Politics and Culture in Early Modern Europe. Essays in Honor of H. E. Koenigsberger.* Cambridge: Cambridge University Press, 1987.

Mackinnon, James. *Luther and The Reformation.* 4 vols. London: Longmans, Green, 1925–30.

Maclean, A. H. "George Lawson and John Locke." *Cambridge Historical Journal* 9 (1947): 68–77.

MacNeill, Duncan H. *George Buchanan on the Powers of the Crown in Scotland.* Glasgow: Glasgow University Press, 1964.

Macpherson, Crawford B. "Capitalism and the Changing Concept of Property." In *Feudalism, Capitalism and Beyond,* edited by Eugene Kamenka and R. S. Neale, pp. 104–25. New York: St Martin's Press, 1975.
- *Democratic Theory: Essays in Retrieval.* Oxford: Oxford University Press, 1973.
- "The Maximization of Democracy." In Laslett and Runciman *Philosophy, Politics and Society\,* edited by Peter Laslett and W. G. Runciman, series 3, pp. 83–103. Oxford: Basil Blackwell, 1967.

Mahoney, Edward P., ed. *Philosophy and Humanism. Renaissance Essays in Honor of Paul Oskar Kristeller.* New York: Columbia University Press, 1976.

Maitland, Frederick William. *Roman Canon Law in the Church of England: Six Essays.* London: Methuen, 1898.

Maitland, W. *The Constitutional History of England.* Cambridge: Cambridge University Press, 1920.

Major, James Russell. "The Assembly at Paris in the Summer of 1575." *Studia Gratiana* 15 (1972): 699–715. In James Russell Major. *The Monarchy, the Estates and the Aristocracy* ... London: Variorum, 1988.
- "The French Monarchy as seen through the Estates General." *Studies in the Renaissance* 9 (1962): 113–25.
- "French Representative Assemblies: Research Opportunities and Research Published." In *Studies in Medieval and Renaissance History,* edited by William M. Bowsky, pp. 183–219. Lincoln: University of Nebraska Press, 1964.

- *The Monarchy, the Estates and the Aristocracy in Renaissance France.* London: Variorum, 1988.
- "The Renaissance Monarchy: A Contribution to the Periodization of History." *Emory University Quarterly* 13 (1957): 112–24. In James Russell Major. *The Monarchy, the Estates and the Aristocracy* ... London: Variorum, 1988.
- "The Renaissance Monarchy as Seen by Erasmus, More, Seyssel and Machiavelli." In *Action and Interpretation*, edited by Christopher Hookway and Philip Pettit, pp. 17–31. Cambridge: Cambridge University Press, 1978. Also in James Russell Major. *The Monarchy, the Estates and the Aristocracy* ... London: Variorum, 1988.
- *Representative Institutions in Renaissance France, 1421–1599.* Madison: University of Wisconsin Press, 1960.

Major, John. "De auctoritate concilii supra pontificem maximum." In Jean Gerson. *Opera omnia*, edited by Louis du Pin, vol. 2, pp. 1131–45. Antwerp, 1706.
- "De potestate papae in temporalibus." In Jean Gerson. *Opera omnia*, edited by Louis du Pin, vol. 2, pp. 1145–64. Antwerp, 1706.
- "De statu et potestate ecclesiae." In Jean Gerson. *Opera omnia*, edited by Louis du Pin, vol. 2, pp. 1121–30. Antwerp, 1706.
- "A Disputation on the Authority of a Council." Translated by J. K. Cameron. In *Advocates of Reform* ... , edited by M. Spinka, pp. 175–84. London: Student Christian Movement Press, 1953.
- *Expositiones Lucentis in Quattuor Evangelia.* Paris, 1529.
- *A History of Greater Britain, as well England as Scotland.* Translated and edited by Archibald Constable. Edinburgh: Edinburgh University Press, 1892.
- *In Mattheum ad literam expositio.* Paris, 1518.
- *In quartum Sententiarum questiones utillissimae.* Paris, 1519.

Major, John M. *Sir Thomas Elyot and Renaissance Humanism.* Lincoln: University of Nebraska Press, 1964.

Malament, Barbara, ed. *After the Reformation. Essays in Honor of J. H. Hayter.* London: University of Pennsylvania Press, 1980.

Mallett, Michael. *Mercenaries and their Masters.* London: Bodley Head, 1974.

Manetti, Giannozzo. "On the Dignity of Man." In *Two Views of Man*, edited by Bernard Murchland, pp. 61–103. New York: F. Unger, 1966.

Manschrech, Clyde L. *Melanchthon, the Quiet Reformer.* New York: Abingdon Press, 1958.
- "The Role of Melanchthon in the Adiaphora Controversy." *Archiv für Reformationgeschichte* 48 (1957): 165–82.

Mansfield, Harvey C., Jr. *Machiavelli's New Modes and Orders: A Study of the "Discourses on Livy."* Ithaca: Cornell University Press, 1978.
- *The Spirit of Liberalism.* Cambridge, MA: Harvard University Press, 1978.

Mansi, G. D., ed. *Sacrorum conciliorum nova et amplissima collectio.* 31 vols. Florence, 1759–98. Reprint. Graz: Akademische Druckmund Verlaganstalt, 1961.

Maravall, Jose Antonio. *Carlo V y el pensamiento politico del Renacimiento.* Madrid: Instituto de Estudios Politicos, 1960.
- *Las Comunidades de Castilla. Una primera revolucion moderna.* Madrid: Revista de occidente, 1968.
- *La philosophie politique espagnole au XVII<sup>e</sup> siècle dans ses rapports avec l'esprit de la Contre-Réforme.* Translated by Louis Cazes and Pierre Mesnard. Paris: J. Vrin, 1955.
- *Le teoria espanola de Estado en el siglo XVII.* Madrid: Instituto de Estudios Politicos, 1944.
Marcolungo, Ferdinando L., ed. *Scienza e filosofia in Dilthey/Giuseppi Zamboni.* Padua: Antenore, 1975.
Marcos, T. Andres. *Los imperialismos de Juan Gines Sepúlveda en su Democrates alter.* Madrid: Instituto de Estudios Politicos, 1947.
Marcus, de Grandval. *De optima politica tam ecclesiastica quam civili.* Paris, 1512.
Margolin, Jean Claude. "La civilité puérile selon Érasme et Mathurin Cordier." In Margolin, *Ragione e "Civilitas,"* edited by Jean Claude Margolin et al., pp. 19–45. Milan: Franco Angeli, 1986.
Margolin, Jean Claude, et al., eds. *Ragione e "Civilitas."* Milan: Franco Angeli, 1986.
Margull, H. J., ed. *The Councils of the Church; History and Analysis.* Philadelphia: Fortress Press, 1966.
Margull, H. J., ed. *Die Okumenischer Konzile de Christenheit.* Stuttgart: W. Kohlhammer, 1961.
Mariana, Juan de. *De rege et regis institutione libri III.* Toledo, 1599.
- *The King and the Education of the King.* Translated by George Albert Moore. Washington: Catholic University of America Press, 1948.
- *Tractatus VII.* Cologne, 1609.
Markus, R. A. *Saeculum: History and Society in the Theology of St Augustine.* Cambridge: Cambridge University Press, 1970.
Markus, R. A., ed. *Augustine: A Collection of Critical Essays.* New York: Anchor Books, 1972.
Marnix, Philippe de. "Letter to William of Orange (March, 1580)." In *Archives.* Ed. Prinsterer. Series 1, vol. 7, pp. 276–86.
Marongiu, A. "The Theory of Democracy and Consent in the Fourteenth Century." In *Lordship and Community ...* , edited by F. Cheyette, pp. 404–21. New York: Holt, Rinehart and Winston, 1968.
Marrone, John. "The Absolute and Ordained Powers of the Pope: An Unedited Text of Henry of Ghent." *Mediaeval Studies* 36 (1974): 23–27.
Marshall, William. "Preface." In Marsiglio of Padua. *The Defence of Peace*, translated by William Marshall. London, 1525.
Marsiglio of Padua. *The Defence of Peace.* Translated by William Marshall. London, 1525. Cf. Gewirth, Alan.
Martène, E., and V. Durand, eds. *Thesaurus novus anecdotorum.* 5 vols. Paris, 1717.

– *Veterum scriptorum et monumentorum historicum, dogmaticorum, moralium amplissima collectio*. 9 vols. Paris, 1724–33.
Martin, Kingsley. *French Liberal Thought in the Eighteenth Century*. London and New York: Harper and Row, 1962.
Martin, Victor. "Comment s'est formée la doctrine de la supériorité du concile sur le pape." *Revue des sciences religieuses* 17 (1937): 121–42; 261–89; 405–27.
– *Les Origines du Gallicisme*. 2 vols. Paris: Bloud & Gay, 1935.
Martines, Lauro. *Lawyers and Statecraft in Renaissance Florence*. Princeton: Princeton University Press, 1988.
– *The Social World of the Florentine Humanists, 1390–1460*. Princeton: Princeton University Press, 1963.
Martyr, Peter. *Most learned and fruitful Commentaries ... upon the Epistles of St Paul to the Romans*. Translated by H. B. London, 1568.
– *A Commentary upon the Book of Judges*. London, 1564.
Marvel, Andrew. *The Rehearsal Transposed*. Edited by D. I. B. Smith. Oxford: Oxford University Press, 1971.
Mason, R. "Kingship, Tyranny and the Right to Resist in Fifteenth Century Scotland." *Scottish Historical Review* 66 (1987): 125–51.
– "Rex Stoicus, George Buchanan, James VI and the Scottish Policy." In *New Perspectives ...* , edited by J. Dwyer et al., pp. 9–33. Edinburgh: John Donald, 1982.
Massaut, Jean-Pierre. *Jesse Clichtoves: l'humanisme et la réforme du clergé*. 2 vols. Paris: Belles Lettres, 1968.
Masselin, Jean. *Journal de États généraux de France tenus à Tours en 1484*. Edited by A. Bernier. Paris, 1835.
Masson, Papire. *Responsio ad Maledicta Hotmani*. Paris, 1575.
Masterson, E. "Suárez on the Origin of Civil Authority." *Irish Theological Studies* 16 (1921): 309–30.
Matharel, Antoine. *Ad Franc. Hotmani: Franco-Galliam ... responsio*. Lyons, 1575.
Mathie, William. "Justice and Equity: An Inquiry into the Meaning and Role of Equity in the Hobbesian Account of Justice and Politics." In *Hobbes's "Science of Natural Justice"*, edited by C. Walton and P. J. Johnson, pp. 257–76. Dordrecht: Martinus Nijhoff, 1987.
Matteis, M. C. *La "teologica politica communale" di Remigio de' Girolami*. Bologna: Patron, 1977.
Mattingley, Garrett. "Some Revisions of the Political History of the Renaissance." In *The Renaissance*, edited by Tinsley Helton, pp. 3–25. Madison: University of Wisconsin Press, 1961.
Maurer, Armand. *St Thomas and Historicity*. Milwaukee: Marquette University Press, 1979.
Maxwell, John. *Sacro-Sancta Regum Majestas, or the Sacred and Royall Prerogatives of Christian Kings*. Oxford, 1644.
May, Larry. "Hobbes on Equity and Justice." In *Hobbes' "Science of Natural Justice,"*

edited by C. Walton and P. J. Johnson, pp. 241–52. Dordrecht: Martinus Nijhoff, 1987.
- "Hobbes's Contract Theory." *Journal of the History of Philosophy* 18 (1980): 195–207.

Mayer, Theodor, ed. *Die Weltz zur Zeit des Konstanzer Konzils: Reichman Vortrage in Herbst 1964.* Constance: J. Thorbeke, 1965.

Mayer, Thomas F. "Marco Mantova: A Bronze Age Conciliarist." *Annuarium Historiae Conciliorum* 14 (1984): 385–408.
- "Thomas Starkey, an Unknown Conciliarist at the Court of Henry VIII." *Journal of the History of Ideas* 49 (1988): 207–27.
- *Thomas Starkey and the Commonweal: Humanist Politics and Religion in the Reign of Henry VIII.* Cambridge: Cambridge University Press, 1989.
- "Thomas Starkey's Aristocratic Reform Programme." *History of Political Thought* 7 (1986): 439–61.

Mazzeo, Joseph A. *Renaissance and Revolution: The Remaking of European Thought.* New York: Pantheon Books, 1967.
- *Renaissance and Seventeenth-Century Studies.* New York: Columbia University Press, 1964.

McConica, James Kelsey. *English Humanists and Reformation Politics.* Oxford: Oxford University Press, 1965.
- "Erasmus and the 'Julius': A Humanist Reflects on the Church." In *The Pursuit of Holiness...*, edited by Charles E. Trinkans and Heiko Oberman, pp. 444–71. Leiden: E. J. Brill, 1972.

McCoy, C. N. R. "Note on the Problem of the Origin of Political Authority." *The Thomist* 16 (1953): 71–81.

McDonnell, Kevin. "Does William of Ockham Have a Theory of Natural Law?" *Franciscan Studies* 34 (1974): 383–92.

McDonough, Thomas M. *The Law and the Gospel in Luther.* Oxford: Oxford University Press, 1963.

McFarlane, K. B. *Wycliffe and English Nonconformity.* Harmondsworth: Penguin, 1972.

McGowan, J. P. *Pierre d'Ailly and the Council of Constance.* Washington: Catholic University of America Press, 1936.

McGrade, Arthur S. "The Coherence of Hooker's Polity: The Books on Ecclesiastical Power." *Journal of the History of Ideas* 24 (1963): 163–82.
- "Introduction." In *Richard Hooker...*, edited by Arthur S. McGrade and Brian Vickers. London: Sidgwick and Jackson, 1975.
- "Ockham and the Birth of Individual Rights." In *Authority and Power...*, edited by Brian Tierney and Peter Linehan, pp. 149–65. Cambridge: Cambridge University Press, 1980.
- *The Political Thought of William of Ockham.* Cambridge: Cambridge University Press, 1974.
- "Repentance and Spiritual Power: Book VI of Richard Hooker's *Of the Laws of Ecclesiastical Polity.*" *Journal of Ecclesiastical History* 20 (1978): 163–76.

- "Rights, Natural Rights and the Philosophy of Law." In *The Cambridge History of Later Medieval Philosophy* ... , edited by Norman Kretzmann et al., pp. 738–56. Cambridge: Cambridge University Press, 1982.
- "The State of Nature and the Origin of the State." In *The Cambridge History of Later Medieval Philosophy*, edited by Norman Kretzman et al., pp. 738–56. Cambridge: Cambridge University Press, 1982.

McGrade, Arthur S., and Brian Vickers, eds. *Richard Hooker: Of the Laws of Ecclesiastical Polity: An Abridged Edition.* London: Sidgwick and Jackson, 1975.

McGrath, Alister E. "John Calvin and Late Medieval Thought." *Archiv für Reformationgeschichte* 77 (1986), 58–78.

McIlwain, Charles H. *Constitutionalism, Ancient and Modern.* Ithaca: Cornell University Press, 1940. Rev. ed. Ithaca: Cornell University Press, 1947.

McIlwain, Charles H., ed. *The Political Works of James I.* Cambridge, MA: Harvard University Press, 1918.

McKenzie, Lionel A. "Rousseau's Debate with Machiavelli in the *Social Contract*." *Journal of the History of Ideas* 43 (1982): 209–28.

McKeon, Richard P. "The Development of the Concept of Property in Political Philosophy: A Study of the Background of the Constitution." *Ethics* 48 (1938): 297–366.

- "Philosophy and History in the Development of Human Rights." In *Ethics and Social Justice*, edited by Howard E. Keifer and Milton Kennedy, pp. 300–32. Albany: State University of New York Press, 1970.

McKitterick, Rosamund. "Some Carolingian Lawbooks and Their Function." In *Authority and Power* ... , edited by Brian Tierney and Peter Linehan, pp. 13–28. Cambridge: Cambridge University Press, 1980.

McLelland, Joseph C., ed. *Peter Martyr Vermigli and Italian Reform.* Waterloo: Wilfrid Laurier University Press, 1980.

McMullin, Ernan, ed. *Construction and Constraint: The Shaping of Scientific Rationality.* South Bend: University of Notre Dame Press, 1988.

McMurrin, S., ed. *The Tanner Lectures on Human Values.* Vol. 7. Salt Lake City: University of Utah Press, 1986.

McNeil, David O. *Guillaume Budé and Humanism in the Reign of Francis I.* Geneva: Droz, 1975.

McNeill, John T. "The Democratic Element in Calvin's Thought." *Church History* 18 (1949): 153–71.

- *The History and Character of Calvinism.* New York: Oxford University Press, 1967.
- "Natural Law in the Thought of Luther." *Church History* 10 (1941): 211–27.

Meek, Ronald. *Social Science and the Ignoble Savage.* Cambridge: Cambridge University Press, 1978.

Meijering, E. P. *Calvin wider die Neugierde.* Nieukoop: De Graaf, 1980.

Mejknecht, A. J. "Le Concile de Bâle, aperçu général sur ses sources." *Revue d'Histoire Ecclésiastique* 65 (1970): 465–73.

Meinecke, Friedrich. *Die Idee der Staatsrason in der neuren Geschichte.* Munich: R. Oldenburg, 1924.

Melanchthon, Philipp. "Commentarii in Aliquot Politicos Libros Aristotelis." In Philipp Melanchthon. *Philippi Melancthonis Opera ... omnia,* edited by C. G. Breschneider, vol. 16, pp. 416–50. Halle-Brunswick: C.A. Schwetsche, 1834–60.
- "Commentarii in epistolam Pauli ad Romanos." In Philipp Melanchthon. *Philippi Melancthonis Opera ... omnia,* edited by C. G. Breschneider, vol. 15, pp. 497–796. Halle-Brunswick: C. A. Schwetschke, 1834–60.
- *Melanchthon on Christian Doctrine: Loci communes: 1555.* Translated and edited by Clyde L. Manschreck. New York: Oxford University Press, 1965.
- *Philippi Melanchthonis Opera quae supersunt omnia.* Edited by C. G. Breschneider. 28 vols. Halle-Brunswick: C. A. Schwetschke, 1834–60.
- "Philosophiae moralia epitome." In Philip Melanchthon. *Philippi Melanchthonis Opera ... omnia,* edited by C. G. Breschneider, vol. 16, pp. 20–163. Halle-Brunswick: C. A. Schwetsche, 1834–60.
- "Prolegomena in Officiis Ciceronis." In Philipp Melanchthon. *Philippi Melanchthonis Opera ... omnia,* edited by C. G. Breschneider, vol. 16, pp. 532–680. Halle-Brunswick: C.A. Schwetsche, 1834–60.

*Mélanges Roger Secrétan.* Montreux: University of Lausanne, Faculty of Law, 1964.

Melden, A. I. *Free Action.* London: Routledge & Kegan Paul, 1961.

Mendenhall, George. *Law and Covenant in Israel and the Ancient Near East.* Pittsburgh: Biblical Colloquium, 1955.

Mendle, J. M. *Dangerous Positions: Mixed Government, the Estates of the Realm and the Answer to the XIX Propositions.* Montgomery: Alabama University Press, 1985.

Mercati, Angelo. "La prima relazione del Cardinale Nicolo de Romanis sulla sua legazione in Inghilterra." In *Essays in History Presented to Reginald Law Poole,* edited by H. W. C. Davis, pp. 277–89. Oxford: Clarendon Press, 1927.

Mercier, Charles. "L'esprit de Calvin et la démocratie." *Revue d'Histoire Ecclésiastique de Louvain* 30 (1934): 5–53.
- "Les théories politiques des Calvinistes dans les Pays-Bas à la fin du XVI$^e$ siècle et au début du XVII$^e$ siècle." *Revue d'Histoire Ecclésiastique de Louvain* 29 (1933): 25–73.
- "Les théories politiques des Calvinistes en France au cours des guerres de religion." *Bulletin de la Société d'Histoire de Protestantisme français* 83 (1934): 225–60.

Merkl, Peter H. *Political Continuity and Change.* New York: Harper and Row, 1967.

Merzbacher, Friedrich. "Die ecclesiologische Konzeption des Kardinale Francesco Zabarella (1360–1417)." In *Festschrift Karl Pivec,* edited by Anton Haidacher and Hans E. Mayer, pp. 279–87. Innsbruck: N.P. 1966.
- "Die Kirchen und Staatsgewelt bei Jacques Almain." In *Speculum iuris et ecclesiarum ... ,* edited by Hans Lentze and Inge Gampl, pp. 301–12. Vienna: Herder, 1967.

Mesnard, Pierre. *L'essor de la philosophie politique au XVI$^e$ siècle.* 3d ed. Paris: J. Vrin, 1969.
- "François Hotman (1524–1590) et le complexe de Tribonien." *Bulletin de la Société de l'Histoire de Protestantisme français* 101 (1955): 117–37.

Methuen, Eric. *Das Basler Konzil als Forschungen der europäischer Geschichte.* Opladen: Wesdeutscher Verlag, 1985.
- *Nikolai von Kues 1401–1464.* Münster: Aschendorff, 1964.
Mew, P. "Conventions of Thin Ice." *Philosophical Quarterly* 21 (1971): 352–56.
Mezieres, Philippe de. *Le Songe du Vieil Pèlerin.* Edited by G. W. Coopland. Cambridge: Cambridge University Press, 1969.
Michaelis, Gottfried. *Richard Hooker als politische Denker.* Berlin: Verlag dr. Emil Ebering, 1933.
Michaels, Leonard, and Christopher Ricks, eds. *The State of the Language.* Berkeley, Los Angeles, London: University of California Press, 1980.
Michaud, Hélène. *La Grande Chancellerie et les écritures royales au seizième siècle (1505–1589).* Paris: Presses universitaires de France, 1967.
Midgley, Mary. *Beast and Man. The Roots of Human Nature.* Ithaca: Cornell University Press, 1978.
Miethke, Jurgen. *Ockhams Weg zur Sozial philosophie.* Berlin: De Gruyter, 1969.
- "Papste, Ortsbischof und Universität in dem Pariser Theologenprozessen des 13. Jahrhundert." In *Die Auseinandersetzungen an der Pariser Universität,* edited by Albert Zimmermann, pp. 52–94. Berlin: De Gruyter, 1976.
- "Repräsentation und Delegation in den politischer Schriften Wilhelm von Ockham." In *Der Begriff der Repräsentatio ... ,* edited by Albert Zimmermann, pp. 163–85. Berlin: De Gruyter, 1971.
- "Die Rolle der Bettelorden im Umbrugh der politischer Theorie an der Wende zum 14. Jahrhundert." In *Stellung und Wirksamkeit ... ,* edited by Kaspar Elm, pp. 119–53. Berlin: Duncker & Humblot, 1981.
- "Zur Bedeutung der Ekklesiologie für die politische Theorie im späterem Mittelalter. In *Soziale Ordnungen ... ,* edited by Albert Zimmermann, pp. 369–88. Berlin: De Gruyter, 1979–80.
Miethke, Jurgen, ed. *Das Publikum politischer Theorie im 14. Jahrhundert zu den Rezeptionbedlingungen politischer Philosophie im späterem Mittelalter.* Munich: Schriften des Historischen Kollegs, 1992.
Migne, J.-P., ed. *Patrologia cursus completus. Series latina.* 227 vols. Paris: Garnier Fratres, 1879–90.
Miller, David, and Larry Siedentop. *The Nature of Political Theory.* Oxford: Clarendon Press, 1983.
Milsom, S. F. C. *Historical Foundations of the Common Law.* London: Butterworth, 1969.
- *The Legal Framework of English Feudalism.* Cambridge: Cambridge University Press, 1976.
Milton, John. *Complete Prose Works of John Milton.* Edited by Douglas Bush et al. 2 vols. New Haven: Yale University Press, 1959–80.
- "Of Reformation." In John Milton. *Complete Prose Works ... ,* edited by Douglas Bush et al., vol. 1, pp. 517–617. New Haven: Yale University Press, 1959–80.
- "The Tenure of Kings and Magistrates." In John Milton. *Complete Prose*

*Works* ... , edited by Douglas Bush et al., vol. 3, pp. 189–258. New Haven: Yale University Press, 1959–80.

Minio-Paluello, L. "Remigio Girolami's *De Bono Communi:* Florence at the Time of Dante's Banishment and the Philosopher's Answer to the Crisis." *Italian Studies* 2 (1956): 56–71.

Minogue, Kenneth. "Method in Intellectual History: Quentin Skinner's Foundations." *Philosophy* 56 (1981): 533–62. Also in *Meaning and Context* ... , edited by James Tully, pp. 176–93. Princeton: Princeton University Press, 1989.

Mitchell, Rosamund J. *John Tiptoft (1427–1470).* London: Longman's, 1938.

– *The Laurels and the Tiara; Pope Pius II, 1458–1464.* London: Harvill Press, 1962.

Mitteis, Heinrich. *The State in the Middle Ages.* Translated by H. F. Orton. Amsterdam: North Holland Publishing Co., 1975.

Moeller, Bernd. *Imperial Cities and the Reformation.* Translated by H. C. Erik Midelfort and Mark Edwards, Jr. Philadelphia: University of Pennsylvania Press, 1972.

– "Zwinglis Disputationen: Studien zu den Anfangen der Kirchenbildung und des Synodalwesens im Protestantismus." *Zeitschrift der Savigny-Stiftung für Rechtgeschichte, kanonistische Abteilung* 56 (1970) and 60 (1974).

Moldo, A., and J. A. Tedeschi, eds. *Renaissance Studies in Honor of Hans Baron.* De Kalb: Northwestern University Press, 1971.

Molina, Luis de. *De iustitia et iure.* 2 vols. Mainz, 1659.

Molina Melia, Antonio. *Iglesia y estado en el siglo de oro español. El pensiamento de Francisco Suárez.* Valencia: University of Valencia Press, 1977.

Mollat, Guillaume. *Les Papes d'Avignon 1305–1378.* 9th ed. Paris: Letouzey & Ané, 1949.

– *The Popes at Avignon, 1305–1378.* Translated by Janet Love. London: Thomas Nelson & Sons, 1963.

Momigliano, A. *Essays in Ancient and Modern Historiography.* Oxford: Basil Blackwell, 1977.

Mommsen, T., ed. *Digesta.* 21st ed. Zurich: Weidmannes, 1970.

Mommsen, T., P. Kruger, R. Schoell, and E. Knoll, eds. *Corpus iuris civilis.* 12$^{th}$ ed. 3 vols. 1911. Reprint. Berlin: N.p., 1954.

Mommsen, Wolfgang J., ed. *Stadburgertum und Adel in der Reformation / The Nobility and the Reformation.* Stuttgart: Klett-Cotta, 1979.

Monahan, Arthur P. *Consent, Coercion, and Limit. The Medieval Origins of Parliamentary Democracy.* Kingston and Montreal: McGill-Queen's University Press, 1987.

– "The Demise of Natural Law: Real or Imaginary?" *The Vital Nexus* 1, no. 2 (November 1991) 63–73.

Monfasini, John. *George of Trebisond.* Leiden: E. J. Brill, 1976.

Monier, Raymond. *Les Institutions centrales du Comté de Flandres de la fin du neuvième siècle à 1304.* Paris: Domat-Montchrestien, 1949.

Montaigne, Michel de. "Essays." In *The Complete Works of Montaigne*, translated by Donald M. Frame, pp. 1–857. London: Hamish Hamilton, 1957.
- *Essais.* Edited by Alexandre Micha. Paris: Garnier-Flammarion, 1969.
- *The Complete Works of Montaigne.* Translated by Donald M. Frame. London: Hamish Hamilton, 1957.

Monter, E. William. *Calvin's Geneva.* New York: Wiley, 1967.
- *Studies in Genevan Government.* Geneva: Droz, 1964.

*Monumenta Germaniae historica.*
- *Auctorum.* 15 vols. Berlin: Weidmann, 1877–1919.
- *Constitutiones.* 2 vols. Hanover: Hahnian, 1963.
- *Fontes.* Hanover: Hahnian, 1933– .
- *Legum.* 5 vols. New York: Kraus Reprint, 1965.
- *Libelli.* 3 vols. Hanover: Hahnian, 1891–1917.
- *Scriptores.* 30 vols. New York: Kraus Reprint, 1963–64.

Moore, Robert Ian. *The Birth of Popular Heresy.* London: Edward Arnold, 1975.
- *The Formation of a Persecuting Society: Power and Deviance in Western Europe, 950–1250.* Oxford: Basil Blackwell, 1987.
- *The Origins of European Dissent.* London: Edward Arnold, 1977.

Moorman, John. *A History of the Franciscan Order from its Origin to the Year 1517.* Oxford: Oxford University Press, 1968.

More, Thomas. *The Apology of Sir Thomas More*, edited by Arthur I. Taft. Appendix, pp. 201–53. London: Oxford University Press, 1930.
- *The Complete Works of St Thomas More.* Edited by Edward Surtz and J. H. Hexter. New Haven: Yale University Press, 1963– .
- "Utopia." In Thomas More. *The Complete Works* ... , vol. 4. Edited by Edward Surtz and J. H. Hexter. New Haven: Yale University Press, 1963– .
- *The Dialogue Concerning Tyndale.* Edited by W. E. Campbell. London: Eyre & Spottiswoode, 1927.

Moreley, Jean. *Traicté de la discipline et police chrétienne.* Lyon, 1562.

Morgan, Edmund S. *Inventing the People: The Rise of Popular Sovereignty in England and America.* New York: Norton, 1988.

Morino, C. *Church and State in the Teaching of St Ambrose.* Washington: Catholic University of America Press, 1969.

Morison, Richard. *Apomaxis calumniarum.* London, 1537.
- *An Exhortation to styrre all Englyshmen to the Defence of their Countreye.* London, 1539.
- *An Invective ayenste the Great and Detestable Vice, Treason.* Amsterdam: Theatrum Orbis Terrarum, 1972.
- *A Lamentation in which is shewed what Ruine and Destruction cometh of Seditious Rebellion.* London, 1536.
- *A Remedy for Sedition.* London, 1536.

[Mornay, Phillipe du Plessis.] *Vindiciae contra Tyrannos.* Edinburgh [Basle], 1579.

Morrall, John B. *Gerson and the Great Schism.* Manchester: Manchester University Press, 1960.

- "Some Notes on a Recent Interpretation of William of Ockham's Political Philosophy." *Franciscan Studies* 9 (1949): 335–69.
Morrill, John S. *Seventeenth-Century Britain, 1603–1714.* Hamden: Archon Books, 1980.
Morris, Christopher. *Political Thought in England: Tyndale to Hooker.* Oxford: Oxford University Press, 1953.
Morris, Colin. *The Discovery of the Individual 1050–1200.* London: Society for the Promotion of Christian Knowledge, 1972.
Morrisey, Thomas E. "The Decree 'Haec Sancta' and Cardinal Zabarella." *Annuarium Historiae Conciliorum* 10 (1978): 145–76.
Morrison, Karl F. *Tradition and Authority in the Western Church, 300–1140.* Princeton: Princeton University Press, 1969.
Morrow, Glenn R. *Plato's Cretan City.* Princeton: Princeton University Press, 1960.
Mosse, C. "La Conception du citoyen dans la *Politique* d'Aristote." *Eirene* 6 (1967): 16–39.
Mosse, George L. *Calvinism, Authoritarian or Democrat?* New York: Rinehart, 1957.
- *The Holy Pretence: A Study in Christianity and Reason of State from William Perkins to John Winthrop.* Oxford: Basil Blackwell, 1957.
- *The Struggle for Sovereignty in England from the Reign of Queen Elizabeth to the Petition of Right.* East Lansing: University of Michigan Press, 1950.
Mousnier, R. "L'Évolution des Institutions Monarchiques en France et ses Relations avec l'État Social." *Le Dix-Septième Siècle* 58–59 (1963): 57–72.
Mousnier, R., et al. *Le Conseil du roi de Louis XII à la Révolution.* Paris: Presses universitaires de France, 1970.
Moynihan, James M. *Papal Immunity and Liability in the Writings of the Medieval Canonists.* Rome: Gregorian University, 1961.
Mozley, J. F. *William Tyndale.* London: Macmillan, 1937.
Mueller, William Arthur. *Church and State in Luther and Calvin.* Nashville: Broadman Press, 1954.
Mujica, P. *Bibliografía suáreziana.* Granada: Universidad de Granada, Catedra Suárez, 1948.
Mugnier-Pollet, Lucien. *La philosophie politique de Spinoza.* Paris: J. Vrin, 1976.
Muldoon, James. "Boniface VIII's Forty Years of Experience in the Law." *The Jurist* 31 (1971): 449–77.
- "A Canonistic Contribution to the Formation of International Law." *The Jurist* 28 (1968): 265–72.
- "The Contribution of the Medieval Canon Lawyers to the Formation of International Law." *Traditio* 28 (1972): 483–97.
- "'Extra Ecclesiam non est imperium?' The Canonists and the Legitimacy of Secular Power." *Studia Gratiana* 9 (1966): 551–80.
- "John Wyclif and the Rights of the Infidels: The Requerimiento Re-Examined." *The Americas* 36 (1980): 301–16.
- *Popes, Lawyers and Infidels: The Church and the Non-Christian World 1250–1550.* Liverpool: Liverpool University Press, 1979.

- "The Remonstrance of the Irish Princes and the Canon Law Tradition of the Just War." *American Journal of Legal History* 22 (1978): 309–25.
Muldoon, James, ed. *The Expansion of Europe: The First Phase.* Philadelphia: University of Pennsylvania Press, 1977.
Mulgan, R. G. "Aristotle's Sovereign." *Political Studies* 18 (1960): 518–22.
Muller, James A. *Stephen Gardiner and the Tudor Reaction.* New York: Macmillan, 1926.
Mulligan, L., J. Richards, and J. Graham. "Intentions and Conventions: Quentin Skinner's Method for the Study of the History of Ideas." *Political Studies* 27 (1979): 84–98.
Mumford, Lewis. *The City in History: Its Origins, Its Transformations, and Its Prospects.* New York: Harcourt, Brace & World, 1961.
Mundy, John H. *Europe in the High Middle Ages, 1150–1309.* London: Longmans, 1973.
- "In Praise of Italy: The Italian Republics." *Speculum* 64 (1989): 815–34.
Mundy, John H., and K. M. Woody, eds. *The Council of Constance. The Unification of the Church.* Translated by Louise Ropes Loomis. New York: Columbia University Press, 1961.
Muñoz, Honorio. *Vitoria and the Conquest of America.* Manila: Santo Thomas University Press, 1935.
Müntzer, Thomas. "Sermon before the Princes." In *Spiritual and Anabaptist Writers*, edited by George Huntston Williams, pp. 49–70. London: SCM Press, 1957.
Munz, Peter. *Frederick Barbarossa: A Study in Medieval Politics.* London: Eyre & Spottiswoode, 1969.
- *The Place of Hooker in the History of Thought.* London: Routledge & Kegan Paul, 1952.
Muratori, Ludovico, ed. *Rerum Italicarum Scriptores.* 25 vols. Milan: 1723–51.
Murbt, Carl, and Kurt Aland, eds. *Quellen zur Geschichte des Papstums und des Romischen Katholicismus.* 2 vols. Tübingen: N.P., 1967.
Murchland, Bernard, ed. *Two Views of Man.* New York: F. Unger, 1966.
Murdoch, John E. "From Social into Intellectual Factors: An Aspect of the Unitary Character of Late Medieval Learning." In *The Cultural Context of Medieval Learning*, edited by John E. Murdoch and E. D. Scylla, pp. 271–348. Dordrecht: D. Reidel, 1975.
Murdoch, John E., and E. D. Sylla, eds. *The Cultural Context of Medieval Learning.* Dordrecht: D. Reidel, 1975.
Murray, Alexander C. *Germanic Kinship Structure. Studies in Law and Society in Antiquity and the Early Middle Ages.* Toronto: Pontifical Institute of Mediaeval Studies, 1983.
Mussato, Albertino. *L'ecerinide.* Edited by Luigi Padrin. Bologna: Nicola Zanichelli, 1900.
Myers, A. R. *Parliaments and Estates in Europe to 1789.* London: Thames and Hudson, 1975.

Myers, Henry, and Herwig Wolfram. *Medieval Kingship*. Chicago: Nelson-Hall, 1982.
Naef, Henri. *La Conjuration d'Amboise et Génève*. Geneva: A. Kundig, 1923.
Naszalyi, Aemilio. *Doctrina Francisci de Victoria de statu*. Rome: Scuola Salesiana del libro, 1937.
- *El Estado segun Francisco de Vitoria*. Translated by I. G. Menendez-Reigada. Madrid: Ediciónes Cultura Hispánica, 1948.
Neale, J. E. *The Age of Catherine de Medici*. London: Jonathan Cape, 1943.
- *Elizabeth I and her Parliaments, 1559–1581*. London: Jonathan Cape, 1955.
Nederman, Cary J. "Aristotle as Authority: Alternative Aristotelian Sources of Late Medieval Political Theory." *History of European Ideas* 8 (1977): 31–44.
- "Bracton on Kingship Revisited." *History of Political Thought* 5 (1984): 61–77.
- "A Duty to Kill: John of Salisbury's Theory of Tyrannicide." *Review of Politics* 50 (1988): 365–89.
- "Knowledge, Consent and the Critique of Marsilio of Padua's *Defensor Pacis*." *Political Studies* 39 (1991): 19–35.
- "Nature, Sin and the Origins of Society: The Ciceronian Tradition in Medieval Political Thought." *Journal of the History of Ideas* 49 (1988): 3–26.
- "Royal Taxation and the English Church: The Origins of William of Ockham's *An princeps*." *Journal of Ecclesiastical History* 37 (1986): 377–88.
Nedham, Marchabout. *Interest Will Not Lie or a View of England's True Interest*. London, 1659.
Needham, Joseph. *The Grand Titration: Science and Society in East and West*. London: Allen & Unwin, 1969.
Nelson, John S., ed. *What Should Political Theory Be Now?* Albany: State University of New York Press, 1983.
Nenna, Giovanni Battista. *Nennio, or A Treatise of Nobility*. Translated by William Jones. London, 1595.
Neuman, Franz L. "On the Limits of Justifiable Obedience." In *Conflict of Loyalties*, edited by R. M. MacIver. New York: Harper and Brothers, 1952.
[Nevile, Henry.] *The Works of the Famous Nicolas Machiavel*. London, 1675.
New, John F. *Anglican and Puritan: The Basis of Their Opposition, 1558–1640*. London: A. & C. Black, 1964.
Nicholas of Cusa. *De auctoritate presidendi in concilio generali*. Edited by Gerhard Kallen. Heidelberg: F. Meiner, 1935.
- "De Concordantia Catholica." Edited by Gerhard Kallen. In Nicholas of Cusa. *Nicolai Cusani Opera omnia*, vol. 14. Hamburg: F. Meiner, 1963–68.
- *Nicolai Cusani Opera omnia*. 16 vols. Hamburg: F. Meiner, 1963–68.
Nicolas of Clamanges. *La Traité de la Ruine de l'Église de Nicolas de Clamanges et la Traduction française de 1564*. Edited and translated by A. Colville. Paris: E. Droz, 1936.
Nicolas d'Oresme. *The De Moneta of Nicolas Oresme and English Mint Documents*. Translated by Charles Johnson. London: Thomas Nelson, 1956.

- *Nicole Oresme and the Astrologers. A Study of his Livre de divinacions.* Edited and translated by G. W. Coopland. Cambridge: Cambridge University Press, 1952.
- "Quaestio contra divinatores horoscopias de Nicole Oresme." Edited by S. Caroti. *Archives d'Histoire doctrinale et littéraire du Moyen Âge* 43 (1976): 201–310.

Niem, Dietrich von. *Dialog über Union und Reform der Kirche, mit einer zweiten Fassung aus dem Jahre 1415.* Edited by H. Heimpel. Leipzig and Berlin: Teubner, 1933.

Niesel, Wilhelm. *The Theology of Calvin.* Translated by Harold Knight. Philadelphia: Westminster Press, 1956.

Nisbet, Robert A. *Social Change and History. Aspects of the Western Theory of Development.* New York: Oxford University Press, 1969.

Noonan, John T. *The Scholastic Analysis of Usury.* Cambridge, MA: Harvard University Press, 1957.

Nobbes, D. *Theocracy and Toleration: A Study of the Dispute in Dutch Calvinism from 1600 to 1650.* Cambridge: Cambridge University Press, 1938.

Norena, Carlos G. *Juan Luis Vives.* The Hague: Martinus Nijhof, 1970.

Norr, Knut W. *Kirche und Konzil bei N. de Tudeschis.* Cologne: Böhlau, 1964.

Notestein, Wallace, Frances Helen Relf, and Hartley Simpson, eds. *Commons Debates 1621.* 7 vols. New Haven: Yale University Press, 1935.

Novars, David. *The Making of Walton's "Lives".* Ithaca: Cornell University Press, 1958.

Nussbaum, Arthur. *A Concise History of the Law of Nations.* New York: Macmillan, 1954.

Oakley, Francis. "Almain and Major: Conciliar Theory on the Eve of the Reformation." *American Historical Review* 70 (1965): 673–90. Reprinted in Francis Oakley. *Natural Law, Conciliarism and Consent ...* London: Variorum, 1984.
- "Christian Obedience and Authority." In *The Cambridge History of Medieval Political Thought, 1450–1700,* edited by James H. Burns, pp. 159–92. Cambridge: Cambridge University Press, 1991.
- "Christian Theology and the Newtonian Science: The Rise of the Concept of the Laws of Nature." *Church History* 30 (1961) 433–57. Reprinted in Francis Oakley. *Natural Law, Conciliarism and Consent ...* London: Variorum, 1984.
- "Conciliarism at the Fifth Lateran Council?" *Church History* 41 (1972): 452–63. Reprinted in Francis Oakley. *Natural Law, Conciliarism and Consent ...* London: Variorum: 1984.
- *Council over Pope? Towards a Provisional Ecclesiology.* London: Herder and Herder, 1969.
- "Disobedience, Consent, Political Obligation." *History of Political Thought* 9 (1988): 211–21.
- "Figgis, Constance and the Divines of Paris." *American Historical Review* 75

(1969): 368–66. Reprinted in Francis Oakley. *Natural Law, Conciliarism and Consent* ... London: Variorum, 1984.
- "Gerson and d'Ailly: An Admonition." *Speculum* 40 (1965): 74–83. Reprinted in Francis Oakley. *Natural Law, Conciliarism and Consent* ... London: Variorum, 1984.
- "The 'Hidden' and 'Revealed' Wills of James I: More Political Theology." *Studia Gratiana* 15 (1972): 363–75.
- "Jacobean Political Theology: The Absolute and Ordinary Powers of the King." *Journal of the History of Ideas* 29 (1968): 323–46.
- "Legitimation by Consent: The Question of the Medieval Roots." *Viator* 14 (1983): 303–35.
- "Medieval Theories of Natural Law: William of Ockham and the Significance of the Voluntarist Tradition." *Natural Law Forum* 6 (1961): 65–83.
- *Natural Law, Conciliarism and Consent in the Late Middle Ages*. London: Variorum, 1984.
- "Natural Law, the *Corpus Mysticum* and Consent in Conciliar Thought from John of Paris to Matthias Ugonius." *Speculum* 56 (1981): 786–810. Reprinted in Francis Oakley. *Natural Law, Conciliarism and Consent* ... London: Variorum, 1984.
- *Omnipotence, Covenant, & Order: an Excursion in the History of Ideas from Abelard to Leibniz*. Ithaca, NY: Cornell University Press, 1984.
- "On the Road from Constance to 1688: The Political Thought of John Major and George Buchanan." *Journal of British Studies* 1 (1962): 1–31. Reprinted in Francis Oakley. *Natural Law, Conciliarism and Consent* ... London: Variorum, 1984.
- *The Political Thought of Pierre d'Ailly: The Voluntarist Tradition*. New Haven: Yale University Press, 1964.
- "Religious and Ecclesiastical Life on the Eve of the Reformation." In *Reformation Europe* ... , edited by Steven E. Ozment, pp. 5–32. St Louis: Center for Reformation Research, 1982. Reprinted in Francis Oakley. *Natural Law, Conciliarism and Consent* ... London: Variorum, 1984.
- "The Tractatus de Fide et Ecclesia, Romano pontifice et Concilia Generali of Johannes Breviscoxe." *Annuarium Historiae Conciliorum* 10 (1978): 99–130.
- *The Western Church in the Later Middle Ages*. Ithaca and London: Cornell University Press, 1979.

Oakeshott, Michael, ed. *Rationalism in Politics*. London: Methuen, 1962.

Oakley, Thomas P. *English Penitential Discipline and Anglo-Saxon Law in Their Joint Influence*. New York: Columbia University Press, 1923.

Oberman, Heiko. "From Ockham to Luther." *Concilium* 17 (1966): 126–30.
- "'Et tibi dabo claves regni coelorum.' Kirche und Konzil von Augustin bis Luther; Tendenzen und Ergebnisse." *Nederlands Theologisch Tijschrift* 39 (1975): 97–118.
- *The Harvest of Medieval Theology: Gabriel Biel and Late Medieval Nominalism*. Cambridge, MA: Harvard University Press, 1963.

- *Luther: between God and the Devil.* New Haven: Yale University Press, 1989.
- *Masters of the Reformation: The Emergence of a New Intellectual Climate in Europe.* Cambridge: Cambridge University Press, 1981. Translation of Heiko Oberman. *Werden und Wertung* ... Tübingen: Mohr, 1977.
- "The Shape of Late Medieval Thought: The Birthpangs of the Modern Era." In *The Pursuit of Holiness* ... , edited by Charles E. Trinkans and Heiko Oberman, pp. 3–25. Leiden: E. J. Brill, 1972.
- *Werden und Wertung der Reformation. Vom Wegestreit zum Glaubenskampf.* Tübingen: Mohr, 1977.

Oberman, Heiko, ed. *Forerunners of the Reformation: The Shape of Late Medieval Thought.* Translated by Paul L. Nylus. London: Butterworth, 1967.
- *Gregor von Rimini: Werk und Wirkung bis zur Reformation.* Berlin: De Gruyter, 1981.

Oberman, Heiko, and Thomas A. Brady, Jr., eds. *Itinerarium Italicum.* Leiden: E. J. Brill, 1978.

O'Callaghan, James F. *A History of Medieval Spain.* Ithaca: Cornell University Press, 1975.

O'Connell, Marvin R. *Thomas Stapleton and the Counter-Reformation.* New Haven: Yale University Press, 1964.

Oestreich, Gerhard. *Neostoicism and the Early Modern State.* Edited by Brigitta Oestreich and H. G. Koenigsberger. Translated by David McLintock. Cambridge: Cambridge University Press, 1982.

Offer, H. S. "Empire and Papacy: The Last Struggle." *Transactions of the Royal Historical Society,* 5th series, vol. 6 (1956): 21–47.
- "The Three Modes of Natural Law in Ockham: A Revision of the Text." *Franciscan Studies* 37 (1977): 207–18.

Ogle, Arthur. *The Tragedy in the Lollards' Tower.* Oxford: Oxford University Press, 1949.

Okin, Susan Moller. "The Sovereign and his Counsellours: Hobbes's Re-evaluation of Parliament." *Political Theory* 10 (1982): 49–73.

Olivecrona, Karl. "Appropriation in the State of Nature: Locke on the Origin of Property." *Journal of the History of Ideas* 35 (1974): 211–30.
- *Law as Fact.* 2d ed. London: Stevens, 1971.
- "Locke's Theory of Appropriation." *Philosophical Quarterly* 24 (1974) 220–34.

Olivier-Martin, François. *Histoire des droits français des origines à la Révolution.* Paris: Domat Montchrestien, 1948.

O'Malley, John W. *Giles of Viterbo on Church and Reform: A Study in Renaissance Thought.* Leiden: E. J. Brill, 1968.
- "Historical Thought and the Reform Crisis of the Early Sixteenth Century." *Theological Studies* 28 (1967): 531–48.
- "Recent Studies in Church History." *Catholic Historical Review* 55 (1969–70): 394–437.

O'Rahilly, A. "Some Theology about Tyranny." *Irish Theological Quarterly* 15 (1920): 301–20.

- "The Sovereignty of the People." In *Studies*. Dublin: 1921.
Orton, H. F. *The State in the Middle Ages: a Comparative Constitutional History of Feudal Europe*. Amsterdam: North Holland Publishing Co., 1975. A translation of Heinrich Mitteis. *Der Staat des höhen Mittelalters: Grundlinien einer vergleichen Verfassungeschichte des Lehnzeitalters*. 4th ed. Weimar: H. Böhlau Nachfolger, 1953.
Osorio, Hieronymus. *A Discourse of Civill and Christian Nobilitie*. Translated by William Blandie. London, 1576.
- "De regis institutione, et disciplina." In Hieronymus Osorio. *Opera omnia*, vol. 1, pp. 253–562. Rome, 1592.
- *Opera omnia*. 4 vols. Rome, 1592.
Otto of Freising. *The Deeds of Frederick Barbarossa*. Translated and edited by Charles C. Mierow and Richard Emery. New York: Columbia University Press, 1953.
Ourliac, P. "La Sociologie du concile de Bâle." *Revue d'histoire ecclésiastique* 56 (1961): 2–32.
Ouy, G. "Gerson et l'Angleterre à propos d'un texte polémique retrouvé du Chancelier de Paris contre l'Université d'Oxford, 1396." In *Humanism in France ...* , edited by A. H. T. Levi, pp. 43–81. Manchester: Manchester University Press, 1970.
Oyer, John S. *Lutheran Reformers against Anabaptists. Luther, Melanchthon and Melius, and the Anabaptists of Central Europe*. The Hague: Martinus Nijhoff, 1964.
Ozment, Steven E. *The Age of Reform: 1250–1550. An Intellectual and Religious History of Late Medieval and Reformation Europe*. New Haven and London: Yale University Press, 1980.
- *Homo Spiritualis. A Comparative Study of the Anthropology of Johannes Tauler, Jean Gerson and Martin Luther, 1509–16, in the Context of Their Theological Thought*. Leiden: E. J. Brill, 1949.
- "Homo viator: Luther and Late Medieval Theology." In *The Reformation in Medieval Perspective*, edited by Steven E. Ozment, pp. 142–54. Chicago: Quadrangle Books, 1971.
- *Mysticism and Dissent: Religious Ideology and Social Protest in the Sixteenth Century*. New Haven: Yale University Press, 1973.
- "Mysticism, Nominalism and Dissent." In *The Pursuit of Holiness ...* , edited by Charles E. Trinkans and Heiko Oberman, pp. 67–92. Leiden: E. J. Brill, 1972.
- *The Reformation in the Cities: The Appeal of Protestantism to Sixteenth-Century Germany and Switzerland*. New Haven: Yale University Press, 1975.
- "The University and the Church. Patterns of Reform in John Gerson." *Medievalia et Humanistica*, n.s. 1 (1970): 111–26.
Ozment, Steven E., ed. *Reformation Europe: A Guide to Research*. St Louis: Center for Reformation Research, 1982.
- *The Reformation in Medieval Perspective*. Chicago: Quadrangle Books, 1971.

- *Religion and Culture in the Renaissance and Reformation*. Kirksville: Sixteenth Century Journal Publishers, 1989.
Packard, Sidney R. *Twelfth-Century Europe: An Interpretive Essay*. Amherst: University of Massachusetts Press, 1973.
Packull, Werner O. *Mysticism and the Early South German-Austrian Anabaptist Movement, 1521–1531*. Scottdale: Herald Press, 1977.
Pagden, Anthony. "Dispossessing the Barbarian: The Language of Spanish Thomism and the Debate over the Property Rights of the American Indians." In *The Languages of Political Theory* ... , edited by Anthony Pagden, pp. 79–98. Cambridge: Cambridge University Press, 1987.
- *The Fall of Natural Man*. Cambridge: Cambridge University Press, 1982.
- *The Languages of Political Theory in Early Modern Europe*. Cambridge: Cambridge University Press, 1990.
- *Spanish Imperialism and the Political Imagination: Studies in European and Spanish-American Social and Political Theory 1513–1830*. New Haven: Yale University Press, 1990.
Pagden, Anthony, ed. *The Languages of Political Theory in Early Modern Europe*. Cambridge: Cambridge University Press, 1987.
Pagels, Elaine. "The Roots and Origins of Human Rights." In *Human Dignity*, edited by Alice Henkin, pp. 1–8. New York: Aspen Institute for Humanistic Studies, 1979.
Palacios Rubios, Juan Lopez de. *De la Islas del mar Océano*. Edited by Silvio Zavala. Mexico City: Fondo de cultura económica, 1954.
Palmieri, Matteo. *Della vita civile: di optimo cive de Bartolomeo Sacchi detto il Platina*. Edited by Felice Battaglia. Bologna: N. Zanichelli, 1944.
Panella, Emilio. "Del bene commune al bene del commune." *Memorie domenicane*, n.s. 16 (1985): 1–186.
Panofsky, Erwin. *Renaissance and Renascences in Western Art*. Stockholm: Almquist & Wiksell, 1960.
Pantin, W. A. *The English Church in the Fourteenth Century*. Cambridge: Cambridge University Press, 1955.
Paradisi, B. "Il pensiero politico dei giuristi medievale." In *Storia delle idee politiche, economiche e sociali* ... , edited by L. Firpo, vol. 2, pp. 1–160. Turpin: Unione tipografico-editrice torinese, 1973.
Parekh, Bhiklu, and R. N. Berks. "The History of Political Ideas: A Critique of Q. Skinner's Methodology." *Journal of the History of Ideas* 34 (1973): 163–84.
Parel, Anthony J. "Thomistic Natural Law and Historicity." *Vital Nexus* 1.2 (1991) 75 –90.
Parel, Anthony J., ed. *The Political Calculus*. Toronto: University of Toronto Press, 1972.
Parel, Anthony J., and Thomas Flanagan, eds. *Theories of Property: Aristotle to the Present*. Waterloo: Wilfrid Laurier University Press, 1979.
Parker, T. H. L. *John Calvin: A Biography*. Philadelphia: Westminster Press, 1975.

Parker, T. M. *Christianity and the State in the Light of History*. London: Adams and Charles Black, 1955.
- "The Conciliar Movement." In *Trends in Medieval Thought*, edited by Beryl Smalley, pp. 127–39. Oxford: Oxford University Press, 1965.
Parks, George B. *The English Traveller to Italy: The Middle Ages (to 1525)*. Stanford: Stanford University Press, 1954.
Parry, J. H. *The Spanish Theory of Empire in the Sixteenth Century*. Cambridge: Cambridge University Press, 1940.
Partner, Peter. *The Lands of St Peter: The Papal State in the Middle Ages and the Early Renaissance*. London: Eyre, Methuen, 1972.
- *The Papal State under Martin V. The Administration and Government of the Temporal Power in the Early Fifteenth Century*. London: British School at Rome, 1958.
Party, Geraint. *John Locke*. London: Allen & Unwin, 1978.
Paruta, Paolo. "Discorsi Politiche." In Paolo Paruta. *Opere Politiche*, edited by C. Monzani, vol. 2, pp. 1–371. Florence, 1852.
- *Opera Politiche*. Edited by C. Monzani. 2 vols. Florence, 1852.
Pas, P. "La Doctrine de la double justice au Concile de Trente." *Epheremides Theologicae Lovanienses* 30 (1954): 5–53.
Pascoe, L. B. "Gerson and the Donation of Constantine: Growth and Development within the Church." *Viator* 5 (1974): 469–85.
- "Jean Gerson: The Ecclesia primitiva and Reform." *Traditio* 30 (1974): 379–409.
- "Jean Gerson: Mysticism, Conciliarism, and Reform." *Annuarium Historiae Conciliorum* 6 (1974): 135–53.
- *Jean Gerson: Principles of Church Reform*. Leiden: E. J. Brill, 1973.
Pasquier, Etienne. *Écrits politiques*. Edited by Dorothea Thickett. Geneva: Ambilly, 1966.
- "Exhortatio aux princes et seigneurs du conseil privé du roi." In Étienne Pasquier. *Écrits politiques*, edited by Dorothea Thickett, pp. 33–90. Geneva: Ambilly, 1966.
- *Lettres familières*. Edited by Dorothea Thickett. Geneva: Droz, 1974.
- *Pourparlers du prince*. Paris, 1560.
- *Les Recherches de la France*. Paris, 1611.
Passmore, John. "The Idea of a History of Philosophy." *History and Theory* 4 (1965), Supplement 5.
Pateman, Carole. *Participation and Democratic Theory*. Cambridge: Cambridge University Press, 1970.
Pater, Calvin Augustine. *Karlstadt as the Father of the Baptist Movements: The Emergence of Lay Protestantism*. Toronto: University of Toronto Press, 1984.
Patrizi, Francesco. *De institutione reipublicae*. Paris, 1585.
- *De regno et regis institutione*. Paris, 1567.
Patry, Raoul. *Philippe du Plessis-Mornay: un huguenot homme d'état*. Paris: Fischbacher, 1933.

Pelikan, Jaroslav. *Spirit versus Structure: Luther and the Institutions of the Church.* New York: Harper & Row, 1968.
Pennington, Kenneth J., Jr. "Bartolomé de Las Casas and the Tradition of Medieval Law." *Church History* 39 (1970): 149–61.
Pennock, J. Roland and John W. Chapman, eds. *Constitutionalism.* New York: New York University Press, 1986.
- *Human Rights.* Edited by J. Roland Pennock and John W. Chapman. *Nomos,* vol. 23. New York and London: New York University Press, 1981.
Perez, J. *La révolution des Comunidades de Castile.* Bordeaux: Feret, 1970.
Perkins, William. *The Works of that Famous and Worthie Minister of Christ in the University of Cambridge, M. W. Perkins.* 3 vols. Cambridge, 1608–1631.
Perouse, G. *Le cardinal, Louis Aleman, Président du concile de Bâle et la fin du grand schisme.* Paris: A. Picard, 1904.
Perrin, John W. "Azo, Roman Law and Sovereign European States." *Studia Gratiana* 15 (1972): 87–101.
- "Legatus, the Lawyers and the Terminology of Power in Roman Law." *Studia Gratiana* 10 (1967): 461–89.
Persons, Robert. *An Answere to the Fifth Part of Reportes.* Saint Omer, 1606.
Peter Comestor. "Historia Scholastica, in Genesim." In *Patrologia ... Latina,* edited by J.-P. Migne, vol. 198, cols. 1050–1142. Paris: Garnier Fratres, 1879–90.
Peterson, D. S. "Conciliarism, Republicanism and Corporatism: The 1415–1420 Constitution of the Florentine Clergy." *Renaissance Quarterly* 42 (1989): 183–226.
Petrarch, Francesco. *De viris illustribus.* Edited by Guido Martellotti. Florence: G. C. Sansoni, 1964.
- *Rerum memorandum libri.* Edited by Giuseppe Billanovich. Florence: G. C. Sansoni, 1945.
Petry, Ray C. "Unitive Reform Principles of the Late Medieval Conciliarists." *Church History* 31 (1962): 164–81.
Philips, G. "La Justification Luthérienne et le Concile de Trente." *Epheremides Theologiae Lovanienses* 40 (1971): 340–58.
Phillips, Margaret Mann. *The "Adages" of Erasmus: A Study with Translations.* Cambridge: Cambridge University Press, 1964.
- *Erasmus and the Northern Renaissance.* New York: Macmillan, 1949.
Phillips, Mark. *Francesco Guicciardini: The Historian's Craft.* Toronto: University of Toronto Press, 1977.
Philippus de Leyden. *De cura reipublicae et sorte principantis.* Edited by R. Fruin and P. C. Molhuysen. Gravenhage: Martinus Nijhof, 1900. 2d rev. ed. 1971.
Piaia, G. "La fondazione filosofica dell teoria conciliare in Francesco Zabarella." In *Scienza e filosofia ... ,* edited by Ferdinando L. Marcolungo, pp. 431–61. Padua: Antenore, 1975.
- *Marsiglio da Padova nella riforma e nella controriforma: Fortuna ed interpretazione.* Padua: Antenore, 1977.

Pico della Mirandola, Giovanni. *De hominis dignitate.* Edited by Eugenio Garin. Florence: Vallechi, 1942.
- "Oration on the Dignity of Man." Translated by Elizabeth Forbes. In *The Renaissance Philosophy of Man*, edited by Ernst Cassirer et al., pp. 223–54. Chicago: University of Chicago Press, 1948.
Piccolomini, Aeneas Sylvius (Pius II). *Aeneas Silvius in Europam.* Memmingen, 1440.
- *De gestis concilii Basiliensis commentariorum libri II.* Edited and translated by Denys Hay and W. K. Smith. Oxford: Clarendon Press, 1967.
- "De liberorum educatione." In Aeneas Sylvius Piccolomini. *Opera quae extant omnia*, pp. 965–92. Frankfurt, Minerva, 1967.
- "De ortu et auctoritate imperii romani." In Gerhard Kallen. *Aeneas Silvius Piccolomini als Publizist. In de Epistola De Ortu et auctoritate Imperii Romani.* Cologne: Petrarca-Haus, 1939.
- *Memoirs of a Renaissance Pope. The Commentaries of Pius II. An Abridgment.* Translated by Florence A. Gragg. Edited by Leona C. Gabel. London: George Allen & Unwin, 1960.
- *Opera quae extant omnia.* Frankfurt: Minerva, 1967.
Pickthorn, Kenneth. *Early Tudor Government: Henry VIII.* Cambridge: Cambridge University Press, 1934.
Picot, Georges. *Histoire des États généraux considérés au point de vue de leur influence sur le gouvernement de la France de 1355 à 1614.* 4 vols. Paris: Hachette et cie., 1872.
Picotti, Giovanni. "La pubblicazione i primi effeti dell 'Execrabilis' de Pio II." *Archivo della Societa Romana di storia patria* 38 (1914): 33–74.
Pillement, G. *Pedro de Luna, le dernier pape d'Avignon.* Paris: Hachette, 1955.
Pilny, Josepha. *Jerome de Prague; un orateur progressiste du Moyen Âge.* Geneva: Perret-Gentil, 1974.
Pineas, Rainer. "John Bale's Nondramatic Works of Religious Controversy." *Studies in the Renaissance* 9 (1962): 218–33.
- "Robert Barnes' Polemical Use of History." *Bibliothèque d'Humanisme* 26 (1964): 5–69.
- *Thomas More and Tudor Polemics.* Bloomington: Indiana University Press, 1968.
- "William Tyndale's Use of History as a Weapon of Religious Controversy." *Harvard Theological Review* 55 (1962): 122–41.
Pinette, G. L. "Freedom in Huguenot Doctrine." *Archiv für Reformationgeschichte* 50 (1959): 200–34.
Pintacuda, F. de Michelis. "Pour une histoire de l'idée de tolérance du 15$^e$ au 17$^e$ siècle." *Revue d'Histoire et Philosophie Religieuse* 65 (1985): 132–51.
Pirenne, Henri. *Medieval Cities: Their Origins and the Revival of Trade.* Translated by Frank D. Halsey. Princeton: Princeton University Press, 1952.
Pitkin, Hannah. *The Concept of Representation.* Berkeley: University of California Press, 1967.

- "Obligation and Consent." In *Philosophy, Politics and Society*, edited by Peter Laslett, W. G. Runciman, and Quentin Skinner, Series 4, pp. 45–85. Oxford: Oxford University Press, 1972.
Plamenatz, John. *Man and Society.* 2 vols. New York: McGraw-Hill, 1963.
Planitz, H. *Die deutsche Stadt im Mittelalter.* Graz, Cologne: Böhlau-Verlag, 1954.
Plinval, Georges de. "Autour du *De Legibus.*" *Revue des Études Latines* 47 (1969): 294–309.
Plucknett, Theodore F. T. *A Concise History of the Common Law.* 5th ed. London: Butterworth & Co., 1956.
Pocock, J. G. A. *The Ancient Constitution and the Feudal Law.* Cambridge: Cambridge University Press, 1957.
- *The Machiavellian Moment.* Princeton: Princeton University Press, 1975.
- "The Origins of the Study of the Past." *Comparative Studies in Society and History* 4 (1961–62): 226–32.
- "Political Ideas as Political Events. Political Philosophers as Historical Actors." in *Political Theory and Political Education*, edited by Melvin Richter, pp. 139–58. Princeton: Princeton University Press, 1980.
- *Politics, Language, and Time. Essays on Political Thought and History.* New York: Athenaeum, 1971.
Podlech, A. "Repräsentation." *Geschichte Grundbegriffe* 5 (1984): 509–47.
Pole, Reginald. *Defence of the Unity of the Church.* Translated by Joseph G. Dwyer. Westminster: Newman Press, 1965.
- *Pro ecclesiasticae unitatis defensione libri quattuor.* Rome, 1538.
"La politique: dialogue traitant de la puissance, autorité et du devoir des princes." In [Simon Goulart.] *Mémoires de l'état de France sous Charles neufième*, vol. 3, pp. 66a–116b. Middelburg [Geneva], 1578.
Pollet, Vincent-Marie. "La doctrine de Cajetan sur l'Église." *Angelicum* 11 (1935): 223–44.
Pollock, Sir Frederick, and Frederick William Maitland. *The History of English Law before the Time of Edward I.* 2d ed. Cambridge: Cambridge University Press, 1898. Reprint. Cambridge: Cambridge University Press, 1968.
Ponet, John. "A Short Treatise of Political Power." In Winthrop S. Hudson. *John Ponet ...* , pp. 246ff. Chicago: University of Chicago Press, 1942.
Pontano, Giovanni. "De fortuna." In Giovanni Pontano. *Opera omnia*, vol. 1, pp. 497–584. Basle, 1538.
- "De principe." In *Prosatori latini del quattrocento*, edited by Eugenio Garin, pp. 1023–63. Milan: R. Ricciardi, 1952.
- *Opera omnia*, 3 vols. Basle, 1538.
- Poole, Stafford. *In Defence of Indians.* De Kalb: Northern Illinois University Press, 1974.
Popkin, Richard H. *The History of Scepticism from Erasmus to Descartes.* 2d ed. New York: Harper and Row, 1968.

Porter, H. C. *Reformation and Reaction in Tudor Cambridge*. Cambridge: Cambridge University Press, 1968.
Possevino, Antonio. *Judicium ... Joannis Bodini, Philippi Mornaei et Nicolei Machiavelli quibusdam scriptis*. Lyons, 1593.
Post, Gaines. "Bracton on Kingship." *Tulane Law Review* 42 (1968): 519–54.
– "Law and Politics in the Middle Ages: The Medieval State as a Work of Art." In *Perspectives in Medieval History*, edited by Katherine Fischer Drew and Floyd Seyward Lear, pp. 64–67. Chicago: University of Chicago Press, 1963.
– "A Roman Legal Theory of Consent, 'quod omnes tangit,' in Medieval Representation." *Wisconsin Law Review* 31 (1950): 61–90.
– "A Romano-Canonical Maxim, 'quod omnes tangit,' in Bracton and in Early Parliaments." *Traditio* 4 (1946): 197–225. Reprinted in Gaines Post. *Studies ...* , pp. 163–238. Princeton, NJ: Princeton University Press, 1964.
– *Studies in Medieval Legal Thought*. Princeton: Princeton University Press, 1964.
Post, R. R. *The Modern Devotion: Confrontation with Reformation and Humanism*. Leiden: E. J. Brill, 1968.
Postel, Guillaume. *De orbis terrae concordia libri quattuor*. Basle, 1544.
Posthumus Meyjes, G. H. M. *Jean Gerson et l'Assemblée de Vincennes (1324)*. Leiden: E. J. Brill, 1981.
Poujol, Jacques. "Jean Ferrault on the King's Privileges: A Study of the Medieval Sources of Renaissance Political Theory in France." *Studies in the Renaissance* 5 (1958): 15–26.
Pounds, Norman J. G. *An Historical Geography of Europe, 430 B.C.–1330 A.D.* Cambridge: Cambridge University Press, 1973.
Powell, James M., ed. and trans. *The Liber Augustalis or Constitutions of Malfi Promulgated by the Emperor Frederick II for the Kingdom of Sicily in 1231*. Syracuse: Syracuse University Press, 1971.
Powicke, F. M., and C. R. Cheney, eds. *Councils and Synods, with Other Documents relating to the English Church, II, A.D. 1205–1313*. Part I. 1205–1265; Part II 1265–1313. Oxford: Clarendon Press, 1964.
Prentout, Henri. *Les États provinciaux de Normandie*. 3 vols. Caen: E. Lanier, 1925–27.
"Préparatifs ... pour les massacres." In [Simon Goulart.] *Mémoires de l'état de France sous Charles neufième*, 2d ed., vol. 1, pp. 265a–468b. Middelburg [Geneva], 1578.
Prescott, Orville. *Lords of Italy: Portraits from the Middle Ages*. New York: Harper and Row, 1971.
Prestwick, Menna, ed. *International Calvinism*. Oxford: Oxford University Press, 1985.
Preus, James S. *From Shadow to Promise: Old Testament Interpretation from Augustine to the Young Luther*. Cambridge, MA: Harvard University Press, Belknap Press, 1969.

Price, Robert. "William of Ockham and *suppositio personalis.*" *Franciscan Studies* 30 (1970): 131–40.
Price, Russell. "The Senses of Virtù in Machiavelli." *European Studies Review* 3 (1973): 315–45.
Prynne, William. *The Sovereigne Power of Parliaments and Kingdomes.* London, 1643.
Ptolemy of Lucca. *Annales ab anno Salutis MLX ad MCCCI.* Louvain, 1619.
– "De regimine principum." In Thomas Aquinas. *Opuscula omnia,* edited by Jean Perrier, vol. 1, Appendix 1, pp. 269–426. Paris: Lethellieux, 1949.
– *Determinatio compendiosa de iurisdictione imperii, auctore anonymo ut videtur Tholomeo Lucensi O.P.* Edited by Marius Krammer. Hanover, Leipzig: Hanianus, 1909.
– "Historica ecclesiastica." In *Rerum Italicarum Scriptores,* edited by Ludovico Muratori, vol. 11, 741–1242. Milan, 1723–51.
Pufendorff, Samuel von. *De Jure Naturae et Gentium Libri Octo.* Lund, Sweden, 1672.
– *On the Duty of Man and Citizen.* Edited by James Tully. Cambridge: Cambridge University Press, 1991.
– *Of the Laws of Nature and Nations.* Translated by Basil Kennett. London, 1710.
– *On the Law of Nature and Nations.* Edited and translated by C. H. and W. A. Oldfather. Oxford: Clarendon Press, 1934.
Puig Peña, Federico. *La Influencia de Francisco de Vitoria en la Obra de Hugo Grocio. Los principios del derecho internacional a la luz de la España del siglo XVI.* Madrid: Tip. de Archivos, 1934.
Pullan, B. *A History of Early Renaissance Italy.* London: Allen Lane, 1973.
Purcell, Maureen. *Papal Crusading Policy.* Leiden: E. J. Brill, 1975.
Putnam, George H. *The Censorship of the Church of Rome.* 2 vols. New York: B. Blom, 1967.
Quaglioni, Diego. "'Regimen ad populum' e 'regimen regis' in Egidio Romano e Bartolo da Sassoferrato." *Bullettino dell' Istituto Storico Italiano per il Medio Evo* 87 (1978): 201–28.
– "Il 'Tractatus de tyrannia' di Bartolo." *Il pensiero politico* 10 (1977): 268–84.
– *Politica e diritto nel Trecento italiano.* Florence: L. S. Olschki, 1983.
– "Un 'Tractatus de tyranno:' il commento di Baldo degli Ubaldi (1327?–1400) alla rex Decernius, c. De sacrosanctis ecclesiis (C.1, 2, 16)." *Il pensiero politico* 13 (1980): 64–77.
"Question, à savoir s'il est loisible aux sujets de se défendre contre le magistrat pour maintenir la religion vraiment chrétienne." In [Simon Goulart.] *Mémoires de l'état de France sous Charles neufième,* 2d ed., vol. 2, pp. 239a–246a. Middelburg [Geneva], 1578.
Quillet, Jeannine. *Les clefs du pouvoir au moyen âge.* Paris: Flammarion, 1971.
– *La philosophie politique de Marsile de Padoue.* Paris: J. Vrin, 1970.
– *La philosophie politique du 'Songe du Vergier' (1378): Sources doctrinales.* Paris: J. Vrin, 1977.

Quinn, David B., ed. *Essays on the History of the North American Discovery and Exploration.* Arlington: University of Texas Press, 1988.
Quirk, Robert E. "Some Notes on a Controversial Controversy: Juan Gines de Sepúlveda and Natural Servitude." *Hispanic Historical Review* 34 (1954): 357–64.
Raab, Felix. *The English Face of Machiavelli.* London: Routledge & Kegan Paul, 1964.
Rabb, Theodore K. "Coherence, Synthesis, and Quality in History." *Journal of Interdisciplinary History* 12 (1981): 315–32.
Rabil, Albert. *Erasmus and the New Testament: The Mind of a Christian Humanist.* San Antonio: Trinity University Press, 1972.
Radouant, Réné. *Guillaume du Vair: L'homme et l'orateur jusqu'à la fin des troubles de la Ligue (1556–1596).* Paris: Lecène, Oudin, 1908.
Rager, John Clement. *Political Philosophy of Blessed Cardinal Bellarmine.* Washington: Catholic University of America Press, 1926.
Raleigh, (Sir) Walter. "Maxims of State." In Sir Walter Raleigh. *The Works ... ,* vol. 8, pp. 1–34. Oxford: Oxford University Press, 1829.
– *The Works of Sir Walter Raleigh.* 8 vols. Oxford: Oxford University Press, 1829.
Ramos, Demetrio, et al. *Francisco de Vitoria y la Escuela de Salamanca: La Ética en la Conquista de America.* Madrid: Consejo Superior de Investigaciónes Científicas, 1984.
Ranum, Orest. *Paris in the Age of Absolutism.* New York: Wiley, 1968.
Rapp, Francis. *L'Église et la vie religieuse en Occident à la fin du Moyen Âge.* Paris: Presses universitaires de France, 1971.
Rathe, C. Edward. "Innocent Gentillet and the First 'Anti-Machiavel.'" *Bibliothèque d'Humanisme et Renaissance* 27 (1965): 186–225.
Raybaud, L.-P., "La royauté d'après les oeuvres de Mateo Zampari." In *Le Prince dans la France ... ,* edited by C. Bontemps et al., pp. 145–204. Paris: Presses universitaires de France, 1965.
Rebuffi, Pierre. *Commentarius in constitutiones seu ordinantes regius.* 2 vols. Lyons, 1613.
Redondo, A. *Antonio de Guevara (1480?–1545) et l'Espagne de son temps.* Geneva: Droz, 1975.
Reeves, Marjorie. "Marsiglio of Padua and Dante Alighieri." In *Trends in Medieval Political Thought,* edited by Beryl Smalley, pp. 86–104. Oxford: Oxford University Press, 165.
– *The Influence of Prophecy in the Later Middle Ages: A Study in Joachimism.* Oxford: Clarendon Press, 1969.
Reid, W. Stanford. "The Book of Discipline: Church and State in the Scottish Reformation." *Fides et Historia* 18 (1986): 35–44.
– "John Knox's Theology of Political Government." *Sixteenth Century Journal* 19 (1988): 529–40.
Reik, Miriam M. *The Golden Lands of Thomas Hobbes.* Detroit: Wayne State University Press, 1977.

Reinard, W. "Nepotismus: Der Funktionwandel einer papstgeschichtlicher Konstanten." *Zeitschrift für Kirchengeschichte* 89 (1975): 145–85.
Remigio de' Girolami. *De bono pacis.* Edited by Charles T. Davis. *Studi Danteschi* 36 (1959): 123–36.
- "De bono communi" and "De bono pacis." In M. C. Matteis. *La "teologia politica communale" di Remigio de' Girolami,* pp. 1–94. Bologna: Patron, 1977.
- "De bono communi" and "De bono pacis." In Emilio Banella. "Del bene commune al bene del commune." *Memorie domenicane,* n.s. 16 (1985): 1–186 at 123–83.
- "The Common Good." Extracts in L. Minio-Paluello. "Remigius Girolami's *De Bono Communi*: Florence at the Time of Dante's Banishment and the Philosopher's Answer to the Crisis." *Italian Studies* 2 (1956): 56–71.
Renaudet, Augustin. *Le Concile gallican de Pise-Milan. Documents Florentins (1510–1512).* Paris: H. Champion, 1922.
- *Humanisme et Renaissance.* Geneva: E. Droz, 1958.
- "Paris de 1494 à 1517: Église et Université; Réformes religieuses; Culture et critique humaniste." In *Courants religieux et humanisme ... ,* pp. 1–24. Paris: Presses universitaires de France, 1959.
- *Préréforme et humanisme à Paris pendant les premières guerres d'Italie (1494–1517).* 2d ed. Paris: Librairie d'Argences, 1953.
Renouard, Y. *The Avignon Papacy, 1305–1403.* Translated by Denis Bethel. London: Faber & Faber, 1970.
Renwick, A. M. *The Story of the Scottish Reformation.* London: Inter-Varsity Fellowship, 1960.
Reu, M. *The Augsburg Confession: A Collection of Sources with an Historical Introduction.* Chicago: Wartburg Publishing House, 1930.
*Le Reveille-matin des François et de leurs voisins.* Edinburgh [Basle?], 1574.
Reydellet, M. *La Royauté dans la Littérature Latine de Sidione Apollinaire à Isidore de Sevile.* Rome: École française de Rome, 1981.
Reynolds, Beatrice. *Proponents of Limited Monarchy in Sixteenth Century France: Francis Hotman and Jean Bodin.* New York: Columbia University Press, 1931.
Reynolds, E. E. *Saint John Fisher.* London: Burns & Oates, 1955.
Rheinstein, Max, ed. *Max Weber on Law in Economy and Society.* Cambridge, MA: Harvard University Press, 1966.
Ribadeneyra, Pedro. *Religion and the Virtues of the Christian Prince against Machiavelli.* Translated and edited by George Albert Moore. Chevy Chase: Silver Dollar Press, 1949.
Rice, Eugene F. "The Humanist Idea of a Christian Antiquity: Lefèvre d'Étaples and His Circle." *Studies in the Renaissance* 9 (1962): 126–60.
- *The Renaissance Idea of Wisdom.* Cambridge, MA: Harvard University Press, 1958.
Richardson, H. G., and G. O. Sayles. *The Governance of Medieval England.* Edinburgh: Edinburgh University Press, 1963.
- *Law and Legislation from Ethelbert to Magna Carta.* Edinburgh: Edinburgh University Press, 1966.

Richter, Melvin, ed. *Political Theory and Political Education*. Princeton: Princeton University Press, 1980.
Ridley, Jasper. *John Knox*. Oxford: Oxford University Press, 1962.
Ridolfi, R. *The Life of Francesco Guicciardini*. Translated by Cecil Grayson. London: Routledge & Kegan Paul, 1967.
– *The Life of Girolamo Savonarola*. Translated by Cecil Grayson. London: Routledge & Kegan Paul, 1959.
– *The Life of Niccolo Machiavelli*. Translated by Cecil Grayson. London: Routledge & Kegan Paul, 1963.
Riesenberg, Peter. "Civism and Roman Law in Fourteenth-Century Italian Society." *Explorations in Economic History* 7 (1969): 237–54.
– *Inalienability of Sovereignty in Medieval Political Thought*. London: AMS Press, 1956.
Riley, Patrick. "The General Will before Rousseau." *Political Theory* 6 (1978): 485–516.
– *The General Will before Rousseau. The Transformation of the Divine into the Civic*. Princeton: Princeton University Press, 1986.
– *The Political Writings of Leibniz*. Cambridge: Cambridge University Press, 1972.
Rinuccini, Alamanni. "Dialogus de libertate." Edited by Francesco Adorno. In *Atti e Memorie dell'academia Toscana di scienze et lettere La Colombaria*. Vol. 22, pp. 265–303. 1957.
Ritter, Gerhard. "Romantic and Revolutionary Elements in German Theology on the Eve of the Reformation." In *The Reformation in Medieval Perspective*, edited by Steven E. Ozment, pp. 15–49. Chicago: Quadrangle Books, 1971.
Rivera Damas, Arturo. *Pensamiento Político de Hostiensis. Estudio Juridico-historico sobre las Relaciónes entre el Sacerdocio y el Imperio en los escritos de Enrique de Susa*. Zurich: Pas, 1964.
Rivière, Jean. *Le problème de l'Église et de l'État au temps de Philippe le Bel*. Louvain and Paris: E. Champion, 1926.
Roberts, Agnes E. "Pierre d'Ailly and the Council of Constance: A Study in 'Ockhamite' Theory and Practice." *Transactions of the Royal Historical Society* 18 (1935): 123–42.
Roberts, Agnes J., ed. *The Laws of the Kings of England from Edmund to Henry I*. Cambridge: Cambridge University Press, 1925.
Robey, David. "P. P. Vergerio the Elder: Republicanism and Civic Values in the Work of an Early Humanist." *Past and Present* 58 (1973): 3–37.
Roca, C. Alberto. *La doctrina suáreciana en la indepencia de America y otros essayos*. Montevideo: University of Montevideo Press, 1979.
Rocaberti de Perelada, Juan Thomas, ed. *Bibliotheca maxima pontificia*. 21 vols. Rome: I. F. Buagni, 1697–99.
Rodes, Robert E., Jr. *Ecclesiastical Administration in Medieval England: The Saxons to the Reformation*. Notre Dame: University of Notre Dame Press, 1977.
Roger, John C. *The Political Philosophy of Blessed Cardinal Bellarmine*. Washington: Catholic University of America Press, 1926.

Rogge, Joachim. "Zwingli the Statesman." In *Huldruch Zwingli* ... , edited by E. J. Furcha. pp. 44–61. Montreal: Faculty of Religious Studies, McGill University, 1985.
Rohan, Henry de. *De l'Interest des Princes et Estates de la Chrétienté*. Paris, 1638.
– *A Treatise of the Interest of the Princes and States of Christendome*. Translated by Henry Hunt. London, 1640.
Rolandino of Padua. "Patavini Chronica." Edited by Philipp Jaffe. *Monumenta Germaniae historica: Scriptores*, vol. 19, pp. 32–147. New York: Kraus Reprint, 1963–64.
Romeyer, B. "La Théorie Suarezienne d'un état de nature pure." *Archive de Philosophie* 18 (1949): 37–63.
Romier, Lucien. *Catholiques et Huguenots à la cour de Charles IX*. Paris: Perrin et cie., 1924.
– *Les Origines politiques des guerres de religion*. 2 vols. Paris: Perrin et cie., 1913–14.
– *Le royaume de Catherine de Medicis. La France à la veille des guerres de religion*. 2 vols. Paris: Perrin et cie., 1925.
Rommen, Heinrich. *Die Staatslehre des Franz Suarez, S.J.* Berlin: M. Gladbach, 1927.
Romualdo of Salerno. "Annales." Edited by W. Arndt. *Monumenta Germaniae historica: Scriptores*, vol. 19, pp. 398–461. New York: Kraus Reprint, 1963–64.
Ronzy, Pierre. *Un humaniste italianisant. Papire Masson (1544–1611)*. Paris: E. Champion, 1924.
Roover, Raymond de. *Business, Banking, and Economic Thought in Late Medieval and Early Modern Europe*. Edited by Julius Kirschner. Chicago: University of Chicago Press, 1974.
Rorty, Richard. "The Historiography of Philosophy." In *Philosophy in History* ... , edited by Richard Rorty et al., pp. 49–76. Cambridge: Cambridge University Press, 1985.
– *Philosophy and the Mirror of Nature*. Princeton, NJ: Princeton University Press, 1979.
Rorty, Richard, J. B. Schneewind, and Quentin Skinner, eds. *Philosophy in History. Essays on the Historiography of Philosophy*. Cambridge: Cambridge University Press, 1985.
[Rose, Guillaume.] *De iusta reipublicae Christianae in reges impios et haereticos authoritate*. Antwerp, 1592.
Rosenstock-Huessy, Eugen. *Die europäischen Revolutionen*. 3d rev. ed. Stuttgart: W. Kohlhammer, 1960.
– *The Driving Power of Western Civilization: The Christian Revolution of the Middle Ages*. Boston: Beacon Press, 1949.
Rott, Jean-Georges, and Simon Verhaus, eds. *Anabaptistes et dissidents au XVIᵉ siècle*. Baden-Baden: V. Koerner, 1987.
Rousseau, G. S. "The *Discorsi* of Machiavelli: History and Theory." *Cahiers d'histoire mondiale* 9 (1965–66): 143–61.
Rousseau, Jean-Jacques. "On Social Contract or Principles of Political Right."

Edited by Alan Ritter and Julia Conway Bondanella. Translated by Julia Conway Bondanella. In *Rousseau's Political Writings*, pp. 84–189. New York, London: W.W. Norton, 1988.

Rowe, J. G., ed. *Aspects of Late Medieval Government and Society*. Toronto: University of Toronto Press, 1986.

Rowe, J. G. and W. H. Stockdale, eds. *Florilegium Historiale: Essays Presented to Wallace K. Ferguson*. Toronto: University of Toronto Press, 1971.

Royer, J. P. *L'Église et le royaume de France au XIV$^e$ siècle d'après le Songe du Vergier et la jurisprudence du Parlement*. Paris: Librairie générale de droit et de jurisprudence, 1969.

Rubenstein, Nicolai. "The Beginnings of Political Thought in Florence." *Journal of the Warburg and Courtauld Institutes* 5 (1942): 198–227.

– "Florence and the Despots: Some Aspects of Florentine Diplomacy in the Fourteenth Century." *Transactions of the Royal Historical Society* (1952): 21–45.

– "Florentine Constitutionalism and Medici Ascendancy in the Fifteenth Century." In *Florentine Studies* ... , edited by Nicolai Rubenstein, pp. 442–62. London: Faber & Faber, 1968.

– *The Government of Florence under the Medici 1434–1494*. Oxford: Oxford University Press, 1966.

– "The History of the Word *Politicus* in Early Modern Europe." In *Languages of Political Theory* ... , edited by Anthony Pagden, pp. 41–56. Cambridge: Cambridge University Press, 1987.

– "Italian Political Thought 1450–1530." In *The Cambridge History of Medieval Political Thought* ... , edited by James H. Burns, pp. 30–65. Cambridge: Cambridge University Press, 1991.

– "Introduction" to Francesco Guicciardini. *Maxims and Reflections* ... , translated by Mario Domandi. New York: Harper and Row, 1965.

– "Marsilius of Padua and Italian Political Thought of his Time." In *Europe in the Late Middle Ages*, edited by J. R. Hale et al., pp. 44–75. Evanston: Northeastern University Press, 1965.

– "Notes on the word *statu* in Florence before Machiavelli." In *Florilegium Historiale* ... , edited by J. G. Rowe and W. H. Stockdale, pp. 313–26. Toronto: University of Toronto Press, 1971.

– "Politics and Constitution in Florence at the End of the Fifteenth Century." In *Italian Renaissance Studies* ... , edited by E. F. Jacob, pp. 148–83. London: Faber & Faber, 1960.

– "Some Ideas on Municipal Progress and Decline in the Italy of the Communes." In *Fritz Saxl* ... , edited by Donald James Gordon, pp. 148–83. London: T. Nelson, 1957.

Rubenstein, Nicolai, ed. *Florentine Studies. Politics and Society in Renaissance Florence*. London: Faber & Faber, 1968.

Rueger, Sofia. "Gerson, the Conciliar Movement and the Right of Resistance (1642–1644)." *Journal of the History of Ideas* 25 (1964): 467–80.

Rufinus. *Die Summa des Magister Rufinus.* Edited by H. Singer. Paderborn: N.P., 1902.
Ruggiers, Paul G. *Florence in the Age of Dante.* Norman: University of Oklahoma Press, 1964.
Rummer, J. "A Fourteenth-Century Legal Opinion." *Quarterly Journal of the Library of Congress* 25 (1968): 179–93.
Runciman, Sir James Cochran Stevenson. *A History of the Crusades.* 3 vols. Cambridge: Cambridge University Press, 1951–54.
Rupp, E. Gordon. *Luther's Progress to the Diet of Worms, 1521.* London: Wilcox & Follett, 1951.
– *The Righteousness of God: Luther Studies.* London: Hodder and Stoughton, 1953.
– *Studies in the Making of the English Protestant Tradition.* Cambridge: Cambridge University Press, 1949.
Rupp, E. Gordon, and A. N. Marlow, eds. *Luther and Erasmus: Free Will and Salvation.* Philadelphia: Westminster Press, 1969.
Russell, Conrad. *Parliaments and English Politics, 1621–1629.* Oxford: Clarendon Press, 1979.
– "The Theory of Treason in the Trial of Stratford." *English Historical Review* 80 (1965): 30–50.
Russell, Conrad, ed. *The Origins of the English Civil War.* London: Macmillan, 1973.
Russell, Frederick H. *The Just War in the Middle Ages.* Cambridge: Cambridge University Press, 1975.
Russell, Jeffrey Burton. *Dissent and Reform in the Early Middle Ages.* Berkeley: University of California Press, 1965.
Russell, Jeffrey Burton, ed. *Religious Dissent in the Middle Ages.* New York: Wiley, 1971.
Russell, Josiah Cox. *Late Ancient and Medieval Population.* Transactions of the American Philosophical Society. New Series 48 (3), 1958.
Sabine, George H. *A History of Political Theory.* 3d ed. London: George G. Harrop, 1963.
Sabrie, J. B. *De l'humanisme au rationalisme, Pierre Charron (1541–1603), l'homme, l'oeuvre, l'influence.* Paris: F. Alcan, 1913. Reissue. Paris: Slatkine, 1970.
Sacksteder, William. *Hobbes Studies (1879–1979): A Bibliography.* Bowling Green: Philosophy Documentation Centre, 1982.
Sadoleto, Jacopo. "De pueris recti instituendis." in Jacopo Sadoleto. *Sadoleto on Education.* Translated and edited by E. T. Campagnac and K. Forbes. London: Humphrey Milford, 1916.
– *Sadoleto on Education.* Translated and edited by E. T. Campagnac and K. Forbes. London: Humphrey Milford, 1916.
Saenger, Paul. "John of Paris, Principal Author of the *Quaestio de potestate papae (Rex Pacificus).*" *Speculum* 56 (1981): 41–55.

St German, Christopher. *An Answer to a Letter.* London, 1535.
- *A Dialogue in English betwixt a Doctor of Divinity and a Student of the Laws of England.* London, 1530.
- *A Little Treatise Called the New Additions.* London, 1531.
- "A Treatise concerning the Division between the Spirituality and the Temporality." In Thomas More. *The Apology of Sir Thomas More, Knight,* edited by Arthur I. Taft, Appendix, pp. 21–53. London: Oxford University Press, 1930.
St Leger, J. *The "Etiamsi daremus" of Hugo Grotius. A Study in the Origins of International Law.* Rome: Pontificium Athenaeum Internationale "Angelicum," 1962.
*St Thomas Aquinas 1274–1974: Commemorative Studies,* pp. 261–82. Toronto: Pontifical Institute of Medieval Studies, 1974.
Salamonio, Mario. *Patritii romani de principatu libri septem.* Rome, 1544.
Salmon, J. H. M. "An Alternative Theory of Popular Resistance: Buchanan, Rossaeus, and Locke." In J. H. M. Salmon. *Renaissance and Revolt ... ,* pp. 136–54. Cambridge: Cambridge University Press, 1987.
- "Bodin and the Monarchomachs." In J. H. M. Salmon. *Renaissance and Revolt ... ,* pp. 119–35. Cambridge: Cambridge University Press, 1989.
- "Catholic Resistance Theory, Ultramontanism, and the Royalist Response, 1560–1620." In *The Cambridge History of Medieval Political Thought ... ,* edited by James H. Burns, pp. 219–53. Cambridge: Cambridge University Press, 1991.
- *The French Religious Wars in English Political Thought.* Oxford: Clarendon Press, 1959.
- "Gallicanism and Anglicanism in the Age of the Counter-Reformation." In J. H. M. Salmon. *Renaissance and Revolt ... ,* pp. 155–88. Cambridge: Cambridge University Press, 1987.
- "The Paris Sixteen, 1584–1594: The Social Analysis of a Revolutionary Movement." *Journal of Modern History* 44 (1972): 540–76.
- "Protestant Jurists and Theologians in Early Modern France: The Family of Cappel." In *Die Rolle der Juristen ... ,* edited by Roman Schnurr, pp. 357–79. Berlin: Duncker & Humblot, 1986.
- *Renaissance and Revolt: Essays in the Intellectual and Social History of Early Modern France.* Cambridge: Cambridge University Press, 1987.
- *Society in Crisis: France in the Sixteenth Century.* New York: St Martin's Press, 1975.
Salmon, J. H. M., ed. *The French Wars of Religion. How Important Were Religious Factors?* Boston: Heath & Co., 1967.
Salutati, Coluccio. *Epistolario.* Edited by Francesco Novati. 5 vols. Rome: N.P., 1891–1911.
- *Tractatus de tyrannis: kritische Ausgabe mit einer historisch-juristischen Einleitung.* Edited by Francesco Ercole. Berlin: Dr Walter Rothschild, 1914.
- "A Treatise on Tyrants." Translated by Ephraim Emerton. In *Humanism and Tyranny ... ,* edited by Ephraim Emerton, pp. 70–116. Cambridge, MA: Harvard University Press, 1925.

Salzman, Philip C. "Political Organizations among Nomadic Peoples." *Proceedings of the American Philosophical Society* 3 (1967): 115-31.
Sampson, Richard. *Oratio qua docet ... ut obediant.* London, 1534.
Sanderlin, George. *Bartolomé de Las Casas. A Selection of His Writings.* New York: Alfred A. Knopf, 1971.
Sandquist, T. A., and Michael R. Powicke, eds. *Essays in Medieval History for Presentation to Bertie Wilkinson.* Toronto: University of Toronto Press, 1969.
Saunders, Jason Lewis. *Justus Lipsius. The Philosophy of Renaissance Stoicism.* New York: Liberal Arts Press, 1955.
Savonarola, Girolamo. *Compendium totius philosophiae.* Venice, 1542.
- "De politia et regno." In Girolamo Savonarola. *Compendium totius philosophiae*, pp. 576-99. Venice, 1542.
- *Prediche sapra Aggeo.* Edited by Luigi Firpo. Rome: Edizione nationale, 1965.
- "Trattata circa il reggimento e governo dell citta di Firenze." In Girolamo Savonarola. *Prediche sapra Aggeo*, edited by Luigi Firpo, pp. 433-87. Rome: Edizione nationale, 1965.
Sawada, P. A. "Two Anonymous Tudor Treatises on the General Council." *Journal of Ecclesiastical History* 12 (1961): 197-214.
Sawyer, P. H., and I. N. Wood, eds. *Early Medieval Kingship.* Leeds: The Editors, 1977.
Sayles, D. O. *The Functions of the Medieval Parliament of England.* Leiden: E. J. Brill, 1987.
Sayles, George O. *Law and Legislation from Ethelbert to Magna Carta.* Edinburgh: Edinburgh University Press, 1966.
Sayre, R. A. *The Essays of Montaigne: A Critical Exploration.* London: Weidenfeld and Nicolson, 1972.
Scarisbrick, J. J. *Henry VIII.* London: Eyre & Spottiswoode, 1968.
- *The Reformation and the English People.* Oxford: Basil Blackwell, 1984.
Schafer, Carl. *Die Staatslehre des Johannes Gerson.* Beilefeld: Bayer & Hausknecht, 1935.
Schalk, F. "Melanchthon et l'humanisme." In *Courants religieux et humanisme ...* , pp. 73-82. Paris: Presses universitaires de France, 1959.
Schardius, S., ed. *De iurisdictione, auctoritate, et praeeminentia imperiali ac potestate ecclesiastica.* Basle, 1566.
Scheible, Heinz. *Das Widerstandsrecht als Problem der deutschen Protestanten, 1523-1546.* Gütersloh: G. Mohn, 1969.
Schelven, A. A. van. "Beza's De Iure Magistratum in Subditas." *Archiv für Reformationgeschichte* 45 (1954): 62-83.
Schellhase, Kenneth C. *Tacitus in Renaissance Political Thought.* Chicago: University of Chicago Press, 1976.
Schenk, W. *Reginald Pole, Cardinal of England.* London: Longmans, Green, 1950.
Schlatter, R. *Private Property.* London: Allen & Unwin, 1951.
"The Schleitheim Confession of Faith." In *The Protestant Reformation*, edited by Hans J. Hillerbrand, pp. 129-36. London: Macmillan, 1968.

Schlick, Moritz. *Problems of Ethics*. Translated by David Rynin. New York: Prentice-Hall, 1939.
Schmauss, Michael, et al. *Handbuch der Dogmengeschichte*. Freiburg-im-Breisgau: Herder, 1971. *Gesellschaft für Altere Deutsche Geschichteskunde neues Archiv* 33 (1908): 285–343; 34 (1908): 723–56.
Schmicker, Robert ed. *Calviniana: Ideas and Influence of Jean Calvin*. Kirksville: Sixteenth Century Journal Press, 1988.
Schmidt, Heinrich Richard. *Reichsstadte, Reich, und Reformation: Korporative Religionspolitik, 1521/30*. Stuttgart: F. Steiner Verlag, 1986.
Schmitt, J.-C. *Mort d'une hérésie: L'église et les clercs face aux beguines et aux beghards du Rhin supérieur du XIV$^e$ au XV$^e$ siècles*. Paris: Mouton, 1978.
Schmitt, Charles B., ed. *The Cambridge History of Renaissance Philosophy*. Cambridge: Cambridge University Press, 1988.
Schmutz, Richard A. "Medieval Papal Representatives: Legates, Nuncios, and Judges-Delegate." *Studia Gratiana* 15 (1972): 441–63.
Schachenburg, Rudolf. "Community Co-Operation in the New Testament." *Concilium* 7 (1972); 9–19.
Schneider, Hans. *Der Konziliarismus als Problem der neueren katholischen Theologie; Die Geschichte der Ausburg der Konstanzer Dekrete von Febronius bis zur Gegenswart*. Berlin: De Gruyter, 1976.
Schnurr, Roman. *Individualismus und Absolutissimus. Zur politischen Theorie vor Thomas Hobbes*. Berlin: Duncker & Humblot, 1963.
Schnurr, Roman, ed. *Die Rolle der Juristen bei der Entstehung des modernes Staates*. Berlin: Duncker & Humblot, 1986.
– *Staatsräson: Studien zur Geschichte eines politischen Begriffe*. Berlin: Duncken & Humblot, 1975.
Schochet, Gordon Joel, ed. *Life, Liberty and Property. Essays on Locke's Political Ideas*. Belmont: Wadsworth, 1971.
– *Patriarchalism in Political Thought*. Oxford: Basil Blackwell, 1975.
– "Political Thought and Political Action: A Symposium on Quentin Skinner: II. Quentin Skinner's Method." *Political Theory* 2 (1974): 261–96.
Schoenberger, Cynthia Grant. "The Development of the Lutheran Theory of Resistance, 1523–1530." *The Sixteenth Century Journal* 8 (1977): 61–76.
– "Luther on Resistance to Authority." *Journal of the History of Ideas* 40 (1979): 3–20.
Schoenstedt, Friedrich. *Der Tyrannenmord im Spätmittelalter: Studien zur Geschichte des Tyrannengriffes und der Tyrannenmord-theorie insbesondere in Frankreich*. Berlin: Junker und Dunnhaupt, 1938.
Schrey, H. H., ed. *Reich Gottes und Welt. Die Lehre Luthers von den 2 Reichen*. Darmstadt: Wissenschaftliche Buchsellschaft, 1969.
Schroeder, H. J., ed. and trans. *The Disciplinary Decrees of the General Councils*. St Louis: B. Herder, 1937.
Schroeder, H. J, trans. *Canons and Decrees of the Council of Trent*. London: Burns and Oates, 1941.

Schulz, Fritz. "Bracton on Kingship." *English Historical Review* 60 (1945): 136–76.
– *History of Roman Legal Science*. Oxford: Clarendon Press, 1946.
– *Principles of Roman Law*. Oxford: Clarendon Press, 1936.
Schussler, H. *Der Primat der Heiligen Schrift als theologisches und kanonistisches Problem im Spätmittelalter*. Wiesbaden: Steiner, 1977.
Schwaiger, Georg von. "Suprema Potestas; Papstlicher Primat und Autorität der Allgemeinem Konzilien im Spiegel der Geschichte." In *Konzil und Papst* ... , edited by Georg von Schwaiger, pp. 611–78. Paderborn, Munich: Schoningh, 1975.
Schwaiger, Georg von, ed. *Konzil und Papste. Festschrift für H. Tuchle*. Paderborn, Munich: Schoningh, 1975.
Schwartz, Edward, and Johannes Staub, eds. *Acta conciliorum oecumenicorum*. 4 vols. Berlin: Walter de Gruyter, 1927–74.
Scipioni, Luigi I. *Vescovo e populo: L'esercizio dell'autorita nella chiesa primitiva*. Milan: Guiffrè, 1977.
Scott, James Brown, ed. *Francisco de Vitoria and His Law of Nations*. Vol. 1 of *The Spanish Origin of International Law*. 2 vols. Oxford: Clarendon Press, 1934.
Scott, Samuel Parsons, trans. *Las Siete Partidas*. Chicago: Commerce Clearing House, 1931.
Scribner, Robert W. "Civic Unity and the Reformation in Erfurt." *Past and Present* 66 (1975): 29–60. Reprint in *Stadtburgertum und Adel* ... , edited by Wolfgang J. Mommsen. Stuttgart: Klett-Cotta, 1979.
Scribner, Robert W. *Popular Culture and Popular Movements in Reformation Germany*. London: Hambledon, 1987.
Scribner, Robert W., and Gerhard Benecke, eds. and trans. *The German Peasant War of 1525: New Viewpoints*. London: Allen & Unwin, 1979.
*Scritti di sociologiae politico in honore di Luigi Sturzo*. Bologna: N. Zanichelli, 1953–54.
Seaver, Paul. "The English Reformation." In *Reformation Europe* ... , edited by Steven E. Ozment, pp. 271–96. St Louis: Center for Reformation Research, 1982.
Seller, Abednego. *The History of Passive Obedience since the Reformation*. Amsterdam, 1689.
Seneca. "Epistle 90." In *Ad Lucilium Epistolae Morales*. Translated by Richard M. Gummere. Vol. 2. Cambridge, MA: Harvard University Press. 1970.
Sepúlveda, J. Gines de. *Democrates alter*. Edited by A. Losada. Madrid: Consejo Superior de Investigaciónes Científicas, Instituto Francisco de Vitoria, 1951.
– *Tratados politicos de J. Gines de Sepúlveda*. Translated by A. Losada. Madrid: Consejo Superior de Investigaciónes Científicas, Instituto Francisco de Vitoria, 1963.
Sextus Empiricus. *Against the Logicians*. Translated by R. G. Bury. London: W. Heineman, 1935.
Seyssel, Claude de. *Les Luenges du Roy Louis XII de ce nom*. Paris, 1508.

- *La Monarchie de France et deux autres fragments politiques*. Edited by J. Poujol. Paris: Libraire d'Argences, 1961.
- *The Monarchy of France*. Translated by J. H. Hexter. New Haven: Yale University Press, 1981.

Shapiro, Ian. *The Evolution of Rights in Liberal Theory*. Cambridge: Cambridge University Press, 1986.
- "Realism in the Study of the History of Ideas." *History of Political Thought* 3 (1982): 535–78.

Shaw, S. Duncan. "Thomas Livingston, a Conciliarist." *Records of the Scottish Historical Society* 12 (1955): 120–55.

Sheedy, Anna T. *Bartolus on Social Conditions in the Fourteenth Century*. New York: Columbia University Press, 1942.

Sheils, W. J., ed. *Persecution and Toleration*. Oxford: Basil Blackwell, 1984.

Shennan, J. H. *Government and Society in France, 1461–1661*. New York: Barnes & Noble, 1969.
- *The Origins of the Modern European State 1450–1725*. London: Hutchison, 1974.
- *The Parlement of Paris*. London: Eyre & Spottiswoode, 1968.

Shirley, F. J. *Richard Hooker and Contemporary Political Ideas*. London: Society for the Promotion of Christian Knowledge, 1949.

Shoenberger, Cynthia G. *The Confession of Magdeburg and the Lutheran Doctrine of Resistance*. New York: Columbia University Press, 1972.

Sider, Ronald J. *Andreas Bodenstein von Karlstadt: The Development of His Thought*. Leiden: E. J. Brill, 1974.

Sieben, H. J. *Die Konzilsidee der alten Kirche*. Paderborn: Schoningh, 1979.
- *Dei Konzilsidee des lateinischen Mittelalters, 847–1378*. Paderborn: Schoningh, 1984.
- *Traktate und Theorien zum Konzil: Von Beginn des grossen Schismas bis zum Vorabend der Reformation, 1378–1521*. Frankfurt: Knecht, 1983.

Siggins, Ian D. Kingston. *Martin Luther's Doctrine of Christ*. New Haven: Yale University Press, 1970.

Sigmund, Paul E. "Cusanus' *Concordantia*: A Re-interpretation." *Political Studies* 10 (1962): 180–97.
- "The Influence of Marsilius of Padua on XVth Century Conciliarism." *Journal of the History of Ideas* 23 (1962): 392–402.
- *Natural Law in Political Thought*. Cambridge, MA: Winthrop, 1971.
- *Nicholas of Cusa and Medieval Political Thought*. Cambridge, MA: Harvard University Press, 1963.

Sikes, J. G. "John de Pouilli and Peter de la Paix." *English Historical Review* 49 (1934): 219–40.

Simon, Joan. *Education and Society in Tudor England*. Cambridge: Cambridge University Press, 1966.

Simon, Y. R. *The Nature and Function of Authority*. Milwaukee: Bruce, 1940.
- *The Philosophy of Democratic Government*. Chicago: University of Chicago Press, 1951.

Sismondi, J. C. L. S. de. *Histoires des Républiques Italiennes du moyen âge*. 2d ed. 16 vols. Paris, 1826.
Simone, Franco. *The French Renaissance. Medieval Tradition and Italian Influence in Shaping the Renaissance in France*. Translated by H. Gaston Hall. London: Macmillan, 1969.
Simons, Menno. *The Complete Writings of Menno Simons*. Translated by Leonard Verduin. Edited by John Christian Wenger. Scottdale: Herald Press, 1956.
– *Opera omnia theologica or Alle de Godtgeleerde Werke van Menno Symons*. Edited by Hendrick Jansz Herrison. Amsterdam, 1681.
Singleton, Charles S., ed. *Art, Science and History in the Renaissance*. Baltimore: Johns Hopkins University Press, 1967.
Sisson, C. J. *The Judicious Marriage of Mr Hooker and the Birth of the "Laws of Ecclesiastical Polity."* Cambridge: Cambridge University Press, 1940.
Skelton, John. *The Complete Poems*. Edited by Philip Henderson. London: J. M. Dent & Sons, 1931.
Skinner, Quentin. "Conquest and Consent: Thomas Hobbes and the Engagement Controversy." In *The Interregnum* ... , edited by G. E. Aylmer, pp. 79–98. London: Macmillan, 1972.
– "Conventions and the Understanding of Speech Acts." *Philosophical Quarterly* 20 (1970): 118–38.
– "The Empirical Theorists of Political Thought and Action." *Political Theory* 2 (1974): 227–303.
– *The Foundations of Modern Political Thought*. Vol. 1 *The Renaissance*. Vol. 2. *The Age of Reformation*. Cambridge: Cambridge University Press, 1978.
– "Hermeneutics and the Role of History." *New Literary History* 7 (1975): 209–32.
– "History and Ideology in the English Revolution." *Historical Journal* 8 (1965): 151–78.
– "The Idea of Negative Liberty: Philosophical and Historical Perspectives." In *Philosophy in History* ... , edited by Richard Rorty et al., pp. 193–221. Cambridge: Cambridge University Press, 1985.
– "Language and Social Change." In *State of the Language*, edited by Leonard Michaels and Christopher Ricks, pp. 562–78. Berkeley, Los Angeles, London: University of California Press, 1980.
– "The Limits of Historical Explanations." *Philosophy* 41 (1966): 199–215.
– *Machiavelli*. Oxford: Oxford University Press, 1981.
– "Machiavelli on the Maintenance of Liberty." *Politics* 18 (1983): 3–15.
– "Meaning and Understanding in the History of Ideas." *History and Theory* 8 (1969): 3–53.
– "The Modern State: Acquisition of a Concept." In *Political Innovation* ... , edited by Terence Ball et al., pp. 90–131. Cambridge: Cambridge University Press, 1989.
– "More's Utopia." *Past and Present* 38 (1967): 153–68.
– "More's *Utopia* and the Language of Renaissance Humanism." In Pagden, *The*

*Languages of Political Theory* ... , edited by Anthony Pagden, pp. 123–57. Cambridge: Cambridge University Press, 1987.
- "Motives, Intentions and the Interpretation of Texts." *New Literary History* 3 (1972): 393–408.
- "On Performing and Explaining Linguistic Actions." *Philosophical Quarterly* 21 (1971): 1–21.
- "The Origins of Calvinist Theory of Revolution." In *After the Reformation* ... , edited by Barbara Malament, pp. 309–30. London: University of Pennsylvania Press, 1980.
- "The Paradoxes of Political Liberty." In *The Tanner Lectures on Human Values*, edited by S. McMurrin, vol. 7, pp. 225–50. Salt Lake City: University of Utah Press, 1986.
- "Political Philosophy." In *The Cambridge History of Renaissance Philosophy*, edited by Charles B. Schmitt, pp. 389–452. Cambridge: Cambridge University Press, 1988.
- "A Reply to my Critics." In *Meaning and Context* ... , edited by James Tully, pp. 231–88. Princeton: Princeton University Press, 1989.
- "'Social Meaning' and the Explanation of Social Action." In *Philosophy, Politics and Society*, edited by Peter Laslett and W. G. Runciman, series 4, pp. 136–57. Oxford: Oxford University Press, 1972.
- "Some Problems in the Analysis of Political Thought and Action." *Political Theory* 2 (1974): 277–303.
- "The State." In *Political Innovation* ... , edited by Terence Ball et al., pp. 90–131. Cambridge: Cambridge University Press, 1989.

Skinner, Quentin, ed. *The Return of Grand Theory in the Human Sciences*. Cambridge: Cambridge University Press, 1985.

Sleiden, Johann. *Sleidanes Commentaries, concerning the state of Religion and common wealth, during the raigne of the Emperour Charles the Fifth*. Translated by John Daus. London, 1560.

Smalley, Beryl. *The Becket Conflict and the Schools*. Oxford: Basil Blackwell, 1978.

Smalley, Beryl, ed. *Trends in Medieval Political Thought*. Oxford: Oxford University Press, 1965.

Smith, Henry Nash. *Virgin Land: The American West as Symbol and Myth*. Cambridge, MA: Harvard University Press, 1950.

Smith, John Holland. *The Great Schism, 1378*. New York: Weybright and Talley, 1970.

Smith, Lacey Baldwin. *Tudor Prelates and Politics, 1536–1558*. Princeton: Princeton University Press, 1953.
- Smith, Preserved. *The Life and Letters of Martin Luther*. Boston, New York: Houghton Mifflin, 1911.

Smith, Sir Thomas. *De republica anglorum*. Edited by L. Alston. Cambridge: Cambridge University Press, 1906.

- *A Discourse of the Common Weal of the Realme of England.* Edited by Elizabeth Lamond. Cambridge: Cambridge University Press, 1906.
Snow, V. F. *Parliament in Elizabethan England: John Hooker's "Order and Usage."* New Haven: Yale University Press, 1977.
Société de l'histoire du protestantisme français. *Actes de colloque L'amiral de Coligny et son temps (Paris, 24–28 octobre, 1972).* Papers from a Conference on St Bartholomew's Day, 400 Years After. Paris: Société de l'histoire du protestantisme français, 1974.
- Soder, Josef. *Francisco Suárez und das Volkerrecht.* Frankfurt am Main: Minerva, 1973.
Soman, Alfred, ed. *The Massacre of St Bartholomew. Reappraisals and Documents.* The Hague: Martinus Nijhoff, 1975.
Sommerville, J. "From Suárez to Filmer: A Reappraisal." *Historical Journal* 25 (1982): 425–40.
- *Politics and Ideology in England, 1603–1640.* London: Longman, 1986.
- "Richard Hooker, Hadrian Saravia, and the Advent of the Divine Right of Kings." *History of Political Thought* 4 (1983): 229–45.
"Somnium Viridarii de jurisdictione regia et sacerdotali." In *Monarchia s. Romani imperii ...* , edited by Melchior Goldast, vol. 1, pp,. 58–229. [1614]. Graz: Akademische Cruck-u Verlagsanstadt, 1960.
Soto, Domingo de. *Libri decem de iustitia et iure.* Lyons, 1569.
Souchon, M. *Die Papstwahlen in der Zeit des grossen Schismas: Entwicklung und Verfassungkampfe des Kardinalates von 1378–1417.* 2 vols. Brunswick: B. Goeritz, 1898–99.
Southern, R. W. *Western Views of Islam in the Middle Ages.* Cambridge, MA: Harvard University Press, 1962.
- *Western Society and the Church in the Middle Ages.* Harmondsworth: Penguin Books, 1970.
Southern, R. W., ed. *Essays in Medieval History. Selected from the Transactions of the Royal Historical Society on the Occasion of its Centenary.* London: Macmillan, 1968.
- *Medieval Humanism and Other Studies.* Oxford: Basil Blackwell, 1970.
Southgate, W. M. "Erasmus: Christian Humanism and Political Theory." *History* 40 (1955): 240–54.
Speed Hill, William, ed. *Studies in Richard Hooker. Essays Preliminary to an Edition of his Works.* Cleveland: Case Western Reserve University Press, 1972.
Spinka, M. *John Hus, a Biography.* Princeton: Princeton University Press, 1968.
- *John Hus and the Czech Reform.* Chicago: University of Chicago Press, 1941.
Spinka, M., ed. *Advocates of Reform. From Wyclif to Erasmus.* London: Student Christian Movement Press, 1953.
- Spitz, David, ed. *Essays in the Liberal Idea of Freedom.* Tucson: University of Arizona Press, 1964.
Spitz, Lewis W. *Conrad Celtis, the German Arch-Humanist.* Cambridge: Cambridge University Press, 1957.

- "Luther's Ecclesiology and His Concept of the Prince as *Notsbischof.*" *Church History* 22 (1953): 113–41.
- *The Religious Renascence of the German Humanists.* Cambridge: Cambridge University Press, 1963.
Spitz, Lewis W., ed. *Political Thought and Social Change.* New York: Atherton Press, 1967.
- *The Reformation: Basic Interpretations, Problems in European Civilization.* 2d ed. Lexington: D.C. Heath, 1972.
Stankiewicz, W. J. *Politics and Religion in Seventeenth-Century France.* Berkeley: University of California Press, 1960.
Starkey, David. *The Reign of Henry VIII. Personalities and Politics.* London: G. Philip, 1985.
Starkey, Thomas. *A Dialogue between Reginald Pole and Thomas Lupset.* Edited by Kathleen M. Burton. London: Chatto & Windus, 1948.
- *An Exhortation to the People, Instructing them to Unity and Obedience.* London, 1536.
Starnes, Colin. *The New Republic. A Commentary on Book I of More's Utopia Showing its Relation to Plato's Republic.* Waterloo, ON: Wilfrid Laurier University Press, 1990.
"Statement of Grievances presented to the Diet of Worms." In *Manifestations of Discontent ,,, ,* edited by Gerald Strauss, pp. 52–63. Bloomington: Indiana University Press, 1971.
Stauffenger, Roger. *Église et société: Génève au XVII$^e$ siècle.* 2 vols. Geneva: Droz, 1983.
Staupitz, Johann von. "Eternal Predestination and Its Execution in Time." Translated by Paul L. Nyhus. In *Forerunners of the Reformation ... ,* edited by Heiko Oberman, pp. 175–203. London: Butterworth, 1967.
Stayer, James M. *Anabaptists and the Sword.* Lawrence: University of Kansas Press, 1972.
- "Christianity in One City: Anabaptist Münster, 1534–1535." In *Radical Tendencies in the Reformation ... ,* edited by Hans J. Hillerbrand, pp. 117–34. St Louis: Sixteenth Century Journal Publishers, 1988.
Stein, Peter. *Legal Evolution. The Story of an Idea.* New York: Cambridge University Press, 1980.
- *Regulae iuris: From Juristic Rules to Legal Maxims.* Edinburgh: Edinburgh University Press, 1966.
Steinmetz, David C. "Calvin and Melanchthon on Romans 13: 1–7." *Ex Auditu* 2 (1986): 74–81.
- "Libertas Christiana: Studies in the Theology of John Pupper of Goch (d.1475)." *Harvard Theological Review* 65 (1972): 191–230.
- *Misericordia Dei: The Theology of Johannes von Staupitz in Its Late Medieval Setting.* Leiden: E. J. Brill, 1968.

- "The Theology of Calvin and Calvinism." In *Reformation Europe* ... , edited by Steven E. Ozment, pp. 211–32. St Louis: Center for Reformation Research, 1982.
Stenton, Doris M. *English Justice between the Norman Conquest and the Great Charter, 1066–1215*. Philadelphia: American Philosophical Society, 1964.
Stephens, W. P. *The Theology of Huldrych Zwingli*. Oxford: Oxford University Press, 1986.
Stephenson, Carl. *Borough and Town: A Study of Urban Origins in England*. Cambridge, MA: Harvard University Press, 1933.
Stern, Laurent. "Hermeneutics and Intellectual History." *Journal of the History of Ideas* 46 (1985): 287–96.
Sternberger, D. *Machiavellis "Principe" und der Begriff des Politischen*. Wiesbaden: Steiner, 1974.
- *Die Wahl des Parlamente und anderer Staatsorgane: ein Handbuch*. Berlin: De Gruyter, 1969– .
Stewart, Pamela D. *Innocent Gentillet e la sua polemica antemachiavellica*. Florence: Casalini libri, 1969.
Stickler, Alfons M. "Papal Infallibility—A Thirteenth-Century Invention." *Catholic Historical Review* 60 (1974): 427–41.
- "Rejoinder to Professor Tierney." *Catholic Historical Review* 61 (1975): 274–77.
Stieber, Joachim W. *Pope Eugenius IV, The Council of Basle and the Secular and Ecclesiastical Authorities in the Empire. The Conflict over Supreme Authority and Power in the Church*. Leiden: E. J. Brill, 1978.
Stone, Lawrence. *The Past and the Present*. Boston: Routledge & Kegan Paul, 1981.
- *The Past and the Present Revisited*. London: Routledge & Kegan Paul, 1987.
Stones, E. L. G. "The Text of the Writ 'Quod Omnes Tangit' in Stubbs's Selected Charters." *English Historical Review* 83 (1968): 759–60.
Stout, Harry S. "Marsilius of Padua and the Henrician Reformation." *Church History* 43 (1974): 308–18.
Strauss, Gerald. *Law, Resistance and the State: The Opposition to Roman Law in Reformation Germany*. Princeton: Princeton University Press, 1986.
- *Nuremberg in the Sixteenth Century*. New York: Wiley, 1966.
- *Pre-Reformation Germany*. London: Macmillan, 1972.
Strauss, Gerald, ed. *Manifestations of Discontent in Germany on the Eve of the Reformation*. Bloomington: Indiana University Press, 1971.
Strauss, Leo. *Natural Right and History*. Chicago: University of Chicago Press, 1953.
- *Thoughts on Machiavelli*. Glencoe: The Free Press, 1958.
Strayer, Joseph R. *On the Medieval Origins of the Modern State*. Princeton: Princeton University Pres, 1970.
- *The Reign of Philip the Fair*. Princeton: Princeton University Press, 1980.
Strayer, Joseph R., and Donald E. Oueller, eds. *Post Scripta. Essays in Medieval Law*

*and the Emergence of the European State in Honor of Gaines Post.* Studia Gratiana 15. Rome: Libraria Ateneo Salesiano, 1972.
Streeter, B. *The Primitive Church.* New York: Macmillan, 1929.
Strohl, H. "Le droit à la résistance d'après les conceptions Protestantes." *Revue d'histoire et de philosophie religieuses* 10 (1930): 126–44.
Struever, Nancy S. *The Language of History in the Renaissance.* Princeton: Princeton University Press, 1970.
Stump, P. "The Reform of Papal Taxation at the Council of Constance, 1414–1418." *Speculum* 64 (1989): 69–105.
Sturm, Johann. *De educatione principum.* Strasbourg, 1551.
Suárez, Francisco. "De civile potestate." In Francisco Suárez. *De legibus,* edited by Luciano Perena et al., vol. 3, pp. 1–16. Madrid: Consejo Superior de Investagiónes Científicas, 1975.
– *Defensio fidei catholicae et apostolicae adversus anglicanae sectae errores.* 2 vols. Naples: ex typis Fibreniansis, 1872.
– *De legibus.* Edited by Luciano Perena et al. 8 vols. Madrid: Consejo Superiore de Investigaciónes Científicas, 1971–81.
– *De opere sex dierum et de anima.* Lyon, 1621.
– "De opera sex dierum," *Opera omnia.* Edited by D. M. Andre. 28 vols. Paris: L. Vives, 1856–78.
– *Opuscula theologica.* Madrid, 1599.
– *Selections from Three Works of Francisco Suárez.* Translated by Gwladys L. Williams, Ammi Brown, John Waldron, and Henry Davis. Oxford: Clarendon Press, 1944.
– *Tractatus de legibus ac Deo legislatore.* Antwerp: Joannis Keerberqius, 1613.
– *Tractatus de Legibus ac Deo Legislatore.* 2 vols. Naples: ex typis Fibreniansis, 1872.
Suerbaum, Werner. *Vom antiken zum frühmittelalterlichen Staatsbegriff. Über Verwendung und Bedeutung von Res Publica, Regnum, Imperium und Status von Cicero bis Jordanis.* 3d ed. Muenster Westfalen: Aschendorff, 1977.
Sullivan, Donald. "Nicholas of Cusa as Reformer: The Papal Legation to the Germanies, 1451–1452." *Mediaeval Studies* 36 (1974): 382–428.
Surtz, Edward. *The Works and Days of John Fisher.* Cambridge, MA: Harvard University Press, 1967.
Sutherland, Donald. "Conquest and Law." *Studia Gratiana* 15 (1972): 35–51.
Sutherland, N. M. *Catherine de Medici and the Ancien Régime.* London: Historical Association, 1966.
– *The French Secretaries of State in the Age of Catherine de Medici.* London: Athlone Press, 1962.
– *The Massacre of St Bartholomew and the European Conflict 1559–1572.* London: Macmillan, 1973.
Swanson, R. N. "The Problem of the Cardinalate in the Great Schism." In *Authority and Power ... ,* edited by Brian Tierney and Peter Linehan, pp. 225–35. Cambridge: Cambridge University Press, 1980.

- *Universities, Academics and the Great Schism.* Cambridge: Cambridge University Press, 1979.
- "The University of Cologne and the Great Schism." *Journal of Ecclesiastical History* 28 (1977): 1-15.
- "The University of St Andrews and the Great Schism, 1410-1419." *Journal of Ecclesiastical History* 26 (1975): 236-42.

Sweeney, Ross, and Anthony Chodorow, eds. *Popes, Teachers, and Canon Law in the Middle Ages.* Ithaca: Cornell University Press, 1989.

Sweezy, Paul, et al. *The Transition from Feudalism to Capitalism.* London: NLB, 1976.

Sylvester, R. S., ed. *St Thomas More: Action and Contemplation.* New Haven: Yale University Press, 1972.

Sylvester, R. S., and E. P. Morc' Hador, eds. *Essential Articles for the Study of Thomas More.* Hamden: Archon Books, 1977.

Talbert, E. W. *The Problem of Order.* Chapel Hill: University of North Carolina University Press, 1962.

Tannenbaum, Frank. *Slave and Citizen.* New York: Alfred A. Knopf, 1947.

Tarcov, Nathan. "Quentin Skinner's Method and Machiavelli's Prince." *Ethics* 92 (1981): 692-710.

Tarlton, Charles D. "History, Meaning, and Revisionism in the Study of Political Thought." *History and Theory* 12 (1973): 307-28.

Taverner, Rycharde. *The Garden of Wysedome.* London, 1539.

Taylor, Charles. "Philosophy and Its History." In *Philosophy in History ...* , edited by Richard Rorty et al., pp. 17-30. Cambridge: Cambridge University Press, 1985.

- *Human Agency and Language.* Philosophical Papers. Cambridge: Cambridge University Press, 1985.
- *Philosophy and the Human Sciences.* Philosophical Papers 2. Cambridge: Cambridge University Press, 1985.
- *Sources of the Self: The Making of the Modern Identity.* Cambridge, MA: Harvard University Press, 1989.

Tecklenburg-Johns, C. *Luthers Konzilsidee in ihrer historischen Bedigtheit und ihrem reformatischen Neansatz.* Berlin: A. Topelmann, 1966.

Tedeschi, John A., ed. *Italian Reformation Studies in Honor of Laelius Socinus.* Florence: Félice le Monnier, 1965.

Tellenbach, Gerd. *Church, State and Christian Society at the Time of the Investiture Contest.* Translated by R. F. Bennett. Oxford: Basil Blackwell, 1940.

Templin, J. Alton. "The Individual and Society in the Thought of Calvin." *Calvin Theological Journal* 23 (1988): 161-77.

Thomas Aquinas. "De regimine principum ad regem Cypri." In Thomas Aquinas. *Opuscula philosophica*, edited by Raymond Spiazzi. Turin: Marietti, 1954.

- *In libros Peri hermeneias expositio.* Quebec: Université Laval, 1945.

- *On Kingship*. Translated and edited by G. B. Phelan and I. T. Eschmann. Toronto: Pontifical Institute of Mediaeval Studies, 1949.
- *Opuscula omnia*. Edited by Jean Perrier. 2 vols. Paris: Lethellieux, 1949.
- *Opuscula Philosophica*. Edited by Raymond Spiazzi. Turin: Marietti, 1954.
- Summa theologiae. Edited by Thomas Gilby. 61 vols. London: Eyre and Spottiswode, 1964–81.

Thomas de Vio (Cardinalis Cajetanus). *De comparatione auctoritati papae et concilii.* Edited by V. M. Paller. Rome: Institutum Angelicum, 1936.
- *In summae theologiae sancti Thomae Aquinatis*. Rome, 1571.
- *Opuscula omnia*. Venice, 1588.

Thompson, Martyn P. "The History of Fundamental Law in Political Thought from the French Wars of Religion to the American Revolution." *American Historical Review* 91 (1986): 1103–28.

Thompson, M., and H. M. Hopfl. "The History of Contract as a Motif in Political Thought." *American Historical Review* 84 (1979): 919–44.

Thomson, John A. F. *The Later Lollards, 1414–1520*. Oxford: Oxford University Press, 1965.
- "Papalism and Conciliarism in Antonio Rosselli's Monarchia." *Mediaeval Studies* 37 (1975): 445–58.
- *Popes and Princes, 1417–1517*. London: Allen & Unwin, 1980.

Thomson, S. Harrison. "Luther and Bohemia." *Archiv für Reformationgeschichte* 44 (1953): 160–80.

Thorne, Samuel. *Bracton on the Laws and Customs of England*. Cambridge, MA: Harvard University Press, 1977.

Tierney, Brian. "Aristotle, Aquinas and the Ideal State." *Proceedings of the Patristic, Medieval, and Renaissance Conference* 4 (1979): 1–11.
- "Bracton on Government." *Speculum* 38 (1963): 295–317. Reprinted in Brian Tierney. *Church Law* ... London: Variorum, 1979.
- *Church Law and Constitutional Thought in the Middle Ages*. London: Variorum, 1979.
- "Divided Sovereignty at Constance: A Problem of Medieval and Early Modern Political Theory." *Annuarium Historiae Conciliorum* 7 (1975): 238–56.
- *Foundations of the Conciliar Theory: The Contribution of the Medieval Canonists from Gratian to the Great Schism*. Cambridge: Cambridge University Press, 1955.
- "Hermeneutics and History: The Problem of Haec Sancta." In *Essays in Medieval History* ... , edited by T. A. Sandquist and Michael R. Powicke, pp. 354–70. Toronto: University of Toronto Press, 1969. Reprinted in Brian Tierney. *Church Law* .... London: Variorum, 1979.
- "Hierarchy, Consent, and the "Western Tradition"." *Political Theory* 15 (1987): 646–52.
- "Hostiensis and Collegiality." *Proceedings of the Fourth International Congress of Medieval Canon Law*. Pp. 401–09. Vatican City, 1976.
- "Infallibility and the Medieval Canonists: A Discussion with Alfons Stickler." *Catholic Historical Review* 61 (1975): 265–73.

- "Medieval Canon Law and Western Constitutionalism." *Catholic Historical Review* 52 (1966): 1–17.
- "Ockham, the Conciliar Theory and the Canonists." *Journal of the History of Ideas* 15 (1954) 40–70. Reprint. Philadelphia: Facet Books, 1971. Also in Brian Tierney. *Church Law* ... London: Variorum, 1979.
- "On the History of Papal Infallibility: A Discussion with Remigius Baumer." *Theoligsche Revue* 70 (1974): 185–94.
- *The Origins of Papal Infallibility.* 2d impression with Postcript. Leiden: E. J. Brill, 1988.
- "Pope and Council: Some New Decretist Texts." *Mediaeval Studies* 19 (1957): 197–218. Reprint in Brian Tierney. *Church Law* ... London: Variorum, 1979.
- *Popes, Teachers and Canon Law in the Middle Ages.* Edited by James Ross Sweeney and Stanley Chodorow. Ithaca: Cornell University Press, 1990.
- "Public Expediency and Natural Law; A Fourteenth-Century Discussion on the Origins of Government and Property." In *Authority and Power* ... , edited by Brian Tierney and Peter Linehan, pp. 167–82. Cambridge: Cambridge University Pres, 1980.
- "'Tria quippe distinquit judicia ...' A Note on Innocent III's Decretal *Per venerabilem.*" *Speculum* 37 (1962): 48–59.
- "Tuck on Rights. Some Medieval Problems." *History of Political Thought* 4 (1983): 429–41.
- "Villey, Ockham and the Origin of Individual Rights." In *The Weightier Matters of Law* ... , edited by John Witte and Frank S. Alexander, pp. 1–31. Atlanta: Scholars Press, 1988.

Tierney, Brian, and Peter Linehan, eds. *Authority and Power: Studies in Medieval Law and Government.* Cambridge: Cambridge University Press, 1980.

Tjernagel, N. S. *Henry VIII and the Lutherans. A Study in Anglo-Lutheran Relations from 1521 to 1547.* St Louis: Concordia Publishing House, 1965.

*Le Tocsin, contre les massacreurs et auteurs des confusions en France.* Rheims, 1577.

Todd, John M., ed. *Problems of Authority: The Papers Read at an Anglo-French Symposium.* London and Baltimore: Helicon, 1962.

Tonkin, J. *The Church and the Secular Order in Reformation Thought.* New York: Columbia University Press, 1971.

Torquemada, Juan de (Turrecremata). *Summa de ecclesia.* Venice: Michael Tranezinus, 1561.
- *De potestate papae et concilii generalis tractatus nobilis.* Edited by J. Friedrich. Cologne, 1871.
- *Oratio synodalis de primatu.* Edited by E. Candal. Rome: Pontificium Institutum Orientalium Studiorum, 1954.

Torrance, T. F. *The Hermeneutics of John Calvin.* Edinburgh: Scottish Academic Press, 1988.
- *Kingdom and Church. A Study in the Theology of the Reformation.* Edinburgh: Oliver and Boyd, 1956.

Torre, Felipe de la. *Institución de un Roy Cristiano, Colegida principalmente de la Santa Escritura.* Antwerp, 1556.

Toussaint, Joseph. "Philippe le Bon et le Concile de Bâle (1431–1449)." *Bulletin de l'Academie Royale de Belgique* 107 (1942): 1–126.

– *Les Relations Diplomatiques de Philippe le Bon avec le Concile de Bâle 1441–1449.* Leuven: Bibliothèque de l'Université, 1942.

Traboulay, David. "16th century Scholasticism and the Colonization of America: Francisco de Vitoria and His Influence." *Zeitschrift für Missionswissenschaft und Religionswissenschaft* 70 (1986): 15–37.

Tracy, James D. *The Politics of Erasmus: A Pacifist Intellectual and His Political Milieu.* Toronto: University of Toronto Press, 1979.

Trapp, Damasus. "Augustinian Theology of the Fourteenth Century: Notes on Editions, Marginalia, Opinions and Booklore." *Augustiniana* 6 (1956): 146–274.

Trevor-Roper, Hugh R. *Archbishop Laud, 1573–1645.* 2d ed. London: Archon Books, 1962.

– *George Buchanan and the Ancient Scottish Constitution. English Historical Review.* Supplement 3. 1966.

Trexler, Richard C. "Rome on the Eve of the Great Schism." *Speculum* 42 (1967): 489–509.

Tribe, Keith. *Land, Labour and Economic Discourse.* London: Routledge & Kegan Paul, 1978.

Trinkaus, Charles E. *In Our Image and Likeness: Humanity and Divinity in Italian Humanist Thought.* 2 vols. Chicago: University of Chicago Press, 1970.

Trinkaus, Charles E., and Heiko Oberman, eds. *The Pursuit of Holiness in Late Medieval and Renaissance Religion.* Leiden: E. J. Brill, 1972.

Troeltsch, Ernst. *The Social Teaching of the Christian Churches.* Translated by Olive Wyon. 2 vols. New York: Macmillan, 1931.

"A True Warning to all Worthy Men of Antwerp." In *Texts Concerning the Revolt of the Netherlands,* edited by E. H. Kossman and A. F. Mellink, pp. 228–31. Cambridge: Cambridge University Press, 1974.

Truyol Serra, Antonio. *La conception de la paix chez Vitoria.* Paris: J. Vrin, 1987.

Tuck, Richard. *Natural Rights Theories: Their Origin and Development.* Cambridge: Cambridge University Press, 1979.

– "Why is Authority Such a Problem?" In *Philosophy, Politics and Society,* edited by Peter Laslett et al., series 4, pp. 194–207. Oxford: Oxford University Press, 1972.

Tudeschis, Nicolaus de (Panormitanus). *Commentario secundae partis in Primum Decretalium librum.* Venice, 1591.

– *Super tertio decretalium.* Lyon, 1599.

Tully, James. *A Discourse on Property: John Locke and his Adversaries.* Cambridge: Cambridge University Press, 1980.

Tully, James, ed. *Meaning and Context: Quentin Skinner and His Critics.* Princeton: Princeton University Press, 1989.

- "The Pen is a Mighty Sword. Quentin Skinner's Analysis of Politics." *British Journal of Political Science* 13 (1983): 489–509. Reprint in *Meaning and Context* ... , edited by James Tully, pp. 7–25. Princeton: Princeton University Press, 1989.
Turley, Thomas. "Infallibilists in the Curia of Pope John XXII." *Journal of Medieval History* 1 (1975): 71–101.
Tyacke, Nicholas. *Anti-Calvinists: The Rise of English Arminianism, 1540–1640*. Oxford: Oxford University Press, 1987.
- "Puritanism, Arminianism and Counter-Revolution." In *The Origins of the English Civil War*, edited by Conrad Russell, pp. 119–43. London: Macmillan, 1973.
Tyndale, William. *An Answer to Thomas More's Dialogue*. Edited by Henry Walter. Cambridge: Cambridge University Press, 1850.
- *Doctrinal Treatises and Introductions to Different Portions of the Holy Scriptures*. Edited by Henry Walter. Cambridge: Cambridge University Press, 1848.
- "The Obedience of a Christian Man." In William Tyndale. *Doctrinal Treatises*, edited by Henry Walter, pp. 127–344. Cambridge: Cambridge University Press, 1848.
- *The Obedience of a Christian Man*. Amsterdam: Theatrum Orbis Terrarum, 1970.
- *The Works of William Tyndale*. Edited by G. E. Duffield et al. Appleford: Sutton Courtenay Press, 1964.
Tyrell, Joseph M. *A History of the Estates of Poitou*. The Hague: Mouton, 1968.
Ullmann, B. L. *The Humanism of Coluccio Salutati*. Florence: L. S. Olschke, 1957.
Ullmann, Walter. "De Bartoli Sententia: Concilium repraesentat mentem populi." In *Bartolo da Sassoferrato: Studi e Documenti*, vol. 2, pp. 705–33. Milan: Guiffrè, 1962.
- "Boniface VIII and His Contemporary Scholarship." *Journal of Theological Studies* 27 (1976): 58–87.
- "Cardinal Humbert and the Ecclesia Romana." *Studi Gregoriani* 4 (1952): 111–27.
- "The Development of the Medieval Idea of Sovereignty." *English Historical Review* 64 (1949): 1–33.
- *A History of Political Thought: The Middle Ages*. Baltimore: Penguin Books, 1965.
- "John Baconthorpe as a Canonist." In C. N. L. Brooke et al.. *Church and Government* ... , pp. 223–46. Cambridge: Cambridge University Press, 1976.
- "John of Salisbury's *Policraticus* in the Later Middle Ages." In *Geschichtsschreibung und geistiges Leben im Mittelalter* ... , edited by K. Hauck and H. Mordek, pp. 519–46. Cologne: Böhlau, 1978.
- "Julius II and the Schismatic Cardinals." *Studies in Church History* 9 (1972): 177–93.
- *Jurisprudence in the Middle Ages*. London: Variorum, 1980. *Law and Politics in the Middle Ages: An Introduction to the Sources of Medieval Political Ideas*. Ithac: Cornell University Press, 1975.

- "The Legal Validity of the Papal Electoral Pacts." *Ephemerides juris canonici* 12 (1956): 253–69.
- *Medieval Foundations of Renaissance Humanism.* Ithaca: Cornell University Press, 1977.
- *The Medieval Idea of Law as Represented by Lucas de Pennā: A Study in Fourteenth-Century Legal Scholarship.* London: Methuen, 1946.
- *The Origins of the Great Schism. A Study in Fourteenth-Century Ecclesiastical History.* London: Burns, Oates and Washbourne, 1948.

Ulmann, Karl. *Reformers before the Reformation.* Translated by Robert Menzies. 2 vols. Edinburgh: N.p., 1855.

Ulpian. "Digesta." In *Corpus iuris civilis.* Edited by T. Mommsen, P. Kruger, R. Schoell, and E. Knoll. 3 vols. 12th ed. 1911. Reprinted Berlin: 1954.

Unger, Roberto M. *Knowledge and Politics.* New York: Free Press, 1975.
- *Law in Modern Society: Toward a Criticism of Social Theory.* New York: Free Press, 1976.

Utley, F. L., ed. *The Forward Movement of the Fourteenth Century.* Columbus: Ohio State University Press, 1966.

Vagedes, Arnulf. *Das Konzil über dem Papst? Die Stellungnahmer de Nikolaus von Kues und des Panormitanus zum Streit zurschen dem Konzil von Basel und Eugen IV.* 2 vols. Paderborn: Schoningh, 1981.

Vahle, Hermann. "Calvinismus und Demokratie im Spiegelder Forschung." *Archiv für Reformationsgeschichte* 66 (1975): 182–212.

Vajta, Vilmos ed. *Luther and Melanchthon.* Philadelphia: Muhlenberg Press, 1961.

Valeri, Nino. *L'Italia nell' Eta dei Principati al 1343 al 1516.* Milan: Mondadori, 1949.
- *La Liberta e la Pace. Orientamenti Politici del Rinascimento Italiano.* Turin: Societa d'Erasmo, 1942.

Valla, Lorenzo. *Opera omnia.* Edited by Eugenio Garin. 2 vols. Turin: Bottego d'Erasmo, 1962.

Valla, Lorenzo. "In Praise of Saint Thomas Aquinas." Translated by M. Esther Hanley. In *Renaissance Philosophy*, edited by Leonard A. Kennedy, pp. 17–27. The Hague: Mouton, 1973.
- *The Treatise of Lorenzo Valla on the Donation of Constantine.* Edited and translated by Christopher B. Coleman. New Haven: Yale University Press, 1922.

Valois, Noel. *La France et la Grand Schisme d'Occident.* 4 vols. Paris: A. Picard, 1896–1902.
- *Le Pape et le concile (1378–1450).* 2 vols. Paris: A. Picard, 1909.

Van Cleve Thomas C. *The Emperor Frederick II of Hohenstaufen: Immutator Mundi.* Oxford: Oxford University Press, 1972.

Van Eijl, Edmond J. M., ed. *Facultas S. Theologia Lovanensis, 1432–1797: Bijdragen tot haar geschiednis.* Louvain: Louvain University Press, 1977.

Van Engen, J. "The Christian Middle Ages as an Historiographical Problem." *American Historical Review* 91 (1986): 519–52.

Vaughan, C. E. *Studies in the History of Political Philosophy before and after Rousseau.* Edited by A. E. Little. 2 vols. Manchester: Manchester University Press, 1925.
Vegio, Maffeo. *De educatione liberorum.* Edited by Maria W. Fanning. 2 vols. Washington: Catholic University of America Press, 1933–36.
Verbeecke, L. "Droit et morale chez Jean Gerson." *Revue historique de droit français et étranger,* 4th sér. 33 (1954): 413–27.
Verbeke, Gerald. *The Presence of Stoicism in Medieval Thought.* Washington: The Catholic University of American Press, 1983.
Verbeke, L., and D. Verheist, eds. *Aquinas and the Problems of His Time.* The Hague: Martinus Nijhoff, 1976.
Vereeke, L. "La Réforme de l'église au concile de Vienne, 1311–1312." *Studia moralia* 14 (1976): 283–335.
Vergerio, Pietro Paolo. "De monarchia sive de optimo principatu." In Pietro Paolo Vergerio. *Epistolario Pier Paulo Vergerio,* edited by Leonardo Smith, pp. 447–50. Rome: Tipografia del Senato, 1934.
– *Epistolario Pier Paulo Vergerio.* Edited by Leonardo Smith. Rome: Tipografia del Senato, 1934.
– "On Good Manners." Trans. W. H. Woodward. In Woodward. *Vittorino de Feltre and Other Humanist Educators,* pp. 96–118. New York. Columbia University Press, 1963.
Verlinden, Charles. *L'esclavage dans l'Europe médiévale.* Vol. 2, *Italie, colonies italiennes du Levant, Levant latin, Empire byzantin.* Ghent: University of Ghent, 1977.
Vermigli, Peter Martyr. *Commentaries ... upon the Epistle of St Paul to the Romans.* Translated by H. B. London: 1568.
– *The Political Thought of Peter Martyr Vermigli.* Edited by Robert M. Kingdon. Geneva: Droz, 1980.
Vernadscky, George. *Medieval Russian Laws.* New York: Columbia University Press, 1947.
Vespasiano da Bisticci. "The Lives of Illustrious Men of the Fifteenth Century." Translated as *Renaissance Princes, Popes and Prelates* by William George and Emily Waters. Introduction by Myron P. Gilmore. New York: Harper and Row, 1963.
Vignaux, Paul. *Justification et prédestination au XIV$^e$ siècle: Duns Scot, Pierre d'Auriole, Guillaume d'Occam, Grégoire de Rimini.* Paris: J. Vrin, 1934.
– "On Luther and Ockham." In *The Reformation in Medieval Perspective.* Edited by Stephen E. Ozment. Pp. 107–18. Chicago: Quadrangle Books, 1971.
Vile, M. J. C. *Constitutionalism and the Separation of Powers.* Oxford: Clarendon Press, 1967.
Villani, Giovanni. "Croniche." In Giovanni Villani. *Chroniche di Giovanni, Matteo e Filippo Villani,* edited by D. A. Racheli. 2 vols. Trieste: 1857–58.
– *Croniche di Giovanni, Matteo e Filippo Villani.* Edited by D. A. Racheli. 2 vols. Trieste, 1857–58.

- Villey, Michel. "'Contrat-Obligation-Société.' Du langage juridique romain au langage juridique moderne." In *Die Rolle der Juristen* ... , edited by Roman Schnurr, pp. 51–64. Berlin: Duncker & Humblot, 1986.
- *Critique de la pensée juridique moderne. Douze autres essais.* Paris: Dalloz, 1976.
- *La Croisade: essai sur la formation d'une théorie juridique.* Paris: J. Vrin, 1942.
- "Le droit de l'individu chez Hobbes." *Archives de philosophie du droit* 13 (1968): 209–31.
- *Le droit et les droits de l'homme.* Paris: Presses universitaires de France, 1983.
- "Les fondateurs de l'école du droit natural moderne au XVIIème siècle." *Archives de philosophie du droit* 6 (1961): 73–105.
- *La formation de la pensée juridique moderne.* 5th ed. Paris: Montchrestien, 1975.
- "La génèse du droit subjectif chez Guillaume d'Occam." *Archives de philosophie du droit* 9 (1964): 97–127.

Villoslada, Ricardo G. "El Concilio de Constanza su historia y teología en los estudios mas recentes." *Archivum Historiae Pontificiae* 3 (1965): 317–30.
- *La Universidad de Paris durante los Estudios de Francisco de Vitoria, O.P.: 1507–1522.* Rome: Gregorian University, 1938.

Vincke, J. *Schriftstucke zum Pisaner Konzil; ein Kampf um die offentliche Meinung.* Bonn: P. Hanstein, 1942.

*Vindiciae contra tyrannos sive de principis in populum, populique in principem, legitima potestate.* Edinburgh, 1579.

Viner, Jacob. *Studies in the Theory of International Trade.* London: Allen & Unwin, 1937.

Vinogradoff, Paul. *Roman Law in Medieval Europe.* 2d ed. Oxford: Oxford University Press, 1929.

Visser, Derek. "Junius: the Author of the *Vindiciae contra Tyrannos.*" *Tijdschrift voor Geschiedenis* 84 (1971): 510–25.

Vitoria, Francisco de. *Comentarios a la Secunda secundae de Santa Tomas.* Edited by Vicente Beltrán de Heredia. 6 vols. Salamanca: N.P., 1932–52.
- *Francisco de Vitoria and His Law of Nations.* Edited by James Brown Scott. Oxford: Clarendon Press, 1934.
- *De Indis et de iure belli relectiones.* Edited by Ernest Nys. Translated by John Pawley Bate. Washington: Carnegie Institution of Washington, 1917.
- *Leçon sur le pouvoir politique.* Translated by Maurice Barbier. Paris: J. Vrin, 1980.
- *Les leçons de Vitoria sur les problèmes de la colonisation et de la guerre.* Translated by Jean Baumel. Montpellier: Imprimerie de la presse, 1936.
- *Political Writings.* Edited by Anthony Pagden and Jeremy Lawrence. New York: Cambridge University Press, 1992.
- *Releccion "De dominio."* Edited and translated by Jaime Brufau Prats. Granada: Universita, 1964.
- *Relecciones teologicas.* Edited by Luis G. Alonso Getino. 3 vols. Madrid: Asociación Francisco de Vitoria, 1933–36.
- *Relectio de Indis, o Libertad de los Indios.* Edited and translated by L. Perena and

J. M. Perez Prendes. Madrid: Consejo Superior de Investigaciónes Científicas, 1967.
- "Relectio Concerning Civil Power." Translated by Gwladys L. Williams. In *The Spanish Origin of International Law*, edited by James Brown Scott, vol. 1. Oxford: Clarendon Press, 1934.
- *Relectio de iure belli.* Edited by L. Perena et al. Madrid: Consejo Superior de Investigaciónes Científicas, 1981.
- "De potestate civile." In Francisco de Vitoria. *Relecciones teologicas*, edited by Luis G. Alonso Getino, vol. 2, pp. 169–210. Madrid: Asociación Francisco de Vitoria, 1933–36.
- "De potestate ecclesiae." In Francisco de Vitoria. *Relecciones teologicas*, edited by Luis G. Alonso Getino, vol. 2, pp. 1–168. Madrid: Asociación Francisco de Vitoria, 1933–36.
- "De potestate papae et concilii." In Francisco de Vitoria. *Relecciones teologicas*, edited by Luis G. Alonso Getino, vol. 2, pp. 211–80. Madrid: Asociación Francisco de Vitoria, 1933–36.
- "De Indis recenter inventis." In Francisco de Vitoria. *Relecciones teologicas*, edited by Luis G. Alonso Getino, vol. 2, pp. 281–438. Madrid: Asociación Francisco de Vitoria, 1933–36.

Vives, Juan Luis. *De Indis et de iure belli relectiones.* Edited by J. Baumel. Translated by J. P. Bate. Washington: Carnegie Institution of Washington, 1917.
- *On Education.* Translated and edited by Foster Watson. Cambridge: Cambridge University Press, 1913.
- *Joannis Ludovici Vives Valentini opera omnia.* 8 vols. Valencia, 1782–90. Reprint. London: Gregg Press, 1964.

Vodola, E. F. "*Fides et culpa*: The Use of Roman Law in Ecclesiastical Ideology." In *Authority and Power ...* , edited by Brian Tierney and Peter Linehan, pp. 83–98. Cambridge: Cambridge University Press, 1980.

Voegelin, Eric. *Order and History.* 5 vols. Baton Rouge 17: Louisiana State University Press, 1956–87.

Voigt, Georg. *Enea Silvio de' Piccolomini, als papst Pius der Zweite, und sein Zeitalter.* 3 vols. Berlin: G. Reimer, 1856–63. Reprint. Berlin: De Gruyter, 1967.

Vooght, Paul de. "Le Cardinal Cesatini et le Concile de Constance." In *Das Konzil von Konstanz ...* , edited by A. Franzen and W. Müller, pp. 357–81. Freiburg: Herder, 1964.
- "Le concile oecuménique de Constance et le conciliarisme." *Istina* 9 (1963): 57–86.
- "Le conciliarisme aux conciles de Constance et de Bâle." In B. Botte et al. *Le Concile et Conciles*, pp. 143–81. Paris: Chevetogne, 1960.
- "Le Conciliarisme aux conciles de Constance et de Bâle (Compléments et précisions)." *Irenikon* 36 (1963): 61–75.
- "Les Controverses sur des pouvoirs du concile et l'autorité du pape au Concile de Constance." *Revue théologique de Louvain* 1 (1970): 45–75.

- *L'Hérésie de Jean Hus*. Louvain: Publications universitaires de Louvain, 1960.
- *Les pouvoirs du concile et l'autorité du Pape au concile de Constance. Le décret Haec sancta synodus de 6 avril, 1415*. Paris: Éditions de Cerf 1965.
- *Les Sources de la doctrine chrétienne, d'après les théologiens du XIV$^e$ siècle et du début du XV$^e$ siècle avec le texte intégral des XII premières questions de la Summa inédite de Gerard de Bologne*. Bruges: Desclée, de Brouwer, 1954.

Wagner, Henry Raup. *The Life and Writings of Bartolomé de las Casas*. Albuquerque: University of New Mexico Press, 1967.

Wahl, J. A. "Baldus de Ubaldis and the Foundations of the Nation-State." *Manuscripta* 21 (1977): 80–96.
- "Baldus de Ubaldis: A Study in Reluctant Conciliarism." *Manuscripta* 18 (1974): 21–29.

Waley, Daniel. *The Italian City Republics*. London: Weidenfeld & Nicolson, 1969.
- *The Papal State in the Thirteenth Century*. London: Macmillan, 1961.

Walker, D. P. *Spiritual and Demonic Magic from Ficino to Campanella*. London: Warburg Institute, University of London, 1958.
- *The Ancient Theology: Studies in Christian Platonism from the Fifth to the Eighteenth Century*. Ithaca: Cornell University Press, 1972.

Wallace, Dewey D. *Puritans and Predestination: Grace in English Protestant Theology, 1525–1695*. Chapel Hill: University of North Carolina Press, 1982.

Wallace, John M. "The Engagement Controversy, 1649–52, an Annotated List of Pamphlets." *Bulletin of the New York Public Library* 68 (1964): 384–405.

Wallace-Hadrill, J. M. *The Barbarian West, 400–1000*. 3d ed. London: Hutchinson University Press, 1985.
- *Early Germanic Kingship in England and on the Continent*. Rev. ed. Oxford: Clarendon Press, 1971.

Walsh, K. *A Fourteenth-Century Scholar and Primate: Richard Fitz-Ralph in Oxford, Avignon and Armagh*. Oxford: Oxford University Press, 1981.

Walther, Helmut G. *Imperiales Königtum, Konziliarismus und Volkssouveränität: Studien zu den Grenzen des Mittelalterlichen Souveränitätsgedankens*. Munich: Fink, 1976.

Walton, C. and P. J. Johnson, eds. *Hobbes' "Science of Natural Justice."* Dordrecht; Martinus Nijhoff, 1987.

Walton, R. *Zwingli's Theocracy*. Toronto: University of Toronto Press, 1967.

Walzer, Michael. *Just and Unjust Wars*. New York: Basic Books, 1977.
- "Puritanism as a Revolutionary Ideology." *History and Theory* 3 (1963): 59–90.
- *The Revolution of the Saints: A Study in the Origins of Radical Politics*. Cambridge, MA: Harvard University Press, 1965.
- *Radical Principles*. New York: Basic Books, 1980.

Ward, A. W., G. W. Prothero, and Stanley Leathes, eds. *The Cambridge Modern History*. 13 vols. Cambridge: Cambridge University Press, 1902–12. Reprint, 1969.

Waring, Luther H. *The Political Theories of Martin Luther.* New York: G.P. Putnam's Sons, 1910.
Warren, W. L. *Henry II.* Berkeley and Los Angeles: University of California Press, 1973.
Warrender, Howard. *The Political Philosophy of Hobbes: His Theory of Obligation.* Oxford: Oxford University Press, 1957.
Watanabe, Miramichi. "Authority and Consent in Church Government: Panormitanus, Aeneas Silvius, Cusanus." *Journal of the History of Ideas* 23 (1972): 217–36.
– "Duke Sigmund and Gregor Heimburg." In Kurt Ebert. *Festschrift Nikolaus Grass,* vol. 1, pp. 559–73. Innsbruck: Universitätsverlag Wagner, 1986.
– "The Episcopal Election of 1430 in Trier and Nicholas of Cusa." *Church History* 39 (1970): 299–316.
– "Gregor Heimberg and Early Humanism in Germany." In *Philosophy and Humanism,* edited by Edward P. Mahoney, pp. 406–22. New York: Columbia University Press, 1976.
– "Nikolaus von Cues, Richard Fleming, Thomas Livingston." *Mittelungen und Forschungsbeitrage der Cusanus Gesellschaft* 6 (1967): 167–77.
– *The Political Ideas of Nicolas of Cusa, with Special Reference to His* De Concordantia Catholica. Geneva: Ambilly-Annemasse, 1963.
Watkins, Frederick. *The Political Tradition in the West.* Cambridge, MA: Harvard University Press, 1962.
Watson, G. "The Natural Law and Stoicism." In *Problems in Stoicism,* edited by A. A. Long, pp. 216–38. London: Athlone Press, 1971.
Watson, Philip S. *Let God be God! An Interpretation of the Theology of Martin Luther.* London: Epworth Press, 1947.
Watt, H. *John Knox in Controversy.* London: T. Nelson and Sons, 1950.
Watt, J. A. "The Constitutional Law of the College of Cardinals from Hostiensis to Joannes Andreae." *Mediaeval Studies* 33: (1971) 127–57.
– "Hostiensis on *Per venerabilem: the Role of the College of Cardinals.*" In *Authority and Power...,* edited by Brian Tierney and Peter Linehan, pp. 99–113. Cambridge: Cambridge University Press, 1980.
Weber, Max. *Economy and Society: An Outline of Interpretive Sociology.* Edited by Guenther Roth and Claus Wittich. 3 vols. New York: Bedminster, 1968.
– *Roscher and Knies: The Logical Problems of Historical Economics.* Translated by Guy Oakes. New York: Free Press, 1975.
Weckmann, Luis. *Las Bulas Alejandrinas de 1493 y la Teoria Politica del Papado Medieval.* Mexico City: Editorial Jus, 1949.
Wegan, M. "La distinction 'Ius et Usus Iuris'." *Revue de droit canonique* 29 (1979): 93–113.
Weigand, W. *Die Naturrechtslehre der Legister und Dekretisten von Irnerius bis Accursius und von Gratien bis Johannes Teutonicus.* Munich, 1967.
Weill, Georges. *Les théories sur le pouvoir royal en France pendant les Guerres de Religion.* Paris: Hachette, 1891.

Weinreb, Lloyd L. *Natural Law and Justice.* Cambridge, MA: Harvard University Press, 1987.
Weinstein, Donald. "Critical Issues in the Study of Civil Religion in Renaissance Florence." In *The Pursuit of Holiness ...* , edited by Charles E. Trinkaus and Heiko Oberman, pp. 265–70. Leiden: E. J. Brill, 1972.
– *Savonarola and Florence: Prophecy and Patriotism in the Renaissance.* Princeton: Princeton University Press, 1970.
Weiss, Roberto. "Cornelio Vitelli in France and England," *Journal of the Warburg Institute* 2 (1938–9): 219–26.
– *The Dawn of Humanism in Italy.* London: H. K. Lewis, 1947.
– *Humanism in England during the Fifteenth Century.* 2d ed. Oxford: Basil Blackwell, 1957.
– *The Renaissance Discovery of Classical Antiquity.* Oxford: Basil Blackwell, 1969.
– *The Spread of Italian Humanism.* London: Hutchison, 1964.
Wellens, Robert. *Les États Généraux des Pays-Bas, des origines à la fin du règne de Philippe le Beau, 1464–1506.* Heule: UGA, 1974.
*Die Welt zur Zeit des Konstanzer Konzils; Reichman Vortrage im Herbst 1964.* Edited by Theodor Mayer. Constance: J. Thorbecke, 1965.
Weltsch, R. E. *Archibishop John of Jenstein (1348–1400). Papalism, Humanism and Reform in Pre-Hussite Prague.* The Hague: Mouton, 1968.
Welzel, H. *Naturrecht und materiale Gereichtigheit.* 4th ed. Gottingen: Vanderhoeck & Ruprecht, 1962.
– Wendel, François. *Calvin: The Origins and Development of His Religious Thought.* Translated by Philip Moiret. London: Collins, 1963.
Werner, K. F. "Les Nations et le sentiment national dans l'Europe médiévale." *Revue historique* 244 (1970): 285–304.
West Haddan, Arthur, and William Stubbs, eds. *Councils and Ecclesiastical Documents Relating to Great Britain and Ireland.* 3 vols. Oxford: Clarendon Press, 1869–78. Reprint. 1964.
Weston, Corinne Comstock. "Beginnings of the Classical Theory of the English Constitution." *Proceedings of the American Philosophical Society* 100 (1956): 156ff.
– *English Constitutional Theory and the House of Lords 1596–1832.* New York: AMS Press, 1970.
– *The Grand Controversy over Legal Sovereignty in Stuart England.* Cambridge: Cambridge University Press, 1981.
– "The Theory of Mixed Monarchy under Charles I and After." *English Historical Review* 75 (1960): 426–43.
Weyrauch, Erdmann. *Konfessionelle Krise und soziale Stabilität: Das Interim in Strasburg (1548–1562).* Stuttgart: E. Ulmer, 1978.
White, Lynn. *Medieval Technology and Social Change.* Oxford: Clarendon Press, 1961.
White, Stephen D. "'Pactum ... legem vincit et amor judicium.' The Settlement of Disputes by Compromise in Eleventh-Century Western France." *American Journal of Legal History* 22 (1978): 281–308.

Whitfield, J. H. *Discourses on Machiavelli*. Cambridge: Cambridge University Press, 1969.
Wieacker, F. *Privatrechtsgeschichte der Neuzeit.* 2d ed. Göttingen: Vanderhoeck & Ruprecht, 1967.
Wilcox, Donald J. *The Development of Florentine Humanist Historiography in the Fifteenth Century.* Cambridge, MA: Harvard University Press, 1969.
Wilenius, Reijo. *The Social and Political Theory of Francisco Suárez.* Helsinki: Societas Philosophica Fennica, 1963.
Wilentz, Sean, ed. *Rites of Power: Symbolism, Ritual and Politics in the Middle Ages.* Philadelphia: University of Pennsylvania Press, 1985.
Wilks, Michael. "Corporation and Representation in the Defensor pacis." *Studia Gratiana* 15 (1972): 251–92.
– *The Problem of Sovereignty in the Later Middle Ages.* Cambridge: Cambridge University Press, 1963.
William Durant the Younger. *De modo generali concilii celebrandi tractatus.* Edited by J. Crespin. Lyons, 1531.
– *Tractatus de modo generali concilii celebrandi.* Edited by F. Clousier. Paris, 1671. Reprint. London: Gregg, n.d.
William of Ockham. *Breveloquium de potestate papae.* Edited by L. Baudry. Paris: J. Vrin, 1937.
– "Dialogus." In *Monarchia s. Romani imperii ...* , edited by Melchior Goldast, vol. 2, pp. 392–957. Frankfurt, 1614. Graz: Akademische Cruck-u Verlagsanstadt, 1960.
– *De imperatorum et pontificum potestate.* Edited by C. Kenneth Brampton. Oxford: Oxford University Press, 1927.
– "Octo quaestiones de potestate papae." In William of Ockham, *Opera politica*, edited by J. G. Sikes, vol. 1, pp. 1–221. Manchester: Manchester University Press, 1949.
– *Guillielmi de Ockham Opera politica.* Edited by J. G. Sikes. 2 vols. Manchester: Manchester University Press, 1940– .
William of Orange. *The Apologie of Prince William of Orange Against the Proclamation of the King of Spaine.* Edited by H. Wansink. Leiden: E. J. Brill, 1969.
Williams, George Huntston, ed. *The Radical Reformation.* London: Weidenfeld and Nicolson, 1962.
– *Spiritual and Anabaptist Writers.* London: SCM Press, 1957.
Williams, Schafer, ed. *The Gregorian Epoch: Reformation, Revolution, Reaction?* Boston: D. C. Heath, 1964.
Wilpert, Paul, ed. *Lex et sacramentum in Mittelalter.* Miscellanea medievallia. Vol. 6. Berlin: De Gruyter, 1969.
Wimpfeling, Jacob. "Agatharchia, id est, bonus principatus: vel epitoma boni principi." In Jacob Wimpfeling. *De instruendo principe ... imago*, edited by M. A. Pitsillio, pp. 181–206. Strasbourg, 1606.
– *De instruendo principe ... imago.* Edited by M. A. Pitsillio. Strasbourg, 1606.
Winters, Peter J. *Die 'Politik' des Johannes Althusius und ihre Zeitgenossischen Quellen.*

*Zur Grundlegung der politischen Wissenschaft im 16 und im beginnenden 17. Jahrhundert.* Fribourg: Rombach, 1963.
Wiser, James L. *Political Philosophy: A History of the Search for Order.* Englewood Cliffs: Prentice-Hall, 1983.
Witt, John de (Pieter de la Court). *The True Interest and Political Maxims of the Republick of Holland and West-Friesland.* London, 1702.
Witt, Ronald G. "The Rebirth of the Concept of Republican Liberty in Italy." In *Renaissance Studies...*, edited by A. Moldo and J. A. Tedeschi, pp. 173–199. De Kalb: Northwestern University Press, 1971.
Witte, Charles-Martial de. "Les bulles pontificales et l'expansion portugaise au XV$^e$ siècle." *Revue d'histoire ecclésiastique* 48 (1953): 683–718; 49 (1954): 438–61; 51 (1956): 413–53; 908–36; 53 (1958): 5–46; 443–71.
Witte, John, and Frank S. Alexander, eds. *The Weightier Matters of Law. Essays on Law and Religion.* Atlanta: Scholars Press, 1988.
Wittram, R. *Die französische Politik auf dem Basler Konzil.* Riga: G. Loffler, 1927.
Wohfeil, Rainer, ed. *Reformation oder frühbergerliche Revolution.* Munich: Nymphenburger Verlagshandlung, 1973.
Wolf, William J. *No Cross, No Crown: A Study of the Atonement.* New York Doubleday, 1957.
Wolfe, Martin. *The Fiscal System of Renaissance France.* New Haven: Yale University Press, 1972.
Wolgast, E. "Reform, Reformation." *Geschischte Grundbegriffe* 5 (1984): 313–60.
Wolin, Sheldon. "Paradigms and Political Theories." In *Politics and Experience...*, edited by Preston King and B. C. Parekh, pp. 125–52. Cambridge: Cambridge University Press, 1968.
– *Politics and Vision: Continuity and Innovation in Western Political Thought.* Boston: Little, Brown, 1960.
Wolter, Udo. *Ius Canonicum in Iure Civile.* Cologne: Böhlau, 1975.
Wolzendorff, Kurt. *Staatsrecht und Naturrecht in der Lehre von Widestandsrecht des Volkes gegen rechtswidrige ausubung der Staatsgewalt.* Breslau: M. and H. Markus, 1916.
Wood, Charles T. "Personality, Politics, and Constitutional Progress: The Lessons of Edward II." *Studia Gratiana* 15 (1972): 519–36.
Wood, Charles T., ed. *Philip the Fair and Boniface VIII.* 2d ed. New York: Holt, Rinehart and Winston, 1971.
Wood, Diana. *Clement VI: The Pontificate and Ideas of an Avignon Pope.* Cambridge: Cambridge University Press, 1989.
Wood, Neal. "The Economic Dimension of Cicero's Political Thought: Property and the State." *Canadian Journal of Political Science* 16 (1983): 739–56.
– *An Introduction to Cicero's Social and Political Thought.* Berkeley: University of California Press, 1987.
– "Machiavelli's Concept of 'Virtù' Reconsidered." *Political Studies* 15 (1967): 159–72.

Woolf, Cecil N. Sidney. *Bartolus of Sassoferrato*. Cambridge: Cambridge University Press, 1913.
Wormald, P. "*Les Scripta* and *Verbum Regis:* Legislation and Germanic Kingship from Euric to Cnut." In *Early Medieval Kingship*, edited by P. H. Sawyer and I. N. Wood, pp. 105–38. Leeds: The Editors, 1977.
Wormald, P., D. Bullough, and R. Collins, eds. *Ideal and Reality in Frankish and Anglo-Saxon Society: Studies Presented to J. M. Wallace-Hadrill*. Oxford: Basil Blackwell, 1983.
Wormuth, Francis. *The Origins of Modern Constitutionalism*. New York: Harper, 1949.
– *The Royal Prerogative 1603–1649: A Study in English Political and Constitutional Ideas*. Ithaca: Cornell University Press, 1939.
Wright, Herbert Francis. *Vitoria and the State*. Washington: Catholic University of America Press, 1932.
Wright, Herbert Francis, ed. *Suárez and the State, Francesco Suárez. Addresses in Commemoration of His Contribution to International Law and Politics*. Washington: Catholic University of America Press, 1933.
Wright, J. Robert. *The Church and the English Crown, 1305–1334*. Toronto: Pontifical Institute of Mediaeval Studies, 1980.
Wyclif, John. "The Church and Her Members." In *John Wyclif. Select English Works ...*, edited by Thomas Arnold, vol. 3, pp. 338–65. Oxford; Clarendon Press, 1869–71.
– *Select English Works of John Wyclif*. Edited by Thomas Arnold. 3 vols. Oxford: Clarendon Press, 1869–71.
Wyduckel, Dieter. *Princeps Legibus Solutus. Eine Untersuchung zur frühmodernen Rechts-und Staatslehre*. Berlin: Dunker & Humblot, 1979.
Wyrwa, Tadeusz. *La pensée politique à l'époque de l'humanisme et de la renaissance*. Paris: Libraire Polonaise, 1978.
Yates, Frances A. *Giordano Bruno and the Hermetic Tradition*. London: Routledge & Kegan Paul, 1964.
Yolton, John, ed. *John Locke: Problems and Perspectives*. Cambridge: Cambridge University Press, 1969.
– "Locke on the Law of Nature." *Philosophical Review* 67 (1958): 477–98.
Yost, John K. "German Protestant Humanism and the Early English Reformation: Richard Taverner and Official Translation." *Bibliothèque d'humanisme and renaissance* 32 (1970): 613–25.
Young, Margaret L. M. *Guillaume des Auletz: A Study of his Life and Works*. Geneva: E. Droz, 1961.
Zagorin, Perez. *A History of Political Thought in the English Revolution*. London: Routledge and Kegan Paul, 1954.
Zaitchik, Alan. "Hobbes's Reply to the Fool. The Problem of Consent and Obligation." *Political Theory* 10 (1982): 245–66.
Zampini, Matteo. *Of the French Monarchy and Absolute Power and also a Treatise of the Three States and their Power*. London, 1680.

Zaret, David. *The Heavenly Contract: Ideology and Organization in Pre-revolutionary Puritanism*. Chicago: University of Chicago Press, 1985.
Zarka, Yves-Charles. "Personne civile et représentation politique chez Hobbes." *Archives de Philosophie* 48 (1985): 287–310.
Zasius, Ulrich. "Consilia, sive iuris responsa." In Ulrich Zasius. *Opera omnia*, vol. 6, pp. 9–576. Aalen: Scientia Verlag, 1964–66.
– *Opera omnia*. 7 vols. Aalen: Scientia Verlag, 1964–66.
– "Usus feudorum epitome." In Ulrich Zasius. *Opera omnia*, vol. 4, pp. 243–342. Aalen: Scientia Verlag, 1964–66.
Zavala, Silvio. *Las Instituciónes Jurídicas en la Conquista de America*. Mexico City: Editorial Porrua, 1971.
– *The Political Philosophy of the Conquest of the Americas*. Translated by Teener Hall. Mexico City: Editorial Cultura, 1953.
Zeeveld, W. Gordon. *Foundations of Tudor Policy*. Cambridge, MA: Harvard University Press, 1948.
Zeller, Gaston. *Les Institutions de la France au XVI$^e$ Siècle*. Paris: Presses universitaires de France, 1948.
Zeydel, Edwin H. *Sebastian Brant*. New York: Twayne, 1967.
Zimmermann, Albert, ed. *Die Auseinandersetzungen an der Pariser Universität*. Berlin: De Gruyter, 1976.
– *Der Begriff der Repraesentatio im Mittelalter; Stellvertretung, Symbol, Zeichen, Bild*. Berlin: De Gruyter, 1971.
– *Soziale Ordnungen im Selbstverstandniz des Mittelalter*. Berlin: De Gruyter, 1979–80.
Zimmermann, Harald. *Papstabsetzungen des Mittelalters*. Graz: Böhlau, 1968.
Zuckerman, Charles. "The Relationship of Theories of Universals to Theories of Church Government in the Middle Ages: A Critique of Previous Views." *Journal of the History of Ideas* 35 (1975): 579–94.
Zwingli, Huldrich. "Der Hirt." In Huldrich Zwingli. *Samtliche Werke*, edited by E. Egli et al., vol. 3, pp. 1–68. Berlin, Leipzig: C. A. Schwetschke and Son, 1904–63.
– *Samtliche Werke*. Edited by E. Egli et al. 13 vols. Berlin, Leipzig: C. A. Schwetschke and Sons, 1904–63.
Zwölfer, Richard. "Die Reform der Kirchenverfassung auf dem Konzil zu Basel." *Basler Zeitschrift für Geschichte und Altertumskunde* 28 (1929): 141–247; 29 (1930): 1–58.

# Index

absolute monarchy, 283, 285
Acacianism, 60
Acciavoli, Donato, 39
Adam, 204; and Eve, 133, 133 n.13, 134, 162, 179, 236
Aegidius of Rome, 5 n.1, 19, 57, 86, 101, 134 n.16, 140, 141, 288; on absolute and ordinary powers of pope, 27
Aeneas Silvius Piccolomini (Pius II), 99, 107, 140, 147, 162, 175
Aethopians, 130
d'Ailly, Pierre, 39 n.55, 76–90, 91–93, 94, 95, 99, 101, 102, 109, 111, 113, 192
Albert the Great, 141
Alciato, Andrea, 47, 48
Almain, Jacques, 109, 109 n.131, 110, 113 n.149, 114–21, 143
Althusius, 49, 124 n.189, 132, 132 n.11
Ambrose, St, 120, 131 n.7
Anabaptism, 227, 238, 247, 252
Anastasius II, pope, 59, 62, 62 n.26
anti-Medici coup of 1494, 39
Aragon, 165
Arezzo, 14
Aristotle, xix, 16, 17, 18 n.6, 19 n.11, 42, 94, 96, 132, 133, 134, 136, 136 n.20, 139, 146, 150, 189, 190, 191, 192, 236, 240, 252, 254, 254 n.171, 264, 280, 286, 290, 291; compatible with Christianity? 286; conception of state, 30; doctrine of causality, 139; *Ethics*, 8, 37 n.54, 39, 290; natural philosophy, 191; on personal immortality, 291; philosophy of nature, 134; *Politics*, 3, 8, 21, 37 n.54, 39, 132, 224, 251, 280; on reason and law, 279

Augsburg Confession, 210
Augustine, St, 8, 46, 89, 101, 120, 131 n.7, 133, 140 n.31, 145, 146, 149 n.62, 162, 178, 197, 199, 200, 202, 204, 236, 238, 245, 255, 279, 280; *City of God*, 200; conception of human nature, 37; doctrine of the peace of order, 240; 'two cities', 295; view on fallen human nature, 135, 135 n.18
Austin, John, 225 n.94
authority: all directly from God, 200, 240; derived from people, 257; in individuals in state of nature, 154; limited, 243
Avignon, 48, 53
Avignon papacy, 73
Azo and Lothair, 261

Babylonian Captivity, 53
Baldus de Ubaldis, 22 n.17, 23–32, 52, 169 n.115, 265; student of Bartolus of Sassoferrato, 24
Barnes, Robert, 195, 199, 200
Baron, Hans, 32, 33, 238 n.119
Bartolus of Sassoferrato, 18, 20, 21–23, 24, 28, 30, 31, 33, 48, 52, 104 n.118, 166, 166 n.110, 169 n.115, 181, 261, 265
Battle of Villalar, 142
Baume, Pierre de la, 221
Beaton, Cardinal, 231
Begenhagen, Johann, 209
believers: have right of self-defence, 229
Bellarmine, Robert, 5 n.1, 11, 128, 128 n.1, 129, 130, 154, 160, 161, 167 n.111, 180 n.152, 207
Belleforest, François de, 257
Benedict XI, pope, 70

Benedict XII, pope 91
Bern, 219
Bernardi, Giovanni, 99
Beza, Theodore, 108, 124, 216, 223, 226 n.87, 229, 232 n.106, 239–49, 250, 254, 256, 259, 263, 264, 265, 270, 271, 272
Biel, Gabriel, 192, 193
bishop of Rome: one among equals, 101
bishops: all equal in rank, 101; election of, 59; rights of, 73
Black, Antony, 129 n.4
Blanchard, Jean: chancellor of University of Paris, 78
Bodin, Jean, 11, 32, 49, 124 n.189, 132, 132 n.11, 260, 280, 296
Boèce, Hector, 122 n.180
Boehner, Philotheus, 191 n.5
Bohatec, Josef, 234 n.109
Bologna, 21, 32
Bolognese legists, 23
Bonaventure, St, 101
Boniface II, pope, 70
Boniface VIII, pope, 19, 22, 52, 60, 65, 66, 68, 69, 71, 114; held office illegally, 60
Boniface IX, pope, 91
Bourges, 48, 243, 256; school of legal studies, 48 n.85
Bracciolini, Poggio, 32
Brethren of the Common Life, 192
Brück, Gregory, 210, 212
Bruni, Leonardo, 32, 33, 34, 37; every citizen equal in liberty, 35; favoured republican form of government at Florence, 34; Florence founded by republican Romans, 36; political freedom the basis for political greatness, 35; rejected contemplation as highest human activity, 36; wanted citizen army, 35
Bucer, Martin, 213, 219, 220 n.71, 220 n.74, 224, 242, 248, 265
Buchanan, George, 108, 108 n.128, 109, 110, 113 n.149, 114, 121–26, 194, 205, 289
Budé, Guillaume: polemic on scholastic jurisprudence, 48
Bullinger, Heinrich, 232, 232 n.106
Burgos, 147
Burns, J. H., 121 n.178

Caesars, the, 17, 21
Cain, 140 n.31
Cajetan. See de Vio, Thomas
Calvin, 18, 81 n.61, 82 n.66, 185, 202, 216, 217–39, 240, 242, 242 n.129, 250, 253, 254, 279, 293, 294, 297; civic reformer, 224; his definition of law, 238
Calvinist resistance literature, 243
Calvinist theologians, 57 n.18
Cambria, bishopric of, 77
Canning, Joseph P., 22 n.17
Canterbury convocation, 273
cardinals, 69, 74, 76; advisory to pope, 70; aristocratic element in ecclesiastical polity, 93; cannot depose pope, 98; choose pope, 86, 102; delegated elective power by whole church, 116; derive authority from whole church 98; elected from all provinces, 87; elective function of, 57; have rights over pope, 71; the inherited senate of Apostles, 82; and pope, 58; represent *congregatio fidelium*, 69; represent whole church, 86; representative body, 79; role in choosing pope, 74; role in church, 67; share in *plenitudo potestatis*, 69, 82
cardinals and pope: like canons and bishop, 69
Cargill Thompson, W. D. S., 197 n.19, 285, 285 n.268, 288 n.276
Carstadt, Andreas, 205
Cartesian philosophy, xxiv
Carthage, 39
Castile, 142, 165
Castilian junta, 146
Castrillo, Alonzo de, 146, 152, 154
Catherine de Medici, 239
Catherine of Aragon, 273
Cato: advocate of republicanism, 17
cause of polity, the community as a whole, 177
Celestine V, pope, 60, 65, 69
Charlemagne, 14, 17, 27
Charles I, of England, 258
Charles V, of France, 76
Charles V, Holy Roman emperor, 141, 141 n.41, 146 n.56, 151, 155 n.76, 156, 208, 216, 225
Chenevière, Marc-Édouard, 234 n.109, 238 n.119
Christ, conferred authority directly on Peter, 79
Christendom, 50, 54 n.11, 96, 100
Christianity: means for returning to original state of perfection, 147
Christian polity: can sometimes attack barbarians, 151
Christian republic, 79

Christians: must accept tyranny, 209
church: can protect its own wellbeing, 92, 119; a corporation, 65, 66; could have chosen first pope, 116; has means to preserve its unity, 90; has no special status in a polity, 218; indefectibility of, 62; a kind of political society, 115; leaders, should be elected, 103; made up of pope plus cardinals, 63; members confer authority on pope, 67; a monarchy, 119; universal is indefectible, 63; as a whole, 63, 67; whole body of faithful, 120; as a whole superior to pope, 63
church council and pope, 58
Church of England, 163 n.95
Church of Rome, 62, 63, 72, 75, 79, 82; pope is head of, 72
church universal 3
Cicero, 123 n.183, 140, 141, 141 n.38; advocate of republicanism, 17; emphasized political value of rhetoric, 34; ideal of *vir virtutis*, 34; influence on medieval political thought, 8 n.4
citizens: self interest of a benefit to the polity, 33
citizenship, 146; integral to human nature, 30
city-state, 219; and independence, 15
civic good: identified with glory, 58
civil authority: established by consent, 240; responsible for religious orthodoxy, 240
*civitas sibi princeps*, 23
Clement, Jacques, O.P., 161, 166
Clement VII, pope, 40, 77, 273
clergy: have no special status in polity, 217, 235
clerics, as civil servants, 50
coercion, xx, 169, 202, 264; element of law, 278; essential feature of state, 136 n.18; needed in polity, 154; only in polity, 179; providential corrective to Fall, 280; result of Original Sin, 280
Coimbra, 167
Coleman, Janet, 298
Colet, John, 11, 46; just-war theory 46 n.79
Coligny, Admiral, 239
college of cardinals, 81, 95, 97, 113, 113 n.149, 179; elect pope, 116. *See also* cardinals
College of Navarre, 90
College of St Jacques, 141, 147
collegial rule, 223
Comenius, 234 n.109

Comestor, Peter, 140
common good, 18, 30, 41–42, 203, 267, 291; final cause of polity, 139; understood by superior individuals, 88
common goods: immediate and mediate, 170; mode of possession of in early church, 131 n.10
common possession: part of natural law, 131; in state of nature, 131
common understanding, 175
common welfare, 262
*communero* movement, 142
community: mystical body, 179; must be able to resist own destruction, 80; not simple collection of individuals, 177
community of the church: source of papal authority, 86
commutative justice, 170
Condé, Prince de, 239
Condren Conal, xxiv n.18
*congregatio fidelium*, 20, 74, 96, 103, 189, 194, 196, 217, 235
conquest of the Americas, 148
*conquistadores*, 132
Conrad of Gelhausen, 76
conscience, 237
consent, xx, 103, 105, 157; basis of political authority, 281; connected with freedom, 102 n.109; entailed by liberty, 264; expressed or tacit, 282; expressed through representation, 269; feature of coronation, 289; given necessarily, 84; ground of political society, 280; necessary to establish polity, 139; needed for lawful rule, 244; need not be expressed, 284; of the governed, 49; of naturally free individuals, 271; rational act to form polity, 178; sign of natural reason, 101; tacit or active, 23
consent of cardinals: promised by pope as condition of consecration, 82
consent theory, 265
Constantine, emperor, 56 n.15, 61, 94
constitutional democracy, 6
constitutionalism, 9; in church, 66, 72
*Constitutum Sylvestri*, 56 n.15
Contarini, Gasparo, 39
contract: basis of polity, 244; between ruler and people, 245, 254, 255, 261, 285; distinction between social and political, 137
core concepts, xviii
coronation oath, 261; contract between ruler and people, 254; limits ruler, 124

corporate character of church, 93
corporational authority: requires consent, 81
corporation of church, seat of full power, 97
corporation theory, 52, 66, 67, 69, 75, 77–79, 80, 95, 125, 181, 292; applied to episcopacy, 97; meaning of head of, 67
corruption of the people: cause of loss of republican liberty, 41
cortès, 142, 163, 243; had power to levy taxes, 165; represents people, 165
council: can depose pope, 118, 118 n.169, 119
Council of Basle, 52, 98, 99, 99 n.104, 100, 107, 107 n.127, 113 n.149, 115, 116, 120, 122, 128, 140 n.32, 166, 193
Council of Chalcedon, 106
Council of Constance, 52, 76, 82, 87, 88, 89, 91, 94, 95, 99, 105, 112, 113 n.149, 116, 120, 193
Council of Nicaea, 61
Council of Pisa, 76, 90, 91, 93, 95, 110, 114, 115, 118, 121; council over pope, 105, 106, 111, 112, 113, 114, 116, 117, 119, 120, 122, 143, 292; represents whole church, 116
Counter-Reformation, 6, 130, 166, 207, 208, 278
covenant: between God and His people, 124, 265; between God and lesser magistrates, 265; between God and political authorities, 265; between ruler and lesser magistrates, 270; between ruler and people, 265, 266, 271; of two kinds, 265
Crockaert, Pierre, 141, 148
Crusades, the, 152
custom, 21–22, 28, 170, 173; binds by silent allowance, 282; can abrogate written law, 172; not part of natural law, 173; rests on consent, 23
Cyprian, 101

Daniel, prophet, 229, 230
Dante Alighieri, 8, 17, 18, 129 n.4
Darius, 231
Decretalists, 24 n.23, 52, 57, 64, 66, 75, 79
Decretists, 52, 56, 57, 62, 63, 64, 65, 75, 79
defence: prime reason for forming polity, 162

defender of the faith, 273
definition of law: Calvin, 238
delegation of authority: constituted a polity, 139
demarchs of Athens, 229
de Muglio, Pietro, 33
deposition, 266, 283
de Soto, Domingo, 129, 129 n.3, 143, 175, 177 n.145, 292
de Vio, Thomas (Cajetan), 110, 114, 115, 116, 117 n.161, 118, 118 n.170, 119, 120, 128, 129, 130, 142–45, 152, 153, 175, 180 n.15, 275, 280; pope over council, 118; tripartite distinction re pope, 119
*dictatores*, 33, 37, 81, 82
Diet of Roncaglia, 22
Diet of Worms, 142 n.41, 194, 208, 209
Dioscorus, 106
direct democracy, 13, 15
disobedience, sinful, 197
distributive justice, 170
divine law, 29, 94
divine omnipotence, 286, 287
divine power: ordinary and absolute, 179 n.149
divine right of kings, 83, 178, 180, 181, 285
divine will, 237
doctors of theology: have authority as teachers and experts, 88; role at general council, 88
doctrine of original sin, 133
doge, 38
dominion, 80; over material things and lower animals, 182; as royal power, 276; of ruler, 282
*dominus mundi*, 4, 17
Donation of Constantine, 47, 53, 94
double contract theory, 138
Du Hames, N., 216 n.69
dukes of Saxony, 219
Durantis, Guilielmus the Younger, 68, 70–73, 97, 103

early Christian communities: held goods in common, 131 n.10
*ecclesia*, for Luther, 196
*ecclesia fidelium*, 75
ecclesiastical authority: established by God, 55; in ruler, 289
*ecclesia universa*, 62, 65, 75
economic development, 13
Edinburgh, 260

electors of empire: represent its units, 102
election procedure, 223
elective consent, 102
Elizabeth I, of England, 121, 232, 274
emperor: can be resisted, 212, 213; can call general council, 106; chosen by electors of empire, 102; *miles papae*, 212
English common law, 289
English Marian exiles, 216
English monarch, limited by law, 283
ephors, 229, 255, 263, 265; can oppose tyrants, 229, 266 n.208; elected by people, 229; of Sparta, 229, 234; of Sparta more powerful than king, 263; responsible to people, 229. *See also* lesser magistrates
*epikeia*, 94
episcopal authority, 72
episcopate: limit on papal authority, 72
equality: before the law, 35; of individual citizens, 15
Erasmus, 11, 46, 46 n.78, 114; hatred of war, 46 n.78
Er furt, 194; University of, 192, 194
estates general, 10, 243, 249, 259, 260, 262
eternal law: two categories of for Hobbes, 277
Eugene IV, pope, 99, 99 n.104, 107
European community, 7 n.3
'execrabilis': papal bull, 107

Fall, the, 134, 139, 153 n.71, 173, 179, 187, 189, 204, 238, 280, 281
fallen nature, 187
Farel, Guillaume, 220 n.71, 221 n.75
Fernandez-Santamaria, J. A., 153 n.71
Fasolt, Constantin, 71 n.45
feudal system, 13
Ficino, Marsilio, 37
Filmer, Robert, 249
fixed-term rule, 15
Flood, the, 140 n.31, 153 n.71, 204
Florence, 17, 24, 31, 32, 33, 34, 35, 38, 40; collapse of, 37; founded by Sulla's veterans, 34; offered honour to all citizens, 36
Florentine: humanists, 32; political thought, 32; republicanism, 39, surpressed, 41
Francesco de Toledo, 166
Franciscan spiritualists, 176
Franklin, Julian H., 257 n.179, 260 n.187
Frederick I, Barbarossa, 17, 22

Frederick II, 52
free: as legal status, 23
free agents: can alienate anything of their own, 283
free choice, 175
freedom, 6, 13; natural characteristic of humans, 182, 183
free individuals:. choose ruler, 281; have property rights, 176
French monarch: limited by custom, 259; originated by election, 261
Fuller, Lon, xviii, xvii n.8
fullness of power: not in pope alone, 81; rests in whole community of church, 98. *See also plenitudo potestatis*

Garden of Eden, 133, 133 n.13, 140, 162, 236
Gardiner, Stephen, 291, 292 n.282
general church council, 58, 61, 63, 65, 72, 75, 76; authority directly from God, 113; authorizes church statutes, 103; bridle on papacy, 107; can depose pope, 60; can function as ordinary judge, 118; cannot err in faith and morals, 117; cannot legislate without pope, 104; democratic element, 81; represents church *propinquissime*, 117 n.163; represents people, 125 n.191; represents whole church, 80, 81, 87, 120; seat of authority of whole church, 97; should be convened every ten years, 72; should contain more than bishops, 87; superior to pope, 56, 64, 65, 105. *See also* council over pope
general will: not will of all, 177
Geneva, 218, 219, 220, 221 n.75, 222, 224, 225, 226 n.87, 239, 241, 243, 250, 256, 260; Council of Sixty of, 222; Council of Two Hundred of, 221 n.75, 222
Geneva Bible, 233 n.108
German Diet, 270
Gerson, Jean, 39 n.55, 76, 89, 90–95, 101, 102, 109, 110, 111, 113, 148, 192, 267
Gerson-les-Barbery, 90
Gianotti, Donato, 39, 40; fervent republican, 39
Gierke, Otto, 51, 128
Gilby, Thomas, 169 n.118
Gilson, Etienne, xxiv, 191 n.4
Glasgow, 109, 215
Glossators, 24

God: only papal superior, 119; primary cause of all power, 178; primary efficient cause of political authority, 139; transfers political power to whole people, 178–79
Goodman, Christopher, 233 n.108, 242, 248, 255 n.174, 265
government: necessary consequence of Fall, 280
Gratian, 3, 55 n.14, 56 n.15, 56, 56 n.17, 57, 58, 59, 62, 62 n.26, 63, 64, 71, 73, 118, 118 n.170, 131; *Decretum*, 54, 54 n.14
greater part, 113. See also *maior pars*; *valentior pars*
Great Schism, 5, 53, 56, 58, 64, 68, 73, 75, 76, 80, 84, 86, 87, 89, 90, 91, 94, 95, 96, 98, 99, 185, 294
Grebel, Conrad, 206
Gregorian Reform, 52, 58, 62, 64
Gregorio de Valencia, 166
Gregory of Rimini, 192
Grotius, Hugo, 32, 49, 132
Guicciardini, Francesco, 33, 39, 43, 44, 45; critic of Machiavelli, 40; republican, 39, 40
Guido de Baysio, 75, 98
Gwilliam, Thomas, 231, 232

'*haec sancta*': papal bull, 105
Hart, H. L. A., xviii
Heidelberg, 242 n.130
Helvetic Confederation, 219
Henry III, of France, 161, 166
Henry VIII, of England, 107, 185, 231, 273
Henry of Langenstein, 76
heresy, papal, 55 n.14, 59, 75; of Anastasius II, 62
Hermogenianus, 131
Hesiod, 140, 141
Hobbes, Thomas, xv, 10 n.14, 11, 132, 137, 139, 162, 183 n.159, 183 n.161, 202, 284
Hoffmann, Hasso, 51 n.3
Holcot, Robert, 192
Holy Roman emperor, 8, 14, 17, 21, 22, 25, 76, 219; his authority derived originally from people, 26 n.25; confirmed by church, 26; had divine origin, character and jurisdiction, 26; had ordinary and absolute powers, 27; held authority from God, 26; universal ruler, 25; was *dominus mundi*, 26

Holy Roman Empire, 15, 16, 21, 22, 23, 25, 208, 252
Honorius, pope, 62 n.26
Hooker, Richard, 273–93
Hopfl, Harro, 217 n.70, 226 n.87, 234 n.112
Hostiensis, 66, 69, 82
Hotman, François, 11, 126, 243, 245, 245 n.142, 256–60, 261, 262, 263, 280, 281, 282
Hubert, cardinal, 57, 63
Hugh of St. Victor, 101, 140
Huguccio, 56, 59, 63, 98
Huguenot political thought, 180, 216, 256, 260, 264; as resistance theory, 81 n.61, 82 n.66, 126
human history: three stages of, 136
humanism, 6; emphasis on individual, 127; emphasis on liberty, 127; philological techniques, 47; political thinking, 9
humans: born free, 182; free and equal, 102, 267; free by nature, 267, 271; have natural need for society, 280; naturally free and social, 138; naturally social, 30, 132, 161, 175, 176, 179; originally lived like beasts, 140, 141
Hus, John, 89, 91

idolatry, 233 n.108
imperial jurisdiction: confirmed by Christ, 26
imperial law: justifies resistance, 212
*imperium*: of Roman people, 31
impersonationist theory of representation, 104
independent city-states, 28
Indians: naturally servile, 150; not mentally inferior, 156
Indians of America, 132
individual rights, 131, 244, 267; inalienable, 284
individuals: are equal, 30, 123; are free in state of nature, 174, 280; cannot act politically, 245; cannot oppose tyranny, 255; cannot resist, 249, 270
infallibility, 105
infidel peoples, 149 n.62
influence, xxiv n.18, 5 n.1
innate sinfulness of humans, 264
Inquisition at Lisbon, 121
institutional church: has no scriptural warrant, 191
Inverness, 231

Isidore of Seville, 48 n.84, 131
Israelite monarchy, 281
Italian city-states, 9, 13, 19
Italian kingdom, 17
Italians: loved freedom, 18
*ius civile*, 153
*ius communicationis*, 157
*ius divinum*, 28
*ius gentium*, 27, 28, 29, 131, 153, 180 n.152; basis for universalizible features of polity, 27
*ius gladii*, 213, 262
*ius naturae*, 28. *See* law of nature
Ivo of Chartres, 56 n.15

James I, of England, 170, 178, 181, 285, 288, 288 n.275
James III, of Scotland, 125
James VI, of Scotland, 122, 170. *See also* James I, of England
Jerome, St, 120
Joannus Monachus, 68–70, 71, 82, 97
Johannes Teutonicus, 63, 72
John XXII, pope, 68, 94, 95
John Chrysostom, 124
John of Paris, 9, 20, 21, 39 n.55, 65–68, 69, 79, 81, 82, 95, 97, 98, 101, 115, 129 n.3, 160 n.89, 177 n.145, 201, 252, 268, 292
John of Salisbury, 41, 89, 163, 163 n.10, 215, 281
John of Saxony, 208, 210
Jonas, Justus, 209, 211
Juan de Segovia, 98, 128, 128 n.1
Julianus, emperor, 173
Julius II, pope, 110, 114, 118
Julius Caesar, 34, 36
justice: three types of, legal, commutative, and distributive, 170
Justinian Code, 46
just war theory, 46, 149, 155, 155 n.62

Kant, Immanuel, xviii
king: apex of spiritual and temporal power, 291; governor over people, 111; has veto over parliament, 288; minister of God to govern justly, 265; not really sovereign, 246
Kingdon, Robert, 250, 251 n.161, 254 n.171
king in council, 125
kingship: best combined with aristocracy and democracy, 81; best form of polity, 81; can be changed by popular consent, 163. *See also* mixed form of government
Knox, John, 11, 110, 216 n.69, 231, 232, 233 nn.107,108, 242, 255 n.174
Kristeller, Oscar, 32

laity: excluded from papal election, 58; not full-fledged members of church, 93; represented by ranks of clergy, 103
las Casas, Bartolomé de, 150, 159 n.84
Latin as *lingua franca*, 7
law: defined as coercive power, 45; defined by Suárez, 168; and edicts of rulers, must be approved, 260; has essentially theological component, 237; international, 148; nature of, 167, 227; as scientific, 48; types of, 277
law of nature, 134 n.16, 235, 244, 284 n.266, everyone born free under, 131
leaders: chosen, do not succeed by heredity, 259
legal justice, 170
legal positivism, 225 n.84
*leges imperii*, 259
legitimate authority: is limited, 207
Leibniz, Gottfried, 108 n.130
Leo I, pope, 40, 106, 254
Leopold of Bebenburg, 239 n.109
lesser magistrates, 30 n.29, 126, 207, 213, 223, 226, 228, 232, 232 n.106, 242, 243, 247, 261, 263; can assist people, 239; can hold rulers to account, 270; can resist for religion, 252; can resist tyranny, 230, 243, 249, 252, 253; can restrain higher ones, 255; delegates of the people, 246; elected by people, 270; have responsibilities to aid, 213; maintain religion, 241; must sustain godly rule, 213; popular, 238 n.119; popular representatives, 270; represent popular authority, 246; servants of the people, 246; various kinds, 270
Leuven University, 128
Lewy, Guenter, 140 n.33, 162 n.93
*lex digna*, 254
*lex regia*, 26, 26 n.5, 27, 271
l'Hôpital, Michel de, 257 n.179
Lhuyd, Humphrey, 122 n.180
Liberius, pope, 62 n.26
liberty, 6; most precious possession, 31; natural to humans, 263, 265

limit, xx, 54, 64, 92, 118, 125, 127, 167, 181, 207, 235, 265; on authority, 110–11; on authority based on natural law, 181; concept of, 238; conditioned by purpose, 54; imposed by representatives of people, 260; on monarchy, 259, 259 n.183, 283; on papal authority, 69, 72, 110; of political authority, 49, 238
limited monarchy, of England, 285
*loci communes*, 250, 251
Locke, John, xv, xxiii, 67 n.35, 108, 137, 139, 183 n.159, 183 n.160, 244, 267, 268, 276 n.243, 284; theory of property similar to that of John of Paris, 67 n.35
Lombard, Peter, 141
Lombardy, 14, 15, 21
Losada, Angelo, 159 n.84
Louis XII, of France, 110, 114, 118
Louis of Anjou, 77
Louis of Nassau, 216 n.69
Lucca, 33
Ludiche, Johann, 211
Ludwig of Bavaria, 19 n.11, 68, 73
Luther, Martin, 20, 48, 107, 153, 181, 185, 186, 187, 189, 191, 192, 193, 194, 195–213, 217, 218, 225, 227, 234 n.109, 235, 236, 254, 279, 284, 293, 294, 297; and *zwei-reiche*, 197
Lutheran political thought, 195, 197, 215, 217, 254
Lutheran theologians, 57 n.18
Lyons, 91

McGrade, Stephen, 276 n.243, 277 n.248
Machiavelli, Nicolo, 33, 39, 41, 42; admired early Roman republicanism, 42; civil discord valuable, 47; defended republican liberty in *Discourses*, 44; dependence on mercenary troops a defect, 43; *Discourses*, 40, 42, 43, 44; excessive private wealth a sign of civic decadence, 43; human behaviour follows fixed pattern, 44; ideal of political liberty, 42; image of *vir virtutis*, 43; new set of civic virtues, 43; on *vir virtutis*, 41; *The Prince*, 36, 38, 40, 41, 43, 44; rejected Christian virtues, 43; value of religious practices, 43
Magdeburg, 229, 241, 242
Magdeburg Confession, 216, 218, 225, 232 n.106, 241, 242, 242 n.130, 245 n.142, 248

magisterial authority: defends the people, 234
magistracies: in ancient Rome, 48
magistrate: cannot be resisted, 228; constituted by the people, 263; derives authority from God, 252; exercises *imperium*, 261; has popular consent, 240; representative of people, 268; authority from God, not people, 238
*maior pars*, 125, 125 n.193
*maior singulis, minor universis*, 112, 246, 272
Major, John, 108, 108 n.128, 109–14, 109 n.131, 119 n.172, 121, 124, 126, 192, 194, 231, 269, 296
Major, J. Russell, 146 n.56
majority support, 269
Marc Antony, 36
Marcellinus, pope, 62 n.26
Marcus, 47
Mariana, Juan de, 137, 161–66, 173, 182, 207, 240, 280
Marsilius of Padua, 8, 9, 18, 19, 19 n.14, 20, 31, 45, 68, 71, 96, 125 n.193, 129 n.4, 132, 169, 169 n.118, 199, 202, 234 n.109, 274, 277, 294; republicanism, 9
Marxism, 6
Mary, queen of Scots, 121, 122, 233, 233 n.108
Mary of Lorraine, 233 n.108
Mary Tudor, 107, 232, 249
Maximilian, emperor, 118
Medici, Lorenzo de, 40, 41
Medici: expelled from Venice in 1527, 40; returned to Venice in 1529–30, 41
Melanchthon, Philipp, 126, 194, 195, 197, 199, 200, 206, 209, 210, 211, 214, 215, 234 n.109, 248, 250, 254
mercenary troops: bad for state, 33
Milan, 14
Mill, John Stuart, 183
Mirandola, Pico della, 37
mirror for princes, 4, 18, 38, 39 n.55
mixed form of government, 81, 163–64, 164 n.101, 224. *See also* kingship
Modestenus, 47
Molina, Luis de, 128, 128 n.1, 130, 166, 176 n.144, 283
monarchy, absolute, 180; best form of polity, 31, 37, 146
monotheism, 50
Montaigu College, 114
More, Sir Thomas, 11, 36, 46; rejected

Italian humanist model of civic virtue, 46; *Utopia*, 36, 45 n.75, 46
Mornay, Philippe de, 11, 108, 124, 126, 243, 243 n.135, 244, 245 n.142, 246, 246 n.144, 247, 260–72, 280, 281, 282, 289, 296
*mos docendi Gallicus*, 48
Moses, 283 n.108
Muldoon, James, 149 n.62
Muñoz, Honorio, 149, 149 n.76
Müntzer, Thomas, 206
mutual agreement: constitutes polity, 264
mutual oath: between people and ruler, 245, 245 n.142
mutual obligation: between ruler and people, 271

natural law, 29, 94, 100, 102, 123 n.183, 131, 146, 151, 152, 153, 167, 168, 170, 173, 175, 180 n.152, 191, 203, 237, 238, 248, 263, 264, 266, 278, 285; affords no one dominion over another, 152; applies to all humans, 170; common to all, 131; distinction between positive and negative aspects of, 173, 175, 179; guarantees church unity, 90; guarantees freedom to all individuals, 152; negative aspects of, 173, morally neutral, 173; originally provided for common ownership, 174; positive aspects of, 173
natural liberty, 244
natural-rights theory, xxi n.13, 183, 265, 283, 298
Navarre, 114
Neapolitan jurists, 27
Nebuchadnezzar, 287
necessary forms: of law, xviii
necessity: knows no law, 104, 104 n.119
Nederman, Cary, 298
neo-Platonism, 50, 91, 100; as theology, 101
Nero, 36
Nicholas V, pope, 99
Nicholas of Cusa, 76, 98–107
Nimrod, 140 n.3, 145
Noah, 204
Nogaret, Philippe, 66
northern Renaissance, 45 n.76
Nuremberg, 213

Oakley, Francis, 53 n.9, 89 n.76, 92 n.82, 112 n.143, 113 n.149, 125 n.193, 286

obedience: owed only to legitimate authority, 213, 254; owed to tyrants, 199, 228
obligations: entail rights, 295
officeholder: distinct from private citizen, 215; distinction between office and, 58, 58 n.21, 63, 67
officers of kingdom: distinct from officers of king, 262
oligarchy, in Florence, 33
oratory: cause of political society, 123 n.183
original compact, 282
Original Sin, 133 n.15, 135, 138, 139, 162, 176, 177, 188, 189–92, 202, 236, 280; corrupted human reason, 236
original society: humanist account of, 123; not a polity, 147
origin of political society, 284
Osiander, Andreas, 213
Otto I, 17
Otto of Freising, 14
ownership (*dominium*), 176
Oxford, 190, 191
Ozment, Stephen, 6 n.2

*pactum societatis*: distinct from *pactum subjectionis*, 163
Padua, 17, 19, 20, 24, 95; University of, 99
Panormitanus, 213
papacy, 15, 16, 19, 25; controls procedure for electing pope, 116; has divine origin, character, and jurisdiction, 26; not indefectible, 62; vacancy in, 69, 75
papal absolutism, 65, 70
papal authority: abuse of, 55, 56, 58, subject to control and resistance; settled directly by God on individual, 143
papal deposition, 67, 80; possible on practical grounds, 106
papal election, 58
papal heresy, 106
papal immunity, 54 n.12, 55
papal intervention: *ratione peccati*, 29
papal jurisdiction: over temporal matters, 26, 29
papal monarchy, 57, 68, 75, 86, 292
papal negligence: grounds for deposition, 105
papal power: supreme on earth, 55
papal resignation, 60; and deposition, 61, 65, 65 n.33
Paris, 18, 109, 110, 147, 161, 190, 191, 192; University of, 65, 76, 89, 90, 107,

109–10, 112, 114, 121, 141, 143, 160 n.89, 194
parlement, 262, 270; of France, 262, must ratify laws, 262; of Paris, 260, 262
*parlementum*: meaning, 259
parliament, 10
*pars potior*, 96. *See also maior pars*: *valentior pars*
particular church: can call general council, 120
Pascoe, L. B., 92 n.81
Patrizi, Francisco, 39; condemned use of mercenary troops, 40
Paul, St, 124, 131 n.7, 164 n.103, 162, 178, 200, 205, 210, 213, 214, 226, 228, 254, 255
Pavia, 24
Peace of Lodi, 38
peace of the community: common good, 18
Peasant Revolt, 205
people: agree to accept ruler and laws, 267; alienate power to ruler, 283; appoint ruler, 112, 164; assign authority to elected ruler, 124; can control tyranny, 164; can depose tyrant, 112, 119; can legislate on own behalf, 28; cannot alienate sovereignty, 272; cannot revise original compact, 283; cause of temporal authority, 143; of church, confer authority on pope, 67; delegate and can withdraw authority, 137; delegate authority to lesser magistrates, 269; do not cause ruler's power but specify ruler, 144; have contract with ruler, 270; have inalienable right to consent, 102; have natural-law right to choose form of polity, 143; have power to legislate, 29; hold ultimate sovereignty, 245; identified in Venice with leading citizens, 38; judge tyrannical ruler, 182; "make the king," 271; originally without ruler or laws, 267; own their sovereignty, 272; place sword in ruler's hands, 267; role in church, 87; role in polity, 225; of Rome, 34; secondary cause of political authority, 139; source of ruler's authority, 289; superior to ruler, 112, 124; transfer power to ruler via consent, 289; transfer right of election to representatives, 102
personal liberty, 14
Perugia, 24

Peter, St, 55, 57, 62 n.26, 71, 79, 83, 116, 119, 179
Petit, Jean, 89, 91
Petrarch, 32, 34; restored *studia humanitatis*, 37
Petrus de Vinea, 52
Philip II, of Spain, 161
Philip III, of Spain, 161
Philip of Hesse, 210, 213, 216, 248
Philip the Bold, 91
Philip the Fair, of France, 22, 60, 65, 66, 68, 114; called for general council, 61
Phillipps, Margaret Mann, 45 n.76
Photinus, 60
Pirkheimer, Willibald, 194
Pisa, 14, 24
Pius II, pope. *See* Aeneas Silvius Piccolomini.
Plato, xvii, 16, 18 n.6, 42, 45, 240, 251; *Gorgias*, xvii; ideal society a simple arcadian model, 45 n.75; *Laws*, 39; metaphysics, xvii; *Republic*, 38, 44, 45; wealth and culture entail warfare, 45
*plenitudo potestatis*, 29, 69, 71, 73, 75, 81, 82, 84, 97, 115, 288, 292
podestà-type rule, 15, 38,
Poissy, 239
*police, la*, 259
political authority: aims at public welfare, 271; based on agreement, 138, 283; based on conquest, 281; based on natural law, 153; can promote religion, 157; derives from popular consent, 244; directed to spiritual good, 289; directly from God, 281, 292; from either God or people, 281; in the people, 20–21, 22, 136, 264; is natural, 146; no individual has it by nature over any other, 182; obliged to promote true religion, 289, 290; perfects humans, 135; protects individual property rights, 267; punishment for sin, 135; to be endured, 135
political contract: does not create authority, 139; natural and conventional, 138–39
political glory, 9
political society: aims at common good, 291; essentially a religious institution, 291; needs consent, 280; origin of, 132, 244; origin requires agreement, 136 n.18; origin requires free consent,

## Index 441

136; public welfare protected by, 268; reason for creating, 135
polity: an artificial grouping, 147; caused by use of reason, 280; choice of form precedes forming, 144; consequence of and response to sin, 145, 146; eclipsed by coming of Christianity, 147; entails mutual agreement by individuals, 162; final cause of, 244; form distinct from establishing, 269; not formed by convention, 152; of any kind can protect its unity, 90
Ponet, John, 108, 108 n.128, 242, 248, 255 n.174, 264
pope: above all earthly authority, 59, 60, 64, 85, 288; abuse of authority, 59; alone can call general council, 92, 104, 120; the anti-Christ, 212; authority is spiritual, 85; can authorize deposition of unbelieving ruler, 157; can be corrected by general council, 80; can be tried and deposed, 67; can depose a tyrant for good of church, 182; can err, 83, 85; cannot legislate alone, 72, 106; cannot overrule general council, 72; and cardinals, 69, 82; comparable to bishop, 71; *curator* or *dispensator*, 67; deposes himself, 59, 61; deposition of, 59, 60, 61; distinction between his sacramental and jurisdictional status, 101; does not own church's possessions, 79; does not possess temporal jurisdiction, 156, 160; elected by cardinals, 86; election of, 60; greatest power on earth, 85; has no ownership rights over individual goods, 268; heretical, 62 n.26; holds office until deposed, 118; lacks temporal coercive power, 85; minister or servant of faithful, 111; must assist in promulgating dogma, 104; must control himself, 56; not *dominus*, 66–67; not subject to any individual, 112, 115, 116; only one member in general council, 106; relation to universal church, 75; removable for sufficient cause, 67; represents the church, 103; represents the church *remote*, 117 n.163; role in appointing emperor, 26; single authoritative head, 54; superior to other faithful distributively, 105; supreme authority, 67, 288; supreme in jurisdiction and status, 67; voluntary submission of, 56 n.17; and whole church, 66

popular authority, 84
popular consent, 11, 13, 22–23, 28, 59, 83, 92, 101, 112, 127, 152, 163, 167, 173, 178, 179, 240, 244, 246, 261, 262, 269, 278, 279, 282, 283, 289; basis for republican polity, 241; basis of political authority, 279; cause of political authority, 129, 268; in empire, 102; entails absolute transfer of authority, 137; essential to enact law, 241, 279; ground of royal dominion, 288; involved in custom, 172; linked with representation, 83; via custom, 28
popular government, 35
popular magistrates, 229
popular sovereignty, 9, 19, 107 n.122, 284, 291; position of Baldus close to, 29
*populus*: not a fictive entity for Baldus, 30; a specific type of corporation, 30
Portugal, 130
Portuguese, 159
positive law, 153, 168, 278; contrary to divine and/or natural law not to be obeyed, 218; related to natural law, 168, 170; rests on consent, 23
post-Glossators, 21, 24
poverty: Franciscan conception of, 30
power, xx; absolute and ordinary distinguishable, 27, 86; all ordained directly by God, 265; distinct from authority, 154; distinction between ordinary and absolute, 285–86, 287, 288; not in only one person, 213; of God is ordinary and absolute, 179 n.149; of the keys, derives from whole church, 117; of the pope, conferred by whole church, 97; to punish derives from whole people, not individuals, 154; to restrain ruler should exist in people, 165
prepolitical phase, 140
*presbyters*, 217; for Luther, 196
priesthood of the faithful, 189, 217
*prima sedes a nemine judicatur*, 54
prince: can resist emperor, 210; cannot resist emperor, 209, 210; minister of the people, 31
*princeps legibus solutus*, xxi, 69, 70, 80, 246
private property, xx n.9, 170, 175, 268; based on practical needs, 174; Lockean concept of, xxiii–xxiv; origins in *ius gentium*, 131; ownership (*dominium*), 174; political society protects, 268; private wealth, devotion to a cause of

civic miseries, 40; of two kinds: over goods, over persons, 174
*privilegium fori*, 104
property rights: include moral rights, 268
Protestant League, 210
Pseudo-Dionsyius, 92
Ptolemy of Lucca, 18, 31, 31 n.30, 33, 40, 42, 133; favoured republicanism, 18; thought kingship despotic, 18
public official: can be killed by private individual, 214
public welfare: the supreme law, 123
Puritanism, 275, 276, 277, 283, 289, 292
Puy, bishopric of, 77

*quod omnes tangit*, 71, 72, 87, 93, 93 n.87, 103, 103 n.113, 225

Ratisbon, 125
realism, xvii
reason: basis for political authority, 153; and conscience, 237; greatest gift of God to humans, 279
rebellion: unjustifiable, 288
Red Sea, 233 n.108
Reformation: in Scotland, 107
Reformation political thought, 107, 110, 122, 126, 129, 132, 136, 178, 180–81, 186, 197, 205, 217, 223, 235, 251, 289, 293; rejects direct role for people, 152
*regnum*, 201
*regnum Italicum*, 8, 34
Remigio de' Girolami, 17, 33, 40, 42
representation, xx n.9, 84, 92, 103, 105; in church council, 112; involves delegation and election, 87; of church, distinction between *remote* (pope) and *propinquissime* (council), 117 n.163; as personification, 84
representative, 246
representative bodies: can limit ruler's authority, 262
representative democracy, 20, 270
representatives, 260, 262; of people, 266, 269, have conditional commitment to ruler, 272
republican constitutionalism, 13
republicanism, 16, 19, 21; best form of government, 18; end of in Italy, 38
republican triumphalism, 9
resistance: always evil, never legitimate, 200; by lesser magistrates, 216; can be active, 253; denied to individuals, 247; distinct from anarchy, 248; forbidden, 199, 208, 217; forbidden by Scripture, 197; forbidden to individual, 245; in defence of true religion, 261; justified by private law, 255 n.174; legitimacy of, 9, 206, 211, 213, 215, 260, 266; legitimacy of for individual, 215; purely passive, 226; to imperial authority, 214; to magistrates is resistance to God, 239; to tyranny lies with lesser magistrates, 230
resistance theory, 11, 57 n.18, 207, 210 n.51, 218, 226 n.87, 235, 239, 241, 243, 247, 248, 251, 253, 254, 255, 255 n.174, 263, 275; of Calvin, 225, 226; Lutheran, 30 n.29; none in Hooker, 279, 283
*rex est imperator in regno suo*, 22 n.19
*rex singulis major, universo minor*, 112, 246, 272
Ridley, Jasper, 232 n.106
rights (*ius, iura*), xx, xx n.9, 176; equal for women and men, 172; of city-states to resist emperor and pope, 29; of the people, 268, primary, 160; of selfdefence, inalienable in state of nature, 154; rooted in state of nature, 284; to choose leader belong to whole church, 80; to life is inalienable, 183
Rinucci, Alamanno, 39
Roman church, 3; not whole congregation of the faithful, 64
Roman Code, 17, 21, 22, 24, 25, 28, 29, 48, 102, 138, 253, 254, 256, 262, 265
Roman consul(s), 253
Rome, 17, 21, 31, 38, 53, 142, 161, 167, 210, 273; diocese of, 63; early republicanism, 42
Rousseau, Jean-Jacques, 162, 177
royal authority: begins in consent of individuals, 163; limited, 265, 289; over church, 275
Rubianus, Crotus, 194
Rufinus, 56 n.16
ruler, above law, 285; accountable to subjects, 122–23; acts for common good, 111; an administrator, 246, 272; an agent for people, 272; appointed by popular election, 124, 268, 292; bound by compact with people, 285; can coerce for spiritual good, 289; can veto law, 283; a god on earth, 288; has absolute commitment to people, 271; has abso-

lute power, 288; has clerical role, 291; has delegated authority, 272; has jurisdiction not ownership, 156, 268; has limited authority from people, 124; *minor universis, maior singulis*, 112, 246, 272; must obey laws of land, 165, 203, 246, 272, 285; must respect rights of subjects, 165; a personification, 84; a president, 262; a public person, 111; responsible for maintaining religion, 218; self-preservation of, 42
rulership: originally in Roman people, 26
Russian revolution, 6

*sacerdotium*, 201; an institutional reality, 196; for Luther, 196
Sacred Scripture: Deut., 233 n.108; Judges, 250; Judges 1:36, 253; Judges 19, 251; Matt. 23:24, 295; Matt. 28:29, 156; 1 Peter 2, 196; Romans 13, 197, 213, 217, 226 n.87, 227, 235, 245, 250, 254, 294; Samuel, 163, 269
St Andrew's, 109, 231, 232
St Bartholomew's Day Massacre, 161, 242, 243, 247, 249, 256, 258, 260
Salamanca, 142, 143, 149; University of, 148, 167
Salamonio, Mario, 31, 40, 47
Salutati, Coluccio, 32, 33, 34, 36, 37, 166; committed republican, 34; favoured single ruler, 34; monarchism of rejected by Bruni, 37 n.51; rejected tyrannicide, 34
Santo Junta General de Reino, 142
Savonarola, Girolamo, 31
Saul, 269; made king by popular consent, 269; selected by God, 269
scepticism, xxi
Schmalkaldic League, 212, 225
Schmalkaldic War, 216
Scottish monarchy, 111
secular authority: not immediately from God, 119
sedition: never permissible, 215
Selden, John, 283, 298
self-defence: legitimate, 213, 214
Seneca, 140, 141
senate: in early church, 82 n.66
Sens, 114
separation of church and state, 289
Sepúlveda, Juan Gines de, 150, 159 n.84
Servetus, Septimius, Roman emperor, 240, 241, 264

Seyssel, Claude de, 11, 146, 259, 261; forerunner of Hotman and Mornay, 11
Siete Partidas, Las, 166
Sigmund, Paul E., 106 n.126
*signori*, 26
single authority: dangerous, 265
Skinner, Quentin, xxii, xxiii, xxiv, 5 n.1, 32, 37 nn.52, 54, 44 n.71, 45 n.76, 109 n.131, 121 n.178, 124 n.189, 128, 128 n.1, 129, 129 n.4, 130, 136 n.19, 160 n.89, 177 n.145, 180 n.152, 229 n.94, 238 n.119, 244 n.138, 240 n.125, 243 n.135, 251 n.161, 255 n.174, 266, 266 n.208, 297
slavery, 131, 131 n.7, 164, 176; sanctioned by positive law, 174
Sleidan, Johann, 254 n.171
social: distinct from political, 132, 136-37, 280
social contract, 137, 138, 139, 163, 180, 283, 284, 285; distinct from political one, 137; explains natural character of polity, 138; occurred before political one, 137-38
society: natural, 280
Society of Jesus (Jesuits), 166, 167, 167 n.111
Socrates, 45
*sola Scriptura*, xiii n.1, 196
Solway Moss, 231
Sommerville, J. P., 177 n.145, 180 n.152, 183 n.159
sovereignty, 25; limitation of, 9; of people, 225; theory of, 29
Spain: could intervene against tyranny, 157-58; could preach Gospel to infidels, 157; could protect Indian converts, 157; could remove indigenous rulers, 111 n.136; had Christian missionary obligations, 157; had spiritual responsibilities in Americas, 150, 151
Spalatin, Georg, 211
Spanish conquest of Americas, 9, 131-32; 149, 149 n.62, 155, 155 n.76
Spanish hegemony: in Americas, spurious claims for, 156
Spanish monarchy: rested on popular consent, 163
Sparta, 263
Spengler, Lazarus, 212
spiritual: superior to temporal, 201
spiritual authority: of political ruler rests on

popular consent, 292; under closer scrutiny than temporal, 85
spiritual sphere: can coerce only spiritually, 202
Standonck, Jean, 114
state, xx, xx n.9; has religious responsibilities, 151; modern concept of, as having rights, 30
state of innocence, 133 n.15, 136 n.18, 179; distinct from state of nature, 131, 131 n.8
state of nature, 123, 132, 133, 134, 139, 140, 147, 161, 162, 167, 173, 174, 175, 176, 179–80, 238, 268, 280, 285; no dominion in, 136 n.18; no private property in, 141; perfect, 146; strife-torn, 279
*status ecclesiae*, 80
Stoicism, 132, 133, 139, 162
Stoic notion of human equality, 46
Storch, Nicolas, 206
Strasbourg, 219, 220 n.71, 220 n.74, 224, 242 n.129, 250, 253, 254 n.171
*studia humanitatis*, 48
Suárez, Francisco, 5 n.1, 32, 128, 129, 130, 133 n.15, 134 n.16, 136 n.18, 136 n.19, 137, 154, 160, 163 n.95, 164 n.102, 166–84, 207, 275, 276, 276 n.245, 280, 283, 284, 298; resistance theory, 181
subjectivism, 4
subjects: must obey rulers, 217, 227; should avoid gratuitous public activity, 227
*Summa Parisiensis*, 56 n.16
superiority, distinction between distributive and collective, 105
superior part, 113
Sylvester, pope, 56 n.15

Tacitus, 258
temporal authority: cannot coerce spiritually, 202; from people, 292; has place in general councils, 88; has religious obligations, 149, 213; not superior to whole people, 116
temporal sphere: governed by natural law, 203
theocracy, 222
Thomas Aquinas, 5 n.1, 9, 17, 18, 21, 28, 39 n.55, 81, 86 n.70, 89, 127, 131 n.8, 133, 136, 136 n.20, 140, 141, 142, 145, 148, 153, 160, 162 n.93, 163, 164 n.103, 166 n.110, 168, 169,
169 n.118, 173, 174, 181, 190, 191, 215, 240, 252, 265, 277, 277 n.248, 280, 287; conception of society not organic, 140; followers of, 9; on reason and law, 279
three estates, 270
Tiberius, Roman emperor, 36
Tierney, Brian, 24 n.23, 56 n.16, 62, 66 n.34
Todi, 33
Toledo, University of, 161
Torgau Declaration, 210, 211, 212, 216
Trajan, Roman emperor, 126, 254
transferred right to elect: not wholly alienated, 102
Trevor-Roper, George, 121 n.178, 126
tribunes, Roman, 18, 229, 234
Trier, 99
Trutveller, Jodorus, 192
Tubingen, University of, 192
Tuck, Richard, 183 n.154, 297
Tully, James, xxii n.15
Tuscany, 14, 15, 21
two spheres: church and state, 50
Tyndale, William, 195, 198, 199, 200
tyrannical magistrate: reduces himself to private citizen, 213
tyrannicide, 81, 89, 112 n.143, 161, 166, 167, 181, 207, 213, 215, 247; legitimate only for public official, 215; specific form of resistance, 249
tyranny, 203, 207, 223, 265; can be resisted, 213; dissolves obligation to obey, 137; distinction between seizure and use, 181, 248, 253; papal, 31, 34; response to sinfulness of subjects, 204
tyrant: can be resisted, 215, 231, 261; derives authority from God, 199, 247; exceeds authority and thus not real ruler, 229; has legitimate authority, 253; has place in divine plan as punishment, 218; *ipso facto* violates agreement with people, 137; must be obeyed, 228; ordained by God, 255; punishable by God, 239; self-reduced to status of citizen, 228

Ulpian, 46, 131, 153
unbelief: does not vitiate political legitimacy, 156
*universitas*, 81, 96, 97, 177 n.145
*universitas ecclesiae*, 82, 88, 104, 106
*universitas fidelium*, 62, 72, 74

*Index* 445

university chancellor: rights of, 78
Urban IV, pope, 27

*valentior pars*, 96. See greater part, *maior pars*
Valla, Lorenzo, 47, 48; on Roman legal texts, 46
Valladolid, 148, 151
Venice, 37 n.54, 38, 39, 40; constitution of 1297, 38; great council appointed ruler, 38; had mixed form of polity, 39; a republican oligarchy, 38
Vergerio, Pier Paulo, 32, 39
Vergil, Polydor, 253
Vermigli, Peter Martyr, 124 n.188, 126, 249–56, 259
*via antiqua*, 191
*via cessionis*, 77, 91, 99
*via concilii*, 77, 91, 93
*via media*, 292
*via moderna*, 141, 191, 236, 279; as scepticism, 236
vicariate, status of, 25
Vienna, 91
Villey, François, 297
Viret, Pierre, 232 n.107
virtù: as worldly magnificence, 45
*vir virtutis*, 38, 41
*vis vi repellere licet*, 209, 215, 248
Vitoria, Francisco de, 5 n.1, 128 n.1, 129, 130, 131, 131 n.7, 137, 141, 143, 147–60, 173, 175, 177 n.145, 240, 246 n.146: criticized Spain's policies, 149
Vives, Juan Luis, 46, 128, 136, 146–47, 152, 162, 175

Volterra, 35
voluntariness, 171
von Gunsburg, Eberlin, 195
von Hutten, Ulrich, 48
von Manderscheid, Ulrich, 99
von Staupitz, Johann, 192, 193
von Usinger, Arnold, 192

Waldensians, 129 n.3
Wenzel, Holy Roman emperor, 210
whole body: of church, 292; of faithful, 63; of people, not every citizen, 245
whole church, 56 n.16, 57, 58; has no causal role in choosing pope, 143
Wilenius, Reijo, 167 n.111, 173 n.134
William of Moerbeke, 96, 132
William of Ockham, 5 n.1, 8, 9, 64, 68, 71, 87, 92, 141, 160 n.89, 191, 191 n.5, 192; on corporation, 30
Williams, George H., 205, 205 n.43
Wimpfeling, Jacob, 194
Winzerus, 125 n.191
Wishart, George, 231, 232
Wittenberg, 186, 195, 205, 273; University of, 194
Wyclif, John, 89

Zabarella, Franciscus, cardinal, 76, 82, 95–98, 122 n.191
Zasius, Ulrich, 48
Zirkulardisputation of 1539, 212
Zurich, 206, 218, 219, 232, 232 n.106, 233
Zwilling, Gabriel, 205
Zwingli, Huldrich, 206, 218, 219, 229, 232, 233, 234, 234 n.109